World Religions

Western Traditions

World Religions
Western Traditions

Third Edition

Edited by

Willard G. Oxtoby

Amir Hussain

OXFORD
UNIVERSITY PRESS

8 Sampson Mews, Suite 204, Don Mills, Ontario M3C 0H5
www.oupcanada.com

Oxford University Press is a department of the University of Oxford.
It furthers the University's objective of excellence in research, scholarship,
and education by publishing worldwide in

Oxford   New York

Auckland   Cape Town   Dar es Salaam   Hong Kong   Karachi
Kuala Lumpur   Madrid   Melbourne   Mexico City   Nairobi
New Delhi   Shanghai   Taipei   Toronto

With offices in

Argentina   Austria   Brazil   Chile   Czech Republic   France   Greece
Guatemala   Hungary   Italy   Japan   Poland   Portugal   Singapore
South Korea   Switzerland   Thailand   Turkey   Ukraine   Vietnam

Oxford is a trade mark of Oxford University Press
in the UK and in certain other countries

Published in Canada
by Oxford University Press

Library and Archives Canada Cataloguing in Publication

World religions : western traditions / edited by Willard G. Oxtoby, Amir Hussain. — 3rd ed.

Includes bibliographical references and index.
ISBN 978-0-19-542717-2

1. Religions. I. Oxtoby, Willard G. (Willard Gurdon), 1933-2003 II. Hussain, Amir

BL80.2.W672 2010   291   C2010-902169-X

Cover image: Mel Curtis/Getty Images

Contents

1 About Religion 2
Roy C. Amore and Amir Hussain

2 Religions of the Ancient World 28
Michael Desrochers

3 Jewish Traditions 66
Alan F. Segal

4 Christian Traditions 164
Willard G. Oxtoby and Roy C. Amore

Contributors

ROY C. AMORE has extensive research experience in Asia. His books include *Two Masters, One Message*, comparing the lives and teachings of Christ and Buddha, and *Lustful Maidens and Ascetic Kings: Buddhist and Hindu Stories of Life*. He is professor in the Department of Political Science and associate dean, administration, Faculty of Arts and Social Sciences, at the University of Windsor and is currently writing a book on religion and politics.

KEN DERRY received his PhD from the University of Toronto's Centre for the Study Religion with a thesis on religion, violence, and First Nations literature. Since 1996 he has been teaching courses on religion, culture, literature, and film at the University of Toronto.

MICHAEL DESROCHERS received his PhD from UCLA in the history of Mesopotamia. Currently an adjunct professor of history at California State University Dominguez Hills, he is at work on two book-length projects: an overview of the religions of antiquity and an examination of historical irony.

AMIR HUSSAIN is professor in the Department of Theological Studies at Loyola Marymount University in Los Angeles, where he teaches courses on Islam and world religions. A Canadian of Pakistani origin, he is the author of *Oil and Water: Two Faiths, One God*, an introduction to Islam for North Americans.

The late WILLARD G. OXTOBY, the original editor of this work, was professor emeritus at the University of Toronto, where he launched the graduate program in the study of religion. His books include *Experiencing India: European Descriptions and Impressions* and *The Meaning of Other Faiths*.

ALAN F. SEGAL is professor of religion and Ingeborg Rennert professor of Jewish studies at Barnard College, Columbia University. He has written extensively in the fields of comparative religion, Judaism, and early Christianity. His books include *Rebecca's Children*, *Paul the Convert*, and *Life after Death: A History of the Afterlife in Western Religion*.

Important Features
of This Edition

T his third edition of *World Religions: Western Traditions* incorporates several features introduced in the single-volume *Concise Introduction to World Religions* (2007). Perhaps the most significant improvement over earlier versions of the full two-volume set is the fact that all the major traditions are now presented in the same way, following an organizational pattern that moves from Origins through Crystallization, Differentiation, Practice, and Cultural Expressions to Interaction and Adaptation. Other highlights include:

- New introductory and concluding chapters by Roy Amore (editor of the companion Eastern Traditions book) and Amir Hussain, common to both volumes;

- Four new contributors writing on Religions of the Ancient World, Muslim Traditions, Indigenous Traditions, and New Religions and Movements

- New pedagogy, including 'Traditions at a Glance' boxes, 'Sites' boxes, recommended websites, and bolded key terms (defined in end-of-chapter glossaries);

- Boxed excerpts from scripture and other essential texts; and

- A striking new four-colour design.

To better reflect the richness and diversity of each religious tradition and its adherents, the text has been completely redesigned in a vibrant four-colour palette, with a thoroughly revamped art program that features an expanded range of beautiful, meticulously chosen photographs, now in full colour.

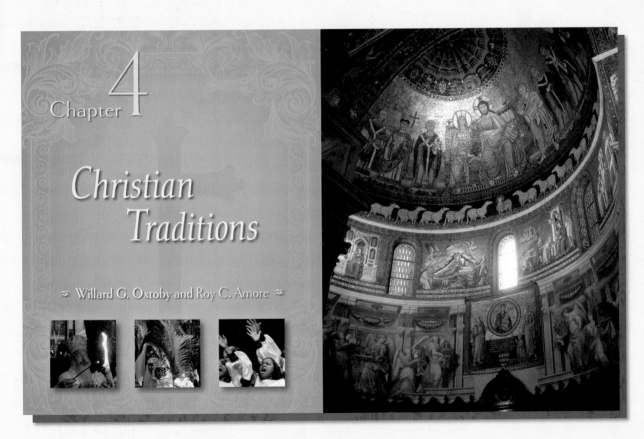

Chapter 4

Christian
Traditions

∾ Willard G. Oxtoby and Roy C. Amore ∾

Traditions at a Glance boxes give readers a summary of the basics at the start of each chapter.

Traditions at a Glance

Numbers
Approximately 14 million

Distribution
7 million in the Americas (mostly US, Canada, and Buenos Aires, Argentina); 3 million in Asia (mostly in Israel); 4 million in Europe (mostly in Russia, Ukraine, France, and England)

Principal Historical Periods
1700 BCE–70 CE   Biblical
c. 70–700   Talmudic
700–1700   Medieval
1700–present   Modern

Principal Founders
The patriarchs and matriarchs: Abraham and his wife Sarah (legendary, c. 1700 BCE); Isaac (their son) and his wife Rebecca; Jacob (their son; also called Israel) and his wives Leah and Rachel (father and mothers, with Bilhah and Zilpah, of the children of Israel). Also Moses (legendary prophet who received the Ten Commandments on Mount Sinai, c. 1200 BCE); Saul, David, and Solomon (semi-legendary kings, c. 1000–900 BCE).

Leaders
Ezra helped build the second Temple, 515 BCE. Yochanan ben Zakkai founded the first rabbinic academy, 70 CE. Judah the Prince produced the *Mishnah*, 220 CE. David Ben Gurion was the first prime minister of the state of Israel, 1948.

Deity
One God, called 'Lord' or 'God' in English. His name is never spoken in Hebrew.

Authoritative Texts
The Hebrew Bible, the *Talmud*, and the *Midrash* (commentaries).

Noteworthy Doctrines
All the righteous of the world can be saved; God has commanded the Jews to observe special laws, including dietary laws and dress codes.

the community since the late eighteenth century, when Jews began to achieve legal rights, gain in affluence, and take part in the intellectual life of European societies. The ritual used to be a relatively simple matter between the rabbi and the youngster and could be conducted on any of the days when the Torah is normally read in the synagogue (Monday, Thursday, and Saturday). Now it is almost always part of the Sabbath service and the whole congregation takes part in it.

Whatever the tradition of the congregation, families devote a great deal of thought to ensuring

Sites

Bethlehem The traditional birthplace of Jesus.

Nazareth Jesus' home in youth and manhood.

Jerusalem The site of Jesus' crucifixion and centre of the earliest Jewish Christian community; capital of the Latin Christian Kingdom in the Holy Land from 1099 to 1187.

Rome The capital of the Roman Empire, where Peter introduced Christianity and the Roman Catholic Church eventually established its headquarters in Vatican City—the world's smallest independent country.

Anatolia A region (corresponding to modern-day Turkey), evangelized by Paul, that became an important centre of the early Church; the location of the famous councils of Chalcedon, Nicaea, and Constantinople.

Constantinople The capital of the Byzantine Empire and headquarters of the Orthodox Church; conquered by the Ottoman Turks in 1453 and renamed Istanbul.

Wittenberg The German town where Martin Luther posted his 95 theses, beginning the Protestant Reformation.

Worms The German city where an imperial council ('diet') tried Luther for political subversion.

Trent (Trentino in Italian) Site of the Council of Trent (1545–63) and centre of the Catholic Church's response to Protestantism, known as the Counter-Reformation.

Geneva The city in which John Calvin attempted to translate his vision of Christianity into a practising community.

Münster A town in northwestern Germany that became a centre of the Anabaptist movement.

Valladolid City in Spain; the site of a great debate in 1550 in which Bartolomé de las Casas defended the rights of the indigenous peoples of the New World.

Salt Lake City, Utah Founded by the Mormons in 1847; the headquarters of the Church of Jesus Christ of Latter-day Saints.

Sites boxes draw attention to locations of special significance to each tradition.

Timelines help to place religious developments in historical context.

Muslim Traditions   269

Timeline

622	Muhammad's *hijrah* from Mecca to Medina
632	Muhammad dies; leadership passes to the caliph
642	Birth of al-Hasan al-Basri, early Sufi ascetic (d. 728)
661	Damascus established as capital of Umayyad caliphate
680	Death of Husayn at Karbala', commemorated as martyrdom by Shi'is
711	Arab armies reach Spain
762	Baghdad established as 'Abbasid capital
922	al-Hallaj (born c. 858) executed for claiming to be one with the Truth
1058	Birth of al-Ghazali, theological synthesizer of faith and reason (d. 1111)
1071	Seljuq Turks defeat Byzantines in eastern Anatolia
1165	Birth of Ibn 'Arabi, philosopher of the mystical unity of being (d. 1240)
1207	Birth of Jalal al-Din Rumi, Persian mystical poet (d. 1273)
1258	Baghdad falls to Mongol invaders
1492	Christian forces take Granada, the last Muslim stronghold in Spain
1529	Ottoman Turks reach Vienna (again in 1683)
1602	Muslims officially expelled from Spain
1703	Birth of Ibn 'Abd al-Wahhab, leader of traditionalist revival in Arabia (d. 1792)
1924	Atatürk, Turkish modernizer and secularizer, abolishes the caliphate
1930	Iqbal proposes a Muslim state in India
1947	Pakistan established as an Islamic state
1979	Ayatollah Khomeini establishes a revolutionary Islamic regime in Iran
2001	Osama bin Laden launches terrorist attacks on America
2004	Madrid train station bombings
2005	London transit bombings

structure called the Ka'ba, believed to have been built by Abraham and his son Ishmael.

The Life of Muhammad (570–632 CE)

Muhammad was born into the Quraysh tribe around the year 570. His father died before his birth and his mother died a few years later.

Muhammad thus grew up an orphan and was cared for first by his paternal grandfather, 'Abd al-Muttalib, and then, after his grandfather's death, by his uncle Abu Talib.

Little is known about Muhammad's youth. He worked as a merchant for a rich widow, Khadijah, whom he married in his mid-twenties. Muhammad is described in the early biographical sources as a contemplative, honest, and mild-mannered

292   World Religions: Western Traditions

Map 5.1   Language and Culture in the Spread of Islam

Muslims moved into North Africa in the second half of the seventh century. Before that time North Africa had been first an important Roman province and then an equally important home of Latin Christianity. With its indigenous Berber, Phoenician, Roman, and Byzantine populations, North Africa was rich in cultural and religious diversity, and it has always maintained a distinct religious and cultural identity that reflects its ancient heritage.

The Umayyads had established their capital in Damascus in 661. With the shift of the capital from Damascus to Baghdad under the 'Abbasids in 762, the main orientation of the eastern Islamic domains became more Persian than Arab, more Asian than Mediterranean. Meanwhile, the centre of Arab Islamic culture shifted from Syria to the western Mediterranean: to Qayrawan, the capital of North Africa, in what is today Tunisia; and to Córdoba, Islam's western capital, in Spain, which rivalled Baghdad and Cairo in its cultural splendour. North African mystics, scholars, and philosophers were all instrumental in this remarkable achievement. In the nineteenth and twentieth centuries, North African religious scholars and particularly Sufi masters played a crucial role in the region's struggle for independence from European colonial powers. They helped to preserve

Informative maps provide useful reference points.

Document Boxes

Document boxes provide a generous selection of excerpts from scripture and other important writings.

Focus Boxes

Focus boxes offer additional information on selected subjects.

End-of-chapter glossaries enhance understanding of key concepts: **further readings** and **recommended websites** provide excellent starting points for further research.

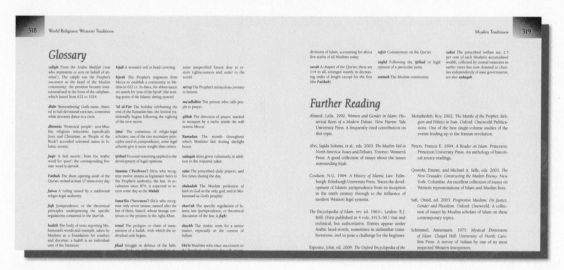

 Extensive ancillary package.

For Instructors: an Instructor's Manual, a Test Generator, and PowerPoint slides.

For Students: A Student Study Guide.

COMPANION WEBSITE

The late Willard G. Oxtoby and Amir Hussain

World Religions: Western Traditions, Third Edition
ISBN 13: 9780195427172

Inspection copy request

Ordering information

Contact & Comments

About the Book

The third edition of *World Religions: Western Traditions* contributed volume examines in detail the major Western religious traditions, namely Judaism, Zoroastrianism, Christianity, Islam, and religions of the ancient world. The text traces each tradition in depth from its origins, through its development, to the religion's meaning and practice in today's society. Comprehensive and accessible, the new third edition offers a thorough and engaging introduction to the Western faiths.

Readership : First- and second-year university and college full-year courses on world religions, and one-semester courses on Western religions, offered out of religion or history departments.

Instructor Resources

You need a password to access these resources. Please contact your local Sales and Editorial Representative for more information.

Instructors should contact their Oxford University Press sales representative for details on the supplements and for login and password information.

Foreword

Will Oxtoby seemed to know everything there was to know about the world's religions. Having majored in philosophy, he completed his PhD in Near Eastern Studies at Princeton and, after learning Hebrew and Arabic, began his career as a Bible professor at McGill. Before long, however, he was enticed into the Persian gardens of Zoroastrianism. Exploring the relationships between Zoroastrianism and early Second Temple period Judaism required him to learn Avestan, the classical Persian language, which in turn required a working knowledge of Sanskrit. By the time he began teaching the history of religion at Yale, he already had half the world's traditions within his purview. He had also developed strong views on the teaching of religion.

He put those views into practice as the founding director of the University of Toronto's Centre for the Study of Religions. Will himself had begun his exploration of other faiths from a Presbyterian perspective, and he wanted to emphasize that anyone with strong roots in a particular religious tradition cannot help bringing certain assumptions to the study of other traditions. In this respect, the believer and the non-believer start from a similar place: both may find it difficult to appreciate an unfamiliar tradition from the insider's point of view.

Will also wanted his students to understand that the truths of religion do not reveal themselves to the casual eye. Close observation is required even when the observer is an insider to the faith. And a capacity for critical analysis is no less essential for those exploring their own traditions than a sympathetic openness to difference is for outsiders seeking to understand religious experiences that they do not share.

In a sense, Will's entire career reflected his conviction that religion plays a central role in the lives of most people around the world, and that we cannot understand others without understanding their faiths. He also believed that it is only by making the effort to understand other religions that we can truly begin to understand our own.

Will was among the first to identify Iran's Islamic revolution as an event of worldwide religious significance—an early expression of a much broader revitalization of religion that was likely to bring with it dangers as well as rewards. A decade later, he recognized the collapse of the Soviet Union as another event of enormous religious importance, and not just because it opened the way for a religious revival in Eastern Europe. It was significant, Will suggested, because the demise of an explicitly atheistic, Marxist-inspired state could be attributed—at least in part—to a contradiction within Marxism. Marx himself had justly criticized religion as an instrument of oppression, serving the authoritarian state. Yet some of the fundamental principles on which Marx based his critique would be quite at home in any number of religions, and in many ways Marxism itself could be seen as a religion (especially one of the Western Abrahamic variety). The communist system had gained power by promising to end tyranny and alleviate human misery. Having done the very opposite, it was justly condemned by its own principles.

In the course of his career, Will came to believe ever more deeply in the plurality of truth. With that belief came the conviction that human efforts to understand truth must be plural as well. In Will's view, truth was not the possession of any single religion or school of thought: it was something that emerged in the process of comparison and dialogue. Thus every religion must be recognized as having its own purchase on truth, and every individual—believer, unbeliever, and everyone in between—as having a potentially valid perspective; then all those perspectives have to become part of a wide-open, ongoing dialogue. The spirit behind such dialogue Will called pluralism, and it was in that spirit that these textbooks were conceived.

Alan F. Segal
Barnard College
Columbia University

Preface

I first met Will Oxtoby in 1987, as a student in his undergraduate course on world religions at the University of Toronto; eventually, I became one of many teaching assistants for that course. I also took numerous other courses with Will, and he supervised my MA as well as my PhD dissertation. Whereas I came from a working-class background (both my parents were factory workers), Will had a consummate academic pedigree. The son and grandson of scholars, he held degrees from Stanford and Princeton and teaching appointments at McGill, Harvard, Yale, and the University of Toronto. He was also an outstanding researcher. But I think that Will's true excellence was as a teacher. It is no coincidence that the publication for which he will be best remembered is a textbook.

Will wrote and edited several chapters of the original *World Religions: Eastern Traditions* and *World Religions: Western Traditions*. The work was first used in draft form for students in his world religions class in 1994–5. After some fine tuning, it was published in 1996 and then revised for the second edition in 2002. The project was Will's gift to those who did not have the privilege of studying with him.

Will believed that only those who loved classroom teaching should write textbooks. Therefore every author he recruited had to be an excellent teacher. He also made sure that his fellow authors were not just academic authorities but sympathetic observers, if not members, of the traditions they were writing about

This third edition of the *Western Traditions* volume, like the new *Eastern* volume edited by Roy C. Amore, takes advantage of the improved chapter structure and enhanced colour format of the single-volume *Concise Introduction to World Religions* (2007). The two new volumes also share both their opening and concluding chapters, on the nature of religion and current trends respectively. New contributors have been recruited, but the criteria that Will laid down have not been forgotten. Together, Roy Amore and I have tried to stay true to his vision. In his original foreword, Will wrote that people often used to ask him why he would waste his life on something as unimportant as religion, but that after the Islamic revolution in Iran no one ever asked that question again. I have had the same experience: since the terrorist attacks of 9/11, not a single student has raised the issue of relevance. On the contrary, the study of world religions is more important today than ever before.

Acknowledgements

At Oxford University Press I would like to thank Katherine Skene for her encouragement, Jennifer Mueller for her developmental guidance, and Sally Livingston for her hands-on editorial work. I also need to thank Roy Amore for all his help in making this volume a reality and a tribute to Will's legacy. Of course, my thanks to Ken Derry, Michael Desrochers, and Alan Segal for their fine contributions.

With Roy Amore, I am also grateful to the following reviewers and those reviewers who wish to remain anonymous, whose comments helped to shape this volume:

Martin Adam, University of Victoria

Edward Chung, University of Prince Edward Island

Husain Khimjee, Wilfrid Laurier University

Edward Smith, University of Guelph

Marie Taylor, Lakehead University

Ayse Tuzlak, University of Calgary

Amir Hussain
March 2010
Loyola Marymount University
Los Angeles

World Religions

Western Traditions

Chapter 1

About Religion

Roy C. Amore ✸ Amir Hussain

ꙮ Looking Both Ways from Stonehenge: Basic Human Religion

Standing on the west side of **Stonehenge**, we watch the sun rise through the circle of massive standing stones. Within the outer circle is a grouping of paired stones capped by lintels and arranged in a horseshoe pattern, opening towards the rising sun. At the centre of the horseshoe lies a flat stone that was once thought to have served as an altar for sacrifices. Today, however, it is believed that the centre stone originally stood upright, marking the spot where an observer would stand to watch the movements of the sun and stars.

The Stonehenge we know today is what remains of a structure erected between 3,500 and 4,000 years ago. But the site had already been used as a burial ground for centuries before that time: researchers believe that the remains of as many as 240 people, probably from a single ruling family, were interred there between roughly 3000 and 2500 BCE.[1] The structure itself is generally believed to have been used for ceremonial purposes, and its orientation—towards the point where the sun rises at the summer solstice—is what has led many to think it might have been designed to serve as a kind of astronomical observatory.

Ignoring the crowd of tourists, we position ourselves behind the central stone to note the position of the rising sun in relation to the 'heel stone' on the horizon more than 60 metres away. Today, on the morning of the summer solstice, the sun rises in the northeast, just to the left of the heel stone. It's easy to imagine that this day—the longest of the year and the only one on which the sun rises to the north side of the heel stone—would have been the occasion for some kind of ceremony in ancient times; that the entire community would have gathered at dawn to watch as someone with special authority—perhaps a priest, perhaps the local chief or ruler—confirmed the position of the rising sun. It's also easy to imagine the sense of order in the universe that would have come from knowing exactly when and where the sun would change course.

Tomorrow the sun will rise behind the heel stone, and it will continue its (apparent) journey towards the south for the next six months. Then in late December, at the winter solstice, the sun will appear to reverse course and begin travelling northwards again. Many centuries after people first gathered at Stonehenge, the Romans would celebrate this day as marking the annual 'rebirth' of the sun—the high point of the festival they called Saturnalia. And in the fourth century CE, the Christians in Rome would choose this same time of the year to celebrate the birth of their risen lord. Christmas was to combine the unrestrained revelry of the Roman midwinter festival, marked by feasting, gift-giving, and general merriment, with the celebration of the coming to earth of a deity incarnate.

Looking Back from Stonehenge

There are a few concepts, shared by virtually all human cultures, that seem fundamental to what we call religion: powerful gods, sacred places, a life of some kind after death, the presence in the physical world of spirits that interact with humans in various ways. These concepts are so old and so widespread that no one can say where or when they first emerged.

Three Worlds

Historically, it seems that humans around the globe have imagined the world to consist of three levels—sky, earth, and underworld. The uppermost level, the sky, has typically been considered the home of the greatest deities. Exactly how this concept developed is impossible to know, but we can guess that the awesome power of storms was one contributing factor. Another was very likely

◀ Stonehenge (© Nick Hawkes/Alamy).

The 'high place' at Petra, Jordan (Roy C. Amore).

the apparent movement of the sun, the stars, and the planets across the sky. Observing the varying patterns could well have led early humans to believe that the heavenly bodies were living entities animated by their own individual spirits—in effect, gods and goddesses.

The very highest level, in the heavens above the clouds and stars, was thought to be the home of the highest deity, typically referred to by names such as Sky Father, Creator, or King of Heaven. This deity—invariably male—was the forerunner of the god of the monotheistic religions. Under the earth lived the spirits of serpents (surviving as the cobras, or **nagas**, in the religions of India) or reptilian monsters (surviving in dragon lore); perhaps because they were associated with dark and hidden places, they were usually imagined as evil. Finally, between the sky and the underworld

lay the earth: the intermediate level where humans lived.

Sacred Places

Around the world, there are certain types of places where humans tend to feel they are in the presence of some unusual energy or power. Such places are regarded as set apart from the everyday world and are treated with special respect. Among these sacred places (the word 'sacred' means 'set aside') are mountains and hilltops—the places closest to the sky-dwelling deities. In the ancient Middle East, for instance, worship was often conducted at ritual centres known simply as '**high places**'. People gathered at these sites to win the favour of the deities by offering them food, drink, praise, and prayer. One widely known example is the altar area on the cliff above the ancient city of Petra in Jordan (familiar to many people from the Indiana Jones films).

Great rivers and waterfalls are often regarded as sacred as well. And in Japan virtually every feature of the natural landscape—from great mountains and waterfalls to trees and stones—was traditionally believed to be animated by its own god or spirit (*kami*).

Animal Spirits

Another common and long-standing human tendency has been to attribute spirits to animals, either individually or as members of a family with a kind of collective guardian spirit. For this reason, traditional hunting societies have typically sought to ensure that the animals they kill for food are treated with the proper respect, lest other members of those species be frightened away or refuse to let themselves be caught.

In addition, body parts from the most impressive animals—bulls, bears, lions, eagles—have often been used as 'power objects', to help make contact with the spirits of these animals. In many cultures, people have attributed magical properties to objects such as bear claws or eagle feathers, wearing them as amulets or hanging them in the doorways of their homes for protection from evil spirits.

Death and Burial

From ancient times, humans have taken great care with the burial of their dead. The body might be positioned with the head facing east, the 'first direction', where the sun rises, or placed in the fetal position, suggesting a hope for rebirth into a different realm. These burial positions in themselves would not be enough to prove a belief in an afterlife; however, most such graves have also contained, along with the remains of the dead, 'grave goods' of various kinds. Some of these provisions for the afterlife likely belonged to the person in life; some appear to be specially made replicas; and some are rare, presumably costly items such

A reconstruction of an Egyptian burial from the fourth century BCE at the British Museum in London; the naturally preserved body of a man is surrounded by a variety of grave goods (Alex Segre/Alamy).

as precious stones. Apparently the living were willing to sacrifice important resources to help the dead in the afterlife.

The belief that deceased ancestors can play a role in guiding the living members of their families appears to be especially widespread. Traditions such as the Japanese **Obon**, the Mexican **Day of the Dead**, and the Christian **All Saints Day** and **Hallowe'en** all reflect the belief that the souls of the dead return to earth once a year to share a ritual meal with the living.

Why Are Humans Religious?

The reasons why humans tend to be religious are far too numerous and complex to be reduced to a single answer. All we can say with any certainty is that religion seems to grow out of human experiences: from the fear of death to the hope for a good afterlife, from the uncertainty surrounding natural events to the sense of control over nature provided by a priest who could predict the change of seasons and the movement of the planets. Religion emerges through the experience of good or bad powers that are sensed in dreams, in sacred spaces, and in certain humans and animals.

Religion has many emotional dimensions, including fear, awe, love, and hate. But it also has intellectual dimensions, including curiosity about what causes things to happen, a sense of order in the universe that suggests the presence of a creator, and the drive to make sense out of human experience.

The nature of religious belief and practice has changed through the centuries, so we must guard against taking the religion of any particular time and place as the norm. What we can safely say is that religion is such an ancient aspect of human experience that it has become part of human nature. For this reason some scholars have given our species, *Homo sapiens*, a second name: *Homo religiosus*.

❧ TEN WAVES OF RELIGION

Most of the chapters in this book focus on individual religions, but it may be useful to begin with a broader perspective. What follows is a brief overview of some of the major developments in the history of what the late Canadian scholar Wilfred Cantwell Smith called 'religion in the singular', meaning the history of human religiosity in the broadest sense.

Looking forward from ancient Stonehenge, we can see a number of patterns emerge in different parts of the world, some of them almost simultaneously. Around 500 BCE, for example, several new religious traditions began to form under the

leadership of a great prophet or sage. And by the first century of the Common Era, the concept of a god born in human form was taking root in many parts of the world.

The history of religion is complex, and any attempt to explain broad patterns and trends runs the risk of oversimplification. Even so, if we want to understand how apparently similar ideas might have taken root in cultures that are otherwise very different, it may be useful to think of the way, over time, an island is shaped by the waves that break on its shores. At the most fundamental level, every wave adds some sand and takes some away, so that the contours of the shoreline are constantly changing. In addition, however, great storms occasionally carry the seeds of new vegetation from one island to another, modifying the environment of the second island and creating new conditions that will support other new species, some of which may be very similar to those already living on the first island.

In the same way, some religious ideas may actually have been carried from their places of origin to other cultures, while others may have developed more or less independently, in response to changing environmental—or social, or economic—conditions.

Just as a great storm will bring new plants to the shore, some of which will take root and eventually choke out earlier arrivals, so from time to time major 'waves' have introduced new religious concepts and practices to different human cultures. Where the soil and climate were suitable, the new elements were able to take root, and in time some of them may have replaced older ones.

Countless small waves have undoubtedly caused additional changes of local importance, but we will focus on the big waves, the ones that have brought similar changes to several traditions around the world. Although the following discussion identifies ten such waves, they are by no means the only ones: other scholars would likely propose somewhat different lists.

Wave 1: Shamanism

One very early wave appears to have carried the ritual specialist—in essence, a kind of priest—that we know today as a **shaman**. (Other terms include 'medicine man', 'soul doctor', and 'witchdoctor'.) The word 'shaman' comes from a specific central Asian culture, but it has become the generic term for a person who acts as an intermediary between humans and the spirit world.

Hunting Rituals

Many ancient cave drawings depict hunting scenes in which a human figure seems to be performing a dance of some kind. Based on what we know of later hunting societies, we can guess that the figure is a shaman performing a ritual either to ensure a successful hunt or to appease the spirits of the hunted species.

It's not hard to imagine why such societies would have sought ways to influence the outcome of the hunt. Indeed, it seems that the more dangerous the endeavour, the more likely humans were to surround it with rituals. As the anthropologist Bronislaw Malinowski pointed out in his book *Magic, Science and Religion*, the Trobriand Islanders he studied did not perform any special ceremonies before fishing in the lagoon, but they never failed to perform rituals before setting out to fish in the open ocean. This suggests that religious behaviour is, at least in part, a way of coping with dangerous situations.

In addition, though, as we have seen, early humans believed that the spirits of the animals they hunted had to be appeased. Thus a special ritual might be performed to mark the first goose kill of the season, in the hope that other geese would not be frightened away from the hunting grounds.

Such rituals reflect humans' concern over the future food supply, but they also reveal something about the nature of human belief in spirits. From very ancient times, it seems, humans have believed that the spirit—whether of an animal killed

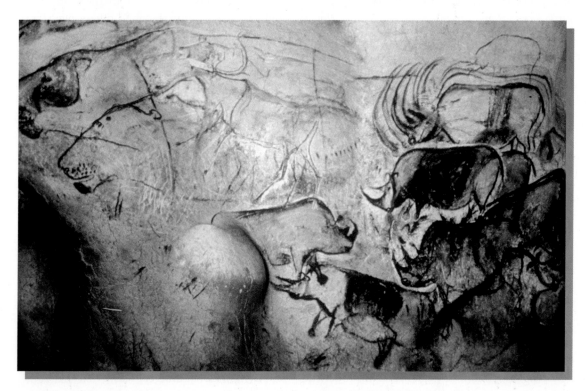

Animal images from the Chauvet cave in southern France, dated c. 30,000 BCE (AP photo/Jean Clottes).

for food or of a human being—survives death and can communicate with others of its kind.

Coping with Unfriendly Spirits

The spirits associated with natural phenomena—from animals to storms or mountains and rivers—have typically been believed to behave towards humans just as humans behave towards one another. Strategies for dealing with unfriendly spirits, therefore, are usually based on what works with humans.

Many cultures have believed wild, uninhabited areas to be guarded by resident spirits. In some cases these spirits have taken the form of monsters or mythical beasts; in others, of 'little people' such as trolls (common in the folklore of Scandinavia, for example).

Unfriendly spirits were of particular concern to those who ventured into the forest as hunters or gatherers, but they were not confined to the wilderness. Pain and disease of all kinds—from toothache to appendicitis to mental illness—were also attributed to possession by malevolent spirits or demons. In Sri Lanka, those suffering from certain illnesses were advised to have a shaman sacrifice a chicken as an offering to the 'graveyard demon', effectively bribing him to go away; in such cases a second chicken, still alive, would be given to the shaman who performed the ritual. Another approach was to frighten the demon away, either by threatening to invoke another, stronger spiritual power, such as the spirit guide of the shaman, to drive him off, or by making threatening gestures or loud noises. The firecrackers still used in some East Asian rituals are examples of the latter approach.

The Shaman

The most important resource of all, however, has been the shaman. Shamans are still active in a number of cultures today. The way they operate varies, but certain patterns seem to be almost universal, which in itself suggests that the way of the shaman is very ancient. Sometimes the child of a shaman will follow in the parent's footsteps, but more often a shaman will be 'called' to the role by his or her psychic abilities, as manifested in some extraordinary vision or revelation, or perhaps a near-death experience.

Candidates for the role of shaman face a long and rigorous apprenticeship that often includes a vision quest, in the course of which they are likely to confront terrifying apparitions. Typically the questor will acquire a guiding spirit, sometimes the spirit of a particular animal (perhaps a bear or an eagle, whose claws or feathers the shaman may wear to draw strength from its special powers) and sometimes a more human-like spirit (a god or goddess). This spirit then continues to serve as a guide and protector throughout the shaman's life.

To communicate with the spirit world, the shaman enters a trance state (often induced by rhythmic chanting or drumming). According to Mircea Eliade in his classic *Shamanism: Archaic Techniques of Ecstasy*, contact is then made in one of two ways. In the first, the shaman's soul leaves his body (which may appear lifeless) and travels to the realm where the spirits live; this way is described as 'ecstatic' (from a Greek root meaning to 'stand outside'). In the second, the shaman calls the spirit into her own body and is possessed by it; in such cases the shaman may take on the voice and personality of the spirit, or mimic its way of moving.

In either case, after regaining normal consciousness the shaman announces what he has learned about the problem at hand and what should be done about it. Typically, the problem is traced to the anger of a particular spirit; the shaman then explains the reason for that anger and what must be done to appease the spirit: in most cases the appropriate response is to perform a ritual sacrifice of some kind.

Wave 2: Connecting to the Cosmos

Our second wave is the one that inspired the building of structures like Stonehenge. People of the Neolithic ('new rock') era went to extraordinary lengths to create sacred areas by assembling huge stones in complex patterns. In some cases the motivation may have been political: perhaps a leader wanted to demonstrate his power over the people under his command. In others, however, the main reason undoubtedly had something to do with religion—for instance, the need for a public space where the rituals essential to the society—weddings, puberty rites, funerals—could be performed.

Discerning the Cosmic Cycles

Ritual centres such as Stonehenge may also have served purposes that we might think of as scientific or technical, but that their builders would have associated with religion. One very important function of priests was to track the seasons and determine the best time for seasonal activities such as

Stonehenge (David MacDonald).

planting. In addition to tracking the north–south movements of the sun, the people of the Neolithic era paid careful attention to the phases of the moon and the rising positions of certain constellations. The horizon was divided into segments named after the planet or constellation associated with that section. What we now call astrology developed as a way of understanding the cycle of the seasons and how humans fitted into it, collectively and individually. In ancient times no important decision would have been made without consulting an expert in the movements of the sun, moon, planets, and constellations. Even in modern times, many people, including political leaders, consult an astrologer before making major decisions.

Hilltop Tombs

We suggested earlier that two powerful reasons behind human religion are the fear of death and the idea of an afterlife. Ancient cultures around the world appear to have favoured high places as burial sites. Where there were no hills, artificial ones were sometimes built, at least for the most important members of the society. The pyramids of Egypt and the stupas of Asia are both examples of this practice. In the pyramids, shafts extending from the burial chambers towards important stars connected the deceased with the cosmos. Similarly in Buddhist stupas, a wooden pole— later, a vertical stone structure—extended above the burial mound to connect the earth with the heavens. Scholars refer to this kind of symbolic link between earth and sky as an *axis mundi* ('world axis').

Animals and Gods

Another common feature of Neolithic religion was a tendency to associate certain animals with specific deities. One very early example comes from the ancient (c. 7000–5000 BCE) city of Catalhoyuk ('forked mound'), near Konya in modern Turkey, where a small sculpture was found of a woman flanked by two large felines. James Mellaart, the archaeologist who first excavated the site in the 1960s, believed she represented a mother goddess seated on a throne. Although this interpretation has been disputed,[2] we know that the ancient Egyptians had a cat goddess named Bast who was revered as a symbol of both motherliness and hunting prowess. And the fierce Hindu goddess Durga is usually depicted riding either a lion or a tiger. (One Christmas card from modern India shows the Virgin Mary riding a tiger in the same fashion.)

A statue of the Hindu bull god Nandi at Lepakshi, Andrha Pradesh (© Hornbil Images / Alamy).

The Bull God

A similar pattern of association links the most powerful male deities with the strength and virility of the bull. In Greek mythology, the great god Zeus took the form of a white bull when he abducted the Phoenician princess Europa. A creature known as the minotaur—half man, half bull—was said to have been kept in a labyrinth beneath the ancient palace of Knossos, on the island of Crete, where frescos show people leaping over the horns of a bull. Greek temples often displayed bull horns near their altars. And in India a bull named Nandi is the sacred mount of the great god Shiva.

The association of the bull with the creator god can even be seen in Judaism, which strictly forbade the use of any image to represent its invisible God. When Moses returns from the mountain and finds that his brother Aaron, the first high priest, has allowed the people to worship an image of a golden calf or bullock, he denounces this practice as idolatry. Centuries later, one of Solomon's sons is severely chastised for installing bull images in the temples he has built.

Wave 3: Temple Religion

A third wave brought larger temples, more elaborate sacrificial rituals, and, with the latter, the development of a priestly class endowed with unusual power, prestige, and wealth. This wave played an enormous role in shaping many traditions, including Judaism, Chinese religion, and Hinduism, beginning roughly three thousand years ago.

Indo-European Priests

'Indo-European' is a modern term referring to a language family and cultural system that eventually stretched from India all the way through Europe; it does not designate any particular ethnic group. The Indo-European (IE) cultural system has been one of the most important in human history. It may have originated in the region around the Black Sea, but that is only one of many theories that scholars have proposed.

From the vocabulary of 'proto-IE', as reconstructed by linguists, it is clear that the IE people hunted, practised metallurgy, rode horses, drove chariots, and waged war, among other things. Farming, however, appears not to have been part

The Sacrifice

When they divided the Man [*Purusha*, the primal Person sacrificed by the gods to create the world], into how many parts did they disperse him? What became of his mouth, what of his arms, what were his two thighs and his two feet called? His mouth was the brahmin, his arms were made into the nobles, his two thighs were the populace, and from his feet the servants were born (Doniger O'Flaherty 1975: 26).

Three times a year all your males shall appear before the Lord your God at the place which he will choose: at the feast of unleavened bread, at the feast of weeks, and at the feast of booths. They shall not appear before the Lord empty-handed: All shall give as they are able, according to the blessing of the Lord your God that he has given you (from Moses' instructions to the people of Israel; Deuteronomy 16:16–17).

of their culture: the fact that the IE vocabulary related to agriculture differs from one place to another suggests that in farming the Indo-Europeans simply adopted existing local practices.

Everywhere the IE warriors conquered, they set up a social system with four basic divisions, the top three of which consisted of priests, warriors, and middle-class commoners. In India these groups are known respectively as the brahmins, kshatriyas, and vaishyas. In ancient times each of these groups had a special clothing colour; thus today in India *varna* ('colour') is still the standard term for 'class'. The priests performed rituals, kept the calendar, taught the young, and advised the kings; within the warrior class, the top clans were the rulers; while the middle-class 'commoners' earned their living as merchants or farmers. Finally, all local people, no matter how wealthy or accomplished, were relegated to the servant (shudra) class.

The four-level social system was given mythic status in the *Rig Veda*, according to which the world came into being through the sacrifice of a 'cosmic person' (*Purusha*). Out of his mouth came the brahmin priests, whose job was to chant the

sacred hymns and syllables. The warriors came from his arms, the middle class from his thighs, and the servants from his feet. Even today, this ancient hymn continues to buttress the social class structure of India.

Over a period of about a thousand years, beginning around 2500 BCE, the Indo-Europeans took control of the territories that are now Afghanistan, northwest India, Pakistan, Turkey, Greece, Rome, central Europe, and, for a while, even Egypt. Their religious culture was similar to most of its counterparts four to five thousand years ago, with many deities, including a 'sky father' (a name that survives in Greek Zeus Pater, Latin Jupiter, and Sanskrit Dyaus Pitar) and a storm god (Indra in India, Thor in Scandinavia); they sang hymns to female deities, such as the goddess of dawn; and they had a hereditary priesthood to offer sacrifices to the gods.

Although the IE people did not necessarily invent the system of hereditary priesthood, they certainly contributed to its spread. In addition to Hindu brahmins, examples include the ancient Roman priests and Celtic Druids. These priests enjoyed great power and prestige, and sometimes were resented by non-priests. (One ancient Indian text includes a parody in which dogs, acting like priests, dance around a fire chanting '*Om* let us eat, *om* let us drink'.[3])

Priests and Temples Elsewhere

We actually know when the first Jewish temple was built. After David had been chosen as king of both the northern kingdom of Israel and the southern kingdom of Judah, he captured the Jebusite city now known as Jerusalem. He transformed the city into a proper capital, complete with a grand palace for himself and an organized priesthood. His son Solomon took the next step, building the first temple in the mid-tenth century BCE. The priests attached to the temple soon made it the only site where sacrificial rituals could be performed.

The Jewish priesthood was hereditary. All those who served in the temple as assistants to the priests were required to be Levites (from the tribe of Levi), and priests themselves had to be not only Levites but direct descendants of Aaron, the brother of Moses who was the original high priest.

Priests became a powerful social class in many other parts of the world as well, including Africa, Asia, and the Americas. In some cultures they were a hereditary class, and in others they were recruited. Typically, the role of priest was reserved for males, females being considered impure because of the menstrual cycle; the Vestal Virgins of ancient Rome, who tended the sacred fires and performed rituals, were among the very few exceptions to the general rule.

Wave 4: Prophetic Religion

The word 'prophet' derives from Greek and has two related meanings, one referring to a person who speaks on behalf of a deity and one referring to a person who foresees or predicts the future. The terms are often conflated because prophets delivering messages from the deity often warned of disasters to come if God's will was not obeyed. The site of the temple at Delphi, Greece, where a virgin priestess under the inspiration of Apollo delivered prophecies, had been considered sacred for centuries, maybe millennia, before the glory days of classical Greece. It must have seemed a natural spot for making contact with the divine and receiving sacred knowledge: high up a mountainside, close to the gods, with a natural cave that resembled the entrance to a womb (*delphys* in Greek, representing the mysterious female energy) and a standing stone or *omphalos* (navel of the earth), representing the male energy and the connection between heaven and earth.

This sacred site dates back at least three thousand years, to a time before the rise of classical

The ruins of the temple at Delphi (Steven Vidler/Eurasia Press/Corbis).

Greece, when the oracle was believed to be inspired not by Apollo but by the earth goddess Gaia. Eventually males took control of the sacred site, but even in classical times the virgin priestesses would prepare themselves to receive Apollo's message by bathing in an artesian spring and breathing intoxicating fumes from a fissure in the earth—both water and fumes issuing from Gaia, the earth.

Those wishing to consult the oracle had to climb the mountain, make known their request, pay a fee, and sacrifice a black goat before their question would be put to the oracle. The priestess would take her place over the fissure and, in an ecstatic trance, deliver Apollo's message, which was typically unintelligible and had to be translated into ordinary language by a male priest. Interpreting the real-world significance of a prophecy was not so simple, however. In one famous case, a Greek leader who asked what would happen if he went to war with another state was told that a great country would fall; accordingly, he went to war—but the country that fell was his own. Similarly in the Oedipus myth, the oracle's prophecy that the infant would grow up to kill his father and marry his mother was fulfilled in spite of the measures taken to avoid that fate.

Abrahamic Prophetic Traditions

In 586 BCE the people of Israel were forcibly removed from their homeland and exiled to Babylon. The centuries that followed the 'Babylonian captivity' were the defining period for the concept of prophecy as it developed in the three monotheistic traditions that trace their origins to the prophet Abraham. Often, the Jewish prophets' messages were directed towards the people of Israel as a whole, warning of the disasters that loomed if they did not follow God's demands.

Christianity saw Jesus and certain events surrounding his life as the fulfillment of Hebrew prophecies. And Islam in turn recognized the Hebrew prophets, beginning with Abraham and including Jesus, as the forerunners of the Prophet Muhammad, the last and greatest of all, the messenger (*rasul*) who received God's final revelations. Muslims understand Muhammad to have been the 'seal of the prophets': no other prophet will follow him, since he has delivered the message of God in its entirety. As with earlier prophetic traditions, the Day of Judgment (or Day of Doom) and the concepts of heaven and hell are central to Islam.

Zarathustra, Prophet of the Wise Lord

Zarathustra (or Zoroaster) was a prophet figure who lived more than 2,500 years ago, probably in the region of eastern Iran or Afghanistan. Although we know little about his life, he left behind a collection of poems devoted to a 'wise lord' called Ahura Mazda. The religion that developed around his teachings, which came to be known as Zoroastrianism, played an important part in the development of monotheism.

The concepts of heaven and hell also owe a lot to the Zoroastrians, who believed that evil-doers were condemned to hell at their death, but that eventually a great day of judgment would come when the souls of all the dead would be made to pass through a fiery wall. Those who had been virtuous in life would pass through the fire without pain, while the rest would be cleansed of their remaining sin and permitted to enter paradise (a term believed to derive from a Persian word meaning garden).

The threat of hell and the promise of heaven were powerful tools for any prophet seeking to persuade people to behave as they believed the deity demanded.

Wave 5: The Energy God

Yet another important wave of change arrived around 2,500 years ago. Among the ideas it carried was one that, although it has never been the focus of a major tradition, continues to inspire important minorities in cultures around the world. That

Divine Energy

The Dao that can be told of
Is not the Absolute Dao;
The Names that can be given
Are not Absolute Names.
The Nameless is the origin of Heaven and Earth;
The Named is the Mother of All Things
   (from Laozi in the *Daodejing*; Lin Yutang 1948: 41).

This finest essence, the whole universe has it as its Self: That is the Real: That is the Self: That *you* are, Svetaketu! (from the *Chandogya Upanishad* 6.9; Zaehner 1966: 110).

idea concerns the nature of the divine and where it is to be found. Specifically, it suggests that the divine is neither a 'sky-father' nor an 'earth-mother', but a force, an energy, that is found by looking within. This is not a god that issues commandments, answers prayers, or in any way interacts with humans as a human. It does not create in the usual fashion of gods, or direct the course of history, or dictate the fate of individuals. In fact, some have suggested that it may have more in common with the principles of modern physics than with the traditional gods of most religions. This divinity simply exists—or rather, 'underlies' everything that exists.

Among the traditions that developed in the wake of this wave were the Daoism of China, the Upanishadic wisdom of India, and the pre-Socratic philosophy of the early Greek world.

Finding the Dao Within

The sage who became known as Laozi ('Master Lao') lived in northern China around 600 BCE. According to legend, he worked for the government as an archivist. At night students would visit his home to hear his words of wisdom about life, especially how to live in harmony with one's inner nature. But Lao had what we might call a

mid-life crisis. Dissatisfied with his job and the social and political life of his time, he is said to have left home and set out to the west, riding on a water buffalo (an event that became a favourite subject for artists). Apparently he had not even said goodbye to his students, but one of them happened to be working as a guard at the border. Shocked to learn that his master was leaving China, he begged Lao to record his teachings before leaving.

So Lao paused at the border long enough to write down the fundamentals of his thought in a series of beautiful, if cryptic, verses that were eventually collected in a small volume called **Daodejing** (or *Tao De Ching*), meaning the book (*jing*) about the *Dao* and its power (*de*). It became and remains one of the world's most influential books.

What did Laozi write that has spoken to so many through the millennia? He begins with what became one of the most famous opening lines in history: 'The *Dao* that can be described is not the eternal *Dao*. The name that can be named is not the eternal name.' In general usage the word *Dao* means 'the way', but here it refers to the mysterious energy that underlies all things. Laozi is warning readers that words cannot adequately describe the *Dao*. Ogden Nash, a twentieth-century poet noted

Laozi and the water buffalo; a sculpture from the Song dynasty (960–1279) (Burnstein Collection/Corbis).

for combining insight and humour, captured the same idea this way: 'Whatever the mind comes at, God is not that.'

In traditional cultures, people talk about the characteristics of various deities—their loving nature, or anger, or jealousy, or desire for a particular kind of behaviour. But the absolute, the eternal *Dao*, has no such attributes. Thus Laozi uses poetic imagery to give us some insights into its nature. Unlike Athena, Zeus, Yahweh, or Indra, the *Dao* does not have a 'personality', and there is no reason for humans to fear, love, or appease it.

Rather, Laozi says, the *Dao* is like water: it will take on the shape of whatever container we pour it into. Falling from the sky, it may seem content to lie in the hollow made by the footprint of an ox in the muddy road. Raining on the rocky mountaintop, it tumbles all the way down. Water seems malleable, passive and without a will of its own. Yet a mountain will be worn down by

the water over time. The water in the ox hoofprint will evaporate and return to the sky, to fall again when the time is right.

'That Is You': Sitting near the Sages of Old India

A worldview similar to that of Daoism took shape in northern India around the same time. The texts it produced, known as the **Upanishads** (a Sanskrit term meaning literally 'sitting-up-near' the master), were reserved for the most advanced students when they were composed, between roughly 1500 and 600 BCE.

What the Daoist sages called the *Dao* the Upanishadic masters called *sat* (usually translated in English as 'being', 'truth', or 'the real'). In one Upanishad there is the story of a young man named Svetaketu who has just completed his studies with the brahmin priests. Back at home, his father, who is a king and therefore a member of the warrior class, asks Svetaketu what his priestly teachers taught him about the original source of all things. When Svetaketu admits that he was not taught about that subject, his father undertakes to instruct him in the secret wisdom.

The first lesson has to do with the need for sleep and food; then the real teaching begins. The father has Svetaketu bring a bowl of water and taste it. Then he has him put a lump of sea salt into the water. The next morning Svetaketu sees that the lump of salt is no longer visible; he tastes the water and finds it salty. We can imagine his impatience at being instructed in something he already knows. But his father has a bigger point in mind. He tells Svetaketu that just as the salt is invisible yet present in the water, so also there is a hidden essence present throughout the world. That hidden essence, the force that energizes everything, is the highest reality, the father says, and that reality is you (*tat tvam asi*; 'that you are'). The Upanishadic master is initiating his son into a new religious worldview that understands 'god' as an energy hidden within and sustaining everything. And that great energy, that ultimate reality, '*tat tvam asi*'—that is you.

The First Principle: Greek Philosophy before Socrates

The same wave influenced Greek thought around 2,500 years ago as well. The Greek-speaking philosophers of Ionia (now southwestern Turkey) began to ask the same questions as Svetaketu's father: What is the first principle, the first cause, the source from which all else comes? Starting from the science of the day, which held there to be four primal elements—earth, air, fire, and water—they wanted to determine which of those four came first. Although their methods were those of philosophy rather than scientific experimentation, their attempt to understand the causal principle underlying all things—without bringing in a god as the final cause—marked a major advance towards the development of the scientific worldview.

Later Theistic Mysticism

European religious thought eventually reflected the influence of this wave as well. German Christian mystics such as Jacob Böhme (1575–1624) would use terms such as *Ungrund* ('ungrounded') or *Urgrund* ('original ground') to refer to the divine as primal cause. Christian, Jewish, and Muslim mystics alike believed in a god beyond the reaches of human understanding.

Wave 6: Purity and Monasticism

At almost the same time that the 'energy god' worldview was establishing itself in China, India, and Greek culture, another spiritual development of great importance was forming in India. The earliest historical records come from the region of what is now northern India around 2,500 years ago, but the tradition itself claims to have much older roots. Its followers typically sought spiritual enlightenment through asceticism—intense bodily discipline. Their ethic was one of non-violence towards all creatures, and their goal was to perfect the human potential for purity of mind.

Ganges Spirituality

English has no specific term for the new type of religion that came into bloom in the region of the Ganges river around 500 BCE. By that time the Indo-European cultural system, including the religion of the brahmin priests, was firmly established in what is now northern India. We can never know for certain what earlier traditions that religion displaced, since the written sources we rely on were the products of the brahmins themselves. However, linguistic and archaeological data lend support to the theory that two of the world's great living religions—Jainism and Buddhism—were rooted in the pre-brahminic traditions of the Ganges region.

Along the banks of the river were many camps where spiritual masters of various persuasions operated what were in effect open-air seminaries. Though some of the teachers were brahmins, others were committed to the idea that it was wrong to harm any living creature. Their followers rejected the killing of animals for food, and some even objected to farming, because hoeing and plowing would harm organisms living in the soil. While the brahmin masters continued to perform their animal sacrifices, the masters committed to the principle of non-harm (*ahimsa*) denounced that tradition. Some of the latter—among them the Jaina master Mahavira—went so far as to require their disciples to cover their mouths and noses and strain their drinking water, in order to avoid causing harm to microscopic insects.

Leaving the world of day-to-day life to follow the path of spiritual enlightenment through rigorous ascetic discipline, the students who gathered around these masters took vows of poverty and celibacy, and considered themselves to have 'departed the world'. The Buddhist and Jaina monastic traditions trace their roots to these ascetics, and it is possible that Indian monasticism played a role in the development of Western monasticism as well.

One more difference between the Indo-European and 'Gangetic' cultural systems is worth mentioning here. In the IE system, priests were recruited only from the brahmin social class. In the Ganges tradition, by contrast, the notion of a hereditary priesthood is rejected entirely: anyone, however humble, can choose to lead the life of a holy person. As the Buddha would teach his followers, the status of the 'true brahmin' is not a birthright, but must be earned through meritorious conduct.

Wave 7: Mystery Religion

'Mystery religion' refers to a wave of Greek and Roman traditions in which the core teachings and rituals were kept secret from outsiders and revealed only to those prepared to undergo initiation in the hope of securing blessings during this life and a heavenly paradise in the afterlife. Such religions became so popular during the Roman period that they presented a threat to the power and influence of the official Roman priesthood (not to be confused with the Roman Catholic priesthood).

The Eleusinian mystery tradition may be the oldest. Named for an ancient Greek town called Eleusis, it grew out of the myth of the young Persephone or Kore ('girl') who is abducted by the god of the dead (Hades) and taken down into the underworld. With the disappearance of this young girl—a potent symbol of growth and fertility—everything on earth begins to die. This imperils not only humans but the gods themselves, who depend on humans to feed them through sacrifices. The girl's mother, Demeter, is therefore allowed to descend into the underworld and bring her back.

Scholars understand the Persephone myth to be based on the seasonal cycles of stagnation during the winter and renewal in the spring. Members of her cult believed that by identifying themselves with the dying and rising goddess through the celebration of seasonal rituals, they too would triumph over death.

Initiates into the mysteries associated with the god Dionysus were also following a very ancient tradition. Through rituals that included the drinking of wine, ecstatic dancing, and, perhaps, the eating of mind-altering plants, participants were able to enter into ecstatic states of consciousness in which they believed that their god would ensure a pleasant afterlife. Another popular mystery cult, dedicated to the goddess Isis, had Egyptian origins.

Many scholars have suggested that mystery cults such as these may have influenced the development of Christianity. The early Christians were initiated into the new cult by undergoing baptism. They then joined an inner circle of people whose faith centred on the death and resurrection of Jesus and who hoped that by following Christ they would secure blessings during this life and a place in heaven after death. Although Christianity developed out of Judaism, its theological structure does seem to have been influenced, however indirectly, by the mystery wave of religion.

Wave 8: God on Earth

The Avatar

Long before the word 'avatar' came into use in computer games, *avatara* was a Sanskrit theological term for the 'coming down' of a god to earth. In the earlier stages of religion there were many stories of gods and goddesses who came down to earth, but there are two major differences in the avatar stories.

First, the avatar is a god in a truly human form—as a later Christian creed put it, 'fully God and fully man'—whereas the ancient gods

Avatar Gods

> For the protection of the good,
> For the destruction of evildoers,
> For the setting up of righteousness,
> I come into being, age after age.
>   (Krishna to Arjuna in the *Bhagavad Gita*; Zaehner 1966: 267).
>
> Have this mind among yourselves, which you have in Christ Jesus, who, though he was in the form of God, did not count equality with God a thing to be grasped, but emptied himself, taking the form of a servant, being born in the likeness of men. And being found in human form he humbled himself. . . . (St Paul to the Christians of Philippi; Philippians 2:6–7).

came down to earth as gods. For example, in the ancient Indian story of Princess Dhamayanti, the father of a beautiful princess holds a party to which he invites all the marriageable princes from various kingdoms. Four gods also attend the party, however, all disguised as the handsome prince Nala, whom the princess already plans to choose. She is disturbed to see five look-alikes, but is finally able to distinguish the four imposters from the real Prince Nala because the gods do not sweat and are floating slightly above the ground. She marries the human prince, and they live happily ever after.

Unlike the gods at Dhamayanti's party, the avatar gods walk on the ground, perspire, get hungry, sleep, and are in every way human. They are incarnated in a human womb, are born, grow up, teach, save the world from evil, and eventually die. As a Christian layman once told me, 'You have to understand that we Christians worship a god in diapers.' His choice of words was unusual, but his theology was solid, and it leads us to the second major change brought by the avatar wave.

This second innovation is the fact that the avatar god is a saviour figure in at least two ways. Not only does he save the world from some evil power, such as Satan or a demonic king, but he saves those who put their faith in him from hell and ensures that they have a place in heaven. In the religions of the avatar wave, the ritual of sacrifice is replaced by the ritual of placing faith in the saviour god.

The biography of the saviour gods follows a well-known pattern. Typically, the avatar god has a special, non-sexual conception. His mother is chosen to bear him because she is exceptionally pure, and an angel or prophet announces to her that the child she is carrying has a special destiny. The saviour's birth, usually in a rustic setting, is surrounded by miracles, which often include a fortuitous star or constellation pattern in the night sky. Wise persons foresee the child's greatness. An evil king tries to kill the baby, but kills another baby, or babies, instead. The child has special powers, and as an adult is able to work miracles. He typically marries and has a child before embarking on his religious mission. His death represents a triumph over evil and the cosmos responds with earthquakes and other natural signs. Upon dying, he returns to the heavens to preside over a paradise in which his followers hope to join him after they die.

The avatar wave hit Asia and the Middle East approximately two thousand years ago. Among Hindus its impact was reflected in the worship of Krishna; among Buddhists in the veneration of Amitabha Buddha (the figure who would become Amida in Japan), and among Jews in the rise of Christianity.

Krishna, Avatara of Vishnu

In some Hindu stories Vishnu is the ultimate deity, the god who lies at the origin of everything there is, including the creator god Brahman. Vishnu lies on his cosmic serpent, sometimes identified with the Milky Way, and out of his navel grows a lotus plant. From the lotus Brahman is born as the first of all creations; then the universe and all its material and spiritual energies follow. This is not exactly a mythic version of the big bang theory, but it comes close. Life evolves, over an unimaginable number of years, out of the divine energy at the centre of the universe. After the universe has run its allotted course, the process reverses from evolution to involution. Over an equally long period of time, eventually all things return into Vishnu, as if crossing the event horizon into a black hole. There all energy lies dormant as Vishnu sleeps, before the whole process begins again.

Another storyline about Vishnu sees him as the protector of the world. When earth gets into trouble, he comes down to save us. The first five *avataras* of Vishnu took the form of animals, and they protected the world from natural disasters in its formative millennia. The next four avatars are humans, the most important of whom is Krishna. His exploits are narrated in several different Hindu sources. The most famous is the *Bhagavad Gita*—the 'Song of the Lord', a small section of the epic *Mahabharata*. The latter tells of a great war between two houses of the royal family. Krishna is a relative of both houses and is recruited by both armies, but chooses to fight for neither. Instead, he agrees to drive the chariot of Arjuna, one of the five princes who lead one army.

At the beginning of the Gita, just before the battle, Arjuna asks Krishna to drive the chariot into the neutral zone between the two great armies, so that he can get a better look at the enemy. But when he sees his adversaries more closely, he loses his will to fight, telling Krishna that he recognizes among them his cousins, his old teachers, and others he remembers from childhood.

Krishna counsels him to take up his bow and fight, for that is his duty as a warrior. Arjuna has misgivings, however, and they begin a long conversation about morality or duty (dharma) and the eternal soul that cannot die even though the body may be killed in battle. Krishna teaches with such great authority that soon Arjuna asks how he knows so much. Krishna replies that he is a god of gods, that he is the energy behind all the categories of spirits and gods. When Arjuna asks for proof, Krishna grants him the eye of a god, with which he sees the splendours and mysteries of the universe as a god would.

In the end, Arjuna accepts the divinity of his chariot-driving cousin, acts on his advice, fights alongside his brothers, and wins the war. More important, however, is what Arjuna learns from Krishna about the many ways to lead a good religious life. These include the *yoga* (way) of good works (*karma yoga*), the way of deep spiritual wisdom (*jnana yoga*), and the way of faithful devotion to Krishna (*bhakti yoga*). Of these, the path of faithful devotion is the most highly recommended because it is the easiest and the most certain. The real saving power comes not from the wisdom or discipline of the individual, but from the saving power of the god. Krishna promises that those who practise devotion to him will go to his heaven when they die.

Another source offers stories about other parts of Krishna's life. We learn from it that Krishna was born under the rule of an evil king who was secretly part of a demonic plot to take over the world. One day King Kamsa is driving the wedding chariot of a female relative when an old man—a prophet figure—yells out to the king and tells him he is assisting in the marriage of a woman whose eighth child will grow up to kill him. The king is about to call off the wedding, but the bride pleads with him to reconsider, even promising that when she has children, Kamsa can do with them as he wishes. Kamsa agrees, the marriage takes place, and he proceeds to kill her children as they are born. On the night of the fateful eighth birth, the father is told in a dream to take the baby to safety with relatives across the river. This he does, replacing his child with a baby girl born the same evening.

When the king's guards hear the baby crying, they awaken the king, who smashes the infant's head on the ground. As the baby's soul rises towards heaven, it tells Kamsa that the baby who will grow up to kill him is still alive. That child is Krishna, and when he grows up he fulfills his destiny, saving the world from the evil represented by Kamsa and his demons.

Amitabha, the Buddha of Saving Grace

The avatar wave gave Buddhism the story of Amitabha Buddha, in which a prince intent on achieving buddhahood makes forty-eight vows, a number of which focus on helping others towards the same goal. Among them is a promise to establish a paradise free of all suffering, disease, and ill will, in which those who put their trust in Amitabha Buddha will be reborn after their death. His followers hope that if they sincerely profess their faith in his saving power, they will be rewarded with rebirth in that 'Pure Land'.

Jesus the Christ: God Come Down

The Christian doctrine of the trinity affirms that the one God exists in three persons: those of the father, the son, and the holy spirit. In formulating this doctrine, the Christians departed radically from the theology proclaimed by Abraham and Moses. There is no room in Jewish thought for an avatar god, but that was the direction in which Christian

thought developed. The prologue to the Gospel of John identifies Jesus with the divine Logos—the word of God that was present before creation. The New Testament says that Jesus 'emptied himself of divinity' and came down for the salvation of the world. His conception is through the spirit of god rather than by normal sexual intercourse. An angel announces the significance of the pregnancy to his mother. The birth is associated with a special star. Shepherds overhear the angels rejoicing and come to revere the infant, according to Luke's gospel. In Matthew's gospel, magi from the East follow a special star and bring gifts to the child.

For Christians, Jesus became the ultimate god who had died on the cross on behalf of his followers and rose on the third day. By participating in the sacred rituals—the sacraments of baptism and the eucharist—and placing their trust in Jesus as Lord, Christians could expect to go to heaven after their death.

So Christianity starts with the Hebrew scriptures and the monotheism of Moses and incorporates into them the avatar pattern, as well as elements of the mystery traditions, to form a new religion. Many Jews resisted these changes, but some accepted them in the belief that God had in fact offered the world a new dispensation.

Wave 9: Scriptural Religion

The ninth wave is hard to date. The earliest scriptures we have are the Zoroastrian Avesta of Persia, the Hindu Vedas, and the Torah of Judaism, all of which took shape approximately three thousand years ago. This wave came much later, however, when different groups began to insist that their particular scriptures were the literal words of God, and to make adherence to those scriptures the focus of their religious life.

The scripturalism wave manifested itself in Rabbinic Judaism in the centuries following the destruction of the Jerusalem temple in 70 CE. It emerged in full force with the rise of Islam, destined

The Word of God

We have sent it down as an Arabic Qur'an, in order that you may learn wisdom (from the Qur'an, 12:2).

In the beginning was the Word, and the Word was with God, and the Word was God. The same was in the beginning with God. All things were made by him, and without him was not any thing made that was made (John 1:1–3, KJV).

And the Word was made flesh and dwelt among us (John 1:14, KJV).

to become one of the two most influential religions of all time. It also played a large role in Protestant Christianity, in which the authority of scripture replaced that of tradition and the papacy.

Living by Torah

During the Jews' exile in Babylon the priests were not able to perform the traditional temple rituals, and so the Jews turned to the rabbis—scholars of the Torah with special expertise in Jewish law and ritual. In this way scripture began to play a more important role in Jewish life, a role that became even more important after the destruction of the second temple in 70 CE. Since that time, Jewish religious life has centred on interpretation of the scripture.

The Word of God

Two or three generations passed after the death of Jesus before the gospels were written, and the Christian canon did not take shape until well into the third century CE. But once the books of the canon were fixed, the Church came to emphasize scripture as a divinely inspired source of faith and practice. The Bible became as central to Christianity as the Torah was to Judaism. Christians commonly refer to the scripture as the word of God, and some believe that the Bible was literally dictated by God to its human authors.

God's Final Prophet

The scriptural wave reached its greatest height in Islam. The *surahs* that make up the Qur'an are believed to be the sacred words of God as revealed to the Prophet Muhammad by an angel, recorded by scribes, and compiled as a collection after his death. In its essence, therefore, the Qur'an is considered to be an oral text, meant to be recited—always in the original Arabic—rather than read. Nevertheless, the written Qur'an is treated with great respect. No other book is to be placed on top of the Qur'an, and before opening the book, the reader is expected to be in the same state of ritual purity required to perform the daily prayers.

The Lotus Sutra

The teachings of the Buddha were transmitted orally for centuries before they were first written down, some two thousand years ago. Although Buddhists revered these texts, their practice did not centre on them. Later, the Mahayana and Vajrayana schools added many more texts to their respective canons, but Buddhists in general did not attribute any special properties to the scriptures themselves. That changed in the 1200s, when a Japanese monk named Nichiren instructed his followers to place their faith in the power of his favourite scripture, the *Lotus Sutra*, and chant their homage to it, just as followers of the Pure Land school chanted homage to Amitabha/Amida Buddha.

Creation through the Word of God

A number of scriptural traditions have maintained that their scriptures were in existence before the creation of the world. The medieval book of Jewish mysticism known as the *Zohar*, for example, teaches that the Torah played a role in the creation of the world. The prologue to the Gospel of John in the New Testament talks about creation through the Word (*logos* in Greek). And Islam understands the Qur'an to have existed in the mind of God before creation.

This idea has ancient roots. In old Israel, Egypt, India, and elsewhere, it was assumed that the deities would not have performed the physical work of creation themselves, like ordinary humans: rather, like kings, they would have commanded that the work be done: 'Let there be light.' Thus the divine word took on a special role in later theologies. In traditional Hindu thought the goddess of speech, Vac, played this role. How could the scriptures—the actual words of the Torah, Bible, or Qur'an—be present in the mind of God at the time of creation, thousands of years before the historical events they describe? The answer for believers is that God knows the future. Outsiders might argue that this calls into question the concept of free will: If the deity knows everything in advance, how can humans be free to choose? What use is it to try to persuade people to do the right thing if the deity has already determined what each of them will do? Such questions have led to lively theological debates in many religious traditions.

Wave 10: Fundamentalism

Our final wave began to take shape in the mid-twentieth century and is still unfolding today. In time it may prove to have been merely a sub-wave of scripturalism. Nevertheless, for those of us living in the aftermath of 9/11, it often seems as if the current wave of violent religious fundamentalism represents something new in the human experience.

The term 'fundamentalism' was first used in the early twentieth century to refer to a variety of American Protestantism characterized by a fervent belief in the absolute, literal truth of the Bible. Adherents of this type of Protestantism reject all forms of secularism that they perceive as inconsistent with biblical tradition. Thus many send their children to religious schools because the public system teaches 'secular' values; some even refuse to vote because the democratic system is a human creation not mentioned in scripture. Not surprisingly, Protestant fundamentalists reject the authority of science and strongly object to the concept of evolution and the idea that the universe is billions of years old. In addition, many scholars have noted that fundamentalist groups tend to be male-dominated and to understand male–female relations and roles from a hierarchical, patriarchal perspective.

Similar movements exist within most religious traditions. Yet however convinced these groups are that their god is the only true one, and that their way of believing and worshipping is the only true way, the majority of their adherents have no desire to force their convictions on others. At the same time, within all these groups there are militant minorities who are prepared to use violence, whether to convert others, to defend the true believers, or to take revenge on perceived enemies. To understand how this wave has taken shape and is developing today, we will look at both regular religious fundamentalism and the more militant varieties in our concluding chapter.

A re-enactment of the crucifixion at a Christian rally in Washington, DC (Erik Freeland/Corbis).

🌿 WHY STUDY RELIGION?

The first and most obvious reason to study religion is that it exists. Not all humans would lay claim to religious beliefs, but humans in general have been religious from time immemorial.

A closely related reason is that religion has played such an important role in human affairs. People go to war over religious identities, make great art to serve religious communities or express their spirituality. People spend significant amounts of their time, money, and energy on religious activities and institutions. People seek to change social norms, or to prevent change, out of religious conviction. In short, religion so pervades the human world that it demands our attention regardless of whether it plays a direct role in our own personal life.

It is also common to study religion for more personal reasons. You may want to know more about the tradition you, or someone close to you, grew up in. You may want to study other religions in order to understand other people's beliefs, or to look at your own beliefs from a different perspective. You may also want to arm yourself with knowledge in order to bring others around to your way of thinking, or to defend your beliefs against the arguments of those who might try to convert you to theirs.

Insider versus Outsider

Most people learn about their own religion from their parents, their teachers at religious schools, or other members of the same religious community. Naturally, people tend to accept the teachings of their religion as true and assume that the teachings of other religions are false, or at least less true. As 'insiders' we may find it disturbing when 'outsiders' challenge our beliefs or suggest that the history of 'our religion' may not be exactly as we have been taught.

One of the advantages of a book such as this is that it helps us appreciate our own traditions from both insider and outsider points of view. When approaching an unfamiliar religious tradition, outsiders need to be sensitive to the ways in which it serves the needs of its followers. For their part, insiders need to understand how their own tradition looks from the outside.

The insider–outsider matter is more complex than we might imagine, for there are many kinds of insiders. Is your Muslim friend a Sunni or a Shi'i? If a Shi'i, does she belong to the Twelver branch or one of the Sevener branches? Which variety of Buddhism does your classmate practise—Theravada, Mahayana, or Vajrayana? If Mahayana, which school? Is your Christian neighbour Protestant, Catholic, or Orthodox? A Protestant may well be an 'outsider' to Catholic Christianity. A Zen Buddhist could have trouble seeing any connection between his practice and an elaborate Vajrayana ritual. Because each religion has many subdivisions, in these volumes we will speak of traditions in the plural. We hope our readers will keep in mind the diversity behind the monolithic labels.

Some Practical Matters

The East–West division of our two volumes is quite conventional, but it is problematic for several reasons. For one thing, the so-called 'Western' religions arose in what we now term the Middle East: they are Western only in the sense that they were widely adopted in the West. A related problem is that there is no clear dividing line between East and West. As the late Will Oxtoby pointed out in an earlier edition of this text, 'the East was everything to the east of Europe' until well into the twentieth century:

> The Orient began where the Orient Express ran: Istanbul. For some purposes, it even included North Africa and began with Morocco. . . . A century ago, Islam was thought to be an Eastern religion, and Westerners who studied it were called orientalists.

For those of us living in the twenty-first century, though, the biggest problem with the East–West division is that all the religions discussed in these volumes are now found throughout the world. Thus our Eastern volume focuses on traditions that developed in the East and are still centred there, while its Western counterpart focuses mainly on those that developed in the Middle East and now predominate in the Middle East, Europe, Africa, and the Americas.

For dates we use BCE ('Before the Common Era') rather than BC ('Before Christ'), and CE ('Common Era') rather than AD ('Anno Domini', Latin for 'in the year of our lord'). For dates that are obviously in the Common Era, the 'CE' will be implied.

Finally, it is difficult to decide whether a book like this should use diacritical marks on foreign words. Scholars of religion writing for other scholars typically use diacritics for precision in transliterating foreign terms into English. Since this is an introductory text, we have chosen not to use diacritics because students often find them more confusing than helpful. Anyone who wishes to do more research on a religious tradition will soon encounter them, however.

Whether or not you are religious yourself, we invite you to delve into the study of several religious traditions that have played central roles both in the lives of individual humans and in the civilizations they have built around the world.

Glossary

All Saints Day A Christian festival honouring all the departed saints; held in the West on 1 November.

Daodejing The Daoist 'Classic of the Way and Power', compiled roughly 2,500 years ago and traditionally attributed to Laozi.

Day of the Dead A Mexican festival honouring the dead.

Hallowe'en Now a popular secular holiday, held on 31 October; originally celebrated as the 'Eve' of All Saints Day.

high places Sacred areas located on hill- or mountain tops; such places existed throughout the ancient Near East.

naga A mythical cobra living in the underworld, often associated with water and fertility in Indian religions.

Obon A Japanese festival honouring ancestors.

shaman A type of priest, widespread among hunter-gatherer societies, who communicates with the spirit world on behalf of the people.

Stonehenge One of several ancient rock structures thought to have been constructed for ritual purposes.

Upanishads Hindu religious texts thought to have been composed between 1500 and 600 BCE.

References

Ballter, Michael. 2005. *The Goddess and the Bull: Catalhoyuk: An Archaeological Journey to the Dawn of Civilization*. New York: Free Press.

Doniger O'Flaherty, Wendy. 1975. *Hindu Myths: A Sourcebook Translated from the Sanskrit*. Harmondsworth: Penguin Classics.

Eliade, Mircea. [1951] 1964. *Shamanism: Archaic Techniques of Ecstasy*. Translated by Willard R. Trask. Princeton: Princeton University Press.

Lin, Yutang. 1948. *The Wisdom of Laotse*. New York: The Modern Library.

Malinowski, Bronislaw. 1948. *Magic, Science and Religion*. Boston: Beacon Press.

Zaehner, R.C., ed. 1966. *Hindu Scriptures*. London: Everyman's Library.

Notes

1. Marc Kaufman, 'Researchers Say Stonehenge Was a Family Burial Ground', *Washington Post*, 30 May 2008: A1.

2. Michael Ballter, *The Goddess and the Bull: Catalhoyuk: An Archaeological Journey to the Dawn of Civilization* (New York: Free Press, 2005).

3. Chandogya Upanishad I, xii, in R.C. Zaehner, ed. *Hindu Scriptures* (London: Everyman's Library, 1966), 84.

Chapter 2

Religions of the Ancient World

ꙮ Michael Desrochers ꙮ

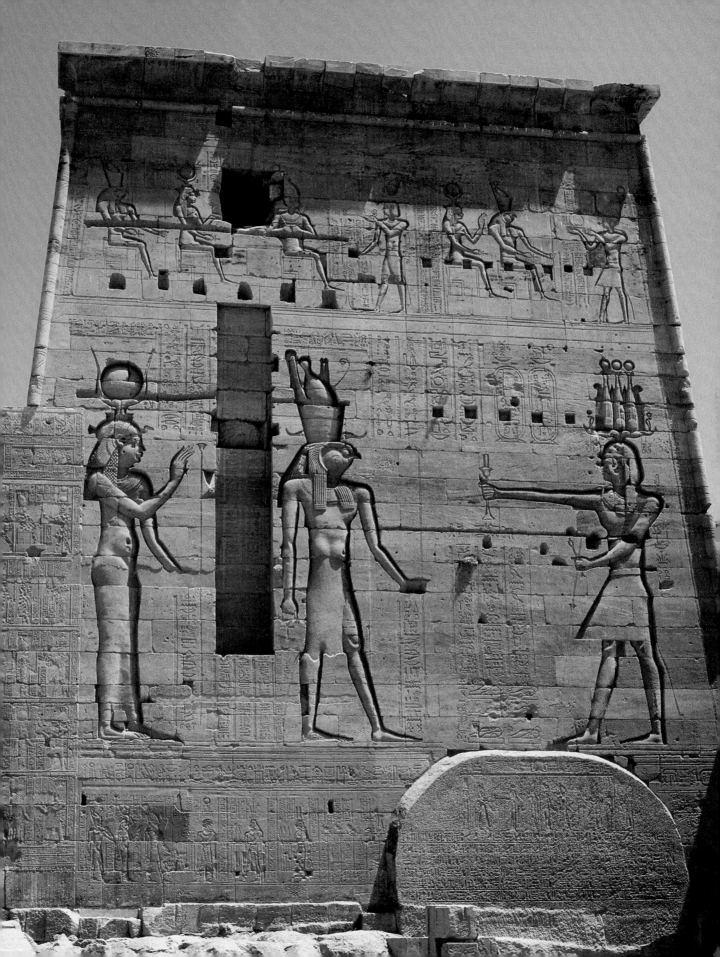

What is it that we are talking about when we discuss religion? Are our concepts of 'religion' in any way comparable to those of the ancient Greeks, Egyptians, and Mesopotamians? It's difficult to say, especially since none of those peoples had a single-word equivalent to the term 'religion'. We know that our word comes from the Latin *religio*. But even the Romans disagreed on its derivation. Some claimed that the word derived from *religare* ('to bind'), as in the unbreakable bond between humans and gods, while others found its roots in *relegere* ('to go over again'), as in the meticulous repetition of a sacred ritual. In fact, the two notions were complementary. The community sought to ensure the continuing support of its gods by faithfully adhering to ancestral customs, and each community had its own religious traditions, hence its own religion, as long as it participated in what the Roman philosopher Cicero called 'the pious cult of the gods'—piety being defined as 'justice towards the gods' (Scheid 2003: 23 and 26). In both cases, the emphasis was on the community rather than the individual.

A Greek phrase meaning 'to honour the gods by participating in customary practices' clearly approximates the Roman *religio*. A comparable Mesopotamian phrase translates as 'fear of god', an attitude of reverence for the divine manifested in cultic observances. The Mesopotamian verb translated as 'to be pious' also meant 'to remember' and 'to be wise'. For the Egyptians—described by the Greek historian **Herodotus** as the most pious people of the ancient world—the true religious practitioners were those who met the following standards spelled out in the New Kingdom mortuary text known as the ***Book of the Dead***:

> who raise up truth to the Lord of All,
> who judge poor and rich,
> who propitiate the gods with the breath of
> your mouths,
> who give god's offerings to the gods and
> invocation-offerings to the dead,
> who live on truth and gulp down truth,
> whose hearts have no lies,
> who detest falsehood.
> (Raymond Faulkner, trans., in von Das-
> sow 1994: 116)

This understanding of religion combined ethical conduct, doing justice to other humans, with the proper piety towards the gods.

A Roman grammarian of the second century CE defined religious people as those who participated in the state's traditional rituals and who avoided superstition ('superstitio'). Superstition was 'irrational' behaviour and might include anything from intentional disregard of standard state practices to improper pursuit of secret knowledge, placation of gods based on fear of their malevolence rather than trust in their beneficence, or overly emotional engagement with a particular god.

When Christians co-opted the term *religio* in the fourth century CE, they redefined it to refer solely to their own 'true' faith in a single god, reclassifying the old traditions as false—not religion but superstition. In 384 CE, Symmachus, the prefect of Rome, attempted to defend the original, non-specific meaning of *religio*, arguing that 'everyone has his customs, everyone his own rites; the Divine Mind has designated different guardians and different cults to different cities' (Schaff and Wace 1885: 415). Four decades later, however, the *Theodosian Code* (a compilation of all the laws enacted since the first Christian emperor, Constantine), outlawed traditional modes of piety as superstitions and legally defined religion from the single perspective of the Christian church.

◀ Reliefs from the Temple of Isis at Philae in southern Egypt show Ptolemy XII (right), ruler of Egypt in the mid-first century BCE, extending an offering to Isis and her son, the falcon-headed god Horus (Michele Burgess/Corbis).

Traditions at a Glance

In the Western context, the term 'ancient world' refers to the general region of the Near East and the Mediterranean as it existed in 'antiquity'—the roughly four thousand years from the late fourth millennium BCE to the early centuries of the Common Era. In that time many religious traditions emerged and evolved, sometimes independently and sometimes intersecting with one another.

Principal Historical Periods (early dates are approximate)

Mesopotamia

3200–2300 BCE	Early Dynastic (Sumerian era)
2300–2150 BCE	Akkadian dynasty
2100–2000 BCE	Third dynasty of Ur ('Sumerian Renaissance')
1900–1600 BCE	Old Babylonian period (age of Hammurabi)
1600–900 BCE	Middle Babylonian period
900–609 BCE	Assyrian Empire
609–538 BCE	Neo-Babylonian Empire (Chaldean dynasty)
538 BCE–	under 'foreign' rule (Achaemenids, Seleucids, Parthians, Sassanians)

Egypt

3100–2700 BCE	Early Dynastic (Archaic)
2700–2200 BCE	Old Kingdom (Pyramid age)
2000–1750 BCE	Middle Kingdom
1550–1050 BCE	New Kingdom
1050–664 BCE	Third Intermediate period
664–332 BCE	Late period
332–30 BCE	Ptolemaic (Greco–Macedonian) period
30 BCE–311 CE	Roman period

Greece

800–500 BCE	Archaic era
500–404 BCE	Classical era
404–336 BCE	Post-classical era
336–146 BCE	Hellenistic era
146 BCE–	Roman era

Rome

509–30 BCE	Republic
30 BCE–284 CE	Early Empire
284 CE–debatable	Later Empire

Persia

559–331 BCE	Achaemenid dynasty
247 BCE–224 CE	Arsacid dynasty
224–651 CE	Sassanian dynasty

Founders and Principal Leaders
The only ancient tradition to identify itself with a specific founder or leader was Zoroastrianism (and even today scholars disagree on the life and contributions of Zarathustra/Zoroaster).

Names of the Deity
Each tradition recognized hundreds, if not thousands, of deities, many of which also had multiple aspects, expressed in various epithets.

Authoritative Texts
None of the ancient traditions had a central text even remotely comparable to the scriptures of the Abrahamic religions. However, certain texts did become essential components of a canonic tradition: *Gilgamesh* in Mesopotamia and Homer's *Iliad* in Greece, for example.

Noteworthy Doctrines
All the ancient traditions were polytheistic, worshipping multiple gods, and all of them sought to promote moral/ethical behaviour. In practice, however, they all placed equal or greater emphasis on ritual of various types.

❧ ANTIQUITY

Geographically, 'antiquity' or 'the ancient world' encompassed a vast territory centred on south-western Asia, southern Europe, and North Africa but radiating as far as western and central Europe, Nubia and Ethiopia, central Asia, and Arabia. The major regions of southwestern Asia were Anatolia (roughly equivalent to modern Turkey), Syria (roughly modern Syria, Lebanon, and Jordan), Mesopotamia (Iraq), and Iran. Anatolia and Iran were primarily highlands. Syria included coastal lowlands, mountain valleys, grasslands, and desert. Mesopotamia, the land 'between the rivers', was the Tigris–Euphrates floodplain. For two millennia, North Africa was basically Egypt, the narrow floodplain on either side of the Nile, but it eventually came to include all the land along the south shore of the Mediterranean Sea. Finally, Southern Europe consisted of the Greek, Italian, and Iberian peninsulas—the Greek and Iberian being relatively infertile areas for which the Mediterranean offered significant compensation.

This varied landscape supported three basic types of communities: desert or highland pastoralists tending herds, agriculturalists dispersed across the countryside in rural villages, and concentrated urban centres. Over time, communities were organized on incrementally larger scales: urban states, territorial states, and eventually universal states/empires.

Map 2.1   Classical World of Greece and Rome

Map 2.2   Ancient Near East

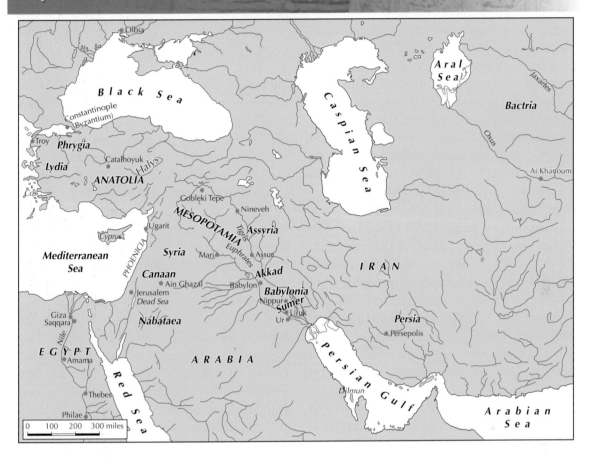

The great age of territorial states was the mid-second millennium BCE. Anatolia, Egypt, and Mesopotamia intersected and interacted in Syria, the land adjacent to the northeastern Mediterranean. That region remained central to the rivalries among the great first-millennium empires—Assyrian (ninth–seventh centuries), Neo-Babylonian (seventh–sixth), Achaemenid Persian (sixth–fourth), Alexander plus Hellenistic (e.g., Ptolemaic Egypt) (fourth–first), and finally Roman (third century BCE–fifth century CE)—and its development reflected the cross-fertilization of peoples, goods, ideas, and cultures. It was not coincidental that the land where Judaism and Christianity emerged was adjacent to the most heavily travelled crossroads, or that both approached their 'definitive' forms in the time of the last great empire of the ancient world.

The end of antiquity, at whichever date historians choose to place it, was marked by continuing antagonism between the western and eastern spheres. Even after the collapse of imperial institutions in the western Mediterranean during the fifth century CE, the Eastern Roman Empire kept up a struggle with the latest Iran-based (Sassanian) empire. That particular conflict served to weaken both empires, leaving them vulnerable to Arab forces and thereby contributing to the rise of Islam.

The earliest historically documented civilization was that of the **Sumerian** people of southern Mesopotamia. The Sumerians were followed by a succession of Semitic peoples: Akkadians, Amorites, Assyrians, and Aramaeans. In those early civilizations, identity was a matter of place. One became a Mesopotamian by moving into the region between the Tigris and the Euphrates; an Egyptian by moving into the valley of the Nile. The situation was quite different, however, with the Greeks (or Hellenes, as they called themselves). One did not become a Greek by moving into Greece. One was a Greek wherever Greeks lived: Greek mainland, Aegean Sea islands, Asia Minor (western coast of Turkey), Black Sea coast, Sicily, southern Italy, coastal eastern Spain, coastal North Africa. As for Rome, the Roman identity was initially reserved for residents of the city. As city expanded into empire, only citizens of that empire were classified as Romans. In 212 CE everyone within the empire gained citizenship.

At the heart of every empire was a constellation of cities. Then, as now, urbanites typically considered themselves superior to their rural counterparts: city-dwellers were urbane, sophisticated, and civilized, whereas those in the countryside—*paganus* in Latin—were unsophisticated, even barbarian. It was this association of the rural with cultural inferiority that, in the time of the late Roman Empire, would lead the triumphant Christian church to disparage the practitioners of traditional religions as unsophisticated, uneducated 'pagans'.

The four-thousand-year span (3500 BCE–500 CE) of antiquity can be broken down in several ways. Archaeologists, for instance, base their divisions on technology (Stone, Bronze, and Iron ages), while historians use periods (typically based on changing political regimes or large-scale cultural shifts). Thus Egypt's long history is broken down into multiple periods: Early Dynastic/Archaic, Old Kingdom, First Intermediate, Middle Kingdom, Second Intermediate, New Kingdom, Third Intermediate, Late, Ptolemaic, and Roman, each ruled by particular dynasties. As important as

chronology is, however, the brevity of this chapter demands a broader approach, focusing on examples from many places and times.

Prehistoric Beginnings

The origins of anatomically modern humans have recently been pushed back as far as 170,000 years ago. Some scholars believe that human symbolic behaviour—such as the association of red ochre with burials—can be traced to an equally distant time. The spectacular cave paintings created over a span of some twenty millennia—from roughly 30,000 to 10,000 BCE—seem to include many symbolic elements, even if there is no consensus on how they should be interpreted. Three more recent sites in southwestern Asia offer somewhat clearer evidence of symbolic behaviour in the period from approximately 9500 to 5000 BCE.

Gobleki Tepe in eastern Turkey represents the period of transition from hunting-gathering to agriculture. Excavations there have uncovered no evidence of residential buildings, but they have revealed several large structures apparently used only for ceremonial activities. Two large central pillars in the shape of a T are ringed by eight additional pillars connected by benches and incised with images of animals such as wild cattle and vultures, perhaps representing the threatening power of nature. While its purpose and meaning cannot be determined with any certainty, this hilltop complex includes several features closely associated with religion: imposing ritual architecture, suggestions of communal participation in socially binding ceremonies, perhaps including periodic public feasts, and natural imagery laden with symbolic meaning. Further testimony to Gobleki's 'sacred' nature is found in the fact that the site was deliberately buried beneath tonnes of earth when it was abandoned around 8000 BCE.

Catalhoyuk, introduced in Chapter 1, was an early agricultural town, inhabited from approximately 7400 to 6000 BCE, also in Turkey. Its growth evidently coincided with the desertion of other settlements in the region, and its unusual structure may reflect a new approach to social integration, prompted by the need to absorb disparate groups of people. Here the structures are clearly residential, but divided into two distinct zones: a drab domestic area and a 'sacred' area with platforms superimposed over burials and walls painted with scenes of humans baiting wild animals and often adorned with bulls' heads. Red ochre marked burials, platforms, plastered animal heads, and thresholds.

Its excavator believes that Catalhoyuk was as much a ritual centre as it was a centre of production, and as much a cemetery as a settlement. Many of the homes contain evidence of numerous burials and appear to have undergone frequent rebuilding. In effect, they are archives, holding

A seated female figure, attended by felines (probably leopards), from Catalhoyuk (SuperStock/SuperStock). Similar animals were later associated with goddesses in a variety of religious traditions. The heads of both the female figure and the animal to her right are modern reconstructions. The original heads have not been found, but evidence from later prehistoric sites in the ancient Near East suggests that they may have been removed and buried shortly after the sculpture was completed.

bones and material objects that appear to have functioned as symbolic texts, preserving transgenerational memory, with ancestors brought back to life, temporarily, with each rebuilding. Catalhoyuk exemplifies many features of religious significance: the association between religion and integration at both the family and community levels, boundaries, rituals, and memorialization, in addition to figurines and a repertoire of symbols used in the region for several millennia.

Excavations at the 'Ain Ghazal site in Jordan revealed burials not of human remains but of three dozen plaster statues and busts with prominent eyes. What they represent (gods, ancestral ghosts, worshippers?) is unclear, as is the reason for their burial (to facilitate rebirth? or simply to make room for the next generation of statues?), but they clearly suggest public ceremony of some kind. Archaeologists have also identified several T-shaped buildings from the site's later habitation phases as neighbourhood 'temples'; and a larger 'temple', on a bluff overlooking the settlement, likely served the entire community.

These sites reflect several dimensions of what we call religion: ritual, symbolism, community participation. The fact that those three dimensions persisted as enduring traditions suggests that they played central roles in human life.

DEITIES

Antiquity was home to tens of thousands of gods, many of whom we will never know. Most people recognize the names of the major Greek deities and their Roman counterparts: Zeus–Jupiter, Hera–Juno, Aphrodite–Venus, Ares–Mars, Athena–Minerva, Poseidon–Neptune, Artemis–Diana, Hermes–Mercury, Hephaestus–Vulcan, Demeter–Ceres, plus Apollo and Dionysus. These are the twelve great deities who, according to the ancient Greeks, inhabited Mount Olympus. But twelve is a paltry number compared to the hundreds and even thousands of gods invoked by other ancient civilizations. The Canaanite city of Ugarit alone made offerings to more than 100 gods; the Babylonian epic of creation, **Enuma Elish,** describes Babylon as the meeting place of 300 gods from 'on high' and 300 more from 'below'; **Hittites** worshipped 'the thousand gods of Hatti'; Egyptian texts and monuments named more than 1,500 deities; the Mesopotamians had some 2,500 deities; and one Sumerian text refers to 3,600 gods (3,600 being a symbolic figure signifying totality).

Not all these gods were equally god-like, of course. Divinity was a kind of continuum along which great gods, secondary gods, minor gods, demigods such as heroes, personified abstractions, and special groups such as nymphs, the dead, and divinized emperors all occupied different locations. Even among the great gods—the twelve Olympians, for instance, or the 'seven great gods' of Mesopotamia—one was supreme: Olympian Zeus, Enlil in Mesopotamia (until he was supplanted by Marduk), Teshub for the **Hurrians** and Hittites, the Canaanite El.

The defining characteristic of these gods was their supreme power, which for much of antiquity was associated with the fiercest forces of nature—in particular, storms. The most powerful humans being rulers, the supreme gods were rulers as well. Secondary gods played supporting roles, acting as

The *Epic of Gilgamesh*

There was an actual third-millennium BCE Sumerian king named Gilgamesh. Proclaimed a god shortly after his death, he became the subject of a series of tales. During the Old Babylonian period the stories were reorganized into a single composition that would be recast throughout later Mesopotamian history and would eventually spread across the ancient Near East. Unfortunately, no complete copy of the text has survived, but the two main versions—the Old Babylonian and the first-millennium BCE Standard—contain the basics of the plot.

The story opens with the citizens of the city of Uruk appealing to the gods for relief from their oppressive king. The gods respond by creating a wild, 'uncivilized' man named Enkidu to serve as a counterweight to Gilgamesh. The two become friends, however, and decide to gain lasting fame by killing the demon known as the Guardian of the Cedar Forest. The plan succeeds, but the fact that they kill the creature as it begs for its life turns what might have been an honourable victory into an act of murder.

The news of their adventure attracts the interest of Ishtar, the goddess of love and fertility. When Gilgamesh rejects her amorous advances, she shows her other side, as the goddess of destruction. She threatens to open the gates to the underworld and unleash the restive spirits on the world unless her father sends the Bull of Heaven to punish Gilgamesh and his people. Accordingly, the bull is sent, only to be slain by Gilgamesh and Enkidu. Then Enkidu makes a fatal mistake: instead of offering the animal as a sacrifice, he tears off its thighbone and hurls it at the gods. For this sacrilege Enkidu must die.

Enkidu's death transforms Gilgamesh, for now he has to face his own mortality—a reality that this son of a goddess has not previously considered. He sets out to discover the secret of immortality. Though several characters along the way warn him that he will not find the object of his quest, he is undaunted. Finally he reaches the island where the immortal Utnapishtim lives with his wife—the only survivors of the annihilating flood sent by the god Enlil in his rage against humans. Utnapishtim tells Gilgamesh the story of the flood, revealing that he did not achieve his immortality but was given it as a divine gift. In parting, Utnapishtim gives Gilgamesh the gift of a plant called 'Old Man Grown Young'—an early version of the fountain of youth. But Gilgamesh loses even that consolation prize when a snake steals it from him. In the end he returns home, chastened, wiser, and resigned to spending the rest of his life striving to be the best possible ruler, husband, and father he can.

judges dispensing justice to humans or as counsellors to the sovereign god, seeking to contain his 'stormy' power. Minor gods served as a kind of staff, carrying out unpleasant tasks for the more powerful deities. In Greece these lower-level gods, known as *daimones*, were understood to be agents of calamity and punishment.

While Athens was named for Olympian Athena, nearby Marathon, the site of the Athenians' victory over the Persians, was named for a hero named Marathon. **Gilgamesh** and Romulus were heroes elevated to gods in Mesopotamia and Rome, respectively, while the Greek **Asclepius** was worshipped as a hero in his homeland and eventually became a major god with shrines throughout the Mediterranean world. Herakles (Hercules) also was deified after performing his extraordinary labours and was widely worshipped as a benefactor and protector.

Among the mortals who were elevated to divinity were Alexander the Great and Augustus Caesar. Their status was comparable to that of the Egyptian rulers who identified themselves as the 'son of Re' or 'Horus' or various Mesopotamian kings who referred to themselves as the 'first-born son of Enlil'.

Athens erected public altars to such deified abstractions as Mercy and Concord. Rome built temples for Hope, Harmony, and Victory. Athena, goddess of wisdom, was the daughter of Zeus and Metis ('Crafty Intelligence'). Mnemosyne ('Memory') was the mother of the Muses. Ma'at ('Order') was an important Egyptian goddess, in perennial conflict with her rival Isfet ('Chaos'). Then there were various 'little' gods of specialized functions and limited powers, including the Roman gods 'Grain blight' and 'Ploughing wide furrows' and the Egyptian underworld deities 'Devourer of sinners' and 'Existing on maggots'.

The polytheistic nature of the ancient world is evident in the fourth-century BCE sacrificial calendars of the Greek town of Erchia, located near Athens, which list 59 sacrifices, to Olympian deities, Athenian state gods, local gods, and family gods, along with a number of otherwise unknown heroes and heroines, including the tribal hero from whom the Erchians claimed to descend.

Many gods had multiple identities. Zeus, for instance, was not only Zeus Olympios, the supreme god who dwelt on Mount Olympus, but also Zeus Stratios, leader of armies; Zeus Eleutherios, securer of freedom; Zeus Ourios, provider of favourable winds to sailors; Zeus Agoraios, overseer of marketplace transactions and oaths; Zeus Herkeios and Ktesios, protector of household land and property; Zeus Apomysios, who chased flies from sacrifices; and Zeus Hymettios, associated with Mount Hymettus. Were these nine different Zeuses or the same god identified by different locales and epithets? Apollo Smintheus ('mouse god') regulated plagues; Apollo Pythios was the god of oracles; Apollo Loxias was the god who 'spoke evasively'; Apollo Delios was patron of the island of Delos. As the patroness of marriage, the consort of Zeus was known as Hera Teleia; her Roman counterpart Juno Lucina supervised childbirth. Were the members of Juno's entourage—Vaticanus, who made infants cry; Cucina, who cared for infants in their cradles; and Potina, who gave drink to infants—separate deities or subordinate qualities of Juno herself? The same could be asked of the six powers—Order, Truth, Intelligence, Sovereignty, Health, and Immortality—who supported **Ahura Mazda** ('Wise Lord'), the supreme Zoroastrian god.

The earliest gods corresponded to natural phenomena: sun, moon, planets, heaven, grain, fresh water, storm. Mesopotamia's Enlil was 'Lord Wind'. The Sumerian goddess Inanna, depicted in the fourth millennium BCE as a reed gatepost, guarded the storehouses on which a community's survival depended. As the Tigris–Euphrates floodplain became urbanized in the late fourth millennium BCE, the deified elements of nature acquired social and political functions. Each city had its own patron deity, typically accompanied by a spouse and counsellors. Over time the gods of several cities or districts were connected to one another through complex family relationships, eventually leading to the development of a pantheon ('totality of gods').

The early patron gods were the equivalent of petty rulers, but as the more successful cities came to dominate their regions, their gods were elevated accordingly. For instance, the status of Marduk, the previously unimportant patron god of Babylon, received an important boost under Hammurabi (r. 1792–1750 BCE) and thereafter continued to rise until, in the Babylonian creation epic (composed towards the end of the second millennium BCE) he became the supreme ruler of the Mesopotamian pantheon. Egypt's New Kingdom rulers similarly elevated **Amun**, the patron of their home city of Thebes, linking him, as **Amun-Re,** with the sun-god Re, the dominant god of the Old Kingdom. Like feudal lords, numerous deities—each with a different local base and area of responsibility, under the direction of one pre-eminent leader and assisted by numerous divine servants—collectively ensured societal order. Multiplicity secured unity.

Greek gods were recognizably human, but on a grand scale. In stories they personified the extremes of human emotions and behaviours, and physical representations of them exemplified the human ideals of beauty, grace, and power. Egypt's earliest depictions of gods showed them in animal form, and throughout their history Egyptians portrayed their gods in various forms: as animals, humans, and sometimes hybrids of the two. While Mesopotamians initially used emblematic animals or symbols to represent their gods, by the late third millennium BCE the deities were represented as recognizably human both in myth and in visual form (statues, figurines, cylinder seals).

Anthropomorphic (human-shaped) statues were the prototypical representations of the di-

A wall frieze on the 'Ishtar gate' in Babylon, constructed c. 580 BCE, represented the god Marduk as a walking dragon; from a modern reconstruction in the Pergamon Museum, Berlin (Bildarchiv Preussicher Kulturbesitz/Art Resource NY).

vine, but some societies refused to depict their gods in any recognizable form. Among them were the Nabataeans—incorporated into the Roman province of Arabia in the second century CE—who used abstract symbols to represent their god Dushara, and the Syrians, whose sun-god Elagabal was represented by a large black stone. Another deity associated with a black stone was Cybele (the Magna Mater or Great Mother).

Although Babylonians fashioned statues of Marduk, they also described him as 'impossible to conceive, impossible to visualize'. In some cases the very names of the gods or the epithets attached to them identified their principal characteristics. Even so, most gods shared a number of characteristics in common. Thus Mesopotamian gods were described in terms that emphasized their transcendent power and knowledge: all-powerful, majestic, perfect, unsurpassable, exceptionally wise. A work from the second millennium BCE known as the *Babylonian Theodicy* declared: 'The divine mind, like the centre of heaven, is remote. Knowledge of it is difficult; humans do not know it.'

Intrinsic to Mesopotamian deities was *melammu* (literally, 'luminous power'), or 'divine splendour', an awesome and fearsome supernatural brilliance emanating from the gods, portrayed as a halo surrounding their heads. At Marduk's birth, the 'auras of the gods' clothed his body and encircled his head. The narrator of the Roman poet Ovid's *Fasti*, while praying to the goddess **Vesta**, 'felt the influence of celestial divinity, and the glad earth gleamed with a purple light' (Feeney 1998: 99). A comparable Egyptian term was *akhu*, 'radiant power'. Amun was praised: 'How great is your power! Your appearance is noble. You have surrounded me with your radiance' (Assmann 2001: 117). Egyptians placed under the heads of the deceased a disk-shaped object inscribed with an incantation (a **Pyramid Text**) in the belief that this would enflame head and body, thereby stimulating the process of divinization. Gilded veneers made Mesopotamian statues of deities appear to scintillate; and the Assyrians depicted gods with flames emerging from their heads and torsos.

In the third-millennium BCE, the Sumerians began to organize their thousands of gods in lists, typically with two columns: names in the left column and descriptions in the right. Eventually, bilingual lists were created, correlating Sumerian with Semitic gods: Sumerian Inanna was linked with Semitic Ishtar, for example. By the mid-second millennium BCE Mesopotamians were producing multilingual lists, recording multiple names for the same god. As political boundaries expanded and contact among different peoples increased, correlations among the gods of different cultures became increasingly frequent. A thirteenth-century BCE Hittite prayer addressed a goddess: 'You are queen of all the lands. In the land of Hatti you go by the name of the Sun-goddess of Arinna, but in the land which you made cedar [i.e., Syria], you go by the name Hepat' (David P. Wright in Johnston , ed., 2004: 190).

Berossus, a Babylonian priest in the third century BCE, wrote that the Persian ruler Artaxerxes II erected a statue of Aphrodite Anaitis (Greek for Persian Anahita) in Babylon and encouraged her worship throughout the Persian Empire. In the fifth century BCE, the Greek historian Herodotus had already equated certain Egyptian gods with their closest counterparts in the Greek pantheon. Especially after Alexander's conquests in the fourth century BCE, the Greeks identified foreign gods with their own: Zeus with Amun and Marduk, Aphrodite with Ishtar, Demeter and Hermes with the Egyptian deities **Isis** and Thoth. Some scholars see this trend as marking a fusion of religious traditions and call it syncretism; others see it simply as a reflection of the need for peoples from different traditions to communicate with one another. Whatever the motivation, the second-century CE Roman satirist Apuleius captured the phenomenon in his *Metamorphoses* (also known as *The Golden Ass*):

The unparalleled divine power is worshipped by the whole world in varied forms, with different rites and diverse names. The first-born Phrygians call me Mother of the Gods

[Cybele]. . .; indigenous Athenians, Minerva [Athena]. . .; the wave-washed Cypriots, Venus [Aphrodite] of Paphos; the archers of Crete, Dictynna Diana [Artemis]; the trilingual Sicilians, Stygian Proserpina; the Eleusinians, the most ancient goddess Ceres [Demeter]; different people call me Juno, or Bellona, or Hecate, or Rhamnusia; those warmed by the first rays of the rising god of the sun—the Ethiopians, Arians [i.e., Africans], and Egyptians steeped in ancient learning—worship me with my own rites and call me by my real name: Isis (Beard et al. 1998: vol. 2, 299).

If, as this passage suggests, all that differed were the names, how many goddesses were there—eleven or one?

🌿 MYTH

Myth served numerous functions in the ancient world. It entertained, acculturated, moralized, explicated, startled, inspired, mocked, mirrored. It offered insight into human nature, social and political relations, and cosmic operations. It even attempted to translate into human terms the seemingly untranslatable. Myth touched on the everyday even as it addressed the ultimate human questions: how the world originated (cosmogony); how it was structured (cosmology); how the gods came into being (theogony); the nature of the gods (theology); how humans came into existence (anthropogony); the purpose of human life; the relationship between fate and free will; how the gods could be seen as just when they allowed evil to exist in the world (theodicy); the end of life and what would come next (eschatology).

In their myths the ancients used analogy to address several of the 'big' questions, especially those concerning origins and identity. There was no creation *ex nihilo* (out of nothing). Creation represented the transformation of shapeless preexistence ('before two things had developed') into

Egypt's boy-king Tutankhaton/Tutankhamun (c. 1341–1323 BCE), depicted as the sun-god Re emerging from the primeval blue lotus, signifying the (re)emergence of life (Sandro Vannini/Corbis).

substantial existence, of potentiality into actuality. Creation gave shape to the amorphous, which both Egyptians and Mesopotamians envisioned as primeval waters. To explain how that transformation came about, both of those civilizations used two analogical models. The first was nature, especially as seen in the daily circuit of the sun and the annual changes of season. Since life in Egypt depended on the Nile and its annual inundation, one Egyptian creation story envisioned an earthen mound with a lotus plant emerging from the receding primeval waters. By the time of the New Kingdom, sun and lotus were merged iconographically.

The second analogical model for creation was human behaviour. Thus some things came into being through sexual intercourse, some through the spoken word, and some through labour. One Egyptian creation myth personified the undifferentiated waters as a primeval god named Atum ('completed'). But in fact he was far from complete: aware of his lone(li)ness, he impregnated himself and gave birth to twin gods, a male named Shu ('air') and a female named Tefnut ('moisture'); also known, respectively, as Ankh ('life') and Ma'at ('order'). Life was perpetual recurrence while order was perpetual sameness. Androgynous Atum passed on to his sexually dimorphic offspring his 'life force' (*ka*), which they in turn implanted in their children Geb ('earth') and Nut ('sky'). In this way singularity became duality became plurality, which in time became complexity and diversity, including deadly competition. In fact, it was the rivalry among the fourth-generation descendants of Geb and Nut—**Osiris** and Seth, with their sister-consorts Isis and Nephthys—that formed the basis of Egypt's most pervasive myth. (Osiris is murdered by Seth, but is temporarily resurrected by Isis, who manages to conceive their son Horus before Osiris returns forever to the underworld; when Horus is grown, he takes up the struggle with Seth.) Eventually Atum was further differentiated into Re, the sun-god whose daily passage represented eternal recurrence; Heka, transformational power; Sia, imagination; and Hu, the word that turned image into creature. The creator, 'the one who made himself into millions', initiated differentiation and multiplication.

Another Egyptian creator-deity was Ptah, the city-god of Memphis, who brought everything into existence through thought and speech. In the beginning was the thought; then came the word. Creation stories multiplied to the point that every late Egyptian temple had a different creation story in which its own god played the role of creator. Isis was 'mistress of the word in the beginning'. Another goddess created the entire world by proclaiming

From the Mesopotamian Creation Epic, *Enuma Elish*

Enuma Elish (*the first two words of the piece, translated as 'when on high'*) *was probably composed towards the end of the second millennium* BCE *as a kind of literary propaganda in support of Babylonian claims to supremacy in Mesopotamia. Crediting Marduk, the patron of Babylon, with the defeat of the primordial creatures whose remains he uses to fashion the universe (essentially by naming everything), it elevates him to the position of supreme god and in so doing legitimizes Babylon's rise to dominance. The opening lines (I: 1–10), which allude to pre-existent potentiality, include references to several of the concepts that were also fundamental to Egyptian creation myths: procreation, naming, fashioning, and land emerging from primeval waters (the female Tiamat represents salt water; the male Apsu, fresh underground water).*

When on high heaven had yet no name,
Nor below had earth received its name,
Primordial Apsu, their begetter,
And fashioner Tiamat, who bore them all,
Mingled their waters together;
No pastures had yet formed, no reedbeds had emerged;
No single god had yet appeared,
No name spoken, no destiny decreed;
Then the gods within them came to life.
Their names pronounced, Lahmu and Lahamu emerged.

just seven magic words. Words—the union of name and object—were the basis of identity.

Ancient Cosmology

In Greek accounts, such as **Hesiod**'s *Theogony*, as in their Mesopotamian and Egyptian counterparts, the first order of creation was the divine. Cosmogony started with theogony. Next came cosmology, the organization of the universe. Egyptians, Greeks, and Mesopotamians all envisioned a tripartite cosmos: heaven, earth, and a **netherworld** of some kind. According to a Mesopotamian text known as *Atrahasis*, the process of organization began with a lottery in which Anu won heaven, Enlil the earth, and Ea the underground waters.

Cosmic order was the goal, but conflict was the norm. So threatening was **Tiamat** (who gave birth to a brood of sea monsters) that Marduk killed her and fashioned the universe out of her carcass. In Greece, Zeus led his generation of gods in overthrowing the older Titans, headed by his father Cronus, who in his time had overturned his own progenitor, Uranus. Similarly in Egypt, the rivalry that led Seth to murder his brother Osiris continued with Horus, the son of the murdered Osiris. We have already noted the ongoing struggle between order and chaos in the persons of Ma'at and Isfet. And the sun-god Re, whose light represented life, descended into the netherworld every night to do battle with the monster Apophis, who symbolized evil because he threatened the source of life itself.

In a world where order was so tenuous, it was essential to establish institutions, protocols, and responsibilities for the gods. One Sumerian myth listed 94 components of the cosmic state, including kingship, governorship, power, knowledge, triumph, rebellion, godhood, priesthood, temple servant, sanctuary, truth, slander, righteousness, dishonesty, and justice (that is, political and religious institutions and ethical standards). Within this cosmic state, every god was assigned a specific responsibility. The goddess Ninti, whose name literally meant 'Lady (*nin*) rib (*ti*)', had the single duty of nursing the sore rib of Enki, the Sumerian god of wisdom. One god was assigned to serve as the divine inspector of canals, another as the divine architect, yet another as the guardian of boundaries. Such appointments were made permanent when they were inscribed on the Tablet of Destinies, which played a role in several myths. In one, the goddess Inanna stole Enki's tablet by getting him drunk. In another, the cosmic state ceased operating when the tablet was hidden. After defeating Tiamat, Marduk secured the tablet, which legitimized both his claim to kingship of the gods and his decrees for reorganizing the cosmos.

In cloudless Egypt, the most visible manifestation of order was the sun's daily course across the sky. As Re's earthly representative, the king was responsible for ensuring order. Thus each day his regimen re-enacted the sun's routine. Egypt's temples were not only the homes of particular gods but models of the cosmos itself. The walls that enclosed them separated order from chaos; processional passageways replicated the course of the sun; dim inner sanctums corresponded to the primeval darkness from which life and order emerged. In maintaining their kingdom's temples, Egyptian rulers secured *ma'at*, the continuing order of the cosmos.

In Mesopotamia, the more important gods might have enjoyed their work, but the lesser gods faced eternal drudgery on their behalf. Eventually they rebelled, forcing the major gods to find substitutes. Thus humans were created, formed of clay lubricated with the blood of a rebel leader named We. Humans (*awilum*) were partially divine (*ilum*), but they were flawed from the start because their progenitor We had challenged the cosmic order. Just as their life-source had been put to death for his 'original sin', humans would some day die and become spirit (*etemmu*). At the same time, because humans had inherited the mind (*temu*) of their dead ancestor, they knew that they were created to serve the gods, to toil daily on their behalf.

Name and ancestry defined human nature; divine will determined human function.

There are relatively few Egyptian accounts of the creation of humans. Among them are two **Coffin Texts** (inscribed on the coffins of elite but non-royal Egyptians during the Middle Kingdom). The account in Coffin Text 1130 is essentially a play on words: 'I created gods from my sweat while humans [*rmt*] are the tears [*rmwt*] of my eye' (Assmann 2001: 177). Coffin Text 714 explains that the creator wept because the other gods were angry at him. Tears streaming, he became temporarily blind, unable to see what his tears had produced. Humans were thus the imperfect products of blind anger and self-pity—quintessential 'human' qualities.

Classical myth also regarded humanity as flawed from the beginning. One tradition, recounted in Ovid's *Metamorphoses*, traced human ancestry to the Titans, the representatives of brute force, barbarism, and chaos, who were defeated by the Olympians, the advocates of law, civilization, and order. Thus humans were variously described as sprouting from soil irrigated by the Titans' blood, materializing out of their incinerated remains, or being formed from their flesh and blood and brought to life by the lightning bolt of Zeus. Ovid reproved humans for being—like the Titans—'contemptuous of the gods'.

Another set of traditions associated human beginnings with an 'original offence' of some kind. When Prometheus ('Forethought'), who fashioned humans from water and earth, stole fire for them, he gave them the ability to offer sacrifices to the gods, but that ability was tainted inasmuch as it was the result of a transgression. Similarly, Pandora ('Allgift') brought into the world a 'box' ('Pandora's box' was actually a jar) entrusted to her by Hermes, who instructed her never to open it; but she disobeyed: she opened the jar and let loose all the evils that would afflict humans for ever after. So dismal was Hesiod's view of humanity that, in his *Works and Days*, he lamented the contrast between the humans of his time, the so-called 'Iron

Race', condemned to toil and misery, and those of the first 'Golden Race', who neither toiled nor aged but feasted and lived like gods. Decline was inherent in the human condition.

Greek literature, in particular, confronted the fundamental flaws that humans could not overcome. In myth, epic, tragedy, and history, Greeks examined the consequences of Zeus' remark to Athena, at the beginning of **Homer**'s *Odyssey*, that greed and folly double the suffering that is the lot of humans. Humans always wanted more than they had and consistently overrated their own intelligence. They ignored divine warnings, thought they could deceive the gods, and refused to accept the limits imposed on them. Greek authors delineated those limits and demonstrated the tragic consequences of ignoring them.

The ancient Mesopotamian myths reflect a similar view of human nature. In *Atrahasis,* for instance, humans do not recognize any limit on procreation. Their numbers multiply so rapidly that Enlil, his divine rest disturbed by their din, sends a great flood to drown them all and relents—allowing the hero Atrahasis and his family to survive—only when Ea offers two solutions for limiting population growth: miscarriage and death. (There is an echo of this story in the *Epic of Gilgamesh* when the hero encounters Utnapishtim, another flood survivor who owes his life to the intercession of Ea.) The same pattern appears in Greece, where the Olympians were said to have sent a 'liquidating' flood in retaliation for a deceitful sacrifice. In this case the survivors, Deucalion and Pyrrha, revived humanity (*laos*) by tossing stones (*laas*) over their shoulders.

According to Egyptian myth, humans and gods originally lived together until some humans rebelled against their subservient status. Enraged at this betrayal, Re wanted to annihilate the entire species, but was advised by other gods to vent his wrath only against the rebels. Accordingly, Re dispatched the goddess **Hathor** to punish the offenders; but she flew into an uncontrollable rage and began killing humans indiscriminately. To prevent complete annihilation of the humans, Re tricked Hathor by mixing ochre into beer until it resembled blood. Bloodthirsty Hathor consumed the beer and became inebriated, losing her focus and ferocity. The surviving humans were thus spared, but before long they attracted the wrath of Re once again. This time, instead of punishing them, Re decided on separation, leaving the earth and moving all the gods to the heavens.

Like the later biblical story of the 'paradise lost', this myth explains humanity's separation from the divine as the consequence of the deity's displeasure with human behaviour, although in this case, instead of expelling the humans, the gods removed themselves. At the same time, it confronts the conflict between justice and power. Similarly in *Gilgamesh*, Enlil thunders when he learns that humans have survived his flood. But the other gods, upset because human sacrifices had ceased during the flood, chastise him: 'How could you so lack judgment as to inundate [all humans]? Punish [only] transgressors; punish [only] wrong-doers.' Cosmic justice was indispensable to limit otherwise unlimited cosmic power. But the criticism directed at Enlil also applied to Gilgamesh, who had abused his powers as the earthly ruler of Uruk.

If the *Gilgamesh* myth sought, on one level, to temper power, power also used myth for its own purposes. Nothing so effectively legitimized a ruler as association with a god. Ancient societies held that kingship 'came down from heaven', and their rulers functioned either as divine agents or as gods themselves. In one New Kingdom myth explaining the ancestry of a future king, the supreme god, Amun, became attracted to a human queen and—disguising himself as her actual husband—did 'all he desired with her'. Before the queen even knew she was pregnant, the child was named by Amun and fashioned in his image by the potter-god Khnum. Thoth, the divine messenger, then announced to the queen that she would bear Amun's offspring. Attended by deities, the queen gave birth to the child, who was raised among the gods and, when sufficiently socialized, presented to the Egyptians as their new king. Centuries later, Alexander the Great, identified as the son of Zeus–Amun when he entered Egypt, circulated a similar story, claiming that a god had visited his mother at his conception.

In turn, that Alexandrian model made its way to Rome. No ruler was more astute in the use of myth to justify his political regime than Octavian, better known as Augustus Caesar. Augustus transformed foundation myth into legitimation myth. Rome's principal foundation myth centred on the legend of Romulus, whose choice of the Palatine hill as the site of the future city was validated by the appearance of twelve vultures. Accordingly, Octavian made it known that twelve vultures had also appeared to him clearly implying that he would re-establish Rome (as he in fact did at the conclusion of the civil wars in 28 BCE).

Throughout his reign Augustus used religious props, including a second foundation myth that was the subject of the greatest literary work of the Augustan Age. Virgil's *Aeneid* traced Rome's origins to Aeneas, a refugee from Troy who was the son of a human father and a divine mother identified as Aphrodite/Venus (Augustus' clan, the Julians, had long claimed Aeneas and Venus as ancestors).

In another vein, Augustus boasted that he had restored 82 temples and (re)built another 14 during his reign. As *pontifex maximus* ('high priest'), he was expected to live next to the house of the Vestal Virgins, the guardians of Rome's hearth, but he didn't want to give up his home. Therefore he rededicated his home as public property and turned part of it into a shrine to Vesta. In this way he not only brought Rome's hearth, the symbol of the empire's divine favour, into his own home, but reinforced his connection with the foundation myth, in which the fire of Vesta was first transferred from Troy to Italy by Aeneas and then brought into Rome by Romulus. Augustus also rebuilt the neighbouring temple of the goddess called Magna Mater or Cybele, whose cult

The Magna Mater (Cybele)

Worship of the Magna Mater ('Great Mother') had a long and distinguished history. The origins of her cult are most commonly traced to seventh-century BCE Phrygia (a land in western Anatolia), but its roots went back at least as far as the neo-Hittites of the early first millennium BCE and quite possibly to the Hittites of the mid-second millennium BCE. From Phrygia the cult spread to Greece in the sixth century BCE and from there to Rome. By the second century CE her sanctuaries covered the breadth of the Roman Empire and beyond, from the Vatican hill to Lugdunum in Gaul (Lyon, France) to Ai Khanoum in northern Afghanistan.

In Phrygia she was known simply as Matar, Mother, but one of her epithets, associating her with mountains, was *kubileya*, which the Greeks rendered as Kybele/Cybele. She was the only Phrygian deity to be depicted iconographically. In many of those depictions she is accompanied by a lion—a symbol of her power.

had originated near Troy and had been introduced into Rome from Greece in 204 BCE.

Finally, the name 'Augustus' itself was part of the emperor's plan to legitimize his rule. Until he took the name for himself (in 27 BCE), 'August' had been an epithet attached to places touched by a god and subsequently consecrated by priests known as augurs. By renaming himself Augustus, Octavian emphasized his heaven-sent good fortune. Sacrifices were offered to both his *genius* (the personification of his innate qualities) and his *numen* (divine power). He would be elevated to divine status on his death in 14 CE, when a senator—his vision sharpened by an extremely large bribe from the widow of Augustus—declared under oath that he had witnessed Augustus physically ascend to heaven.

exchange for crops, progeny, economic security, health, and safety—practical benefits in a world where subsistence was hard and most people were lucky to live to thirty. The means through which humans performed their part in this exchange was ritual.

A third-century BCE plate from Ai Khanoum, Afghanistan, shows Cybele, under the watchful gaze of the Greek sun-god Helios, riding in a lion-drawn chariot driven by Nike (the winged goddess of victory) towards a typical Iranian fire altar (Thierry Ollivier/Museé Guimet).

🌿 PRACTICE

Ritual

'Pious' humans fed, clothed, and sheltered their gods; bestowed gifts on them; glorified and obeyed them in

A Roman statue of Cybele/Magna Mater from the first century CE, in the collection of the Getty Villa (Marshall Astor). Here she sits on a throne accompanied by a lion. Her headdress in the shape of a city wall symbolizes her relationship with the urbanized Roman Empire, which, as her horn of plenty suggests, benefits from her role as provider. It has been suggested that the statue's face may be that of Livia, the wife of Augustus.

though they were not consumed. So close was the association between ritual and mystery the Egyptians referred to ritual itself as *shetau*, 'mystery'. Most rituals were performed in secret, away from public scrutiny, and required the meticulous performance of a sequence of steps that simultaneously imitated the cosmic order and helped to secure it by pleasing the gods.

The foremost ritual act was the sacrifice (from the Latin meaning 'to make sacred'; the Mesopotamian equivalent meant 'gift', and the Greek 'to make smoke'). Sacrifice transformed a profane object into a holy one. Sacrificial offerings ranged from simple foods (fruits, vegetables, honeyed barley cakes) and libations of wine, milk, or oil to animals, ritually slaughtered by priests and then cooked and eaten by devotees. As in Mesopotamia, animal sacrifice was the central ritual of Greek and Roman religion, the highlight of public festivals. Sacrifices were performed on altars, more important than temples to Greeks and Romans. Since the smoke from the sacrifices had to rise to heaven to reach the gods, altars were open to the elements. In Greece and Rome, temples were treasuries housing the gifts offered to the gods by their devotees, either in thanks for favours granted or in fulfillment of vows ('votive' gifts). Temples themselves were state-supported gifts. Altars and temples were parts of a sanctuary, an area separated from its surroundings by a sacred boundary. Everything within the boundary belonged to the god.

Temples provided a place for gods to spend their time on earth. In Mesopotamia and Egypt, gods dwelt in their temples as living statues, entering them through 'Opening of the Mouth' rituals. Priests began each day by greeting and worshipping the divine statue in its inner sanctum, then anointing and dressing it; Egypt's clothing rite alone required 45 separate steps.

Finally, in the most important of all the daily rituals, the statue was offered the first of two (in Mesopotamia) or three (in Egypt) daily meals, which mysteriously nourished the gods even

Typically a festival would begin with a procession in which the god's statue was displayed to the public, followed by hymns to the deity, the sacrifice ritual, games or competitions while the sacrificial animals cooked, and a communal banquet. The first three stages were solemn while the last two were celebratory. Humans revelled in one another's company, confirmed communal bonds, re-established connections with the gods, and acknowledged the pre-eminence of the divine. The Greek philosopher Democritus pronounced that a life without festivals was a long road without inns. In Athens the religious calendar set aside 170 festival days every year.

Except during public festivals, ritual was the exclusive prerogative of priests. In Mesopotamia and Egypt, priests were originally private citizens appointed for limited periods of service, but in time priesthood became a full-time profession. Priests were scrupulous in the performance of their duties, which included ensuring the absolute integrity of sanctuaries. Egyptian priests, 'pure ones', were circumcised, dressed in white, and observed food taboos; to remove physical pollution and restore spiritual purity, they washed themselves several times each day, often in basins located at temple entrances. Mesopotamians, too, ritually removed surface and internal impurities in 'bathing houses' before entering temple grounds. Such ritual cleansing was referred to as 'making holy'; sometimes it was reinforced with pleasant-smelling incense.

Anyone entering a sacred place had to be pure, both morally and physically. When a wealthy local benefactor of a North African town dedicated a shrine to Asclepius during the early Roman Empire, he set the following conditions: 'Whoever wishes to ascend into the shrine, let him abstain from women, pork, bean, barber, and public bath for three days; do not enter the enclosure wearing shoes' (Rives 2007: 102). The Greek physician Hippocrates wrote, 'We mark out the boundaries of the temples and the groves of the gods, so that no one may pass them unless he is pure, and when we enter them we are sprinkled with holy water' (Adams, n.d.). The entrance to the Egyptian temple at Edfu warned: 'Whoever enters by this door must beware of entering impurely, for god loves purity more than millions of rituals'. Inside the temple were further injunctions: 'Do not utter falsehood in his house, do not covet things, do not slander, do not accept bribes, do not be partial as between a poor man and a great, . . . do not reveal what you have seen in

the mysteries of the temple' (Herman te Velde, in Sasson, ed., 1995: 1733).

Women in Ancient Religion

There were as many goddesses in the ancient world as there were gods, so it is no surprise that women had significant roles and responsibilities in ancient religion. Women identified in particular with the goddesses associated with marriage, pregnancy, and birth, and in Greece and Rome they celebrated their own festivals. Women served female deities, maidens attending virgin goddesses and matrons attending Demeter and other mother-goddesses. Sumerian women held high priestly office. The highest-ranking priestess was literally the 'lady goddess'. Sargon of Mesopotamia, in the late third millennium BCE, installed his daughter, Enheduana, as high priestess of the moon-god of Ur. So integral were women to their religion that Mesopotamians dismissed as uncivilized any people whose god knew no priestess.

Greek priestesses kept the keys to temples, groomed cult statues, led prayers, and even took part in sacrifices—activities for which the typical Greek woman would be responsible in her own home. Finally, according to Strabo, a celebrated Greek geographer and historian of the first century CE, women's religious influence was paramount even in places where they had no official role: 'All agree that women are the chief founders of religion; it is women who encourage men to more attentive worship of the gods, to festivals, and to supplications' (Connelly 2007: 166–7).

Divination

An Assyrian incantation text refers to the gods as 'draw[ing] the cosmic designs'. In such a universe, the ability to 'divine' the gods' wishes and plans was crucial, especially for rulers. Gods communicated their designs, but rarely in a form that was immediately obvious. Humans almost always had to work to uncover and interpret them.

The exceptions to that rule were cases of inspiration or revelation—a phenomenon typically associated with the holy scriptures of Judaism, Christianity, and Islam. Among the ancient texts that claimed divine inspiration was the *Iliad*, whose opening line—'Sing, goddess, of Achilles' wrath'—suggests that Homer was merely the mouthpiece for a divine muse. Mesopotamians also claimed to receive revelations, which arrived in dreams. A note at the end of a Babylonian composition stated that it had been revealed to the author by **Erra,** the god of violence, during the night: 'When [the author] recited it upon waking, not one word did he omit, not one word did he add. Erra heard and approved' (*Erra* V: 42–5; trans. M. Desrochers).

The significance of prophecy lay above all in its impact on the state. For the Romans the most important prophecies were the Sibylline Oracles, associated with the Sibyl (from the Greek for 'prophetess') of Cumae, a Greek colony near Naples. By the late third century BCE the Sibylline Oracles had been relocated to Rome, where they were guarded by priests. All other prophecies, whatever their source, had to be 'tested' against the Sibylline oracles in order to establish their legitimacy. Our knowledge of Mesopotamian prophecy derives mainly from some eighty prophecies found in two official archives, one from the Old Babylonian period and the other from the Assyrian Empire. The latter refers to a number of prophets, most of them women, whose names associated them with Ishtar. Prophecies reported to rulers, because they touched on the affairs of king or state, needed confirmation via other forms of divination, especially extispicy (examination of the inner organs [exta], especially livers, of sacrificed animals).

The word 'oracle' (from the Latin for 'to speak') may refer not only to gods' answers to questions

The *Iliad*

The *Iliad*, composed by Homer in the eighth century BCE, describes the events of several days towards the end of the ten-year war between the Greeks and Trojans. The war pits not only humans but also gods against one another: Hera, Poseidon, and Athena, for instance, favour the Greeks, while Apollo, Ares, and Aphrodite side with the Trojans. The gods—who do not have to face death—are depicted as considerably less noble than the human characters, all of whom must either die or mourn the deaths of their loved ones. Lying, browbeating, carping, threatening, promiscuous, and generally petty, the gods are hardly suitable models for humans to emulate. Their dominant characteristic is their vastly superior power, most evident in Zeus, who also manifests an apparent lack of concern for human death and anguish.

The human who most resembles the gods is Achilles, the most powerful Greek warrior, whose father was human but whose mother was a minor goddess. The *Iliad* is his story above all. It is his 'wrath' that the first line of the poem refers to, and when it is aroused, Achilles projects the power of a god. In the concluding chapters, he is truly uncontrollable, willing to go to his own prophesied death if only he can unleash his fury on as many Trojans and gods as possible. Even after he kills Hector, the greatest and most noble of the Trojan heroes and the specific target of his 'mankillings', Achilles' wrath is undiminished. He straddles Hector's corpse, abusing it and refusing to release it for burial. His anger still seethes when Priam, Hector's aging father, crawls in terror towards him to plead for the release of his son's body. Reminded of his own father by Priam, Achilles sets aside his wrath and releases the body. This act of compassion serves to tame Achilles' 'god-like' anger and to restore his humanity.

but also to the places where they were delivered or the people through whom the gods spoke. Egyptian festival processions, in which gods' statues made public appearances, provided opportunities for individuals to ask them 'yes–no' questions. The answers were relayed via movement: 'yes' if the statue advanced, 'no' if it retreated. Rulers' questions concerned issues of state, especially military campaigns, while commoners asked about daily concerns: what crop to plant, who had committed a theft, whether a sick child would recover.

The best-known oracle of antiquity was at Delphi in Greece, where the god Apollo spoke through the priestess called the Pythia. On 'oracle days', enquirers would pay a substantial fee to line up with a sacrificial goat, on which a priest sprinkled water: if the animal shook off the water, Apollo would hear the enquiry. On entering the temple, the enquirer presented a question to a priest who passed it on to the Pythia. Apollo then spoke through her. Responses were often ambiguous, and questioners were expected to put considerable effort into interpreting them.

Most of what we know about the questions posed to the Pythia comes from Herodotus and **Plutarch**, both of whom were interested primarily in matters of state. Evidence of other types of questions is available, however, on lead tablets from the oracle of Zeus at Dodona. The majority of the queries recorded on those tablets reflect the everyday concerns of ordinary people—the same kinds of concerns we find in Egypt or Mesopotamia: should I wed? will he love me in return? is it really my child? did I misplace my blankets or were they stolen? Plutarch himself complained of the trivial, mundane questions posed to the Pythia in his day.

In Mesopotamia and Rome, virtually anything could contain a message from the gods: stars, storms, smoke, oily water, sacrificed animals, chance meetings, even human hair. Divination was a matter of reading between the lines, noticing unusual phenomena, recognizing anomalies and finding significance in them.

Omens were divine messages understood as warnings. Mesopotamians recorded two types of omen: diagnostic and predictive. Diagnostic omens were based on physical or behavioural characteristics: a mole on the right thigh, for instance, might indicate prosperity, while a generous person could expect to be treated generously. Predictive omens, by contrast, hinted at one's fate or *shimtu* ('that which has been decreed'). Sometimes these omens were discovered through observation of natural phenomena: movements of the stars, unusual births, thunder on a cloudless day, a sudden appearance of birds. Assyrian rulers required that every unusual sighting throughout the empire be reported to the court.

Predictive omens could also be solicited, however, by various means. Pouring oil on water was one common method. Eventually, lengthy treatises were written explaining how different effects should be interpreted. For example: 'If I pour oil on water and the oil sinks, surfaces, and covers the water: [then] for the campaign, disaster; for the sick person, the hand of god is heavy [he will die].' Examination of a sheep's liver was the most common method of divination in Mesopotamia (and was eventually transmitted to the Roman world), but the most influential (and enduring) was astrology, translating the 'heavenly writing' of the gods.

The divine 'inscriptions' that recorded human destiny were analogous to royal decrees. Yet in the same way that citizens could appeal to rulers to reconsider their decisions, humans could appeal to gods to reconsider theirs. One could pray to Ishtar, for instance, to use her power to transform an unfortunate *shimtu* into a favourable one. More commonly one resorted to incantations or rituals to ward off or drive away (exorcize) evil, or to remove its effects. An Egyptian text called the *Instruction for [King] Merikare* even suggested that the creator gave humans magic specifically as a weapon to ward off whatever evil might come their way.

Three Sumerian statuettes, c. 2900–2370 BCE, show male worshippers with their hands clasped over their chests in prayer (David Lees/CORBIS). Their large eyes—a feature of many Mesopotamian sculptures—were meant to represent the awe that worshippers felt in the presence of the gods.

ETHICS

An important part of the function of an Egyptian tomb was to serve as monument to the virtue of the deceased. During the Old Kingdom, the tombs of high-ranking Egyptians often bore 'autobiographical' inscriptions attesting to their virtue. In later periods, however, the dead had to prove their virtue to a divine tribunal that included Osiris and **Anubis**, the jackal-headed god who acted as the divine undertaker. The third member of this tribunal was Ma'at, the goddess of truth, justice, and order, who used the scales of justice to weigh the heart of the deceased against her own 'feather of truth'. Presented with a list of eighty possible

'sins'—offences against social norms—the deceased was expected to respond with avowals of innocence. Each lie or transgression caused the heart's side of the scale to sink. If it sank too far, the deceased would disappear forever into the maws of a monster, but if the heart stayed level with Ma'at's feather, the person would gain eternal life among the gods.

Autobiographical tomb inscriptions emphasized the values central to human social interaction: responsibility, compassion, and justice. An early Mesopotamian ruler named Urukagina introduced a series of reforms, at the end of which he declared that the fundamental responsibility of a ruler was to protect widows and orphans from 'the strong man'. Hammurabi of Babylon's so-called 'law code' proclaimed that he 'brought justice to the land'. And a famous Egyptian story from the Middle Kingdom praises the wisdom of an 'eloquent peasant' who urges the powerful to 'Speak and perform justice, for it is mighty. It is great; it endures; its worth is proven; it leads one to be revered' (Lichtheim 1973: 181).

Several Egyptian texts, known as 'instructions', were designed to inculcate the fundamental values of the society: self-control, acceptance of limits, trust in other humans and, above all, the gods. Social superiors should be obeyed and social inferiors treated with generosity. Above all, Egyptian society valued balance.

In Greece the message was much the same, summed up in Apollo's Delphic admonition: 'Nothing in excess.' The *Histories* of Herodotus offered numerous instances of the dire consequences of excess, and Greek tragedians made careers of demonstrating those consequences on the stage. Cosmic justice would ensure that every transgression was eventually punished. Retribution was inescapable. If the perpetrator of an offence was not punished, a descendant would be.

A major figure in Herodotus was Croesus, king of Lydia, a powerful state in western Anatolia. When the rising Persian Empire began to encroach on his domain in the mid-sixth century BCE, Croesus asked Apollo's oracle at Delphi about

An Egyptian Tomb Inscription

The following text is from an Old Kingdom tomb at Saqqara, the most important royal mortuary before it was replaced by Giza. (The words 'to the naked' were missing from the inscription and were supplied by the translator.)

I spoke truly, I did right;

. . .

I judged between two so as to content both;
I rescued the weak from one stronger
As much as I had power.
I gave bread to the hungry, clothes <to the naked>;
I brought the boatless to land;
I buried him who had no son;
I made a boat for him who lacked one.
I respected my father, I pleased my mother,
I raised their children.
So says he whose nickname is Sheshi.
    (Lichtheim 1973: 17)

the consequences of waging war against Cyrus. Informed that 'a great empire would be destroyed' if he went into battle, the ambitious Croesus closed his inner ear to the oracle's ambiguity. Taking the oracle's answer as a guarantee of victory, Croesus fought Cyrus, only to be defeated. Afterwards, when he complained that Apollo had misguided him, the Pythia responded that Croesus should

Counsels of Wisdom

The following extract (lines 135–45) comes from a Mesopotamian text summarizing proper religious behaviour and its rewards. It is thought to date from the mid-second millennium BCE.

Praise your god every day.
Prayer and sacrifice complement incense.
Generously offer gifts to your god,
For this is piety towards the gods.
Prayer, supplication, and prostration
Will be repaid a hundredfold;
You will find favour with your god.
Reverence secures grace,
Sacrifice prolongs life,
And prayer atones for guilt.
Whoever honours the gods is despised by none.

have asked which empire would be defeated. Croesus' failure to ask the question was his responsibility, not Apollo's. Humans were responsible for their own actions and for the consequences of those actions. If improper actions incurred punishment, then appropriate actions could reap rewards. As a Mesopotamian text known as the 'Moral Canon' explained:

> If he is just, and nevertheless things go
>   wrong, later on things will get better.
> If he speaks according to justice, he will
>   have good recompense.
> If he loves what is good, only goodness will
>   follow him all the time.
> If he is merciful, he will die in abundance.
> If he is concerned about helping others,
>   the gods will follow him all the time.
>   (Giorgio Buccellati, trans., in Sasson, ed.,
>   1995:1690–1)

How humans treated one another was no less important than how they treated the gods. Social order depended on the former, cosmic order on the latter.

Could the stain of sin, once committed, be removed? In Mesopotamia, two types of incantation were available for the purpose of purification. Approximately two hundred sins required purification, among them ignoring food taboos, slandering, bearing false witness, oppressing the weak, dishonouring parents, stealing, committing adultery, murdering, swearing false oaths, scorning the gods, and failing to name the god while making offerings. In one way or another, all these sins involved disrespect, either towards the gods or towards other humans. The list is strikingly similar to the sins listed in the Egyptian *Book of the Dead*.

❧ WISDOM LITERATURE

To question the justice of the gods was a sin. Yet how else can humans respond when faced with

Isis nursing the infant Horus; bronze, 600–300 BCE (Gianni Dagli Orti/CORBIS).

apparent injustice, especially the suffering and death of an innocent child? In a time when three of four newborns never reached adulthood, it is little wonder that the most popular deities were associated with female fertility and childbirth. Foremost among them was Isis, whose devotion to her son Horus made her a symbol of motherhood not only in her Egyptian homeland but throughout the ancient world.

One memorable scene in Egyptian myth has Isis, on finding her child near death, accuse Re of imperious disregard of suffering and death: stung by her attack, Re restores Horus to health. Many human mothers sought Isis' intercession for their children, and when that failed they must have been tempted to accuse their gods of similar disregard.

Even the most pious must sometimes have wondered whether their devotion would ever be rewarded. Disappointed hopes gave rise to a literary genre called 'wisdom literature'. In one of these texts, known as the *Babylonian Theodicy*, a speaker who has faithfully fulfilled all his religious obligations, exactly as prescribed in the *Counsels of Wisdom*, expresses his frustration.

> Those who neglect the god go the way of
>   prosperity,
> While those who pray to the goddess are
>   impoverished and dispossessed.
> In my youth I sought the will of my god;
> With prostration and prayer I followed my
>   goddess,
> But I was bearing a profitless corvée
>   [forced labour] as a yoke.
> My god decreed instead of wealth destitution.
>   (Lambert 1960: 75–7)

In another Mesopotamian text (*Ludlul bel nemeqi*; 'I will praise the lord of wisdom'), a Job-like 'righteous sufferer' has performed all the prescribed rituals, to no avail. Here he laments the impossibility of understanding the ways of the gods:

> I wish I knew that these things were
>   pleasing to one's god!
> What is proper to oneself is an offence to
>   one's god;
> What in one's heart seems despicable is
>   proper to one's god.
> Who knows the will of the gods in heaven?
> Who understands the plans of the
>   underworld gods?
> Where have mortals learned the way of a god?
>   (Lambert 1960: 41)

The 'wisdom' conveyed by these texts, of course, is resignation to the inscrutable will and superior power of the gods.

Similar themes ran through Greek literature. No figure was more tragic than Sophocles' Oedipus, a good man and good ruler but, being human, of limited knowledge and power. At the close of *Oedipus Tyrannus*, the chorus asks, 'What god, what dark power leapt beyond all bounds, /beyond belief, to crush your wretched life?' (Robert Fagles, trans. 1984). And a character in Euripides' play *Heracles* accuses Zeus of being heartless or unjust. Yet in his *Phoenician Women* the playwright has Oedipus conclude that humans have no choice but to endure whatever the gods decree.

THEOLOGY

Theology began whenever it was that humans first began posing questions about the gods. The early 'god lists', identifying and correlating the gods, marked an early step in its development. Another major step came in the first millennium BCE, when Egyptian and Mesopotamian priests set about establishing a canon of core texts for their respective religious-literary traditions. Attached to late Egyptian temples were the House of Life and the House of Books, in which priests passed on their knowledge to neophytes and preserved the sacred writings, written in hieroglyphs (Greek for 'holy writing', from the Egyptian 'words of the god'). Egyptian temple libraries contained 42 indispensable books—42 being the number of Egyptian provinces, hence symbolic of perfection or totality. Among them were books explaining how to inscribe texts on temple walls. The priests who began the process of codifying their cultic knowledge in this way were transforming the 'words of god' into holy scripture.

A major shift in thinking about the gods has been attributed to the sixth-century BCE Greek poet, philosopher, and social critic named Xenophanes. Only fragments of his work have survived, but in them he rejects the anthropomorphic view of the divine, according to which 'mortals suppose that gods are born, wear their own clothes and have voice and body'. He was particularly contemptuous of those—notably Homer and Hesiod—who 'attributed to the gods all sorts of things which are matters of reproach and censure among men: theft, adultery, and

From the *Instruction for Merikare*

Dating to approximately 2100 BCE, the Instruction for [King] Merikare *purports to be a manual for rulers, emphasizing—in an obvious echo of Old Kingdom tomb autobiographies as well as the judgment of the dead in the* Book of the Dead—*the ethics of justice above all. The first part of this extract refers to the omniscience of the sun-god Re and claims that he prefers the modest offering of an honest person to the lavish offering of an evil person. The conclusion praises Re as the creator god, in lines that call to mind the opening verses of* Genesis *and that also share a number of motifs with Mesopotamia's* Epic of Creation.

While generation succeeds generation,
God who knows characters is hidden;
One cannot oppose the lord of the hand
   [i.e., the sun-god as creator]
He reaches all that the eyes can see.
One should revere the god on his path,
Made of costly stone, fashioned of bronze
   [i.e., the processional statue of the god]
. . .

Make worthy your house of the west [tomb],
Make firm your station in the graveyard,
By being upright, by doing justice,
Upon which men's hearts rely.
The loaf [of bread] of the upright is preferred
To the ox of the evildoer.
Work for god, he will work for you also,
With offerings that make the altar flourish,
With carvings that proclaim your name,
God thinks of him who works for him.

Well tended is mankind—god's cattle,
He made the sky and earth for their sake,

He subdued the water monster,
He made breath for their noses to live.
They are his images, who came from his body.
He shines in the sky for their sake;
He made for them plants and cattle,
Fowls and fish to feed them.
He slew his foes, reduced his children,
When they thought of making rebellion.
He makes daylight for their sake,
He sails by to see them.
He has built his shrine around them,
When they weep he hears.
He has made for them rulers in the egg,
Leaders to raise the back of the weak.
He made for them magic as weapons
To ward off the blow of events,
Guarding them by night and day.
He has slain the traitors among them,
As a man beats his son for his brother's sake.
For god knows every name.
   (Lichtheim 1973: 103–4)

mutual deceit'. In the place of those all-too-human gods Xenophanes proposed a supreme universal god:

One god is greatest among gods and men,
not at all like mortals in body or in thought.

Whole he sees, whole he thinks, and whole he hears.

Always he abides in the same place, not moving at all, nor is it seemly for him to travel to different places at different times.

But completely without effort he shakes all things [keeps everything moving] by the thought of his mind.
   (Lesher 1992: 23, 25, 31, 33)

Cleanthes' *Hymn to Zeus*

The Hymn to Zeus, *though written some two thousand years after* Merikare, *is strikingly similar in theme. Its author, the Stoic philosopher Cleanthes (331–230), places the same emphasis on the universal dominion of a single omniscient god (Zeus, in this case) and his role in dispensing universal justice.*

Noblest of immortals, many-named, always all-powerful
Zeus, first cause and ruler of nature, governing everything with your law,
greetings! For it is right for all mortals to address you:
for we have our origin in you, bearing a likeness to god,
we, alone of all that live and move as mortal creatures on earth.
Therefore I shall praise you constantly; indeed I will always sing of your rule.
This whole universe, spinning around the earth, truly
obeys you wherever you lead, and is readily ruled by you;
such a servant do you have between your unconquerable hands,
the two-edged, fiery, ever-living thunderbolt.
For by its stroke all works of nature <are guided>.
With it you direct the universal reason, which permeates
everything, mingling with the great and the small lights.
Because of this you are so great, the highest king for ever.
Not a single thing takes place on earth without you, god,
nor in the divine celestial sphere nor in the sea,
except what bad people do in their folly.
But you know how to make the uneven even
and to put into order the disorderly; even the unloved is dear to you.
For you have thus joined everything into one, the good with the bad,
that there comes to be one ever-existing rational order for everything.
This all mortals that are bad flee and avoid,
the wretched, who though always desiring to acquire good things,
neither see nor hear god's universal law,
obeying which they could have a good life with understanding.
But they on the contrary rush without regard to the good, each after different things,
some with a belligerent eagerness for glory,
others without discipline intent on profits,
others yet on indulgence and the pleasurable actions of the body.
<They desire the good>, but they are born now to this, then to that,
while striving eagerly that the complete opposite of these things happen.
But all-bountiful Zeus, cloud-wrapped ruler of the thunderbolt,
deliver human beings from their destructive ignorance;
disperse it from their souls; grant that they obtain
the insight on which you rely when governing everything with justice;
so that we, having been honored, may honor you in return,
constantly praising your works, as befits
one who is mortal. For there is no greater privilege for mortals
or for gods than always to praise the universal law of justice.

(Thom 2005: 40–1)

The debates set off by these ideas have yet to end. Anaxagoras, following Xenophanes, wrote that 'All living things, both great and small, are controlled by Mind' (E. Hussey, in Freeman 1996: 227). Protagoras disagreed: 'Concerning the gods I am unable to discover whether they exist or not, or what they are in form; for there are many hindrances to knowledge, the obscurity of the subject and the brevity of life' (W. Guthrie, in Freeman 1996: 227). Other Greeks, such as the Athenian playwright Critias, were downright cynical: 'I believe that a man of shrewd and subtle mind invented for men the fear of gods so that there might be something to frighten the wicked even if they acted, spoke, or thought in secret' (R. Muir, in Freeman 1996: 227). Epimarchus believed that gods were personifications of natural phenomena; Euhemerus that they were former kings and heroes raised to divine status through the constant retelling of their deeds. Some interpreted myths as allegories illustrating philosophical verities. Certainly the most influential Greek thinker was Plato, whose ideas on subjects such as the goodness of god, god as creator (demiurge), divine forces intermediate between god and humans (*daimones*), ethics, the duality of body and spirit, the inferiority of the material world, and the superiority of the spiritual would profoundly affect Western philosophy and theology.

Among the Romans who contributed to the development of theology, the most important was Cicero, but the most interesting was Varro. Borrowing from Greek thought, he suggested that there were three ways of thinking about the gods (*theologiai* in Greek, literally 'words about gods'): mythical, philosophical, and civic/practical (referring to popular understanding and practices). Even though they were mutually incompatible, Varro argued, each served a purpose that rendered it valid in its own sphere.

Death and the Afterlife

Gilgamesh never thought about death until his closest friend died. Enkidu's death threw him into emotional turmoil, and he had to experience the full range of disbelief, rage, and grief before he could accept it. He ordered craftsmen to fashion a statue of Enkidu; had valuable items from his own treasury interred with his friend so that Enkidu could impress the netherworld gods; and held a funeral that included a sacrifice of animals for a banquet at which Gilgamesh ordered further offerings to the gods.

Ancient funeral rites institutionalized the sequence of emotional responses to a death. Greek rites, for instance, included several phases. In the 'laying out' phase, women washed, anointed, and dressed the body, wrapped it in cloth, and placed in its mouth or hand a coin to pay for Charon's ferrying it across the river Styx to the land of the dead; then they positioned the body on a bier where family members paid their final respects. The following night, accompanied by mourners, a family procession 'carried out' the deceased to the burial site, where it was cremated and then interred with offerings of food, wine, and other items deemed useful in the afterlife. The family then returned home for a funeral banquet that typically included animal sacrifices.

Families showed their respect for the dead by maintaining their gravesites and making offerings on the anniversaries of their deaths. These family 'cults of the dead' were complemented by community observances such the Athenian festivals of Genesia and Anthesteria. Rome's comparable festivals were the Parentalia and the Lemuria (the latter was dedicated specifically to those who had not received proper burial).

Roman customs varied over time, alternating between periods of cremation and inhumation. During the Roman Empire, when inhumation was the norm, corpses were placed in sarcophagi ('flesh-eaters') until they decomposed; then the bones would be gathered for placement in ossuaries. Evidence of the reburial of exhumed skeletons as early as 9000 BCE has been found at Kfar HaHoresh, a specialized burial site in the Galilean hills of Israel.

A Tavern-keeper's Advice to Gilgamesh

Essentially, Siduri tells Gilgamesh to 'seize the day'.

You will never find the life you seek.
When the gods created humankind,
they apportioned to them death;
immortal life they kept for themselves.
Gilgamesh, fill your belly,
enjoy yourself day and night!
Take pleasure every day,
dance and be merry day and night!
Wear clean clothes, anoint your head, bathe in water!
Dote on the child who holds your hand;
tender your wife loving embraces.
(*from the Old Babylonian* version of *Gilgamesh*; trans. M. Desrochers)

Forced to recognize his own mortality but still unwilling to accept it, Gilgamesh set out (clad in 'the skin of a lion') to learn how he could become immortal. On the way he met several people who warned him that he would never succeed. Among them was a woman, a tavern-keeper named Siduri, who advised him to make the most of his time on earth.

Mesopotamians, along with other cultures of antiquity, believed that the spirits of the dead lived on, but depictions of the afterlife were so consistently gloomy that no one looked forward to it. Most Greeks and Romans shared that view. In Book 11 of the *Odyssey*, Odysseus makes his way to the underworld. There he meets the spirit of Achilles, who tells him that he would rather be a hired hand toiling on someone else's hardscrabble land than be ruler of the underworld. Surviving funerary inscriptions suggest that most Greeks did not envision any meaningful existence after death.

Some did, however, among them Egyptians, Zoroastrians, certain philosophers, and a minority of Greeks and Romans, all of whom imagined the afterlife as the place of final justice, where individuals would be treated in accordance with their behaviour in this world. That was certainly the message of Egypt's Pyramid and Coffin Texts, as well as the *Book of the Dead*.

Among the 'mysteries' revealed to initiates of the mystery religions—Orphism, the **Eleusinian mysteries**, the cult of Isis—were the keys to safe passage through the netherworld. Egyptian texts similarly offered maps of the underworld. In Zoroastrianism, the evil ended their days in the 'House of the Lie', while the good ascended to Ahura Mazda's 'House of Good Thought'. The latter retained their bodies and therefore would be able (as in Islam) to enjoy sexual intercourse—a promise that would be unavailable to Christians in their heaven, based as it was on Platonic ideals emphasizing the intellect over the corrupt physical body.

The layout of the afterlife varied from society to society. Urban Mesopotamians envisioned an expansive underground city, while Egyptians looked forward to a luxurious country estate. Whatever the society, the land of the afterlife was said to lie in the west, where the sun set, sometimes under the ground, sometimes in the heavens. Since the inhabitants of the underworld could threaten the living, it was important to communicate with them to secure their support. Caves, springs, and tombs were seen as special points of contact with the dead and underworld gods. Sometimes passages to the underworld were dug into the earth. Recent excavations at Tell Mozan in Syria, site of the ancient Hurrian city of Urkesh, have exposed a deep circular pit that has been interpreted as a channel to the underworld: it contained the remains of animals that were presumably sacrificed as offerings to the netherworld powers. Just as the netherworld was imagined as a mirror image of the heavens, the pit with its stairway to the netherworld was a mirror image of the Mesopotamian **ziggurat**, a temple tower understood to represent a 'stairway to heaven'.

Not everyone feared death. The Greek philosopher Epicurus wrote, 'The most terrifying of evils, death, is nothing to us, since when we exist, death does not. But when death is present, then we do not exist'. A favourite epitaph in Roman times consisted of a simple sequence of verbs: 'I was not; I was; I am not; I care not'. The Roman Stoic philosopher Seneca left this epigram: 'Death is either an end or a transition', hence not to be feared (all three cited in Segal 2004: 222–3).

According to the *Book of the Dead*, dissolution awaited all gods. More dramatically, one Coffin Text stated that, after millions of years, Atum and Osiris would return to 'one place', the undifferentiated state that preceded the creation of the differentiated world. In Zoroastrianism, Ahura Mazda/Ohrmazd and his rival Angra Mainyu/Ahriman coexisted for three thousand years before the creation of the world. Creation itself consisted of three three-thousand-year eras. The third era was further subdivided into three separate millennia, each concluding in a violent upheaval that ended with the arrival of a saviour. The ninth and final millennium was further divided into four ages (gold, silver, steel, and mixed iron) of successive decline. The ultimate end would also bring to an end the continuous cosmic battle between good (Ahura Mazda) and evil (Angra Mainyu): the victory of Ahura Mazda would be marked by a general resurrection, in which the dead would rise 'in their lifeless bodies'.

❧ THE END OF ANTIQUITY

A Christian sermon delivered around 400 CE condemned 'antiquity' as 'the mother of all evils'. It reflected the attitude of all three Western monotheisms towards their 'defeated' polytheistic foes. Their victory was taken to be the seal of God's approval, the inevitable outcome of sacred history. Victory is always inevitable to the victors.

The fate of the 'losers' is not necessarily so clear to them. In at least one instance, however, a defender of the Egyptian tradition had a premonition of its end. The author of the late Egyptian text known as the *Asclepius Apocalypse* did not identify any particular threat, but he clearly felt the presence of one:

And yet there will come a time when it will be seen that the piety and unremitting devotion with which Egyptians have worshipped the gods was futile and that all sacred addresses to the gods will be vain and fruitless. For the deity will ascend once more from earth to the heavens and forsake Egypt. This land, once the seat of religion, will then be bereft of divine presence. Foreigners will inhabit this land and not only will the old cults be neglected, but religion, piety, and the cult of the gods will be actively prohibited by law. Of the Egyptian religion only fables will remain and inscribed stones. . . . This Whole, so good that there never was, is, or will be anything better, will be in danger of disappearing for good; the people will regard it as a burden and revile it. They will no longer love this world, this incomparable work of god, this glorious edifice, fashioned from an infinite variety of forms, instrument of the divine will, pouring its favour unstintingly into its work, where in harmonious variety everything worthy of worship, praise, and love shows itself as one and all. Darkness will be preferred to light, death to life. No one will raise his eyes to heaven. The pious will be taken for madmen, the godless for wise, the wicked for good (Assmann 2002: 387).

Historians looking for the event that marked the definitive end of antiquity have many choices: the Roman emperor Theodosius's ban on traditional sacrifices in 392 CE, or his decree, the following year, forbidding anyone 'to go to the sanctuaries, walk through the temples, or raise his eyes to statues created by human labour'; the sack of Rome in 410; the closing of the Academy in Athens by Justinian in 529. Just as beginnings— the very first time a god was given a name, the first

time a structure was erected to serve as a temple, the first time a sacrifice was offered to a god—are impossible to pinpoint, so are endings. In the 470s a prefect of Rome restored an image of Minerva; two decades later a bishop of Rome suppressed the ancient festival of Lupercalia. Meanwhile, despite repeated prohibitions, Christians continued to offer sacrifices to an image of Constantine, the first Christian emperor.

In 389 CE Serena, the adopted niece of Theodosius I and a committed Christian, entered the Augustan temple of Magna Mater (the Great Mother, Cybele), removed a necklace from the cult image of the goddess, and placed it around her own neck. Observing this transfer of religious symbols and power from antiquity to the 'modern' day was Rome's last Vestal Virgin, the priestess responsible for keeping Rome's eternal flame alive, who had taken refuge in the Mother's sanctuary. Her protests met deaf ears, and she was never heard from again. The age of the 'mother of all evils' was over; the reign of the Father had begun.

Sites

MESOPOTAMIA

Assur The centre of the Assyrian Empire (900–609 BCE), whose rulers claimed that Assur had replaced Babylon as the centre of the cosmos.

Babylon Literally the 'gateway of/to the gods', Babylon was for many centuries the political and religious centre of Mesopotamia. Hammurabi (c. 1750 BCE) claimed that, with the construction of his temple complex dedicated to the god Marduk, Babylon had supplanted Nippur as the 'navel of the universe'.

Nippur The religious centre of the Sumerians, who identified Nippur as the centre of the universe.

Ur In southern Mesopotamia; the site of one of the best-preserved ziggurats, dating to the Third Dynasty of Ur.

EGYPT

Akhetaton (modern Amarna) Literally 'the horizon of Aton', Akhetaton, in central Egypt, was a short-lived capital during the religious upheavals of the New Kingdom.

Memphis Located just south of contemporary Cairo, Memphis was the capital of Egypt during the Old Kingdom, when the three great pyramids were constructed at the city's nearby necropolis of Giza/Gizeh.

On The centre of the sun god Re; renamed Heliopolis ('city of the sun') by the Greeks.

Thebes (modern Luxor) The political and religious capital of the New Kingdom. The great temples of Luxor and nearby Karnak were dedicated to Amun-Re. The Valley of the Kings, where New Kingdom rulers were buried, is located on the west bank of the Nile.

GREECE

Athens The cultural heart of the ancient Greek world and the site of the Parthenon, the temple of the city's patroness, Athena.

Delphi Home to the most important oracle in the Greek world, dedicated to Apollo.

Dodona The site of the oldest Greek oracle, dating to prehistoric times; dedicated to Zeus, it was originally associated with a mother goddess.

Eleusis Located just west of Athens, Eleusis was home to the cult of the Eleusinian mysteries.

Olympia The site of the ancient Olympic games. Its sanctuary was home to numerous structures, including temples to Zeus and Hera, as well as a monumental statue of Zeus that was among the 'seven wonders' of the ancient world.

ROME

Rome The religious as well as the political capital of the Roman world, Rome contained hundreds of temples, among them the magnificent Pantheon (eventually converted into a Christian church).

Glossary

Ahura Mazda 'Lord Wisdom' or 'the Wise Lord', the pre-eminent male divinity of early Zoroastrianism. Later Zoroastrian texts refer to him as Ohrmazd.

Amun/Amun-Re The principal Egyptian state god. Initially known as 'the hidden one', he was elevated to the status of a major god during the Middle Kingdom and identified with Re as Amun-Re. Finally, in the New Kingdom, Amun-Re became the ruler of the gods and the physical father of the pharaohs, undergirding both the Egyptian state and the cosmos.

Anubis The jackal-headed deity who was Egypt's principal funerary god during the Old Kingdom. During the Middle Kingdom, Anubis became a subordinate of Osiris.

Asclepius (also written Asklepios and Aesculapius) was a god of healing, worshipped throughout the classical Mediterranean world. His most important cult centres were at Epidaurus in Greece and Pergamum in Asia Minor. In Roman times, those seeking cures would spend the night in one of his temples, where he was expected to appear in a dream and either cure them immediately or advise them on a course of treatment. In the *Asclepius Apocalypse* he is the character chosen to comment on Egypt's ills.

Atrahasis A long narrative poem from Mesopotamia, composed during the Old Babylonian period and named for its hero, Atrahasis (meaning 'exceptionally wise'). It includes mythological accounts of the creation of humans, their almost complete annihilation via a flood, and the re-creation of humanity through the life cycle of birth, marriage, and death.

Book of the Dead A New Kingdom collection of spells (based on the earlier **Coffin Texts**) designed to ensure the resurrection of the dead and their security in the afterlife. 'Book of the Dead' is a modern designation; the actual title translates as 'the coming forth by day'.

Coffin Texts Texts (essentially spells, based on the earlier **Pyramid Texts**) inscribed on the coffins of non-royal elite Egyptians during the Middle Kingdom, intended to protect the dead traversing the netherworld and to secure an afterlife comparable to that of the (divinized) dead rulers.

Eleusinian mysteries The tradition centred on the myth of Persephone's abduction to the underworld by Hades. Initiates took part in rituals designed to ensure a favourable stay in the netherworld. Unlike most Greek ritual traditions, the Eleusinian cult was non-exclusive, equally accepting of males and females, slaves and free citizens.

Enuma Elish The Mesopotamian creation epic, written in the late second millennium BCE, in which the Babylonian hero-god Marduk triumphs over the forces of chaos, 'creates' and orders the universe, and becomes ruler of the Mesopotamian pantheon. The title (literally, 'when on high') comes from the first two words of the composition.

Erra (or Irra) Mesopotamian god of violence, responsible for war and plagues; in a late Mesopotamian story known as *Erra and Ishum*, he threatened to destroy Babylonia for no reason other than to demonstrate power.

Gilgamesh Historical ruler of the city of Uruk, c. 2700 BCE, who became the subject of a series of Sumerian stories that were reformulated during the Old Babylonian period into a unified narrative commonly known as the *Epic of Gilgamesh*; Book XI recounts the story of the flood.

Hathor Egyptian cow goddess associated both with creation (love, sex, and fertility) and with violent destructive power.

Herodotus The fifth-century BCE Greek known as the 'Father of History', who in his *Histories* described the religious practices of numerous peoples.

Hesiod The eighth-century BCE author of *Works and Days* and *Theogony*; one of the two primary sources for the 'standard' portraits of the Greek gods (the other was Homer).

Hittites A people of mixed origin (Indo-European and Hurrian, among others) who turned their homeland of Hatti (Anatolia/eastern Turkey) into a major power between the seventeenth and twelfth centuries BCE. Many of their myths passed into the Greek world.

Homer The eighth-century BCE author of the *Iliad* and the *Odyssey*; the other primary source for the 'standard' portraits of the Greek gods (see also Hesiod).

Hurrians A people who lived in the regions of northern Mesopotamia and Syria from the early third to the late second millennia BCE, speaking a language unrelated to those of their Semitic and Indo-European neighbours but whose gods and religious practices were highly influential, especially on the Hittites.

Isis The best known of all Egyptian goddesses. She was first mentioned in Old Kingdom texts, where she was associated with rulers in both life and death (her name translates as 'throne'). In later myth she was the devoted sister and wife of Osiris and the loving mother of Horus. During the Ptolemaic and Roman eras, Isis took on the functions of numerous other deities and became a universal goddess, worshipped throughout the Mediterranean world.

netherworld Also known as the afterworld or afterlife, the netherworld was the region that the spirits of the dead entered. While 'netherworld' envisions the land of the dead as lying beneath the earth, the land of the dead could also be located in the heavens.

Osiris The Egyptian god, depicted as a mummy wearing a crown, elevated to the position of ruler of the realm of the dead during the Middle Kingdom. New Kingdom texts portray him as the pre-eminent judge of the dead, a belief that gained in significance in the later periods of Egyptian history and presumably influenced the understanding of divine judgment in Judaism and Christianity.

Plutarch (46–120 CE) A leading citizen of the Greek city of Chaeronea, not far from Delphi, Plutarch served as a magistrate, an ambassador to many Mediterranean lands, and, most important, as the senior priest of Apollo at Delphi. A prolific author, he is best known for his *Parallel Lives* (of famous Greeks and Romans). The *Moralia* is a collection of shorter pieces, including 'On the Decline of the Oracles' and 'On the Worship of Isis and Osiris'—the most complete version of the principal Egyptian myth.

Pyramid Texts Incantations (literally, 'utterances') originally carved on the walls of the royal burial suites of several late Old Kingdom rulers; recited by priests during the burial ritual, and later funerary cult rituals, to guarantee the resurrection and well-being of dead rulers.

Sumer The urban civilization of southernmost Mesopotamia (Sumer) in the late fourth millennium BCE; Sumerian religion was the substratum of Mesopotamian religion.

Tiamat The female monster who represented primeval chaos/disorder and was subdued by Marduk in **Enuma Elish**. The name 'Tiamat' is related to *tehom*, the Hebrew word usually translated as 'the void' or 'nothing' in the first verses of *Genesis*.

Vesta The Roman goddess of household and hearth, worshipped by women in particular and served by priestesses known as the Vestal Virgins, who maintained the sacred fire that secured the safety of Rome itself.

ziggurat A Mesopotamian temple tower in the form of a stepped pyramid. The most famous ziggurat was the Tower of Babel, but the best example is in the ruins of Ur. Unlike the pyramids of Egypt, built to house the remains of kings, the ziggurat was a virtual mountain, at the top of which was a sanctuary where worshippers could commune with the gods (believed to reside on mountaintops).

Further Reading

Mesopotamia

Bottéro, Jean. 2001. *Religion in Ancient Mesopotamia*. Chicago: University of Chicago Press. A sophisticated, topical overview of Mesopotamian religion.

Dalley, Stephanie. 2000. *Myths from Mesopotamia: Creation, the Flood, Gilgamesh, and Others*. Revised edn. New York: Oxford University Press. A collection of the key texts of Mesopotamia in translation.

Jacobsen, Thorkild. 1976. *The Treasures of Darkness: A History of Mesopotamian Religion*. New Haven: Yale University Press. A chronological treatment of the subject, based in large part on Jacobsen's sensitive translations and interpretation of numerous early texts.

Egypt

Assmann, Jan. *The Mind of Egypt*. 2002. New York: Metropolitan Books. A challenging examination of continuity and, especially, change in Egyptian religion.

David, Rosalie. 2002. *Religion and Magic in Ancient Egypt*. London: Penguin Books. A straightforward presentation of 3,000 years of Egyptian religion.

Pinch, Geraldine. 2002. *Egyptian Mythology: A Guide to the Gods, Goddesses, and Traditions of Ancient Egypt*. Oxford: Oxford University Press. A basic but comprehensive survey.

Wilkinson, Richard H. 2003. *The Complete Gods and Goddesses of Ancient Egypt*. London: Thames & Hudson. An illustrated guide to Egyptian gods and goddesses, in encyclopedia form.

Greece

Burkert, Walter. 1985. *Greek Religion*. Cambridge: Harvard University Press. A classic text on Greek religion.

Buxton, Richard. 2004. *The Complete World of Greek Mythology*. London: Thames & Hudson. An illustrated guide to Greek gods and goddesses, in encyclopedia form.

Connelly, Joan Breton. 2007. *Portrait of Priestess: Women and Ritual in Ancient Greece*. Princeton, NJ: Princeton University Press. A groundbreaking examination of the role of women in Greek religion.

Mikalson, Jon D. 2005. *Ancient Greek Religion*. Oxford: Blackwell. A solid introduction, arranged by topic.

Ogden, Daniel, ed. 2007. *A Companion to Greek Religion*. Oxford: Blackwell. A collection of articles on eight major aspects of Greek religion, based on recent research; includes an excellent bibliography.

Rome

Beard, Mary et al. 1998. *Religions of Rome*. 2 vols. Cambridge: Cambridge University Press. Volume I offers a sophisticated analysis of Roman religion during both the Republican and Imperial periods; volume II offers hundreds of primary documents.

Rives, James B. 2007. *Religion in the Roman Empire*. Oxford: Blackwell. A topical introduction, appropriate for upper-division students.

Iran

Boyce, Mary. 1979. *Zoroastrians: Their Religious Beliefs and Practices*. Oxford: Routledge & Kegan Paul Ltd. Although some of her interpretations are not necessarily accepted today, Boyce is recognized as a leading scholar of Zoroastrianism.

Oxtoby, Willard G. 2002. 'The Zoroastrian Tradition,' in *World Religions: Western Traditions*. 2nd edn. Toronto: Oxford University Press. Still the best brief introduction to the subject.

General

Hinnels, John R., ed. 2007. *A Handbook of Ancient Religions*. Cambridge: Cambridge University Press. Eleven chapters on 'ancient' religions, including Indian, Chinese, Aztecan, and Incan, in addition to those of the ancient Near East and the Classical world.

Johnston, Sarah Iles, ed. 2004. *Religions of the Ancient World: A Guide*. Cambridge: Harvard University Press. A single-volume compendium that includes sections on eleven major aspects of religion, the histories of eleven religious traditions, and comparative examinations of twenty important topics.

Sasson, Jack M., ed. 1995. *Civilizations of the Ancient Near East*. Volume III. New York: Charles Scribner's Sons. Contributions by experts in the fields of Mesopotamian, Egyptian, Hittite, Canaanite, ancient Arabian, and Iranian religions; primarily for advanced students, but many chapters should be accessible to introductory students.

Recommended Websites

Mesopotamia

www.etana.org
> ETANA (Electronic Tools and Ancient Near Eastern Archives) offers a range of materials for advanced students.

Egypt

www.egyptology.com
> Still the best elementary-level introduction to Egypt on the web.

www.egyptologyforum.org
> Sponsored by the Egyptologists' Electronic Forum; particularly valuable for its guide to Internet resources for ancient Egyptian texts.

Greece and Rome

www.perseus.tufts.edu
> The Perseus Digital Library provides texts in Greek, Latin, and English for advanced students.

Iran

www.fas.harvard.edu/~iranian/Zoroastrianism
> Maintained by Prods Oktor Skjaervø; includes a detailed up-to-date assessment of Zoroastrianism as well as a wealth of documents

General

www.fordham.edu.halsall/ancient/asbook.HTML
> The Internet Ancient History Sourcebook provides easy access to Egyptian, Mesopotamian, Persian, Greek, and Roman texts as well as many from ancient Israel and early Christianity.

www.ancientopedia.com
> Offers articles on Mesopotamian, Egyptian, Greek, Roman, and Persian history and culture, including religion.

References

Adams, Francis, n.d. Translation of Hippocrates, 'On the Sacred Disease'. Accessed 12 Feb. 2010 at <http://classics.mit.edu/Hippocrates/sacred>.

Assmann, Jan. 2001. *The Search for God in Ancient Egypt*. Ithaca: Cornell University Press.

———. 2002. *The Mind of Egypt*. New York: Metropolitan Books.

Beard, Mary et al. 1998. *Religions of Rome*. 2 vols. Cambridge: Cambridge University Press.

Connelly, Joan Breton. 2007. *Portrait of a Priestess: Women and Ritual in Ancient Greece*. Princeton, NJ: Princeton University Press.

Feeney, Denis. 1998. *Literature and Religion at Rome: Cultures, Contexts, and Beliefs*. Cambridge: Cambridge University Press.

Freeman, Charles. 1996. *Egypt, Greece, and Rome: Civilizations of the Ancient Mediterranean*. Oxford: Oxford University Press.

Johnston, Sarah Iles, ed. 2004. *Religions of the Ancient World: A Guide*. Cambridge: Harvard University Press.

Lambert, W.G. 1960. *Babylonian Wisdom Literature*. Oxford: Oxford University Press.

Lesher, J.H. 1992. *Xenophanes of Colophon*. Toronto: University of Toronto Press.

Lichtheim, Miriam. 1973–80. *Ancient Egyptian Literature*. 3 vols. Berkeley: University of California Press.

Rives, James B. 2007. *Religion in the Roman Empire*. Oxford: Blackwell.

Sasson, Jack M., ed. 1995. *Civilizations of the Ancient Near East*. Vol. III. New York: Charles Scribner's Sons.

Schaff, Philip, and Wace, Henry, eds. 1885. *Nicene and Post-Nicene Fathers*. Series II, Volume X. Edinburgh: T & T Clark. Accessed 12 Feb. 2010 at <www.ccel.org/ccel/schaff/npnf210.html>.

Scheid, John. 2003. *An Introduction to Roman Religion*. Bloomington: Indiana University Press.

Segal, Alan F. 2004. *Life after Death: A History of the Afterlife in Western Religions*. New York: Doubleday.

Thom, Johan. 2005. *Cleanthes' Hymn to Zeus*. Tubingen, Germany: Mohr Siebeck.

von Dassow, Eva, ed. 1994. *The Egyptian Book of the Dead: The Book of Going Forth by Day*. San Francisco: Chronicle Books.

Chapter 3

Jewish Traditions

❧ Alan F. Segal ❧

Judaism is quintessentially a historical religion. It sees human history as a reflection of the desires and demands of God, and it understands itself to have been founded more than 3,200 years ago at Mount Sinai, when a divine revelation was delivered through Moses to the people Israel. The covenant, or agreement, with God that was sealed at Mount Sinai established a set of moral and ritual obligations that continue to govern Judaism today.

A Ritual Initiation

Those obligations are reaffirmed every Saturday in the rituals that mark the coming of age of thirteen-year-olds. The details of the **Bar Mitzvah** and Bat Mitzvah ceremonies (the Aramaic terms mean 'son of the commandment' and 'daughter of the commandment', respectively) reflect several of the features that Jews consider most significant in their tradition generally.

The coming-of-age ritual is a regular part of every congregation's weekly worship. Saturday for Jews is the day of rest, called the **Sabbath**. It is a day for prayer and public assembly in the **synagogue**, the Jewish house of worship and community meeting. The teenager reads two selections from the Hebrew Bible: one from the **Pentateuch** (the five books of Moses, which make up the first section of the Bible) and one from the second section, called the *Prophets*. (The third section, called the *Writings*, is a collection of assorted works.)

The idea that adulthood begins at thirteen is based on an ancient concept of legal majority that has nothing to do with attaining adult status in the modern world: it will still be several years until a thirteen-year-old is allowed to drive a car or cast a vote. Rather, what the ceremony signifies is arrival at the age of ritual and moral responsibility. Thus the young person's presence may be counted towards the *minyan*, the quorum of ten necessary to begin group prayer, and he or she may be called to read aloud from the sacred scripture and recite the blessings that are part of every synagogue service.

The scripture from which the Bat or Bar Mitzvah reads in public for the first time is the **Torah**. In the broadest sense, the Torah (i.e., religious law) can include both the entire Hebrew Bible and all the commentaries on it, but here the term refers specifically to the five books of Moses. The Torah that is proclaimed in synagogues is written entirely in ancient Hebrew, painstakingly transcribed by hand onto a scroll that is treated with the utmost respect. In order to read from it, the candidate must have learned both the ancient script in which the text is written and the traditional melodies to which the words are chanted. The Torah is considered the ultimate repository of religious truth, and Jews are expected to study as well as observe it throughout their lives.

The blessings recited by the young person express the values of the community, which responds by reaffirming them. The Bar or Bat Mitzvah then gives thanks for the scripture that has served as a guide for the people Israel. The city of Jerusalem and the dynasty of David are mentioned, and finally the Sabbath itself is extolled for the beauty and quietude it brings. In its response to the blessings, the congregation notes that the only way in which Jews are different from anyone else is that they have been given the special responsibility of studying and keeping the Torah.

In other respects the coming-of-age ceremony may differ significantly from one congregation to another. Some conduct their services almost entirely in the local language (English, French, etc.). Others prefer a service largely or even wholly in Hebrew. Some insist that candidates prepare by studying Hebrew and learning the traditional chants. Others also include or even substitute essay-writing, social action, and good works for some of the traditional requirements. Although the most traditional synagogues continue to insist

◀ Praying at the Western Wall in Jerusalem. The lower part of the wall dates from Roman times, when it stood as the enclosure of the Temple precincts (Anne B. Keiser/National Geographic/Getty Images).

Timeline

c. 1280 BCE	Moses leads the Exodus from Egypt
c. 1000 BCE	David takes Jerusalem and makes it his capital
922 BCE	Northern kingdom separates following Solomon's death
c. 800 BCE	Amos initiates literary prophecy
722 BCE	Assyrians conquer northern kingdom and disperse its people
621 BCE	Josiah centralizes worship at the Temple in Jerusalem in Deuteronomic reform
586 BCE	Babylonians conquer Jerusalem and deport its leaders
538 BCE	Persians conquer Babylon, permitting exiles to return
164 BCE	Rededication of the Temple after Maccabean uprising
70 CE	Romans lay siege to Jerusalem and destroy the Temple
c. 220	The *Mishnah* of Rabbi Judah ha-Nasi
c. 500	The Babylonian *Talmud*
882	Birth of Saadia, *Gaon* in Babylonia (d. 942)
1040	Birth of Rashi, commentator on Bible and *Talmud* (d. 1105)
1135	Birth of Moses Maimonides, author of *The Guide of the Perplexed* (d. 1204)
1250	Birth of Moses of León, author of the *Zohar* (d. 1305)
1492	Jews expelled from Spain
1666	Sabbatai Zvi is promoted as the messiah
1698	Birth of Israel ben Eliezer, the Baal Shem Tov, in Poland (d. 1759)
1729	Birth of Moses Mendelssohn, pioneer of Reform in Germany (d. 1786)
1881	Severe pogroms in Russia spur Jewish emigration
1889	Conservative Judaism separates from Reform in the United States
1897	Theodor Herzl and the first Zionist Congress
1938	German synagogues vandalized in prelude to the Holocaust
1948	Establishment of the state of Israel

that only males can be called to the Torah, they are the minority in North America today, and many of them now offer similar (though not exactly equivalent) ceremonies to celebrate girls' coming of age.

After the service the young person's family usually holds a luncheon or dinner for relatives and friends to celebrate his or her success and the family's good fortune. These events may be simple, centring on the religious dimensions of the day, but they can be almost as lavish as a wedding reception, with a catered feast and a dance orchestra.

Behind the Bar Mitzvah ritual has always been a rite of passage to maturity, but it has taken on a new significance both for the family and for

Traditions at a Glance

Numbers
Approximately 14 million

Distribution
7 million in the Americas (mostly US, Canada, and Buenos Aires, Argentina); 3 million in Asia (mostly in Israel); 4 million in Europe (mostly in Russia, Ukraine, France, and England)

Principal Historical Periods

1700 BCE–70 CE	Biblical
c. 70–700	Talmudic
700–1700	Medieval
1700–present	Modern

Principal Founders
The patriarchs and matriarchs: Abraham and his wife Sarah (legendary, c. 1700 BCE); Isaac (their son) and his wife Rebecca; Jacob (their son; also called Israel) and his wives Leah and Rachel (father and mothers, with Bilhah and Zilpah, of the children of Israel). Also Moses (legendary prophet who received the Ten Commandments on Mount Sinai, c. 1200 BCE); Saul, David, and Solomon (semi-legendary kings, c. 1000–900 BCE).

Leaders
Ezra helped build the second Temple, 515 BCE. Yochanan ben Zakkai founded the first rabbinic academy, 70 CE. Judah the Prince produced the *Mishnah*, 220 CE. David Ben Gurion was the first prime minister of the state of Israel, 1948.

Deity
One God, called 'Lord' or 'God' in English. His name is never spoken in Hebrew.

Authoritative Texts
The Hebrew Bible, the *Talmud*, and the *Midrash* (commentaries).

Noteworthy Doctrines
All the righteous of the world can be saved; God has commanded the Jews to observe special laws, including dietary laws and dress codes.

the community since the late eighteenth century, when Jews began to achieve legal rights, gain in affluence, and take part in the intellectual life of European societies. The ritual used to be a relatively simple matter between the rabbi and the youngster and could be conducted on any of the days when the Torah is normally read in the synagogue (Monday, Thursday, and Saturday). Now it is almost always part of the Sabbath service and the whole congregation takes part in it.

Whatever the tradition of the congregation, families devote a great deal of thought to ensuring

A young man reads from the Torah during his Bar Mitzvah ceremony (Nancy Louie/istockphoto).

that their sons and daughters learn as much as possible about the tradition and appreciate the meaning of the event. Moreover, Jews' understanding of what Torah entails is much more complex and varied than it was in the era that is the subject of the first five books of the Hebrew Bible. Today some in the community emphasize the moral meaning of the Bar Mitzvah ceremony over its ritual components, preserving the tradition by renewing it in ways that are meaningful in the contemporary world. We will see other examples of such renewal in the course of this chapter.

Defining Judaism

The diversity of Judaism today is the product of historical circumstance. In the course of its development Judaism gave rise to two other world religions. Christianity and Islam, like Judaism, trace their spiritual lineage to the biblical patriarch Abraham. Judaism is by far the smallest of the three traditions, with a worldwide population just 1 to 2 per cent the size of its Christian and Muslim counterparts. Yet its historical influence is far greater than its small numbers would suggest, for it was with the Jewish people that monotheism—the belief in one God—originated.

Christians and Muslims readily acknowledge their debt to the ideas and practices of ancient Judaism. Each of the Abrahamic faiths sees itself as continuing and fulfilling the mission of ancient Israel. Each lays claim to the historical pedigree that the Hebrew Bible gives to 'the people of the LORD'. But because they are preoccupied with their own interpretations, Christians and Muslims often fail to appreciate the distinctive interpretations of their shared heritage that have developed in Judaism over the past two millennia. It will be our task in this chapter to sketch that development.

Is the Jewish heritage by definition religious? The answer is yes and no. Yes, because it is possible to join the Jewish community through conversion, and many people have done so. On the other hand, the tradition is far more commonly inherited than chosen, and for that reason Judaism is frequently considered an 'ethnic' religion.

Some Jews have said yes to their ethnic identity while saying no to the religion. A substantial number of North Americans, Europeans, and Israelis identify themselves as Jews but do not take part in the religious tradition. Rather, they see themselves as members of a cultural community with distinctive literary and artistic traditions, foods and folkways, and roles in their various social and historical milieus. Religion, to them, is a part of their culture, but not necessarily the defining part.

Neither is biological descent. The idea that the Jews constitute a genetic race, which was central to their persecution in the twentieth century, simply cannot be substantiated. Ever since the time of the ancient Hebrew kingdoms, people of diverse origins have converted or married into the community. Thus any attempt to identify someone as Jewish on the basis of biological heredity is bound to fail.

It is impossible to arrive at an exact count of the world's Jewish population, partly because of these differences in definition. In all, Jews probably number just under 14 million worldwide today. Approximately half live in Israel now. The next largest population of Jews is in the Americas, mostly the United States and Canada, but with significant populations in Argentina and Brazil. The rest live mainly in Europe, especially France, England, Ukraine, and Russia (though Jews from the former USSR and its sphere of influence have immigrated to Israel, Europe, and North America in large numbers in recent years). The world population of Jews in the early twenty-first century is almost one-third smaller than it was in 1939. In that year the Second World War began, and by the time it was over in 1945, roughly 6 million European Jews had been put to death by the Nazis—the political party that ruled Germany—in what is widely known today as the **Holocaust**.

Israel aside, the main centres of Jewish culture today are in some European cities and, in particular, the large urban areas of eastern North America. About half of all Jews are unaffiliated with any synagogue. The other half span the range from liberal and unobservant to intensely traditional and deeply observant. In the United States and Canada, there are three major groupings: Reform, Conservative, and Orthodox. To understand Judaism, it is important to note that for the most part the divisions reflect differences in ritual practice rather than belief or doctrine. The exact divisions depend on the history of Judaism in each specific country. By contrast, in Christianity differences in belief and doctrine used to be the defining issues separating one denomination from another.

Jews believe that God expects all human beings to follow the same fundamental moral code, which was revealed in a covenant given to Noah after the primeval flood and is accessible to the entire human race through reason. In addition, however, Jews understand themselves to be bound by a subsequent covenant, delivered through the prophet Moses at Mount Sinai. God took the Israelite people out of Egypt and, when he did, he again claimed them as his people. They responded that the LORD would be their God (*Jeremiah* 7: 23, 11: 4, 30: 22). The promise was confirmed at Mount Sinai, where the Hebrews (or Israelites, as they were known then) were commanded to follow a number of special rules that set them apart from all other peoples. For this reason Jews today think of themselves as God's special people: not in the sense that they are preferred above any other, but in the sense that they have been saved from slavery and elected to fulfill a special responsibility, to serve as God's priests in the world (*Leviticus* 19: 2; 26: 12).

ORIGINS

The Biblical Period

The history of Israel, as it is recorded in the Torah, is history written from a special perspective. It is the history of a people as they understand and follow a God who has chosen them to serve as his instrument. Some of that history is well known because the foundation of Hebrew religious literature, the Hebrew Bible, is sacred scripture for Christians and Muslims as well. Its interpretations differ not only *vis-à-vis* the other communities but within Judaism.

The liberal wing of Judaism accepts modern historical principles and reserves the right to question the historical accuracy of the biblical text, just as some modern Christian and Muslim scholars do, distinguishing between myth, legend, and history. On the other hand, the traditional wing of Judaism believes every word in the text to be literally true. They take the text to have been dictated to Moses and the various prophets by divine inspiration. The student must be sensitive and alert to a range of opposing perspectives on the same events.

The earliest known references to Israel in secular historical records date from the thirteenth century BCE. The key moment comes when we can begin to match the Israelites' narratives with accounts of the same people and events in the texts of their neighbours. Archaeologists have recovered an Egyptian stela (a monumental stone) dating from about 1206 BCE inscribed with a hymn describing the victories of the Egyptian pharaoh Mer-ne-Ptah:

> Great joy has arisen in Egypt;
> Jubilation has gone forth in the towns of
>   Egypt.
> They talk about the victories which
>   Mer-ne-Ptah Hotep-hir-Maat made in
>   Tehenu:
> 'How amiable is he, the victorious ruler!
> How exalted is the king among the
>   gods!' . . .
> The princes are prostrate, saying:
>   'Mercy!' . . .
> Plundered is Canaan with every evil . . .
> Israel is laid waste, his seed is not . . .
> All lands together, they are pacified.
>   (Wilson 1950: 365–81)

The hieroglyphic expression referring to Israel here designates a wandering people rather than a people with a territory or fixed borders. This is consistent with other semitic-language texts, a century or so earlier, that mention Hapiru (possibly 'Hebrews'? but meaning 'migratory people') or Shoshu, an Egyptian word meaning a migratory tribe. Whatever the historical value of the Hebrews' own legends, then, it seems they were identifiable to others as the people Israel by the end of the thirteenth century BCE. This is where we will draw the line between biblical legend and biblical history.

It would be naive to suggest that every subsequent detail in the Hebrew biblical narrative can be accepted as history without question. Historical inquiry becomes a matter of puzzling out what most likely happened, regardless of what the sources themselves may say. Not surprisingly, the results of such exercises are sometimes quite at odds with traditional pious understanding of the Bible as factual in every detail.

Creation in Genesis

The first eleven chapters of *Genesis* describe the primeval history of the universe. In Chapter 1, God creates heaven and earth. Interestingly, the text does not actually state that the universe was created from nothing. What it says is that before creation, everything was chaotic and primal waters covered the earth. God 'divided the light from the darkness' and created different things on each of the first six 'days', in a process that culminated in the creation of humanity, male and female. Then, on the seventh day, God rested, setting the pattern of a weekly Sabbath. Because the text describes the order of time as proceeding from evening to morning, Jews celebrate the Sabbath starting at sundown on Friday night and ending at sundown on Saturday.

Chapter 2 of *Genesis*, however, tells a different story. Here God causes a mist to rise from the ground, out of which vegetation sprouts. He then creates the primal man, Adam, and plants a garden in Eden, where he places the man before creating the animals and, finally, the woman, Eve.

Religious traditionalists sometimes worry that such inconsistencies obscure God's plan; therefore they try to rationalize or smooth them over. In fact, there are passages in the Bible itself that suggest efforts to interpret earlier material. The author of *Isaiah* 45, for instance, unlike the author of *Genesis* 1, explicitly says that God created the darkness as well as the light:

> So that [people] from the rising and the
>   setting sun
> may know that there is none but I:
> I am the LORD, there is no other;

I make the light, I create darkness,
author alike of prosperity and trouble.
I, the LORD, do all these things.
　(*Isaiah* 45: 6–7)

The writer of *Isaiah* 45 in the fifth century BCE felt it necessary to emphasize that God was the creator of good and evil, darkness and light, in order to underline the distinction between the teachings of the Hebrews and those of the Zoroastrians.

Modern biblical scholars take a different view of these textual inconsistencies. Instead of treating them as problems for human understanding of God's plan, they see them as clues to the composition of the text. Thus they suggest that the three interpretations of the chaos before creation came from different sources, and that the contradiction was allowed to stand because the compiler of the biblical text was reluctant to change any of them. Thus (as we shall see in more detail below), the first chapter is now ascribed to a priestly writer known as the P narrator, while the second chapter is believed to be part of an ancient Hebrew epic compiled by the king's court and commonly designated JE. *Isaiah* 45, so-called 2 *Isaiah*, was written in the Persian period by a prophet who felt that further interpretation was necessary. *Genesis* 1 offers an ordered view of creation. Everything is arranged according to the days of the week. But there is also a priestly hierarchy. First is God, the creator, who creates by means of his word. Second is the Sabbath, the period of rest built right into the universe. And third is humanity, male and female, created at the last moment before the Sabbath in the image and likeness of God.

Another voice in the biblical narrative (the D writer) has Moses lecturing to the people:

Take ye therefore good heed unto yourselves . . . lest you lift up your eyes unto the heavens, and when you see the sun and the moon and the stars, even all the host of the heavens, you be drawn away and worship them and serve them, which the LORD your God has allotted unto all the people under all the heavens (*Deuteronomy* 4: 15–19).

The earliest interpretations of the creation story within the Bible itself take it to mean that humanity should never worship created objects like the sun, the moon, and the stars, that God created everything, and that there are not separate gods for the good and the bad.

The Primal Couple

Genesis 2 ends with God's creation of man and woman. 'Adam' is the Hebrew word for 'man' in the sense of humanity, but here it appears as the proper name of the individual created as well. Thus 'Adam' has connotations similar to those of 'Everyman' in English. 'Eve', according to the biblical text and most interpreters, is derived from the word for 'living'.

In *Genesis* 2 Adam and Eve stand naked without shame, in a state of perfect innocence, peace, and harmony. *Genesis* 3 shows how easily this state can be reversed. In a play on words, the childlike nakedness (in Hebrew, *'arom*) of the primal couple is contrasted with the shrewdness (in Hebrew, *'arum*) of the serpent who presents them with the temptation to become like God by eating the fruit of the Tree of the Knowledge of Good and Evil.

The characters are sketched in just a few words. Adam is unwary and trusting and speaks in very simple sentences; Eve is curious and evidently intelligent, speaking in complex sentences that show her thinking through problems. In fact, the couple do not lack understanding or intelligence before they eat the forbidden fruit: what they lack is moral sense, or the ability to make moral distinctions. After all, the tree is not the 'tree of knowledge'; it is the 'tree of the knowledge of good and evil'.

Indeed, it is Eve's sharp intelligence that appears to lead to her downfall. Easily tempted by the serpent, she eats the fruit (not specifically identified as an apple) and Adam follows her lead without protest, even though both understand that they are disobeying a direct order from God.

The shame and guilt they experience afterwards are two aspects of the 'knowledge of good and evil'—that is, the moral capacity—acquired by eating the forbidden fruit.

The Eden story explains the conditions of human life through narrative rather than philosophical argument. Thus pain and evil are the consequences of human disobedience and lack of moral discernment. Even though Adam and Eve have been banished from the paradise that was the immediate presence of God, he continues to show his loving care while expelling them. The narrative purports to explain a wide variety of phenomena: from why snakes crawl on the ground and why women have pain in childbirth, to why people have to work for a living and why we die. Some of these matters are natural, some are cultural, and others are ultimate issues of human existence. We call such stories 'etiological' because they offer to explain the causes or reasons behind our present circumstances.

According to later Jewish tradition, the transgression committed by the primal couple was not so great as to cast a permanent cloud over human nature or to require further atonement. By contrast, the dominant Christian interpretation sees their disobedience as the 'original sin' and insists that there is a deep and sinister relationship between sexuality, sin, death, and Satan (the great enemy of God, with whom the snake would sometimes be identified). Finally, it is important to keep in mind that not all the consequences of the Adam and Eve story were negative for humans. Among the positive benefits is the fact that humans ever since have had the moral capacity to choose the good and to keep God's laws. Making the correct choices is one of the Bible's major themes.

The Israelite Narratives

The first eleven chapters of *Genesis* provide the background that, ultimately, explains why God had to choose a specific people and establish a covenant with them to convey his ideas to the human race. In this series of narratives, humans repeatedly show how badly they govern themselves when left free to follow their own conscience. In fact, they so foul the earth with violence and corruption that God must find a way to destroy their evil society.

The story of the flood was virtually universal in the mythologies of the ancient Near East. Thus the Hebrews merely adopted a theme that was probably familiar to all the peoples with whom they came in contact. In the dominant Mesopotamian accounts, the gods cause the flood because they are disturbed by the din of human life (some scholars have suggested that this story points to overpopulation). In the Hebrew version of the story, however, the motivation is moral: to punish the evil that humans have perpetrated and clear the way for a fresh start, God floods the earth, allowing only Noah and the creatures in his ark to survive.

But human judgment is no better after the flood than before it. When the king of Babylon attempts to approach God's level by building a tower to heaven, God responds by confounding human language. Not until *Genesis* 12 is there any sign of hope that humanity can be redeemed. Finally, in that chapter, God chooses Abraham to serve as an example of a righteous life. Thus, the primeval history is a prologue to the major action of the Hebrew Bible, which is the story of the people Israel in their relationship to God.

The word 'myth' has come to connote falsity, and even today people are more likely to apply it to the narratives of other cultures than to their own. This is especially true of Israelite culture, which for many years was believed to have rejected any sort of mythology in favour of belief in the one God.

Israelite culture could be considered antimythological to the extent that it rejected the various fertility cults and nature gods of its neighbours. Throughout the Bible, the Israelites maintain that there is only one God, and that the forces of nature are under his control. On the other hand, scholars of religion regard myth as a genre that attempts to express a specific culture's sense of the ultimate order of things. And in that context it is possible to see the Hebrew view of the relationship between God and the people Israel itself as a myth expressing the ultimate meaning of life for Hebrew culture.

Abraham

The narratives of the **patriarchs and matriarchs**—the tribal ancestors of the Hebrews—mark the transition from the imaginative paradigms of myth and allegory to the anecdotal detail of legend. While there is no evidence outside the Bible that Abraham and Sarah, Isaac and Rebecca, Jacob and his wives, Joseph, Moses, and the rest ever existed, we can plausibly situate them in the culture of the ancient Near East as it is documented in archaeological records from places like Mesopotamia and Egypt.

In the past these neighbouring cultures were known to the West almost solely through the Bible's references to them, but modern archaeological and textual research has brought to light many details of the patriarchs' world. We now have records of ancient peoples living on the Mesopotamian plain (between the Tigris and Euphrates rivers, in modern Iraq) and in Egypt whose history goes back 2,000 years before the Hebrews. Mesopotamian texts composed after 1800 BCE suggest that the stories of the patriarchs do contain some historically accurate threads. For instance, the names of Abraham's ancestors resemble place names mentioned in northern Mesopotamian records between the nineteenth and twelfth centuries BCE. According to the biblical account, Abram (his original name, changed to Abraham in his old age) is told by God to leave his home in Ur of the Chaldees, in southern Mesopotamia, and move first to Haran, in northern Mesopotamia and eventually to the land of Canaan, which is located mainly in the hill country known today either as the West Bank or as Judea and Samaria.

From the perspective of the twenty-first century, the Jews are ancient people, but the Hebrews of Abraham's time (and their descendants, the

Israelites and Judeans) saw themselves as a people newly born through the specific command of their God. Even so, by the beginning of the Common Era the Jews' history as a people was long and eventful enough for the Romans to recognize them as an ancient people and to respect the legitimacy of their religion.

Covenant

The central organizing concept in the ancient Hebrews' religion was the covenant (in Hebrew, **berith**). A theological term, 'covenant' means much the same thing that 'contract' does today. The purpose of life for those bound by the covenant is defined by the special contractual relationship into which first Abraham, then Jacob and Moses and the people of Israel, enter with God, since the covenant specifies exactly how God desires Abraham's descendants to behave. God promises Abraham that he and his descendants will have the land of Canaan for their own—but the land is not a free gift. Both sides must live according to specific obligations.

When Abraham asks for some assurance that the divine promise will be fulfilled, God appears to him in a vision and instructs him to 'Bring . . . a heifer three years old, a she-goat three years old, a ram three years old, a turtledove, and a young pigeon.' Abraham obeys, cuts the animals in two, and lays 'each half over against the other'. Then, after 'the sun had gone down and it was dark, behold, a smoking fire pot and a flaming torch passed between these pieces. On that day the LORD made a covenant with Abram, saying, 'To your descendants I give this land' (*Genesis* 15: 8–10, 17–18).

The flaming torch, signifying the presence of God, passes between the pieces of the animals to signify that God has sworn a solemn oath. This ceremony is believed to reflect the treaty-making practices of the ancient Near East. (Apparently, the cutting-up of the animals symbolized the laying of a curse on anyone who violated the oath.) Thus God's providence is expressed in the form of a treaty between two great chiefs: Abraham, the ancestor of all the people of Israel, and Yahweh, the God who promises to oversee the destiny of his descendants, provided they conform to the model of behaviour laid out in the covenant.

The theme of obedience to God's will is emphasized a few chapters later, in *Genesis* 22, when God calls on Abraham to sacrifice his son Isaac as a burnt offering. Abraham binds his son, prepares the fire, and is grasping his knife when at the last moment an angel intervenes, telling him to spare the boy and sacrifice an animal instead. Indicating God's opposition to the human sacrifice practised by the Canaanites, this story also helps to justify the building of the Temple at Jerusalem, which was identified as Mount Moriah (2 *Chronicles* 3: 1), the place where the sacrifice supposedly took place.

The idea that the laws governing a particular society have divine sanction was in no way unusual. All the great cultures of the Near East at the time of the Hebrews, and for centuries before them, attributed their legal systems to various gods. The Babylonian king Hammurabi (r. 1792–1750 BCE), for example, was said to have been selected by the god of wisdom to establish his famous code of law. However, Hammurabi's code was also seen as his own great achievement. The Hebrews were distinctive in regarding their law as having been given to them directly by God.

The two other patriarchs—Abraham's son Isaac and Isaac's son Jacob—are similarly portrayed as making covenants with God, as is Moses, centuries later, at Sinai. These accounts of the legendary early leaders parallel the ceremonial covenant-making of the part-legendary, part-historical Hebrew kings David, Solomon, and Josiah, and the scribe Ezra. Each of these great figures in biblical history renews the covenant between himself, his people, and his God.

Finally, the nature of the rewards promised in return for faithful adherence to the covenant reflect the values and perspectives of Hebrew society at the time when these narratives were written. The ultimate rewards are offspring and a homeland,

but in addition Abraham himself is assured of a long life and a peaceful death (*Genesis* 15: 15). It is also worth noting the absence of any reference to the prospect of a reward after death. The ancient Hebrews understood ultimate rewards in concrete terms: an easy death after a long and comfortable life, with many descendants to carry on afterward. The early part of the Hebrew Bible offers no indication of interest in the disposition of souls after death.

Moses and the Exodus

The narratives of the patriarchs as national ancestors in *Genesis* are followed by the dramatic account of Moses as leader and lawgiver in *Exodus*. Whereas the stories of the patriarchs are situated in a period of migration from Mesopotamia into the land of Canaan, the Moses narratives place him at the head of a migration from the other centre of ancient Near Eastern civilization, Egypt. In reality, these two migrations may have overlapped, some of the Hebrew ancestors coming from the direction of Egypt via the Sinai Peninsula and others from the east and north, from the direction of Mesopotamia. In the Bible, however, the two migrations are described as occurring in strict chronological and historical sequence. Thus the descendants of Abraham are first sent to Egypt and then, after 400 years of oppression, are led home by Moses. In arranging their material in this way, the compilers emphasized the linearity of Hebrew thought and its dogged historicism, in which God is seen as the author of every consecutive event.

The Divine Name

Chapter 3 of *Exodus* relates an encounter that Moses has with God during a visit to the wilderness before his people's escape from Egypt. In that account, Moses has a vision of God as a flame in a bush that burns without being consumed. God then identifies himself as the God of the patriarchal lineage—Abraham, Isaac, and Jacob—and gives his personal name, represented in Hebrew by the four letters YHWH.

Conventionally, scholars write this Hebrew word as 'Yahweh'. Without the vowels to go between those consonants, it is impossible to know how that name would have been pronounced, although the text of *Exodus* 3: 14, in which YHWH tells Moses 'I am who I am', suggests a connection with the Hebrew verb *hayah*, 'to be'. Thus the statement 'I am who I am' may mean 'I am the one who causes things to happen.' If this interpretation is correct, God's own name, Yahweh, may originally have meant something like 'he who causes to be'. It was not unusual for gods in the ancient Near East to be named after their primary features. If that was the case with the Hebrew God, embedded in this etymology are far-reaching intuitions about the uniqueness of events. God causes history, as well as the endless seasonal repetition that characterizes the concept of time in the agricultural calendar.

Over the centuries, partly because of the commandment not to take God's name in vain, it came to be considered blasphemous to pronounce the name at all. However, traditional Judaism also forbade any tampering with the Hebrew scriptural text, in which the sequence YHWH appears frequently. Therefore Jews reading aloud from the scripture would substitute the Hebrew word *adonay* (a title similar to 'lord') wherever the four letters YHWH were written. English translations usually print the substitute term entirely in small capital letters, as LORD or GOD.

The name 'Jehovah' is a variation on the same theme, formed by combining the four Hebrew consonants YHWH with the vowels from the word *adonay*. 'Jehovah' is used only in Christian circles; it gained currency in the sixteenth century, when Protestants with limited knowledge of Hebrew began turning to the ancient biblical texts in their campaign against the abuses they perceived in the institutional Church of Rome.

In some branches of Judaism today, not even the four Hebrew consonants are written: instead, the name is represented by a double *y*, or an *h* with an apostrophe. Similarly, the English words 'God' and 'Lord' are not written in full, but as 'G–d' and 'L–rd'. In spoken usage, the Hebrew expression *ha-Shem*, 'the Name', is substituted for YHWH or Adonai.

The Exodus

When the **Exodus** story begins, the Hebrews are in Egypt, working on construction projects in the eastern part of the Nile Delta. The work amounts to slave labour, and God tells Moses to request the Hebrews' release from the Egyptian pharaoh. When the pharaoh refuses, God sends plagues on the Egyptians but spares the Hebrews, enabling them to escape from Egypt. They cross the Yam Suf—traditionally translated as 'Red Sea', but literally the Reed Sea—which swamps their pursuers, and reach the barren Sinai Peninsula.

In time all Jewish people, whatever their individual origins, would come to identify with the Exodus story, which they understood as a metaphor of the transition from slavery to freedom as a people under God's special providence, with a destiny and a purpose. To this day they commemorate their participation in the event during the **Passover** festival.

It is during the forty years of nomadic life in the wilderness, under the leadership of Moses, that the legal foundations of Israelite society are laid. Moses meets with God at Mount Sinai and receives the Ten Commandments as the core of Israel's law, written on stone tablets 'with the finger of God' (*Exodus* 31: 18).

The Ten Commandments, presented in *Exodus* 20: 2–17 and again in *Deuteronomy* 5: 6–21 (the term 'Deuteronomy' means 'second law'), are stipulations of a covenant. In the covenantal renewal ceremony that is described in *Deuteronomy*, there is a communal oath taking: all the people, not just the leaders, swear to obey its terms.

The foundations of Israelite ritual life are also laid during the wilderness period, when the children of Israel were wandering in the desert. Moses' brother, Aaron, becomes the archetypal priest. In the absence of a permanent Temple,

In the shadow of Mount Sinai. There is no archaeological proof that this peak on Egypt's Sinai Peninsula is the one where Moses received the Ten Commandments, but it has been associated with the event since at least the fourth century (Andrew Leyerle).

Hebrew worship is instituted in an elaborate tent called the Tabernacle. Kept in the Tabernacle as the central cult object is a chest called the Ark of the Covenant, which serves as the throne for God's invisible presence. No image is placed on this base, for the deity is not to be represented by any three-dimensional image. However, two winged beasts called the cherubim are depicted on the top, and God is sometimes imagined as riding between their wings. The prohibition against depicting God himself marked a sharp contrast to the image-rich practices of all the Israelites' neighbours. When Moses discovers that Aaron has capitulated to popular sentiment and erected a statue of a golden calf for the people to worship, Moses proclaims God's denunciation of such idolatry.

The Israelite Kings

The Israelites proceed from nomadic to settled life in the land of Canaan under Moses' successors, beginning with Joshua. The book of *Joshua* recounts some spectacular victories over the Canaanites. But the following book, *Judges*, suggests that it was no easy task to displace the Canaanites, with their heavily fortified cities and well-equipped armies.

At first the Israelites are able to gain only a few positions in the hill country for themselves, and for a time they are even tempted to emulate the Canaanites in their worship of a fertility god named Ba'al. But Yahweh denounces the Canaanite religious practices of ritual prostitution and child sacrifice, and he demands that the Israelites repudiate them, promising the Hebrews progeny and long life if they obey his covenant.

The Ten Commandments, *Exodus* 20: 2–17

I am the LORD your God who brought you out of Egypt, out of the land of slavery.

You shall have no other god to set against me.

You shall not make a carved image for yourself nor the likeness of anything in the heavens above, or on the earth below, or in the waters under the earth. You shall not bow down to them or worship them; for I, the LORD your God, am a jealous god. I punish the children for the sins of the fathers to the third and fourth generations of those who hate me. But I keep faith with thousands, with those who love me and keep my commandments.

You shall not make wrong use of the name of the LORD your God: The LORD will not leave unpunished the man who misuses his name.

Remember to keep the sabbath day holy. You have six days to labour and do all your work. But the seventh day is a sabbath of the LORD your God; that day you shall not do any work, you, your son or your daughter, your slave or your slave-girl, your cattle or the alien within your gates; for in six days the LORD made heaven and earth, the sea, and all that is in them, and on the seventh day he rested. Therefore the LORD blessed the sabbath day and declared it holy.

Honour your father and mother, that you may live long in the land which the LORD your God is giving you.

You shall not commit murder.

You shall not commit adultery.

You shall not steal.

You shall not give false evidence against your neighbour.

You shall not covet your neighbour's house; you shall not covet your neighbour's wife, his slave, his slave-girl, his ox, his ass, or anything that belongs to him.

The greatest threat the Israelites face, however, comes from the Philistines, who arrive on the coastal plain at about the same time as the Israelites emerge from the desert and become their principal rivals. Although 'Philistine' now connotes a lack of culture, the biblical Philistines were related to the Mycenaean Greeks and far more advanced than the Hebrew shepherds, especially in iron technology. The Romans would eventually name the region Palaestina, after the Philistines.

In this period the Israelites lived as a loose tribal confederation informally ruled by chieftains known as *shofetim* (often translated as 'judges'). There was no official process for electing or appointing the judges: their leadership was charismatic, meaning that it depended entirely on popular acceptance. Evidently there were local elders and priests too, but in moments of crisis the people looked to the judges for leadership. By modern historical standards, the judges—Deborah, Samson, Shamgar, Jephthah, and Ehud, to name only a few—are all legendary characters, but the accounts in the book of *Judges* describe them as chosen by God to save the Israelites from threats of foreign domination.

In the two generations coming shortly after 1000 BCE, Israelite society experienced a shift to a centralized monarchy. Kingship was a new institution, created to deal with the threats posed by the Canaanites and especially the Philistines. According to the story narrated in *1 and 2 Samuel*, God chooses first Saul, then David, and finally David's successors to be kings because the Israelites need relief from the Philistine menace. At first God is reluctant to appoint a king, but both the people and the times seem to demand one. Ultimately God places the government squarely in the hands of a dynasty founded by the unlikely figure of David.

We first meet David, the youngest son of Jesse, as an inexperienced youth fit only to look after the sheep. But God strengthens David's hand to the point that he is able to defeat the Philistines' champion, Goliath, and unify the northern and southern tribes as a single Israelite people. The Bible leaves us with the impression that the Philistines disappear, although we know from the archaeological evidence that their cities continued to exist as more or less powerful entities throughout the entire period of Israelite settlement. Then David captures Jerusalem from the Jebusites and makes it his capital, often referred to as 'the City of David'.

David's successor is Solomon—his son by Bathsheba, his favourite wife. Solomon undertakes a number of ambitious construction projects throughout the kingdom, including a lavish Temple to Yahweh on the hill called **Zion**, a rock-outcrop ridge on the uphill side of Jerusalem. But his build-up of the central government and his use of conscript labour have the effect of alienating the ten northern tribes.

On Solomon's death, about 921 BCE, the kingdom breaks up. The northern tribes follow a usurper named Jeroboam. Eventually they make Samaria their capital and take the name Ephraim or 'Israel' for themselves. In inscriptions in foreign capitals they are often known as the 'Sons of Omri', after a powerful later king. The southern kingdom of Judah is usually known as the 'Sons of David' on foreign inscriptions. The northern kingdom continues for two centuries until they are overrun and dispersed by Assyrian invaders in 722 BCE, after which they become known as the 'ten lost tribes'. The southern tribes, centring on Jerusalem and using the name Judah, continue until 586 BCE, when the city was invaded by Babylon and its leaders were sent into exile. In the centuries that followed the Babylonian conquest, the people longed for a restoration of the Davidic kingship as a sign of God's continuing loyalty to his covenant people.

The Five Books of Moses

In the northern and southern Israelite regions, the stories of Abraham and Jacob functioned to unify their populations, who all claimed descent from these patriarchs. The idea of a family connection to Jacob originated among the ten Hebrew tribes in the northern kingdom, and Jacob's alternative name, Israel, became the name of the people. Meanwhile, the idea of a family connection to Abraham, who lived south of Jerusalem, served to bond the remaining two Hebrew tribes in the southern kingdom of Judah. When the kingdom was unified under David, each region, north and south, came to understand the other's stories as part of its own heritage. Eventually, scribes living in the south incorporated all the stories into a single narrative told from the perspective of the Davidic monarchy.

The kingship as an institution was able to put its imprint on many of the early traditions of Israel because it was the power behind the collection of the stories. Later generations would look back to the accomplishments of King David, followed by those of King Solomon, as manifestations of divine favour. As founder of the Judean dynasty, David was idealized for his military shrewdness. He was also depicted as talented in music, so that the hymn collection of the Jerusalem Temple, the contents of the book of *Psalms*, came to be attributed to him.

With the reign of Solomon, the scribes attached to the court and the Temple began to see their little country as having at last established a reputation in the wider world. And indeed it had, although the immediate reason appears to have been a short-lived power vacuum created by the simultaneous declines of the Egyptian and Mesopotamian empires. Solomon enters into marriages with foreign princesses, thereby cementing political alliances, and plays host to a visiting queen from Sheba, a region to the south in Arabia later fabled for its aromatic incense. Solomon is portrayed as the paragon of wisdom, and the biblical collection of *Proverbs* is attributed to him.

But the United Kingdom of Israel did not last long. Solomon's son Rehoboam made the decision to impose the Jerusalem government's policies on the northern tribes, which led them to secede under Jeroboam. The breach was never healed. But after the northern tribes were dispersed by the Assyrians in 722 BCE, the southern kingdom continued as a state for another century and a half, until it was conquered by the Babylonians in 586 BCE.

Besides the accounts produced within the governing circles in the society, many ancient traditions were collected and transmitted by priests. The clearest examples can be seen in the books of *Leviticus* and *Numbers*, centring on the priestly law code in *Leviticus* 18–26. These traditions were also included in the five books of Moses, in the late monarchy and the exile. The priestly writers were responsible for editing the books into the form we know today.

All the editorial voices mentioned so far—northern, southern, even priestly—put their individual stamps on the biblical account of the transmission of the law at Sinai. It is the crucial event defining the Israelite people, and today it still gives the Jewish religion its special character. For the Orthodox community, it was at Sinai that the entire corpus of the five books was given, from the story of creation to the farewell address of Moses before he dies at the threshold of the promised land. It was all given by special revelation, directly from God to Moses.

Various editors and transmitters of the text, from their own perspectives, sought to emphasize that the covenant between Israel and God entails a social contract. The Ten Commandments emphasize human social responsibilities, as does the Book of the Covenant, the extended law code that immediately follows the commandments. Similarly, the priestly narrators, interested in the ritual and liturgical aspects of the covenant ceremony, portray Moses as an intermediary between God and the people.

Critical study of the Bible in modern times has meant a major shift in the questions asked of the first five books of the Bible. For centuries, tradition had ascribed their composition to Moses, acting under divine inspiration or dictation. Faced with a discrepancy or difficulty in the received text, a traditional commentator would typically ask what God intended the text to mean. Modern interpreters, by contrast, have tended to ask who would have chosen to make a particular statement, and why. In this context discrepancies are seen not as challenges to faith but as clues for investigation.

Modern Theories of the Composition of the Bible

One of the first to suggest that the Pentateuch, the five books of Moses, might be a composite creation was the eighteenth-century French physician Jean Astruc, who called attention to differences in the names used to refer to God. He suggested that material by one author, who consistently referred to God as Yahweh, had been intermixed with that of another, who regularly referred to God as Elohim. Other investigators began to notice stylistic differences within the text, and in the second half of the nineteenth century a theory of four major blocks of material in the Pentateuch was articulated by the German scholar Julius Wellhausen.

Wellhausen's theory, known as the **Documentary Hypothesis**, has been vehemently criticized by traditional Jews, Christians, and Muslims alike, who reject its humanizing assumptions. It has also been criticized by many liberal and radical scholars, who may share those assumptions but who disagree on details of composition and compilation. Still, the broad outlines identified in the Documentary Hypothesis continue to shape much contemporary scholarship and serve as a basis for further research. In that sense, it stands as one of the great intellectual achievements of the nineteenth century.

The nineteenth-century Bible scholars imagined individual people writing specific documents at specific times. Now we know that each source represents the perspective of a particular oral tradition, later written down by a group of scribes working under the auspices of a particular institution in the society—such as the royal bureaucracy or the Temple bureaucracy—and that in each case oral traditions were included in their editorial efforts, a process that continued over several generations.

The hypothetical author or school associated with use of the name Yahweh is called the Yahwist. The material of this source is identified by the letter J, because the name 'Yahweh' is spelled with J in German, the language of the scholars who first put forward the hypothesis. The Yahwist, who emphasized southern localities and the role of Abraham, is thought to have worked in the southern kingdom of Judea, probably beginning before the division of the kingdoms in the late tenth century BCE.

The second source is called E, or the Elohist, for its use of the generic term 'Elohim' to refer to God. E wrote in the northern kingdom after its separation, probably starting during the ninth century BCE, and emphasized northern local traditions. E refers to the sacred mountain as Horeb, not Sinai, and to the people displaced by the Israelites as Amorites rather than Canaanites. God is a more awesome and remote entity for E than for J, and the covenant relationship is less nationalistic.

In many places, however, the two strands, J and E, have been woven together to create a great Hebrew epic known as JE, which can be recognized by its use of the term 'the LORD God' to speak of the divinity. The Garden of Eden story beginning in *Genesis* 2 is a good example of JE, whereas *Genesis* 1 represents a priestly prologue to the whole story.

According to *2 Kings* 22: 8, a copy of the book of the law was found during the reign of Josiah, in 621 BCE, in the course of repairs to the Temple in Jerusalem. On the authority of that book, altars elsewhere in the kingdom were suppressed and worship was centralized at the Jerusalem Temple for the first time. Since the earliest known reference to the restriction of worship to a single location comes in *Deuteronomy* 12: 13, it is assumed that the book that was found was *Deuteronomy* and that it, the D source, was a new production.

Ostensibly, *Deuteronomy* is a sermon by Moses, which would place its composition some 600 years earlier. But its vocabulary and concerns are those of Josiah's day, when the prophet Jeremiah was active. Indeed, when Moses speaks of himself as a prophet in *Deuteronomy* 18: 15, he suggests a set of role expectations characteristic of the prophetic movement as it is thought to have existed in the eighth and seventh centuries BCE but not earlier. Central to the D source is a rewards-and-punishments theology of national morality.

In some ways the most striking aspect of the Documentary Hypothesis is its suggestion that P, the priestly source, was a late contribution to the body of writings that make up the Pentateuch. It is another voice that had been developing independently in the society. In its present form, it is thought to come from 586–539 BCE, the period after the Jerusalem Temple had been destroyed and the Judean leadership sent into exile by the Babylonians, for it contains numerous descriptions and measurements of the Temple and its furnishings. As long as the Temple stood, there would have been no need for these details, but with the Temple in ruins, P offers a literary blueprint for its restoration.

Israelite Society

The complex textual history makes it difficult to form a clear picture of ordinary life in the biblical period. In the case of gender relations, for instance, we do not know whether the stories reflect conditions in the actual patriarchal period or in the kingship period when they were written. Yet some contemporary interpreters use biblical models to govern their own behaviour and to force others to comply. When interpreters say that the Bible restricts marriage to one woman and one man, they seem to forget that the patriarchs and many Israelites took several wives and concubines, as late as the time of Jesus.

There are a few basic respects in which the biblical accounts probably do reflect social reality, since the details are consistent across the centuries. Marriage, for instance, was almost universal among Hebrews; men were allowed several wives if they could afford to support them; and children were highly prized (offspring are referred to again and again as rewards for faithful observance of the covenant with Yahweh). On the whole, tilling the land and securing it from harm were men's responsibilities, while raising children and running the household were women's. The nature of the interaction between men and women is not so clear, however.

The relationship between Abraham and Sarah is depicted as cooperative and very direct. Certainly Sarah is able to affect many decisions within the household. And David is portrayed as indulging his wives even in the highly charged political atmosphere of his old age, when the succession to his throne was paramount in all his children's minds. But these characters represent the elite of their society, and the power that women at that level enjoyed was conferred on them by their husbands. A woman without a husband (or father, or son) to provide for her depended entirely on the protection provided by Yahweh's laws (*Exodus* 22: 22; *Deuteronomy* 10: 18).

Women often play a part in the exposition of important themes. For example, the military victory of the judge Deborah over the Canaanites helps to illustrate God's control over history. He chooses the least likely characters as champions—women,

left-handers, lowly shepherds, inexperienced youths—precisely in order to show that it is he, not the individual, who determines victory and defeat. Deborah's gender thus functions exactly as the young David's weakness does, to demonstrate God's power.

God's complete control over history is also reflected in many birth stories. Often, when a special birth is to be announced, the prospective mother is said to be barren. Since failure to bear children would undermine the covenant, God intervenes directly to prepare the mother's womb so that she can deliver the child who will benefit the people. Later, Greek stories of heroes born from the union of gods and humans would apparently play a role in the New Testament doctrine of the virgin birth of Jesus. But the Hebrew Bible chose a different way to mark a special or revelatory birth.

Somewhat easier to reconstruct than the personal life of the Israelites is their legal system. The Hebrews appear in many instances to have put more emphasis on fairness than their more civilized neighbours. Incarceration was a frequent punishment among the latter, but virtually unknown among the Israelites. A large number of Hebrew laws allow for penalties of monetary restitution rather than bodily mutilation. Restitution is quite frequently substituted for crimes that in neighbouring countries were punished by death. By Greek and Roman times, the use of monetary compensation for loss was evidently universal.

On the other hand, for crimes like murder or adultery, Hebrew society consistently demanded capital punishment, whereas in other nations the punishment depended on the rank of the perpetrator. In most Mesopotamian nations, an aristocrat could make restitution for the death of a commoner, but a commoner would suffer capital punishment for the same crime. Hebrew law made no such distinction in status. It also demanded capital punishment for adultery on the part of a wife, because violation of the marriage vow represented an offence against the deity before whom it was sworn. The common double standard of the ancient world, where the punishments for infidelity differed significantly between men and women, was exacerbated by the fact that men were permitted to have more than one wife.

Slavery was practised throughout the ancient world, but was somewhat less offensive in Hebrew society than elsewhere, at least in some respects. For example, the Israelites were forbidden to enslave their debtors for any more than a fixed term. Thus a man—and his family—could be enslaved to work off the value of an unpaid debt. But the period of enslavement was not indefinite. When the debt was discharged, at puberty in the case of a young female slave, or at the next sabbatical year (when the fields lay fallow), Hebrew slaves had to be set free.

The Prophets

Perhaps as important as the voices of the priests and legal experts in the Hebrew Bible are those of the prophets. Since both Christianity and Islam also associate themselves with prophetic insight, the prophetic movement may be said to have influenced more people than any other religious movement in human history.

Hebrew prophecy appears to have grown out of ancient Near Eastern traditions of spirit possession. Such experiences are described as 'ecstatic' because they involve a kind of psychological displacement, so that practitioners 'stand outside' the bounds of normal awareness and conduct. A number of ecstatic prophets—among them Elijah, Elisha, and Micaiah ben Imlah—are mentioned in the Bible from the time of the Hebrew settlement of the land through the early monarchy, but the period of the major prophets, whose visions and predictions are preserved in the Bible, does not begin until about 750 BCE.

How the prophets received their messages is unknown. It is possible that they actively sought to induce visions; however, they present themselves as the intermediaries used by God to communicate with his people, and the words they deliver are understood to be God's, not their own. The prophetic writings surviving from (or ascribed to) the period between the ninth and fifth centuries BCE are notable for their rational clarity, their social criticism, and their poetic intensity. These literary prophets (all of them men) appear in a variety of contexts, sometimes speaking from within the administration of the monarchy and sometimes as social critics standing outside it. Whatever their social location, the message they deliver is always the same: that the people are not living up to God's covenant and that they will soon be punished if they do not change their ways.

The writings of the prophets refer to the concept of the covenant not in the narrow technical language of treaties, but in the broader language of metaphor. The prophet Amos delivers the words of Yahweh: 'You only have I known of all the families on earth. Therefore I will punish you for all your iniquities.' The word 'know' in this context has a specific meaning in ancient Hebrew, referring to recognition of a covenant obligation. Yahweh, as Amos presents him here, may sound like a kind of despot, but in fact he is stating a grievance and seeking redress because Israel has defaulted on its contract with him.

In the eyes of the prophets, marriage contracts are also covenants. They have stipulations and are enforced by an oath. The accusations of seduction and adultery in *Hosea* gain their force by describing the covenant between Israel and Yahweh as a troubled marriage. The prophet presents Israel as the wayward wife of Yahweh, who will win her back and even forgive her adultery. Metaphorically, the prophets are describing the people's worship of the Canaanite fertility gods with the term 'adultery':

Therefore, behold, I will allure her, and bring her into the wilderness, and speak tenderly to her. And there I will give her her vineyards, and make the Valley of Achor a door of hope. And there she shall answer as in the days of her youth, as at the time when she came out of the land of Egypt. And in

From the Prophets

It has been told you, mortal, what is good and what the LORD requires of you: only to act justly, to love mercy, and to walk humbly before your God (*Micah* 6: 8).

He shall not judge by what his eyes see, or decide by what his ears hear; but with righteousness he shall judge the poor, and decide with equity for the meek of the earth; and he shall smite the earth with the rod of his mouth, and with the breath of his lips he shall slay the wicked (*Isaiah* 11: 3–4).

In the days to come the mountain of the LORD's house shall be set over all other mountains, lifted high above the hills. All the nations shall come streaming to it, and many peoples shall come and say, 'Come, let us climb up on to the mountain of the LORD, to the house of the God of Jacob, that he may teach us his ways, and we may walk in his paths.' For [Torah] issues from Zion, and out of Jerusalem comes the word of the LORD; he will be judge between nations, arbiter among many peoples. They shall beat their swords into mattocks and their spears into pruning-knives; nation shall not lift sword against nation nor ever again be trained for war (*Isaiah* 2: 2–4, also *Micah* 4: 1–3).

that day, says the LORD, you will call me, 'My husband', and no longer will you call me, 'My ba'al.' For I will remove the names of the ba'als from her mouth, and they shall be mentioned by name no more. . . . And I will betroth you to me forever; I will betroth you to me in righteousness and in justice, in steadfast love, and in mercy. I will betroth you to me in faithfulness; and you shall know the LORD (*Hosea* 2: 14–20).

If the people give up their sinful relationship with the Canaanites' goddesses and gods, their sexual rituals of fertility and their abhorred child sacrifice, Yahweh will reconcile with them. The force of this prophetic writing depends on the prophet's effective use of the metaphors of love and betrothal for covenantal obligation. Since the name of the Canaanite god, Ba'al, also means 'husband', it too becomes part of the extended metaphor of adultery. Through the ages, the Hebrew tradition's great sin of idolatry has continued to be identified with adultery.

Despite the prophets' warnings, however, the nation continued its drift towards ruin. The literary prophets recorded the destruction of the northern and southern kingdoms. Some of them had been critics of the establishment; others belonged to it. But their eloquence, as well as their successful predictions of national destruction, convinced later Israelite society that they all spoke the word of Yahweh.

The Babylonian Exile

In 586 BCE the Judean kingdom fell; Solomon's Temple was razed, to lie in ruins for three generations; and the Hebrews' leaders were sent into exile in Babylon. As much as any single event, the **Exile** marks the transition of the Hebrew tradition from the national cult of an ancient kingdom to the religious heritage of a widely dispersed people. From the sixth century BCE on, we can speak of Jews (i.e., 'Judeans') and Judaism, rather than of Hebrews or Israelites and Hebrew or Israelite religion.

The catastrophes that followed the Babylonian invasion mark the disruption of many ancient Israelite institutions. As in the case of many historical transitions, not everything happened overnight, but the Exile gave focus and impetus to a number of significant social and religious changes.

The heritage was no longer that of a national state but of a subject or minority population. Especially among Jews dispersed abroad, life was now more urban than agricultural, so that many of the old agriculturally based laws and rituals needed to be rethought. In the absence of the Temple, the focus shifted away from formal worship towards congregational life. At some time during the Exile, the institution known as the synagogue was born, and Temple worship never regained its former importance even after the Temple was rebuilt. Aramaic gradually replaced Hebrew as the vernacular language, and although Hebrew remained the language of ritual, it took on an antiquarian flavour. The longing for restoration of Yahweh's sovereignty expressed itself in a variety of ways, including visions of a deliverer king (messianism) or a cosmic battle followed by judgment at the end of the age (apocalypticism).

Even to Jews who lived at a distance from Jerusalem, the Temple there symbolized their covenant:

By the waters of Babylon, there we sat down and wept, when we remembered Zion. On the willows there we hung up our lyres.

For there our captors required of us songs, and our tormentors, mirth, saying, 'Sing us one of the songs of Zion!'

How shall we sing the LORD's song in a foreign land?

If I forget you, O Jerusalem, let my right hand wither! Let my tongue cleave to the roof of my mouth, if I do not remember you, if I do not set Jerusalem above my highest joy!

(*Psalm* 137: 1–6)

The destruction of the Temple brought on a crisis of confidence. The problem was not that Yahweh's dominion was limited to the region of Judah, for he was also lord of all creation, but that he had been worshipped in a single place for so long. Did the destruction of that building mean that Yahweh

had finally abandoned his people? The author of *Lamentations* 5: 20–2 expressed the general fear:

Why dost thou forget us for ever, why dost thou so long forsake us?

Restore us to thyself, O LORD, that we may be restored! Renew our days as of old!

Or hast thou utterly rejected us? Art thou exceedingly angry with us?

The nation needed a sign that God had not permanently rejected it. As if in response, the prophet Ezekiel describes the appearance in a storm cloud of a heavenly chariot driven by the glory of God. Abandoning the Temple just before its destruction, the divine radiance approaches Babylonia. Thus the answer to *Psalm* 137's despair is that Yahweh's song *can* be sung in a foreign land because he has come into exile with his people:

Like the bow in a cloud on a rainy day, such was the appearance of the splendor all around. This was the appearance of the likeness of the glory of the Lord. When I saw it, I fell on my face, and I heard the voice of someone speaking (*Ezekiel* 1: 28).

When Cyrus the Persian conquered Babylon in 538 BCE, therefore, he was seen by the Israelites living there as part of God's plan (see *Ezra* 1: 1; *Isaiah* 41: 2, 44: 28, 45: 1). In his own statements Cyrus did not present himself as the bringer of a new order to the world, but as the restorer of the ancient regimes destroyed by the Babylonians, and hence the champion of all the old gods. He allowed the traditional priests of Babylonia's god Marduk to practise their own religion. And he allowed the Jews to go back to Judea to re-establish their Temple. The account in *Ezra* suggests that Cyrus himself is a worshipper of Yahweh:

In the first year of Cyrus king of Persia, that the word of the LORD by the mouth of Jeremiah might be accomplished, the LORD stirred up the spirit of Cyrus king of Persia so that he made a proclamation throughout all his kingdom and also put it in writing: 'Thus says Cyrus king of Persia: 'The LORD, the God of heaven, has given me all the kingdoms of the earth, and he has charged me to build him a house at Jerusalem, which is in Judah. Whoever is among you of all his people, may his God be with him, and let him go up to Jerusalem, which is in Judah, and rebuild the house of the LORD, the God of Israel—he is the God who is in Jerusalem' (*Ezra* 1: 1–3).

The covenant is being reformulated by the demands of history: The Israelites have learned something about the world from their sojourn in exile. Now Yahweh must direct all of world history, not just the destiny of Judah. Cyrus, the Emperor of Persia, was not a devotee of Yahweh. But his decision to allow the return to Jerusalem was in keeping with his policy of patronizing the priesthoods and cults of the old order. The writer of *Isaiah* 45 is so impressed with Cyrus's rise to power that he calls him the 'messiah' (the anointed one), designated by Yahweh to serve as the instrument through which Israel's destiny will be fulfilled.

The Second Commonwealth

Not all the Jews wanted to return to Judah under the new Persian regime (538–331 BCE), however. Many artisans and aristocrats were prospering in Babylon and chose to stay there, forming the nucleus of a community that would play a major role in the composition of the Babylonian *Talmud* in the early centuries of the Common Era.

With prophetic rhetoric, a postexilic author of later chapters in *Isaiah* declares the theme of homecoming. He maintains that God is on the verge of repeating all his past deliverances:

Comfort, comfort my people, says your
    God.

Speak tenderly to Jerusalem, and cry to her
    that her warfare is ended, that her iniqui-
    ty is pardoned, that she has received from
    the LORD's hand double for all her sins.
    (*Isaiah* 40: 1–2)

The exiles are to be drawn from the far corners of the earth. The new in-gathering will be like a new Exodus, bringing the people of Israel across water and fire. *Isaiah* (43: 15–19) says that, just as at the Red Sea (*Exodus* 15: 3), Yahweh will appear as a warrior doing battle. New heavens and a new earth will be created. This new Israelite commonwealth will be a fresh beginning:

Arise, shine; for your light has come, and
    the glory of the Lord has risen upon you.
For behold, darkness shall cover the earth,
    and thick darkness the peoples; but the
    LORD will arise upon you, and his glory
    will be seen upon you.
And nations shall come to your light, and
    kings to the brightness of your rising.
    (*Isaiah* 60: 1–3)

Isaiah's words are among the most stirring biblical passages. Unfortunately, the condition of the returning exiles was still poor. Archaeological evidence suggests that the buildings were small and decayed quickly. In fact, the beginnings of the postexilic community, or 'second commonwealth', were so meagre that very little is known of events in that period.

The fate of the succession of Judean kings is unclear. The heir to the throne, who adopted the Babylonian name Sin-Ab-Usuru, or Sheshbazzar in Hebrew, arrived in Jerusalem shortly after the return began. Thereafter the descendants of David were called *nasi* ('prince') rather than *melekh* ('king'), perhaps in deference to the Persian Empire, which ruled the country from the east. Zerubbabel, another descendant of David's line, apparently arrived in Judea to succeed Sheshbazzar. The second Temple was then completed in

515 BCE. After that date, all references to Zerubbabel and the kingship cease.

The mysterious disappearance of the Davidic king stimulated legends about a future king. One object of speculation was *2 Samuel* 7, which promised that the Davidic kingship would continue forever. Thus the idea was born that a king of David's line would return and bring with him a perfect order. Until this time, the term 'messiah' had always referred to the current anointed priest or king. Centuries later, it came to be understood as meaning a future king, since there was no anointed, divinely sanctioned king in the line of David on the throne, although the priestly line continued intact.

Ezra and Nehemiah, who established a stable government in Judea, arrived there as court officials of the Persian Empire. Their dates are not known for certain, but the government they set up was explicitly based on the covenantal blueprint outlined in the first five books of Moses. In describing the 'constitutional assembly' convened by Ezra, for instance, Nehemiah attempts to turn the harvest festival known as **Sukkoth** ('Booths' or 'Tabernacles') into a covenant-renewal ceremony, even though he is aware that the crops are now promised to Persian overlords. Such a ceremony could not inaugurate independence. Instead, covenant renewal was at best a national day for the Jewish area called Judah under Persian rule.

An inhabitant of this region, the former tribal territory of Judah, was known as a *yehudi*, a Judean. This is the root of the English word 'Jew'. But under the Persians and then the Greeks, *yehudi* was usually a territorial rather than a religious designation. The term gained its modern meaning, referring to a member of the Jewish religion, only in the first and second centuries CE. The shift, occurring just as the New Testament was being written, gave it a particular ambiguity then. Even so, ethnicity already had religious overtones in the Persian period.

Endogamy—marriage only within a particular group—is the most common marriage system in human society. In the Hebrew case, however, it is also part of a larger symbolic system in which the holiness of the people is protected by concentric circles of exclusion, culminating in the absolute purity of the high priest as he enters the inner sanctum of the Temple on Yom Kippur, the Day of Atonement.

One reason the Hebrews had prohibited intermarriage appears to have been the Canaanites' practice of child sacrifice, which continued even into Roman times. Worshippers of Yahweh were expected to marry within Abraham's family, so that their numbers would grow through the gift of progeny—the very opposite of Canaanite child sacrifice. In time, however, the practice of conversion developed, permitting foreigners to become Jews. The biblical book of *Ruth* identifies a woman of the neighbouring Moabites as an ancestor of King David. In this romance, the emphasis is on marriage *into* the family—rather than intermarriage, marriage out of the family. The fact that David's ancestor enters the family Israel from outside legitimizes the practice for later generations. From now on, the people of the covenant are defined ideologically, not just genealogically.

In the absence of a king, most of the affairs of state came under the purview of the priests. To refer to this system of government as theocracy would be incorrect, for God did not rule directly. Rather, the ruling priests claimed to be carrying out God's purposes. Some of the priests became political bureaucrats.

A notable achievement of this period was the editing of the first five books of the Bible by the priestly aristocracy. Put together in a single work consisting of five scrolls, the document came to be known as the Torah, a word originally signifying a priestly ordinance and reflecting the editorial contributions of the priests. The priestly editors did not fundamentally alter the original epic stories, but they often combined conflicting accounts of the same events in order to make a seeming whole. Gathering past traditions for posterity was a common practice across the Persian Empire in countries seeking to preserve the traditions disrupted by the Assyrians and Babylonians.

The Torah became the foundation document of the nation in the period of the second commonwealth in somewhat the same way that the collected body of British law came to serve as Britain's constitution. Because of the conventions in which covenants were written, however, the Hebrew constitution came complete with a creation myth, a national epic, and a narrative history.

Hellenistic Judaism

The Persian Empire fell to Alexander the Great in 331 BCE. That conquest marked the end of the Hellenic age—the time of the city states in classical Greece—and the beginning of the Hellenistic (from *hellenizo*, meaning 'I speak Greek' or even 'I learn to speak Greek'). It was in this period that Greek was adopted by many peoples of the eastern Mediterranean, where it remained the most important language of trade even after the Romans arrived.

The common culture of this period had little to do with the values of ancient Athens. Increasing trade and cultural contact fostered a cosmopolitan outlook that gradually eroded the Judeans' connections to the traditions of their forefathers. This was especially true for the Jews—now the majority—who lived outside the ancient land of Israel, throughout the Mediterranean and Mesopotamia. The reality of the **Diaspora** (from the Greek for 'sowing of seed', hence 'dispersal') meant that Judaism had to evolve new ways of understanding and explaining itself.

The Jewish community of Alexandria in Egypt adopted Greek names as well as Greek styles of architecture and dress. By the early third century BCE, knowledge of Hebrew had declined to the point that the Bible had to be translated into Greek. According to legend, the translation was the product of seventy scholars who, although working independently, by a miracle produced identical drafts. The edition is therefore called the **Septuagint** (from the Latin for 'seventy').

This story was only a legend, but it served to establish both the religious authority of the Septuagint itself and the legitimacy of biblical translation generally. (By contrast, Islam holds that only the original Arabic Qur'an is authentic; any translation is considered to be only an interpretation.)

Translation brought the Bible to a community with a new set of cultural expectations. For the Jews in Alexandria, the Greek Bible was less the covenant charter of the Hebrew state than it was an object of meditation and literary study. Thus the editors of the Septuagint took the three divisions of Hebrew scripture—*Law*, *Prophets*, and *Writings*—and rearranged them in four genres (law, history, poetry, and prophecy). In the process, various conflicting versions of the same stories were juxtaposed, and the discrepancies between them became more evident than they had been in the Hebrew original.

Even the community still living in Judea was touched by Hellenization, although it may have kept more of its native ways. The district of Judea was very small—closer in size to modern metropolitan Jerusalem than the modern state of Israel. Surrounded by Greek-influenced societies, it could hardly ignore Hellenistic culture. Examples of Hellenistic influence include the amphitheatre and gymnasium constructed in Jerusalem in the second century BCE. In addition, several records identify women as the leaders of congregations and the benefactors of buildings; these women likely benefitted from a general improvement in the status of women—at least among the upper classes—in the late Hellenistic world.

Hellenization proceeded at different rates in different classes, accentuating divisions and exacerbating conflicts among the social classes of Judea. The two groups traditionally charged with leadership within the community—the priests and the rural aristocrats—sought out Greek educational institutions. A developing trades class also learned rudimentary Greek for use in international exchange. These Jews felt that Greek philosophy and culture did not interfere with their Jewishness.

In their early contact with Jewish traditions, the Greeks seem to have been favourably impressed. Hecataeus of Abdera, who travelled and wrote in the fifth century BCE, praised Moses as one 'who did not make any kind of picture of gods, as he did not believe that God was in human form'. Theophrastus, writing in the fourth century BCE, described the Jews as a 'race of philosophers', and many schools of Greek philosophy were sympathetic to the principle of monotheism. Not all responses to Judaism were positive, however. Most anti-Jewish comments by Greek (and Roman) writers merely express a general dislike of foreigners, but xenophobia would cross the line into anti-Semitism in the first century. According to the Jewish historian Flavius Josephus, Apion—an educator who wanted to keep Jews out of the great schools of Alexandria—claimed that the Jews of Jerusalem worshipped an ass's head made of gold.

The Maccabean Revolt

For over a century, Judea was under the control of the Ptolemies—the Greek dynasty (descended from one of Alexander's generals) that had ruled Egypt since 305 BCE. In 198 BCE, however, the territory passed into the hands of a rival Greek dynasty called the Seleucids, the rulers of Syria. Identifying the Hebrews' Yahweh with the supreme god of the Hellenized world, the Seleucids transformed Jerusalem's Temple into a cult place of Zeus in 168 BCE. The Seleucid king, Antiochus IV, raided it for its riches, then moved troops into the Temple area and suspended the local Torah constitution. He may not have intended specifically to crush the Judeans' religion; his motives may have been primarily economic and political. But from the Judeans' perspective, any threat to their community amounted to an attack on their religion.

In 166 BCE a general revolt broke out, led by a group of resistance fighters called the Maccabees (derived from 'hammer', the Hebrew nickname of their leader, Judah). Though its immediate objective was to expel the Seleucids, this action also reflected a dispute within the Jewish community, between traditionalists and those who favoured assimilation to the dominant Hellenistic culture. In *1 Maccabees* the traditionalists accuse the Hellenizers of 'abandon[ing] themselves to evil ways': repudiating the covenant, intermarrying with gentiles, and even 'remov[ing] their marks of circumcision' (*1 Maccabees* 1: 11–15). Those who favoured assimilation probably thought it would advance the political and economic interests of Jerusalem. In the less Hellenized rural areas, however, they were seen as undermining the religious basis of Judean life and violating the Torah constitution. Worse yet, the main proponents of Hellenization were the priests.

The Maccabees prevailed, recapturing Jerusalem from the Seleucids and expanding the Jewish state to its pre-exilic boundaries. The rededication of the Temple, in 164 BCE, brought the divided community together and is commemorated in the minor holiday called Hanukkah. Thereafter, however, the rebel leaders set themselves up as client kings of the Seleucids and Romans, readily adopting Hellenistic culture. Their descendants, known as the Hasmonean dynasty, ruled in shaky independence for more than a century, from 165 BCE until 64 BCE, when the Roman general Pompey captured Jerusalem and brought Judea under Roman occupation.

Dynamics of Hellenism

The Maccabean revolt was a watershed. Once the Hellenization process came into conflict with the traditional constitution of Israel, the Torah, it could no longer be tolerated. But the converse was also true: Greek ideas, no matter how foreign, could be incorporated into Judaism as long as conflict with Torah could be avoided. Life under a foreign empire was possible as long as the political situation allowed for the Israelite constitution to operate as well. Thus a second, subtler phase of Hellenization began, in which Judaism began to adapt Hellenistic ideas and use them for uniquely Judean purposes.

First-Century Sects

Hellenistic society was not merely cosmopolitan but individualistic, and Hellenistic culture encouraged opposing concepts of truth. These qualities were reflected in Hellenistic Judaism, which comprised a variety of sects. Any attempt to impose a single orthodoxy would have led to wholesale defections, but accommodating diversity promoted stability. As in North American party politics today, power was effectively balanced between two major groups—the Sadducees and Pharisees—who together ran the Sanhedrin, a communal council with juridical functions. Representing the upper and middle classes respectively, both these groups faced challenges from two smaller, more radical sects: the Essenes and the Zealots.

Sadducees

The Sadducees represented the upper stratum of Judean society—the aristocracy that embraced Hellenization. The upper class both politically and occupationally, they were also the party of the priestly establishment and the custodians of the Temple, in charge of its operations. They insisted on a narrow, literal interpretation of the law.

Pharisees

The Pharisees represented the middle classes. Some were landowners, some were skilled workers (tent-makers, carpenters, glass-blowers), and many were professional scribes serving the aristocratic Sadducees. From time to time the Pharisees also held power in the Temple, but they were more at home in the synagogues of Judea.

In contrast to the Sadducees, the Pharisees were disposed to interpret the scriptural text broadly, though they tried to establish principles and procedures for scriptural interpretation. They were also punctilious about rules of purity and tithing, which distinguished members in good standing from the general populace. Special groups called *havuroth* ('brotherhoods') were even more strict about these matters, and although they did not withdraw from the general population, they tended to live near their fellowship brothers. Disdaining the Sadducean priests as purely cultic functionaries, the *havuroth* considered themselves to be the proper custodians of the law.

The Christian writers of the New Testament, not surprisingly, were critical of the Pharisees, depicting them as hypocrites more interested in

Josephus on Jewish Sects

Josephus (37–c. 100 CE) came from a priestly family in Jerusalem and was well acquainted with the religious landscape of his day.

Now at this time there were three schools of thought among the Jews, which held different opinions concerning human affairs; the first being that of the Pharisees, the second that of the Sadducees, and the third that of the Essenes. As for the Pharisees, they say that certain events are the work of fate, but not all; as to other events, it depends upon ourselves whether they shall take place or not. The sect of Essenes, however, declare that Fate is mistress of all things, and that nothing befalls men unless it be in accordance with her decree. But the Sadducees do away with Fate, holding that there is no such thing and that human actions are not achieved in accordance with her decree, but that all things lie within our power, so that we ourselves are responsible for our well-being, while we suffer misfortune through our own thoughtlessness (Josephus, *Jewish Antiquities*, 13: 171–3, in Thackeray, trans., 1927–65: 311–13).

the outward forms of ritual than in the inner substance of righteousness. From the Pharisees' own perspective, however, paying attention to external forms was a way of making the sacred law part of everyday life.

Essenes

The Essenes are widely believed to have been the authors of the Dead Sea Scrolls—a collection of manuscripts from the Maccabean and early Roman period discovered in 1947 near the Dead Sea at Qumran. They were a group of rigorously observant priests under the leadership of a man they called the Teacher of Righteousness, or Righteous Teacher. When a candidate they disapproved of was appointed high priest, they left Jerusalem and retired to the desert. There, they established a centre of priestly purity in preparation for what they believed to be the coming **apocalypse**: the final battle between the forces of darkness and light at the end of time.

Reading the past described in the Torah as the model of their future, the Essenes produced a genre of commentary known as *pesher*, applying the text to the events of their own time. They thought of themselves as the new children of Israel, waiting to take the promised land back from the Hellenized Jews and gentiles—the new Canaanites—after a second forty years in the desert.

Zealots

At the far end of the political spectrum were several groups that rejected Roman authority under any circumstances. Most of what we know about these groups comes from Josephus, who describes them as bandits. But in fact their motives appear to have been purely political.

The most famous of these revolutionaries were the Zealots (also characterized by Josephus as 'the Fourth Philosophy'), who came together expressly to liberate Judea from Roman control. Beginning in the northern region called Galilee in 66 CE, the revolt was effectively crushed with the destruction of Jerusalem in 70, but a group of perhaps a thousand rebels defended the fortress of **Masada** for another four years.

Masada was a natural high mesa near the Dead Sea, fitted out by Herod the Great as a self-sufficient, fortified palace, which the Zealots captured from the Romans shortly after the revolt began. It remained the almost impregnable headquarters of the Zealot movement until the rest of Judea had fallen. But after a four-year siege, it too was finally conquered in 73. When the Romans entered the fortress they found all the remaining defenders—men, women, and children—dead by their own hands. According to Josephus, the mass suicide followed a stirring speech by Eleazar:

> But since we had a generous hope that deluded us, as if we might perhaps have been able to avenge ourselves on our enemies . . . let us make haste to die bravely. Let us pity ourselves, our children, and our wives, while it is in our own power to show pity to them; for we were born to die, as well as those were whom we have begotten. . . . But certainly our hands are still at liberty, and have a sword in them. Let them then be subservient to us in our glorious design; let us die before we become slaves of our enemies, and let us go out of the world, together with our children, and our wives, in a state of freedom (Whiston 1802, 3: 471–2).

The emergence of the Zealots upset the balance between the Sadducees and the Pharisees. The revolt against Rome left Jerusalem and the Temple in ruins and also destroyed Qumran. It was from the ashes of these disasters that the **rabbinic movement** would emerge to carry on the traditions of Pharisaism.

Samaritans

Although the Samaritans were descendants of the northern Israelites, their ancestors are thought to have begun marrying outside the Hebrew faith around the end of the eighth century BCE. By the

Hellenistic period they were becoming a separate group on the fringes of Judaism. Rejecting the *Prophets* and *Writings* of the Hebrew Bible, they accepted only the first five books of Moses as canonical, and their version of those books differed significantly from the Hebrew Pentateuch in that it contained several references to a messianic figure expected to be a prophet like Moses.

Christians

Christianity also began as a sect within Judaism, and it is the only Jewish sect of its day whose origins are well known. If we understand Christianity better by considering it as a first-century Jewish sect, therefore, we also understand the first-century Jewish sects better by considering Christianity as one of them.

The Christian message that, with repentance, all are equal before God was typical of all sectarian apocalypticism in first-century Judea. The Christian practices of public repentance, purification through baptism, and chaste communal living were likewise typical of the other contemporary apocalyptic groups. Furthermore, like all the Jewish sects of the time, the Christians posed a problem for the Romans and their upper-level Jewish administrators in that their movement had a clear political dimension. Yet these similarities only emphasize the striking difference between Christianity and Essenism, for example. Essenism was limited to a priestly elite whose members were preoccupied with the cultic purity rules that allowed them to approach God's holy places. Christianity, by contrast, was primarily interested in reaching out to the distressed or sinful.

Jewish Thought in the Hellenistic Period

Attitudes in the Diaspora

Philo was an Alexandrian Jewish philosopher whose writings reflect in sophisticated form views current across the Diaspora in the first century. His work indicates that the Torah remained fundamental, but that Diaspora thinkers were particularly interested in showing that it was in harmony with Greek philosophy on essential issues. Thus, for example, Philo argued that the biblical narrative of the Garden of Eden was not literally true, but should be understood as an allegory of the development of the soul's moral virtues. In this respect Philo seems strikingly modern. Like the Sadducees, however, he insisted on a literal interpretation of many of the laws in the Bible.

The Concept of God

From the beginning, Jewish thought has centred on the assumption of a single, all-powerful creator God who for his own reasons has chosen Israel to carry his message to the world. That God is the sole master of the universe is affirmed in the *Shema* of *Deuteronomy* 6: 4: 'Hear, O Israel, the LORD is our God, the LORD is One.' Contact with Greek culture challenged this idea of God. By this time most Greek philosophers had come to see the universe as dependent on a single principle—variously identified as love, or beauty, or the good—and to think of the traditional gods in allegorical rather than literal terms. Furthermore, the Greeks understood change as a kind of imperfection—and since the idea of creation implied change, in their view the ultimate good could not be a creator. Rather, creation had to be the work of a semi-divine intermediary power called a demiurge. Under the influence of Greek thought, Hellenistic Jewish philosophers like Philo reasoned that there must be some intermediary power to carry out Yahweh's work on this earth. Among the powers they envisioned was the **logos**: a kind of instrumental divine intelligence.

The notion of an intermediary was taken up by Christianity, in which Jesus was said to have a double nature, divine and human at the same time. The idea that God's essence contained a son as well as a father represented a fundamental alteration of the unitary divinity envisioned by Judaism.

The idea that the people Israel were chosen by God is at the centre of their national history. Though not explicitly articulated as a doctrine in Judaism, it is assumed both in the Hebrew

From the *Psalms*

LORD, what is humanity that you are mindful of it,
Or mortals that you take notice of them?
Human life is but a breath of wind,
Their days are a shadow that passes away.
    (*Psalm* 144: 3–4)

Yahweh, hear my prayer, listen to my cry for help, do not stay deaf to my crying, for I find shelter
    with you.
I am your guest, [but] only for a time, a nomad like all my ancestors.
Look away, let me draw breath, before I go away and am no more!
    (*Psalm* 39: 12–13)

But remember this: wise men must die; stupid men, brutish men, all perish.
The grave is their eternal home, their dwelling for all time to come; they may give their own names
    to estates, but they must leave their riches to others.
For men are like oxen whose life cannot last, they are like cattle whose time is short.
    (*Psalm* 49: 10–12)

Bible and in later commentaries on it. Still, as the prophets had pointed out, Yahweh was the Lord not only of Israel, but of all creation. In the Hellenistic era, Christians presented a competing claim for the role of God's chosen people—with a significant difference. Whereas Judaism emphasized the responsibilities entailed by the covenant, under which the Jews were to transmit God's law to all humanity, Christianity emphasized the fulfillment of the covenant's promises, without the obligation to obey the ordinances of Jewish law.

Resurrection

The Jewish Bible abounds in predictions regarding the fate of the world at the end of this age. Yet it says almost nothing about the destiny of the individual at the end of this life. Doctrine concerning the end of the age is termed **eschatology**, from the Greek for 'study of the end'. A genre of Jewish literature that emerged in the later prophetic books (second century BCE) and flourished in the Hellenistic era, continuing even into the Byzantine period of the first several centuries CE, is termed 'apocalyptic', from the Greek for 'unveiling' (the Latin equivalent is 'revelation'). Most apocalyptic literature is eschatological in nature and visionary in presentation. Whereas the prophets had claimed to report Yahweh's words, the apocalyptists generally claimed to report their own visions: 'I saw, and behold . . .'.

The elements that make up the visions represent a kind of code. Sometimes the code is explained and sometimes it is not: the passages without explanations left the field wide open for reinterpretation over the centuries. By and large, the subject of these texts appears to be the fate either of Israel as a whole or of a particularly faithful subgroup.

Regarding the individual, the ancient Hebrews were not preoccupied with the prospect of a continuing existence after death—perhaps in part because they made no strict distinction between body and soul, and therefore had no basis for thinking that something separate from the body might survive death. (The Hebrew word *nefesh*, which is often translated as 'soul', is better translated as 'person'.)

The original answer to the question of where personality goes after death was Sheol, an underground place similar to the Greek Hades, where the individual resides in greatly attenuated form. Sheol is not equivalent to either heaven or hell; rather, it is a pit, a place of weakness and estrangement from God, to which all the dead go and from which the spirits of the dead issue on the rare occasions when they can be seen on the earth. Occasionally, the psalmists and prophets appear to suggest that the righteous live in God's presence, but what this means is unclear:

> Where can I escape from thy spirit? Where can I flee from thy presence?
> If I climb up to heaven, thou art there; if I make my bed in Sheol, again I find thee. . . .
> If I say, 'Surely darkness will steal over me, night will close around me', darkness is no darkness for thee and night is luminous as day; to thee both dark and light are one.
> (*Psalm* 139: 7–8, 11–12)

> All our days go by under the shadow of thy wrath; our years die away like a murmur.
> Seventy years is the span of life, eighty if our strength holds; the hurrying years are labour and sorrow, so quickly they pass and are forgotten. . . .
> Teach us to order our days rightly, that we may enter the gate of wisdom.
> (*Psalm* 90: 9–10, 12)

What mattered was not to continue as a spirit, but to live on in one's descendants. Nothing in Hebrew thought anticipates the post-biblical idea of paradise or resurrection as a reward for a righteous human life. The book of *Ecclesiastes* is particularly clear about the finality of death:

> For the fate of the sons of men and the fate of beasts is the same; as one dies, so dies the other. They all have the same breath, and man has no advantage over the beasts; for all is vanity.
> (*Ecclesiastes* 3: 19)

There is a passage in *Job* that has often been read as a prediction of resurrection, but a more plausible interpretation would see Job as seeking an advocate who will vindicate his challenge to the justice of God while he is still alive:

> For I know that my Redeemer (or Vindicator) lives, and at last he will stand upon the earth;
> And after my skin has been thus destroyed, then from my flesh I shall see God, whom I shall see on my side, and my eyes shall behold, and not another.
> (*Job* 19: 25–6)

Job, like *Ecclesiastes*, seems almost to argue explicitly against any simple belief in immortality—in direct contradiction to the way the book is usually understood today. And while *Ezekiel* 37 describes the resurrection of buried bones, this image is clearly identified as a metaphor referring to national renewal, not personal immortality.

Judaism did eventually develop a doctrine of resurrection, however. This development is traced to the second century BCE, around the time of the Maccabean revolt—likely the first occasion when Jews were asked to risk death specifically for their religion. The evidence is the first unequivocal biblical reference to resurrection, in the book of *Daniel*. (Although this text purports to have been written during the Babylonian period, most—if not all—of it is now assigned to a much later date.) The reference is in *Daniel* 12: 2:

> And many of those who sleep in the dust of the earth shall awake, some to everlasting life, and some to shame and everlasting

contempt. And those who are wise shall shine like the brightness of the firmament; and those who turn many to righteousness, like the stars for ever and ever.

In *Daniel's* vision, the righteous martyrs who died in order to remain true to God's Torah will be restored to everlasting life, while those who persecuted them will endure everlasting punishment. Until the late first century, the idea of resurrection was still a novelty, subject to debate. The Sadducees rejected it entirely, while the Pharisees accepted it, as did the Christians. (The willingness of Jesus' followers to believe in his resurrection would have been consistent with the idea of resurrection for martyrs.)

The Messiah

The term 'messiah' comes from the Hebrew *mashiah*, meaning 'anointed one'; anointing (pouring oil over the head) was a standard Hebrew inauguration ritual signifying divine sanction, usually of a new king. Like the doctrine of resurrection, the idea of a messiah is a concept that emerged and developed in the context of Israel's historical experience. In Hellenistic times it came to mean an ideal future king, priest, or prophet who would lead Israel to victory, but until the collapse of the Judean monarchy in the sixth century BCE, the term almost always referred to the current king. A rare exception, suggesting recognition of divinely sanctioned special service, is a reference to the Persian king Cyrus—who made possible the return from Babylon—as Yahweh's anointed in *Isaiah* 45.

Before the Exile, a few passages from the prophets predicted that God would raise up an ideal king some time in the future. As long as Hebrew kings reigned, however, the term 'messiah' was reserved for them. Thus the expected king is referred to either as the son of David (*Isaiah* 11; *Ezekiel* 34; *Micah* 5) or the 'branch', a new shoot of the Davidic family tree (*Jeremiah* 23).

It was in the Persian period following the return from Exile, after the last heir to the Davidic throne disappeared without a historical trace, that the idea of a future king began to take on a new significance. One basis for hope was a promise in 2 *Samuel* 7 that Israel would never fail to have a king of the Davidic line.

The precise nature of the hopes associated with the future king varied. Thus the Essenes expected a priestly messiah, while Philo, who refers in a veiled way to the messiah, looked forward to a future victory over evil and unjust rulers (*On Rewards* 115–19). And the apocalyptic literature associated the messiah with a divine overturning of the existing order, exemplifying God's sovereign control of events and rewarding the piety of the faithful who had trusted in God.

At one place in the apocalyptic literature a messiah's death is envisioned, but only as a natural part of a sequence of eras. In 2 *Esdras* (or *4 Ezra*) 7: 28–30, God's kingdom is to be established by the messiah and his supporters, all of whom are to live for 400 years. When all die at the end of this period, the world will return to chaos, but eventually the righteous will be resurrected. Nowhere in this literature is there any hint of the Christian idea that the messiah will die for humanity's sins. Whatever suffering may be involved, the messiah is the one who is expected finally to bring God's justice to the world.

Together, the disastrous wars against Rome and the spread of Christianity made the rabbis wary of messianic movements, for they exposed the community to internal and external threats. The rabbinic view was summed up in the advice of Rabbi Yochanan ben Zakkai (first century CE) that, on hearing reports of the messiah, a farmer should first finish planting his tree and only then go to see whether the reports were true (Avot of Rabbi Nathan 31b). The message was clear: while one must not give up hope that the messiah will come, it would be foolhardy to give easy credence to anyone fomenting rebellion or heresy.

Messianism remained an ideal in Judaism through the centuries, its fire dimmed but not extinguished by failed attempts and questionable claimants. Two late examples—Sabbatai Zvi in the seventeenth century and Jacob Frank in the eighteenth—will be discussed later in this chapter.

CRYSTALLIZATION

The Rabbinic Movement

The fall of Jerusalem to the Romans in 70 marked a turning-point in the history of Judaism comparable to the Exile of the sixth century BCE. Once again the Temple was destroyed, and this time it was not rebuilt. Institutions and practices associated with Temple worship—such as animal sacrifice—vanished from Jewish life (the only group to continue animal sacrifice were the Samaritans), and the Sadducees, having lost both their power base and their *raison d'être*, disappeared. So too did the Essenes, whose base at Qumran had been razed by the Romans on their way to besiege the desert fortress of Masada after the sack of Jerusalem. And Rome would tolerate the Zealots no longer.

In this way it fell to the Pharisees to preserve Judaism. Although they too disappeared in time, their traditions became the base on which the institutions of rabbinic Judaism were built. Thereafter, the chief custodians of the Jewish heritage would not be the priests but the teachers and legal specialists known as **rabbis**.

The Bar Cochba revolt of 132–5, a century after Jesus' death, contained strong messianic overtones. When the revolt was quelled, the death of its messianic leader gave rise to a tradition (clearly reminiscent of the early Christians' response to Jesus' death) that the suffering and death of the messiah are necessary for the end to come.

Politically, the Pharisaic-rabbinic movement soon worked out a *modus vivendi* with the Romans. The rabbis conceded that the Jewish community in any location would be subject to the law of the host community. Palestinian Jewish community government was re-established, and although this body had no significant political power, limited local power was eventually granted to the Patriarch (the highest position in Palestine).

Gradually, during and after the second century, what had been one of two Jewish sects vying for power transformed itself into a legal and religious establishment that consciously sought to avoid sectarian divisions. The resulting stability

From Sacrifice to Loving-kindness

Yochanan ben Zakkai was a famous rabbi who helped Judaism make the transition from a religion based around the Temple to a religion based on prayer and acts of loving-kindness in the first century CE.

Once as Rabbi Yochanan ben Zakkai was coming from Jerusalem, Rabbi Joshua followed after him and saw the Temple in ruins.

'Woe unto us,' Rabbi Joshua cried, 'for the place where the iniquities of Israel were atoned is destroyed!'

'My son,' Rabbi Yochanan ben Zakkai said to him, 'do not grieve. We have another atonement as effective as this. And what is it? It is acts of loving-kindness, as it is said: "I desire mercy and not sacrifice"' [Hosea 6: 6] (*The Fathers According to Rabbi Nathan 6*).

was advantageous to Rome because it minimized the risk of dissent and facilitated the collection of taxes and duties.

As the tradition from which Christianity emerged, Judaism might be expected to have stayed closer to the original culture. But in fact rabbinic Judaism, like Christianity, can be seen as both a continuation and a transformation of the biblical tradition. The rabbinic movement was not a hereditary priesthood. All that was required for ordination was the appropriate education, which was available to any male at the local school (the institution of the *yeshiva*, meaning 'sitting' or 'session', evolved over the centuries); as soon as the student had completed his studies to the satisfaction of the teachers, he was ordained a rabbi, though many continued to study the Torah for years afterwards.

The rabbis directed a new attention to religious observance in everyday life, and in so doing they provided the structure that Jewish society needed. Now that the Jews were a subject people, the religious law became the principal means of fulfilling the covenant with God. Disputes over matters such as the right to decree a new month based on sightings of a new moon, which characterized the rabbinic movement, were far less serious than the sectarian issues that had divided Sadducees, Essenes, and Pharisees in the past.

The Temple rituals used in the past to achieve reconciliation between God and Israel were replaced by good deeds and 'acts of loving-kindness'. In the absence of the sacred space within the Temple, the table of every Jew was made sacred through the elaboration of purity rules. In addition, some aspects of the Temple service were transferred to the synagogue. Finally, the community's traditions had to be recorded in texts. The challenge paralleled the one that had faced the priestly writers in the time of the Exile. The Judaism that we know today may be based on the rabbinic Judaism of late antiquity but that Judaism, in turn, was the product of a natural development as the culture of the ancient Hebrews evolved to accommodate the wider world.

The Synagogue

The locus of public worship in rabbinic times was no longer the Temple but the synagogue (from the Greek for 'assembly' or 'gathering'; the word originally referred to the congregation, not the building). Jews continued to pray three times a day, as dictated by the Bible, and to attend special services in commemoration of the special services in the Temple. But Jewish prayer never again revolved around a central Temple. Nor did it take place solely in synagogues: the traditional order of prayer may also be followed at work or at home. It is not unusual to see observant Jews standing in a quiet place reciting their prayers during the day while travelling.

Synagogues may have come into being as far back as the destruction of the first Temple in 586 BCE, but they became especially important as places of assembly, study, and prayer in the Diaspora. After 70 CE, many of the activities that used to take place at the Temple—such as the blowing of the *shofar* (a trumpet made of a ram's horn)—were transferred to the synagogue, along with much of the Temple liturgy (augmented over the years by prayers, poems, and psalms written by rabbinic Jews).

In the first century, as ever afterwards, synagogues often met in the homes of wealthy patrons or patronesses, some of whom exercised considerable leadership, and some even bequeathed their houses to the congregation after their death. (Many of the earliest Christian congregations began in the same way.) There are ruins of synagogue buildings dating from the late first century, and we have literary evidence that synagogues existed even before that: Philo indicates that Alexandria had myriad synagogues, although no traces of them have been found.

The early synagogue buildings were evidently of two kinds: the longhouse (a long rectangular room) and the basilica (modelled on a popular style of Roman municipal architecture). There is also some evidence that buildings designed for other purposes could be pressed into service as synagogues.

At first no special provisions were made to accommodate women. The reason for this is not clear: perhaps women fulfilled their religious duties at home, or perhaps the custom of separation by gender during worship had not yet taken hold (although Josephus refers to segregation in Essene worship in the first century). Dedicatory inscriptions identifying individual women as benefactors of synagogue buildings, with titles such as 'leader' or 'matriarch', do not necessarily mean that those women attended the synagogue, since wealthy Greco-Roman women normally stayed out of public view.

The specific architectural details that characterize synagogues today began to appear by the third century. The congregation prayed facing Jerusalem, the site of the Temple. Cut or painted in the wall in front of them was a niche over which the Torah was placed during the service. Thus, most synagogues in Western countries face east. For prayer at home, many Jews mark the direction with a plaque reading 'Mizrah' ('east' in Hebrew).

At first the Torah scrolls were housed in other buildings for safekeeping and study, and were taken to the synagogue only for services. There is some evidence that in the Hellenistic period, the Torah scrolls were sometimes transported in a model of the ancient Ark of the Covenant, then imagined as a four-wheeled cart with a model Temple on top. This practice may have been influenced by a Greek custom in which the sacred objects of a cult were periodically paraded through the city in a model temple on wheels.

Eventually the Torah niche became an elaborate piece of furniture called the holy ark, permanently housing the Torah scrolls at the front of the synagogue. In later tradition there is a lamp above the ark, the *ner tamid* ('eternal lamp'), which is tended

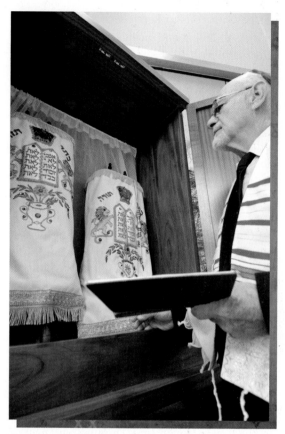

A rabbi with the Torah scrolls in a modern ark (Mike Cherim/istockphoto).

continuously in commemoration of the lamps in the Temple. Also part of synagogue architecture is the *bema* (Greek for 'rostrum'), from which the Torah is read. When placed in the centre of the congregation, this rostrum makes worship a kind of theatre in the round. When placed at the front with the ark containing the Torah, it forms a stage. Both arrangements can still be seen in modern synagogues.

The use of the seven-branched **menorah** ('candlestick' or 'lamp stand') in both ancient and modern synagogues dates back to the days of the Temple. In fact, the Victory Arch of Titus in the Roman Forum depicts Roman soldiers carrying off a large seven-branched menorah as booty from the destruction of the Jerusalem Temple. At that time the menorah became a symbol of Jewish culture and sovereignty; today it is the official symbol of the state of Israel.

The six-pointed star, called the *Magen David* ('shield of David'), was first used as a specifically Jewish symbol only in the Middle Ages. In the Hellenistic period it was simply a decorative motif used in synagogues. It probably became more popular in the Islamic period because Islamic culture, and Jews who were influenced by it, preferred geometric patterns to human or animal images that might be taken as idolatry.

Earlier mosaics and frescoes often included such images, however. Although three-dimensional sculpted forms were avoided, synagogue buildings in Galilee have mosaic floors depicting the zodiac and the seasons, with the sun in the centre represented as a young man standing in a Roman chariot drawn by four horses. In any other context, this figure would have been easily identified as Apollo or Helios, the god of the sun.

There is some evidence that when pious Jews used ordinary objects bearing depictions of human form, such as the moulded figures often found on spoons or jars, they made a small symbolic cut on the object so that the figure would not be complete. In antiquity, synagogue decorations also included depictions of the Temple façade and rams' horns, and especially flora associated with the Sukkoth harvest festival, such as palm, myrtle, willow, and pomegranate. Evidently, flat representations of Greek gods, especially when made to be walked upon, did not run the risk of idolatry posed by the pagans' three-dimensional statues.

The arts of the classical world were sometimes put to use for Jewish decorative purposes in Roman and Byzantine synagogues. The third-century synagogue at Dura-Europos in northeastern Syria had wall paintings (now preserved in the Damascus museum) depicting biblical stories. God is not portrayed directly, but his presence is symbolized by a hand appearing from the heavens, and characters from Abraham through Ezekiel are depicted in Hellenistic dress.

Scripture and Commentary

The period after 70, when the rabbinic practices and institutions were taking shape, marks the beginning of 'classical Judaism'. The interpretations of the covenant obligations developed at that time have remained standard for Jews throughout the world to the present day.

As in the sixth century BCE, the loss of the Temple raised the scriptural texts to a new level of authority. The centrality of the *Law* (ascribed to Moses but not completed until about 400 BCE) and the *Prophets* (probably stabilized around 200 BCE) in the first century is clear in a famous passage from the Christian gospel of Matthew, in which Jesus identifies the love of God and the love of neighbour as the essential commandments: 'On these commandments hang all the law and the prophets' (*Matthew* 22: 40). Another statement of the latter commandment, often cited as 'do unto others as you would have them do unto you' (*Matthew* 7: 12), is also presented as the fundamental message of the Jewish law and prophets. And a variation on the same 'golden rule', ascribed to the scholar Hillel, who lived a few decades before Jesus, describes it in the same way. But these two collections were not the only religious literature considered important. Among the other works chosen for translation in the Septuagint were the book of *Psalms*, the Temple hymn collection, 'wisdom' writings such as *Job* and *Proverbs*, and a variety of apocalyptic and historical texts. With the diversity of sectarian emphases, the number of writings that might be candidates for scriptural status was growing.

Tradition reports that the contents of the third portion of the Hebrew canon, the sacred *Writings*, were finally determined by the rabbis at Yavneh— a centre for rabbinical study near the Mediterranean coast—in about the year 90. To be included in the collection, a text had to have been composed in Hebrew in the period before the Exile. Because the book of *Daniel* appeared to meet these criteria, it was included, even though it is now believed to date only from the second century BCE, whereas the more straightforward account of the same period in *Maccabees* was ineligible because it was known only in Greek.

In this way the Bible came to consist of three sections: the *Law* (Torah), the *Prophets* (Hebrew *Nevi'im*), and the sacred *Writings* (Hebrew *Ketuvim*). Jews often refer to the complete corpus as the **Tanakh**—an acronym based on their titles (T–N–KH).

After the biblical corpus had been fixed, the rabbis proceeded to collect and add to the body of Bible interpretation, known as **midrash** ('interpretation' or 'commentary'). Most midrashic commentaries are line-by-line interpretations following the sequence of the biblical text, although they may also be ordered by the lectionary cycle (the schedule of biblical readings every week) traditionally used in the synagogue.

The early *midrashim* include three books of legal discussions from the first and second centuries, when the Pharisees made imaginative use of exegetic principles to derive rulings about contemporary customs from the written text of the Bible. But they also claimed that their interpretation was present from the very beginning.

These three books—the *Mekhilta* for *Exodus*, and *Sifra* for *Leviticus*, and *Sifre* for *Numbers* and *Deuteronomy*—contain a wealth of information about the context in which the legal discussions were held. But the process of commenting continued for centuries, so it is sometimes difficult to tell what era a particular tradition comes from. The rabbinic writers of *midrash* took it as their task to understand the full significance of the biblical text. Part of that task entailed resolving the frequent contradictions between one passage and another. We have already noted one classic example

The Essence of Judaism

The following excerpts come from a tractate (treatise) in the Mishnah *entitled* Pirke Aboth. *The title is commonly translated as 'The Ethics of the Fathers' or 'The Sayings of the Fathers', but a more accurate translation would be 'The Chapters of the Ancestors'.*

1: 1. Moses received the Torah on Sinai and handed it down to Joshua, and Joshua to the elders, and the elders to the prophets, and the prophets handed it down to the men of the Great Assembly. They said three things: be deliberate in judgment, raise up many disciples, and make a fence around the Torah.

1: 2. Simeon the Just was one of the last members of the Great Assembly. He used to say: 'Upon three things the world stands—on the Torah, on the Temple service, and on acts of kindness.'

1: 12. Hillel and Shammai received Torah from them. Hillel says: 'Be one of Aaron's disciples, loving peace and pursuing it, loving mankind and bringing them near to the Torah.'

1: 14. He used to say: 'If I am not for myself, who then will be for me? And if I am for myself alone, what am I? And if not now, when?'

1: 18. Rabban Simeon ben Gamaliel says: 'On three things the world stands: on justice, on truth, and on peace, as it is written, 'Execute the judgment of truth and peace in your gates' [*Zechariah* 8: 16].'

2: 8. Rabban Yochanan ben Zakkai received Torah from Hillel and Shammai. He used to say: 'If you have learned much Torah, do not take credit for yourself, for this was the purpose of your creation.'

of inconsistency in the accounts of the creation, where the first humans appear to be created twice—once in *Genesis* 1: 26, where the man and woman are created together, and again in *Genesis* 2: 22, where God creates the woman Eve out of Adam's rib. One midrashic solution to this puzzle suggests that Chapter 2 describes the events of the sixth day of Chapter 1, and that Eve is actually Adam's second wife, created because the woman created in Chapter 1 proved unsatisfactory; this first 'wife', known as Lilith, eventually figures as a demon in Jewish folklore.

This is just one of many stories proposed by the rabbis to explain problematic passages. None of them is actually present in the Bible; but since the rabbis adopted them to reconcile seeming contradictions in the text, they can all be considered part of the Torah in an extended sense.

Another, later type of *midrash*, known as homiletical, is believed to present discussions generated by rabbinic sermons. Thus there is no single authoritative interpretation of any biblical passage. Jewish biblical commentary is a communal and composite literature, bringing together the commentaries of various important rabbis in a centuries-long effort to uncover the implications of every biblical verse and relate the Bible to the understanding and the concerns of the time.

The *Mishnah*

A major achievement in the rabbis' restructuring of the tradition was their codification of the Jewish legal heritage. Forms that had been passed down orally in the Pharisaic tradition were now organized and written down. This basic legal literature consists of two parts: the **Mishnah** and the *Talmud*.

Unlike the midrashic commentaries, which follow the structure of the books that made up the Hebrew canon, the *Mishnah* was an entirely new kind of text, with its own topical arrangement in six 'orders' or divisions: Seeds (agriculture), Festivals, Women, Damages, Holy Things (ritual), and Purifications. Summarizing the Pharisaic-rabbinic movement interpretation of the traditional law, the *Mishnah* is the oldest datable rabbinic document, produced shortly before 220 by Rabbi Judah, known as 'ha-Nasi' ('the prince').

The authority of the *Mishnah* was based on the notion that alongside the five books of Moses there was another body of precedent and interpretation that had been passed down orally from Moses. This doctrine of an 'oral law' allowed the rabbis to assert that their own interpretations were no less God-given than the doctrines written explicitly in the Torah constitution. Whether the oral law was so called because it was originally not allowed to be written down or merely because it had started its existence in oral form is unclear. In any event, all the 'oral law' may be found today in sacred books studied by the rabbinic community.

The Pharisees long ago claimed that this oral tradition had been passed only to them; that only they were entitled to determine its meaning; and that their interpretation represented the true continuation of the prophetic tradition. This was the Pharisees' pretext for taking over the governance of the community from the priests, whom they looked down on as mere functionaries. The development of Pharisaic traditions is reflected in two first-century schools of interpretation, one led by Hillel and the other by Shammai. The earliest stages likely involved the codification of laws on the issues of most interest to the Pharisees—Sabbath law, purity, and tithing. But the early rabbis also took a keen interest in marriage and divorce, for rules of personal status defined membership in the Jewish community.

Even though the Temple no longer existed, much of the oral legal tradition addressed matters directly associated with it, such as purity laws and the sacrificial system. This material was subjected to the same careful analysis as the other parts of the law, presumably to establish the Pharisees' right to control a new Temple, should one be built. Although the failure of the Bar Cochba revolt of 132–5 CE made it painfully clear that the Temple would not be rebuilt anytime soon, the rabbinic commentary on Temple law continued, in preparation for the eventual messianic age.

By the second century it was taken for granted that the Pharisaic–rabbinic movement had always been dominant in Judaism. The rabbis' authority was projected backward onto traditions that had developed in totally different circumstances, some when Pharisaism was merely one of several competing sects representing conflicting perspectives in Hellenistic Judaism. Now schools and factions within the rabbinic movement itself competed with one another, each proposing its own rules for scriptural exegesis. Tradition recorded their competing views, and often admits that more than one of them may have merit.

Although the *Mishnah* of Rabbi Judah the Prince is highly honoured and is quoted as authoritative, it is not the only repository of the traditions compiled by the first generations of the rabbis, who are often called the **Tannaim** (Aramaic for 'repeaters' or 'teachers'). These alternative traditions are found in a book called the *Tosefta* (Aramaic for 'addition'), and the precedents they provide are considered equally valuable in rabbinic discussions.

The *Talmud*

By about 220, the formerly open and growing body of interpretation that the Pharisees claimed to have received orally from Moses had, like the Bible, become a fixed, written text. And, like the Bible, the *Mishnah* of Rabbi Judah itself now became the subject of passage-by-passage commentary. With its six 'orders' subdivided into a total of 63 tractates (treatises), the *Mishnah* became the skeleton of the collection known as the *Talmud*.

The *Mishnah* itself is no longer than a desk dictionary. There are two different *Talmuds*, however, each of which is closer to the size of a multi-volume encyclopedia. Each *Talmud* consists of the Hebrew *Mishnah* of Rabbi Judah

Rabbinic Humour

Rabbinic humour was sharp. Sometimes it was directed at ignoramuses, women, and gentiles, but often the target was the the rabbis' own irrational pretensions. The following examples come from the Talmuds *and the midrash.*

Rabbah and R. Zerah joined together in a Purim feast. They became drunk, and he cut R. Zerah's throat. On the next day, he prayed on his behalf and revived him. The following year he said, 'Will your honour come and we will have Purim together?' He replied, 'No. A miracle does not take place on every occasion' (b. Meg. 7b).

'Teach us to number our days' [*Psalm* 90: 12]. R. Joshua said: 'If we knew exactly the number of our days, we could repent before we die.' R. Eliezer said: 'Repent one day before you die.' His disciples said: 'Who knows when he will die?' 'All the more, then, let him repent today for perhaps he will die tomorrow. The result will be that all his life will be spent in repentance' (Midrash Psalms on Psalm 90: 12 197a, section 16).

The Rabbis taught: The father has the following obligations towards his son: He must circumcise him, redeem him, teach him the Torah, take a wife unto him, and teach him a trade. Some say he must teach him to swim also. Rabbi Yehuda said: 'He that does not teach his son a trade, teaches him to rob.' Teaches him to rob? How is that?—we may say: as though he taught him to rob.

R. Eliezer used every argument to substantiate his opinion, but they [the other rabbis] would not accept them. He said, 'If the law is as I have argued, may this carob tree argue for me.' The carob tree uprooted itself and moved a hundred cubits from its place. Some say it moved four hundred cubits. They said, 'From a tree no proof can be brought.' Then he said, 'May the canal prove it.' The water of the canal flowed backwards. They said, 'From a canal no proof may be brought.' Then he said, 'May the walls of this House of Study prove it.' Then the walls of the house bent inwards, as if they were about to fall. R. Joshua rebuked the walls and said to them, 'If the learned dispute about the law, what has that to do with you?' So, to honour R. Joshua, the walls did not fall down, but to honour R. Eliezer, they did not become straight again. Then R. Eliezer said, 'If I am right, may the heavens prove it.' Then a heavenly voice said, 'What have you against R. Eliezer? The law is always with him.' Then R. Joshua got up and said, 'It is not in heaven' [*Deuteronomy* 30: 12]. What did he mean by this? R. Jeremiah said, 'The Torah was given to us at Sinai. We do not attend to this heavenly voice. For it was already written in the Torah at Mt Sinai that "By the majority you are to decide" [*Exodus* 23: 2].' R. Nathan met Elijah and asked him what God did in that hour. Elijah replied, 'He laughed and said, "My children have defeated me"' (b. Baba Metzia 59b).

Why was man created on Friday? So that, if he becomes haughty, one can say to him, 'The gnat was created before you' (b. Sanhedrin 38a).

An idolater asked R. Yochanan b. Zakkai: 'These rites that you perform look like a kind of witchcraft. You bring a heifer, burn it, pound it, and take its ashes. If one of you is defiled by a dead body you sprinkle upon him two or three drops and you say to him: "You are clean!"' R. Yochanan asked him: 'Has a demon of madness ever possessed you?' 'No,' he replied. 'Have you ever seen a man possessed by this demon of madness?' 'Yes,' he said. 'And what do you do in such a case?' 'We bring roots,' he replied, 'and make them smoke under him. Then we sprinkle water upon the demon and it flees.' Said R. Yochanan to him, 'Let your ears hear what you utter with your mouth! Precisely so is this spirit a spirit of uncleanness, as it is written, "And also I will cause the prophets and the unclean spirits to pass out of the land" [*Zechariah* 13: 2]. Water of purification is sprinkled upon the unclean and the spirit flees.' When the idolater had gone, R. Yochanan's disciples said to their master, 'Master, you have put off this man with a mere makeshift argument. But what explanation will you give to us?' Said he to them, 'By your life! It is not the dead that defiles nor the water that purifies. The Holy One, Blessed be He, merely says: "I have laid down a statute, I have issued a decree. You are not allowed to transgress my decree," as it is written, "This is the statute of the law" [*Numbers* 19: 2]' (Numbers Rabbah 19: 8).

together with one of the two bodies of commentary, known as a ***Gemarah*** (from a Hebrew word meaning 'completion').

One *Gemarah* comes from the Jewish community in Palestine, the other from the Jewish community in Babylonia. The *Mishnah* and the Palestinian *Gemarah* form the *Palestinian Talmud*; this material is also often referred to as the *Jerusalem Talmud*, though it was likely produced in the Galilee region north of Jerusalem. The same *Mishnah* and the other *Gemarah*, produced in Babylonia, form the *Babylonian Talmud*.

The *Mishnah* is in Hebrew, the language of the past, of liturgy and scholarly study (the Christian equivalent would be Church Latin); both *gemarahs*, however, are in Aramaic, a vernacular language of the time related to Hebrew. (Jesus and most of his generation of Jews spoke Aramaic fluently and knew some Hebrew. Jews also often spoke Greek and even knew a little Latin. But Aramaic gradually took over as the spoken language of the Jews living in Palestine and became one of the languages spoken by the Jews in Babylonia.)

Typically, a selection from the *Talmud* starts with a short passage from the *Mishnah* followed by the text of the related *Gemarah*, which can be many times the length of the *Mishnah* text to which it is attached. In printed editions, such as the standard Vilna edition of 1880–6, the *Mishnah* and *Gemarah* are printed in a small column in the centre of the page, surrounded by later additions and commentaries, together with various other study aids such as cross-references.

The *Jerusalem Talmud* is an interesting source of history, lore, and tradition in Judaism, but it was produced under difficult circumstances. Not only was the economy in decline, but with the Christianization of the Roman Empire, Jews were increasingly subject to discriminatory laws, including a law enacted about 425 that abolished the office of the Patriarch (the head of the leading Palestinian academy).

In Babylonia, by contrast, the ruling Sasanian Persians were relatively tolerant of the Jewish community. Perhaps as a consequence, the legal discussions undertaken there were more acute and substantial than their Palestinian counterparts, and the *Babylonian Talmud* became the more authoritative version for the Jewish community as a whole. At first Palestine was in charge of the ritual calendar: thus the arrival of each new month was determined in Palestine (by direct observation of the moon) and the news was then communicated to other lands. When the calendar eventually came to be calculated mathematically, the Babylonian community embarked on an independent ritual life. This change formalized the primacy of the Babylonian Talmudic academies, which had been gaining in talent and prestige for generations.

The Babylonian *Gemarah* records the discussions of more than 2,000 sages arguing over specific ways to resolve issues by reference to the text of the *Mishnah*. In contrast to the ordered discussions of the *Mishnah*, the *Gemarah* discussions tend to be quite complex and far-ranging, even free-associational. Nevertheless, brief technical terms identify the formal characteristics of the specific arguments that are about to be mounted.

Since the text of the *Mishnah* is a law code, much of the *Gemarah*, which comments on it, is strictly legal in nature. Not every legal discussion produces a prescription for a specific legal procedure, but those that do form part of the body of religious law known as **halakha** ('the way' or 'procedure', or more specifically, the proper legal procedure for living life).

There is another style of expansion that is more anecdotal; it is referred to as **aggadah** ('narrative'). *Halakha* directives are explicit statements arrived at through legal analysis; *aggadah* teaches a moral lesson, often by telling a story or interpreting the meaning of a word.

Jews conventionally regard the topically arranged legal material of the *Talmud* as *halakha* and the expansion on the narratives of the Bible in the *midrash* as *aggadah*, because they emphasize law and story, respectively. Strictly speaking, however, examples of both genres can be found in each collection, though in vastly different proportions. As a result, the terms *halakha* and *aggadah* are often used very loosely. Sometimes the words refer to particular legal or folkloric techniques of analyzing ancient text, sometimes to specific books of the oral law in which these techniques are used.

The Status of Torah

The same elasticity of definition characterizes rabbinic and Jewish understandings of the term 'torah'. In the period of the first Temple, 'torah' apparently referred only to the laws that governed priestly behaviour. Starting with the book of *Deuteronomy*, however, it was used to refer first to a written book of law and then to the Pentateuch. In biblical times, books were written on scrolls. This form has been retained for the copy of the sacred text used in synagogue recitation. Called a **Sefer Torah** ('book of the Torah'), it is written by hand on parchment and mounted on wooden rollers. For other uses, however, the Pentateuch is bound as a book (the form that replaced scrolls in late antiquity) called a **Humash**, from the Hebrew word for 'five'.

In a broader sense, the 'Torah' is the entire Hebrew Bible, the Tanakh, and in some cases the term may even be extended to include the books of the oral law—the *Midrash*, *Mishnah*, and *Talmud*. That is because every discussion of holy law and procedure, whether it be moral, ritual, or ceremonial, is considered part of the same divine revelation, continuing over the millennia. Thus the word 'Torah' can refer to any revelatory or canonical literature. In rabbinic parlance, the *Talmud* and the commentaries on it, produced in various lands by various experts over the centuries, are part of Torah, although they are also called *Torah she ba'al peh*, 'oral Torah'.

The study of Torah continued unabated while the *Talmud* was being completed. Together, the two principal rabbinic academies in Babylonia, located in the towns of Sura and Pumbeditha, were the intellectual centre of the Jewish world from the fourth to the ninth century and even after. There, the leader of the *yeshiva* or Talmudic academy, known by the honorific term **gaon** ('excellency'), often enjoyed greater power and respect than the ostensible head of the Jewish community, the exilarch. This was because the *gaon* supervised the rabbinic enterprise of legal interpretation.

The one major threat to the primacy of the *gaon* was the rebellion of the **Karaites** ('scripturalists'), a group of Jews who rejected the authority of the *Talmud* and its interpreters and considered only the Bible to be canonical. The eighth-century founder of Karaism, Anan ben David, also rejected the popular holiday of Hanukkah, along with every other festival that was not specifically mentioned in the Bible. In its emphasis on simplicity (bordering on asceticism), Karaism had more in common with Islam than with the elaborate intellectual pursuits of the rabbis. In fact, it flourished in Muslim lands because of the culture's affinity for simple piety.

Further Development of Jewish Law

According to tradition, the compilation of the *Talmud* was completed by the end of the sixth century, though scholars think that the composition continued for some time after that. In any event, once the *Talmud* had reached its canonical form, the ongoing development of Jewish law took three principal forms. One was the passage-by-passage commentary on the Talmudic text, which included the *Gemarah* as well as the *Mishnah*. Jewish intellectuals all over the world and across the centuries have written legal commentaries on some aspect of the legal tradition, and they continue to do so today. Although the *Talmud* itself was closed to further growth, every printed edition of the text now includes a selection of the most important commentaries in the margins and footnotes. These *Tosafot* (Hebrew for 'additions' or 'footnotes') are not to be confused with the *Tosefta* of the Tannaim, which are printed in a separate volume.

Perhaps the most famous of all the commentators on the *Talmud* was Rabbi Shlomo ben Yitzhak (1040–1105), who lived in Troyes, north of Paris. As is common with rabbinic writers, he is known by the acronym of his title and name: Rashi (R–Sh–Y). His commentaries are invaluable for understanding the simple sense of difficult Talmudic passages. Rashi also wrote commentaries on biblical books, which are considered landmarks in Jewish scriptural interpretation, and is an important source of evidence on medieval French.

The second development of the legal tradition was a collection of rulings made by expert rabbis in response to questions posed by individual communities. This *Teshuvah* ('an answer') or (in Latin) *responsum* ('a response') literature always took the form of public letters. It is possible that the letters of Paul in the New Testament are early examples of this genre, since they contain Paul's answers to questions asked by the early church communities. Although Paul is now part of Christian rather than Jewish tradition, the questions he addresses are of the same type as the ones that Jews have asked over the centuries. The tradition continues today, but only in the Orthodox community, where the most highly revered rabbis extend Talmudic reasoning to issues raised by modern advances in medical technology, such as the use of birth control and the artificial prolongation of life. However, their rulings do not affect Conservative and Reform Jews, who feel that the individual's own judgment supersedes that even of great legal authorities. The third post-Talmudic development was the periodic codification of the growing legal heritage. Essentially, a legal code serves two purposes: to classify legal material topically and logically, and to establish what should be done in various situations. To create a code requires the ability both to simplify complex material, so as to make it understandable to lay persons, and to interpret theoretical discussion so as to decide how the law will be put into practice.

Although Rabbi Judah's *Mishnah* resembled a code, it did not always address the practical question of how the law should be carried out in specific cases. In the medieval world further codes were formulated. Two influential medieval codes were the **Mishneh Torah** ('A Copy of the Torah'; c. 1180) of Moses Maimonides and the *Arba'a Turim* ('Four Rows') of Jacob ben Asher (c. 1270–1340). Following the outline of that work, Joseph Karo, a sixteenth-century Spanish Jew who migrated to Palestine, brought diverse legal opinions together in a massive compilation entitled *Bet Yosef* ('House of Joseph') and later produced a condensation of this work under the title *Shulhan Arukh* ('Spread Table', an allusion to *Psalm* 23). The latter work is still consulted today by Jews seeking a practical guide to Torah observance, without the intricate legal discussions and hypothetical solutions to possible contradictions in the law that one finds in the *Talmud* and commentaries.

Applying Legal Principles

Originally the civil law of the Israelites, the Torah thus became the religious law of rabbinic Judaism and the guide to moral conduct for Jews far removed in time and space from the ancient state. For such an ancient law to adapt and stay relevant to later ages, a healthy tradition of study and commentary was essential.

Rabbinic Judaism gave enormous emphasis to proper ethical conduct. The tradition called for numerous specific actions of both a ritual and a moral nature, but it recognized that no two circumstances are ever fully identical. Therefore every situation must be analyzed individually. The study of the *Talmud* essentially provided training in the principles of ethical analysis from every conceivable perspective.

'An eye for an eye, a tooth for a tooth,' says the book of *Exodus*. As harsh as this principle may sound today, it may well have been unusually humane in the second millennium BCE, when some societies would put a serf to death for injuring his master. The Bible limited the penalty to the extent of the injury. By the rabbinic period, however, even this relatively lenient principle was considered too severe—what the Romans called a *lex talionis* ('law of retaliation'). After very little debate, the rabbis concluded that compensation for loss of a body part, for example, should take the form of a financial payment.

To a modern interpreter, this shift from physical to fiscal punishment was clearly the product of moral development over time leading the Israelite people to see the original injunction as unjust. Most Orthodox Jews, however, holding the scripture to be incapable of error, maintain that the *Exodus* verse called for financial compensation all along: in their view, the development required was in the human interpretation of the text, in which the rabbis were guided by the Holy Spirit.

For centuries Jewish exegetes have applied the principles of Torah to the problems of everyday life. In the Hellenistic period, for instance, many people were reluctant to lend money when a sabbatical year (the year when fields lie fallow) was approaching, for fear that they would not be repaid. Even though the Torah does not speak specifically about this problem, the rabbis were confident that the solution to it could be found in scripture. In this case the solution—known as a *takkanah* ('remediation') and attributed to Hillel—was for the court itself to take over debts for the sabbatical year. Thus lenders could feel confident that they would recover their principal, and debtors could arrange the loans they needed to continue in operation.

Law is continually amplified in response to new situations. For guidance in dealing with these new situations, people looked to the rabbis as an elite group of professional specialists in precedent and tradition. But rabbinic law was hardly unanimous or monolithic. Currently, for example, Jewish law does not have a single answer on whether a woman may seek an abortion. The biblical precedent is found in the same passage from *Exodus* that gave us 'an eye for an eye':

> When men fight, and one of them pushes a pregnant woman and a miscarriage results, but no other damage ensues, the one responsible shall be fined according as the woman's husband may exact from him, the payment to be based on reckoning. But if other damage ensues, the penalty shall be life for life, eye for eye, tooth for tooth, hand for hand, foot for foot, burn for burn, wound for wound, bruise for bruise (*Exodus* 21: 22–5).

Rabbinic interpretation takes this to mean that the death of a fetus is a tort but not in itself a capital crime. If the life of a mother is endangered, it is certainly permissible to abort the pregnancy.

According to rabbinic law, a fetus is not a person, with all the rights that personhood entails, until it has been born and shown its viability by surviving a certain amount of time (normally a month) after birth.

Even so, whether abortion is acceptable in any particular case depends on subtle distinctions in rabbinic discourse. To avoid overstepping the bounds, some Jews would never perform an abortion, and others would do so only if the life of the mother is truly endangered. Others, interpreting more broadly, might perform an abortion if the mother reports that she is psychologically unfit for motherhood. Reform Jews would say that it is important to consult the rabbinic rulings of the past, but that past rulings are not automatically binding on contemporary life. They might extend one principle or another discussed by the rabbis and follow it to a conclusion never reached in the past, then justify their decision on the basis of what a rabbi operating under similar principles might do today.

Purity and Community

Some of the most arcane laws of the Torah involve ritual purity. When the rabbis turned their attention to these laws they were codifying a complex symbolic system. Today, purity laws are generally understood as serving a hygienic function for primitive societies because they tended to prohibit contact with harmful substances, such as corpses or human excreta, and control behaviour around them. In various cultures, however, some completely harmless substances may be taboo, while some harmful ones may be central to ritual events. The same is true of the Hebrew rules, some of which have no obvious medical value.

Hebrew society, like many non-Western societies, had a series of food taboos. Probably the best known is the commandment not to touch—let alone eat—the meat from pigs (pork, ham, bacon, etc.). Other forbidden foods include blood and any carnivorous bird or mammal. Shellfish (clams, shrimp, lobster, etc.) are also prohibited.

Another rule forbids eating meat and milk together, but this one is rabbinic, not biblical. Although the Bible forbids Jews to eat a young goat boiled in its mother's milk (*Exodus* 23: 19), it says nothing about keeping meat and milk strictly separate. The latter rule was introduced by the rabbis as a safeguard against violating the biblical rules. This practice of setting up rules to prevent inadvertent violations of the law is known as 'making a fence around the Torah'.

Some of the dietary rules followed in Jewish homes today originated in Temple rituals. Among them is the rule that, to be ritually acceptable as food, an animal must have been slaughtered in a particular way that was traditionally believed to minimize its suffering; this rule originally applied to the animals used in sacrifice rituals. The prohibition against eating blood—which God gave to all humanity, not just the Jews, as a sign that only God had control over life—was now understood as a sign of the sanctity of every Jewish home. The rules required that only properly tithed produce (that is, one-tenth having been reserved for the priests) be eaten, especially in countries other than Judea, where tithing obligations did not apply. There are also special rules for the Passover holiday, such as a prohibition on bread containing leavening (yeast, etc.). (Kosher regulations will be discussed in more detail later.)

Another series of rules, rooted in the Bible, forbade willful contact with 'polluting' substances such as menstrual blood and semen. Touching these unclean or 'polluting' substances was not a sin in itself—such contact was inevitable—but the resulting pollution had to be removed by visiting a *mikveh* (ritual bathhouse) for a purifying immersion ceremony. Other purity laws required that both spouses undergo ritual immersion after sexual intercourse, and prohibited intercourse entirely for the first two weeks of every menstrual cycle. Since converts to Judaism are required to begin the regimen of ritual immersion, Christian baptism is widely thought to have grown out of the Jewish practice.

Purity laws served as symbolic social boundary markers, separating the pious from the less pious. At the same time they served to separate Jews from the host society, imposing a high degree of group coherence. The rules proliferated as Pharisaism became rabbinism. Thus even though Jews were not forbidden to have contact with gentiles, the proliferation of dietary and purity laws made everyday social relations increasingly difficult. And since gentiles did not observe the purity rules, sexual relationships with them were naturally ruled out unless they converted to Judaism. The rules had the double effect of idealizing the vanished Temple, which had demanded the highest purity, and of recognizing that, in its absence, the final stage in the purification process—the sacrifice ritual—was no longer possible. The rabbis built on some of the older Pharisaic rules to establish a new understanding of ritual purity within the home that continues to this day in Orthodox Judaism. In biblical society, the priests had been a separate hereditary class that maintained a high degree of ritual purity. In one sense, with the Temple gone, priesthood lapsed. In another sense, however, maintaining ritual purity became the obligation of every Jew, whether descended from a priestly family or not. And rabbinic Judaism thought of the community as having a priestly role among the nations of the world.

Repentance

The rabbis also put great emphasis on the concept of repentance. Although they had no doubt that righteousness was God's will, they did not design a 'scoreboard' religion in which good deeds could be totalled against bad. Rather, they taught that human life is constantly balanced between good and evil deeds, and that for this reason the need for repentance (Hebrew *teshuvah*, literally 'turning' or 'returning') is constant. Without sincere individual repentance, even the solemn rituals of Yom Kippur (the day of atonement) are merely external forms. God effects atonement only when the individual sincerely repents. There are several stages to repentance. First, one must admit to having done wrong. The rabbis acknowledge that sin is committed not by deliberately evil people, but by people who know right from wrong and seek to do the right, but who have an ability to rationalize their behaviour that prevents them from seeing where they go wrong. Thus the very first stage of repentance is to acknowledge openly the wrong one has done. This confession is critical for everything that comes afterwards.

The next stage in repentance should be true sorrow for one's misdeeds, but this does not follow automatically from the first stage. People may admit their sins without actually feeling sorry for having committed them. Or they may rationalize their sins as necessary under the pressure of circumstances. True repentance means acknowledging that all these thought patterns are traps.

One must promise never to repeat the sin and take steps to fulfill that undertaking. But repentance means more than feeling sad and promising to change one's behaviour. It also means ensuring that anyone harmed by one's actions receives the appropriate compensation.

Some crimes, such as murder, may require the death of the perpetrator as compensation, even though it cannot bring back the life of the victim. A person who truly repents and is willing to accept death may enter God's presence as a forgiven sinner. But in fact the rabbis rarely had the authority to pronounce a death sentence because of the legal strictures they put in place for capital trials: few situations were clear-cut enough for the capital penalty to be imposed.

If God can forgive the sincere penitent, human beings must do the same. A person who has been wronged may seek restitution, but is obliged to respond with forgiveness once the wrong-doer has completed all the stages of repentance. By the same token, wrongdoers must have completed all those stages in order for God to accept their repentance on Yom Kippur. Rabbinic Judaism has been characterized as a religion of works, but it still leaves enormous scope for divine grace. It emphasizes God's availability for forgiveness as well as the human need to achieve it. Once the Temple and its sacrificial rituals were no longer part of Jewish life, therefore, the rabbis ruled that marriage and death were also occasions for individuals to repent. But repentance can take place at any time.

The rabbis developed a very sophisticated notion of intention. Just as English common law recognizes several degrees of intention in murder cases, so the rabbis recognized the role that subtle differences in intention play in determining the significance of any action. To find someone guilty of murder, they usually required a degree of intentionality that would be very difficult to ascertain in court. This was possible because they believed God to be a witness to every human action.

Thus even in cases where lack of evidence makes it impossible for a human court to determine the truth, it is assumed that God is a righteous judge and will always ensure an appropriate outcome: if a wrong has been done, God will see that the wrongdoer is punished. This brings us to a subtle but important distinction. Although rabbinic law resembles a national law code, it is distinctive in that it assumes God to be a constant participant in the legal process. Sometimes people find rabbinic writing legalistic. But this is a category mistake. The fact is that a great deal of rabbinic writing *is* law, albeit highly theological law.

Commandments for Jews and Gentiles

Rabbinic thought had a clear notion of the Torah, both written and oral, as God's gift to the Jews. The next logical question for the rabbis to answer was what God intended for the gentile nations (in Hebrew, *goyim*). Did they too have a part in the divine plan, with their own privileges and responsibilities? By what standards should their conduct be judged?

In attempting to answer these questions, the rabbis began to articulate a theory of universalism. Of course, even the biblical writers had understood that God was Lord of the whole world, not just of the people Israel. This understanding is dramatically expressed in the *Genesis* creation story. In their day, various pre-exilic prophets had drawn the gentiles into their scenarios as instruments of punishment that God would use to settle scores with a sinful Israel. Other prophets had pronounced against certain nations in God's name for overstepping the limits of the punitive roles assigned to them. Post-exilic writers, especially in the apocalyptic genre, had envisioned the glorification of Israel and the subjugation of the gentile nations as a long-delayed demonstration of God's loyalty to his people. The longer that intervention was delayed, the more dramatic it was expected to be when it finally came.

In the biblical account, the covenants that Yahweh makes with Abraham and Moses establish specific privileges and responsibilities for the people of Israel. The Ten Commandments given to Moses are at the heart of the law, but in the classic rabbinic interpretation of Torah, more than 600 other commandments, *mitzvoth* (the plural of **mitzvah**), were delivered orally at Sinai. The conventional total is 613; the rabbis of the Middle Ages delighted in enumerating all of them.

It was the covenant with Abraham that marked the formation of a distinct Israelite people. But there was an earlier covenant—the one that God made with Noah, the survivor of the primeval flood, and sealed with the rainbow. The rabbis linked the salvation of the gentiles explicitly to this covenant, for in it God promises mercy and deliverance to all humanity. They also believed that in it God gave to everyone a number of laws known as the Noachide (or Noahic) commandments.

The number of the Noachide commandments vary from six to ten (different rabbinic commentaries cite different numbers), but they are conventionally said to be seven. They consist of prohibitions against blasphemy, idolatry, bloodshed, incest, theft, and the eating of flesh from living animals. Often added to these is recognition of the true God.

The rabbis derived these ordinances from what they took to be scriptural revelation intended to let the whole human race know the meaning of righteousness. Above all, though, the Noachide commandments are consonant with universal human reason. They are universally recognizable moral imperatives, like 'natural' laws. In medieval Judaism, rabbinic commentators seeking to understand God's plan for Christianity and Islam—religions founded on biblical and Jewish principles but far greater in numbers and power—looked to the Noachide commandments for guidance. Since Islam was strictly monotheistic and rejected the making of images, the rabbis came to see it as consistent with the Noachide commandments. Some of them saw Christianity in the same light. But others balked at Christianity's trinitarian doctrine and its rich Roman and Eastern traditions of devotion to *eikons* or 'images'.

Some rabbis, especially those living in Christian countries, pointed out that even though Christianity associates a mortal and his image with God—a heresy in both Judaism and Islam known as 'associationism'—righteous Christians could still count on eternal life because the Noachide commandments do not specifically prohibit it for gentiles. Other rabbis, many of them living in Muslim lands, believed, (as did the Muslims) that Christianity represented an outright violation of monotheism since Islam insists that nothing can share the divine status of God.

Rabbinic Judaism encouraged toleration and respect for Christianity and Islam based on the universalistic principle that all the Abrahamic faiths worshipped the same God. Christians and Muslims similarly developed legal arguments for the toleration of Jews, although these were based on the fact that Judaism was the foundation of their own faiths. Of course, the formal acceptance of Judaism did not prevent centuries of intolerance towards Jews (though persecution was much more prevalent in Christian than in Muslim lands). Nor did Jews always live up to the rabbis' universalistic notions regarding the other Abrahamic faiths.

Jews never explicitly rejected the idea of conversion to Judaism, and today they readily accept sincere converts. Some non-Jews may find it hard

The Rabbis on Gentiles

The Tannaim (the early rabbis) argued over the status of gentiles, but eventually they decided that the righteous of all nations have a place in the world to come.

Rabbi Eliezer said: 'All the nations will have no share in the world to come, even as it is said, "The wicked shall go into Sheol, and all the nations that forget God" [*Psalm* 9: 17]. The wicked shall go into Sheol—these are the wicked among Israel.' Rabbi Joshua said to him: 'If the verse had said, "The wicked shall go into Sheol with all the nations," and had stopped there, I should have agreed with you, but as it goes on to say "who forget God," it means there are righteous men among the nations who have a share in the world to come' (Tosefta Sanhedrin 13: 2).

Rabbi Jeremiah said: 'Whence can you know that the gentile that practices the law is equal to the high priest? Because it is said, "which, if a man do, he shall live through them" [*Leviticus* 18: 5]. And it says, "This is the Torah of man" [*2 Samuel* 7: 19]. It does not say, "the law of the priests, Levites, Israelites," but "This is the law of man, O Lord God." And it does not say, "Open the gates and let the priests and Levites and Israel enter," but it says: "Open the gates that the righteous may enter" [*Isaiah* 26: 2]. And it says, "This is the gate of the Lord, the righteous shall enter it." It does not say, "The priests and the Levites and Israel shall enter it," but it says, "The righteous shall enter it" [*Psalm* 118: 20]. And it does not say, "Rejoice ye, priests, Levites, and Israelites," but it says, "Rejoice ye righteous"[*Psalm* 33: 1]. And it does not say, "Do good, O Lord, to the priests and the Levites and the Israelites," but it says, "Do good, O Lord, to the good" [*Psalm* 124: 4]. So even a gentile, if he practises the Torah, is equal to the high priest' (Sifra 86b; b. Baba Kamma 38a).

to understand why devout Jews do not bear witness to their faith by proselytizing, but Jews see no need to convert others in order to ensure their salvation: for them it is enough to preach the righteousness that makes all people, Jewish or gentile, equal in the eyes of God. The decision to convert is entirely personal, reserved for those who sincerely wish to join their fate with that of the people Israel.

DIFFERENTIATION

The Medieval Period

By convention, the Jews of the premodern world were divided geographically into two groups, **Sephardim** and **Ashkenazim**. The former lived in the region of the Mediterranean, while the latter lived in central and eastern Europe, away from the Mediterranean. (A handful of much smaller communities belonging to neither group are discussed on p. 126.)

By the medieval period, Sepharad was identified primarily with Spain, which with Portugal came to dominate Sephardic intellectual history. European Jewish settlement in the New World began with Sephardim from Spain, Portugal, and Italy—the pioneering lands of exploration and colonial empire-building. There have been important Sephardic centres in Italy and the Turkish Empire, and Jews across North Africa and the Middle East can all be counted among the Sephardim.

Ashkenaz was identified primarily with Germany, but in time, as persecution forced its members to migrate, came to include Poland, Hungary,

Romania, and Russia as well. Some Ashkenazim settled in France and England over the centuries before their descendants moved to North America. In the medieval period all Ashkenazim lived as minorities under Christian domination, and after the middle of the nineteenth century, Ashkenazic Jews, so often uprooted in Europe, migrated to the New World in numbers so great that the earlier Sephardic immigrants became almost invisible. North American Jews are today overwhelmingly Ashkenazic in custom and culture. Jews from Muslim lands have been much more likely to settle in Israel. As a consequence, the Israeli population today is more or less balanced between Sephardim and Ashkenazim.

In the Middle Ages, Jewish cultural and intellectual life fared better in the Islamic world than in Christian Europe. The prophet Muhammad had been deeply influenced by Christian and Jewish teachers before his experience of revelation. Therefore Islam remained officially tolerant of both Christians and Jews, who as 'People of the Book' were entitled to certain legal rights, including the right to practise their own religion.

Not all Muslim rulers lived up to Islam's principles, however. In most places Jews were subject to discriminatory legislation forcing them to pay special taxes, wear special garments, live in special quarters, stay off the roads when Muslims approached, and so on. Nevertheless, in every place conquered by the Muslims—from Spain in the eighth century to Anatolia in the fifteenth—the new rulers were welcomed as liberators by Jewish communities that had suffered under Christian oppression.

Medieval Jewish Philosophy

Medieval Jewish philosophy flourished primarily in Muslim lands, where intellectual life had been deeply influenced by Greek philosophy.

Saadia

The earliest notable Jewish philosopher of the medieval period was Saadia (882–942), who became

---

Marital Customs

Marital customs in Jewish communities depended to a significant degree on the culture of the larger society in which the Jewish community was situated. Thus in Muslim-controlled regions, Jewish men who could afford to support more than one wife continued to practise polygamy, as the ancient Hebrews had; however, the Jewish marriage contract included a number of safeguards for women that were not necessarily available to women in the host society.

Over the centuries, changes in the status of women have required the use of a rare but important rabbinic legal instrument called the *takkanah* ('repair', here with the sense of 'repeal'). The most famous *takkanah* on the subject of marriage banned the practice of polygamy and is usually attributed to Rabbenu Gershom of Mainz (c. 960–1028), who is also credited with a *takkanah* forbidding a husband to divorce his wife against her will. The polygamy *takkanah* was essentially directed at Jews living in Christian lands (Jews living under Islamic law may still have more than one wife today). It is possible, however, that the *takkanah* had little practical effect: some scholars suggest that the practice of polygamy simply died out in the West, more or less by common agreement.

The variations in customs across the Jewish world would become an important issue in the modern state of Israel, where a single legal system had to be created for Jews from many different societies, on the basis of Jewish law, British mandatory law, and Turkish law. So Israel is not so much governed by Jewish law as influenced by it, having developed its own traditions of civil and criminal law. Bigamy was outlawed in 1951 by a civil law designed to protect the rights of women, but immigrants who had already been legally married to more than one wife in their country of origin were exempted.

A *Techina* (Devotional Prayer) for Women

Women developed special devotional prayers (called Techinot) *for themselves, to be recited as they did the usual preparations for the Sabbath and holidays. Here is one that women have traditionally said as they place a loaf of challah (a braided bread) in the oven on Fridays so that there will be a special bread to bless for the Sabbath.*

This the woman says when she puts the Sabbath loaf into the oven:

Lord of all the world, in your hand is all blessing. I come now to revere your holiness, and I pray you to bestow your blessing on the baked goods. Send an angel to guard the baking, so that all will be well baked, will rise nicely, and will not burn, to honor the holy Sabbath (which you have chosen so that Israel your children may rest thereon) and over which one recites the holy blessing—as you blessed the dough of Sarah and Rebecca our mothers. My Lord God, listen to my voice; you are the God who hears the voices of those who call to you with the whole heart. May you be praised to eternity (Umansky and Ashton 1992: 55).

the *gaon*, or principal, of the important rabbinic academy of Sura in Babylonia. He translated the Hebrew Bible into Arabic and defended rabbinic Judaism against the teachings of the Karaites.

A major theme in all Jewish philosophical writings was the tension between reason and revelation. But Saadia believed there was no such conflict: whenever biblical events or texts appeared to contradict rational principles, they should be taken allegorically rather than literally. In this, Saadia was following a tradition that had begun with Philo in Alexandria in the first century. Saadia's best-known philosophical work is *The Book of Beliefs and Opinions* (*Sefer Emunoth veDeoth*), in which he maintains that Judaism alone is the divinely revealed truth. The use of human reason would eventually lead to the same truth, but revelation is a gift from God that makes it available instantaneously.

Yehuda Ha-Levi

Yehuda Ha-Levi (1075–1141) was born in the city of Toledo in Spain shortly after it fell under Christian control. Like all educated Jews of the time, he studied the *Talmud*, but he is known for his poetry

(written in Hebrew using the conventions current in Arabic poetry) and a philosophical work called *The Kuzari*, based on a famous legend according to which the Khazars, a Tatar people living near the Caspian Sea, had converted to Judaism sometime in the eighth century. In Ha-Levi's version of the story, the conversion of the Khazars takes place after their king has listened to presentations by advocates of each of the three great religions—Islam, Judaism, and Christianity. The rabbi cites the notion of *netzah Yisrael* ('the eternity of Israel'; that is, its survival against all odds through the many catastrophes of history) as proof of God's special interest in Israel. He also mentions the unbroken tradition of Judaism, which is much longer than Christian or Islamic tradition, together with the Jews' bravery in allowing themselves to be martyred for their faith.

Ha-Levi even suggests that Islam and Christianity are appropriate preparatory faiths for nations that are not yet capable of the religious and philosophical analysis necessary to accept Judaism. When the nations of the world mature in their faith, they will be ready for Judaism. Though Jews have never actively sought to convert others,

From *The Kuzari*

Yehuda Ha-Levi was quite critical of the pagan philosophers, who attempted to understand the world without the help of the Bible. He much preferred the exercise of reason to be guided by scripture. But he respected the philosophers for having learned so much without biblical guidance.

On fundamental principles, the philosophers hold opinions which are absurd to the intellect, and which the intellect treats with contempt. Such, for example, is their explanation of the revolution of the celestial sphere. They state that the sphere seeks for a perfection which it lacks, namely, to occupy all possible spatial positions. Since it cannot achieve such a state simultaneously in respect of each of its constituent parts, it attempts to achieve it by occupying each possible position in turn. Equally false is their opinion regarding the emanations which flow from the First Cause. They maintain that from an angel's knowledge of the First Cause there arises of necessity another angel, and from the angel's knowledge of itself there arises a sphere; and so the process of emanation advances step by step down through eleven stages till the emanations come to an end with the Active Intellect, from which arises neither an angel nor a sphere. And they hold other views like these, which are less convincing than those advanced in the *Sefer Yezirah*. All these opinions are highly dubious, and it is impossible to find any two philosophers agreeing on them. However, we should not blame the philosophers for this. Rather, they deserve our praise for what they managed to achieve simply through the force of rational argument. Their intentions were good, they established the laws of thought, and they rejected the pleasures of this world. They may, in any case, be granted superiority since they were not obliged to accept our opinions. We, however, are obliged to accept whatever we see with our own eyes, or any well-founded tradition, which is tantamount to seeing for oneself (Alexander 1984: 14–19).

in Ha-Levi's story the rabbi is the most persuasive of the three advocates, which is the reason that the Khazars became Jews.

Maimonides

Moses Maimonides, or Moses ben Maimon (1135–1204), was born in Cordoba, Spain, lived in Egypt, and is undoubtedly the most famous of all Jewish philosophers. In religious texts he is usually known as 'Rambam': R–M–B–M, the acronym of 'Rabbi Moses ben Maimon'.

Maimonides became a refugee at the age of thirteen when the Almohads, a Muslim fundamentalist group from North Africa, took control in Spain. He fled first to Morocco, then to Palestine, which was under the control of the Crusaders, and finally to Egypt. There he found employment—and the freedom to practise his religion—as physician in the court of the Muslim sultan of Egypt, the famous Salah al-Din (Saladin).

Other medieval Jewish philosophers wrote on an impressive range of subjects, scriptural, devotional, and scientific, but Maimonides' accomplishments were truly prodigious. He wrote the famous code of Jewish law, *Mishneh Torah*, in Hebrew; several treatises on medicine; a treatise on logic as well as several on medicine; and a number of **responsa** advising Jewish communities around the world on matters such as false conversion, the concept of resurrection, and the arrival of the messiah.

Perhaps to underline the shift in focus from technical matters in Judaism to a wider concern with religious thought generally, Maimonides

Maimonides' Twelfth Fundamental Principle of Faith

In his commentary on the Mishnah, *called the* Mishneh Torah, *Maimonides included a summary of Judaism under the heading 'Thirteen Principles of Faith'. His twelfth principle, that no one should try to determine the date of the messiah's arrival, was a reflection of the apocalyptic speculation that was widespread among Jews, Christians, and Muslims alike in the twelfth century.*

I believe in perfect faith that the Messiah will come, and we should not consider him as tardy: 'Should he tarry, wait for him' [*Habakkuk* 2: 13]. No date may be fixed for his appearance, nor may the Scriptures be interpreted in such a way as to derive from them the time of his coming.

wrote his most important philosophical treatise, *The Guide of the Perplexed*, in Arabic, although it was quickly translated into Hebrew. Ostensibly a letter of advice addressed to a single student, the *Guide* was aimed at the many acculturated Jews who, living in a cosmopolitan and philosophically sophisticated environment, had begun to question the truth of their own religion.

Maimonides' deep knowledge of Aristotle put him at the forefront of the intellectual life of his day. Earlier medieval philosophers such as Saadia and Ha-Levi had drawn on Neoplatonism, a tradition based on the work of Plato that spoke of abstract ideas, a universe of emanating intellects, and mystical or intuitive insight, which allowed humans to receive an intuition of the highest good. By contrast, the Aristotelian tradition was based on analytic observation of physical phenomena and human behaviour, and most religious thinkers were wary of it because it took a more mechanistic view of the universe.

Aristotle believed the universe to be eternal, not created as the Bible maintains. Nevertheless, Maimonides accepted Aristotle's physics provisionally for the purpose of proving the existence of God. Rambam's greatest contribution was his effort to resolve the tension between faith and knowledge. Like most Jewish philosophers before him, he saw no contradiction between reason and revelation, and held that the Bible should not be taken literally when it attributes human forms and feelings to the divine.

In addition, however, Maimonides argues that the truths revealed through the visions of the prophets represent the perfect union of the intellectual and imaginative faculties, and that all the laws Jews are required to follow are ultimately rational, even if the reasons for them seem beyond human ken.

The last part of *The Guide of the Perplexed* tackles difficult questions regarding God's providence. The rabbis understood that, for the moral system they had designed to make sense, humanity must have free choice: without free will, a system of rewards and punishments based on the moral choices of individual humans would be meaningless. For them, the story of Adam and Eve marked the beginning of that power of choice, and Maimonides did not challenge that position.

Whatever freedom is granted to individual humans, however, appears to take away from God's perfect sovereignty. The rabbis were content to express the problem in paradoxical statements: 'All is foreseen yet free will is given,' they said. Or: 'All is in the hands of heaven except for the fear of heaven'—meaning that God controls everything except whether people respond to him. For the rabbis, this amounted to a statement of faith that God's powers are so great that they will prevail and yet still provide for human will. But the problem did not go away; Arab philosophers and intellectuals agonized over the question of which principle was more fundamental: human free will or God's sovereignty.

Maimonides contributed to this discussion by using Aristotle's cosmology to arrive at a compromise. He asked the question of divine providence in a traditional scholastic way: 'How far does God's knowledge extend into our imperfect world?' For philosophers in the Platonic tradition, who typically thought of divinity as perfect and changeless, such a question immediately posed a new problem: If we suppose that God knows change, does this not compromise divine perfection?

According to Arabic Aristotelian philosophy, God's knowledge of his creation ends at the species level; he knows sparrows as a species, for instance, but his providence does not extend to the individual sparrow. Maimonides suggests that this analysis is correct for all species except humans. What enables God's providence to extend to the individual level in humans, he says, is the human capacity for rational thought. To the extent that humans use their rational facilities, God is able to perceive them as individuals and guide their actions. The prophets, who perfected both their rational and imaginative facilities, are therefore the model for all humans. The more we train and use our rational faculties, the more we value moral behaviour—because true morality is truly rational—and the more capable we are of receiving divine guidance. This does not mean that fully rational humans will never experience sorrow or misfortune. But it does mean that their misfortunes and setbacks are specifically known by God and are somehow part of a divine plan. By contrast, non-rational humans, who are intellectually and morally insensitive, cannot be known to God in this way, as individuals. Therefore what happens to them is accidental in the same way that it is accidental whether a particular sparrow falls prey to a cat or flies free. ('Accidental', for Maimonides, meant non-essential in the way that a person's height is non-essential.)

For Maimonides, rationality is essential to God himself. But God's intelligence is different from ours. In fact, God has no attributes because attributes are accidental. Everything God is, he is essentially. His intelligence is entirely active, a truly creative essence that describes only God. He creates the universe by thinking, and it exists only because he is thinking it.

The same rationality is made accessible to humans through a series of 'emanations' forming the heavenly spheres. Transferred from one sphere to the next through their angelic rulers, the divine rationality eventually reaches the angel responsible for the lunar sphere, the one closest to earth. It is this angel, known as the Active Intellect, who enables the human mind to form thoughts. We need the Active Intellect because our minds in themselves are passive, possessing only the potential for intelligence—*tabulae rasae* ('blank slates') in Latin scholastic parlance.

In order to understand the emanations conveyed by the Active Intellect, however, we need to perfect our intellects through moral and intellectual schooling. The Active Intellect is also the angel of prophecy, which for Maimonides (as we have seen) represents the perfection of the intellectual and imaginative faculties. In this way revelation is explained as the perfection of the rational principle. God's emanations cannot be automatic because God must be free to give prophecy to whomever he wills.

Of course, God can withhold prophecy even from the perfectly trained human, but this would be exceptional. Prophetic powers are the acme and zenith of the intellectual life. The Torah, the perfect embodiment of prophecy, is a special gift to the Jewish people. All those who study and follow the law are, in fact, training to be prophets. But all humans can participate in prophecy to the extent to which they perfect their potentialities. The Greek philosophers, as well as the religions of Christianity and Islam, also and necessarily partake in this truth, though usually to a lesser degree because they have each fallen victim to error in one way or another. So for Maimonides, reason and revelation are identical processes, and they are both identical with the power by which God creates and preserves the universe.

Rambam's great accomplishment was to promote a view of Judaism as thoroughly rational. This view itself was not new, but he provided the intellectual structure to sustain it, and that structure has characterized Jewish self-understanding to this day. Whereas orthodox Islam maintained that reason should retreat before faith, and Christian Aristotelianism, as exemplified by Thomas Aquinas in the thirteenth century, argued that faith must retreat in the face of issues that are proven right or wrong by reason, Maimonides saw all seeming contradictions between reason or science and faith as just that: only apparent and ephemeral. Rationality and good religion are equivalent.

Thus science and religion were in harmony for Maimonides, not in opposition, and Judaism was perfectly consistent with the Aristotelian worldview that the acculturated and affluent Jews shared with the enlightened Islamic society around them. The guidance he offered the 'perplexed' among them was that the principles of 'science' (i.e., learning) need not bring their faith into question. Rather, a correct intellectual understanding of the world and Jewish tradition would show the two to be in perfect agreement.

It cannot be said that Jews universally admired or adopted Maimonides' system. He wrote for an intellectual elite among the Jews of his day in the Islamic world, speakers of Arabic who shared the Aristotelian assumptions of medieval Islamic thinkers. The situation of Jews was very different in Christian lands such as France, where his writing set off a century of fierce controversy punctuated by book burnings and occasional edicts of ostracism by rabbis opposed to Maimonides' enterprise.

On the whole, Maimonides' emphasis on reason has served the Jewish community well in

From Bahya Ibn Paquda's *Duties of the Heart*

Bahya Ibn Paquda was an eleventh-century moralist living in Saraossa, Spain, who sought to express the essence of the law in his book Duties of the Heart. *Written in Arabic, it was translated into Hebrew in the twelfth century.*

You should know, O mortal, that the greatest enemy you have in the world is our evil inclination, which is woven into the powers of your soul and intertwined with the constitution of your spirit, sharing with you the direction of your bodily senses and mental faculties. He rules over the secrets of your soul, over the thoughts you keep hidden away in your mind. He is your counsellor in all your actions—seen and unseen—which you perform out of free choice. He lies in wait for your moments of inattention: you may be asleep to him, but he is always awake to you; you may be unaware of him, but he is never unaware of you. He dons for you the robe of friendship, and bedecks himself with the guise of love for you. He becomes one of your confidants and counsellors, one of the sincerest of your friends. He subtly deceives you, going along with what you want with outward signs and gestures of agreement, but all the while he is shooting at you his deadly arrows in order to destroy you, after the fashion of one of whom Scripture speaks: 'Like a madman shooting deadly darts and arrows, so is the man who deceives his fellow and then says, "I was only joking" [*Proverbs* 26: 18–19]' (Alexander 1984: 98–100).

times of peace and prosperity, when intellectual life has been able to flourish. In times of trial and tribulation, however, Jews have been more likely to turn to mysticism for consolation.

The Early Modern Period

It was the toleration of Jews in Islamic Spain that allowed Maimonides' thought to flourish. But that 'Golden Age' came to a definitive end in 1492, when the Christian monarchs Ferdinand and Isabella took control of Granada, the last remaining Muslim stronghold. The Jewish presence might have been helpful to the Christians in a culture shared with Muslims, but once the Reconquista—the campaign to reconquer Spain and take it back into Christendom—was largely complete, the regime wasted no time in expelling the Jews. When Columbus set out for the New World in August 1492, he had to sail from a small port in southern

Map 3.1   Expulsion and Migration of Jews from Europe, c. 1000–1500 CE

Source: I.R. al Fārūqī and D.E. Sopher, *Historical Atlas of the Religions of the World* (New York: Macmillan, 1974): 148–9.

Spain because all the major ports were clogged by Jews leaving their centuries-old home.

Ferdinand and Isabella were by no means the first Christian monarchs in western Europe to expel Jews. But the effect was particularly devastating for the Iberian Peninsula, where Jewish culture was well-established and highly sophisticated. To avoid expulsion, some Jews converted to Christianity while continuing to practise their ancestral faith in secret. But even the *conversos* ('New Christians') who abandoned Judaism faced persecution by the Spanish Inquisition. An arm of the Church established in Spain in 1478 and dedicated to rooting out Christian heresy, it developed a new specialty in uncovering Jewish beliefs and observances among the *conversos* or Marranos ('pigs'), as they were sometimes derisively called.

Most of the Jews who left Spain found their way to the Ottoman Turkish Empire. When its ruler, Sultan Bayazid II (r. 1481–1512), heard of the Jewish expulsion, he mocked the Spanish monarchs' folly and suggested that Turkey would take advantage of the squandered 'wealth' of Spain. He thereafter encouraged the dispossessed Jews to take shelter in his empire. As a result, some Jews living in contemporary Turkey still speak a dialect of Spanish called Ladino, as well as Turkish.

Jewish Mysticism

The spiritual crisis generated by the expulsion sparked a new interest in mystical practice and pietistic devotion to the ordinary customs of Judaism. Jewish mysticism traces its roots back as far as the biblical prophets themselves. There is some evidence that they may have used various physical techniques to induce ecstatic visions. Hellenistic and medieval Jewish mystical writers, however, claimed to be capable of receiving divine visions solely through their interpretation of the imagery used by the prophets. For these mystics the most interesting biblical passages are the ones where God shows himself to his people in a human form or 'presence' known as the *kavod*,

'glory of God'—a form that was understood to be the principal messenger of God, the angel of the Lord.

In the apocalyptic tradition that followed the age of prophecy, some visions involve human manifestations of the divine. Especially interesting is the so-called 'Son of Man' (apparently a Hebrew expression meaning a 'manlike figure'). Probably an archangel such as Michael or Gabriel, he symbolizes the martyrs of the community in *Daniel* 7: 13: 'I saw in the night visions, and, behold, one like the Son of Man came with the clouds of heaven, and came to the Ancient of Days and they brought him near before Him.' There is good evidence that these images played a crucial role in the conversion of Paul, whose identification of Jesus as the Christ recalls Daniel's identification of the 'Son of Man' as the messiah and the angel of the Lord. Those early mystical traditions were increasingly disturbing to the rabbis, who feared that mystical interpretation of texts would lead to heresy and abrogation of the law.

The earliest and longest phase of Jewish mysticism, stretching from the prophecies of *Ezekiel* through the apocalyptic visions in *Daniel* to the emergence of **Kabbalah** in the twelfth century, is known as Merkabah ('chariot') mysticism. The central aspects of Merkabah mysticism were (1) an anthropomorphic concept of God and a keen interest in matters such as his size, as in the so-called Shiur Koma ('measurement of the body') literature, (2) heavenly ascents, (3) theurgic (magical) spells and motifs, and (4) apocalyptic and revelatory writings.

The central experience was the ecstatic journey of the adept to the heavenly throne room. Although the human-like figure on the throne was usually referred to by a name associated with angels (such as Metatron or Zoharariel), it was understood to represent 'the king in his glory'. These *Hekhaloth* ('Palaces') texts were edited and re-edited throughout the entire first period of Jewish mysticism. In the form in which we have them, they display many of the characteristic concerns of the Hasidei Ashkenaz, a pietist group that flourished in fourteenth-century Germany.

The development of the teaching called Kabbalah ('received tradition') is probably most responsible for the gradual diminution of Merkabah mysticism, though Kabbalah in turn was probably influenced by Islamic Sufi mysticism. In medieval Jewish mysticism, the heavenly journey of the Merkabah mystics came to be understood as symbolizing a journey into the self.

In place of the heavenly palaces, Kabbalah developed a notion of ten *spherot* ('countings' or 'spheres'). By correctly aligning these *spherot* through rituals, pious deeds, and mystical meditation, the Kabbalist can affect the future course of events and participate in the divine plan for the universe.

The *Zohar*

The principal text of Kabbalah is the *Zohar*. Although it purports to be the work of Rabbi Shimon bar Yohai, a famous second-century rabbi, its real author was probably the Spanish Kabbalist Moses ben Shemtov of León (1250–1305). The *Zohar* has a special mystical agenda. It describes God as an unlimited divine principle, *En Sof* ('without end'), who produces the universe indirectly through the series of emanations called the *spherot*.

Sometimes the *spherot* recall the heavenly spheres of philosophical discourse; but sometimes they suggest more imaginative configurations of the different powers of God. They can be envisioned as forming a tree of life or even the primeval, cosmic man, *adam ha-kadmon*. When they are arrayed as the latter, they seem to be related to the earlier notion of a gigantic angelic mediator who somehow embodies the name of God. The correct alignments, or 'unifications', of the *spherot* will bring about the most harmonious balance of divine forces.

The *Zohar* suggests that this insight is implied in the biblical text. In form, then, the *Zohar* resembles a midrashic exposition of scripture; but instead of explaining the sense of a verse, it explains the secret knowledge that could be derived from it:

> He who desires to understand the wisdom of holy unity, let him contemplate the flame which rises from coal or from a candle for the flame rises only when it is attached to a material thing. Come and see: in the rising flame there are two lights, one a white shining light, and the other a dark bluish light that holds on directly to the candle. . . . Come and see: there is no stimulus for the kindling of the blue light that it might provide the basis for the white light save through the people of Israel who . . . unite with it from below and continue in their endurance (*Zohar* III, 290a; Caplan and Ribalow 1952: 161–2).

In this passage, the blue light symbolizes the aspect of divinity *spherah* known as Malkut ('kingship') or **Shekhinah** ('God's indwelling'), which in turn is identified with the spiritual presence of the people Israel. This particular *spherah* (grammatically feminine in Hebrew) has an explicitly feminine identity, and is imagined in sexual union with the masculine aspect of God.

The white light conventionally symbolizes the higher *spherah* of **hesed**, God's aspect of 'loving-kindness'. Thus the passage tells us that even a simple flame reveals something about the relationship between God and Israel: specifically, that the existence and behaviour of Israel are integrally related to God's loving-kindness in the world. The purpose of these manifestations of God's various aspects in the world is to ensure the correct flow of divine effulgence (*shefa*), which is generally thought to be balanced when the upper *spherah* (usually Tiferet, 'beauty') is properly related to the *spherah* Malkut or Shekhinah, the feminine aspect of God that signifies Israel.

The mystic tradition maintains that this balance is affected by human behaviour, ritual and otherwise. Thus, sexual intercourse between Kabbalistically sophisticated spouses, when performed with the proper meditations, could help to align the heavenly dimensions of God. But any properly completed ritual action—like the blessing over wine before a meal—could have a beneficial effect on the universe. In the following passage, the bride and the husband together represent the *spherah* Malkut or Shekhinah, while the husband alone represents Tiferet:

> Rabbi Simeon would sit and study Torah all night when the bride was about to be united with her husband. . . . the companions of the household in the bride's palace are needed on that night when the bride is prepared for her meeting on the morrow with her husband under the bridal canopy. They need to be with her all that night and rejoice with her in the preparations with which she is adorned, studying Torah—progressing from the Pentateuch to the Prophets, and from the Prophets to the writings, and then to the midrashic and mystical interpretations of the verses, for these are her adornments and her finery (*Zohar* I, 8a).

On one level, this passage is a simple description of a bride's preparations for marriage. On another level, it is an allegory of the role that Jewish learning plays in the 'love affair' between God and the world.

Many of the deepest Jewish minds have seen Kabbalah as irrational, even absurd, and condemned it as undermining the fundamental principle of monotheism. Nevertheless, it has appealed to great numbers of people troubled by the suffering that Jews have experienced and the enormous part that evil plays in the world. Kabbalah explains evil as the result of a misalignment of divine effulgence and offers humans the hope that their action will help the divinity in his progress towards the goal of cosmic perfection:

> The story of Jonah [the name literally means 'aggrieved'] may be construed as an allegory of the course of a man's life in this world. Jonah descends into the ship: this is parallel to man's soul descending to enter into his body in this world. Why is the soul called Jonah? For the reason that she becomes subject to all manner of vexation when once she enters into partnership with the body. Thus, a man in this world is as in a ship crossing the vast ocean and like to be broken, as it is written 'so that the ship was like to be broken' (*Zohar* on *Jonah* 1: 4; Scholem 1949: 103).

In this view, the 'vexation' of the body has a purpose: to motivate the soul to strive towards perfection.

Luria and Sabbatai Zvi

Until the sixteenth century, Kabbalah was largely a private contemplative discipline. That changed with Isaac Luria (1534–72), who founded a community of mystics in the hilltop town of Safed in the Galilee region. Luria explained the tragedy of Jewish life in terms of a split in the Godhead that occurs in the process of the creation, when God must contract himself to make room for the universe. When his perfection was removed from the area that was to be the universe, the divine sparks became contaminated with the gross and evil material of creation. The earthly counterpart of this cosmic process was the exile of Israel.

According to Luria, mystics can help God return the divine sparks to their correct place—and in so doing assist in the rectification (*tikkun*) of the universe—through meditation, magic, and acts of piety, including ritual activities. The community that Luria founded in Safed practised asceticism and observed the rules of Judaism with special intensity, hoping that this would assist God in the enterprise of redemption and hasten the coming of the messiah.

Messianic expectations came to a head in 1666, when an adept of Lurianic Kabbalah named Sabbatai Zvi was proclaimed the messiah in Smyrna and attracted a varied following of mystically oriented Jews. Influenced by the quickening of millennial expectations among Christians—who associated the year 1666 with the references in *Revelation* (13: 17–18) to '666', the supposed 'number of the beast'—the followers of the mystical messiah marched on the sultan in Istanbul. At first, the sultan ignored the rag-tag army camped outside the walls; then he had Zvi imprisoned. Finally he offered Zvi the choice between conversion to Islam and death. Zvi chose the former, and most of his followers gave up in despair.

Those who did not repudiate him understood Zvi's choice as a way of fulfilling the Jewish commandments by taking on evil directly and conquering it. This idea, which they called 'the commandment that comes by infraction' (*ha-mitzvah haba`ah b'averah*), gave further impetus to the aspect of mysticism that is called 'antinomian', that is, counter to rule or law. Many of Zvi's most devoted supporters followed his lead, converting to Islam but continuing to practise their ancestral Sephardic traditions in secret, mystical ways. (There are still some members of this sect in modern Turkey, known as the Dönmeh, 'returners'.)

Other supporters carried the movement as far as Germany. A woman known as Glueckl of Hamelin later wrote a memoir in which she described the movement's impact there:

> Our joy, when the letters arrived [from Smyrna] is not to be told. Most of them were addressed to the Sephardim who, as fast they came, took them to their synagogue and read them aloud; young and old, the Germans too hastened to the Sephardic synagogue.

The Sephardic youth came dressed in their best finery and decked in broad green silk ribbons, the gear of Sabbatai Zvi 'with timbrels and with dances' they one and all trooped to the synagogue, and they read the letters forth with joy like the 'joy of the Feast of Water-Drawing.'

Many sold their houses and lands and all their possessions, for any day they hoped to be redeemed. My good father-in-law left his home in Hamelin, abandoned his house and lands all his goodly furniture, and moved to Hildesheim. He sent on to us in Hamburg two enormous casks packed with linens and with peas, beans, dried meats, shredded prunes and like stuff, every manner of food that would keep. For the old man expected to sail any moment from Hamburg to the Holy Land. . . . For three years the casks stood ready, and all this while my father-in-law awaited the signal to depart. But the Most High pleased otherwise (Lowenthal 1977: 46–7).

From the point of view of Orthodox Judaism, the Sabbatians resembled Christians in that they were a mystical and antinomian messianic group who took their original teachings from Judaism but who abandoned it over issues involving Jewish law. Roughly a century later, another group of this type, in Podolia (western Ukraine), became outwardly Christian under the influence of a later Sabbatian named Jacob Frank.

Hasidism

The founder of **Hasidism** was Israel ben Eliezer (1698–1759), better known as the Baal Shem Tov ('master of the Good Name'), the Baal Shem, or simply 'the Besht' (an acronym). Orphaned shortly after his birth in the eastern European region of Bukovina (now northern Romania–Moldavia), he grew up as a ward of the Jewish community and in his youth he delighted in telling stories to children.

From the Memoirs of Glueckl of Hamelin

Glueckl (1646–1724) married a merchant named Hayyim of Hamelin at the age of fourteen. She bore twelve children, became his adviser in business, and, after his death in 1689, carried on the business alone. Her touching memoir offers a rare window into the private life of a Jewish family in the seventeenth century.

In my great grief and for my heart's ease I begin this book the year of creation 5451 [1690–1]—God soon rejoice us and send us His redeemer!

I began writing it, dear children, upon the death of your good father, in the hope of distracting my soul from the burdens laid upon it, and the bitter thought that we have lost our faithful shepherd. In this way, I have managed to live through many wakeful nights, and springing from my bed shortened the sleepless hours.

This, dear children, will be no book of morals. Such I could not write, and our sages have already written many. Moreover, we have our holy Torah, in which we may find and learn all that we need for our long journey through this world to the world to come. It is like a rope which the great and gracious God has thrown to us as we drown in the stormy sea of life, that we may seize hold of it and be saved.

The kernel of the Torah is 'Thou shalt love thy neighbor as thyself.' But in our days we seldom find it so, and few are they who love their fellow men with all their heart—on the contrary, if a man can contrive to ruin his neighbour, nothing pleases him more (Lowenthal 1977: 1–2).

As an adult he worked as a Hebrew teacher, lime quarrier, and small innkeeper—and dabbled in Kabbalah—but above all he wandered from community to community in Podolia (western Ukraine) and Walachia (southern Romania), meeting ordinary people and making disciples. Everyone who met him was impressed by his humility. He appears to have received the title 'Baal Shem' in recognition of his success as a healer, bringing about miraculous cures through the use of God's name. Sometimes he organized impromptu retreats where he preached through informal conversations and humble lessons.

Though the common folk who were his principal audience knew enough Hebrew to say their prayers, they were largely uneducated, and the scholars produced by the rigorous and elitist Talmudic academies of eastern Europe had little to offer them. By contrast, the Baal Shem Tov proclaimed a simple and accessible message: that the best way of communing with God was through humility, good deeds, prayer (ecstatic and otherwise), and joy. He preached the importance of mutual help, forbearance, and other virtues. He himself became the model for a Hasidic leader, a *zaddik* ('righteous person'). He sought the presence of God in everyday life.

Like *aggadah*, Hasidic stories seek to teach a moral lesson, often through the most mundane aspects of ordinary life—in one famous Hasidic tale, a student learns about the divine from watching his master tie his shoes. The stories of Hasidic masters often bear a striking resemblance to the paradoxical exercise of a Zen *koan*.

The Besht's pietistic Judaism became very popular in eighteenth-century eastern Europe. The name given to its adherents, Hasidim ('pious ones'), recalls the virtue of *hesed*, steadfast loyalty or faithfulness owed to the other by each party to the biblical covenant relationship. (In the second

Jewish Communities in Africa and Asia

Beyond the eastern Mediterranean world were a number of Jewish communities that had little or no contact with the currents of either Sephardic or Ashkenazic Jewry. In Ethiopia, the people derogatorily referred to as Falashas ('exiles') survived in isolated villages until modern times. According to their own tradition, they are descendants of the retinue that accompanied the legendary Arabian Queen of Sheba on her visit to King Solomon in the tenth century BCE; but their ancestors are now generally thought to have been Ethiopians who were converted to a form of Judaism practised in southern Arabia in the period shortly before the emergence of Islam. In 1975, the Israeli rabbinate ruled that the Habashim (Ethiopians) qualified for entry into Israel, and since then most have moved there.

Iran has had a historically and intellectually significant Jewish minority since early Islamic times; the ninth-century Karaite Benjamin of Nehavand, for instance, was an Iranian Jew. Since the establishment of modern Israel, Iranian Jews have seen their status become politically more and more sensitive, and some have been wrongly prosecuted as suspected Israeli sympathizers. But this was not salient in 1948, when Iran maintained relations with Israel. The Iranian suspicion of Jews has developed only since the fundamentalist imams came to power in the Islamic revolution of 1979.

Still farther east, India has two historic Jewish communities, one on the southwestern Malabar Coast, in Cochin, and the other on the western coast just south of Mumbai. Their origins are uncertain, but both claim to be related to the legendary ten lost tribes of northern Israel, which were scattered by the Assyrian invasion of 722 BCE. The Cochin community, documented by medieval European and Arab travellers, was probably augmented by some of the Spanish Jews expelled from Spain at the end of the fifteenth century. Its members assimilated to Indian life, and even developed the rudiments of a caste structure in their own community. Soon after Indian and Israeli independence (in 1947 and 1948, respectively), most of one subgroup left for Israel, but the other remained in India because the Indian government would not allow them to take their financial assets out of the country.

The community known as the Bene Israel ('children of Israel'), near Mumbai, appears to have had only a sketchy acquaintance with Jewish tradition until the eighteenth century, when it came into contact with Jews in Cochin and Baghdad, along with some Presbyterian missionaries from Scotland. The Bene Israel wear Indian dress and do not condemn their Hindu neighbours' polytheism. Until recently, they did not allow widows to remarry and thought that the Bible prohibited the eating of beef.

More recently, a tribal people living in northeastern India have also identified themselves as descendants of the ten lost tribes of Israel—an idea that may have originated in the teachings of Christian missionaries. Quite recently, they invited the Orthodox rabbinate of Israel to convert them and took the name Bnei Menashe as their ethnic identity. Whatever their origins, they are now considered fully Jewish, and many of them are moving to Israel.

Finally, the presence of a small community of Jews in the central Chinese city of Kaifeng has been traced to traders from Yemen, Iraq, or Iran who settled in coastal cities in the Middle Ages. In the past, the Kaifeng community appears to have had Torah scrolls, and until a couple of generations ago its members still avoided pork. But the last rabbi died two hundred years ago, and the Communist government's repression of religion accelerated the community's decline in the twentieth century. Even so, approximately 200 families claimed some recollection of their Jewish ancestry in the 1980s, and some Jewish visitors have taken them books about Judaism in the hope of reviving their religious life.

century BCE, Jewish loyalists in the Maccabean uprising were also called 'Hasidim', but their movement was entirely separate from the Baal Shem Tov's.) After the death of the Besht, the Hasidim were led by his disciple Rabbi Ber of Mezeritz, also known as the Maggid ('preacher').

The theory of leadership under the *zaddikim* was first articulated during the Maggid's life. All the subsequent leaders of Hasidism after the Baal Shem Tov were titled Zaddik and were entitled to pass their authority on to their children. Thus a *zaddik* (or 'Rebbe' in **Yiddish**) was both the holder of a hereditary office and a kind of intermediary between the people and God. The popular appeal of Hasidism provoked the opposition of the rabbinic community, characterized by the Hasidim as Mitnagdim ('opponents'). One of the things the Mitnagdim found most suspect about the Hasidim was that they deified their leaders.

When Hasidism spread to Latvia and Lithuania, the centre of rabbinic rationalism in eastern Europe, it changed character again. In those communities Talmudic training was quite common, and, for Hasidism to attract adherents there, it needed Talmudic credentials. It gained those credentials in the person of a respected Belorussian Talmudist named Shneur Zalman (1746–1812), the author of a philosophic tractate known as *Tania* ('As It Is Taught'). Zalman's membership marked a synthesis of Talmudic Judaism with Hasidic pietism. His followers were known by the acronym Habad (or Chabad), representing the names of three *spherot*: Hokhma ('wisdom'), Bina ('insight'), and Da'at ('knowledge'). Because the centre of the movement was the Belorussian town of Lubavitch, they are often called Lubavitcher Hasidim.

Today the followers of Shneur Zalman's descendants, who took the name Schneerson, are centred in Brooklyn in New York City. They proselytize other Jews and for that purpose have opened branches in many countries, including Israel and India. (The Lubavitcher House in Mumbai was one of the targets in the terrorist attacks on that city in November 2008.) To the untrained eye, the Lubavitcher Hasidim may resemble strict Orthodox Jews, but technically they are not Orthodox in either their beliefs or their practices. Since 1994, when Rabbi Menachem Schneerson died without a male heir, the Lubavitcher have been without a leader, which has stimulated some messianic expectations. They are only one of several Hasidic sects, each founded by another early disciple of the Baal Shem Tov, that have often been in sharp competition with one another as well as the Orthodox mainstream, which remains quite hostile to most of the Hasidic program.

PRACTICE

Prayer

The rabbis took a lively interest in the subject of prayer. Among the commandments given in *Deuteronomy* 6: 4–9 is one calling on Israel to speak of the Lord's laws morning and evening. This the rabbis interpreted as a reference to prayer. Accordingly, Jews are instructed to pray before they go to sleep and when they rise.

Public prayer follows the order of the Temple service, which was performed three times a day. Therefore Jews typically pray in the morning, the afternoon, and the evening. Although these prayers may be private, they are quite often performed in a synagogue, preferably with a *minyan* (a group of ten) as a quorum. Jews also pray privately upon retiring and rising. For convenience a number of the daily prayers can be grouped and performed together.

Additional prayers are acceptable any time and virtually anywhere, as long as the setting does not detract from the dignity of the prayer or make it impossible to achieve the proper state of mind or spiritual intention (*kavvanah*).

The Shema

In Jewish liturgy, the following passage (from Deuteronomy 6: 4–9) is called the Shema, after its first word in the Hebrew. It is the watchword of Israel's faith, repeated 'morning and night'.

Hear O Israel, the LORD our God, the LORD is One. You shall love the LORD your God with all your heart and with all your soul and with all your strength. These words which I command you this day are to be kept in your heart. You shall repeat them to your children, speaking of them indoors and outdoors, morning and night. You shall bind them as a sign upon your hand and wear them as signs upon your forehead; you shall write them on the doorposts of your houses and on your gates.

The Content of Prayer

To avoid any risk of idolatry or polytheism, the rabbis forbade Jews to pray to angels or intermediary beings of any kind. In keeping with their emphasis on ethics, the rabbis also insisted that prayer be subject to the same ethical standards that govern every other aspect of Jewish life. Thus it is permissible to pray for God's special favour, but only if the advantage sought would not adversely affect anyone else. To pray for something that might cause harm to others is strictly forbidden. Seeing a plume of smoke in the distance, for instance, a Jew is not allowed to pray that the building on fire not be his own house, because that would amount to praying that the fire be in someone else's house. Jews are not allowed even to pray for the fall of their enemies. By contrast, prayer for the benefit of others is strongly encouraged.

The particular kinds of prayers offered and the specific texts of the prayers have developed over millennia of Jewish history. Although the prayer books of Sephardic and Ashkenazic Jews differ somewhat, on the whole prayer is something that unites Jews the world over. By tradition, the language of prayer is Hebrew, and many prayers end with the word *amen*, meaning 'so be it'.

Kavvanah

Rabbinic law requires that every action, including prayer, be rightly intentioned towards God. This intention, or *kavvanah*, can be defined in a variety of ways. One of the characteristics of the Hasidic movement is the special attention it pays to *kavvanah* in prayer.

Items Worn in Prayer

To help foster the appropriate *kavvanah* for prayer and other ceremonial functions, many Jewish men wear special garments and other articles of dress called for in the Bible. Among those articles is the **tallith** or prayer shawl: a rectangular piece of material with long fringes at the corners as specified by biblical law (*Numbers* 15: 37–41). Based on a standard outer garment from Hellenistic times, the *tallith* today is usually striped in blue and white (though other colours are also possible) and comes in two sizes. Some Jews prefer a very large one that covers the shoulders as well as the neck and can be drawn over the head, like a kind of hood, when the wearer is concentrating in prayer. Others prefer a short *tallith* that is simply draped around the shoulders like a scarf.

Since the Bible calls for the *tallith* to be worn at all times, very Orthodox Jews wear a short 'half *tallith*'—a kind of undershirt with the fringes of the longer garment—under their street clothes. At the other extreme, most Reform Jews have given up the prayer shawl altogether.

Another common item of dress for Jewish males is a skullcap (**kippah** in Hebrew, **yarmulke** in Yiddish), worn in observance of the injunction to cover the head when praying. Since every day brings many occasions that call for a prayer or blessing, more traditional Jews simply wear a head covering all the time. The history of this practice is unclear, though it may have evolved from the use of the *tallith* to veil the head in the presence of divinity. The earliest evidence for use of the *kippah* comes from the Middle Ages, when it was considerably larger than it is today. Devout Orthodox Jews wear a *kippah* at all times, even under ordinary hats or baseball caps, while most Reform Jews do not wear them at all, even in prayer. But a fair number of modern Jewish males, particularly students, now choose to wear skullcaps as a public statement of their Jewish identity. In the spirit of equality, some Jewish women have begun to wear both the *tallith* and the *kippah* as well.

Finally, **tefillin** are traditional prayer garb worn by men on weekdays. They are two small black boxes that hold passages from scripture. Long leather straps attached to the boxes are used to tie one box to the forehead and the other to the upper arm, facing the heart. The usual English term for *tefillin* is '**phylacteries**', from a Greek term meaning 'protective charm', but this is actually misleading, since the boxes have no protective value. Rather, they are intended to fulfill literally the commandment in *Deuteronomy* 6 to bind the words of Torah 'upon the hand and as frontlets between the eyes'. Pious Jews put on *tefillin* for morning prayers every day except Saturday, the Jewish Sabbath. *Tefillin* dating to the time of the Bar Cochba revolt (132–5) have been found in the caves of Judea, so we know that they were already in use in the first century. Orthodox Jews use them regularly as an aid to prayer, in order to concentrate the mind and fulfill the commandment. Reform Jews have suspended their use almost entirely, however.

Blessings

The early rabbis believed that all the gifts God provides should be acknowledged. To that end they designed a formula for expressing gratitude that

A young man at prayer wearing *tefillin* (AFP/Getty Images).

begins 'Blessed art Thou, O Lord our God, King of the Universe' and then continues with words of thanks appropriate to the occasion. Wine and bread in particular are blessed whenever they are offered; it seems likely that the Christian Eucharist grew out of this this custom, as reinterpreted by Jesus. After the meal, a longer formula of praise is customarily chanted or—if a sufficient number of people have eaten together—sung by all present.

Jewish prayer is both a comfort and an expression of joy in God's creation. Some Jews feel that God responds to prayer; others do not, but still feel that the regular sequence of prayers throughout the day is beneficial in concentrating attention on the ethical goals of life.

Sabbath Observance

The Sabbath begins at sunset on Friday and continues until sunset on Saturday. On Friday night many Jews attend synagogue services: Orthodox

Sabbath Blessings for Reading the Torah Scroll

The following prayers and responses are almost always spoken in Hebrew. Although the word translated here as 'Blessed' (Baruch) is sometimes rendered as 'Praised', 'blessing' is an appropriate response for humans to make in response to God's continuous bounty. Note that it is the fact that the Torah was given to the Jews that makes them the 'chosen' people.

Before reading from the Torah:
Reader: Blessed be the Lord, the source of blessing.
Congregation: Blessed be the Lord, the source of blessing, throughout all time.
Reader: Blessed are you, Lord our God, King of the Universe, who has chosen us from among all peoples by giving us His Torah. Blessed are You, Lord who gives the Torah.

After reading from the Torah:
Blessed are You, Lord our God, King of the Universe, who has given us the Torah of Truth, planting within us eternal life. Blessed are You, Lord who gives the Torah.

Before reading from the Prophets:
Blessed are You, Lord our God, King of the Universe, who has chosen the good prophets, and maintained them, whose utterances were truthful. Blessed are You, Lord, who chose the Torah, Moses His servant, Israel His people and prophets of truth and righteousness.

After reading from the Prophets:
Blessed are you, Lord our God, King of the Universe, Rock of all ages, righteous in all generations, steadfast God, who speaks and the deed is accomplished, who decrees and fulfils, whose every word is truth and righteousness. Faithful are you, who is the Lord our God, and faithful are all Your words. None of your words will ever be found empty, for You are a faithful and merciful God and King. Blessed are You, Lord, who are the faithful God in all your promises.

Show compassion for Zion, the habitation of our lives. And bring hope speedily in our days to the humbled soul. Blessed are You, Lord who brings joy to Zion by her descendants.

Bring us joy, Lord our God, through Your prophet Elijah and the kingdom of the House of David Your anointed. May Elijah come soon, to gladden our hearts. May no usurper sit on David's throne, and may no other inherit his glory. For by Your holy name you have promised that his light shall never be extinguished. Blessed are you, Lord shield of David.

For the Torah, for worship, for the prophets, and for this Sabbath day which you have given us for holiness and rest, for dignity and splendour—for everything—do we thank You and bless You. May Your name be blessed continually for every living creature. Blessed are You, Lord who sanctifies the Sabbath.

services tend to be short and close to sunset, but most Conservative and Reform congregations now favour a longer service in the evening, after the Sabbath dinner.

Even though it occurs every week, the Sabbath is undoubtedly the most sacred day in the Jewish calendar, consecrated by special prayers. Observant Jews cease all work by sundown on Friday so that they can experience to the fullest the special quiet of a day devoted entirely to song, prayer, and contemplation.

In the grand six-day creation story in *Genesis*, the Sabbath is built into the order of the universe. This is frequently mentioned in the special prayers for the Sabbath. It serves as a remembrance of the Garden of Eden and a foretaste of the return to Eden that is expected to come with the messiah. The Sabbath is also a primary sign of the enduring covenant with God:

> The Israelite people shall keep the sabbath, observing the sabbath throughout the ages as a covenant for all time: it shall be a sign for all time between Me and the people of Israel: For in six days the LORD made heaven and earth, and on the seventh day He ceased from work and was refreshed (*Exodus* 31: 16–17; also Sabbath prayerbook).

Jews return home early on Friday afternoon so that they can have all the preparations for the Sabbath meal—cooking, cleaning, lighting candles—completed before sundown. The meal itself is typically a special one, served on the best dishes, and accompanied by special prayers celebrating God's work of creation, psalms, hymns, and special Sabbath songs, as well as all the customary blessings of bread and wine. Still, the Sabbath meal is really just an augmented form of an ordinary Jewish meal, for Jews do not eat any food without praising and thanking God. Virtually every action of the day is sanctified by Jewish law. Every action is subject to moral analysis and every religious rite is an object lesson in morality. Denied a country of their own, with their own great religious monuments, the Jewish people instead built up a system that sanctified everyday life and sought the presence of God in it.

On Saturday, synagogue services continue through the morning. The afternoon is devoted to learning or quiet contemplation. Then many Jews return to synagogue in the evening to mark the end of the Sabbath with a boundary-marking observance called Havdalah. Celebrated with wine, a braided candle, and a spice box symbolizing the sweetness of the Sabbath, the Havdalah ('distinction' between the Sabbath and weekdays) service also blesses the promise of the new week and includes a reference to the prophet Elijah, presumably in the hope that he will appear and mark the arrival of the messianic age before the next Sabbath.

Sabbath Restrictions

Orthodox Jews will do nothing on the Sabbath that could be defined as work—from kindling a fire or cooking food to driving a car or playing tennis. In strict observance, they may not even turn on a light or push an elevator button because using electricity falls into the category of building a fire; hence in many modern high-rises and hospitals the elevators are programmed to stop at every floor continuously on the Sabbath. The Orthodox, who seek to live within walking distance of the synagogue, spend the entire Sabbath there. Reform and Conservative Jews also attend their synagogues, but they may drive there, and some will even do secular work, go to the beach, or enjoy a game of golf after services finish.

The ancient rabbis emphasized participation in religious rituals for all Jews, not just religious specialists, which had the effect of strengthening Jewish resistance to acculturation in the Roman and Persian worlds. At the same time, however, they worked to make the rules more livable. One hardship in the rabbinic calendar arose whenever a holiday and the Sabbath fell on consecutive days, making it necessary to prepare food too far in advance. In such cases, a legal fiction called an *eruv* ('mixing', perhaps of the sacred with the profane) was used to change the time frame involved. The *eruv tavshilin*, or 'cooking *eruv*', legitimizes cooking on the festival day preceding a Sabbath by symbolically starting the preparation of the Sabbath food before the festival. This is done with a conscious intent, a declaration, a prayer, and a symbolic act of food preparation and can be performed either individually or by the rabbi on behalf of the entire community.

Similarly, the spatial frame of Sabbath activity can be extended. Ancient Sabbath laws forbade carrying anything between 'private' and 'public' domains or walking farther than 2,000 cubits (0.8 kilometres or 0.55 miles) from one's house. An *eruv hatzerot* ('eruv of courtyards') links various private areas together so that the prohibition on 'public areas' does not apply. This can be accomplished in various ways, but today it is common for an Orthodox Jewish community to use a wire strung around the tops of several telephone poles to encircle the community. Symbolically, this turns the area enclosed by the wire into a walled city, in which carrying is permitted. In New York, Toronto, and elsewhere in North America, many of the large Jewish communities have erected *eruvs* around entire cities or neighbourhoods; one in Washington incorporates the White House. As a result, observant Jews may walk farther than the biblical Sabbath journey of 2,000 cubits while carrying articles, strolling with their babies, or otherwise enjoying the peace of the Sabbath.

Dietary Laws

Jewish dietary laws address three subjects in particular: (1) permitted and prohibited foods, (2) food preparation, and (3) the foods that may be combined in the same meal.

Meat that is not **kosher** (ritually acceptable) may not be eaten under any circumstances. In addition to pork, all land animals and birds that prey on others are excluded, though all fish with fins and scales are permitted. Land animals must have a split hoof and chew the cud; thus beef is a typical Jewish meat dish. In North America chicken has become the classic Sabbath evening meal; kosher chicken soup with matzoh balls (*knaydelach*, 'dumplings', in Yiddish) is a quintessential Ashkenazic dish, popularly known as Jewish penicillin for its abilities to soothe a cold. Chopped chicken liver is another classic Ashkenazic dish.

Since sea creatures must have both scales and fins, sharks, shellfish, invertebrates, and a variety of lower marine forms are all prohibited. North American Jews, most of whom share north European culinary traditions, eat many smoked fish, including lox (smoked salmon), herring, sable, or whitefish, often with cream cheese on a bagel, traditionally for Sunday brunch. Gefilte ('filled') fish is an Ashkenazic dish of ground carp and pike that was originally cooked with vegetables and then stuffed back into the fish skin, but now more often takes the form of dumplings. Sephardic Jews from Spain or Italy, or those from Arab, Iranian, or North African backgrounds, eat various kosher variations on foods from those regions, such as stuffed pitas, falafel (fried chickpea balls), and tabbouleh (bulgur salad).

Kosher slaughtering practice follows the prohibition against eating the blood of animals or birds. Thus every piece of meat is thoroughly drained, washed, and salted to remove any trace of blood. Animals must be slaughtered in such a way that they die immediately without feeling pain. In practice, this means one quick stroke from a very sharp knife with no nicks in it. The animal may not be stunned or hurt before the slaughter, contrary to the common practice in non-kosher slaughterhouses. The carcass is then inspected for a variety of impairments, any of which can disqualify the animal. The meat must also be cut in specific ways so as to remove several parts that are not considered fit for Jewish consumption.

Most contemporary North American slaughterhouses and government regulators do not know or concern themselves with these special practices. Therefore observant Jews consider produce from these sources, as well as meat from animals hunted for sport, to be inhumane and *treif* ('carrion') or non-kosher. Some of the specially trained butchers called *shokhets*, familiar with all the laws, are rabbis themselves, but even they are supervised by rabbis who periodically inspect the premises and seek to confirm that the employees have led observant and moral lives.

At Passover, a time of 'spring cleaning' and fresh beginnings, Jews add to the normal preparation regulations the requirement that food be free of yeast or leaven. All the equipment used to prepare Passover food must be either new or thoroughly cleaned.

Many Jews observe elaborate rules designed to prevent any combination of milk with meat. These rules are based on the biblical injunction not to eat a kid boiled in its mother's milk (*Exodus* 23: 19). In order not to transgress this rule inadvertently, observant Jews who have eaten one of those foods will wait a specified period of time before consuming the other. Observant Jews will never eat a cheeseburger, and after a meat meal they will not have ice cream for dessert, or put milk in their tea or coffee. There are even special requirements for the production of cheese, which is usually made from milk or cream curdled with rennet from a cow's stomach. Many Jews keep two complete sets of dishes, silverware, pots and pans, and cooking utensils for use with milk and with meat. Some also insist on two different dishwashers, sinks, and ovens as well. European Jews classify foods using terms in Yiddish: *flaischich* (meat), *milkich* (dairy), *pareve* or *parve* (neither), and *kosher lepaysach* (kosher for Passover).

Today many younger Jews are simplifying their lives by choosing vegetarianism. Some Jews maintain a kosher home and so are able to entertain observant guests, but eat non-kosher food outside. This practice, of course, does not satisfy the requirements of Jewish law but it is a surprisingly popular compromise. Reform Jews vary widely: most do not observe dietary laws at all, some observe them symbolically by abstaining from shellfish and pork only, and a few observe them in full. Conservative Jews usually try to observe the rabbinic ordinances and will eat in a restaurant only if they can find fish on the menu, since ordinary restaurants do not normally use specifically kosher meats. Orthodox Jews avoid restaurants altogether unless the restaurant has a certificate of *kashrut* ('fitness'); they may even suspect the *kashrut* certificates of some restaurants.

The care with which different people observe the dietary laws is taken as an indicator of their piety, and the distinctions between degrees of care can be quite subtle. Because the laws are so comprehensive, observant Jews need to know exactly what is in commercially packaged foods, particularly where dairy or meat products are concerned. Increasingly, the North American food industry has co-operated, in part because many foodstuffs need little or no special preparation to pass the kosher inspections. There are two large supervisory bodies whose insignia (a small K or U in a circle) can be found on an enormous variety of foodstuffs— even on such unlikely products as Easter eggs and chocolate Santa Clauses. One of the marks of the acceptance of Jews in North American life is the widespread availability of kosher food not only in supermarkets but on airlines, trains, and university campuses. For many people, Jews included, the kosher laws have become the most obvious marker of Jewishness and the principal way of distinguishing Jews from others.

Synagogue Service

The chanting in the synagogue reaches a crescendo with the reading of the Torah scrolls, which is traditionally done on Mondays, Thursdays, the Sabbath (Saturday), and special holidays. The synagogue service today, as in antiquity, is conducted largely by laypersons rather than the rabbi, who is not a priest; however, in North America, Reform and Conservative rabbis have taken on the role of a minister, leading parts of the service and usually giving the weekly sermon.

The basic order of formal service follows the order established at the ancient Temple in Jerusalem, which consisted of song, musical accompaniment, and sacrifice. With the destruction of the Temple the practice of animal sacrifice came to an end, but the other elements of the Temple service were transferred to the synagogue and incorporated into individual piety.

An early example of the rabbinical project to transfer Temple activities into the purview of the synagogue can be seen in the work of Yochanan ben Zakkai (c. 30–90 CE), who issued numerous rulings on matters such as when and where the *shofar* (ram's horn) should be blown. In this way the rabbis appointed the synagogue the successor to the Temple as the pre-eminent place for Jewish prayer. Before the publication of prayerbooks, the order of the service was fluid within the limits established by the rabbis' rulings, but these were probably based on what was already common practice in the community. People recited largely from memory and leaders were free to insert their own personal prayers or texts.

In time, services came to include professional singers called *hazanim*, or 'cantors', who continue to be part of Jewish worship. Today they lead the congregation by singing lines from the prayer books—in effect, marking the progress of the service—while members of the congregation pray quietly (but audibly) at their own rate. The Reform movement adopted a more formal European model in which prayers were recited in unison, but some congregations are now returning to the more traditional Jewish style.

There are three basic chanting traditions: Yemenite (by far the oldest), German, and Spanish. Different cantillations (special marks inserted in printed versions of the Torah to indicate the correct melody to chant) are used for recitations from the Torah and the *Prophets*, as well the solemn holidays of **Rosh Hashanah** and **Yom Kippur**.

A Bar Mitzvah ceremony in any denomination will normally include some chanting. Therefore candidates are given a basic introduction to the chant notations, though many of them simply memorize their parts from recordings. **Cantors** are specially trained in the subject, however. In North America today, modern synagogues usually include a large social hall for the celebrations that follow events such as Bar Mitzvah ceremonies and weddings, as well as a library and classrooms that reflect their traditional role as houses of study. Many also offer temporary shelter for the homeless, especially in winter.

The Annual Festival Cycle

The Jewish calendar is a lunar calendar. Each month starts with the new moon, which is a time for special prayers, and consequently the fourteenth or fifteenth of every month coincides with the full moon. Since twelve lunar months add up to only 354 days, Jews have decided that the lunar calendar must be kept in phase with the solar year through the addition of a leap month, Adar Sheni ('second Adar'), in a fixed schedule of seven years out of every nineteen. The rabbis used to base the calendar on direct observation, taking testimony from witnesses who had seen the new moon. Today astronomical calculations are used and festival dates and leap months are projected far in advance.

Years are now counted from the creation of the universe, which the rabbis calculated by adding up the life spans and time spans mentioned in the biblical text; thus 2010 CE is the year 5771 by Jewish reckoning. Each year begins with a new moon in the fall, usually close to the equinox, following the rules for lunar–solar correction. The holiday is called Rosh Hashanah, 'the head of the year' and inaugurates the 'High Holidays', a time of special meditation and examination of one's moral behaviour during the previous year.

Most of the holidays observed today have their roots in the ancient agricultural and pastoral festivals of the ancient Hebrews, but even in biblical times they were associated with specific events in the historical narrative of the people Israel. Eventually rabbinical interpretation gave them new dimensions of symbolic meaning. The fall holidays were associated with contrition in the Bible and this association has been strengthened since they have been celebrated according to the rabbinic liturgy. Rosh Hashanah and Yom Kippur especially have become spiritual holidays of repentance and contemplation.

Rosh Hashanah and Yom Kippur

Rosh Hashanah (New Year) and Yom Kippur (the Day of Atonement) are celebrated at the time of autumn harvest and were traditionally marked by the blowing of the ram's horn, or *shofar*. In rabbinic observance, the *shofar* allegorically wakes up the congregation from its moral slumber with a reminder to consider carefully the deeds of the past year. On the Day of Atonement, the most solemn day of the year and a strict fast day, the liturgy uses the imagery of the shepherd counting his sheep or the commander counting his troops to describe the yearly judgment of people by God.

Sukkoth

At Sukkoth (the festival of booths or 'tabernacles', derived from the Greek word for a temporary dwelling), which concludes the autumn harvest, many Jews still build a *sukkah*, a small temporary shelter, outside the house and sleep (or at least eat) in it for some or all of the eight-day festival. No doubt this tradition originated in the ancient farmers' practice of camping out in the fields to protect the ripening crops. In the biblical interpretation, however, it recalls the Israelites' reliance on temporary shelters during their migration from Egypt under the leadership of Moses.

Hanukkah

Unlike the other festivals, Hanukkah did not originate in the practices of the ancient Hebrews. It dates from the Hellenistic period, specifically the mid-second century BCE, when the Maccabean Jews drove the Seleucids out of Jerusalem. It celebrates the purification and rededication (*hanukkah*) of the Temple after its profanation by the Seleucids.

The fact that there is no treatise on Hanukkah in the *Mishnah* suggests that the rabbis did not consider it a major part of the Hebrew spiritual tradition. Nevertheless, they managed to give it a spiritual dimension by turning it into a celebration of deliverance through divine intervention: the miraculous eight-day duration of one day's quantity of oil is symbolized by the Hanukkah menorah. As a post-biblical holiday, Hanukkah was long considered of minor importance, but in the twentieth century North American Jews began to pay more attention to it because of its proximity to Christmas. Modern Israelis also celebrate Hanukkah with gusto as a reminder of an earlier victory in the struggle for national liberation from foreign oppression.

Purim

Purim, another minor festival, usually falls in March. Its narrative, taken from the book of *Esther*, recalls the deliverance of the Jews in Persia from destruction at the hands of an evil Persian official named Haman. Speculation on its antecedents focuses on the resemblances between the names Esther and Mordechai and the names of the Babylonian divinities Ishtar and Marduk. The Purim celebrations are reminiscent of the North American Hallowe'en, with costume parties, merrymaking, and gifts of candy. It can also be compared with Mardi Gras, with its late winter date and its indulgent partying.

Passover (Pesach)

The major festival of Passover comes in the spring, the season of agricultural rebirth and renewal. It ritually enacts 'spring cleaning' in the home. All the food to be eaten during the eight days of the festival, for instance, must be prepared on newly cleaned equipment. But its real significance is spiritual, for it commemorates the Exodus—the critical moment when Moses led the Israelites out of slavery in Egypt and towards freedom in the promised land. Like the Sabbath, Passover is closely associated with the home, and is usually celebrated with a family meal called a **seder**. The Passover liturgy, called the **Haggadah** ('narrative'), recounts the story, explains the significance of the symbols associated with it—most notably the unleavened bread eaten in memory of the Israelites' hasty departure, when they had to leave before the bread they were making could be baked—and emphasizes the participation of all Jews, past and present, in that experience of divine deliverance.

A brother and sister read from the Haggadah at the Passover seder (Ira Block/National Geographic/Getty Images).

Shavuoth

Shavuoth ('weeks'), in late spring, can be traced to the barley harvest, and its observance came to be associated with the eating of dairy foods, perhaps because spring is also calving time. In rabbinic Judaism it celebrates the giving of the Torah on Mount Sinai. Coming fifty days after the first day of Passover, it is also known as Pentecost (from the Greek meaning 'fiftieth') and is associated by Christians with the gift of the Holy Spirit.

The Ninth of Ab

The Ninth of Ab means literally the ninth day of the month of Ab. It is a fast day observed in late summer in memory of the destruction of the first and second Temples. The fast continues from sunset to sunset, and includes the avoidance of all luxurious display. Because leather was a luxury item in rabbinic times, Orthodox Jews today avoid wearing leather shoes on the Ninth of Ab; sometimes an entire congregation will attend the synagogue in canvas running shoes.

Life-Cycle Rituals

Common to all the world's religious traditions is the custom of marking certain transitional moments in a person's life—'rites of passage—such as birth, coming of age, marriage, and death. The Jewish tradition is no exception. Since this chapter began with the coming-of-age ceremony, the Bar or Bat Mitzvah, and will conclude with the marriage ceremony, we will focus here on the rituals surrounding birth and death.

Birth

The most characteristic ritual concerned with birth is circumcision: the removal of the male foreskin. As a rule, this is done on the eighth day

From the Passover Haggadah Liturgy

This is the bread of affliction, the poor bread which our fathers ate in the land of Egypt. Let all who are hungry come and eat; let all who are in need come to our Passover seder. Now we are here; next year may we be in Jerusalem. Now we are slaves; next year may we be free!

of life, unless the infant's health is endangered. Normally, the procedure is carried out by a ritual circumciser called a *mohel*, hired for the occasion. These days, the *mohel* may also be a physician, but there are still many 'paramedical' people who have been thoroughly trained in the rabbinic procedure.

Jewish circumcision usually takes place in the home, in the presence of family members who have come together to celebrate the birth. The liturgy emphasizes the parents' commitment to giving the child a proper Jewish education, to prepare him for learning, doing good deeds, marriage, and a life within the community. Because the ritual is in the hands of the individual family, sometimes significant family traditions are included within it. In most cases there is no need for a rabbi, but many families still ask one to attend, to make sure that the ceremony is legally acceptable.

After any birth, male or female, the family normally goes to synagogue and is awarded an *aliyah* ('going up'), one of the honours surrounding the reading of the Torah. The parents recite the blessing over the Torah passage that is to be read; then the rabbi or the service leader asks for special blessings on the child and announces the child's name. Since there are normally seven *aliyoth* each week, there are often several announcements of baby namings, engagements, and so on; sometimes they also include requests for prayers for the sick. In this way, the entire community is kept abreast of the important events in the lives of individual families. These customs, which were largely eliminated by Reform Judaism, are now being reinstated even there because they mean so much to the community.

Marriage

Marriage is universally praised in Judaism. Though some great scholars may be forgiven for remaining single, everyone is encouraged to marry and raise children. Sexual relations within the sanctified bounds of marriage are encouraged both for procreation and for the pleasure they bring to the couple; sexual fulfillment is generally included among the responsibilities that a man owes his wife. Thus Jewish marriages are occasions for great happiness within a context of religious seriousness and sanctity. A marriage can be celebrated almost anywhere: in a home, a synagogue, a hotel, a catering establishment. A rabbi is present in a legal capacity, to make sure that the marriage contract is properly prepared and the proper procedures are followed. Official witnesses to the legal proceedings must also be present. (The same is true for a Jewish divorce.) Although rabbinic specifications are rarely followed exactly in North America today, Orthodox couples will observe Orthodox marriage customs as well as the legal formalities required by the state.

Divorce

Divorce is mentioned several times in the Bible (most explicitly in *Deuteronomy* 24: 1–4) and Judaism accepts it as a legal institution. As in Islam, the grounds for divorce are theoretically quite wide, but in practice divorce is frowned on and hence relatively rare.

Even today, Jewish divorce rates in the Americas are considerably lower than those of the non-Jewish majorities. A divorce must be instigated by the husband, though in some cases a court will ask a husband to divorce his wife upon her request. On the other hand, no woman can be divorced against her will; mutual consent is required. The divorce decree, called a *get* in Hebrew, is presented to the wife by the husband. It regularly includes a financial settlement and provisions for the return of property that rightfully belongs to the wife.

Death

Jews believe that death should be faced resolutely and without illusion. There are several strange and interesting customs, and not a few superstitions, that accompany the bereavement process, but all are directed towards allowing the bereaved to come to terms with the separation from their departed loved ones. Funeral activities can even be conducted in the home, although that is extremely rare in North America today.

The liturgy for the funeral is meant to console the grieving family. It explicitly states that God will resurrect the righteous, that they will shine as the brightness of the firmament, and that they will be bound up in the bonds of life. But even at these moments, Judaism is not specific about how God will fulfill the promise that the dead will live again.

In the Hellenistic period, the remains of the deceased were first placed in sarcophagi (stone coffins) kept above the floor in tombs; approximately a year later, after the flesh had decomposed, the bones were ceremonially interred by the family. This system, known as secondary burial, was standard among gentiles as well as Jews at the time, and was reflected in the Christian account of the tomb where Jesus' body was placed immediately after his death. In modern Judaism, the remains are always placed in a plain coffin, without

The Kaddish Prayer

Reader:
Hallowed and enchanced may He be throughout the world of His own creation. May He cause His sovereignty soon to be accepted, during our life and the life of all Israel. And let us say: Amen.

Congregation and Reader:
May He be praised throughout all time.

Reader:
Glorified and celebrated, lauded and worshiped, acclaimed and honoured, extolled and exalted may the Holy One be, praised beyond all song and psalm, beyond all tributes that mortals can utter. And let us say: Amen.

May the prayers and praise of the whole House of Israel be accepted by our Father in Heaven. And let us say: Amen.

Let there be abundant peace from Heaven, with life's goodness for us and for all the people Israel. And let us say: Amen.

He who brings peace to His universe will bring peace to us and to all the people Israel. And let us say: Amen.

embalming, and interred as soon as possible after the death, though no funerals are held on the Sabbath, that is, between Friday sundown and Saturday sundown.

When a death occurs, community members band together to cook and otherwise help the bereaved family however they can, freeing them from mundane responsibilities so that they can 'sit Shiva' (from the Hebrew for 'seven'). For seven days after the burial, the family will receive visitors who wish to pay their respects. Mirrors are covered, and family members dress in sombre colours and either rip their clothing or wear a short black ribbon with a cut in it to symbolize ripping. The children, traditionally the sons in particular, honour the memory of the dead by reciting a special prayer called the Kaddish every day for a year. Recitation of the Kaddish has been associated with grieving, but the prayer itself never mentions death or dying and only praises God for his many daily miracles.

Religious Education

Though women were often literate in the vernacular language, traditionally education was confined to men until the modern period. Traditional religious education began at about the age of five, and in many places the new students would be displayed to the community in a ceremonial parade. Young children began by learning the Hebrew alphabet, sometimes with the help of cakes baked in the shape of the various letters. The first subject of study during the school years was the Bible, followed by the medieval Bible commentators Abraham ibn Ezra and Rashi.

Advanced education took place in a *yeshiva*, where the young men worked with acknowledged Talmudic masters to understand the difficult text of the *Talmud* and studied a variety of commentaries, starting with Rashi's commentary on the plain meaning of the text. Primary among the other commentaries are the *Tosafot*, the 'additions' that appear in the outside margins of the printed

Talmudic texts, though other commentaries were published separately.

Most contemporary North American Jewish families are less interested in the *Talmud* than traditional Jews but still want their children to learn about Jewish literature, history, customs, and ceremonies, and often Hebrew as well. Most do not adopt the traditional curriculum described above. Rather, children usually attend after-school classes three or even four days a week. In more traditional families boys are also taught the rudiments of Jewish law, including not only its content but its sophisticated methods of reasoning. Today, even in very conservative Jewish households, women receive a similar education. Families who belong to synagogues usually consider the Bar Mitzvah or Bat Mitzvah ceremony a kind of 'elementary school' graduation from the special religious training the child has undergone.

In North America, a significant minority of Jewish parents look to private Jewish day schools to provide an even more thorough religious training. In these cases, the children normally spend about half the day studying Jewish subjects and the other half studying the regular curriculum. Many young people continue their Jewish education after the Bar Mitzvah ceremony. Reform Judaism has instituted a ceremony known as confirmation, usually at the completion of grade nine. Jewish confirmation is another graduation ceremony, held at the late spring holiday of Shavuoth (Pentecost), which roughly coincides with the end of the school year in North America. Shavuoth is especially appropriate because it is associated with the giving of the Torah. But every graduation is also a commencement, as educators in the United States are fond of reminding their audiences, and a young Jew's obligation to learn is lifelong. In Orthodox Jewish homes, the children are supposed to continue studying Jewish texts throughout their lives, working with their parents on Sabbaths and holidays just as they do with their peers during the week.

Pupils at a Hebrew school in Newton, Massachusetts (Michele McDonald/Boston Globe/Landov).

Members of other religious communities admire and sometimes envy the central role that study has in the Jewish tradition. It is pursued in the home; for example, it is not unusual for the leader of a Passover seder to open some aspects of the ceremony for debate and discussion, encouraging the various participants to bring all their acumen to bear on resolving wide-ranging issues suggested by the liturgy. Study is pursued in the community; most North American synagogues sponsor high schools, where issues of Jewish life are discussed in an informal way, usually a few times a week. Extensive continuing and adult education programs cover elementary Hebrew, the prayer book, the musical chant, philosophy, mysticism, and current books of special interest to Jews. The complexity of the rabbinic tradition provides endless food for thought.

Conversion to Judaism

In the time of the Babylonian Exile, and as a direct consequence of it, Hebrew communities began to establish themselves here and there among other populations. Until then only those living in the Hebrew kingdoms would have been considered Israelites; now it was possible to be a Jew while living elsewhere. At the same time, the possibility arose that people of various other origins might wish to be considered Jews.

Whether others could belong became a subject of debate in the postexilic Judean community. The biblical book of *Ruth*, discussed earlier, takes an inclusivist position. And the book of *Jonah* argues that God cares about the people of Nineveh in Assyria. Scholars remain divided, however, concerning how much energy Jews actually devoted to proselytizing in the Persian, Greek, and Roman worlds. We know that conversions took place because there are reports of them and because rabbinic law contains a very detailed set of procedures for accepting converts. Still, there is no evidence of any active mission to convert gentiles.

Perhaps it was the need to live as members of a minority, as guests in foreign nations, that dampened the Jewish urge to proselytize, since any effort to convert the children of the host country would surely have been seen as hostile. Indeed, proselytizing activity in medieval Christian and Islamic lands was punishable by death. In such a climate, active missionary work was necessarily curtailed. Nevertheless, Jews since ancient times have been willing to receive converts who truly desire to join the Jewish people.

Rabbinic Judaism came to specify three conditions for conversion: male circumcision, ritual immersion (or baptism), and acceptance of the commandments. There are many stories of conversion in the rabbinic literature. The rabbis took care to ensure that candidates for conversion were sincere, for insincerity would endanger the community. They verified that converts were willing to cast their lot with this unfortunate and endangered people. With a 'yes' answer to all questions, one was accepted. Usually conversions involved a period of training in the specific responsibilities of an adult Jew.

When a male student is ready, the ceremony of circumcision is performed. Even a man who has already been circumcised must undergo a symbolic shedding of blood. Perhaps the difficulties surrounding this operation have contributed to the fact that conversion has been more common among women than men.

The next requirement is baptism by total bodily immersion. Orthodox Jews, who still rely on ritual immersion for a variety of purifying purposes, build special facilities for the purpose. Men and women visit these baths (*mikvehs*) separately at specific times during the week. When converts begin their new life, the first ritual immersion they undergo symbolizes the purification required for the transition from gentile to Jewish life. Every *mikveh* must contain a certain amount of 'living water' from streams or rainfall.

When a convert enters a *mikveh*, a court of three rabbis is usually convened at the site. The rabbis question the candidate, from behind a curtain if she is a woman. They ask about the convert's willingness to perform Jewish rites and responsibilities. They also allow the convert to demonstrate the knowledge he or she has learned from instruction. Then the candidate submerges him- or herself completely in the *mikveh* several times and on coming up is a Jew in every respect. Converts are named as the son or daughter of Abraham and are given complete Jewish names, indistinguishable from those of other Jews.

Once one has joined the people Israel—whether by birth or by conversion—it is impossible to leave. Jews may reject Judaism or convert to a different faith, but they can never change their Jewish identity.

INTERACTION AND ADAPTATION

Judaism and Modernity

Both the Sabbatian movement and Hasidism may be seen as reform movements within Judaism that emerged in the early modern era. Another early move towards reform may be seen in the writings of the seventeenth-century philosopher Baruch Spinoza. Living in the Netherlands, where Jews had achieved a relatively free and equal life under the tolerant Dutch regime, Spinoza challenged many of the traditional tenets of both Judaism and Christianity.

A more far-reaching desire to reform Judaism, however, developed as Jews came into closer contact with European life. For Jews, the real opportunity to join European society began in the Napoleonic period (1799–1815), when the ideals of the French Revolution—*liberté, égalité, fraternité*—spread throughout Europe. Before this time, Jews in Europe had been living in various degrees of isolation from their host societies, concentrated in enclaves that in some cases were legally separate entities. From the sixteenth century on, such districts came to be known as 'ghettos', after the local name of the Jewish quarter in Venice. Now, as the nineteenth century opened, Jews were swept into the political and cultural unrest sparked by the French Revolution, especially in western Europe.

The Reform Movement

Reform Judaism arose with the belief that Jewish life should parallel that of modern Europe. Many Jews who left the ghetto simply disappeared into European society and converted to Christianity. Others, however, wanted to reform Judaism in such a way that it could have a continuing part in modern European life. This movement reached its most significant form in Germany in the late eighteenth and early nineteenth centuries.

The first and most influential reformer, Moses Mendelssohn (1729–86), whose ideas preceded the French Revolution, may be seen as the father of modern Orthodoxy as well as Reform Judaism, because his formula for the relationship between Jewish identity and European nationality became the model almost everywhere. Mendelssohn was born in a ghetto in Dessau, Germany, and educated in traditional Judaism both at home and in Berlin. While in Berlin, however, he also studied German language and philosophy, and he brought those skills to the translation of the Pentateuch and *Psalms*. He also attracted the attention and friendship of many prominent German intellectuals, including Gotthold Lessing; the character Nathan in Lessing's play *Nathan the Wise* is widely believed to be based on Mendelssohn.

In his treatise *Jerusalem*, Mendelssohn argued that the Jews of Germany should absorb as much as possible of German culture, and should enjoy the same kind of intellectual freedoms that other Germans did. This would in no way affect the essence of Judaism, which Mendelssohn argued was a religion of reason combined with a revealed law. Separating his Jewishness from his personhood, he argued that Judaism was a religion, not a nationality or an ethnicity, and that Jews could be Germans in exactly the same way that Protestants and Catholics were Germans. That argument, of course, depended on the host country's acquiescence. Progress towards toleration and equal rights for German Jews took roughly a century, sometimes helped and sometimes hindered by the lack of a single German political state. And in the twentieth century, Jewish participation in German nationality was rescinded by Hitler, who decided that German nationality should reflect his own misguided racial theories.

There was also a nagging question within the Jewish community: did Jews really want to give up their rights as a semi-autonomous people within Europe? A great many rabbis rightly suspected that emancipation—full participation in German society—would pose a new threat to Jewish survival. In 1807 Napoleon called for an assembly of Jewish rabbis and laymen, modeled on the ancient Sanhedrin, to determine whether the Jews of France were truly committed to French citizenship. The delegates' answers suggested that they wanted the privileges of French nationality, which was what the French state wanted as well. But, as the rabbis had feared, growing freedom brought both increasing dilution of Jewish life and growing numbers of defections to Christianity.

One response to these threats was to pursue religious reform. Mendelssohn himself, in the previous generation, had remained a traditional Jew in all his household observances while conducting himself in public no differently from any other German. But the prospect of such a double life did not appeal to the next generation. Mendelssohn's son Abraham converted to Christianity before his own son Felix Mendelssohn, the great Romantic pianist and composer, reached adulthood.

The Reform movement, which was centred in Germany, sought to minimize the temptations of conversion by creating a new kind of Jewish religious life, more in tune with the times, that came to be known as Reform or (in Britain) Liberal Judaism. They reformed synagogue services to resemble church services, introducing Western musical instruments as well as vernacular prayers and sermons, and cut out numerous repetitions. They even experimented with changing the day of worship from Saturday to Sunday, though most Reform congregations eventually went back to the traditional Friday night and Saturday morning Sabbath observance. Reformers adopted Western dress, and treated traditional Jewish dietary and purity observances as personal or congregational decisions rather than immutable laws.

Taken to North America by German Jews who settled there in the mid-nineteenth century, Reform Judaism continued to modernize and imbibe the intellectual assumptions of the time. The emphasis on freedom of religion and equality of opportunity in North America, however imperfectly those principles were put into practice, served as a great support for reforming Judaism. Inherent in Reform Judaism and characteristic of North America especially is a philosophical preference for ethics over ritual. Emphasizing the moral value of the commandments, it sees ethical behaviour as the essence of Judaism and tends to regard

From American Reform Platforms, 1885 and 1937

For Reform Judaism, reformation is a continuous process. Therefore Reform Jews periodically meet to consider whether their positions and practices need adjusting to meet new needs. The following 'Platforms'—short statements of current positions—show the evolution of Reform beliefs and practices in the United States between 1885 and 1937. Of course, in keeping with the Reform ethos, they are suggestions rather than dictates.

Pittsburgh, Pennsylvania, 1885
We recognize in every religion an attempt to grasp the Infinite One, and in every mode, source or book of revelation held sacred in any religious system the consciousness of the indwelling of God in man. We hold that Judaism presents the highest conception of the God-idea as taught in our holy Scriptures and developed and spiritualized by the Jewish teachers in accordance with the moral and philosophical progress of their respective ages. We maintain that Judaism preserved and defended amid continual struggles and trials and under enforced isolation this God-idea as the central religious truth for the human race.

Columbus, Ohio, 1937
In view of the changes that have taken place in the modern world and the consequent need of stating anew the teaching of Reform Judaism, the Central Conference of American Rabbis makes the following declaration of principles. It presents them not as a fixed creed but as a guide for the progressive elements of Jewry.

   Judaism is the historical religious experience of the Jewish people [and] . . . its message is universal, aiming at the union and perfection of mankind under the sovereignty of God. Reform Judaism recognizes . . . progressive development in religion and consciously applies this principle to spiritual as well as to cultural and social life. . . (Alexander 1984: 137, 138).

various traditions, customs, and ceremonies as non-essential artifacts of a particular historic context, not necessarily eternally valid.

The Reform movement's emphasis on the present rather than the past was clear in the principles set out at a meeting of American Reform rabbis in Pittsburgh in 1885:

- The Bible reflects primitive ideas of its own age, clothing conceptions of divine Providence in miraculous narratives.
- The laws regulating diet, priestly purity, and dress do not conduce to holiness and obstruct modern spiritual elevation.
- We are no longer a nation but a spiritual community and therefore expect no return to Palestine.

Conservative Judaism

Another approach to reform Judaism called itself the *Jüdische Wissenschaft* ('science of Judaism'). It was founded in Germany in 1819 by Leopold Zunz and enlisted scholars like Abraham Geiger and Zecharias Frankel. Instead of actively promoting change, these men preferred to look at the tradition in question to see if its retention could be justified. Frankel, for instance, argued that there were legal and aesthetic grounds for retaining some of the ancient rituals. Unlike some of his colleagues, he was not embarrassed by them.

These scholars were in the forefront of the movement that came to be known in North America as Conservative Judaism. At first the two reform movements were separated primarily by taste and style, but in 1889 the reformers met in Cincinnati at a banquet where the menu included shrimp, which was biblically forbidden to Jews. Those who stayed and ate became identified with the American Reform movement, while those who refused coalesced into the American Conservative movement.

Conservative Judaism takes an intermediate position between Reform and Orthodoxy. If a particular custom can be shown to be fairly recent or secondary, then there is a precedent for further changing or even eliminating it. Since the black caftans worn by Hasidic Jews did not become customary until the fifteenth century or later, they are not obligatory. On the other hand, the order of prayers in the Jewish service goes back at least as far as the first-century Temple service and therefore is seen as firmly established by Jewish law. Hence most Conservative synagogues pray largely, though not entirely, in Hebrew and keep the traditional order of Jewish service.

Nevertheless, some aspects of the liturgy have been modified in response to changing social realities. Thus many expressions that reflect patriarchal assumptions have been changed or eliminated, and most Conservative congregations in the United States and Canada now seat men and women together, allow women to participate in the services as freely as men, and train women to lead worship as cantors and rabbis (as the Reform movement has been doing for decades). Although most Conservative Jews are similar to Reform Jews in their practice, a small minority choose to live a life much closer to Orthodoxy.

Orthodox Judaism

Orthodox Judaism emphasizes the preservation of Jewish tradition. Although many Orthodox Jews in North America have adopted modern styles of dress, they still conduct services in Hebrew, observe Sabbath obligations based on the ancient rules found in the *Talmud*, insist on kosher meals, and maintain traditional distinctions in gender roles, reserving the leadership roles in worship and ritual exclusively for males.

At the same time the Orthodox have to live in the modern world. While they have rejected reform programs and the Conservative *Jüdische Wissenschaft* as betrayals of authentic Judaism, they have tried to find a modern idiom for the preservation of their traditions. Among the most effective spokespersons for this perspective in the nineteenth century was Rabbi Samson Raphael Hirsch. Instead of merely condemning the

From S.R. Hirsch, 'The Dangers of Updating Judaism'

But, above all, what kind of Judaism would that be, if we were allowed to bring it up to date? If the Jew were actually permitted at any given time to bring his Judaism up to date, then he would no longer have any need for it; it would no longer be worthwhile speaking of Judaism. We would take Judaism and throw it out among the other ancient products of delusion and absurdity, and say no more about Judaism and the Jewish religion!

If the Bible is to be for me the word of God, and Judaism and the Jewish law the revealed will of God, am I to be allowed to take my stand on the highway of the ages and the lands and ask every mortal pilgrim on earth for his opinions, born as they are between dream and waking, between error and truth, in order to submit the word of the living God to his approval, in order to mould it to suit his passing whim? And am I to say: 'See here modern, purified Judaism! Here we have the word of the living God, refined, approved and purified by men!' (Grunfeld 1956, 2: 215–6).

reformers, he outlined a positive program for modern Orthodoxy. Essentially he gave credence to the modern world as well as the traditional sources of Jewish identity, calling for both Torah (in the sense of 'Jewish religious truth') and *Derekh Eretz* (literally 'the way of the land'; in this context, European life).

Living in a separate community in the German city of Frankfurt-am-Main, Hirsch maintained that Jews should enjoy many of the advantages of modern European life, but that some separation from that was necessary for Jewish survival. The traditional rituals and observances were the tried-and-true ways of educating a person who is both a good person and a good Jew—a *Yisroel Mensch* ('a humane member of Israel'), as he expressed it. His balanced view of the role of tradition and modernity in a general way set the pattern for the modern Orthodox movement as a whole.

Politically, Israel today is a modern, Western-style democracy. Yet its religious life is officially Orthodox. Even though the principal political parties are secular in their ideology, none of them has been able to hold power for long without the help of one or more of the small ultra-traditionalist religious parties. As the price of its vote, each

religious party demands that it be the only spokesperson for Judaism in Israel, and each makes a number of religious demands on the national life of the country. Thus matters such as marriage and divorce are controlled exclusively by the Orthodox communities. This arrangement continues the practice of the Ottoman Turkish Empire, which ruled Jerusalem for four centuries, from 1517 to 1917, and gave each religio-ethnic community some jurisdiction over personal law.

In North America many individual members of the Reform and Conservative communities are virtually indistinguishable from one another in terms of practice. Where these movements differ is not so much in doctrinal belief as in their attitudes towards accommodation to the host culture. The most significant indicators of a North American congregation's orientation are usually its prayer book, service, and the particular national organization to which it sends its congregational dues.

Twentieth-Century Theology

Historically, periods of acculturation and assimilation have tended to stimulate Jewish theological and philosophical inquiry. In the twentieth century, as in the heyday of Arab–Jewish co-operation in Muslim Spain, Judaism once again entered a period of rich theological expression.

The life of Franz Rosenzweig (1886–1929) is a good example of the kinds of forces that helped to promote Jewish philosophical speculation in Europe and North America. His family—cultured, affluent, and assimilated, without any deep religious commitments—wanted Rosenzweig to become a physician. Instead he embarked on a career in philosophy, and at a crucial point decided that he could be the kind of liberal Christian described by the philosopher G.W.F. Hegel. His path took a new direction, however, following a conversation with a distant relative who had already converted. Rosenzweig decided that if he were going to convert, he should do so 'not as a pagan but a Jew'. To that end he set out to deepen his understanding of Judaism. After attending a Yom Kippur service in a small Orthodox synagogue in Berlin, he decided that Judaism was preferable to Christianity because Jews were already with 'the Father' and therefore had no need to apply to 'the Son' for mediation.

Drafted into the German army in the First World War, he wrote his first and most systematic work, *Der Stern der Erlösung* ('The Star of Redemption') on postcards to his mother. In it he maintains an incipiently existentialist stance, declaring all truth to be subjective. Arguing that both Judaism and Christianity are true in the subjective sense, he maintains that each has a particular role to play in the world. By constantly projecting the purposes of God into the world, the politically powerful countries of Christendom are constantly helping to convert and transform it. Jews, on the other hand, he characterizes as politically powerless but clear-sighted in their ritual and liturgical concerns. They are in eternal communication with God through the eternally repeated rituals of Judaism and the *halakha*, the Jewish law. (Like many Europeans of the early twentieth century, Rosenzweig left Islam out of the equation because the Ottoman regime was perceived to be politically

powerless. Nor did he ever systematically address the great Asian faiths.)

For Rosenzweig, the Jew's covenant with God is eternal and timeless because the rules governing Jewish life have served to insulate Judaism and prevent the dilution of its spiritual power. Christianity, by contrast, has had the job of bringing the word of God to other nations. It enjoys the benefits of its engagement with world, but also risks the diminution and dilution that Judaism has avoided.

Tragically, Rosenzweig developed amyotrophic lateral sclerosis (Lou Gehrig's disease) in the early 1920s and for several years before his death was completely paralyzed, able to communicate only through his wife. A circle of admirers formed a prayer group around him. His personal courage and his understanding of the value of traditional Judaism from the perspective of modern liberal, secular thought attracted a following across the broad spectrum of modern Judaism. On the other hand, his concept of Judaism as standing outside of history, one with the Father eternally, can no longer be sustained in a literal sense: since the Holocaust and the formation of the modern state of Israel, Jews have fully re-entered history.

Rosenzweig's emphasis on his own personal experience and his exclusive focus on Judaism and Christianity have limited the relevance of his work. A more influential religious existentialist, whose theological work has been more significant to religious people everywhere, Jewish and otherwise, is Martin Buber (1878–1965).

Buber was a student of Wilhelm Dilthey and Georg Simmel, two important nineteenth-century German intellectuals, but he also felt the influence of Hasidism through his family and especially his grandfather, Solomon Buber, who was a famous scholar of *midrash*. Buber and Rosenzweig were associates in *Das Jüdische Lehrhaus* ('The Jewish School') in Frankfurt, co-translators of a German translation of the Bible, and close personal friends.

Buber published his most famous work, *Ich und Du* (translated as *I and Thou*), in 1923. Scrutinized, admired, and critiqued by generations of religiously concerned thinkers within Judaism and outside it, this work is as much a poem as a treatise. In it Buber suggests that all human beings have two ways of relating to the world. Most of our interactions are functional, aimed at manipulation and control; these Buber describes as 'I–It experiences'. But there are also moments of epiphany, or 'I–Thou experiences', in which the divine presence can be felt and true dialogue with God is possible.

Both kinds of experience can be had with either objects or persons. But for Buber, behind every I–Thou experience is the presence of God, the Eternal Thou, seeking dialogue. Thus the Bible (like any spiritual book) may record I–Thou experiences, but it cannot produce them in its readers: however carefully we study it, we are just as likely to have an I–Thou experience when examining a piece of mica as when studying the prophet Micah. In this respect Buber disagrees strongly with Rosenzweig, for whom the Bible was a unique source of religious truth. Buber's refusal to grant the Bible any special status as revelation has angered traditional Jews as much as it has pleased other intellectuals and scholars of Western religion.

Buber, unlike Rosenzweig, was forced to come to terms with the Holocaust, but because he was so close to its horrors he did not wish to dwell on them. Instead he proposed that God could sometimes hide his face—enter an eclipse, as he phrased it.

An ardent Zionist, Buber moved to Palestine in 1938, but his advocacy of a binational state, for Jews and Arabs equally, was widely criticized as overly idealistic. On the other hand, his mystical notion of dialogue as a spiritual exercise resonated in the Christian, Muslim, Hindu, and Buddhist worlds. Non-Jewish thinkers with different conceptions of mystical experience sometimes object that he does not provide adequate support for his ideas, but Buber never seems to feel that such critiques were as significant as the recognition that the I–Thou experience exists, and that the divine can be found in the details of everyday life.

In the 1930s, a former Conservative rabbi named Mordecai Kaplan founded a movement known as Reconstructionism. Kaplan attempted to define Judaism as a religious civilization or, in today's terms, a religious culture. He felt that belief in God was important to the people's self-understanding, but was not in fact essential to the definition of the group. He thus translated references to the terms 'God' and 'Lord' with terms such as 'The Eternal'.

For many years, Reconstructionism was a kind of ideological position that attracted followers across the spectrum of North American Judaism. It became a separate entity only in the 1960s, with the founding of a Reconstructionist rabbinical seminary in Philadelphia. Today there are several Reconstructionist synagogues in North America, but they still represent only a very small segment of the community. Ideologically, many Jews who think of themselves as an ethnic group espouse Reconstructionist ideals but remain within a Reform or Conservative synagogue.

Zionism

It was in the mid-nineteenth century, when nationalism became a powerful cultural and political force in Europe, that Jews first began to explore the idea of leaving Europe and returning to their ancient homeland in the Near East. The idea of return was hardly new: medieval Jewish literature frequently evoked the sense of absence from the land of Israel; Yehuda Ha-Levi wrote poetically of his sadness to be in the West (Spain) when his heart was in the East; and the words of the Passover seder, 'next year in Jerusalem', attest to an ongoing spiritual longing for return, either now or in the messianic age. But the nineteenth century introduced several other currents that flowed together to give modern Zionism its impetus.

In the Bible, Zion is the name of a ridgetop in Jerusalem that is said to be God's dwelling place. Today, however, that place is known as the Temple Mount and what tourist guides call Mount Zion is a hill just outside the walls of the Old City of Jerusalem. Even in antiquity the name Zion had broader connotations, including the land surrounding Jerusalem, the people, and their religio-political institutions. The modern movement to return to the ancient land of Israel, to found a nation there on the model of modern European nationalism, is called Zionism.

A significant factor in the emergence of Zionism was the revival of the Hebrew language. In the age of emerging nation-states, the importance of a common language was widely recognized by nationalist theorists. Many Ashkenazic Jews in central Europe spoke Yiddish, but it was not spoken by Jews everywhere and at the time was not considered to have a classical literature. The only language that all Jews had in common was Hebrew, which was still used extensively in prayer and for literary and intellectual purposes but otherwise rarely spoken.

One of the advocates of a Hebrew revival was a Lithuanian named Peretz Smolenskin, who settled in Vienna in 1868 but found himself out of step with the assimilationist spirit there. In 'Am 'Olam ('Eternal People'), which he published in Hebrew in 1883, he argued that to remain a people, the Jews would have to develop practical as well as spiritual ties to Palestine. One immediate step they could take, which would at the same time serve to bind them to one another and to their tradition, was to speak Hebrew. Eliezer Ben Yehudah took on himself the job of creating a modern Hebrew vocabulary. His seventeen-volume dictionary of modern Hebrew was not completed until 1959—nearly forty years after his death.

Another common nineteenth-century current was the desire for political experimentation. Moses Hess was an early socialist thinker whose ideas had an influence on the thought of Karl Marx. In 1862, in his book *Rom und Jerusalem* ('Rome and Jerusalem'), he argued that the Jews as a people needed statehood and called on them to create a polity that would be a model of socialist principles for the world. In the first half of the twentieth century, the collective agricultural settlement known as the *kibbutz* would become a hallmark of Zionist settlement in Palestine.

As the nineteenth century drew to a close, the desire for a haven from persecution was frequently expressed, but perhaps no more dramatically than by Leo Pinsker. Born in 1821 in the Russian part of Poland, Pinsker became a physician in the Ukrainian port of Odessa, where he took an active role in Jewish cultural affairs; in the 1860s he strongly advocated the translation of the Bible and the Jewish prayers into Russian. The *pogrom* (state-supported massacre of Jews) of 1871 challenged his faith in cultural assimilation, however, and in 1881 a more severe *pogrom* galvanized him into writing an anonymous pamphlet in German, *Auto-Emanzipation* ('Self-Emancipation') addressed to Jews who lived to the west. Incisively, Pinsker contended that the Jews were not safe in the countries in which they lived as minorities. Cultural assimilation was not enough: the only safeguard of Jewish security and dignity would be a separate homeland.

The haven-from-persecution theme has been central to the modern Zionist movement. The principal founder of the movement was Theodor Herzl (1860–1904), a Viennese journalist who became committed to the goal of Jewish statehood in response to the Dreyfus Affair: the French political scandal in which a Jewish army officer named Alfred Dreyfus was convicted of treason in 1894 and two years later was found to have been framed. Although Herzl himself had grown up in an assimilated home, he came to believe that anti-Semitism was so entrenched in European society that the only way for Jews to have normal existence would be as a people in their own land and that they would have to have a political state or something approximating it. His Zionistic ambitions were entirely secular and nationalistic; for a time Herzl and Pinsker even contemplated the idea of a Jewish national homeland somewhere other than in the land of biblical Israel.

In the twentieth century, although the Zionist movement coalesced around Herzl's leadership, a number of alternative visions of Zionism were proposed. Asher Ginsberg, a Russian intellectual who wrote under the name Ahad Ha-'Am ('one of the people'), suggested that a Jewish national homeland could be a spiritual centre not only for the Jewish people but for the world. For him, Jewish nationalism meant pride in the moral virtues that the Jewish people had always valued.

From Theodor Herzl, *The Jewish State* (1896)

Herzl believed that anti-Semitism could not be eliminated: to be free of it, therefore, Jews needed a state of their own.

No one can deny the gravity of the situation of the Jews. Wherever they live in perceptible numbers, they are more or less persecuted. . . . Everything tends, in fact, to one and the same conclusion, which is clearly enunciated in that classic Berlin phrase: 'Juden Raus!' (Out with the Jews!)

I shall now put the Question in the briefest possible form: are we to 'get out' now and where to? . . . Let the sovereignty be granted us over a portion of the globe large enough to satisfy the rightful requirements of a nation; the rest we shall manage for ourselves.

The creation of a new State is neither ridiculous nor impossible. We have in our day witnessed the process in connection with nations which were not largely members of the middle class, but poorer, less educated, and consequently weaker than ourselves. The Governments of all countries scourged by Anti-Semitism will be keenly interested in assisting us to obtain the sovereignty we want. . . .

Argentine is one of the most fertile countries in the world, extends over a vast area, has a sparse population and a mild climate. The Argentine Republic would derive considerable profit from the cession of a portion of its territory to us. The present infiltration of Jews has certainly produced some discontent, and it would be necessary to enlighten the Republic on the intrinsic difference of our new movement.

Palestine is our ever-memorable historic home. The very name of Palestine would attract our people with a force of marvellous potency. If His Majesty the Sultan were to give us Palestine, we could in return undertake to regulate the whole finances of Turkey. We should there form a portion of a rampart of Europe against Asia, an outpost of civilization as opposed to barbarism. We should as a neutral State remain in contact with all Europe, which would have to guarantee our existence. The sanctuaries of Christendom would be safeguarded by assigning to them an extra-territorial status such as is well-known to the law of nations. We should form a guard of honor about these sanctuaries, answering for the fulfillment of this duty with our existence. This guard of honor would be the great symbol of the solution of the Jewish Question after eighteen centuries of Jewish suffering. . . .

It might further be said that we ought not to create new distinctions between people; we ought not to raise fresh barriers, we should rather make the old disappear. But men who think in this way are amiable visionaries; and the idea of a native land will still flourish when the dust of their bones will have vanished tracelessly in the winds. Universal brotherhood is not even a beautiful dream. Antagonism is essential to man's greatest efforts. But the Jews, once settled in their own State, would probably have no more enemies (Herzl 1946: 91–3, 95–6, 153).

He pointedly defined his concept of Jewish life against the concept of the *Übermensch* ('superior being') formulated by the German philosopher Friedrich Nietzsche. Although Ahad Ha-'Am was not religious in the traditional sense of the word, he was spiritually attached to the people Israel in a romantic, nationalistic way.

Meanwhile, some Orthodox Jews believed that in the absence of the messiah, the Jews' return to Zion could not be legitimate. They refused to work for the creation of a modern state and, after it came into being in 1948, they refused to acknowledge its existence. Many settled in Israel anyway because it housed many of the important sites of Jewish history and was the only asylum available to them after the Second World War. Even today there are some Orthodox Jews in Israel who live as if the state did not exist, although they accept its subsidies for household life and education.

Of course there are also religious Zionists who fully support the existence of a Jewish state. This movement has accounted for most of the

From Ahad Ha-'Am, 'The Jewish State and the Jewish Problem' (1897)

Ahad Ha-'Am felt that Jews should have their own place to live, but he was not as commited as Herzl to the creation of a Jewish state. Rather, he hoped to see the creation of a 'spiritual centre' from which Jewish culture and values could spread to the rest of the world.

The stream of modern culture, when it mingles with Judaism, destroys Judaism's defences from within, so that Judaism can no longer remain isolated and live a life apart. The spirit of our people strives for further development; it wants to absorb the basic elements of general culture which reach it from the outside world, to digest them and make them part of itself, as it has done in the past at different periods of our history. But the conditions of its life in exile are not conducive to this. In our time culture everywhere clothes itself in the national spirit of each people, and any alien who wants to participate in that culture must annihilate his individuality and be swallowed up by the dominant ethos. Hence Judaism in exile cannot develop its individuality in its own way. When it leaves the ghetto walls, it is in danger of losing its own essential life, or, at the very least, its national unity, of being split up into many kinds of Judaism, each with its different character and life, as there are countries where the Jews are dispersed. . . .

Judaism can, for the present, be content with little. It does not need an independent State, but only the creation in its native land of conditions favourable to its development: a fair-sized settlement of Jews working without hindrance in every branch of culture, from farming and handicrafts to science and literature. . . .

To sum up: Hibbat Ziyyon [love of Zion], no less than 'Zionism', wants a Jewish State and believes in the possibility of founding a Jewish State in the future. But while 'Zionism' looks to the Jewish State to provide a remedy for poverty, as well as complete tranquility and national glory, Hibbat Ziyyon knows that our State will not give us these things until 'universal righteousness sits enthroned and holds sway in the life of nations and states'. Hibbat Ziyyon looks to a Jewish State to provide a 'secure refuge' for Judaism and a cultural bond to unite our nation. 'Zionism', therefore, begins its work with political propaganda; but Hibbat Ziyyon begins with a national culture, because only through that culture and for its sake can a Jewish State be established in a way that will be acceptable and beneficial to the spirit of the Jewish people (Ahad Ha'am 1962: 89).

immigration to Israel from North America in recent decades, and religiously motivated Zionists are represented by several political parties in contemporary Israel.

But religion is by no means essential to the notion of Jewish peoplehood. Many Jews without any religious commitments still feel ethnically or nationally attached to Israel and consider its continued existence important to their Jewish identity.

Furthermore, many Reform Jews in Europe or North America who initially felt somewhat estranged from Zionism because they were completely at home in their own societies eventually came to accept many Zionist premises. Many North American Jews developed strong feelings for Israel at the time of the Six-Day War in 1967, for instance, perceiving it to be surrounded by hostile nations, and those feelings were strengthened in 1973, when the country was attacked on Yom Kippur, the holiest day of the Jewish calendar. Pro-Israel sentiment was somewhat weakened, however, following Israel's invasion of Lebanon in 1982, and opinion regarding its current policies in the West Bank and Gaza is sharply divided.

Judaism in the Americas

Assimilation and acculturation are two distinct social processes that help to account for the differences among Jews in their understanding of their Jewish identity. Assimilation assumes that incorporation into the mainstream necessarily entails a loss of previous identity. Acculturation, by contrast, assumes many possible outcomes of the encounter between two cultures, including the eventual rejection of parts or all of the new culture by the host society. Jews from different European countries have quite different understandings of their Jewish identities. The first wave of Jewish immigration to the Americas—mainly to South America, the Caribbean islands, and the United States—came from Spain and Portugal in the eighteenth century. Most of the Jews in Curaçao today trace their roots to those Sephardic immigrants. In North America, however, their descendants

assimilated long ago. The only traces of their presence are a few Jews with Spanish names like Costas and Seixas (some of whom are descendants of later Sephardic immigrants who had previously settled in places like England or the Netherlands) and a few synagogues, notably the famous Touro Synagogue in Newport, Rhode Island, and the Spanish-Portuguese Synagogue in Manhattan. German Jewish immigration began in the 1840s after the failure of liberal political reforms in Germany. It brought a number of Reform-influenced Jews who considered themselves Germans of the Mosaic persuasion—that is, German nationals who happened to be Jewish in religion. They settled mostly in the United States, often in the same areas where other German immigrants settled, especially the midwest. Unlike the latter, however, the Jewish immigrants tended to be pedlars and shopkeepers rather than farmers.

It was this wave of Jewish settlement in the Americas that produced the great German Jewish mercantile families of the late nineteenth century—families such as the Bambergers (who owned the Macy's department store, among others, and helped to found the Institute for Advanced Study at Princeton) and the Guggenheims (American mining entrepreneurs who founded the Guggenheim Museum and the Guggenheim Fellowship). They brought with them many German customs, including what we know as the Christmas tree (*Tannenbaum*, 'fir tree'—a term with no religious connotation in German). Such customs were associated with nationality rather than religion in Germany because they were based on ancient pre-Christian traditions.

The next and largest wave of Jewish immigration to America arrived from eastern Europe, some from the *shtetlach* (or *shtetls*—Yiddish for 'little towns') and some from the Jewish quarters of the major cities. The 3 million Jews living in areas controlled by Russia had not benefitted from the social changes that allowed for Jewish liberation in western Europe and the Americas. Although a cultural reform movement known as the

Haskalah ('Enlightenment') had flourished during the relatively benign rule of Czar Alexander II (r. 1855–81), his successor, Alexander III (r. 1881–94), openly encouraged pogroms, massacres, and deportations of Jews.

Alexander III's policies were directly responsible for the enormous wave of Jewish immigration that landed mostly on the eastern coasts of Canada and the United States. At first most of the new arrivals went to New York. The German Jews donated massively to help the indigent *Ostjuden* ('eastern Jews'), but were not particularly friendly towards them. Not literate in either German or English, the eastern European immigrants found jobs in the tobacco and clothing sweatshops of the Lower East Side of Manhattan.

In Russia each ethnic group was treated as a separate nationality, and until very recently the passports of Russian Jews continued to identify their nationality as 'Jewish'. Thus Jews arriving from eastern Europe have tended to think of themselves as Jewish by nationality as well as religion. Ironically, some thought they were sacrificing their religion in crossing the Atlantic, because Orthodox rabbis in Europe warned against North America as a place of non-kosher iniquity.

In 1922, new immigration quotas stopped the flow of Jewish immigration to the United States, but Jews continued to arrive in Canada, Cuba, Mexico, and South America. In Canada, Jews settled primarily in urban Quebec and Ontario, but also in Winnipeg. French-speaking Jews from North Africa and the French possessions tended to favour the Montreal area because of its French environment. Some English-speakers also settled in Montreal, while others headed for Ontario and the West.

The doors of the United States remained largely shut to Jews fleeing from Nazi oppression in the 1930s, and Canada too refused most Jewish refugees during the Second World War. Most of the Jews who arrived in North America after 1945 were concentration-camp survivors. They had undergone enormous sacrifices to reach the New World, having survived horrifying deprivation and the near-extermination of their people. Consequently, their feelings about the necessity for Jewish survival—whether in North America or in the new state of Israel—were much more urgent and intense than those of earlier arrivals.

The Holocaust

No event since the destruction of the second Temple and the expulsion from Spain has so affected the Jewish people as the Holocaust. Adolf Hitler, whose National Socialist ('Nazi') party came to power in 1933, was able to convince many Germans that their country's economic woes should be blamed not on the worldwide depression, or on government policy, or on the punishing reparations that it was required to pay after the First World War, but on the nation's Jews.

The Nazis, fearing that the Jewish presence among them would sully their 'racial' superiority, passed a series of laws that were ever more cruel to Jews. They stripped Jews of German nationality. They looted Jewish stores and prevented Jews from practising their livelihoods. They sent Jews to concentration camps to work as slaves. Finally, they erected gas chambers and crematoria to kill the Jews, a program the Nazis called *die Entlösung* ('the Final Solution' to the 'Jewish problem').

A major factor in the success of Hitler's campaign, of course, was European Christianity's long tradition of vilifying the Jews as 'Christ killers'. Those wishing to foment hatred against the Jews for their own purposes could find ample ammunition in the New Testament, whose editors painted Jews in an extremely bad light for their own theological reasons.

It can be argued that Hitler's war against the Jews was the most successful of all his endeavours. For whatever reasons, the Allies did not strike back strongly enough even when they clearly understood what he was doing. There were no Allied raids on the railway tracks that took tens of thousands of Jews to their deaths every day. Worse still, in eastern Europe, especially in Poland, Hitler found some ready accomplices for his work.

In the terrible nightmare of Nazi oppression, to help Jews meant almost certain death. Yet there were many individual Christians who took that risk in order to hide Jews or help them escape, and of those who were found out, many suffered the same fate as the Jews they had tried to help. The 6 million Jewish deaths in the Second World War amounted to between one-quarter and one-third of the total death toll in Europe, sometimes estimated at 22 million. The Holocaust killed roughly a third of all the world's Jews—men, women, and children—in the space of a few years.

Jews shuddered when the enormity of the crime became known. The Jews had always assumed that, even though they might sin, the eternity of the people Israel was a sign of God's continuing favour. How Hitler had come so close to exterminating a whole people—how God could have allowed the wholesale killing of so many innocent, non-combatant men, women, and children—demanded a special answer. In fact, those questions may never be satisfactorily answered. For most Jews the only possible response is to continue interpreting historical events as the unfolding of God's design, in which their people have a special role.

Among those who have tried to formulate answers is the world-famous author Elie Wiesel (b. 1928). Wiesel was a traditional *yeshiva* student in the town of Sighet in Romania when the Nazis arrived. His first novel, *Night*, chronicles the murder of his family and his own survival of the extermination camps. Since then, he has written movingly in fiction and non-fiction of the predicament of modern Jews. The faith he has articulated is ambivalent and often tentative, but in combining doubt with a solid affirmation of Jewish and human values, he seems to speak to the complex feelings shared by many Jews and gentiles alike in contemplating the horrors of the modern world.

'Jews must continue to live so as not to grant to Hitler a posthumous victory,' wrote Emil Fackenheim (1916–2003), a German rabbi and professor who emigrated to Canada in 1938 and to Israel after 1981. In this regard, Fackenheim spoke for a wide spectrum of Jews who feel that Hitler's project to exterminate an entire people must be remembered and must never be repeated, anywhere in the world. The Holocaust has materially changed the significance of Jewish identity in the world. In Fackenheim's view, it is no longer acceptable for Jews to accept martyrdom (which had been considered honourable since the Hellenistic era), no matter how good the cause, because the people Israel must look to its own survival. To the traditional 613 commandments spoken by God to the Jewish people, Fackenheim posited that the Holocaust had added a 614th: from now on, Jews are commanded to live as Jews in the modern world, so that Judaism and Jewishness can never be exterminated as Hitler tried to do.

The State of Israel

For most Jews, the founding of the state of Israel is closely associated with the terrible tragedy of the Holocaust. In no sense did Israel compensate for the lives that were lost—but it did represent the promise of a place in the world where Jews might at last be safe. The Zionist campaign for a haven from persecution succeeded in attracting support not just from Jews but from non-Jewish leaders around the world in the years following the Second World War. The United Nations voted to partition Palestine and create two states, one Jewish and one Arab. The creation of Israel did a great deal to resolve the problem of Jewish refugees in Europe.

For many years, the neighbouring Arab states of Egypt, Jordan, Syria, and Lebanon vied with each other as well as Israel for control of all the area. But they were unable to defeat Israel militarily, and eventually ceded to Palestinians—though not to Israelis—the right to control their own territory. The Palestinians, however, have not been able to agree on a policy to deal with Israel's occupation of the lands gained either in the 1948 or the 1967 war. Many seem willing to negotiate a state in the land of Israel and Palestine. Others refuse to negotiate and have taken up arms against civilians in the Israeli state. Israel, claiming its own need to defend its citizens, has imposed very strenuous controls on the civilian population, to try to prevent bombings, suicide actions, and rocket launches. More than six decades after its creation, Israel still has not managed to resolve some problems fundamental to accommodating an emerging Palestinian nationality. The question of sovereignty and control over the old city of Jerusalem, for example, has been a constant and so far insoluble difficulty.

One can hope that peace negotiations will eventually resume, after all hostilities have shown themselves to be pointless. But it does not lie in the hands of Israel alone to bring this about.

North America

For many years American culture has assumed that assimilation should be the goal of every immigrant, and that all ethnic groups should blend together in one great 'melting pot'. Yet the range of immigrants that the American pot has succeeded in blending is actually quite small, consisting mainly of a few northern European groups (English, Irish, Scottish, Scandinavian). Other European groups have remained largely separate, as have 'visible minorities' such as Blacks and Asians.

One could argue that Jews have much to gain by staying out of the melting pot. Jewish leaders have traditionally railed against intermarriage. And for two generations, most American Jews did marry within their own community. Since 1985, however, roughly 55 per cent of all American Jews have married non-Jewish partners. If enough non-Jewish spouses were to convert, that would help to stabilize the Jewish population. However, some predict that within a few generations the Jewish community will consist only of those most resistant to intermarriage: the Orthodox.

The situation in Canada is slightly different. Like the United States, Canada is a country built on immigration, but Canadians tend to describe their society as a mosaic rather than a melting pot. From earliest times, Canada has contained at least two distinct cultural communities, French and English, and the nation itself was founded on the idea that the different communities have the right to live their own lives. Even before 'multiculturalism'—a type of cultural pluralism—became official policy in the 1970s, new Canadians of other ethnic backgrounds may have experienced somewhat less pressure to assimilate than their counterparts in the US.

Canada's formula has none of the imperatives implicit in the American melting-pot model. In Canada, the concepts of national identity and group rights are different from those in the United States. Moreover, the Canadian Jewish community is younger in that it arrived in great numbers only after the doors of immigration were closed in the United States. For these reasons, the Jewish community is less assimilated in Canada than it is in the United States. But the cultural and social processes that affect Canada and the United States are so similar that one can easily foresee similar outcomes for the Jewish communities in both countries.

Judaism in the Modern World

Modernity has transformed Judaism, allowing it to develop many different denominational groups, for the same reason that denominations developed in the Hellenistic period: to provide Jews with intelligent choices about how to live their lives Jewishly. The modern world, like the Hellenistic one, offers many different ways of living, which appeal to Jews in different ways and demand different ways of being Jewish. Creative Jewish minds have therefore found ways to accommodate these lifestyles within Judaism. A major difference between North American Judaism and Israeli Judaism is often overlooked. North American Jews are part of the democratic life of North America. Having been nurtured in adversity while working for equality, most accept the notion that Jews should not only be good citizens of the state in which they reside and should participate fully in its political and social life, but should also work for the continued cultural pluralism of North America.

Of course there are exceptions to this rule, notably in the more self-contained Orthodox and Hasidic communities. There is also a small but growing minority of Jews who have entirely given up on the idea of accommodation with modern life. These Jews, who call themselves *haredim* ('tremblers', after a verse in *Isaiah* that describes the true worshippers of God), refuse all contact with the modern world. In a sense they are the fundamentalists of the Jewish tradition, and they have steadily been gaining political power under conservative governments. On the whole, however, North American Jews are willing to accept the threat that assimilation poses for Jewish survival because of the undeniable benefits of modern Western democratic life. North American Jews' identity is thus a blend of ethnicity and religion.

A different concept of Judaism has emerged in Israel. For most Israeli Jews—except for the *haredim*—Judaism is a nationality. The majority of Israeli Jews observe the Sabbath because it is the national day of rest, the Jewish holidays because they are national holidays.

But the majority of Israelis do not observe Sabbath regulations in the traditional sense. The beaches of Tel Aviv are just as busy as the beaches of Long Island in New York on a warm sunny Saturday. Although most modern Israelis are willing to give the Orthodox parties the powers necessary to govern, they are unwilling to live their lives by Orthodox standards. Loyalty to Israel may be a religious duty for Jews living in the Diaspora, but for people actually living in the state it is a political and military matter.

So there is another kind of acculturation underway in Israel. Most Israelis, while living in a state that is predominantly Jewish, are in the process of formulating an entirely new way to live Jewishly, a transformation just as sweeping as the one that is taking place among North American Jews.

It is by no means clear whether these different Jewish communities still really understand each other. Israelis see a threatening future for Jewry in American street violence and anti-Semitism, whereas North American Jews see threats in Israel's ethnic polarization and confrontation with the Palestinians. In the mid-1990s, despite moves towards peace with neighbouring Arab states, conflict between Jews and Arabs living under Israeli jurisdiction continued, and the divisions among Jews were deepened by the assassination in 1995 of Israeli prime minister Yitzhak Rabin. Though fragile, the peace process with the Palestine Liberation Organization made remarkable progress towards recognizing the rights of both communities. But no formal agreement was reached with the other major Palestinian national organization, Hamas (the Islamic Resistance Movement). It is doubtful that any agreement will be reached in the foreseeable future because Hamas seems uncompromisingly committed to the destruction of the state of Israel. The administration of George W. Bush (2000–8), despite protestations of support for peace and even a so-called 'roadmap' to achieve it, brought nothing in the way of formal agreements between the Palestinians and the Israelis. And even if a formal agreement were reached, the success of any peace process would ultimately depend on the ability of two peoples who have been bitter adversaries for more than a century to develop mutual trust. Thus the prognosis for the future of Judaism is clouded, regardless of the contributions of the North American Jewish community and the fortitude or diplomatic skills of the Israelis. If there is a Jewish people, it will be because a religious understanding of their history has made it possible for them to survive as Jews.

Hope for the Future: A Jewish Wedding

A more optimistic vision of the future can be seen at any wedding where both the bride and the groom are Jewish, whether by birth or by conversion. Weddings may be performed in homes or synagogues, hotels or catering halls. Whatever the setting, what they have in common is the *huppah*: a tent-like canopy under which the marriage ceremony is conducted. Often the bride and groom are escorted to the *huppah* by their parents, but the bride may also enter in a procession reminiscent of a standard church wedding. In the Orthodox ritual she will circle the groom seven times before the ceremony begins with the bride and groom drinking from a consecrated cup of wine.

The wedding is first of all a legal agreement in which the husband and wife pledge mutual support and aid. The groom declares, 'Be consecrated unto me as my wife according to the laws and traditions of Moses and Israel.' This in itself is enough to complete his legal obligation. But it is quite common in North America to add more promises: 'I will love, honour, and cherish you. I will protect and support you, and I will faithfully care for your needs, as prescribed by Jewish law and tradition.'

The bride often now makes a similar declaration: 'In accepting the wedding ring, I pledge you all my love and devotion, and I take upon myself the fulfillment of all the duties incumbent upon a Jewish wife.' Then the groom will usually give a ring to the bride (or the two will exchange rings). The ring is conventional in the West, but it may be replaced by any gift of sufficient worth to formalize the legal transaction.

After the legal formalities are concluded, seven blessings are recited over a second cup of wine. The blessings recall the creation and the joy of ancient Judah in the celebration of marriages. In fulfillment of the last blessing, which prays for the sound of joy in Judah and Israel, the wedding usually concludes with an enormous feast.

In many ways the Jewish wedding ceremony encapsulates the community's hopes for survival. In consecrating the union of two young Jewish lives, the community thanks God for creation and sustenance, remembers its past, pledges its responsibilities publicly, and prays for its continuation. These themes are particularly poignant today, in the face of an uncertain future.

In ancient times the prophet Hosea likened the covenant between Israel and its God to a wedding. Just as the wedding, in uniting two people, commits them to play their part in the life of their

A bride and groom stand under the *huppah* (David Furst/AFP/Getty Images).

community, so the covenant between God and Israel continues to commit all Jews to play their part in the fulfillment of the Jewish people's special purpose in the world.

Sites

Mount Sinai The place where *Exodus* 20–31 says the children of Israel received the Ten Commandments and the subsequent Book of the Covenant. The mountain called Mount Sinai today may or may not be the same one.

Jerusalem A fortress of the Jebusites that was conquered by David around the year 1000 BCE (2 *Samuel* 5: 5–10); also known as 'The City of David'.

Samaria The capital city of the Northern Kingdom.

Alexandria A city in Egypt, founded by Alexander the Great, which became the home of an important Greek-speaking Jewish community.

Masada The mountain fortress where Jewish Zealots made their last stand against the Romans in 73 CE, three years after the destruction of the Temple in Jerusalem.

Yavne (also known as Jamnia). A small town west of Jerusalem, where the early rabbinic movement fled for safety during the revolt against Rome (70 CE).

Okop, Podolia A small village in the Polish Russian pale of settlement where the founder of the Hasidic movement, Israel ben Eliezer, the Baal Shem Tov, was born in 1698.

Cincinnati, Ohio The capital of the Reform movement in the United States and the location of the principal Reform seminary.

New York City The home of the largest Jewish population in the Americas and headquarters of the (Conservative) Jewish Theological Seminary.

Glossary

aggadah Anecdotal or narrative material in the *Talmud*; see also **halakha**.

apocalypse From the Greek for 'unveiling' (the Latin equivalent is 'revelation'); the final battle between the forces of darkness and light expected at the end of time. Apocalyptic literature flourished in the Hellenistic era.

Ashkenazim Jews of northern and eastern Europe, as distinguished from the Mediterranean Sephardim.

Bar Mitzvah 'Son of the commandments'; the title given to a thirteen-year-old boy when he is initiated into adult ritual responsibilities; some branches of Judaism also celebrate a Bat Mitzvah for girls.

berith Hebrew term for covenant, the special relationship between God and the Jewish people.

cantor The liturgical specialist who leads the musical chants in synagogue services.

Diaspora 'Dispersal', the Jewish world outside the land of ancient Israel; it began with the Babylonian Exile, from which not all Jews returned.

Documentary Hypothesis The theory (1894) that the Pentateuch was not written by one person (Moses) but compiled over a long period of time from multiple sources.

eschatology Doctrine concerning the end of the age, from the Greek for 'study of the end'.

Exile The deportation of Jewish leaders from Jerusalem to Mesopotamia by the conquering Babylonians in 586 BCE; disrupting local Israelite political, ritual, and agricultural institutions, it marked the transition from Israelite religion to Judaism.

Exodus The migration of Hebrews from Egypt under the leadership of Moses, understood in later Hebrew thought as marking the birth of the Israelite nation.

gaon Title of a senior rabbinical authority in Mesopotamia under Persian and Muslim rule.

Gemarah The body of Aramaic commentary attached to the Hebrew text of the *Mishnah*, which together with it makes up the *Talmud* (both the *Jerusalem Talmud* and the *Babylonian Talmud*).

Haggadah The liturgy for the ritual Passover supper.

halakha Material in the *Talmud* of a legal nature; see also **aggadah**.

Hasidim 'Pious ones'; applied to two unrelated groups of loyal or pious Jews: those who resisted Hellenism militarily in second-century BCE Palestine, and the mystically inclined followers of the Baal Shem Tov in eighteenth-century Poland and their descendants today.

hesed Hebrew term for the loyal conduct, sometimes translated as 'mercy' or 'loving-kindness', incumbent on God and on humans as parties to the covenant relationship.

Holocaust 'Burnt offering' or 'burnt sacrifice'; one of the ancient sacrifices mandated in the Hebrew Bible. The term has more recently been applied to the persecution and murder of 6 million European Jews by the Nazis before and during the Second World War (1939–45).

Humash The first five biblical books, the Pentateuch, when bound in book form for private study; in synagogue worship the same text is read from a scroll (see **Sefer Torah**).

Kabbalah The medieval Jewish mystical tradition; its central text is a commentary on scripture called the *Zohar*, compiled by Moses ben Shemtov of León (d. 1305) but attributed to *Rabbi Shimon bar Yohai*, a famous second-century rabbinic mystic and wonder-worker.

Karaites 'Scripturalists', an eighth-century anti-rabbinic movement that rejected the *Talmud* and post-biblical festivals such as Hanukkah, taking only the Bible as authoritative.

kippah 'Dome' or 'cap'; the Hebrew word for skullcap or *yarmulke*.

kosher Term for food that is ritually acceptable, indicating that all rabbinic regulations regarding animal slaughter and the like have been observed in its preparation.

logos 'Word'; a kind of divine intelligence thought to mediate between God and humanity and carry out God's intentions on earth.

Masada The fortress whose Jewish defenders are said to have committed suicide rather than surrender to Rome.

menorah The seven-branched candlestick, a Jewish symbol since ancient times, well before the widespread adoption of the six-pointed star; the nine-branched menorah used at Hanukkah is sometimes called a *hanukiah*.

midrash Commentary on scripture.

minyan The quorum of ten required for a prayer service in the synagogue.

Mishnah The Hebrew summary of the oral law—inherited from Pharisaism and ascribed to Moses—arranged by topic; edited by Rabbi Judah ha-Nasi before 220 CE, it has an authority paralleling that of the written Torah.

Mishneh Torah A topically arranged code of Jewish law written in the twelfth century by Moses Maimonides.

mitzvah A commandment; in the Roman era, the rabbinic movement identified exactly 613 specific commandments contained within the Torah.

Passover The major spring festival of agricultural rebirth and renewal, given a historical dimension by association with the hasty departure of the Israelites from Egypt under Moses' leadership.

patriarchs and matriarchs Ancestors of the Israelite nation in the Hebrew Bible's narratives of origins; 'patriarch' was also a title given to the head of the Jewish community in early rabbinic times.

Pentateuch The first five books of the Hebrew Bible, ascribed by tradition to Moses but regarded by modern scholars as the product of several centuries of later literary activity.

phylacteries The usual English term for *tefillin*.

rabbi A teacher, in Roman times an expert on the interpretation of Torah; since priestly sacrifices ceased with the destruction of the Temple, the rabbi has been the scholarly and spiritual leader of a Jewish congregation.

rabbinic movement The legal teachers and leaders, initially Pharisees, who became the dominant voices in Judaism after the destruction of the Temple and eventually became the rabbis as we know them.

responsa **literature** From the Latin for 'answers' (singular, *responsum*); accumulated correspondence by medieval and recent rabbinical authorities, consisting of rulings on issues of legal interpretation; also known as *Teshuvoth* (singular, *teshuvah*).

Rosh Hashanah The new year festival, generally occurring in September.

Sabbath The seventh day of the week, observed by Jews since ancient times as a day of rest from ordinary activity.

seder 'Order'; the term used for the ritual Passover supper celebrated in the home; the six divisions of the *Mishnah* are also called orders or seders.

Sefer Torah 'Book of the law'; a special copy of the first five books of Moses, hand-lettered on parchment for use in synagogue rituals (see also **Humash**).

Sephardim The Jews of the premodern Mediterranean and Middle East, as opposed to the Ashkenazim of northern and eastern Europe.

Septuagint The Greek translation of the Hebrew scriptures, made in Alexandria in Hellenistic times.

Shekhinah The divine presence or 'dwelling', often described in visionary terms by ancient commentators on *Ezekiel* and by medieval mystics.

Sukkoth The festival of 'Tabernacles', named for the temporary booths or shelters originally constructed by farmers in autumn to protect their ripening crops and given a historical interpretation recalling the migration experience of the Exodus.

synagogue The local place of assembly for congregational worship, which became central to the tradition after the destruction of the Jerusalem Temple.

takkanah 'Remediation'; a principle (attributed to Hillel) that facilitated borrowing by allowing the court to take over farmers' debts in years when their fields were fallow.

tallith A shawl worn for prayer, usually white with blue stripes and with fringes at the corners.

Tanakh The entire Hebrew Bible, consisting of Torah (or law), Nevi'im (or prophets), and Ketuvim (or sacred writings), and named as an acronym of these three terms.

Tannaim The rabbinic authorities whose opinions are recorded in the *Mishnah*, as distinguished from the rabbis (Amoraim) whose opinions appear in the *Gemarah* material of the *Talmud*.

tefillin Small black leather boxes, also termed phylacteries, containing words of scripture, tied to the forehead and forearm by leather thongs.

Torah A word meaning 'teaching' or 'instruction'; applied most specifically to the Law of Moses (the Pentateuch) but may also refer to the entire scripture, including commentaries, and even the entire spiritual thrust of Jewish religion.

yarmulke The Yiddish word for the *kippah* or skullcap worn by Orthodox Jewish males.

yeshiva A traditional school for the study of the scriptures and Jewish law.

Yiddish The language spoken by many central and eastern European Jews in recent centuries; though it is written in Hebrew characters and contains some words derived from Hebrew, it is essentially German in its basic structure and vocabulary.

Yom Kippur The day of atonement, ten days after Rosh Hashanah; the day for the most solemn reflection and examination of one's conduct.

zaddik 'Righteous person', a title conveying the Hasidic ideal for a teacher or spiritual leader.

Zion In biblical times, the hill in Jerusalem where the Temple stood as God's dwelling place; by extension, the land of the Israelites as the place of God's favour; in modern times, the goal of Jewish migration and nation-state settlement.

Further Reading

Abrahams, Israel, ed. 1927. *The Legacy of Israel*. Oxford: Clarendon Press. Chapters on Jewish contributions in various fields of Western culture.

Agus, Jacob B. 1959. The *Evolution of Jewish Thought: From the Time of the Patriarchs to the Opening of the Modern Era*. London: Abelard-Schuman. Good source, especially on the Middle Ages.

Ausubel, Nathan. 1974. *The Book of Jewish Knowledge: An Encyclopedia*. New York: Crown. Handy, simple explanations, understandable to the non-Jewish reader.

Barnavi, Elie, ed. 1992. *A Historical Atlas of the Jewish People: From the Time of the Patriarchs to the Present*. New York: Knopf. Excellent on the Diaspora in medieval and modern times.

Ben-Sasson, Haim H., ed. 1975. *A History of the Jewish People*. London: Weidenfeld and Nicolson. A social and cultural history.

De Breffny, Brian. 1978. *The Synagogue*. London: Weidenfeld & Nicolson; New York: Macmillan. A survey of synagogue architecture.

Casper, Bernard M. 1960. *An Introduction to Jewish Bible Commentary*. London: Thomas Yoseloff. The genre and spirit of *midrash*, especially as pursued in the Middle Ages.

Cohen, Arthur A. 1962. *The Natural and the Supernatural Jew: A Historical and Theological Introduction*. New York: Pantheon. Treats the meaning of modernity for Judaism.

Encyclopedia Judaica, 16 vols. 1971. *Jerusalem: Encyclopedia Judaica*, New York: Macmillan. Some of the articles, such as the one on Jerusalem, are almost books in themselves.

Gaster, Theodor H. 1952. *The Festivals of the Jewish Year*. New York: William Sloane Associates.

Shows how agricultural festivals received historical interpretations.

Glazer, Nathan. 1972. *American Judaism*. 2nd ed. Chicago: University of Chicago Press. A sociological interpretation.

Grollenberg, Luc H., ed. 1956. *Atlas of the Bible*. London: Nelson. Good for the archaeological and historical context of ancient Israel.

Hertzberg, Arthur. 1972. *The Zionist Idea: A Historical Analysis and Reader*. New York: Atheneum. A standard, well-documented source on the Zionist movement.

Idelsohn A.Z. 1932. *Jewish Liturgy and Its Development*. New York: Holt. Written by an expert on Jewish music and chanting.

Kaniel, Michael. 1979. *Judaism*. Poole, Dorset: Blandford. A volume on Jewish art, from a series on world art.

Kanof, Abraham. 1969. *Jewish Ceremonial Art and Religious Observances*. New York: Abrams. Contains pictorial illustrations of items used in worship.

Montefiore, Claude G., and Herbert Loewe, eds. 1938. *A Rabbinic Anthology*. London: Macmillan. A good collection of basic rabbinic texts.

Newman, Louis I., ed. 1934. *The Hasidic Anthology: Tales and Teachings of the Hasidim*. New York: Scribner. Contains many of the most frequently cited Hasidic texts.

Rabinowicz, Harry. 1960. *A Guide to Hasidism*. London: Thomas Yoseloff. A concise survey of Hasidic spirituality.

Scholem, Gershom G. 1974. *Kabbalah*. Jerusalem: Keter. The medieval mystical tradition surveyed by one of its most distinguished modern interpreters.

Schwarz, Leo W., ed. 1956. *Great Ages and Ideas of the Jewish People*. New York: Random House. A survey of religious and social history.

Segal, Alan F. 1986. *Rebecca's Children: Judaism and Christianity in the Roman World*. Cambridge, Mass.: Harvard University Press. Treats the Christian and early rabbinic movements as parallel developments.

Simon, Maurice. 1950. *Jewish Religious Conflicts*. London: Hutchinson. A masterful and readable survey of the development of religious authority across the centuries.

Steinsaltz, Adin. 1989. *The Talmud, the Steinsaltz Edition: A Reference Guide*. New York: Random House. Valuable explanations of technical rabbinic terminology and usage.

Trattner, Ernest R. 1955. *Understanding the Talmud*. New York: Nelson. One of the most lucid introductions.

Wilson, Robert R. 1980. *Prophecy and Society in Ancient Israel*. Philadelphia: Fortress Press. Contextualizes the prophets, making excellent use of sociological and anthropological approaches.

Yerushalmi, Yosef. 1982. *Zakhor: Jewish History and Jewish Memory*. Seattle: University of Washington Press. Themes from the medieval Jewish experience.

Recommended Websites

This list is based on the helpful list put together by Behrman House Publishing:

http://www.behrmanhouse.com/popular_jewish_websites.htm

Israel

www.inisrael.com/3disrael/index.html
   Israel in 3D

www.goisrael.com
   Israel Ministry of Tourism

www.centuryone.com/hstjrslm.html
   Jerusalem history

www.knesset.gov.il/vtour/eng/index.htm
   Knesset Virtual Tour

Education

www.jewishvirtuallibrary.org/index.html
   Jewish Virtual Library

www.jbooks.com
   The Online Jewish Book Community

Jewish History

www.nmajh.org/exhibitions/index.htm
   National Museum of American Jewish History

www.ushmm.com
   United States Holocaust Memorial Museum

www.fordham.edu/halsall/jewish/jewishsbook.html
   Internet Jewish History Sourcebook

www.cjh.org/
   Center for Jewish History

www.americanjewisharchives.org/syna/websites.php
   American Jewish Archives; a list of various website resources for the study of Jewish history and American Jewish history

References

Ahad Ha'am. 1962. *Nationalism and the Jewish Ethic: Basic Writings of Ahad Ha'am*. Ed. Hans Kohn. New York, Schocken.

Alexander, Philip, ed. 1984. *Textual Sources for the History of Judaism*. Manchester: Manchester University Press.

Caplan, Samuel, and Harold U. Ribalow, eds. 1952. *The Great Jewish Books and Their Influence on History*. New York: Horizon.

Grunfeld, Isidor, trans. 1956. *Judaism Eternal: Selected Essays from the Writings of Rabbi Samson Raphael Hirsch*. 2 vols. London: Soncino Press.

Herzl, Theodor. 1946. *The Jewish State*. New York: American Zionist Emergency Council.

Kohn, H., ed. 1962. *Nationalism and the Jewish Ethic: Basic Writings of Ahad Ha-Am*. New York: Herzl Press.

Lowenthal, Marvin, trans. 1977. *The Memoirs of Glückel of Hameln*. New York: Schocken.

Marcus, Ralph, trans. 1961. *Josephus, Antiquities XII–XIV*. Cambridge, Mass.: Harvard University Press.

Schechter, Solomon. 1896. *Studies in Judaism*. 1st series. New York: Macmillan.

Scholem, Gershom G. 1949. Zohar: *The Book of Splendor*. New York: Schocken Books.

Thackeray, H. St. J., trans. 1927. *Josephus in Nine Volumes*. Cambridge, Mass.: Harvard University Press.

Umansky, Ellen, and Dianne Ashton, eds. 1992. *Four Centuries of Jewish Women's Spirituality: A Sourcebook*. Boston: Beacon.

Whiston, William, trans. 1802. *The Genuine Works of Flavius Josephus*. Edinburgh: Thomas and John Turnbull.

Wilson, John A. 1950. 'Egyptian Hymns and Prayers.' In *Ancient Near Eastern Texts Relating to the Old Testament*, ed. James B. Pritchard, 365–81. Princeton: Princeton University Press.

Chapter 4

Christian Traditions

❧ Willard G. Oxtoby and Roy C. Amore ❧

Throughout the Christian world, the year reaches a climax towards the end of December, when the Christmas season marks the birth of the man Christians believe to have been the incarnate son of God, the manifestation of divine nature and purpose in a human life. Christians assert that in Jesus God reached out to conquer humanity's weaknesses.

To identify oneself as a Christian is to declare Jesus the lord and saviour of the world. The heavy emphasis that Christians place on that declaration is crucial for understanding the nature of Christianity, for to be a Christian is to make a commitment of faith in the doctrine that Jesus was the incarnate son of God.

Christians are found in every part of the world and form the world's largest religious community. Estimates place their number at a billion and a half—about one-quarter of the human family. They are the majority in Europe, the Americas, Australia and New Zealand, and many African countries. In the eastern Mediterranean, where Christianity originated, historic Christian communities remain, but as small minorities within their predominantly Muslim societies. In Asia, Christians constitute the majority only in the Philippines, although they are a significant minority (approaching one-third of the population) in Korea.

🌿 ORIGINS

The Life of Jesus

We know very little about the early years of Jesus, before he began his public life around the age of 30. Luke and Matthew recount a series of extraordinary events surrounding his birth in Bethlehem, a small town just southeast of Jerusalem. We are told that his childhood home was in Nazareth, a tiny Jewish village on a rocky hillside in the predominantly Greek-speaking northern region called Galilee, and we assume that he learned the trade of his father (a carpenter or builder). But from his youth we have only one story: at the age

of 12, after spending the High Holidays in Jerusalem with his family, he is said to have become so absorbed in discussing the subtleties of Jewish law with the teachers at the temple that his family started home without him.

His public years begin with his **baptism** by his older cousin, John the Baptist, during which he sees the heavens open and the holy spirit descending like a dove. Interpreting this mystical vision as a call to prophecy or ministry, he withdraws into the 'wilderness' on the eastern side of the Jordan River, on a kind of spiritual retreat. There he is joined by Satan, who offers him a series of temptations, each of which he refuses.

On his return from the wilderness Jesus goes to Capernaum, a town on the northwest shore of the Sea of Galilee, where his mother, Mary, now lives with other family members (perhaps his younger siblings, although Roman Catholic doctrine—which holds Mary to be 'ever virgin'—identifies them as cousins). The reason for leaving Nazareth is never explained, but one theory suggests that it may have had something to do with the death of his father, Joseph.

Soon after his return from the wilderness, Jesus attends a synagogue service in Nazareth and volunteers to do one of the Torah readings. The passage he is given to read speaks of a time to come when the lame shall walk and the blind will see. He then declares to those present that this prophecy is now fulfilled. This episode sets the stage for a series of miracles and at the same time underlines the idea that he has come to fulfill prophecies of the Hebrew Bible.

Jesus recruits twelve male disciples, most of whom make their living as fishermen. Not surprisingly, fishing and the Sea of Galilee figure

◀ Built on foundations that were laid around 220 CE, the basilica of Santa Maria in Trastevere may be the oldest church in Rome (Zeke Livingston). These mosaics date to the thirteenth century.

Timeline

c. 3 BCE	Birth of Jesus
c. 30 CE	Death of Jesus
c. 65	Death of Paul
312	Constantine's vision of the cross
325	First Council of Nicaea
337	Constantine is baptized on his deathbed
c. 384	Augustine's conversion experience
451	Council of Chalcedon
529	Benedict establishes monastery
842	Iconoclastic controversy ends
862	Cyril and Methodius in Moravia
c. 1033	Birth of Anselm (d. 1109)
1054	Break between Rome and Constantinople
1095	Urban II calls for the first crusade
1187	End of the Latin Kingdom of Jerusalem
c. 1225	Birth of Thomas Aquinas (*Summa Theologiae*) (d. 1274)
1517	Luther posts his 95 theses
1534	Henry VIII becomes head of the Church of England
1536	Calvin's *Institutes*
1563	Council of Trent concludes
1738	John Wesley's conversion experience
1781	Immanuel Kant's *Critique of Pure Reason*
1830	*Book of Mormon*
1859	Charles Darwin's, *On the Origin of Species*
1870	First Vatican Council concludes
1910	Publication of *The Fundamentals*
1948	First assembly of the World Council of Churches
1965	Second Vatican Council concludes

prominently in his teaching. He also attracts a number of women followers, among them Mary Magdalene, who play important roles. For the next year or more, Jesus travels the region around Capernaum, working miracles, teaching how to apply Jewish law to everyday life, and telling **parables**, many of which point to an impending **apocalypse** that will lead to a new era of peace and righteousness he calls the kingdom of God. His main venues are synagogues or private houses, but sometimes he preaches to larger crowds who gather to witness his miraculous cures, which include healing the blind and even raising the dead.

When he goes to Jerusalem with his disciples for the high holy days around Passover, he causes a disturbance at the temple by accusing the money changers of cheating on the rate charged to exchange regular Greek and Roman coins for the traditional Hebrew coins required to make offerings. On the Sunday before Passover, he fulfills another prophecy by riding into the town on a donkey. The people honour him by placing palm leaves in the road before he rides by and shouting his praises. A few days later, while praying in a garden outside Jerusalem, he is arrested by a mixed party of Roman soldiers and servants of the temple priests whose authority he has challenged. When one disciple tries to resist, Jesus tells him to put his sword away.

Taken first before the Sanhedrin and then before the Roman governor, Pontius Pilate, Jesus is accused of perverting the people and claiming to be the king of the Jews. Together with several other condemned men, he is paraded through the streets of Jerusalem to the place of execution, a hill called Golgotha, where he is nailed to a cross and left to die. Two days later, on the morning following the Sabbath, some of his women followers go to the tomb where his body was placed on the Friday, only to find it empty. In one account an angel tells the women that God has raised him from the dead; in others he appears to the disciples himself. In any event, it became the Christian belief that he had been resurrected and had gone to sit at the right hand of God in heaven, from where he would soon return to judge all persons and usher in the kingdom of God.

How Jesus understood his mission is not clear. His most frequent term for himself is 'the son of man'. In everyday Aramaic, this was the term for 'human', but it is also one of the terms used in the Hebrew literature to refer to an agent of God who will usher in a new era of justice and righteousness. 'Son of man' is not a synonym of 'messiah', but it has similar connotations, and Christians came to understand Jesus to be the long-awaited messiah. The Greek term *christos* was used as a synonym for 'messiah', and so he came to be known as Jesus the **Christ**, which is usually shortened to Jesus Christ.

The Gospels and Jesus

In Mark's account, a Roman soldier who is standing by as Jesus gasps his last breath is moved to say, 'Truly this was a son of God.'

It is fitting that Mark attributes this comment to a Roman soldier rather than one of Jesus' followers, for the Christian movement soon grew beyond its origins as a Jewish sect. Within a generation of his death, his followers had decided that his message was not for the Jews alone, and that anyone

Children in Asuncion, Paraguay, take part in the annual celebration of Palm Sunday, commemorating Jesus' entry into Jerusalem (AFP/Getty Images).

Traditions at a Glance

Numbers
1.5 billion around the world

Distribution
Christians constitute the majority of the population in Europe and the Americas, Australia, New Zealand, sub-Saharan Africa, and the Philippines; over a third of the population of Lebanon; and almost a third of the population of South Korea.

Principal Historical Periods

c. 3 BCE–c. 30 CE	Lifetime of Jesus
c. 30–c. 120	The New Testament or Apostolic age
c. 120–451	The early Church
1517–c. 1600	The Protestant Reformation
17th century–present	The modern period

Founders
Founded by the followers of Jesus of Nazareth, called the Christ, on the basis of his teachings and resurrection. Among the early founders, the apostles Peter and Paul were especially important.

Deity
One God, called 'God' or 'Lord', who exists in three persons: as Father, Son, and Holy Spirit.

Authoritative Texts
The Christian Bible consists of the Old Testament (the Hebrew Bible) and the New Testament. The Roman Catholic and Orthodox churches include as part of the Old Testament a number of books from the *Septuagint* that Protestants set apart as Apocrypha. In addition, Roman Catholics hold the teaching office (*magisterium*) of the Church to be authoritative.

Noteworthy Doctrines
Jesus is the second person of the Trinity, truly God as well as truly man, and his resurrection is the sign that those who believe in him will have eternal life. The authority of the Church has been passed down from the apostles.

could become a Christian. In that decision lay the seeds of Christianity's development as one of the world's three great missionary religions.

In the accounts of Jesus' life—known as **gospels**, from the Greek *evangel*, meaning 'good news'—he performs miracles. Today, the very stories that apparently impressed people 2,000 years ago may form a barrier to some minds. But the insights into human personality and relationships that permeate his teachings, and the confidence with which he was ready to challenge traditional scriptural and legal interpretations, place Jesus among the world's most astute and perceptive teachers. He commands his followers to love their enemies as well as their friends, and in word and example emphasizes forgiveness to a degree that

Sayings of Jesus

The following passages come from the body of teachings in Matthew *conventionally known as the 'Sermon on the Mount' (*Luke *presents similar material). The translation is from the* New English Bible.

If, when you are bringing your gift to the altar, you suddenly remember that your brother has a grievance against you, leave your gift where it is before the altar. First go and make your peace with your brother, and only then come back and offer your gift (5: 23–4).

You have learned that they were told, 'Eye for eye, tooth for tooth.' But what I tell you is this: Do not set yourself against the man who wrongs you. If someone slaps you on the right cheek, turn and offer him your left. If a man wants to sue you for your shirt, let him have your coat as well. If a man in authority makes you go one mile, go with him two. Give when you are asked to give; and do not turn your back on a man who wants to borrow (5: 38–42).

Pass no judgment, and you will not be judged. For as you judge others, so you will yourselves be judged, and whatever measure you deal out to others will be dealt back to you. Why do you look at the speck of sawdust in your brother's eye, with never a thought for the great plank in your own? Or how can you say to your brother, 'Let me take the speck out of your eye,' when all the time there is that plank in your own? First take the plank out of your own eye, and then you will see clearly to take the speck out of your brother's (7: 1–5).

---

is probably not exceeded in any other religious tradition.

Because Jesus lived at a time when there were no birth records, school transcripts, or employment files, our understanding of him depends on accounts produced a generation and more after his death. The Christian authors of those accounts had some extraordinary (and highly partisan) claims to make: that their teacher had been the long-awaited kingly deliverer, that his humiliating death on the cross was a victorious martyrdom, that he had come back from the dead, had risen to heaven, and would return in triumph. They even asserted that Jesus was the son of God, and that through his sacrifice of himself, he had become the saviour of humanity. Unfortunately for historians of the period, there are few non-Christian sources that might be used either to corroborate or to dispute those claims.

As historical evidence, then, what can the early Christian literature tell us? For more than a century scholars have agreed that, however suspect some of the details may be, it does demonstrate the existence of a community of faith centred on belief in Jesus as the risen lord. Whether or not Jesus actually did or said everything the texts attribute to him, the Christian message was crystallizing into recognizable form by the middle of the first century. The Christian movement was coming into focus, reporting the life of Jesus on earth, but also preaching an interpretation of that life as cosmically significant.

More than three centuries later, when Christianity became the established religion of the Roman Empire, church leaders made a list of the writings they acknowledged to be 'scripture'. That standard list, or **canon**, of books and letters is what Christians know as the New Testament. It includes the gospels attributed to four of Jesus' disciples: Matthew, Mark, Luke, and John. By then, those four accounts had been accepted throughout Christendom. The situation was much more fluid in the late first and early second centuries, when the texts were first written, and they were not the only accounts in circulation. It is helpful to think of each gospel as the product of an individual author with his own particular interpretation and audience in mind. We will treat them in the order in which most modern scholars believe they were written, rather than in the canonical order (which puts Matthew first).

Mark

Mark's account is the simplest, shortest, most straightforward, and most likely the earliest of the four canonical gospels. It starts not with Jesus' birth, but with the beginning of his mature ministry following his baptism by John the Baptist, who prophesies that Jesus will be far greater than John. After a forty-day retreat in the wilderness, during which he wrestles with the temptations of Satan, Jesus launches his ministry in Galilee, proclaiming that the kingdom of God is at hand. His local reputation spreads as he performs healing miracles. He also violates the Sabbath law by picking grain and healing on the day of rest, and when he is challenged for doing so, he takes the notion of Jewish legal authority into his own hands, declaring that the Sabbath is made for people rather than people for the Sabbath. It is in response to this apparent arrogance, Mark suggests, that the Pharisees conspire to do away with him.

Jesus selects from among his male followers a group of twelve (a significant number in Hebrew tradition, symbolizing a complete set) as his inner circle of disciples. Accompanied by them, he continues to heal, teach, and challenge the priorities of religious authority. Eventually he goes to Jerusalem, arriving with an entourage that shouts 'Hosanna' (a cry for divine deliverance in Hebrew prayer) and proclaims the coming of a king in the line of the Hebrew dynastic founder, David. Over the course of a week in Jerusalem, he disputes with the religious authorities, celebrates the Passover with his disciples, is betrayed by one of them (Judas), and is arrested. Brought to trial before Pilate, the Roman governor, Jesus does not deny that he is the king of the Jews and offers no defence.

Jesus is executed on the cross, crying out a quotation from one of the Hebrew psalms, 'My

Sources of the Gospel Narratives

Much of the Gospel material consists of Jesus' teachings. Some of these take the form of parables: narrative stories designed to teach a moral lesson. Others take the form of short sayings that could stand alone, apart from any narrative, as universally applicable proverbs or maxims. In chapters 5 through 7 of his account, Matthew describes Jesus as delivering a collection of these on a mountain in northern Palestine; the material is thus known as the Sermon on the Mount. Luke presents the same material—though in his gospel it is delivered on a plain.

In general, Luke and Matthew overlap to a considerable extent, and it has been assumed that both of them used Mark's narrative as a source for their accounts. Yet some of the material they both include is not found in Mark.

These discrepancies led German scholars in the nineteenth century to postulate that the material not in Mark must have come from a different source, one that both Luke and Matthew used and that has since been lost. This hypothetical document has come to be known as 'Q', from the initial letter of *Quelle*, the German word for 'source'.

God, my God, why have you forsaken me?' As he breathes his last, the Roman centurion identifies him as 'truly' a son of God, and before the Sabbath begins, his body is placed in a tomb, which is sealed by a large stone. The day after the Sabbath, three women followers go to the tomb to anoint the body, only to find the stone rolled away and the body missing; a figure appears to them and informs them that Jesus has risen from the dead and will meet with the disciples. In some manuscripts of Mark's gospel, Jesus appears to the eleven faithful disciples at a meal, commands them to preach the gospel (i.e., the 'good news'), and promises that they too will be healers.

Luke

Luke's account contains two chapters of material not found in *Mark*, detailing events before Jesus' adult baptism and ministry, including visions and portents anticipating the birth of John the Baptist as well as that of Jesus. It reports on Jesus' birth in Bethlehem and describes how shepherds in the fields, informed of the birth of the messiah by angels (divine messengers), come and pay their respects to the infant; Luke does not mention any wise men from the East, however; the *magi* (Persian for 'priests') are in *Matthew*. At a newborn-purification ceremony in the temple, a devout man is inspired to proclaim the infant to be the messiah. Luke's opening chapters also incorporate a number of hymns that were apparently already in use in the early Church.

These omens, portents, and declarations would have served to strengthen the case that Jesus was the long-awaited messiah. Whereas someone reading only Mark's account would likely understand Jesus to have embarked on his ministry following an adult decision marked by baptism, Luke's version of the story emphasizes that Jesus was born into his role and destined for it. Moreover, the signs and portents recounted by Luke would have appealed to gentiles as well as Jews, for such wonders were a standard part of the biographical traditions associated with important teachers and healers in Greco-Roman as well as Hebrew antiquity. In fact, Luke appears to have had a Greek readership in mind, for the gospel is addressed to Theophilus—a Greek name meaning 'One who loves God'— and he presents his Jewish saviour as being important to the gentile world.

Luke also provides more information than Mark regarding the trial and crucifixion of Jesus. In his narrative, the charge against Jesus was that in claiming kingship, he was inciting rebellion. Although the Roman governor, Pilate, himself finds Jesus innocent of any crime, mob pressure demands execution, and Pilate yields to it. In *Luke* the Roman centurion who witnesses the crucifixion declares that Jesus is innocent, not (as in *Mark*) that he is a son of God. And after the discovery of the empty tomb, Jesus appears among his followers and speaks to them. Here again, as in his handling of the infancy narratives, Luke seems to consider signs and portents the most important evidence of Jesus' special role. References to the fulfillment of Jewish expectations are not numerous and appear only in statements attributed to Jesus himself.

Matthew

Matthew's account includes much of the same material as Luke's, but his focus is noticeably different. As a writer, Matthew has clearly designed his narrative to persuade a Jewish audience of the truth of Jesus' claim to be the messiah. It has been suggested that his account of Jesus' escape from the slaughter of infants by King Herod was specifically intended to echo the *Exodus* account of the Israelites' escape from the wrath of the Egyptian pharaoh. Thus in Matthew's narrative—and his alone—King Herod, on hearing of the birth of a child who is to be the king of the Jews, plots to kill every Jewish infant to protect his own reign. An angel warns Jesus' parents to take the child and escape to Egypt, where they remain until the tyrant's death. 'This,' writes Matthew, 'was to fulfill what the Lord had spoken by the prophet, "Out of Egypt have I called my son"'—an explicit reference to a passage from the book of the prophet Hosea: 'When Israel was a child, I loved him, and out of Egypt I called my son.' Many scholars suspect that some details of Matthew's narrative were inspired by the existing Hebrew texts. On the other hand, many conservative Christians over the years have seen the content of the earlier texts as placed there by God expressly so that, when the time came, the words could be reinterpreted to reveal a meaning that had been divinely intended for them all along. Let us consider a few of the more challenging cases.

Matthew begins his account by tracing the genealogy of Jesus as the descendant of King David, in a lineage that runs through Joseph, the husband of Mary. However, Matthew then bypasses this genealogy and declares that Mary was already pregnant with Jesus before her marriage, with a child fathered by the Holy Spirit rather than Joseph. Part of Matthew's purpose in making this unusual claim is to associate Jesus' birth directly with a prophecy from the book of *Isaiah* (7: 14), which he quotes: 'Behold, a virgin shall conceive and bear a son, and his name shall be called Emmanuel (which means, "God with us").'

In citing this passage, Matthew set the stage for one of Christianity's most problematic teachings, for although the Hebrew text of *Isaiah* mentions only a 'young woman', the Greek translation is ambiguous and can be read as 'virgin'. In fact, *Matthew* and *Luke* are the only sources for the doctrine of the virgin birth.

In his determination to link Jesus to Hebrew scripture, Matthew also makes some outright mistakes. To provide a scriptural context for Jesus' use of parables, for instance, he attributes the passage 'I will open my mouth in parables, I will utter what has been hidden since the foundation of the world' to 'the prophet' or (in some manuscripts) 'the prophet Isaiah', when in fact it comes from *Psalm* 78.

The historical episode of deepest significance for Christians is the **Passion** (suffering) and death of Jesus on the cross. Bystanders mock Jesus for having trusted in God, saying that God should rescue him now. Jesus says he is thirsty. His hands and feet are pierced. Soldiers cast lots to divide up his clothing. And Jesus cries out, 'My God, my God, why have you forsaken me?' This phrase comes from the opening line of *Psalm* 22, which also contains several other details of the Passion, including the piercing of hands and feet.

How many of these details would an eyewitness to the crucifixion actually have observed? Jesus may well have cried out that he was forsaken, and quite possibly he had in mind the rest of *Psalm* 22, which concludes by expressing trust in divine deliverance. Did the other events recorded actually 'happen', or were they supplied by association as scripture-conscious narrators like Matthew retold the narrative? This sort of question will probably never be settled to everyone's satisfaction.

If the gospel writers have added associations and details to their stories of Jesus, what did Jesus himself actually intend? On this question Christian opinion varies widely, but some points stand out with clarity. Jesus wanted his fellow Jews to live up to ideals already present in their tradition. Like the Hebrew prophets before him, he placed ethics ahead of ritual. He was ready to challenge traditional interpretations, repeatedly declaring, 'You have heard it said . . . , but I say to you . . . .' He shares a popular expectation that the 'kingdom of God', which will in some way restructure society, is at hand, and he was willing to die a martyr's death for the cause. This much probably was true of the historical Jesus. But his followers soon developed a preaching message that went much further in what it claimed for him.

John

Despite their differences, the three gospels sketched so far (*Matthew*, *Mark*, and *Luke*, in order of their appearance in the New Testament) share a good deal in common when they are contrasted with John's, the fourth gospel. Scholars therefore refer to the first three as the 'synoptic gospels'. The term 'synoptic' (from Greek, 'viewing together') can be confusing. It does not mean that they offer a brief summary or synopsis. Rather, it implies that they have a unified perspective or viewpoint. John's gospel is a biography of another sort.

We have described the gospel accounts as interpretations. Even in Mark's relatively straightforward account, the selection and arrangement of material amounts to an interpretation. And we have seen how careful Matthew was to present Jesus' life as the fulfillment of earlier prophecies. Compared with these narratives, however, John's gospel is a major theological essay.

His purpose is to set out not just the narrative itself but its cosmic significance. Far from simply recounting the teachings and actions of Jesus, John proclaims Jesus' identity as messiah and saviour. Regarding his purpose as a writer, John is candid at the end of his twentieth chapter:

> Now Jesus did many other signs in the presence of the disciples, which are not written in this book. But these are written that you may come to believe that Jesus is the Messiah, the Son of God, and that through believing you may have life in his name (*John* 20: 30–1).

In his opening passage, or prologue, John shows his theological interest at once. 'In the beginning,' he writes (recalling the opening words of *Genesis* in the Hebrew scriptures) 'was the **logos**, and the *logos* was with God, and the *logos* was God; all things were made through him.' *Logos* is a Greek term with an important range of meaning in the philosophy and religion of the Hellenistic world at the time of Jesus. It meant 'word' not just as a vocabulary item, but the whole idea of divine intelligence and purpose. A God who can create the world through his word who can command the world through his word, and who can redeem the world through his word, is what John wants his hearers to appreciate here. This *logos* is the 'word' with a capital W.

A few verses later in the prologue, John declares Jesus to be the **incarnation** of that divine Word: 'The *logos* became flesh and dwelt among us, full of grace and truth; we have beheld his glory, glory as of the only Son from the Father.' For John, the eternal divine purpose has manifested itself as a personal presence in human form, in the recent experience of the community. He goes on to emphasize the distinction that the early Christian movement as a Jewish sect was making between its message and the traditional Jewish law, the contrast between law and gospel: 'For the law was given through Moses; grace and truth came through Jesus Christ.'

Here John is in step with the writings of an early convert, Paul, who probably contributed as much as anyone to the shaping of the early Christian message. Like Paul, John is now using the title 'Christ' (the Greek translation of the Hebrew word for messiah, 'anointed') practically as a second personal name for Jesus. John's view of the significance of Jesus is encapsulated in a frequently quoted passage: 'For God so loved the world that he gave his only Son, that whoever believes in him should not perish but have eternal life' (*John* 3: 16).

As the gospel continues, the idea that Jesus is the messiah becomes something more than John's personal interpretation: Jesus himself repeatedly declares it in his own words. Whereas Mark's Jesus will neither confirm nor deny that he is the long-awaited king, John's Jesus has no such reluctance. Even in the first chapter, when a questioner declares him to be the son of God, Jesus responds: 'Truly, truly I say to you, you will see heaven opened, and the angels of God ascending and descending upon the Son of man.'

Repeatedly throughout John's gospel, Jesus declares himself to be the means of salvation in passages that begin with 'I am':

> I am the bread of life; he who comes to me shall not hunger, and he who believes in me shall never thirst (6: 35).

I am the light of the world; he who follows me will not walk in darkness, but will have the light of life (8: 12).

I am the good shepherd. The good shepherd lays down his life for the sheep (10: 11).

I am the resurrection and the life; he who believes in me, though he die, yet shall he live, and whoever lives and believes in me shall never die (11: 25–6).

I am the way, and the truth, and the life; no one comes to the Father, but by me (14: 6).

I am the vine, you are the branches. He who abides in me, and I in him, he it is that bears much fruit, for apart from me you can do nothing (15: 5).

John's Jesus is more than a teacher with an insight into human nature; he is the definitive link between God and humanity.

Salvation, then, is John's goal for us humans, who need to be delivered from the flaws and constraints of our condition. He is especially concerned with our mortality, and he offers the hope of life. Paul, as we shall see, is also concerned with our sinfulness, and offers the hope of **justification**—being 'set right' with God. In the final analysis, only God can save us from sin and death, that is, from the limitations of our human existence.

A theological issue has been raised, to which subsequent thinkers would devote centuries of reflection. How is it that the transcendent God enters into the human condition to perform these saving acts? Jesus' status as a manifestation of God was eventually spelled out in the doctrine of the **Trinity**, after the middle of the third century, but the link between the divine and the human in Jesus continued to be a doctrinal issue well into the fifth century. And the process by which human sin is conquered or atoned for remained a central doctrinal question throughout the centuries.

From Sect to Church

The small circle of disciples who were left to carry on after Jesus' execution bore little resemblance to the institution that within four centuries would become the state church of the Roman Empire. The disciples were peasants and fishermen from rural Galilee, a small Jewish sect whose teacher had stirred in them the hope that low-status and marginalized people (the poor, women, Samaritans, sinners) had a place in God's plan. They expected the end of the age, and the glorious return of their teacher, to come at any moment.

Various explanations are offered for how early Christianity transformed itself from a small sect within Judaism to an independent missionary religion. Not surprisingly, the New Testament book *Acts of the Apostles*, which is Luke's sequel to his gospel, describes a miraculous event. In *Acts* 2 the disciples have gathered to celebrate the festival of Shavuoth, seven weeks after the Passover crucifixion, when the Holy Spirit appears to them as a rush of wind and fire. Suddenly they are able to speak and be understood in diverse languages— and therefore to preach to all people.

Acts also provides more everyday information about the **apostles**, as the original Christians are called. Chapter 15, for instance, tells of a genuine debate over whether prospective members who are gentiles need to be circumcised as Jews in order to join the movement. This debate would have taken place around the year 49, when the Christians had been preaching for nearly two decades. In *Acts*, Peter and James, Jesus' brother or kinsman, who are depicted as leaders among the apostles, steer a middle course between exclusive Jewish and gentile definitions of the movement. (The answer comes in *Galatians* 2, where the Christians reach a consensus that circumcision is not required.)

In his writings, Luke makes hardly any explicit reference to the Zealot-inspired rebellion against

Roman rule in 66–73—in the course of which the Temple was destroyed—even though it must have been the century's watershed political event for any Jew in Palestine. We may speculate that the Christians would have sought to distance themselves from Jewish nationalist ambitions, and to some extent from identification with Judaism altogether.

Hints of such an effort can be seen in Luke's description of Jesus entering Jerusalem for his final week in the city:

> And when he drew near and saw the city he wept over it, saying, 'Would that even today you knew the things that make for peace! But now they are hid from your eyes. For the days shall come upon you, when your enemies will cast up a bank about you and surround you, and hem you in on every side, and dash you to the ground, you and your children within you, and they will not leave one stone upon another in you . . .' (*Luke* 19: 41–4).

With the destruction of the city fresh in his mind, it is not surprising that Luke depicted Jesus and his followers as mild-mannered in word and deed. But there are hints to the contrary in *Mark* 14 and *Matthew* 26. In their accounts of Jesus' arrest, Mark and Matthew say that the disciples were armed, that they resisted arrest, and that Peter used his sword to cut off the ear of one of the arresting men.

Paul

The principal influence on the direction of the early Church was not one of Jesus' unprepossessing band of twelve, but an educated and sophisticated convert who took the name Paul. A cosmopolitan figure with the privileged status of a Roman citizen, Paul was a Pharisee from the diaspora Jewish community in Tarsus (on the southern coast of what is now Turkey) who had gone to Jerusalem for religio-legal study.

Paul had not known Jesus personally. Yet—as Luke tells it—while Paul was travelling to Damascus for the purpose of persecuting Christians, he experienced a vision of the post-resurrection Jesus that turned his life upside-down. For the next quarter century he travelled tirelessly around the eastern Mediterranean, initially preaching to the diaspora Jewish communities, but eventually reaching out to gentiles as well, teaching that all were heirs in Christ to the promises of God.

Paul corresponded with the scattered communities of Christian converts in letters whose content ranges from personal greetings through liturgical blessings to essays on questions of theology. His letters, written before the gospels themselves were composed, constitute the earliest Christian literature, and their influence on Christian theology can hardly be overestimated.

In his letters, Paul refers to himself as the apostle to the gentiles. He rejects the idea that in order to follow Jesus one must first become a Jew and follow the various regulations of Pharisaism. For Paul, it is not through observance of ritual laws or even correct moral conduct that salvation is attained, but rather through faith in Jesus and the divine grace that comes through him. Divine grace, transmitted through Christ, frees people from bondage to the law of Moses. Paul expresses his sense of this freedom with the certainty of intense personal experience.

At the same time, Paul takes up some broader issues with his gentile audience. To educated citizens of the Greco-Roman world, goodness amounted to virtue, that is, the cultivation of right moral conduct. But action that is morally correct by gentile standards is no more effective than action that is ritually correct by Pharisaic standards. Basically, human beings are inherently self-willed and sinful, as the Church was later to spell out in its doctrine of '**original sin**'. It was in order to liberate humans from their sinful nature, Paul says, that God sent Jesus to die a self-sacrificing death. Fifteen centuries later, the idea that salvation—redemption from sin—depends solely on trusting faith would be central to the Protestant Reformation.

Another major theme in subsequent Christian theology that can be traced to Paul is the contrast between life 'in the spirit'—centred on lasting religious values such as faith, hope, and love—and life 'in the flesh': the pursuit of what passes away, including worldly ambition or pleasure. Whether or not it was Paul's intention, his rejection of 'life in the flesh' was interpreted as meaning that the body must be controlled or repressed—a concept that would become a major issue in later Christian theology.

Thanks to Paul's voyages, Christian communities were established in many of the port cities of the Roman Empire by the time he died, about the year 65. At the beginning of his involvement with Christianity, Paul had assisted the people who stoned the apostle Stephen to death, by holding their coats. Now, at the end, Paul was to become a martyr (etymologically, a 'witness') himself, executed in Rome as part of the emperor Nero's persecution of Christians.

Marcion and the Canon

If we identify Paul as the architect of Christianity, then Marcion (d. c. 160) might be described as the author of a blueprint that was rejected. Marcion, who lived a century after Paul, was a wealthy ship-owner, the son of a bishop, from the region of the Black Sea who made his way to Rome. Although his teachings led to his **excommunication** (formal expulsion) from the Church in 144, this did not deter him from making his views known.

In his theology, Marcion takes Paul's ideas to astonishing lengths. Paul's contrast between law and gospel becomes for Marcion a contrast between the Old Testament and New, not just between one scripture and another but between one god and another. Marcion sees the 'Demiurge', the creator God of the Hebrew scriptures, who gives the law to Moses, as stern and fearsome, capricious, despotic, and cruel. The coming of Jesus reveals an utterly different God, a God of love and mercy, who will take the place of the Demiurge.

In that case, of course, the Hebrew scriptures must be rejected as well. In *Matthew 5*, Jesus says that he comes not to destroy 'the law and the prophets' (i.e., scripture) but to fulfill them. Marcion, however, rejected *Matthew* as well as the entire Hebrew canon. He accepted as scripture only ten letters by Paul and an edited text of Luke's gospel and *Acts*.

Marcion had a following in some circles, particularly in Syria, but it appears to have died out by the fifth century. His principal influence can be seen in the responses he drew from other Christian theologians. Emphatically, they rejected Marcion's view and affirmed that the Christian message was indeed rooted in the faith of ancient Israel. Staking its claim to the heritage of Moses and the prophets, the early Church established its credentials as a religion with a legitimate historical pedigree.

By raising questions about Christianity's Jewish past and scriptural authority, Marcion pushed the Church to ratify the Hebrew scriptures as a part of the Christian message. Thus even though his ideas were rejected, he contributed to the Church's eventual definition of its scriptural canon: the list of writings that make up the Old and New Testaments.

The Gnostics

Paul was not the only writer to distinguish between the spirit and the flesh, nor was Marcion the only one to distinguish between negative and positive divine principles. Another spiritual and doctrinal challenge to early Christianity came from the movement known as **Gnosticism**.

The Gnostics claimed to have privileged, secret knowledge. (The Greek word *gnosis* means 'knowledge'.) To their Christian adherents they offered an inner meaning of Christianity (and to Jewish Gnostics, of Judaism). At first they were not a separate community, but rather a school of thought within the network of the Christian churches.

The Gnostic philosophical narrative is dualistic: the divine powers of good are opposed by demonic forces of evil, and spirit is in a cosmic struggle with matter. In the beginning, the material world was created through the entrapment or fall and fragmentation of spirit into matter. Depending on the particular account, spirit is the victim of temptation or treachery or attack. In any case, there will be battles before the cosmos is redeemed and spirit is restored to its proper place.

The Christian Gnostics understood Jesus as an emissary from the realm of the spirit who took on the appearance of human form for his earthly life but did not take on material existence. In their view, his purpose was to transmit to humans the saving secret knowledge of how to rise above this life to the realm of spirit. This view also implied a practical agenda for religious life: if matter was evil, then physical comforts and satisfactions, even for the purpose of procreation, were to be avoided (or at least ignored) in favour of abstinence, celibacy, and asceticism.

Later Christian centuries knew about Gnostic teachings largely from the arguments against them in the writings of early Christian theologians. Critics of Gnostic teachings, who termed them docetic (from Greek *dokesis*, 'appearance'), argued that to treat Jesus as a spiritual apparition was to rob Christianity of the extraordinary power associated with the doctrine of divine incarnation in human form.

Grounds for a more sympathetic view of Gnostic ideas became available to historians in the mid-twentieth century, when an important collection of Gnostic manuscripts on papyrus was discovered at Nag Hammadi in Egypt. Among the Nag Hammadi texts is the *Gospel of Thomas*, one of many writings, Gnostic and otherwise, that did not win ratification as scripture by the Church at large. Although it was probably written after Jesus' death, it reports his sayings as though he were still alive and does not describe his death. In it the disciples ask, 'Tell us how our end will be.' Jesus replies, 'Have you already discovered the beginning, that you now seek the end?' This may be a cryptic reference to the complex Gnostic teachings about the origin of the world.

One small Gnostic community survives today. Concentrated, until recently, in southern Iraq, the Mandeans (from Aramaic and Syriac *manda*, 'knowledge') came to be known as 'Christians of St John' because of their reverence for John the Baptist. A separate religion of the Gnostic type arose in third-century Iran. Mani, who was raised in Gnostic circles, declared himself to be a prophet, produced scriptural writings, and organized an independent community. Mani was a synthesizer who claimed to sum up the teachings not only of Jesus but of Zoroaster and the Buddha. **Manichaeism**, the tradition of 'the living Mani', spread through much of the Roman Empire and competed with Christianity for adherents in the fourth and fifth centuries. It won converts in Egypt and North Africa, including the theologian Augustine, who was a Manichaean before he turned to Christianity.

The development of Christian doctrine responded to the challenges first of Gnostic and then of Manichaean teachings. Christians came to stress the unity and sovereignty of God, the humanity of Jesus, and the goodness of life in the material world. Nonetheless, some Gnostic ideas, such as the reality of the devil as an antagonist to God and the value of asceticism, continued to find a place in Christianity.

CRYSTALLIZATION

Emerging Church Organization

Although spontaneous at first, the Christian movement became formally organized during the early centuries. Some role specialization developed, with teachers providing leadership in established groups, probably on the pattern of synagogue study, and evangelists spreading the message to form new groups. Before long, formal ordination was required to perform ritual and administrative functions. The most basic ordained position was that of deacon, and women as well as men were so designated in the early Church. During the first two centuries, women apparently performed a variety of ecclesiastical roles, but in later ages even the role of deacon came to be monopolized by men.

Apostle, deacon, and elder (*presbyter* in Latin) are the only leadership roles mentioned in the New Testament, but sometime between the writing of the New Testament books and the early Christian councils the priest emerged as the person in charge of rituals and instruction in Christian congregations. Although the role of deacon survived, deacons were subordinate to priests. The ranking priest in a particular political jurisdiction was known as a **bishop** (from Greek *episkopos*, 'supervisor'). His was the responsibility to ordain deacons and priests, symbolized by 'laying hands' on the head of the inductee. Similarly, although any Christian could induct someone into the faith by performing the symbolic bathing ritual, it was the bishop, making his rounds in his diocese (administrative district), who would confirm the baptism of new initiates.

The hierarchy of priests was further developed to include the role of archbishop: the bishop chosen to supervise all the bishops in a large region. By the third century, four even larger episcopal jurisdictions or 'sees' had gained prominence in the Roman Empire because of the importance of their cities: Alexandria in Egypt, Jerusalem, Antioch in Syria, and Rome in Italy. The bishops of these cities came to be known as **patriarchs**. A fifth patriarch was added in Constantinople when the imperial capital moved there in the fourth century. The boundaries and lines of authority within the Church were drawn along the lines existing in the political arena.

To give legitimacy to their claims of authority, Christians often invoked the apostles. Thus an early affirmation of faith was called the Apostles' Creed, and the ordination lineage of bishops was referred to as apostolic succession. Various nations claimed that their peoples had been converted by the missionary activity of one or another of the apostles—Egypt by Mark, India by Thomas, and Armenia by Thaddeus and Bartholomew.

Saints

Paul referred to all loyal members of the Church collectively as 'saints', but in time that title came to be reserved for individuals who were considered channels of divine grace, or who had distinguished themselves by displaying an unusual degree of piety. Contemporaries of Jesus, including his parents, his faithful disciples, the four gospel writers, and the early missionaries, became saints as a matter of course. Persons who accepted martyrdom—the ultimate sacrifice for the cause—were singled out, as were leading theologians and bishops in the early Christian centuries. The saints even included a pre-Christian figure (John the Baptist) and a non-human (the archangel Michael). Later, the Church would develop elaborate criteria for bestowing the title of saint on a deceased Christian.

Asceticism

In the eastern Mediterranean, people wishing to retreat from society to practise contemplation or austerity moved to the margin of the desert. The Hellenistic Jewish sect widely identified as the Essenes built their community in the desert, near the shores of the Dead Sea. John the Baptist and his movement were associated with the desert. In the gospels, it is to the desert that Jesus withdraws to wrestle with the question of his own calling, and it is in the desert that he resists the devil's temptation.

In India, centuries before Jesus, a Hindu man whose sons were grown and able to care for the family might embark on a new life as a forest-dwelling, contemplative ascetic. Among Buddhists and Jainas, even young men and women were encouraged to depart the householder life and follow the rules for living as monks or nuns for the rest of their lives. There are even suggestions that these Indian spiritual practices might have served as models for early Christian monasticism, since Buddhist inscriptions in India claim contact with the world of the Greeks, but such suggestions remain undocumented.[1]

Several factors likely contributed to the emergence of Christian asceticism. No doubt some of the early ascetics wanted to prepare for the end of the world and the return of Christ, which they expected imminently, and the practice of a strict discipline was widely believed to deepen spiritual experience. During the periods of persecution in the second and third centuries, life in the desert became an alternative to martyrdom. And in more secure periods, to give up comfort or wealth was an effective way to make a public statement repudiating the laxity and complacency of the wider community, particularly after the fourth century, when, with imperial patronage, Christianity became fashionable and even began to acquire some opulent trappings.

The origins of Christian monasticism are traced to Antony, who was said to have lived 105 years (c. 251–356) in Egypt. The account of his life attributed to the Alexandrian theologian Athanasius describes the spiritual temptations that Antony sought to overcome by withdrawing to the solitude of the desert frontier:

> The enemy would suggest filthy thoughts, but Antony would dissipate them by his prayers. The wretched devil even dared to masquerade as a woman by night. It was as though demons were breaking through the four walls of the little chamber and bursting through them in the forms of beasts and reptiles. All at once the place was filled with the phantoms of lions, bears, leopards, bulls, of serpents and asps, of scorpions and wolves. Antony said: 'It is a sign of your helplessness that you ape the forms of brutes' (Meyer 1950: 22–8).

Antony and others who pursued their discipline in solitude were termed hermits, from the Greek *eremos*, 'solitary'. Noteworthy among them was Simeon (c. 390–459) in northern Syria. After having already been a hermit for ten years, in his mid-twenties Simeon built a pillar on which he would sit for the rest of his life, using a basket to haul up the supplies provided by his admirers. At first low, the pillar was gradually raised to a height of 18.5 m (60 ft). Simeon's example of dedication attracted converts and pilgrims, and other 'stylites' (pole-sitters) copied him.

Although the monastic life came to be permanent and corporate, its origins appear to have been temporary and sometimes individual. As the Greek word *monos* ('one', 'alone') suggests, monasticism entailed a life apart from the wider society. In time, however, the 'desert fathers' took up locations near one another for safety and mutual support. Such groupings were at first informal. In Egypt, Pachomius established nine monasteries for men in the first half of the fourth century, and his sister Miryam (Mary) two for women. Basil, a fourth-century bishop of Caesarea in Cappadocia (east-central Turkey), drew up regulations for monks that included vows of poverty and chastity, specified hours of prayer, and assigned manual tasks. Some communities in or near towns or cities dedicated themselves to social service. Monasticism was coming to be formalized as a corporate discipline and an integral part of Christianity.

Persecution and Martyrdom

Roman society had civic gods and rituals that the population at large was expected to support. But the Christian minority stood aloof from the public religion, which they rejected as the worship of idols. From their point of view, they were keeping faith with their heritage of exclusive Hebraic monotheism, but from the Roman perspective they were guilty of insubordination. To the technically justifiable charges of insubordination the state from time to time added false accusations of incest, cannibalism, and black magic—practices that some Romans believed would provoke the gods to mete out punishment in the form of epidemics and natural disasters. As a consequence, Christians in the first and second centuries were sometimes subject to persecution by local mobs.

In the third century, however, the empire was in a crisis of deepening military, administrative, and economic instability. The emperor Decius, seeking to revitalize his shaky regime, commanded public sacrifices to the Roman civic gods, with the penalty of death or imprisonment for anyone who would not comply. Throughout the empire, in the years 250–1, Christians were systematically persecuted as a matter of state policy, and in 257–9 the emperor Valerian conducted another campaign of official persecution. It was in this period that acceptance of martyrdom became the ultimate test of faith for Christians who modelled their own conduct on the self-sacrificing death of their lord, confident that they would be rewarded with eternal life in fellowship with him.

'The blood of the martyrs is the seed of the church,' said Tertullian (c. 160–c. 220), who came from Carthage in North Africa and was the first theologian to write in Latin. He had a point. By making martyrs of Christians, the Roman state helped to build a tradition of bravery and fidelity that the Christians could be proud of. According to a number of accounts, the example of steadfast faith set by the martyrs helped to persuade many pagans to become Christian. The last and fiercest of the official persecutions of the Christians came in 303 under the emperor Diocletian. For the next nine years, Christians were killed, church properties destroyed, and Christian sacred writings burned. But the 'Great Persecution' was no more successful in suppressing the Christians than the earlier campaigns had been.

Imperial Christianity

Constantine

A shift of policy under Diocletian's successor forever changed Christianity's place in the world. Constantine (r. 306–37) gradually abandoned the persecution policy, issuing an edict in 313 that gave Christians liberty to practise their religion, and eventually granting them state support and patronage. What accounted for this dramatic shift?

Eusebius, bishop of Caesarea in Palestine, who lived through the transition, attributed it to God's providence. According to his *Life of Constantine*, the emperor's **conversion** to Christianity was sparked by a vision he experienced on the eve of a decisive battle in 312, in which a cross appeared in the heavens, accompanied by the words 'conquer in this sign'. The following day, his troops won the battle and he gained control of the western half of the empire.

Modern historians have speculated about Constantine's motives, however. The allegedly sudden vision does not square with the gradual pace of change in imperial policy. Christian symbols appeared on Constantine's coinage alongside pagan symbols for some time, and it was several years before the pagan symbols disappeared. Sunday did not become a public holiday until 321, and even then it coincided with popular worship of the sun, a kind of nature monotheism. Finally, even though his mother was a Christian, Constantine himself was not baptized until he was on his deathbed. On the other hand, defenders of his sincerity argue that baptism in his day was understood to bring about a total cleansing from sin that guaranteed salvation: therefore it was typically postponed until the last moment, so that the dying person would enter heaven with the cleanest slate possible.

Whatever his religious motives, Constantine must have been a shrewd enough politician to recognize that the Church as an institution had the potential to serve as a much-needed stabilizing force. The Church was dispersed throughout the empire. It had developed a system of regional government in which local dioceses operated under the supervision of bishops. In response to doctrinal challenges, it seemed to be developing a coherent set of teachings. It had remarkable discipline, both institutional and personal. And—with the exception of the martyrs, whose courage in the Great Persecution was fresh in memory—Christians conformed to imperial policy.

Still, Christianity did not replace paganism overnight. The etymology of the word 'pagan'—from the Latin for 'rural'—hints at the process: Christianity spread in the towns and along the trade routes, while people in more remote areas continued to follow the old ways. (Similarly, the word 'heathen' came from 'heath', meaning a wasteland or wilderness.) The emperor Julian (r. 361–3) even attempted (unsuccessfully) to bring back pagan worship and teaching, though he stopped short of resuming the persecution of Christians. It was only with Theodosius I (r. 379–95) that the empire became officially Christian.

The consequences of official establishment were far-reaching. No longer did Christians risk losing their livelihoods, or even their lives, by associating with the Church; now Church membership was, if anything, a way to get ahead. In time, it became the normal practice to baptize infants and young children; parents undertook to raise their offspring in the faith, and sometimes additional baptismal sponsors, known as godparents, were recruited from outside the family. No longer were bishops chosen and doctrines determined by the Church alone; now rulers oversaw the appointment of bishops and convoked councils.

Creeds and the Trinity

The Church began composing **creeds**—statements of the content of Christian faith—very early in its history. Especially before Constantine put an end to the policy of persecution, such statements served as tests of the seriousness and commitment of individuals joining the movement. The importance attributed to creeds (from the Latin meaning 'belief') has had a lasting influence on Christians' understanding both of themselves and of others. Because they define themselves as people who believe such-and-such about Jesus or about God and the world, they have—often mistakenly—expected other traditions to define themselves in terms of belief as well.

Perhaps as early as 150 but certainly by the early third century, a formulation known as the Apostles' Creed was coming into use, especially in the Latin-speaking western part of the Mediterranean. Although it is named after the first generation of Christians, we have no historical evidence that this formulation was used at their time (if it had been used, it ought to be present in Eastern Christianity to a degree that it is not). But the ascription of this creed to the first Christian generation clearly represents a claim of authority and legitimacy for it. It is frequently recited by congregations in services of worship:

> I believe in God, the Father almighty, maker of heaven and earth; and in Jesus Christ his only Son our Lord, who was conceived by the Holy Spirit, born of the Virgin Mary, suffered under Pontius Pilate, was crucified, dead, and buried. He descended into hell; the third day he rose again from the dead; he ascended into heaven, and sits on the right hand of God the Father almighty; from thence he shall come to judge the living and the dead. I believe in the Holy Spirit; the holy catholic church; the communion of saints; the forgiveness of sins; the resurrection of the body; and the life everlasting.

The other well-known ancient formulation is the Nicene Creed, named for the Council of Nicaea in 325 but ratified in its present form in 381. Somewhat longer than the Apostles' Creed, it covers

The Nicene Creed

We believe in one God, the Father almighty, maker of heaven and earth, and of all things visible and invisible; and in one Lord Jesus Christ, the only-begotten Son of God, begotten of the Father before all worlds, God of God, light of light, very God of very God, begotten not made, being of one substance with the Father, by whom all things were made, who for us men and for our salvation came down from heaven, and was incarnate by the Holy Spirit of the Virgin Mary, and was made man, and was crucified for us under Pontius Pilate. He suffered and was buried, and the third day he rose again according to the scriptures, and ascended into heaven, and sits on the right hand of the Father, and he shall come again with glory to judge both the living and the dead; whose kingdom shall have no end. And we believe in the Holy Spirit, the Lord and giver of life, who proceeds from the Father (and the Son), who with the Father and Son together is worshipped and glorified, who spoke by the prophets. And we believe in one holy catholic and apostolic church. We acknowledge one baptism for the remission of sins. And we look for the resurrection of the dead, and the life of the world to come.

many of the same topics in more detail and is a regular part of services in the Catholic tradition.

Comparing these two texts, we see that the Nicene Creed is more specific about the Holy Spirit and more inclined to mention the Spirit along with God the father and Christ the son as part of a triadic list. These differences reflect the emergence of the explicit doctrine of the Trinity, a central Christian teaching—and a problematical one. Because it is rooted in the monotheistic Judaic tradition, Christianity has resisted asserting a plurality of distinct gods, but it has wanted to recognize a plurality of divine 'persons' or divine manifestations.

Christians today often assume that the doctrine of the Trinity has been present in their tradition from the very beginning, almost as though it had been ordained by God from the foundation of the world. But in fact the Trinity as such is hardly mentioned in the New Testament. The text occasionally speaks of God as father, of Jesus as son, and of God's spirit, but almost nowhere does it put the three together in an explicit list. A passage in

Matthew (28: 19) refers to baptism in the name of the Father, Son, and Holy Spirit, but some scholars believe it to be a late addition. It took the Church several centuries to arrive at a doctrine that would hold the three in balance while preserving the principle of monotheism.

The discussions that took place over that time were similar to the preliminary stages in any research project. At stake was the relationship among the three divine 'persons' or manifestations: God as heavenly father and creator, Jesus as son and redeemer, and the Holy Spirit as a continuing source of inspiration, guidance, and comfort. The theologian Origen (c. 185–c. 254) of Alexandria wrote: 'With regard to the Holy Spirit it is not yet clearly known whether he is to be thought of as begotten or unbegotten, or as being himself a Son of God or not, but these are matters which we must investigate to the best of our power from holy scripture' (Stevenson 1957: 213).

The emerging doctrine of the Trinity dominated discussion in the early fourth century. The early theologians' preoccupation with theoretical distinctions may seem excessive today, but at the time, when Christianity was emerging as the empire's establishment religion, doctrine was a highly political matter. Doctrinal issues were rallying points around which rivalries for Church leadership crystallized. The problem was not so much that the differences between competing views were unbridgeable as that the people involved were unwilling to bridge them.

Because of the political implications, the public was intensely interested in theological issues. The climate in the new capital, Constantinople, was portrayed by one fourth-century bishop as follows:

> If in this city you ask anyone for change, he will discuss with you whether God the Son is begotten or unbegotten. If you ask whether the bread is any good, you will receive the answer that 'God the Father is greater, God the Son is less.' If you say that you need a bath, you will be told that 'there was nothing before God the Son was created' (adapted from Frend 1965: 186–7).

In a time when doctrine is still developing, **orthodoxy**—'right teaching'—does not exist: it can be identified only in retrospect, once we know which view prevailed. Orthodoxy is the consensus that can be affirmed—with the wisdom of hindsight—as having been intended all along.

By the same token, an idea that was generally accepted at one moment might well be heresy a few years later. Around the year 260, Paul of Samosata (a town now in eastern Turkey) was chosen bishop of Antioch, partly because of his theological acumen. He had a binitarian theology of God as father and son. He described God as father, wisdom, and Word, and believed that the Word rested on, but was not identical with, Jesus. But Trinitarian theology was developing, and in 268 the very views that had favoured his appointment were condemned as heretical: accordingly, he was deposed.

In the early fourth century, a priest named Arius (c. 250–c. 336) was put in charge of a major church in Alexandria, Egypt. Likely taking his cue from the prologue to *John*, which seems to suggest that God and the Word (*logos*, here identified with Christ), were distinct, Arius proposed that the son of God was not eternal, but was created within time by the father as part of the creation of the world; in other words, 'there was an existence when the Son was not'. This meant that the son was not eternal by nature, but was subject to change. Another Alexandrian, however, took the opposite view. Athanasius (c. 296–373) asserted the coeternity and coequality of father and son, underlining the power of the son to be a saviour.

Constantine, hoping that a unified Church would promote stability in his empire, called a meeting of the bishops in Nicaea, not far from Constantinople, in 325. The dispute between Arius and Athanasius was part of the agenda, and the decision went against Arius. But the matter was not laid to rest. Arian views continued to attract support, and they continued to surface in various compromise formulas for half a century before they were definitively rejected under the emperor Theodosius I at the Council of Constantinople in 381. Although Arianism survived for a while among the Teutonic tribes beyond its northern boundary of the empire, where it was carried by a Gothic-born missionary named Ulfilas, its influence came to an end with the conversion of the Teutonic Franks to Catholicism in 495.

Meanwhile, no sooner had the dust settled on the debate over the Trinity in 381 than a corollary to Athanasius' position cried out for attention. If, as the new orthodoxy had it, the eternal son was coequal with the father, then how did the eternal divinity of Jesus relate to his historical humanity? Trinitarian doctrine had preoccupied the fourth century; Christological doctrine—doctrine regarding the incarnation of God in Christ—was to become the obsession of the fifth.

Regional divisions developed around three positions on this question. The incarnate Christ could be

- two separate persons, one divine and one human (as the **Nestorian churches**, stretching eastward across Asia, believed);
- one person, with only a divine nature (as the **Monophysites**, from Ethiopia and Egypt to Syria and Armenia, believed); or
- one person, but with both a divine nature and a human nature (as the Greek- and Latin-speaking churches believed).

Each of these positions has continued to find adherents, from the fifth century to the present day.

DIFFERENTIATION

Despite the many controversial issues of the early centuries—Christianity's relationship to Jewish scripture and law, the divine versus human nature of Jesus, the trinitarian understanding of God—the majority of Christians had remained members of a single 'catholic' (universal) church. Gradually, though, the divisions became more serious, and they involved growing numbers of Christians.

Alexandrian versus Antiochene Christology

The split that produced the Nestorian churches was the result in part of political rivalry and in part of a doctrinal dispute between theologians in Alexandria in Egypt and others in Antioch in Syria. The Alexandrians, such as Cyril (d. 444), understood Christ in terms reminiscent of the prologue to *John*: the eternal *logos* or Word was incarnated in the human person of Jesus, and therefore experienced all the changes that he did: birth, the gaining of wisdom, suffering, death.

By contrast, the Antiochenes, such as Theodore of Mopsuestia (in what is today southern Turkey; c. 350–428), argued that the *logos* was an entity distinct from the human Jesus, over whom it exercised a controlling influence. These differences came to a head when the theologians tried to define the status of Mary, the mother of Jesus. For the Alexandrians, Mary was the *theotokos* (in Greek, 'bearer of God'). But for the Antiochenes, she was the *christotokos* ('bearer of Christ'): the mother of the man Jesus but not of the eternal son of God. What was at stake here was not merely doctrine; the allegiance of popular devotion was at stake if one sided with Antioch against the Alexandrian *theotokos* concept.

Nestorianism

Politically, the rivalry was between Cyril, the patriarch of Alexandria, and Nestorius (d. 451), patriarch of Constantinople. (Although Nestorianism was named after him, he was more a sponsor than an author of the Antiochene position.) Soon after his appointment in 428, Nestorius caused a furor by supporting the Antiochenes who rejected the view of Mary as the mother of God. Within three years, at the Council of Ephesus in 431, he was deposed; in 435 the emperor Theodosius II, who had appointed him bishop, condemned his writings; and the following year nestorius was banished to a monastery in southern Egypt.

Despite the victory of the Alexandrians, Nestorian Christianity persisted in the east, eventually spreading from its centre in northeastern Syria (today in southeastern Turkey) across central Asia as far as western China and the southwestern coast of India.

The Monophysites

After the Council of Ephesus in 431, the doctrinal pendulum swung towards the position of Cyril of Alexandria. A key figure in this development was Eutyches, who headed a large monastery near Constantinople and had influential connections at the court of Theodosius II. Eutyches taught that

Map 4.1   Christianity: Major Spheres of Influence

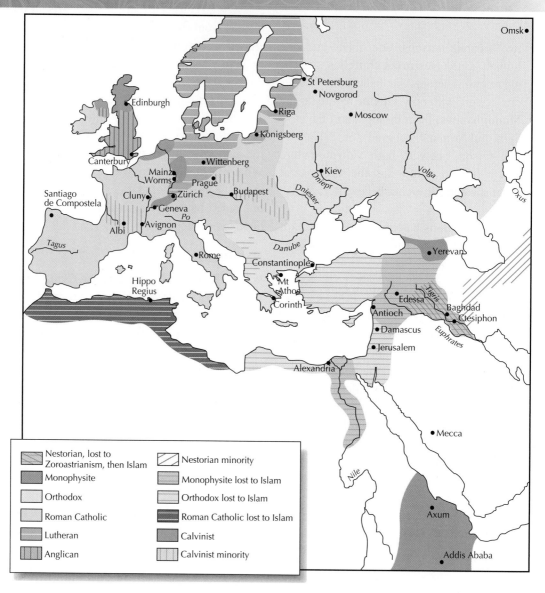

Legend:

- Nestorian, lost to Zoroastrianism, then Islam
- Monophysite
- Orthodox
- Roman Catholic
- Lutheran
- Anglican
- Nestorian minority
- Monophysite lost to Islam
- Orthodox lost to Islam
- Roman Catholic lost to Islam
- Calvinist
- Calvinist minority

with the union of the divine and the human in Jesus the human was fully absorbed into or replaced by the divine. Thus Christ had only one *phusis* (Greek, 'nature')—hence the term 'monophysite'.

In 448 Eutyches was summoned by the pro-Antiochene patriarch to a synod (gathering) of bishops in Constantinople, where he was condemned and deposed for not acknowledging two natures in Christ. By the following year, however, that patriarch had been replaced by a supporter of the Alexandrian position, who convoked what has been called the 'Robber Synod' to reverse the previous year's actions and condemn Eutyches' opponents instead. Then in 450 Theodosius II died. With the loss of imperial favour, Eutyches was expelled from his monastery, and when the new

Christianity in Egypt, Ethiopia, and Armenia

The indigenous Christians of Egypt, the Copts, believe that their faith was taken to Egypt by the gospel writer Mark, and that their ancestors were pioneers, with Anthony, in the development of monasticism. After the Islamic conquest in the seventh century, Egyptians who remained Christian were a minority, but a significant one. The Copts have retained a sense of cultural pride as 'original' Egyptians.

By the fourth century, Coptic Christian influence had extended to Ethiopia. A few centuries later, Ethiopia gave asylum to Muslim emigrants, but it was not subjugated by Islam. It remained Christian, recognizing the authority of the Coptic patriarch in Cairo and maintaining a window on the world through its own priests and monks in Jerusalem. The Ethiopian church has remained essentially Coptic, though it has been formally independent of Cairo since the mid-twentieth century.

In Armenia as in Egypt, legend traces the introduction of Christianity to the missionary activity of the apostles, in this case Thaddeus and Bartholomew. Armenian Christians maintain that their king Tiridates III, who was baptized by Gregory the Illuminator around 301, was the first ruler anywhere to establish Christianity as a state religion.

regime convoked a council at nearby Chalcedon in 451, it repudiated both Eutyches' views and the actions of the Robber Synod, while reconfirming the rejection of Nestorianism in the opposite direction.

The formula produced at Chalcedon steered a middle course between the Nestorians, who compromised the eternal deity of Jesus, and the Monophysites, who compromised his humanity, asserting that the incarnate Christ was one person

The Major Branches of Christianity

Nestorians (about 200,000)
   'Assyrians' of Iraq, Iran, and Turkey
   Nestorian Malabar Christians in India
Monophysites (about 30 million)
   Copts in Egypt
   Ethiopians
   Jacobites or Syrian Orthodox
   Jacobite Malabar Christians in India
   Armenians
Orthodox (at least 150 million)
   Greek
   Bulgarian, Serbian, and Romanian
   Russian and Ukrainian
Catholics (about 900 million)
   Roman Catholics
   Eastern 'Uniate' churches
   (some Anglicans)

Protestants (about 400 million)
   Sixteenth-century divisions
      Lutherans
      Anglicans
      Reformed (Presbyterian) churches
      Anabaptists
      Unitarians
   Seventeenth- and eighteenth-century divisions
      Congregationalists
      Baptists
      Quakers
      Methodists
   Nineteenth-century divisions
      Disciples
      Seventh-Day Adventists
      Jehovah's Witnesses
      Christian Scientists
      Mormons

with both a divine and a human nature. It was acceptable to both the Greek Church in Constantinople and the Latin Church in Rome. But it did not sit well with everyone. During the reign of Justinian (r. 527–65), Christians in three Eastern regions separated themselves from Constantinople. These were the Coptic Christians of Egypt and Ethiopia, the Jacobites of Syria, and the Armenians. All these branches survive to the present day.

Jacobites (Syrian Orthodox)

In Syria, where Antiochene theology and Nestorianism had been strong, Monophysite teachings were promoted in the sixth century through the vigorous activity of a missionary named Jacob, who was nicknamed Baradae ('ragged') because he disguised himself as a beggar to avoid arrest. From Constantinople to Egypt to the frontier of the Persian Empire, Jacob established congregations and organized a hierarchy. The surviving Syrian Orthodox Church, which is Monophysite, calls itself Jacobite in acknowledgement of his influence.

Like the Nestorians, Syrian Monophysites spread their teaching to the Malabar Coast of southwestern India, where it has survived. A Jacobite reform offshoot of 1836, influenced by British missionaries, called itself Mar Thoma (St Thomas) Church because legend says that the apostle Thomas took Christianity to India.

The Greek Orthodox Tradition

The councils of Nicaea in 325, Constantinople in 381, Ephesus in 431, and Chalcedon in 451 are called 'ecumenical', from a Greek word meaning 'world-wide', because they were accepted by both the Eastern Orthodox and Western Catholic branches of Christianity as part of their respective official histories. Partly because of its location, the fourth and last of them, the Council of Chalcedon, was composed almost entirely of Eastern bishops, but in response to the Monophysite challenge it arrived at a formula that was acceptable to Rome as well as Constantinople. Its declaration reads, in part:

> . . . our Lord Jesus Christ, the same perfect in godhead and perfect in manhood; truly God and at the same time truly man of a reasonable soul and a body; consubstantial with the Father according to his godhead, and consubstantial with us according to his manhood, in all things like unto us apart from sin; begotten before all worlds (ages), of the Father according to his godhead, and also in these latter days, on account of us and our salvation, of the virgin Mary, the Mother of God, according to his manhood.

This position, that the incarnate Christ was one person with both a divine and a human nature, still left plenty of room for debate. Chalcedon did not attempt to arrive at a final resolution—only to establish the acceptable limits of debate.

And the debate was certainly not over. In the early seventh century, there was what amounted to a rerun of the Monophysite controversy. In an attempt to win back the Monophysite Christians to the east, it was proposed that Christ had two natures, divine and human, but only one mode of activity (*energia*) or will (*thelema*); hence the name Monothelite for this view. But this effort was repudiated before the end of the century, and by then much of the Monophysite world was converting to Islam in any case. The main portion of the empire in the eastern Mediterranean remained orthodox within the terms of Chalcedon's doctrinal formulation. The Greek-speaking Byzantine (or Eastern Roman) Empire was a comparatively stable and prosperous region in the seventh and eighth centuries, and therefore far more conducive to intellectual life than its Latin-speaking Western counterpart, which was still struggling after the barbarian invasions. Byzantium lasted more than a thousand years after Constantine. Even the slow but steady spread of the Turks, who took control of Constantinople in 1453, did not mean the end of the Greek Church. Formally tolerated under Islam, though now forbidden to proselytize, the Byzantine Church became a self-governing religious community under the Ottoman Turks, with the patriarch as its civil ruler. Greece gained its independence from Turkey in a rebellion that began in 1821, but Constantinople (renamed Istanbul by its new rulers) has remained Turkish.

Characteristic of Byzantium and also of the other Orthodox traditions is a close association of religion with the ruling regime and the national language. Historians refer to the involvement of the emperors in the affairs of the Church as 'caesaropapism', and Orthodox Christianity displayed a number of other features that could be described as imperial.

Theology

Representative of the eastern Mediterranean's cultural sophistication in that age was the Greek theologian John of Damascus (c. 675–c. 749), who for a time followed in his father's footsteps as the representative of the Christians to the Muslim caliph. His major work, *Pege gnoseos* ('Fountain of Wisdom'), is a comprehensive treatise on theological topics.

Medieval Byzantine theology included a rich vein of devotional practice and **mysticism**. Simeon (949–1022), who headed a monastery in Constantinople, wrote of the profundities of the spiritual life. A pervasive theme in his work is God's closeness to the faithful:

> I know that the Immovable comes down;
> I know that the Invisible appears to me;
> I know that he who is far outside the
>   whole creation
> Takes me into himself and hides me in his
>   arms.
>   . . .
> I know that I shall not die, for I am within
>   the Life,
> I have the whole of Life springing up as a
>   fountain within me.
> He is my heart, he is in heaven
>   (McManners 1990: 147–8).

By the fourteenth century a group calling themselves the Hesychasts (from a Greek word meaning 'inner stillness') had developed a devotional practice centred on repetition of a mantra-like formula known as the Jesus Prayer: 'Lord Jesus Christ, son of God, have mercy on me, a sinner.' When their practical spiritual discipline was challenged by Barlaam the Calabrian, a philosopher who held that one could know God directly only in the next life, another great Byzantine theologian came to their defence. Gregory Palamas distinguished between God's essence and his energies, agreeing with Barlaam that God transcends this realm, but arguing that God's energies come through to humans like the radiance of the transfigured Christ described in *Mark* 9 and *Matthew* 17. Palamas held divine transcendence and divine contact with humans in balance: 'He is being and not being; he is everywhere and nowhere; he has many names and cannot be named; he is both in perpetual movement and immovable; he is absolutely everything and nothing of that which is' (Meyendorff 1964: 209).

Christianizing the Slavs

Eastern Orthodoxy is the name used to refer to the form of Christianity that was carried from Byzantium to various peoples in eastern Europe. In the ninth century, Orthodox missionaries to the Slavic peoples made significant headway. Language played an important part in their success, for they used local vernaculars rather than Greek, and this encouraged the development of independent local churches with a strong sense of national identity based on language.

This missionary effort was pioneered by two brothers, Cyril (826–69) and Methodius (c. 815–85). In 862 they travelled to Moravia (the region of today's Czech Republic), where they preached in the vernacular and produced translations of the Bible and the liturgy into Slavonic. When, after Cyril's time, a new alphabet (based on the Greek) was created for Slavic languages such as Bulgarian, Serbian, Ukrainian, and Russian, it was named Cyrillic in his honour. Romania, which was originally colonized by Rome as the province of Dacia, was Christian from the fourth century and adopted the Latin alphabet, but its church was eventually brought into the Eastern Orthodox orbit during a period of Bulgarian rule.

Other parts of eastern Europe were converted by Roman Catholic missionaries, who instituted a Latin liturgy and more centralized Church control. Thus the languages of the mainly Catholic peoples such as the Croats, Slovenes, Czechs, Slovaks, Poles, Lithuanians, and Hungarians use the Latin alphabet. The early centre of Russian Orthodoxy was Kiev, in Ukraine, whose pagan ruler Vladimir apparently converted in order to marry the sister of the Byzantine emperor and thereby form an advantageous alliance. Whatever his motives, he became a vigorous promoter of Christianity, though it seems the methods he used among his subjects may have been more coercive than persuasive. It was only after Kiev fell to Mongol invaders in 1237 that Moscow replaced it as the centre of Russian religion and politics. Russian ecclesiastical and diplomatic interests coincided in the nineteenth century when, as part of its effort to establish a presence in the Holy Land, Moscow established churches and convents while strengthening diplomatic ties with the Turkish Empire. Likewise, Russian political expansion in Siberia was aided by missionaries to the indigenous peoples of the region. From 1917 to 1989 the communist state was hostile to religion of any kind. But Christianity survived, often transmitted from grandmother to grandchild. After 1989, the Russian Orthodox Church slowly reasserted its traditional role as the church favoured by the state, while Catholics and Protestants were allowed more freedom. Since the late 1990s, however, the state has been less than welcoming to foreign missionaries. A 2006 law brought the bank accounts of foreign-backed organizations under scrutiny, in effect cutting off most outside support for missionary work in Russia. In protest against the Catholic Church's 'expansionism', the Russian Orthodox Patriarch Alexy II refused to meet with Pope Benedict XVI during his 2007 trip to Russia. Protestants find their religious life even more restricted in the former Soviet republics of Belarus and Uzbekistan.

Secular Yugoslavia disintegrated in the 1990s into religio-ethnic strife among Catholic Croats, Muslim Bosnians and Albanians, and Orthodox Serbs. Today the leadership of the Serbian Orthodox Church continues to espouse Serbian nationalist policies, while the civil government wants good relations with its neighbours and closer integration with the European Union. To appease the influential Orthodox clergy, the Serbian government has introduced religious instruction in the school system, by Orthodox priests or others they approve. In 2006 a law was passed to return the properties of all religious communities previously nationalized under the Nazi or Communist regimes. The Jewish community alone has requested the denationalization of more than 500 properties confiscated during the Nazi period. So far, however, only the Orthodox Church has regained possession of its properties.

Constantinople and Rome

After the Council of Chalcedon, Greek and Latin Christianity grew further and further apart. The underlying reasons probably had more to do with politics and cultural differences, but once again a theological formulation provided a rallying point. At issue was a single word, *filioque* (Latin, 'and from the son'). Did the Holy Spirit 'proceed' from God the father, as the Greek Church had it in the Nicene Creed, or from the father and the son, as the Latin Church came to maintain? Photius, the patriarch of Constantinople, in 867 denounced both the intrusion of Latin missionaries into Bulgaria, which he took to be Greek territory, and the insertion of *filioque* into the creed. For the next two decades, one party in Constantinople repudiated the term and condemned the **pope**, while its opponents supported the term and condemned Photius.

Behind the theological niceties lay the basic issue of authority, for Rome had added *filioque* to the creed without the consent of a universal Church council. In so doing, it had staked its claim to be the centre of authority against the Greek view of Rome as just one among five equally important patriarchates, and the Roman notion of papal authority against the Greek understanding of authority as vested in councils of bishops. The final break between Rome and Constantinople is conventionally dated to 1054, though it was in the making before then and attempts were made after that date to heal it.

Unlike the Roman Catholic Church, the Orthodox Church venerated **icons**, refused to include *filioque* in the creed, permitted its clergy to marry, used languages other than Latin in Bible readings and the liturgy, and—most important—refused to recognize the supremacy of the Roman pontiff.

Eastern-rite Catholic Churches

Rome's efforts to recruit new adherents among Eastern Orthodox Christians led to the formation of new churches that, even though they were aligned with Rome rather than Constantinople, retained important elements of the Eastern tradition, from the use of local languages (rather than Latin) to immersion baptism. Significantly, they also continued to have married priests, although their higher ecclesiastical officers were generally drawn from the celibate clergy. Since most of the Eastern Catholic churches had Orthodox roots, most of them continue to have Orthodox counterparts today. The exception is the Maronite Church of Lebanon. Named after its fifth-century founder Maron, it has always been part of the Roman Catholic rather than the Orthodox world.

The Latin Tradition

The Papacy

The Church centred in Rome thought of itself as 'catholic', that is, universal. Its interaction with political regimes in the Latin world (the western

Mediterranean and northern Europe) produced the synthesis of religion, culture, and governmental and social structure often referred to as Christendom (the 'domain' of Christianity).

The bishop of Rome had unchallenged ecclesiastical authority in the Latin-speaking West of the empire (as did his Orthodox counterpart in the East). His office was particularly important in part because Rome was the capital of the empire, and in part because of the city's connection with St Peter—the 'rock' on which Jesus was supposed (in *Matthew* 16: 18) to have said he would build his church. Rome was believed to have been the site of Peter's martyrdom, and its bishops traced their institutional lineage to him. By the third century the bishops of Rome, who were called popes (from *papa*, 'father'), were claiming theological primacy as the successors of Peter, and their practical influence in matters of government increased dramatically after the fifth century, when government in the western part of the empire collapsed under the pressure of Germanic invasions. In those chaotic times, the Church was the principal source of organization and continuity. Culturally and religiously, Latin Christianity conquered the populations that were the military victors over Rome.

Augustine

In Constantine's century, Latin-speaking Christians in the western Mediterranean generally shared the doctrines approved by the councils held in the Greek-speaking East. But in the course of time the Latin theologians went their own way. The dominant issue in the East was the nature of divinity in God and Christ, while in the West it was human sinfulness and the possibility of divine redemption.

A landmark figure in this development was Aurelius Augustine (354–430), who was born in what is now Algeria. In his dramatic and passionate life, several currents flow together. He had a pagan father, and studied classical philosophy and rhetoric as well as Neoplatonism, the mystical interpretation of Plato's philosophy. His mother, Monica, had attempted to raise him as a sincere Christian, but he sowed his wild oats in his student years, even having a child with his common-law companion. Between the ages of twenty and thirty he was a Manichaean, but after a vivid conversion experience he returned to the Christian faith in a far more sophisticated form than the one in which he had been raised. He became a priest and a prolific theological writer, and as bishop of Hippo, in North Africa, campaigned actively against heresy.

The questions that had preoccupied Augustine while he was a Manichaean—the struggle between good and evil, spirit and matter, the tension between the spiritual and the carnal—remained in his Christian writing. His ideas shaped medieval Christianity's view of the human self and personality as dependent on God, and his sense of guilt concerning the body's appetites was reflected in the medieval Church's central concern with liberation from sin.

Augustine's best-known work is probably his *Confessions*. Relating his own spiritual struggles, the tension between his conscience and his will, he tells how he came to the Christian faith, and explains how it is in principle possible for anyone to follow the same path to faith in the goodness of God.

It is characteristic of Augustine, after reasoning his way through to a logical conclusion, to show that this conclusion accords with a text from the Bible. This approach set the pattern for much medieval Christian philosophy. In keeping with its role as the 'handmaid of theology', it attempted to show revelation, authority, and faith to be reasonable, and to spell out their consequences.

A famous theological dispute arose between Augustine and a British monk named Pelagius, who encountered Augustine's views in Rome and disagreed. The theological question at issue in the 'faith versus works' debate was how salvation is achieved. Augustine followed Paul in insisting that the only way to salvation was through faith in the grace of God. Pelagius, however, took Jesus' words 'Be therefore perfect as your heavenly father is perfect' to mean that humans could achieve such perfection through their own moral efforts, their 'works'. Pelagius did not actually deny the grace of God, but his critics, including Augustine, charged that he did not give adequate recognition to the role that divine grace plays in overcoming human frailty.

Perhaps Augustine's most influential work was *The City of God*: a monumental theology of history, from biblical to Roman civilization. His thesis is that culture and institutions, even those of the Roman Empire itself, are of no enduring value in the sight of God. The earthly city, with all its

Augustine's Conversion

The quotation at the end of this extract comes from Paul's letter to the Romans:

I was greatly disturbed in spirit, angry at myself with a turbulent indignation because I had not entered thy will and covenant, O my God, while all my bones cried out to me to enter. . . . It was I who willed and I who was also unwilling. In either case, it was I. . . . Suddenly I heard the voice of a boy or a girl—I know not which—coming from the neighbouring house, chanting over and over again, 'Pick it up, read it.' . . . In silence I read the paragraph on which my eyes first fell: 'Not in revelling and drunkenness, not in lust and wantonness, not in quarrels and rivalries. Rather, arm yourselves with the Lord, Jesus Christ; spend no more thought on nature and nature's appetites' (Outler 1955: 170–6).

Pope Gregory I

A remarkable leader, Pope Gregory I 'the Great' (r. 590–604) performed ecclesiastical and imperial administrative duties simultaneously. His reputation was such that the collecting and editing of a repertory of ancient musical melodies, which took place after his death, in the seventh and eighth centuries, was attributed to him. It included over 600 compositions for various parts of the **mass**. Gregorian chant was not the only such collection, but it was the most influential religious source for the later development of European music. The term 'Gregorian' applied to the calendar, however, denotes another Gregory a thousand years later. In 1582, an adjustment under Pope Gregory XIII set the calendar of western Europe ten days ahead of the Julian calendar, which continued to be used by the Orthodox churches.

sins, is part of the divine plan; its kings are divine representatives and rule by divine mandate. But humans must in the end flee the earthly for the heavenly city, to join the community to whom God has promised salvation. The Church both symbolizes this city of God and is the means of reaching it. Christian political theory is based on Augustine in that it sees the Church as transcending the state.

Medieval Christianity

The Middle Ages are generally considered to stretch from the collapse of the Western Roman Empire, around 500, to the beginning of the Renaissance, around 1500. It was during this period that many Christian doctrines and practices became established.

The Monastic Life

Monastic communities developed a highly structured religious discipline in the medieval period. There were all-male communities of monks and all-female communities of nuns. Members of a community were required to make solemn vows of poverty, chastity, and obedience, to stay within the physical precincts of the community, and to follow the community's 'rule' (its code of discipline or body of regulations).

Monks played an important part in both the Greek and Latin traditions. Technically, since monasticism had begun as an alternative to established

religion, monks were laymen rather than priests, but a demanding schedule of prayer and worship was central to their practice. A distinction was drawn between 'religious' (or 'regular') clergy, who followed a monastic rule, and 'secular' clergy, who worked in the world and in the Greek Church (unlike the Roman) were permitted to marry. (Members of ecclesiastical hierarchy were always celibate, however.) An important centre of Byzantine spirituality is Mount Athos, a peninsula in northern Greece that projects into the Aegean Sea. It is dotted by twenty monasteries founded at different times over the last thousand years. The entire peninsula is a preserve of male monks, and no woman is permitted to set foot there.

Monastic Discipline

The Rule of St Benedict is fundamental to monastic discipline. Benedict (c. 480–550) came from Nursia, east of Assisi in Italy. In about 529, he moved with a small band of monks to Monte Cassino, a summit overlooking the route between Rome and Naples. The instructions that he put in place covered every aspect of communal religious life, from spiritual discipline to economic self-sufficiency. Benedict's sister, Scholastica, established a convent for women nearby, and other self-governing monasteries based on Benedict's rule were founded across western Europe.

Daily living in the Middle Ages took a great deal of work, for those inside religious communities no

From the Rule of St Benedict

The regulations that Benedict established in the first half of the sixth century became the model for many other religious communities.

XXIII. *Of excommunication for faults.* If a brother be found contumacious or disobedient, proud or a grumbler, or in any way acting contrary to the holy Rule and despising the orders of his seniors, let him, according to the Lord's commandment, be privately admonished once and twice by his seniors. If he do not then amend, let him be publicly rebuked before all. But if even then he do not correct himself, let him be subjected to excommunication, if he understands the gravity of this penalty. If, however, he is incorrigible, let him undergo corporal chastisement.

XXXIV. *Of the extent of excommunication.* The extent of the excommunication or discipline is to be regulated according to the gravity of the fault; and this is to be decided by the abbot's discretion. If a brother be found guilty of a lighter fault, he shall be excluded from the common table; he shall also intone neither psalm nor antiphon in the oratory, or read a lesson, until he has atoned. He shall take his meals alone, after those of the brethren; if, for example, the brothers have their meal at the sixth hour, he shall have his at the ninth. . . .

XXXIII. *Whether the monks should have anything of their own.* More than any thing else is this vice of property to be cut off root and branch from the monastery. Let no one presume to give or receive anything without the leave of the abbot, or to retain anything as his own. He should have nothing at all: neither a book, nor tablets, nor a pen—nothing at all. For indeed it is not allowed to the monks to have bodies or wills in their own power. But for all things necessary they must look to the Father of the monastery; nor is it allowable to have anything which the abbot has not given or permitted. All things shall be common to all, as it is written: 'Let not any man presume or call anything his own' [*Acts* 4: 32] (Bettenson 1967: 118, 120).

less than for those outside. Monasteries and convents had to support themselves, often through the sale of the products of their own fields and vineyards; thus physical labour was an integral part of any community's rule.

Monks and nuns were also required to attend prayer services at specified hours throughout the day, and most were expected to engage in serious study of the scriptures. In fact, the medieval monasteries played a crucial role as cultural custodians, for their scholars and libraries together preserved much ancient learning that might have otherwise been lost.

By the tenth century, however, many monasteries were attracting criticism for their worldliness.

Some were effectively under the control of the local feudal authorities on whose support they depended; large donations of land and other bequests had made some of them wealthy; and the manual tasks that had once been an integral part of monastic discipline were increasingly performed by servants or serfs.

Cluniac Fathers

Founded in 910 by William the Pious, Duke of Aquitaine, the monastery at Cluny, north of Lyon in France, became the centre of a movement to reform monasticism by bringing its institutions under the control of religious rather than secular authorities. Over the next two and a half centuries, the Cluniac order established a network of more than 300 satellite houses across Europe. Like the Church itself in Constantine's day, the order served as a stabilizing influence at a time of political fragmentation and turbulence.

Cistercians

Within a century of its founding, however, Cluny itself was growing rich. Robert of Molesmes responded in 1098 by founding an austere new order at Cîteaux, north of Cluny near Dijon. The Cistercians (from the Latin for Cîteaux) wore simple undyed wool habits, ate no meat, and worshipped in sparsely decorated churches. Within a century there were 500 Cistercian abbeys. Though the Cistercians had refused lavish endowments, rising land values in the more marginal areas where they established themselves eventually made their order wealthy too.

One group of Cistercians in particular became known for their rule of silence. The Cistercians of the Strict Observance, or Trappists, were founded in the 1600s by Armand de Rancé, abbot of the monastery of La Trappe in Normandy. The best known Trappist in the twentieth century was the mystic Thomas Merton (1915–68), who became interested in Asian spirituality, especially Zen Buddhism, and was active in social protest in the 1960s.

Other Cistercians helped to found spiritual orders of knights such as the Knights Templar, the Knights of St John, and the twelfth-century Teutonic order. Their members made pilgrimages to the Holy Land and took as their biblical model the Maccabees, the Jewish patriots of the second century BCE.

Carthusians

Also influenced by Robert was a German named Bruno, who turned to the religious life in his mid-forties and followed Robert's spiritual direction before founding his own order in 1084. The Carthusian order (named after its base at La Grande Chartreuse, near Grenoble in France), it too demanded a vow of silence and considerable austerity from its members. Like the Benedictine abbey of Fécamp, near the English Channel, the Chartreuse abbey supported itself in part by making and selling a famous liqueur, in this instance the brilliant green one that gave its name to the colour chartreuse.

Mendicant Orders

The monastic response to the secular world had been to withdraw from it—even if that withdrawal turned out to be more a matter of theory than of practice. With the growth of towns and cities in Europe, however, came a significant new problem: urban poverty. To respond to the needs of the urban poor, a new type of religious order emerged. Instead of turning their backs on the world and withdrawing to monasteries, members of the new **mendicant** orders dedicated themselves to pastoral work, serving the people.

There were mendicant orders for women and laypeople as well as men. Their members—called **friars**, from the Latin *frater* ('brother')—either worked or begged for their living, and were not bound to one convent. In England, the chief mendicant orders were identified by the colour of the mantle worn over the habit or religious uniform.

Franciscans

Francis of Assisi (1182–1226) grew up as the privileged son of a wealthy cloth merchant in central Italy, but a serious illness in his twenties led him to rethink his life. On a pilgrimage to Rome, he was so moved by the beggars outside St Peter's Basilica that he exchanged clothes with one of them and spent the day begging for alms. When he returned to Assisi, he dedicated his life to serving the poor. Gradually attracting a small group of like-minded companions, he established a rule of life emphasizing poverty, which received papal approval in 1209. Within a few years, Clara of Assisi had formed a Franciscan women's order known as the Poor Clares. An offshoot of the Franciscans called the Capuchins drew up their own rule in

The Prayer of St Francis

Although this prayer is not found in the writings of St Francis of Assisi, it has been attributed to him by Franciscan oral tradition.

Lord, make me an instrument of your peace. Where there is hatred let me sow love; where there is injury, pardon; where there is doubt, faith; where there is despair, hope; where there is darkness, light; and where there is sadness, joy.

O divine master, grant that I may not so much seek to be consoled as to console; to be understood as to understand; to be loved as to love. For it is in giving that we receive; it is in pardoning that we are pardoned; and it is in dying that we are born to eternal life.

1529 and are still known today for their soup kitchens, which offer free meals in impoverished neighbourhoods.

In 1224 Francis experienced a vision of an angel from whom he received the 'stigmata': wounds in his own body replicating those suffered by Christ on the cross. Proclaimed a saint in 1228—just two years after his death—he quickly became a beloved figure and the subject of many legends, among them several that emphasized his love of the natural world. In one of the most famous tales, he preaches to a flock of birds, telling them how fortunate they are to be provided for by God.

Dominicans

In 1216–17 a priest from northern Spain named Dominic Guzmán received a papal mandate to establish a preaching order dedicated to combatting the 'Albigensian heresy'. (Named for the city of Albi in southwestern France, Albigensianism was a dualistic doctrine, not unlike Manichaeism, centred on a view of existence as a struggle between light and darkness, and was highly critical of Roman Catholicism.) Dominicans such as

Thomas Aquinas (1225–74) rapidly established their influence as itinerant preachers of doctrine in university towns such as Paris.

St Francis preaching to the birds; a detail from the predella of an altarpiece (c. 1295) depicting the stigmatization by the early Renaissance master Giotto di Bondone (Réunion des Musées Nationaux/Art Resource NY).

Carmelites

The Carmelites, or hermits of Mount Carmel, were organized in Palestine in 1154, during the Crusades, and given a rule by the patriarch of Jerusalem. As the numbers of crusaders in the Holy Land declined, the Carmelites established themselves in Europe and England, where they were termed 'White Friars'.

Celibacy

The insistence that priests be celibate became stronger in the Middle Ages and much stronger in Latin Catholicism than in Greek Orthodoxy. Rationales for priestly celibacy included the spiritual benefit of surmounting worldly desires and the practical benefit of freedom from the responsibilities of marriage and parenthood. In addition, since it made a hereditary priesthood impossible, celibacy worked against the tendency for institutional influence to become concentrated in particular families.

Popes and Princes

From the ninth century onward, popes and princes competed for supremacy. When Charlemagne, king of the Franks, was crowned emperor by Pope Leo III in 800, the Franks considered it an endorsement of their German-based kingdom as heir to the political mantle of Rome (though Voltaire, in the eighteenth century, remarked that this 'Holy Roman Empire' was neither holy, nor Roman, nor an empire.) Later in the ninth century, when Charlemagne's dynasty was faltering and the popes were strong, the Church argued that the coronation illustrated the Church's role as king-maker.

In the tenth century, however, ecclesiastical appointments could be bought and sold; princes could confer the offices of abbots and bishops on their own nominees; and even the bishopric of Rome was increasingly under the influence of princes. In 1046 the German (Holy Roman) emperor Henry III marched into Italy, deposed three rival claimants to the papacy, and imposed his own candidate.

Finally, in 1059, Pope Nicholas II took advantage of a fluid political situation to decree that the selection of popes should be decided by an assembly of cardinals (senior clergy of important churches in Rome). And in 1075, Pope Gregory VII not only issued a decree that threatened excommunication (expulsion from the Church) for any prince who invested anyone with an ecclesiastical office, but declared that the pope could depose emperors.

The dispute continued over the next two centuries, but gradually a rationale for defining the relative spheres of popes and princes was developed. Based on the distinction between temporal and spiritual power drawn by Pope Gelasius in 494, the theory of 'two swords' held that the pope is given both the sword of spiritual power and the sword of temporal power but delegates the temporal to a secular ruler, who is therefore accountable to him. In intellectual arguments in the 1050s, the two sides were making relatively simple claims of possession and scriptural precedent; by 1300 they were disputing political philosophy.

Institutionally as well, the Church grew to resemble the secular states with which it competed. It depended on tax revenues, which it was often unable to collect. It was also subject to coups both from within the Church and from outside. In 1303 Pope Boniface VIII was arrested in his family villa, and in 1309 the French-born Pope Clement decided to move the papal court from Rome to Avignon, in southern France, where it remained until 1377. This period is sometimes referred to as the 'Babylonian captivity' of the papacy.

Just after the return to Rome, the Church was once again plunged into turmoil when a disputed papal election produced two claimants to the papal office. This split in the Church, known as the Great Schism, continued for more than a generation. And although it was resolved in theory in 1414, when the council of bishops meeting at

Constance in southern Germany ruled that the papacy was accountable to assemblies such as itself, this ruling was observed only in the breach until more than a century later. Real power during the fifteenth century was largely in the hands of national rulers in different parts of Europe, and the popes themselves increasingly behaved like Renaissance princes.

The Crusades

The Crusades were a series of military campaigns spanning two centuries, in which Latin Christians from western Europe attempted to recover Jerusalem from Muslim control. Part of the impetus for this effort was a long tradition of pilgrimage to the Holy Land, often undertaken as a penance or in fulfillment of a vow, on the part of western European Christians who were also hoping to acquire sacred relics that could be brought back and placed in churches where they could be venerated by the faithful.

In the course of Islam's expansion across the Middle East, the Arab Muslims had captured Jerusalem in 637. The few local people who remained Christian were formally tolerated, in accordance with Islam's policy regarding its fellow Abrahamic religions, and Christians from outside the Islamic world were still free to make pilgrimages to Jerusalem. In the eleventh century, however, Christian pilgrimages to Jerusalem were interrupted by several events. These included the burning of the Church of the Holy Sepulchre by the mad caliph al-Hakim in 1010 and the capture of Jerusalem in 1071 by the Seljuq Turks, who as recent converts to Islam were less accommodating than the Arabs had been. The Byzantine emperors felt threatened and appealed for Western help.

In 1095, in an eloquent address in Claermont, France, Pope Urban II declared it God's will that Western Christians go to the aid of the Eastern Christians and liberate the holy places of Palestine. Thousands of French, Norman, and Flemish knights responded by 'taking the cross' in a public

act signifying their commitment to the cause. The crusaders won some bloody victories, capturing Antioch and Jerusalem (1099) and even Edessa in northeastern Syria.

To hold on to their conquests, small crusader states were organized along the Syro-Palestinian coast. Among those states was the Latin kingdom of Jerusalem, which the crusaders held for nearly a century. They were driven out, however, by Salah al-Din (Saladin) in 1187.

In response to the crusaders' losses, beginning with the fall of Edessa in 1144, further expeditions set out from Europe, but these later crusades were often unfocussed, distracted by objectives short of Jerusalem. The second crusade, for instance, was diverted in 1148 to the unsuccessful siege of Damascus, a city that had been at peace with the kingdom of Jerusalem. On the third crusade, Richard I ('Lion-hearted') of England took Cyprus from the Byzantines in 1192. Troops of the fourth crusade in 1204, bound for Egypt, went instead to Constantinople, plundered the city, and placed a ruler from Flanders on the throne. The Byzantines recaptured the city in 1261, but relations between Western and Eastern Christians did not recover.

In 1228, the Holy Roman emperor Frederick II negotiated the return to the crusaders of Jerusalem, where he had himself crowned king even though he was under an excommunication order. In 1244, however, Jerusalem was once more lost to the Muslims. The Crusades brought out the best and the worst in the people involved: valour and devotion, but also violence and greed. Too often, a religious project turned into a worldly adventure in which many men found scope for their ambitions as warriors. And the people of Venice, in particular, profited from the opportunity to open trade with the East, as well as the looting of Constantinople in 1204; among the spoils the crusaders brought back to their city were four life-sized bronze horse sculptures that have adorned the basilica of San Marco ever since.

Pope Innocent III condemned the crusaders' attacks on fellow Christians. Yet their successes strengthened papal as well as national authority in Europe. They fired the enthusiasm of many people, inspiring chronicles, poetry, and heroic stories, and they broadened Europe's geographical and intellectual horizons, perhaps even preparing the way for later voyages of exploration. But the Latin states in the Holy Land failed militarily, and the attacks on the Byzantines only deepened the divisions between Eastern and Western Christians. Since the colonial era, Muslims have regarded the crusaders as precursors of Western infiltration and intrusion into the territory of the Middle East.

Sainthood

Over the centuries the Church developed criteria for sainthood (including the performance of attested miracles), a canonical list of saints, and a rigorous procedure for screening new nominees for the title. The first person to become a saint by papal decree was a German bishop, in 993.

The saints, collectively, came to be regarded as a kind of heavenly senate or honour society. They were thought to possess merit or virtue, a personal credit in the economy of blessedness, that could be drawn on by believers who wanted them to intercede with God on his or her behalf. By praying to a saint or making a pilgrimage to his or her shrine, one might win release from punishment in the next existence and from guilt in this one. In short, the saints could be powerful allies in the quest for spiritual benefit.

Particular saints are honoured on particular days. Their profile was so high in Latin Christianity that in the sixteenth century Spanish and Portuguese explorers of the New World named islands and features of the coastline for the saints on whose days they arrived at these places.

Certain saints came to be associated with specific conditions or occupations. St Christopher, for example, who was said to have carried the child Jesus across a dangerous river, is one of several patron saints of travellers, and St Cecilia became the patron of musicians because she sang a song to God on her deathbed.

Particular saints also came to be associated with particular symbols. Visitors to Venice, for instance, learn that the lion symbolizes the gospel author St Mark. Similarly, a bishop portrayed carrying a beehive is likely St Ambrose, the fifth-century bishop of Milan, whose name connotes nectar; reportedly, Ambrose's mother dreamed that as a boy he swallowed a bee, which made him sweet of speech. But the beehive is also associated with the twelfth-century St Bernard of Clairvaux, who was called the 'honey-mouthed teacher'. Keys represent the apostle Peter, to whom (in a famous passage in *Matthew* 16) Jesus promises the keys to earth and heaven; but there are at least nine other saints who have also been represented with keys. And the orb appears not only with God but also with Dominic, the twelfth-century founder of the Dominican order whose mission it was to bring light to the world.

In some places the traditions of particular saints include elements of pre-Christian customs and symbolism. The eighth-century English Church historian Bede reports correspondence from Gregory the Great a hundred years before him:

> On the day of the dedication or the festivals of the holy martyrs, whose relics are deposited there, let them make themselves huts from the branches of trees around the churches which have been converted out of shrines, and let them celebrate the solemnity with religious feasts. Do not let them sacrifice animals to the devil, but let them slaughter animals for their own food to the praise of God (*Ecclesiastical History*, ch. 30; Colgrave 1969: 109).

St Ursula was depicted as sailing the Rhine in the fashion of the earlier Teutonic moon goddess Urschel. And St Christopher, 'Christ-bearer', was said to have felt he was bearing the weight of the

St Christopher carrying the Christ child; a woodcut by an unknown artist from a 1423 edition of the *Golden Legend*, a collection of hagiographies compiled around 1260.

universe when he carried the child Jesus on his shoulder, recalling Hercules and Atlas, who bore the weight of the world in classical mythology.

A saint named Josaphat was venerated for his good works in India, but scholars now believe that his name was derived from the Buddhist title Bodhisattva and that the Josaphat legend was based on the story of the Buddha in his days as a Bodhisattva, before his enlightenment. And in southern France the discovery of what was thought to be the headstone marking the grave of a martyred saint inspired calls for the canonization of 'Saint Decimil'—until someone realized that the tombstone was actually a milestone marking an old Roman road.

In 1969 Pope Paul VI eliminated from the roster of saints several whose historical existence had been found questionable, among them St

Christopher. Their status in the Anglican Church, which separated from Rome in the sixteenth century, remained unchanged, however.

The Figure of Mary

Pre-eminent among the Christian saints was Mary, the mother of Jesus. Although she is largely in the background in the gospel accounts of Jesus' public ministry, her role as the virgin mother and her presence at the crucifixion (in *John* 19) made her the object of intense popular devotion, both as the principal feminine point of access to the Trinity and as a model of sorrow-enduring love in her own right. Among the events in her life commemorated first in the Greek east and eventually throughout the Christian world were the annunciation of her pregnancy, her ritual purification following the birth of Jesus, and her death, celebrated in the Orthodox east as the feast of the Dormition ('falling asleep'—that is, death) and in the West as the feast of the Assumption (referring to her 'assumption' into heaven).

At the same time, she became the object of intense theological speculation, not only during the fifth-century Nestorian controversy over her status as *theotokos* ('bearer of God'), but in debates over matters such as her bodily assumption into heaven and the doctrine of the **Immaculate Conception**, according to which she herself was born without the 'stain' of original sin.

A widespread custom among Roman Catholics is the use of the **rosary**, a string of fifty-eight beads and a small **crucifix** (a cross bearing the image of the suffering Christ) to keep track of the sequence of prayers. The rosary has five sequences of ten beads, separated by single beads of a different colour or size. (The English word 'bead' comes from the same origin as the German *beten*, 'to pray'.) The person using the rosary will say one 'Our Father' (also known as the Lord's Prayer) and ten 'Hail Marys' The Hail Mary is a brief prayer whose first phrase is found in the first chapter of Luke's gospel:

Mariology

The status of Mary has tended to be more exalted among Eastern Orthodox and Roman Catholic thinkers than among Protestants. Although Martin Luther seems at times to have affirmed the doctrines of the Immaculate Conception and the Assumption, his reasons may have had less to do with Mary herself than with the implications of those doctrines for the status for Christ. John Calvin praised her as 'holy virgin' but had reservations about her title as 'mother of God'.

By contrast, the Roman Catholic Church placed more emphasis than ever on Mary after the Reformation. In 1854, Pope Pius IX defined as **dogma**—authoritative, indisputable truth—the doctrine of the Immaculate Conception. Nearly a century later, in 1950, Pope Pius XII did the same for the Assumption: the doctrine according to which Mary was taken up bodily to heaven upon her death. The Second Vatican Council (1962–5) did not add to her titles, as some had wished, although Pope Paul VI proclaimed her Mother of the Church in 1964. John Paul II also spoke in traditional terms of Marian piety. Catholic devotion to Mary is somewhat more restrained today than it was in the past, but Pope Benedict XVI is a strong advocate of Marian devotion.

Hail, Mary, full of grace, the Lord is with you; blessed are you among women, and blessed is the fruit of your womb, Jesus. Holy Mary, mother of God, pray for us sinners now and at the hour of our death.

In Latin Europe, artistic depictions of Mary developed a set of conventions all their own. Although some of these conventions can be traced to the cult of the pre-Christian goddess Isis, Mary's role is not limited to that of the devoted young mother. She is also the mature woman who grieves at the martyrdom of her adult son; she is the model of purity and incorruptibility, of devotion and fidelity, of sorrow and compassion. Many statues and paintings of the Virgin Mary present her alone, as a model of selflessness to which all—male as well as female—might aspire.

Many devout Catholics have reported experiencing visions of Mary. Among the most famous was Bernadette Soubirous, a young girl from Lourdes in southwestern France who in 1858 claimed to have seen Mary on sixteen occasions and to have received from her the command to build a church. Lourdes has been an important place of pilgrimage and faith healing ever since.

Evil, Devil, and Angels

Does the devil exist? Today, many Christians who are quite ready to think of God in personal terms are reluctant to suppose that a comparable being exists as his adversary. In 1999 Pope John Paul II advised the faithful to think of hell not as a place but as a condition of spiritual estrangement. Things were different in the Middle Ages. Not only did God have an angelic host, but the devil—Satan, or the Antichrist—commanded a corresponding host of demons.

Belief in evil spirits or demons is nearly universal in traditional religions. Some theorists associate this belief with the fear of threatening forces, including ferocious animals, in the natural world. Others attribute it to the fear that angry ghosts of the dead may return to settle old scores, or to berate the living for ignoring them.

Likewise widespread among societies is the belief in good or protective spirits. In the biblical tradition, the term 'angel' meant 'messenger', usually a male herald. Over time, however, angels in Christianity were increasingly represented as winged and haloed feminine creatures. But the belief remained into modern times that every person is watched over by a guardian angel.

Medieval theologians devoted considerable speculation to angels. Several authors, influenced by Neoplatonic descriptions of the cosmos as consisting of nine emanating spheres, ranked angels in a nine-level hierarchy. Angels were thought to be created, not eternal, and to have will, but not emotion. They know God more fully than humans do but still not completely.

The notion of the devil, a single adversary leading the host of demonic powers, may be as old as monotheism itself. The Greek *diabolos* ('slanderer') matches the name Satan ('accuser' or 'adversary') in Hebrew. He was also called Ba'al-zabul ('mighty lord') corrupted to Ba'al-zabub ('lord of the flies').

A view common since early Christian writers is that the devil started as an angel but that through pride he tried to take over God's role and so fell from grace. This is the implication of the name Lucifer ('bearer of light'): a star that has fallen from heaven. Biblical tradition speaks of humankind (personified as Adam) as having fallen from the paradise of Eden through an act of selfishness, and Christian theology made selfishness central to its notion of innate, or 'original', sin. The notion that the devil had fallen from heaven in a parallel fashion offered plenty of opportunity for moral admonition.

Once fallen, Lucifer presides over the realm of hell, which is the destiny of the wicked after their earthly life. The medieval imagination mapped this realm in often grotesque detail. The torments suffered by the wicked ranged from extreme cold, far from the divine light, to boiling in cauldrons. Whatever morbid pleasure some people may have derived from imagining their own tormentors in similar cauldrons could well have been offset by the fear that they themselves might face punishment for wicked thoughts, if not wicked deeds.

The medieval Christian world seems to have been obsessed with the reality that death comes to us all. Death was unpredictable but always close at hand, especially after more than a third of the population of western Europe was wiped out by plague, the Black Death, in the late 1340s. At the same time it was considered the consequence of sinfulness and marked the beginning of the eternal punishment the sinner could expect to face in the hereafter. Among the rituals that served to remind Christians of the human condition was a 'dance of death' in which the participants dressed as skeletons.

Sin, Heresy, and the Inquisition

To the modern mind, the Latin Christianity of the Middle Ages seems obsessed with sin. Humans were considered subjectively or 'originally' sinful owing to their pride and self-will, but specific actions were also objectified as sins. Medieval theologians believed that such sins contributed to the individual's mortality. Referring to the first New Testament letter of John (*1 John* 5: 16), they drew a distinction between minor 'venial' sins, which could be forgiven, and 'mortal' sins, which were so serious as to deprive the soul of God's grace; to be classified as 'mortal', a sin had to concern a 'grave matter' and be committed both knowingly and willfully. Even mortal sins could be forgiven, however, as long as the sinner confessed to a priest, who could prescribe penance and offer absolution.

For moral edification, the Church also warned the faithful against seven 'deadly sins': pride, covetousness or avarice, lust or lechery, envy, gluttony, anger or wrath, and sloth. A list of seven was established as early as the beginning of the seventh century by Pope Gregory I, although his seventh sin was despair rather than sloth.

There were also seven virtues. Augustine, at the end of the fourth century, was among those who combined four virtues central to Greek philosophy—wisdom, courage, temperance, and justice—with the three primary New Testament virtues of faith, hope, and love, best known from Paul's first letter to the Corinthians (13: 13). (By the late 1800s, 'charity' had been added to that list, but it was originally understood to be included in 'love'.)

Another virtue, not identified as such but useful for survival, was conformity. In the Middle Ages, European society was dominated by the Church, and those who were not baptized into the faith, notably Jews and Muslims, lacked the rights and privileges of the mainstream society. There had also occasionally been Christians—whether dissenting intellectuals or ill-informed peasants—whose differences from the mainstream marked them as heretics. During the eleventh century, increasing numbers of heretics were burned at the stake, though as a rule such sentences were carried out by secular rather than religious authorities. 'Heretic' groups such as the Waldensians of northwestern Italy and the Albigensians or Cathars of southwestern France tended to seek refuge in regions where such authority was less strict.

Church councils in the twelfth century prescribed penalties for heresy, including expulsion from the Church, imprisonment, and confiscation of property. Such penalties were part of the internal legal system that the Latin Church was developing, known as canon law, which covered Church institutions, the conduct of clergy and laity, and adherence to doctrine. Canon law was in place by 1184, when Pope Lucius III instructed bishops to carry out 'episcopal inquisitions' in their dioceses: to investigate allegations of heretical activity, examine the suspects, and turn over any resisters to the secular authorities for punishment.

These measures intensified in the early thirteenth century, with the organization of the Dominican order, initially to combat the Albigensians. In 1233 Pope Gregory IX established a tribunal at Toulouse, which went so far as to remove from Christian cemeteries the remains of persons posthumously charged with heresy.

The Inquisition in Toulouse established a trial procedure that lasted for centuries. Those accused of heresy, even by anonymous informers, were presumed guilty unless they could prove their innocence. Those who confessed were assigned penances and penalties, but those who maintained their innocence were returned to prison to 'discover' their heresy. In 1252 Pope Innocent IV ruled that torture could be used and that heretics handed over to the secular authorities should be executed within five days. The Inquisition was at its most brutal in Spain, where the grand inquisitor Tomás de Torquemada ordered more than two thousand executions and aided the expulsion of the Jews and Muslims from Spain in 1492—the same year that Columbus sailed to America.

Peasant superstition contributed to the medieval tendency to identify certain individuals as witches, practitioners of malevolent magic. Witches were thought to be the devil's agents on earth and to have intimate sexual relations with him. The *Malleus Maleficarum* ('Hammer of Witches'), a handbook for Christian witch-hunting, was published in 1486 by two German Dominicans, Heinrich Kraemer and Johann Sprenger, who two years previously had been authorized by Pope Innocent VIII to eradicate witchcraft from Germany.

Society's efforts to hunt down, prosecute, and execute such individuals by burning demonstrate how devastating the fear of non-conforming behaviour can be. Very often, personal grudges led to accusations of witchcraft. In records of sixteenth- and seventeenth-century witchcraft trials in England, the most frequent charge was that the alleged witch, usually a neighbour, often an old woman, had caused some misfortune to befall the accuser. Widows and women with knowledge of herbal cures were particularly likely to attract accusations of witchcraft. It is also possible that the symptoms of 'demonic possession' suffered by some accusers may have been physiological; records of the witchcraft trials of 1692 in Salem, Massachusetts, have suggested to some modern researchers that the accusers were accidentally poisoned by ergot—a grain fungus that produces a hallucinogen similar to LSD. People who ingest ergot-infected grain often die, but those who survive report strange experiences and wild visions.

Scholastic Philosophy

The dominant expression of thought in western Europe in the Middle Ages is known as scholasticism, a word that means different things to different people. Institutionally, it is described as the work of the clergy in the 'schools', that is, the medieval universities. In emerging universities like those in Paris, Bologna, and Oxford, theology was a central part of the curriculum. The clerical base of scholarship a thousand years ago is reflected in the academic hoods and gowns, similar to monks' robes, that are still common today.

Intellectual definitions of the movement, on the other hand, characterize scholasticism in terms of its assumptions and goals. Faith and reason, for scholastics, are mutually confirming; philosophy is termed the 'handmaid' of theology. The idea that theology is 'faith seeking understanding' can be seen in the early fifth century in Augustine, and in early sixth-century Italy in the government administrator Boethius, who urged his readers: 'As far as you are able, [to] join faith to reason.' He was perhaps the last important layman for a thousand years in Christian philosophy, for in 529 the emperor Justinian closed the Platonic academy in Athens and in that very same year Benedict founded his abbey at Monte Cassino. The centre of gravity shifted to the clergy as custodians of faith and learning.

John Scotus Erigena, who was born in Ireland around 810 and taught in Paris, expanded on Augustine's distinction between authority and reason. For Erigena, scripture is the source of authority, but it is the duty of reason to examine and expound it.

Early scholastic teaching was based on the *lectio*, the reading of scripture. At this early stage the scholastics were seeking to distill and summarize scripture and arrive at a rational grasp of its meaning. As time went on, however, scholastic teaching developed a dialectical structure in which a proposition of doctrine was stated and then objections to it were raised and systematically dealt with.

Anselm

Anselm (c. 1033–1109), a native of the Italian Alps who became archbishop of Canterbury in England, moved away from the principle of scriptural authority, asserting that faith itself has a kind of rationality. One of the formulations for which he is famous is the statement 'I believe so that I may understand.'

The most tantalizing of the medieval proofs for the existence of God is Anselm's '**ontological argument**'. Unlike later proofs that infer God's existence from inspection of the universe, Anselm's reasoning finds it implied in the very idea of God. Characterizing God as 'a being greater than which nothing can be conceived', Anselm argues in the second chapter of his *Proslogion* that such a being must exist not only in the mind but in reality, since if it did not exist, some other being that did exist would be greater. In the next two chapters of the same treatise, Anselm pursues the argument in a second and more substantial form: a being that cannot be conceived not to exist is greater than one that can. Philosophers understand this proposition to mean that all other being is contingent, whereas God's being is necessary.

Readers who may see this line of argumentation as implying existence by definition are not far off the mark. Even in Anselm's own time, there were people, such as the French monk Gaunilon, who held that the idea of perfection did not necessarily imply existence. But it was not until the eighteenth-century Enlightenment that the German philosopher Immanuel Kant made clear the objection that existence is not a description or 'predicate'. As Kant put it, the idea of a perfect being does not of itself cause a perfect being to exist any more than the thought of money actually puts coins into one's pocket.

Nonetheless, Anselm's thinking has resonated for centuries in Christian theology because it expresses the uniqueness and majesty of God's being, which exists not in the way that objects do in the universe, but as the ground and basis of existence of the universe itself. Indeed, some thinkers refused to speak of God as existing, since to do so would amount to diminishing God. The strategy of denying descriptions of the divine in order to move beyond their limitations is known as the *via negativa* or 'negative way' in theology. We have already seen it in Gregory Palamas; it was also used by late medieval Latin mystics.

However much philosophers have been intrigued by the ontological argument, Anselm's main influence on theology lies in his contribution to Christian **atonement** theory. For the Church fathers in the centuries before Anselm, God entered the world to overcome the sin and death that hold humankind in bondage. In their classical atonement theory, it was by becoming incarnate and suffering that God rescued humanity from the power of the demonic.

What propels Anselm's thought in his work *Cur Deus homo* ('Why God Became Human') is more a juridical notion of punishment than an incarnational theology. In his view, to satisfy divine justice, sin must be compensated for; but since those guilty of sin are ordinary humans who cannot fulfill this obligation, Jesus appears to make the payment. Indeed, Jesus' self-sacrifice is the highest human gift to God. For Anselm and his medieval Latin successors, God set the terms and conditions, and he did send his son to help meet them, but Christ's human nature was sufficient to fulfill the obligation. Anselm's view of the atonement contributed to the medieval Latin interpretation of the **Eucharist**—the **sacrament** in which believers consume consecrated bread and wine in commemoration of the Last Supper—as the re-enactment of Christ's sacrifice.

As scholastic thinking developed, so did the philosophical resources at its disposal. The tradition on which early scholastics relied came through Augustine and Boethius. Based on the thought of the Greek philosopher Plato, it was dominated by consideration of abstract ideas. It was in the twelfth century that Latin Christianity discovered the thought of Plato's contemporary Aristotle, which gave more scope for practical considerations and examination of the material world. What people thought of as 'reason' came to consist of more than logic; it became more empirical, taking in the observation of phenomena. Aristotle's thought reached western Europe first through Arabic translations used by Muslims and Jews in medieval Spain, and then in Greek by way of the Byzantines. The first major Latin theologian to take up Aristotle was Albertus Magnus, who taught in Germany in the thirteenth century.

Thomas Aquinas

The greatest of the Aristotelian scholastics was Thomas Aquinas (c. 1225–74), a Dominican from Aquino (near Naples) who taught in Paris. Foremost among his works is his *Summa Theologiae* ('Summation of Theology'). In it and other writings Thomas sharpened the distinction between reason and faith. He believed a number of Christian faith assertions, including the doctrines of the Trinity and the incarnation of God in Christ, to lie beyond reason, in the realm of faith, but that did not mean that they were contrary to reason. Other Christian affirmations, however, such as the existence of God, he did believe to be provable by reason.

Thomas identified five 'ways' of proving God's existence. Most of these describe some feature of the extant world and argue that without a God such a world could not exist.

The first three of Thomas's ways overlap as variations on what philosophers call the '**cosmological argument**' for God's existence. First, change or motion in the universe is evidence that there must be a Prime Mover to sustain the process. Second, the pattern of cause and effect points to God as a First Cause. Third, things have the possibility of existing or not existing, being generated or corrupted, but unless there was a time when there was nothing at all, there must have been some being that existed out of necessity, and that is God.

The fourth of Thomas's 'ways' argues that there are gradations of goodness, truth, and nobility in what we experience, and that therefore there must be a being that is supremely good, supremely true, and supremely noble; in a sense, this is also a type of cosmological argument. Finally, the fifth 'way' consists in the idea that the plan observable in the universe is evidence of a divine planner; this is an example of the **teleological argument** (from Greek *telos*, 'end' or 'purpose'). Thomas was convinced that an understanding of God as creator made it possible to maintain a foothold in a doctrine of biblical authority while exploring the characteristics of the secular world. The tension between these two concerns proved controversial, however. Three years after Thomas's death, the archbishop of Paris formally condemned a list of propositions reminiscent of Thomas's thinking. But the comprehensiveness of Thomas's system proved attractive to later generations. In 1567, at the time of the Catholic Reformation, Pope Pius V declared him 'Doctor of the Church'. And in 1879, in an effort to counteract modern thinking, Pope Leo XIII made Thomism the official theology of the Roman Catholic Church.

Medieval Mystics

The fourteenth-century reaction to Thomas's views included further discussion of the limits of reason in matters of faith. But there was another development afoot that rendered those limits to some extent irrelevant. The late Middle Ages saw a remarkable flowering of mysticism.

To describe something as 'mystical' is not simply to say that it involves mystery. Mysticism is a specific tradition that emphasizes the certainty of profound personal experience. Typically, the mystic is certain of God, not because of some logical proof but because he or she has experienced a moment of vivid, intense awareness. At such a moment one may experience ecstasy (from Greek, 'standing outside oneself'), or displacement from one's ordinary mode of awareness. One characteristic of that experience is a sense of union with the divine through a temporary dissolving or bridging of the gulf that normally separates the human person from God.

The mystic then descends from the heights to more mundane awareness. Accounts of mystic experience are inevitably written from memory, after the moment of ecstasy has passed. A number of medieval Christian mystics nevertheless described in vivid detail what they had experienced.

Medieval mysticism was part of a long tradition of cultivation of the interior life. In Christianity, that life is usually termed spirituality. It complements the ethical life where virtue is practised in one's relationship with others. In spirituality, the heart or conscience opens itself to the divine through prayer and contemplation. For many Christians, spirituality is the essence of religious experience, and credit for it is given to the action of the Holy Spirit on the individual self or soul.

Christian spirituality had roots in the Jewish tradition of contemplation of the mystery of God's presence with his people. It was cultivated by the 'desert' fathers—and mothers—whose ascetic practice was the foundation of medieval monasticism, and was central to the monastic life.

In the Greek world, mysticism was especially influenced by Gregory of Nyssa, who in the fourth century likened the knowledge of God to the soul's groping towards the light, with the desire of love, in a dark night of unattainability and unknowing. In sixth-century Syria, another writer, a convert who had heard the apostle Paul preach in Athens and called himself Dionysius, spoke of a divine reality beyond all names, including such formulations as the Trinity. This Pseudo-Dionysius, whose ideas show the influence of Neoplatonism, negated all forms, proposing a spiritual ascent to the nameless One.

In medieval Europe, the most formidable systematizer of mystical thought was the German Dominican Johannes ('Meister') Eckhart

(c. 1260–1327), who combined the ideas of Gregory and Pseudo-Dionysius with Augustine's psychology of the self. For Eckhart, human beings are created in the image of God, but our divine nature is obscured because our life is finite and creaturely. However, the mind of the spiritual person permits an actualization of the divine nature that the human soul contains. The individual mystic becomes aware of the divinity of his or her being. Eckhart's mysticism is unitive, seeking to dissolve distinctions between self and God.

In the fourteenth century, the Flemish mystic Jan van Ruysbroeck took up the problem of differentiation and related it to the persons of the Trinity. God as Father, he said, is the One. But the other parts of the Trinity are related to the movement of creation in the cosmos and a movement of awareness in the self.

Whereas Eckhart and Ruysbroeck sought to identify the self with the image of God, others saw God in all the nearness of humanity. The French Cistercian Bernard of Clairvaux likened the awareness of God to the awareness of one's beloved. Unity of the spirit with God, he said, is a concurrence of wills, not a union of essences. Like the ecstasy of love, this union is fleeting, but no less intensely experienced:

> To lose yourself so that you are as though you were not, to be unaware of yourself and emptied of yourself, to be, as it were, brought to nothing—this pertains to heavenly exchanges, not to human affection (O'Brien 1964: 122).

Bonaventure (1221–74), an Italian Franciscan who taught at Paris in the thirteenth century, wrote a text entitled *Journey of the Mind to God*. In it meditation on the humanity of Christ becomes the point of experiential contact with the divine. Later, in the writings of St John of the Cross, a sixteenth-century Spanish Carmelite, the soul seeks to purify itself. John speaks of the 'dark night of the soul' when it is purged of its attachments and rises to God in a union described in the language of a pure flame.

Female Mystics

A striking feature of late medieval mysticism was the scope it afforded for women. Though women were forbidden to participate fully in clerical activities, and were limited to supporting roles even in female religious orders, there was no limit to the experiential depth and profundity they could attain in their devotion.

Hildegard of Bingen (1098–1179) was a Benedictine abbess who had a creative life in writing and music but was also involved in politics and diplomacy. Clergy and feudal nobility sought the counsel of 'the Sybil of the Rhine', as she was called. When she became abbess in 1141, she had a vision of tongues of flame from the heavens settling on her, and over the next ten years she wrote a book of visions entitled *Scivias* ('Know the ways [of God]').

Catherine of Siena (1347–80 or 1333–80) in Italy was a member of a Dominican lay order. She was actively involved in the religious politics of the day, but her *Dialogue* records her mystical visions.

Julian of Norwich (c. 1342–c. 1413) was an English mystic who experienced visions one day during a five-hour state of ecstasy, and one vision the next day; after two decades of reflection she wrote a description and analysis of her visions in her *Sixteen Revelations of Divine Love*. To her, evil was a distortion introduced by the human will, serving to reveal by contrast all the more clearly the divine love of God.

Living in the period of transition between the late medieval and early modern, Teresa of Ávila (1515–82), a Spanish Carmelite in the same spiritual milieu as St John of the Cross, decided at the age of forty to seek spiritual perfection. Within two years she experienced her first mystical ecstasy, and over the next fifteen years, while actively working to establish religious houses, she deepened her devotional practice until in 1572 she reached the state of 'spiritual marriage'. The

Two Female Mystics

Hildegard of Bingen

From Scivias (*Know the ways [of God]*), *written between 1141 and 1151, Book II, section 2.6:*

On the Trinity: Just as the flame contains three essences in the one fire, so too, there is one God in three persons. How is this so? The flame consists of shining brightness, purple vigour and fiery glow. It has shining brightness so that it may give light; purple vigour so that it may flourish; and a fiery glow so that it may burn.

In the shining brightness, observe the Father who, in his fatherly devotion, reveals his brightness to the faithful. In the purple vigour contained within it (whereby this same flame manifests its power), understand the Son who, from the Virgin, assumed a body in which Godhead demonstrated its miracles. And in the fiery glow, perceive the Holy Spirit which pours glowingly into the minds of believers.

But where there is neither shining brightness, nor purple vigour, nor fiery glow, there no flame is seen. So too, where neither the Father nor the Son nor the Holy Spirit is honoured, there God is not worthily revered.

And so, just as these three essences are discerned in the one flame, so too, three Persons are to be understood in the unity of Godhead (Bowie and Davies 1990: 53, 75).

Teresa of Ávila

From Chapter 18 of her autobiography:

Previously, . . . the senses were permitted to give some indication of the great joy they feel. But now the soul enjoys incomparably more, and yet has still less power to show it. For there is no power left in the body—and the soul possesses none—by which this joy can be communicated. At such a time anything of the sort would be a great embarrassment, a torment and a disturbance of its repose. If there is really a union of all the faculties, I say, then the soul cannot make it known, even if it wants to—while actually in union I mean. If it can, it is not in union.

How what is called union takes place and what it is, I cannot tell. It is explained in mystical theology, but I cannot use the proper terms; I cannot understand what mind is, or how it differs from soul or spirit. They all seem one to me, though the soul sometimes leaps out of itself like a burning fire that has become one whole flame and increases with great force. The flame leaps very high above the fire. Nevertheless it is not a different thing, but the same flame which is in the fire (Cohen 1957: 122–3).

writings she produced during this period are noteworthy because they treat the life of prayer comprehensively, describing its steps and intermediate stages between 'discursive' prayer (i.e., prayer mentioning specific needs) and ecstasy.

A woman who was not a mystic in the sense of the foregoing but nonetheless a person of intense spiritual visions was Joan of Arc (1412–31), who led a military expedition in 1429 to relieve the French forces under siege by the British at Orléans, south of Paris. Captured the following year, she was charged and convicted of witchcraft and heresy, and burnt at the stake in 1431. On a review of her trial in 1456 she was posthumously declared innocent, and in 1920 she was declared a saint.

The Protestant Reformation

The World after 1450

In the fifteenth century, Christianity was essentially a European phenomenon. Apart from the ancient Eastern churches of Ethiopia and southern India and some remnant minorities in the eastern Mediterranean, Asia and northern Africa had long since turned to Islam. The fall of Constantinople to the Ottoman Turks in 1453 sealed the victory of the Muslims over Byzantine Christians after seven centuries of rivalry.

But the balance of civilizations in the world changed after 1450. A generation after the fall of Constantinople, Christendom's horizons were vastly broadened when the Portuguese navigator Bartolomeu Diaz sailed around southern Africa in 1488, outflanking the Turks who had controlled the overland routes to Asia. Another Portuguese, Vasco da Gama arrived on the shores of India in 1498. From the sixteenth century onward, European colonial powers established a presence in the ports of India, Southeast Asia, and China. In the same years Spanish navigators reached the New World, taking Christianity with them. Ironically, just as European Christianity was poised for this global expansion, it was fragmented by a crisis of institutional and spiritual authority: the challenge of Protestantism.

Luther

By the early sixteenth century, pressure for change in the Latin Church had been building for decades. Princes north of the Alps were challenging the power of the papacy in Rome. The period of cultural rebirth known as Renaissance was well underway, as was the revival of classical learning central to humanism, exemplified in the Dutch scholar Desiderius Erasmus (1466–1536). Condemning complicated scholastic theology, Erasmus urged a return to the simple morality of Jesus

From Erasmus, *The Praise of Folly*

The Dutch classical scholar and humanist Desiderius Erasmus wrote The Praise of Folly *in 1509 after a visit to Rome, while staying in England with his friend Sir Thomas More, whose social critique* Utopia *('Nowhere') was published seven years later.*

[Some questions have] been discussed threadbare. There are others more worthy of great and enlightened theologians (as they call themselves) which can really rouse them to action if they come their way. What was the exact moment of divine generation? Are there several filiations in Christ? Is it a possible proposition that God the Father could hate his Son? Could God have taken on the form of a woman, a devil, a donkey, a gourd, or a flintstone? If so, how could a gourd have preached sermons, performed miracles, and been nailed to the cross? And what would Peter have consecrated if he had consecrated when the body of Christ still hung on the cross? Furthermore at that same time could Christ have been called a man? Shall we be permitted to eat and drink after the resurrection? We're taking due precaution against hunger and thirst while there's time. There are any amount of quibbles even more refined than these, about concepts, relations, instants, formalities, quiddities, and ecceities, which no one could possibly perceive unless like Lynceus he could see through blackest darkness things which don't exist (Radice 1986: 126–7).

through the critical study of scripture in local languages; he also wrote a scathing satire of Catholic doctrine and Church corruption called *Encomium moriae* ('The Praise of Folly', 1509). A few years later, Ulrich von Hutten and Crotus Rubianus published *Letters of Obscure Men* (1513–15), mocking the intricacy and futility of Church regulations.

Literacy was spreading and local vernacular dialects were developing into regional languages. But suggestions that the Bible might be translated into the languages of the people were firmly rejected by the church, which was well aware of the threat that direct access to scripture would pose to its authority. When John Wyclif (1329–84) in England and John Hus (c. 1369–1415) among the Czechs proposed to replace Latin with the vernacular in worship and to translate the Bible into the languages of the people, the church condemned them as heretics.

Although the growing challenges to the Church had been in evidence for decades, it was the stubborn and uninhibited personality of one man that made it possible for the Protestant Reformation to erupt as it did. Martin Luther (1483–1546) was an Augustinian monk and theological scholar at the university in Wittenberg who objected to the Church's practice of selling **indulgences**: releases from the time the soul was required to spend in **purgatory** (a kind of holding area for the departed in the course of their passage from death to the next existence).

The standard way of raising a topic for debate was to post a notice on the church door. Accordingly, Luther tacked up a list of 95 propositions, or

From the *Letters of Obscure Men*

In this extract from their satire, Ulrich von Hutten and Crotus Rubianus take aim at the Church's elaborate dietary rules. Heinrich Schafmaul ('sheep's mouth') writes to ask whether it is a sin to eat an egg with a chicken in it on a fast day.

. . . we were lately sitting in an inn in the Campo dei Fiori, having our supper, and were eating eggs, when on opening one I saw that there was a young chicken within.

This I showed to a comrade; whereupon quoth he to me, 'Eat it up speedily, before the taverner sees it, for . . . if he sees that there is a young fowl in that egg, he will say "Pay me for that fowl!" Little or big, 'tis all one.'

In a trice I gulped down the egg, chicken and all.

And then I remembered that it was Friday!

Whereupon I said to my crony, 'You have made me commit a mortal sin, in eating flesh on the sixth day of the week!'

But he averred that it was not a mortal sin—nor even a venial one, seeing that such a chickling is accounted merely an egg, until it is born.

He told me, too, that it is just the same in the case of cheese, in which there are sometimes grubs, as there are in cherries, peas, and new beans: yet all these may be eaten on Fridays, and even on Apostolic Vigils. But taverners are such rascals that they call them flesh, to get more money.

Then I departed, and thought the matter over.

And by the Lord, Master Ortwin, I am in a mighty quandary, and know not what to do.

I would willingly seek counsel of one of the Courticians [court ministers in Rome], but they are not devout men (Stokes 1909:445–6).

'theses', criticizing not just the sale of indulgences but other aspects of Church practice. Called to defend himself against charges of political subversion at a 'diet' (imperial council) held in 1521 at the German city of Worms, he was offered the opportunity to retract his challenge. But he stood his ground: 'Unless I am convicted by Scripture and plain reason—I do not accept the authority of popes and councils, for they have contradicted each other—my conscience is captive to the Word of God, I cannot and I will not recant anything' (Bainton 1974, 15: 551).

Accordingly, Luther was banished from Germany and excommunicated from the Church. But as the news of his challenge spread, it attracted support from those seeking change in various aspects of spiritual and political life. Before long, that support took on a concrete political form.

Like others, Luther criticized the Church's lavishness and corruption, but the core of his challenge was theological. Seeking to recast Christian understanding of the very nature of sin and redemption, he rejected the transactional notion that Christians could expiate their sins by confessing them and performing the prescribed acts of penance. Instead, Luther argued that in Jesus divine grace reaches out to human beings, saving and redeeming individuals regardless of their merit or performance.

Taking up a key theme in Paul's New Testament letter to the Romans, Luther insisted that humans are justified (made right in their relation to God) by faith alone. For Luther as for Paul, the dialectic was between faith and works. Just as Paul had argued that salvation could not be earned through observance of the Torah commandments, however faithful, Luther argued that the way to redemption had nothing to do with the rituals of confession and penance.

Banished from Germany, Luther disappeared for more than a year. Many thought him dead, but he was actually in hiding under the protection of the elector of Saxony, Frederick the Wise. Luther made use of this period of seclusion to write a series of theological works and to translate the New Testament from the original Greek into a direct, lively German that eventually gave the Luther Bible a profoundly influential place in German literature.

It is doubtful that the Protestant Reformation could have taken place, at least in the form we know, much sooner than it actually did. The technology of printing from movable type had been introduced in Europe only half a century earlier, when the first Latin Bible came off Johann Gutenberg's press in Mainz in 1456. Though prohibitively expensive at first, printed materials soon became economical to produce. Pamphlets outlining the topics of Luther's challenge were quickly disseminated, and Luther's own short tracts appeared in at least 1,300 different printings by 1523. His very readable translation of the Bible had an impact, too (the New Testament appeared in 1522 and the Old Testament in 1534).

When Luther's arguments inspired a dozen nuns to leave the convent in Wittenberg, three of them went back to their families but the other nine had no homes to go to. Luther found husbands for eight of them and married the ninth, Katherina von Bora, himself. It is probable that moral concern, even ideological conviction, played a greater role in their relationship, at least initially, than romance. In the course of time they had six children and also adopted four orphans. In his writing *Concerning Married Life*, Luther suggested that even the most mundane of everyday activities, such as the washing of diapers, can be ennobled by faith. And in setting a pattern for married clergy in Protestantism, he made it possible for clergy to counsel the married people among their flocks on the basis of practical experience as well as theory.

But there were also broader theoretical aspects to Luther's view of clergy and the priesthood, for he effectively took the priesthood off the pedestal of status and authority that it and the institutional Church had enjoyed since the time of Constantine. For Luther, the ultimate authority lay not in institutional tradition but in the Bible and the inner guidance of the Holy Spirit. Thus there was no need for an intermediary between the Christian and God to transmit human petitions or dispense divine grace. The egalitarian concept of universal priesthood, or the 'priesthood of all believers', is central to Protestantism.

In 1524–5, when an uprising broke out among German peasants, Luther refused to endorse all their demands. As a consequence, the more radical among them left Luther for a more strident leader, Thomas Müntzer, who eventually played a major role in the Anabaptist movement, so-called because it held that baptism should be reserved for adults capable of making a mature decision for faith.

Luther also disagreed with the Swiss reformer Huldrych (Ulrich) Zwingli over the interpretation of the Eucharist. Both men rejected the Roman Catholic view of the sacrament as a literal re-enactment of Christ's self-sacrifice. But whereas Luther continued to believe that Jesus was physically present, if unseen, during the rite, Zwingli insisted that the words 'this is my body' meant only 'this represents': in short, that the rite was purely symbolic.

The debate illustrates a recurring issue for Protestants: if the Bible itself is your ultimate authority, by what authority can you decide to take some parts literally and others metaphorically? Luther's biblicism was simple: if the text has Christ say of the bread and wine 'this is my body', then Christ's body must be present in the bread and wine of the Eucharist. Those who, like Zwingli, maintained that 'this is' meant 'this represents' were implicitly committing themselves to a more subtle notion of scriptural authority.

Sixteenth-Century Branches of Protestantism

The Reformation was marked by division and diversity. Early reformers often advocated their breakaway doctrines with an ideological stridency that was no less authoritarian than the church they had rejected. At a practical level, redundancy and confusion developed when independent bodies competed for adherents. A denominationally fragmented Church has been the legacy of the Protestant Reformation down to the present day.

Three main 'establishments' emerged from the sixteenth-century Reformation: Lutheran, Anglican, and Calvinist. (Other branches, such as the Anabaptists and Unitarians, are considered non-establishment.)

Lutherans

The followers of Martin Luther's theological and political leadership flourished in Germany and Scandinavia. Like him, they stressed the authority of scripture and the guidance of the Holy Spirit. Lutheranism allowed ample scope for rational and intellectual argument in the exposition of scripture, but it also encouraged a deep sense of personal piety. Images of God as friend and companion are just as frequent in the texts of Lutheran hymns as images of God as warrior or judge.

In worship and in ecclesiastical organization, Lutherans departed in only some respects from the Roman Church. They retained a Eucharist-like sacrament, but they celebrated it in the vernacular rather than Latin, and they held that Christ's body was present along with the bread and wine but was not produced out of them. The Lutheran priesthood continued to be governed by bishops, but members of the clergy were permitted to marry. (Only in recent years have Lutheran women been ordained as priests.)

In most parts of Germany and Scandinavia, Lutheran Christianity became the state religion. The '**Evangelical**' Church, as it is called in Germany, is dominant in northwestern and northeastern Germany, while Catholicism is stronger in the south. To this day, Germany provides basic funding for churches out of tax revenues. All taxpayers, including non-believers, pay a flat rate, and the money is directed to Evangelical or Catholic treasuries depending on the taxpayer's affiliation. Outside Germany and Scandinavia, Lutheranism has spread through migration and missionary activity.

During the nineteenth century, it was carried to North America by Germans who settled in places such as Pennsylvania, Ohio, Missouri, and Ontario, and by Scandinavians, most of whom settled in Minnesota and Wisconsin. The ethnic character of the North American Lutheran churches has become diluted over time, except in places where it has been refreshed by continuing immigration.

Anglicans

In Germany the Reformation was a popular movement, but in England it was royal policy. Henry VIII (r. 1509–47) wanted a male heir, but his queen, Catherine of Aragon, had borne only a daughter. Hoping that Anne Boleyn would produce a son, in 1527 Henry requested an annulment of his marriage to Catherine on the grounds that she had previously been married to his deceased brother. Although Pope Clement VII refused the request, Henry found some support in European universities. In 1533, therefore, he secretly married Anne and then had the archbishop of Canterbury, Thomas Cranmer, annul the first marriage and pronounce the second valid.

At Henry's instigation, the English parliament in 1534 passed an Act of Supremacy, which proclaimed the king 'the only Supreme Head in earth of the Church of England'. Although the wording implied that the monarch had always had that authority, in fact he had not: the act itself was the first document in which the king replaced the pope as head of the English Church.

But divorce and a male successor were not the only things on Henry's mind. While the break with Rome could be interpreted as the product of high-minded principle, it is more likely that Henry was motivated by the desire to expropriate the Roman Church's vast landholdings. Throughout England, the ruins of the abbeys that Henry confiscated stand as a stark reminder, as do similar ruins elsewhere in northern Europe.

The key Protestant reformer under Henry's son, Edward VI, was Cranmer, the archbishop of Canterbury. Convinced that the austere Calvinist approach to reform imposed in Geneva was correct, Cranmer purged the English Church of its images, candles, and priestly vestments and interpreted the Eucharist as a memorial meal around a table rather than a sacrifice at an altar. The features of Roman Catholic practice that Cranmer eliminated under Edward were all reintroduced under Henry's eldest daughter, the Catholic Mary Tudor (r. 1553–8), but Cranmer made an enduring contribution in the 1549 *Book of Common Prayer*, still a model for Anglican worship.

Cranmer was trapped between the Reformation in which he believed and the monarchy he served. Charged with treason and then heresy, he tried at first to avoid execution by recanting his Protestant views and affirming papal supremacy and Latin Eucharistic theology. But when he was burned at the stake, he held to the flames the hand with which he had written the recantations, declaring, 'This hand has offended.'

When Henry's second daughter, Elizabeth I, succeeded her sister, the Church of England settled into a balanced position. Under Elizabeth the Church took a middle way. For example, the 1559 revision of the *Book of Common Prayer* preserves both Eucharistic theologies: the more Catholic sacrificial concept of 'this is my body, given for you', and the more Protestant memorial reading of 'take, eat in remembrance of me'.

In the end, even though the English Reformation was largely directed from the top down, the church it produced had much in common with the church produced by the grass-roots Lutheran Reformation: an established a state church without links to Rome; a traditional mass as one type of liturgy, but conducted in the vernacular; a hierarchy with bishops, but with clergy who could now marry. The Church of England has remained a state institution, with the monarch as its titular head. The ranking bishop of the Church continues to be the archbishop of Canterbury.

The tradition of the Church of England is known in most parts of the world as Anglican, although in the United States it is called Episcopalian, after its form of government by bishops. Anglicanism has taken root wherever British influence has been dominant, not only in Australia, New Zealand, South Africa, and English-speaking Canada, but also in the former British colonies and protectorates in East Africa, West Africa, the Caribbean, India, and the Polynesian islands.

The diversity of the human community is reflected among the participating bishops at international meetings of the Anglican communion. In recent years, however, the relative liberality of the American and English churches in approving the ordination of homosexual priests has led to a serious disagreement with the more conservative bishops of the former colonies and protectorates.

A tension of much longer standing is the one between what came to be called 'high-church' and 'low-church' Anglicanism. The high-church side can approach Roman Catholicism in its emphasis on ritual, whereas the low-church side is more spontaneous and evangelical.

A notable expression of high-church Anglicanism was the Oxford movement, which began as a response to changes in the legal status of the Church of England. Between 1828 and 1832, laws that had restricted Roman Catholics or required municipal officers to be practising Anglicans were repealed, and some Anglicans feared their Church might lose its established status. The movement's response was to emphasize that the Church was not dependent on the state, but derived its authority and truth from 'catholic' tradition—by which they meant not the Roman Catholic Church but the tradition that began with the apostles.

Between 1833 and 1841 John Keble, John Henry Newman, and others published 90 *Tracts for the Times*, arguing for the continuity of that tradition. The Tractarians, as they came to be called, also promoted a revival of Anglican interest in the aesthetics of the liturgy and the dignity of priesthood. Despite low-church fears of Roman Catholic influence, which were not allayed by the influx of immigrants from Catholic Ireland at the time of the famine, the Oxford movement succeeded in bringing Anglicanism closer to Roman Catholicism. In fact, Newman himself became a Roman Catholic in 1845, and in 1879 he was made a cardinal.

Reformed Churches

From the 1520s to 1560s, the Reformation movement in and around Switzerland departed from Luther's position on several points. While Zwingli in Zürich disputed Luther's Eucharistic theology, Martin Bucer in Strasbourg promoted a more active role for lay people as ministers, elders, deacons, and teachers.

The dominant intellectual leader of the Reformation, however, was John Calvin (1509–64), a lawyer and classical scholar (even a Renaissance humanist) who imposed rigorous norms of doctrine and conduct on the city of Geneva. Calvin's Geneva has been described as a theocracy comparable to Iran under the rule of religio-legal scholars after 1979. Yet to his followers Calvin's trust in God's power and caring providence brought at least as much joy as it did fear.

Calvin's principal theological treatise, first published in 1536 and expanded in subsequent editions, is generally known in English as *Institutes of the Christian Religion*. In form, it is a manual of spiritual discipline or instruction in Christian piety. Calvin echoes Augustine's idea, expressed in the *Confessions*, that humans are created for communion with God and lack rest until they arrive at it. The human approach to God is both intellectual and spiritual; Calvin uses the term 'knowledge' almost synonymously with 'faith'. For Calvin, God is absolutely sovereign, initiating all actions, both creating and redeeming the world. Two implications of this teaching were given a central place by Calvin's interpreters, and the Reformed tradition has struggled to defend them ever since: the idea that humans are so sinful as to be utterly dependent on divine grace for salvation; and the idea that the sovereign God has **predestined** every person to either salvation or damnation. There is a juridical flavour to Calvin's system that recalls

Anselm, and the substitution of Christ as a payment for human sin, as in Anselm's atonement theory, had a central place in Calvin's thought, alongside the work of the Holy Spirit and the authority of scripture. So strong was Calvin's influence that the **Reformed Churches** are often referred to as Calvinist.

From sixteenth-century Geneva, the ideas of the Swiss Reformation spread to other lands, notably France (where the adherents of the Reformation are known as the Huguenots), the Netherlands, Hungary, England, and Scotland. In the Netherlands, Calvin's teaching of predestination was challenged by Jacobus Arminius, who believed that God's sovereignty was compatible with human free will. Arminian views were condemned by an assembly in Dordrecht (Dort) in 1518, which sentenced their supporter, the scholar and jurist Hugo Grotius to life imprisonment. (Grotius escaped in a box of books being shipped to his wife and settled for a time in Paris.)

In the Netherlands and Hungary, the Calvinist churches have been known as 'Reformed' churches, after their theological tradition. In England, the tradition was called Presbyterian, because of its form of government by lay elders or 'presbyters'; for the same reason, the established state Church of Scotland is termed Presbyterian. Reformed Churches do not have bishops; instead, the regional representative assembly, the presbytery, corporately performs the traditional tasks of a bishop, including the supervision, examination, and ordination of candidates for ministry. Through migration Presbyterianism has taken root on other continents. Presbyterians from England and Scotland settled in eastern Canada and the middle Atlantic American states, as well as in New Zealand and Australia. Dutch Reformed settlers carried their tradition to South Africa, New Amsterdam (New York), and Michigan. In the nineteenth and twentieth centuries, Presbyterian missions from Britain and North America reached many parts of Asia and Africa, but in most cases the churches they founded remained small, and in Islamic regions they found most of their recruits among Eastern Orthodox Christians. The Presbyterians did become a sizable minority in Korea, however.

Anabaptists

Each of the three branches of the Reformation named so far was willing, even eager, to take over the governance of the local European society and to replace established institutions by becoming an establishment itself. This was not the case with the somewhat more diverse and less cohesive group who became known as 'Anabaptists'.

The Anabaptists' emphasis on adult rather than infant baptism reflected their voluntaristic conception of Christianity. In their view, baptism should not be imposed: it should be actively sought on the basis of mature personal commitment. The Church should seek to restore the close-knit sense of community of the apostolic era, and should remain apart from political institutions and structures. Anabaptist groups rely on lay preachers rather than trained clergy and have tended to pacifism in times of war. Essentially an antiestablishment movement, the Anabaptist movement emerged in response to dissatisfaction with the pace of change in the first decade of the Reformation. One of the first breaks with the 'establishment' Reformation came in 1525, when some of the more radical followers of Zwingli began administering adult baptism in defiance of Zwingli himself.

A decade later, in the northwestern German town of Münster, Anabaptist efforts to establish the kingdom of God by force prompted a crackdown by Catholic and Protestant authorities alike. Thereafter a former Dutch priest named Menno Simons led the movement into a largely otherworldly and non-violent path. Since there was virtually no chance of removing the authorities, he urged his followers to remove themselves from society. Some of his followers—the Mennonites—settled in the Netherlands, where they enjoyed toleration and by the middle of the nineteenth century had largely assimilated to the secular climate of the Enlightenment. As the movement spread eastward through Germany and Austria to the Ukraine, however, hardship and persecution led some to remove themselves from Europe altogether.

Mennonites who migrated to the Americas settled mainly in Pennsylvania and, later, Ontario and the Canadian prairies. In Pennsylvania, where some arrived as early as 1663, they came to be known as Pennsylvania Dutch (from *Deutsch*, meaning 'German'). Today most Mennonites are fully part of the modern world. Nevertheless, some branches, such as the Old Order Amish farmers in Pennsylvania and Ontario prefer traditional modes of dress and conduct. They continue to farm with the draft animals and simple tools of a century ago, resisting more modern machinery and gadgetry as part of the moral temptation and corruption of the secular world.

Unitarians

Unitarianism rejects the doctrine of the Trinity. So what does it have to do with a tradition that may be strictly defined as faith in Jesus as the son of God? Its relevance lies in the fact that it reflects the experience of those who have struggled intellectually with the doctrine of the Trinity and finally concluded that they could not affirm the divinity of Jesus. Historically, it is only in the context of traditional Christianity that Unitarianism makes sense.

As early as 1527 in Strasbourg, Martin Cellarius preferred to speak of God as a single person. Others expressed similar views. Subsequently, Unitarian communities emerged in several lands, including Poland and Hungary. In England, John Biddle began to publish Unitarian tracts in 1652, but a Unitarian congregation was not organized until 1773–4, when Theophilus Lindsey resigned from the Church of England and opened a Unitarian chapel in London.

In the United States, Unitarianism represented a left-wing theological break with Congregationalism (see p. 217 below). William Ellery Channing preached a sermon in Baltimore in 1819 that American Unitarians have taken as a kind of denominational manifesto. However, Channing did not think of the Unitarians as a separate group and claimed to belong 'not to a sect, but to the community of free minds'.

In North America, Unitarianism has appealed mainly to people of a humanist and rationalist bent, often in university circles. In 1961, the Unitarians merged with a kindred group, the Universalists. Because of its minimal creedal demands, Unitarianism has often been the denomination of choice for Jewish–Christian couples.

Puritanism

Puritanism was not a denomination in itself, but a movement in English and colonial American Protestant churches that flourished from the sixteenth to the mid-seventeenth century. It began as an effort to 'purify' the Church of England of the remnants of Catholic practice that it retained after the accession of Elizabeth I in 1558, when Protestants exiled during the reign of the Catholic Mary I returned to England from Calvinist Geneva.

Among the ideas the exiles introduced from Geneva was the Calvinist theory of predestination. Some Anglican theologians, such as Richard Hooker and William Laud, preferred the free-will arguments of their Dutch contemporary Jacobus Arminius. But the Puritans held firmly to Calvinist theology, committing themselves to a rigorous view of human sinfulness and divine predestination.

Individuals who believed themselves to have been chosen by God for salvation tended to display a strict, sometimes smug, sense of moral vocation that was reflected in the Puritan movement. The poetry of John Milton (*Paradise Lost*) and the *Pilgrim's Progress* of John Bunyan are well-known literary expressions of Puritan ideals, which included moderation in behaviour and moral activism.

A seminal modern interpretation of Calvinist thinking was a 1904–5 essay by the German sociologist Max Weber. In *The Protestant Ethic and the Spirit of Capitalism*, Weber explored the Calvinist incentives for zealous, self-denying action to transform the world of the here and now, however uncertain one's fate in the hereafter might remain. Although Reformation leaders preached other-worldly values and scorned the direct pursuit of riches, doing well could be a by-product of do-ing good. As Weber saw it, Calvinists (including Puritans) who were motivated both to work hard and to live simple lives tended to accumulate sav-ings and thus to play an important role in a cap-italist system. Puritans and English Presbyterians found themselves in substantial agreement in the Westminster Confession of Faith in 1647, and in the 1650s Oliver Cromwell sought to unite the Presbyterians, Congregationalists, and Baptists in a Puritan state church. But the Church of England largely rid itself of Puritanism with the restoration of the monarchy in 1660, and thereafter Puritan-ism ceased to have a coherent existence as a move-ment in England. It had a ripple effect, however, in non-conformist (i.e., non-Anglican Protestant) denominations such as the Congregationalists. By the time Puritanism waned in England, it had al-ready spread to the new world, carried by Puritan immigrants to New England.

Seventeenth-Century Denominations

Congregationalists

The Congregational churches trace their roots to 'separatist' clergy in the time of Elizabeth I, but they did not become a significant force in England until the time of Cromwell, in the mid-1600s. As far as doctrine is concerned, there is little to distinguish Congregationalism from Presbyterian Calvinism. Where they differ is in their form of governance. Carrying the notion of the priesthood of all believers to its logical conclusion, Congrega-tionalists reject the idea of elders and accord each individual congregation the ultimate authority to manage its theological and institutional affairs: for them, the only higher power is God.

In England, Congregational churches formed a Congregational Union in 1832 and were active in political and missionary causes throughout the nineteenth century. But the tradition's strong-hold was Massachusetts, where Congregational-ists founded Harvard University in 1637 in order not 'to leave an illiterate ministry to the churches, when our present ministers shall lie in the dust'. Yale University (1701) and other educational in-stitutions in the American northeast were also founded by Congregationalists.

Baptists

Like the Anabaptists in continental Europe, the English Baptists practised the baptism of mature believers rather than infants. But they were much more intimately connected with the Puritan move-ment in England than with the Anabaptists. They believed that people should choose their religion rather than be born into it, and that the individ-ual's choice ought to be private and beyond any interference by the state. By the 1640s, the Eng-lish Baptist movement had two branches. Calvin-ist, or 'Particular', Baptists reserved redemption for a particular sector of humanity, whereas 'Gen-eral' Baptists proclaimed a general redemption for humanity.

The first Baptist churches in the United States were established as early as 1639, but the Baptist presence remained small until the revival move-ment of 1740–3 known as the Great Awakening. Though the Baptists were not among its principal protagonists, they made massive numerical gains in its wake. They positioned themselves to be-come the largest American Protestant denomina-tion partly through their successful appeal to the Black population; by the middle of the twentieth century, two out of every three African-American Christians were Baptists.

Quakers

George Fox was an English dissenter who in 1646, after three years of seeking, claimed to have found spiritual enlightenment. He began to preach that moral and spiritual peace was not to be had in the institutional churches but in the experience of the 'inner light' of the living Christ. He called his followers Friends of the Truth, but they became known as 'Quakers' after Fox, appearing in court on charges of blasphemy, advised the judge to tremble at the word of the Lord. The judge responded by calling Fox a 'quaker' and the name stuck, although the movement has called itself the Religious Society of Friends since the nineteenth century.

Quakers at worship combine intellectual and spiritual reflection, sitting in silence until moved by the Holy Spirit to speak. Although there is no ritual as such, meetings do follow conventions: roughly twenty minutes are allowed to pass before anyone speaks; senior members of the meeting generally speak first; and declarations are expected to be logical and thoughtful.

Quakers today number only about 100,000 worldwide, but their humanitarian work for peace and refugee-relief causes has earned the movement widespread respect. The Quakers are strongest in Pennsylvania (founded by William Penn in 1682 specifically as a place where Quakers might find religious toleration and free expression), Indiana, and around various university towns.

For all the diversity of their practice, the Congregationalists, Baptists, and Quakers shared one principle: rejection of external human authority—a central theme of the Reformation.

Eighteenth-Century Denominations

Pietism

The term 'Pietism' designates not a denomination but a movement that rippled through various Protestant denominations, including the Lutherans in Germany and the Reformed (Calvinist) churches in the Netherlands, beginning in the late 1600s. Dissatisfied with the doctrinal and institutional rigidity they perceived in the Protestant churches emerging from the Reformation, Pietists sought a spontaneous renewal of faith accompanied by a feeling of certainty of divine forgiveness and acceptance. For many, that feeling of certainty was all the evidence they needed to validate their faith. This position set Pietists against the emerging rationalism of the eighteenth-century Enlightenment but would find intellectual expansion in the emphasis laid on feeling by Schleiermacher (see p. 241). Pietism spread in Lutheran circles both in Europe and in the Americas. In the form articulated by the Moravian Brethren—who traced their origins to the early Czech reformer John Hus—it also influenced the Wesleyan movement in England and contributed to Methodism.

Methodists

In the late 1720s, a number of Anglican students at Oxford formed a group to study the Bible and attend church together. This methodical approach inspired others to nickname them 'Methodists'. Among them were John Wesley (1703–91), his younger brother Charles, and George Whitefield, all three of whom embarked on careers as itinerant preachers. In 1735 John and Charles set out on a mission to evangelize Native Americans in Georgia, but their condemnation of slavery made them unwelcome in the American South and they returned to England in 1738. A few months later, after a visit to a Moravian Pietist community, and three days after his brother Charles's conversion, John Wesley underwent a similar experience, feeling his heart 'strangely warmed', in Pietist fashion.

John Wesley began to preach to public gatherings, often of miners and workers, outside the established churches. In the 53 years until his death, he preached more than 40,000 sermons, averaging 15 a week, and travelled some 320,000 kilometres (200,000 miles), mainly on horseback. Though he had at first hoped his movement would revitalize the Church of England from within, Wesley eventually oversaw the organization of his following as an independent denomination and personally ordained leaders for it. Charles Wesley also became an itinerant preacher, but would be remembered above all for the many hymns he composed.

Revivalism

By the mid-1700s, the Pietist model of spiritual rebirth or conversion had spread to several denominations. Efforts to promote a reawakening of spiritual enthusiasm resulted in a wave of revivals, especially in the American colonies. The 'Great Awakening' of 1740–3 was one such movement, sparked by the Calvinist preaching of a gifted and versatile theologian named Jonathan Edwards after a visit from the Wesleys' associate George Whitefield. Its influence spread from Massachusetts throughout New England and well beyond, altering the shape of American Protestantism as the nation expanded westward.

Itinerant preachers addressing camp meetings—large gatherings, typically held in the open air and sometimes continuing for several days—inspired mass conversions. Although Edwards had preached mainly to Congregationalists and Presbyterians, the Methodists and Baptists were the most successful in making new recruits. The Methodists became the largest Protestant denomination in the American Midwest and, after the Baptists, in the American South as well.

Holiness Churches

In time the main Methodist bodies in America became more organized and conventional, more sedate and mainline. But new independent churches and movements continued to spring from the revivalist roots of Methodism. Because of their emphasis on the experience of receiving the gift of holiness, these congregations are often referred to as **Holiness Churches**. Among them are the Church of the Nazarene and the Church of God (started in Anderson, Indiana).

The intensity of feeling associated with that experience is often expressed physically. Some people roll in the aisles of the meeting (hence the nickname 'holy rollers'); some speak out ecstatically in an exotic prayer language ('speaking in tongues', technically termed '**glossolalia**'). In either case, the group believes such behaviour to be inspired by the Holy Spirit. Though initially a Protestant phenomenon, this **charismatic** activity (from the Greek word for spiritual gifts) has spread to Catholic Christians as well since the 1970s.

Roman Catholicism after 1500

The Catholic Reformation

The Roman Church itself recognized the need to correct the abuses of ecclesiastical power that Luther had condemned. With the Council of Trent (1545–63), the Latin Church embarked on a process of renewal emphasizing discipline, accountability, and faithfulness to ecclesiastical and historical tradition that would come to be known as either the 'Catholic Reformation' or the 'Counter Reformation' (because it was designed to counter the rise of Protestantism).

The Council of Trent

After several delays, the Council of Trent opened in 1545 at the Italian city of Trento, northwest of Venice, and continued on and off until 1563, when it finished with a burst of decisive energy. Although participation was restricted to Catholic bishops, Protestants were in attendance at some of the sessions, and for a time there was even hope for reconciliation and reunion, but a compromise could not be achieved. The decrees formulated at Trent—the adjective for them is 'Tridentine'—would stand as the Roman Catholic Church's self-definition for four centuries. They covered the entire range of issues, practical and theoretical, that had come to a boil in the Reformation.

Historians differ in their assessments of the Roman Catholic response to the Reformation. Protestants see the post-Tridentine era as one of repression, pointing to the *Index of Prohibited Books*, which was institutionalized at Trent, and the revival of the investigative tribunals of the Inquisition as examples. Catholic interpreters do not deny that there was an *Index* or an Inquisition, but they underline the need for discipline and fidelity to truth understood conservatively, as well as to a genuine desire for renewal.

The council acted to enforce discipline and end the abuses and excesses that had so weakened the Church's credibility as an institution. It stood its ground against some of the Protestants' theoretical positions, however. It reaffirmed the authority of institutional tradition alongside scripture. It also upheld the idea of a priesthood with a distinct status and function as intermediaries, reaffirming the tradition of celibacy and creating seminaries for training new priests. In addition, Trent reiterated the Catholic understanding of the mass as a sacrifice. According to the doctrine of **transubstantiation**, the words 'this is my body' and 'this is my blood' are literally and mysteriously effective, transforming the wafer and the wine of the mass into the body and the blood of Christ.

For four centuries after Trent, the Tridentine text of the mass, in Latin, was standard throughout the Catholic world. Since Latin was no longer spoken by the congregation, however, the moment of transubstantiation was indicated by the ringing of a small bell. For the faithful that moment is one of mystery and miracle, but others have dismissed it as a show; the English expression 'hocus-pocus' is thought to have originated in a garbling of the words *hoc est corpus meum*, 'this is my body', pronounced in Latin by the priest.

The Jesuits

Founded shortly before the Council of Trent, in 1540, the Society of Jesus, or Jesuit order, exemplified three of the principal areas of renewal in the Catholic Church after the Reformation: spiritual discipline, education, and missionary expansion. Its founder, Iñigo López (c. 1495–1556), of the northern Spanish town of Loyola, is better known by the name Ignatius, which he used after the age of forty. In his twenties, Iñigo was practically a soldier of fortune, serving with bravado in the retinues of nobles until he was wounded in the leg by a cannonball. He chose painful corrective surgery, in an age without anesthesia. The books available during his convalescence included the lives of saints, which may have influenced his decision to take religious vows of poverty, chastity, and obedience.

It was while following a regimen of prayer and bodily self-denial in 1522–3 that he wrote his *Spiritual Exercises*. A concise manual for Christian meditation, a theological reflection on Christ's incarnation as a divine intervention in human history, and a call to arms to join a spiritual crusade, it is a classic of Catholic piety. An encyclical of Pope Paul III in 1548 gave it the most favourable papal endorsement for any book ever with the possible exception of the Bible, and in 1922 Pope Pius XI designated Ignatius, who had been canonized exactly 300 years earlier, the patron saint of spiritual exercises.

After being rejected for permanent residence in Jerusalem, which was under Turkish control, Ignatius returned to Spain in 1524, where he studied philosophy and gained followers for his spiritual exercises. Because the heresy-hunting climate in Spain put restrictions on his activity, he moved to Paris in 1528 and with six friends formed a society in 1534 vowing strict poverty and service to others. In the next few years they moved to Italy, where several, including Ignatius, were ordained as priests. In 1540, Pope Paul III approved the society as a religious order, which Ignatius led as 'general' until his death sixteen years later.

As time passed, the Jesuits became particularly important as teachers, well known for rigorous intellectual training. Many institutions are named in honour of one or another of the leading figures in the order's first century: in addition to Ignatius himself, these figures include Robert Bellarmine, Peter Canisius, Aloysius Gonzaga, and Francis Xavier.

As a result of their influence as educators, the Jesuits became the confessor priests of royalty in several European courts, both admired and criticized for their intricate reasoning on moral questions ('casuistry'). After the middle of the

From a letter of Marie de l'Incarnation

In 1654, 15 years after her arrival in Quebec, Marie de l'Incarnation wrote to her son describing her mystic relationship with the divine.

The state which I now experience . . . is a completely extraordinary clearness about the ways of the adorable Spirit of the Word Incarnate. I know, experientially in great pureness and certainty, that here is Love Himself intimately joined to me and joining my spirit to His and 'all that He has said has spirit and life, [*John* 6: 63],' in me. Particularly does my soul experience being in this intimate union with Him. . . .

I find myself frequently saying to Him: 'Divine Spirit, guide me in the ways of my Divine Spouse.' I am continuously engaged in this divine exchange in a fashion and a manner so delicate, so simple, and so intense that there is no way of expressing it. It is not an act. It is not a sigh. It is an air so gentle in the centre of the soul where God has His dwelling that . . . I cannot find words to express it. My converse with the adorable Majesty contains only what the Spirit makes me say. It is by Him that I speak because in this language of the spirit in such exchanges as these wherein His Divine Majesty wills to dignify my lowliness I am entirely incapable of doing anything except through his very delicate urging (O'Brien 1964: 297–8).

eighteenth century, however, suspicion of their 'foreign' political influence led to their expulsion from Portugal, France, and Spain, and in 1773 Rome suspended the order in Latin countries. The suspension was never extended to Russia, however, and individual Jesuits continued to teach in Germany and Austria. Rome reinstated the order in 1814.

Catholic Women's Orders

The most prominent Catholic teaching order of women dates from exactly the same period. The Ursulines, founded in 1535 in Italy by Angela Merici, became particularly influential in France and Canada. One of the most famous Ursulines was the mystic Marie Guyard (1599–1672), known as Marie de l'Incarnation. Left a widow before she was 20, she entrusted her young son to her sister and entered the Ursuline convent at Tours at the age of 27. Inspired by the Jesuits' accounts of their mission in New France, in 1639 she travelled to the small French settlement at Quebec, where she established a convent, a school, and a 'seminary' for young Aboriginal women. Her numerous letters are an invaluable source of information on early New France. She also wrote of her personal development as a mystic.

Roman Catholic Missions

Asia

India

Once the Portuguese had opened a trade route to India in the sixteenth century, the king of Portugal sent the Spanish Jesuit Francis Xavier, one of Ignatius's original circle, to evangelize the East Indies. Francis reached India in 1542, made Goa his base, and began to establish communities of converts along the coastlines of India, Sri Lanka, and the Malay Peninsula. Despite chronic seasickness, he travelled on to Japan in 1549 and in 1552 set out for China, but fell ill and died on the way. The Jesuits have attributed 700,000 conversions to Francis.

In 1599 the archbishop of Goa persuaded the indigenous Syriac Church ('the Christians of St Thomas') of the Malabar Coast to repudiate the patriarch of Baghdad and transfer their allegiance to Rome. But fifty years later many of this community, disappointed with the Jesuits' performance, transferred their allegiance to the Syrian Orthodox Church.

Much of the success achieved by missionaries in Portuguese territories has been attributed to the material benefits that came with conversion; access to food, employment, or special privileges induced many economically and socially disadvantaged Hindus to convert (those who did so were sometimes called 'rice Christians'). During the first half of the seventeenth century, however, the Italian Jesuit Robert De Nobili took a different approach, trying to adapt Christianity to the local culture. An aristocrat himself, he set out to reach the brahmin class of Hindus by adopting the discipline of Indian holy men and by not challenging the caste structure of Indian society. He avoided contact with outcastes and advocated the appointment of different missionaries to preach to different Hindu castes. He also studied various Indian languages, including Sanskrit, and wrote books, hymns, and poems in them. He is said to have made 100,000 converts, but other missionaries were critical of his approach. Summoned to appear before the archbishop of Goa to respond to complaints, he was allowed to continue, but the degree to which missionaries should assimilate to local cultures was to remain a perennial subject of debate.

Japan

In Japan, where Francis Xavier spent three years (1549–52), assimilation to the local culture at first produced remarkable success. The Portuguese priests admired the Japanese, especially the military discipline of the feudal class. For their part, the Japanese seem to have found the Jesuits similar to their own Zen monks in discipline and learning, and to have seen Christianity as another Buddhist sect. It was policy to conform to Japanese etiquette, as Alessandro Valignano indicated on his inspection visit to Jesuit missions there in 1579; he stipulated that all local customs not explicitly in contradiction to Christianity should be observed. Especially on the southwestern island of Kyushu, various local Japanese lords, who were eager to build up trade, encouraged the missionaries, espoused Christianity, and imposed it on their realms. An estimated 150,000 Japanese had become Christians by 1582, and by 1615 that figure may have risen as high as 500,000. But Japanese rulers were arising who saw the influence of the missionaries as a threat. In 1587 the shogun Hideyoshi Toyotomi ordered the missionaries banished, though he did not enforce the ban until 1597, when he executed nine missionaries

A descendant of Japan's 'Kakure Kirishitan', or 'Hidden Christians', conducts a ritual in front of holy relics on Ikitsuki Island (KIYOSHI OTA/Reuters/Landov).

and seventeen Japanese Christians. The Tokugawa shogun Hidetada consolidated power in central Japan and, after a few years of anti-Christian edicts, undertook in 1614 to round up and deport the 150 Christian missionaries who were in Japan at the time, but about a third of them managed to find their way back.

The persecution of Christians intensified under Hidetada, reaching a peak in the early 1620s. Torture awaited those who would not comply when asked to step on an image of Christ or Mary. The Roman Catholic Church counts 3,125 as martyrs in this period in Japan. Around Nagasaki, where Christianity had been strongest, resentment of the central Tokugawa government prompted an uprising in 1637–8, but the crushing of this resistance marked the end of Japan's 'Christian century'. Catholic Christianity ceased to be a presence in Japan, although when the country was opened up to renewed foreign contact two centuries later, in 1858, missionaries discovered a small remnant community that had kept the faith alive, if in a garbled form.

China

When the Italian Jesuit missionary Matteo Ricci landed at the southern Chinese port of Macau in 1582, he was far from the first to have taken Christianity to China. We know of two previous waves: one was the Nestorian branch of Christianity, which had travelled overland to Xi'an in 635, and the other a Catholic mission under the Franciscan John of Monte Corvino, which travelled overland to Beijing in 1294. Although no Christian community survived from these earlier waves, there was a monument: a Nestorian inscription on a large standing stone that the Jesuits found in Xi'an almost a thousand years after it had been carved.

Ricci did his best to avoid alienating the Chinese. When he and his Jesuit companions first made their way into southern China after 1582, they wore clothing similar to that of Buddhist monks and conducted themselves unobtrusively. After being ordered in 1589 to leave one southern locale, they apparently acted on the advice of a local convert and presented themselves as Confucian-style scholars rather than Buddhist-style monks.

Ricci and the Jesuits won favour at the imperial court in Beijing by offering the emperor gifts such as lenses and prisms, mechanical clocks, and European maps. Not only were the Jesuits invited to stay, but they received a monthly stipend. Ricci remained in Beijing until his death nine years later. This was a period of active cultural exchange, in which Chinese philosophical and religious texts were translated into Latin and European scientific and mathematical texts were translated into Chinese.

One of Ricci's successors was a German Jesuit named Adam Schall von Bell, who had studied Galileo's astronomy in Rome. He arrived in China in 1619, was given a post in the imperial bureau of astronomy in 1629 with responsibilities for reforming the calendar, and was made chief of the bureau in 1645 after he had helped cure the empress dowager of an illness. In 1650, Schall was able to build a church in Beijing that the emperor even attended. When he was in his mid-seventies, however, Schall was sentenced for plotting against the state, probably because of complaints from jealous Chinese astronomers.

There were complaints from Europeans as well, notably Dominicans and Franciscans, concerning the Jesuits' strategy of accommodating indigenous cultural traditions. Schall's successor, the Flemish Jesuit Ferdinand Verbiest, spent more than thirty years in China, from 1657 until 1688, during which three issues in particular raised questions about the compatibility of Chinese customs and Christianity. First, the Jesuits allowed Chinese converts to take part in rituals honouring Confucius, presumably thereby endorsing his moral system as compatible with Christianity. Second, they permitted converts to continue practising the rituals of 'ancestor worship', in which deceased family members were honoured with prostrations, incense, and food offerings. Third was the question of whether Chinese terms such as 'Tian' ('heaven'), and 'Shangdi' ('the Lord above'), meant the same thing as the Christian term 'God'.

Politically, the Jesuits were walking a tightrope. On the one hand, they wanted to win over the Chinese mandarins and so needed to offer a subtle and judicious endorsement of Chinese culture. On the other hand, they were being challenged by rival orders, notably the Franciscans and Dominicans, who, because of their medieval experience in Europe and recent experience among tribal populations in places such as the Philippines automatically condemned anything that smacked of paganism.

The confrontational evangelism of these orders in China embarrassed the Jesuits. Meanwhile, in 1639, a Dominican complained to Rome about the Jesuits, representing their positions on some points (such as their reluctance to declare Confucius to be in hell) accurately and misrepresenting them on others. Rome essentially agreed, and it took the Jesuits fifteen years to get the charges cleared.

The closing years of the seventeenth century brought renewed suspicion of the Jesuits' strategy of accommodation, this time voiced by French missionaries. The upshot, in 1693, was a ruling by Charles Maigrot, a papal vicar in coastal China, that condemned Ricci's teachings, participation in the Chinese rites, and the use of Chinese terms for God. The emperor, who had just issued an edict of toleration, remained sympathetic to the Jesuits, but when a papal legate—another Frenchman—arrived in China in 1705, he and Maigrot together showed themselves to be so ignorant of Chinese culture that the emperor banished them.

The emperor subsequently gave residence permits only to pro-Ricci missionaries. But with Ricci's death in 1722, any Christian hope for the evangelization of China from the top down came to an end. Within a few years, there were hardly any Christians left among the Chinese literati. Meanwhile, the restrictions imposed by Maigrot were renewed by papal decrees in 1715 and again in 1742, severely curtailing the ability of Catholic missionaries in China to present Christianity in indigenous terms.

Three centuries after Vasco da Gama and Christopher Columbus, Catholic missions in Asia were left with almost nothing apart from the Philippines to show for their efforts. European Christianity had failed to displace the religious traditions, social institutions, and sophisticated intellectual heritages of the Eastern civilizations. In the Western hemisphere, by contrast, the story was just the opposite. Latin America was to become a new heartland of Catholicism.

Catholic Missions in the Americas

Barely a year after Columbus landed at Santo Domingo in 1492, a papal bull effectively divided the non-European world between Spain and Portugal. Africa, Asia, and Brazil went to Portugal, and the rest of Latin America to Spain. From the very beginning, therefore, an intimate relationship existed between the Church and the state in Latin America.

When Hernán Cortés reached Mexico in 1519 and Francisco Pizarro reached Peru in 1532–3, they encountered highly sophisticated social and religious institutions. Yet the great civilizations of the Aztecs and Mayas in Mexico and the Incas in Peru seemed to fall like dominoes before the relatively small European forces. In the past, some historians attributed the Europeans' success to their advantage in weapons, or their use of horses, which the indigenous peoples of the Americas did not have. More recent theories have emphasized the devastating effect of European diseases on populations that had no natural immunity to them.

In Mexico, the Aztec ruler Moctezuma (Montezuma) even welcomed Cortés with gifts. One explanation of that episode suggests that the Aztecs were expecting the god Quetzalcoatl to arrive from the east in the form of a fair-skinned king, and therefore may have perceived Cortés and his men as the fulfillment of their religious expectations. If

Bernardino de Sahagún and Bartolomé de las Casas

Two important exceptions to the standard missionary pattern in Latin America were Bernardino de Sahagún and Bartolomé de las Casas. Sahagún (c. 1490–1590) was a Franciscan who made it his business not only to learn the language of the Aztecs but to document their myths, symbols, and rituals. His *Historia de las cosas de Nueva España* ('History of matters in New Spain') is an invaluable ethnographic record of Mexico at the time of its conquest by Cortés.

Bartolomé de las Casas (1484–1566) arrived in the New World in 1502 and settled in Hispaniola with his father. In 1513 he served as a chaplain with the Spanish forces that conquered Cuba. Like every veteran of that campaign, he was given a parcel of land and a number of local people to work it, effectively as slave labour. But las Casas soon renounced his allotment of serfs and set out to win a hearing for the rights of the indigenous people. He eventually joined the Dominican order and wrote a monumental *Historia de las Indias* ('History of the Indies'), detailing the abuses committed by the Spanish in Mexico, which was published only after his death.

Named bishop of Chiapas in Guatemala in 1544, he denied absolution to any slave-holders in his diocese. And in 1550 he returned to Spain to defend the Latin American indigenous people's case in a great debate—held at the request of the king—on the moral justification for European Christian conquest of the peoples of the New World. The issues that las Casas raised concerning cultural imperialism and the use of force are still relevant today.

that was the case, they were sadly mistaken. The priests and friars who accompanied the conquerors had been sent not to fulfill but to displace and destroy Mexican religion. And Cortés himself required that any Mexican tribe seeking to ally itself with the Spanish destroy its sacred images.

In numerical terms, the missionary effort appears to have been a tremendous success. One Franciscan friar calculated that within ten years he had baptized 200,000 local people, as many as 14,000 in a single day. The authenticity of those conversions is questionable, however.

Some of the clergy spoke no South American language, and therefore had to rely on pictures, symbols, and gestures to convey their message. Nor did conquered populations necessarily abandon their traditions when they accepted Christianity. Behind the Christian altars in Mexico were pagan images; inside early Mexican crucifixes were Aztec cult objects; and in coastal Brazil, where West African blacks were taken as slaves, African tribal deities persist to this day in the guise of Catholic saints in the folk religion known as

candomblé. These are only a few examples of the **syncretism**—the fusion of elements from very different traditions—that characterizes Catholic Christianity in Latin America even today.

As the missionaries, accompanied by civilians and soldiers, extended their reach to Paraguay and Argentina in the south and California in the north, they established autonomous villages known as *reducciones* ('reductions'), where local people were protected from colonial enslavement. The price of that protection included acceptance both of Christianity and of a paternalistic system in which the residents' life and work were strictly laid out for them.

By the end of the colonial era, according to some estimates, the Church controlled half of the productive land under Spanish rule. Today Latin America is home to half the world's Roman Catholics, and from Mexico to Tierra del Fuego, Roman Catholicism is the majority religion. Despite the presence of some rapidly growing Protestant groups, particularly **Pentecostal churches**, Catholic Christianity would seem to have no serious

The Virgin of Guadalupe

Across the Western hemisphere, syncretism has given local people religious figures that they can identify as their own. The most important of these figures in Mexico is the Virgin of Guadalupe, whose cult goes back to a hill near Mexico City that was sacred to the Aztec goddess Tonantzin, who was herself a virgin mother of gods. In 1531 a Christian convert named Juan Diego reported an apparition of a beautiful lady who said she was 'one of his own people' and instructed him to gather roses from the hilltop and present them to the bishop. He wrapped them in a piece of cloth, and when he opened the package before the bishop, an image of the Virgin appeared to be visible on the cloth. Preserved in a basilica at the foot of the hill, the cloth is still venerated today, and the cult that surrounds it is reminiscent of popular piety in medieval Europe.

rival in Latin America. On the other hand, Latin American Catholicism may actually contain within itself the rival that it appears to lack. Interfaith dialogue may be today's agenda for Christians in other religiously diverse regions of the world, such as India or North America, but in Latin America the dialogue is with the indigenous past and is internal to the Christian community.

Catholicism in North America

North America is a region where diverse Roman Catholic influences have met and interacted, some carried by missionaries and others by settlers. The Spanish missionary activity in Latin America, for instance, contributed diverse legacies to North America. Florida was an area of early settlement direct from Spain. Texas and New Mexico were part of Mexico until the mid-nineteenth century. In California, the Franciscans established a chain of missions along the coast, the last and northernmost at Sonoma, north of San Francisco, in 1823.

As Russian settlers had established Fort Ross, with an Orthodox chapel, only a little farther north along the same coast, there was an element of competition between the Spaniards, who had arrived in North America via the Atlantic, and the Russians, who had arrived via Siberia. Arguably, the encounter between the Spanish and the Russians in California marks the moment when Christianity finally encircled the globe.

But the Spanish and Portuguese were not the only missionaries to the New World. To the north were the French. In 1535–6 the French explorer Jacques Cartier had sailed up the St Lawrence River as far as the first rapids. Because he was looking for a route to China, he called the spot—near the site of the future Montreal—Lachine. But a permanent French settlement on the St Lawrence had to await the arrival, in 1603, of Samuel de Champlain, who explored upstream to Ottawa and the Great Lakes.

Missionaries followed: four Récollet friars in 1615 and five Jesuits in 1625. The Jesuit Jacques Marquette arrived in Quebec in 1666 and two years later founded a mission at Sault Ste Marie (i.e., St Mary's rapids) at the northern end of Lake Michigan. With the layman Louis Jolliet, who was a native of New France, he explored southward along the Mississippi River. French missionary activity among the Iroquois and other indigenous peoples was handled largely by the Jesuits. Their respect for local ways played an important part in persuading indigenous people to adopt Christianity. But Native traditions were not eradicated.

In recent years, Native traditions of respect for the creator and the creation (i.e., the natural environment) in particular have been attracting new attention. The other major inroads of European Catholicism in North America were the result of migration. French settlements developed along the St Lawrence, in Acadia (Nova Scotia), and along the lower Mississippi (Louisiana), while the colony of Maryland was established in 1632 by George Calvert, Lord Baltimore, specifically as a refuge for Catholics fleeing persecution in England. In time, other regions, including Atlantic Canada and the future Ontario, would also attract Catholic settlers from the British Isles.

From the mid-nineteenth century on, the growth of industrial cities along the East coast of North America attracted large numbers of immigrants from Ireland and later from Italy. In fact, the ecclesiastical hierarchy of the Catholic Church in North America has tended to mirror the local settlement history. Thus in the past many American bishops were of Irish descent, and their successors are increasingly likely to come from Italian or Hispanic backgrounds. There are also newer Catholic immigrant communities of Portuguese, Filipinos, and others. Modern migration reflects the worldwide spread of Christianity; because of their links with the Western Christian world, Christian minorities are somewhat overrepresented among the migrants from different parts of Asia settling in the West today.

🌿 PRACTICE

The Early Church

The early Christians gathered regularly in one another's homes on Sunday mornings, perhaps choosing that time because of its association with the risen Christ. Spontaneous, even trance-like, activity was accepted as a manifestation of the presence of the Holy Spirit, but the norm was a more formalized ritual consisting of prayer, affirmations of faith, song, scripture reading, preaching, and the Eucharistic service. Many services concluded with a benediction or blessing by the officiating minister or priest.

Christian prayer is reverent and contemplative conversation with the divine, in which practitioners seek to align their attitudes and motivations

with it. Christians can pray individually as well as in groups; indeed, Jesus instructs his disciples not to make a show of prayer, but to pray in privacy. He teaches them what is known as the Lord's Prayer, often referred to by its opening words, 'Our Father' (in Latin, *Pater noster*). This prayer was already in fairly wide use around the end of the first century, when the gospels were produced, and is shared by all branches of Christians.

> Our Father, who art in heaven, hallowed be thy name. Thy kingdom come; thy will be done, on earth as it is in heaven. Give us this day our daily bread, and forgive us our trespasses, as we forgive those who trespass against us. And lead us not into temptation, but deliver us from evil [for thine is the kingdom, and the power, and the glory for ever].[2]

Since most Christians know the Lord's Prayer by heart, it is usually recited in unison during worship. Most of the other prayers included in a service are recited by the officiating priest or minister on behalf of the congregation.

The Eucharist

The Eucharist is also common to all branches of Christianity, although it is referred to by different names. It re-enacts the Passover supper that, according to the synoptic gospels, was Jesus' last meal with his disciples, when he distributed the bread and wine, declaring them to be his body and blood, and asked the disciples to do the same in remembrance of him.

Because Jesus gives thanks before distributing the bread and wine, the ritual is called the Eucharist, from the Greek word for thanksgiving. Roman Catholics commonly refer to the Eucharistic service as the mass, from the final words of the Latin Eucharistic ritual, *Ite, missa est* ('Go; it has been delivered'). Many Protestants refer to the ritual as Holy Communion or the Lord's Supper. Eastern Orthodox Christians frequently refer to the service as the Liturgy, from a Greek word meaning 'service'.

The heart of the ritual is the 'Eucharistic prayer', in which the officiating priest or minister repeats the account of Jesus' last supper and invites the congregation to 'communicate'—to receive communion—by taking a portion of the 'elements' of bread and wine. A communicant who takes the bread only is said to receive communion 'in one kind', whereas dipping the bread into the wine or sipping from a cup extends the communion to 'both kinds'.

Baptism

Baptism is the Christian ritual in which a person is admitted into participation in the community. At the time of Jesus, a baptismal ritual signified the washing away of uncleanness, so that the person could enter a new condition. Various movements practised ritual bathing, including the one with which Jesus' forerunner, John the Baptist, was associated.

As long as Christianity remained a minority religion, joining it entailed some potential personal sacrifice. Therefore its initiation ritual was not something to be undertaken lightly. One was baptized into the faith only after a course of instruction. The content of that instruction was called catechism, and those who received it were catechumens.

Worship in the Greek Church

In the first centuries of Christianity, religious services must have included chanting. The evidence is only fragmentary, but similarities in medieval

Greek Orthodox worshippers at the Church of the Nativity in Bethlehem light their candles from the 'Holy Fire' (AFP/ Getty Images).

Roman Catholic, Greek Orthodox, Muslim, and Jewish melodies and harmonies point to a common background, and the signs used for musical notation in the Byzantine era are virtually identical to those recording Jewish cantorial tradition in medieval Hebrew manuscripts.

Many Christians celebrate the eve of Easter with a vigil service in which a flame symbolizing Jesus' resurrection is passed from candle to candle among the congregation. The ceremony is particularly spectacular in the Greek Orthodox service at the Church of the Holy Sepulchre in Jerusalem. Hundreds of worshippers, each carrying a candle, pack the church's rotunda. A priest is ritually searched to ensure that he is carrying no matches. He then enters the chamber at the centre of the rotunda, which marks the traditional site of Jesus' tomb. After a time he extends his arm from the chamber with a miraculously burning taper. The people closest to him light their candles from his and then share the fire with others, so that within moments the vast rotunda is a sea of flame. Outside the church, the fire is carried by runners to Orthodox congregations elsewhere. This ritual impressively symbolizes the spreading of the Easter light and the going forth of the gospel message.

The Concept of Sacrament

The Latin word *sacramentum* originally meant an oath of allegiance, but it came to be applied to a wide variety of formal Christian actions. In the fifth century Augustine used it to refer to formulas such as the Lord's Prayer and the creeds. In Latin Christianity in the twelfth century, as many as thirty sacraments were enumerated, but in the next century a list of seven emerged that became standard for the Catholic tradition: baptism, confirmation, the Eucharist, penance, anointing the seriously ill, ordination, and marriage. Many Protestants pared the list down to baptism and the Eucharist, as the two ritual actions inaugurated by Jesus. The Anglican prayer book's words, 'an outward and visible sign of an inward and spiritual grace', sum up many Christians' understanding of such rituals.

Pilgrimages and Relics

In the early Church, the bodies of saints and martyrs were interred in churches. This practice marked a break from Jewish tradition, which regarded the dead as unclean and required that they be promptly buried in cemeteries. By the fourth century, it was customary to celebrate the Eucharist with altar cloths that had fragments of saints' bones sewn into their hems. And at the Second Council of Nicaea in 787, it was declared mandatory to have a relic—part of the body or personal paraphernalia of a venerated individual—in order to consecrate a church sanctuary.

The importance of relics in popular piety in the medieval era can hardly be overestimated. As tangible things, they were easy for people with little or no schooling to understand, and the practice of making pilgrimages to see them became common in the Middle Ages. For people whose horizons were typically limited to the fields and towns where they lived and worked, a pilgrimage was an experience to look forward to. It was almost the sole form of tourism in the Middle Ages. Organized groups set out to visit various centres and shrines, many of which contained relics, much as people today sign up for package tours to cultural or recreational destinations. The fourteenth-century English pilgrims travelling to the shrine at Canterbury in Geoffrey Chaucer's *Canterbury Tales* represent a variety of social types (including one who is ready to make a quick profit by producing fraudulent relics).

Possession of relics might bring rewards in the next world, but in the interim, cities or chapels that possessed them could expect tangible economic benefits from the pilgrimage trade. Princes and priests made deals to acquire relics, bought them, fought to capture them, stole them, or fabricated them. One English bishop, kneeling to venerate a bone of Mary Magdalene at a pilgrimage site, is said to have bitten off the end of the bone and taken it home with him.

Rarely did all of a saint's bones remain together in one place. Thus even though Santiago (i.e., St James) de Compostela in northwestern Spain was a major pilgrimage destination, portions of the same saint's body could be visited in half a dozen other places. The most treasured relics were those associated with Jesus himself, especially with his suffering and death. Chips and slivers of wood purported to be from the True Cross were highly prized, as were spines from the Crown of Thorns that was placed on Jesus' head before he was crucified. Various pieces of cloth were preserved for the impressions of Jesus' body they were said to carry: his face en route to the crucifixion on Veronica's veil and his entombed body on a shroud that turned up in France in the fourteenth century and later came to be kept in Turin, Italy.

A relic of Jesus' mother, Mary, venerated at Chartres in France, was known as the *Sainte Chemise* or holy undergarment, which she reportedly wore when giving birth to Jesus. This was by no means the most intimate Christian relic. Since doctrine held that Jesus and Mary alike had been taken bodily into heaven, the only physical relics available were body parts or substances left behind during their lifetimes. Hence another prize held at Chartres was a trimming from the circumcision of the infant Jesus; known as the *Saint Prépuce*, it was only one of several holy foreskins venerated at various sites across Europe. As for Mary, the milk she allegedly spilled while nursing Jesus was preserved in surprisingly large amounts; pilgrims to Bethlehem over the centuries have been able to visit a Latin chapel and bring away packets of soil from the place said to be the site of the event.

Relics carried on one's person were contained in pieces of metal jewellery resembling amulets, with the piece of bone or sliver of the cross visible through glass like the bubble in a carpenter's level. Relics kept in a church for the faithful to venerate were displayed in reliquaries, ornate containers at least the size of a candlestick, often with a crystal window through which the object itself could be seen. Reliquaries made of gold or silver, which could be quite costly, took a variety of forms, from treasure chests to models of church buildings. The most ambitious reliquary, in a sense, is the thirteenth-century sanctuary in Paris known as the *Sainte Chapelle* ('holy chapel'), which was built by Louis IX to house a Crown of Thorns acquired in Constantinople. Its magnificent stained-glass windows are among the truly great treasures of medieval Christian art.

Protestant Worship

Like the various ideologies held among the spectrum of denominations, different Protestant forms of worship express varying degrees of departure from the Roman model. Thus Anglicans will make the sign of the cross on their own bodies (touching face, chest, and shoulders), as Orthodox and Catholic Christians do, but other Protestant denominations make a point of avoiding this gesture.

One central issue was the status of the officiating clergy. For medieval Latin Christianity, the priest was a representative of the divine and practically a dispenser of miracles. Now Protestants, who stressed the human side, made the officiant more a representative and spokesperson for the congregation. Protestants claimed that there is no need for a human intermediary—whether living priest or dead saint—between a Christian and God.

For denominations at the Catholic end of the spectrum, such as the 'high-church' wing of Anglicanism, the clergy were still termed priests and addressed as 'father', though they were no longer required to be celibate. Low-church Anglicans and most other Protestants preferred to call their clergy 'ministers' with reference to their role as leaders of worship or 'pastors' with reference to their role as spiritual counsellors. Protestants gave more responsibility to the laity as preachers and leaders of worship, and a few denominations, such as the Quakers, were led largely by lay people.

Protestants also departed from Rome in their interpretation of the sacramental rituals, particularly the Eucharist. Some Anglicans and Lutherans, who sought to retain a sacrificial understanding of the Eucharist, believed that the body and blood of Christ are present in or together with the bread and wine of the ceremonial meal. In Switzerland, however, reformers such as Zwingli and Calvin established the more common Protestant understanding of the Eucharist less as a sacrifice than as a memorial in which the bread and wine symbolize Christ's body and blood.

The way in which communion is received varies as well. In the denominations closest to the Catholic tradition, the communicants line up near the altar, whereas many Protestant congregations remain seated as elders or ushers serve the bread on trays and the wine in little individual glasses. The materials used as bread and wine have also varied: often, the Catholic tradition has used unleavened wafers for bread, and many Protestant churches use unfermented grape juice instead of wine. In some parts of the world, bread and wine may not be available: thus in the Philippines, for example, some Protestants share rice cakes and fruit juice or cola instead.

In the later Middle Ages, the congregation might rarely have the opportunity to take part in the Eucharist—perhaps as infrequently as twice a year. The Reformation demanded greater participation by the people. In recent years, some Protestant denominations, among them the Anglicans, have made the Eucharist a weekly event. Ironically, though, most have come to celebrate the sacrament less often—in some congregations, only once every three or four months. Instead, they emphasize the reading of scripture and the interpretation of scripture in the minister's sermon.

The first decades of the Reformation in Germany and England saw the development of systematic plans for the reading of consecutive portions of the entire Bible in the daily services of morning and evening worship. Known as 'lectionaries', these plans were not unlike the medieval monastic 'offices' or schedules for the reading of scripture. Each testament was covered twice during the year. The *Genesis* account of creation would thus be read on New Year's Day, but Jesus' crucifixion might come up closer to Christmas than to Good Friday. In the course of time, as it became clear that many people would not be attending church twice a day, more selective plans were designed that scheduled the texts judged more important on consecutive Sundays and tried to cover the highlights of scripture in a three-year cycle. Practice varies quite widely today, but in churches that maintain more formal worship, the norm is to preach from a passage assigned for the day.

Rejecting priestly mediation, Protestants looked for signs of direct activity on the part of the Holy Spirit. Thus the clergy in some denominations cultivated an extemporaneous style of prayer intended to evoke the immediate presence of the Holy Spirit. On the other hand, as we have seen, Quaker meetings tend to be highly formalized.

In the sixteenth and seventeenth centuries, each emerging Protestant movement usually drafted its own affirmation of faith or 'confession'. Since these confessions tended to be rather long, however, many Protestant denominations continued to use either the Apostles' Creed or the Nicene Creed in worship services.

The Christian Year

The liturgical year for Christians is structured around the two main festivals of Christmas and Easter. It begins with **Advent**, the series of four Sundays that precede Christmas. Today, four special candles in the sanctuary, lit cumulatively over the four weeks, often mark the anticipation that characterizes the Advent season.

Christmas

The time of the year when Jesus was actually born is not known. For some time the date was the subject of speculation; one third-century text identified 28 March as the date by reasoning that the world would have to be perfect, with trees in leaf and flowers in bloom, and the day would have to be a Wednesday because in *Genesis* the sun and moon are created on the fourth day. But by the fourth century the date had been more or less set around the midwinter solstice, coinciding with the Roman celebration of the unconquered sun. The Christian idea of a birth that would bring new blessings was easily associated with the annual renewal of the sun's radiance.

Many early Christians paid more attention to the baptism of Jesus than to his birth. This was especially true in the Greek-speaking churches of the eastern Mediterranean. In the Latin West, however, a theological difference appears to have prompted a shift in ritual emphasis to the feast of Jesus' birth. At a time when some Christian teachings maintained that the human side of Jesus' nature was less important than the divine, the Latin Church affirmed the centrality of the incarnation by celebrating the feast of his birth. The word 'Christmas' means 'the mass of Christ'. Thus the solemn significance of the mass figures as a theme even amid the joy and optimism of Christmas.

Christmas today is a blend of religious and cultural elements. Carols and hymns proclaim joy that the Christ-child is born. Greetings and family visits enhance a feeling of community. Some elements of Christmas observance in the English-speaking world come from the midwinter traditions of pre-Christian northern Europe: evergreen trees (Germany), holly and mistletoe (Britain), the yule-log and reindeer (Scandinavia). The same traditions are practised even in such dramatically different climates and seasons as those of the Caribbean, Hawaii, or Australia. The jolly, avuncular figure of Santa Claus goes back to the third-century St Nicholas of Myra, in what is now Turkey, who was a patron saint of sailors before becoming a bearer of children's gifts. Christians themselves consider many of the holiday season's cultural trappings to be secular rather than religious. In theory, they distinguish between the sacred and the secular. The distinction is rooted in the early history of Christianity, which survived three formative centuries as a minority movement before it became the established religion of any state. In Christian history, however, the distinction has not always been easy to apply; sorting out the spheres of church and state was a problem in the Middle Ages and remains one today. And modern Christians who expect states to be secular have had difficulty adjusting to states recently built on religio-communal identity, such as Islamic Pakistan or Jewish Israel.

The feast of the Epiphany comes twelve days after Christmas, on 6 January in the Gregorian calendar. It celebrates both the visit of the 'wise men' (or *magi*) to the infant Jesus and his baptism as an adult. The link between these events may be the fact that both can be understood as manifestations of his mission or lordship; in fact, 'manifestation' is the meaning of the word 'Epiphany' in Greek. In some Christian countries, Christmas gift-giving is delayed until Epiphany or is spread, one gift per day, over the 'twelve days of Christmas'. The date of Epiphany in Latin Christianity corresponds roughly to that of Christmas in the Julian calendar—the calendar followed by the Greek Orthodox.

Easter

Christmas has a fixed date in the calendar because it is related to the solar year. Easter, by contrast, is related to the phases of the moon and therefore has a variable date. The event that Easter commemorates occurred just after the Jewish spring festival of Passover, but the Latin Church eventually fixed its date as the first Sunday after the first full moon after the spring equinox. Thus it can fall anywhere across a range of five weeks from late March to late April. The date of Easter in the Greek Church is calculated in a slightly different way, with the result that it coincides with the Latin Easter only about once in every four years.

Easter, which is the feast of Jesus' resurrection, comes as the conclusion of **Lent**: a period of six and a half weeks of which the last seven days constitute what is called Holy Week. For most Christians Lent is the time of the year for the greatest solemnity, most serious reflection, and most stringent discipline. Eventually, in Latin Christianity, it became common practice to mark Lent by 'giving up' or abstaining from various pleasures, such as meat, with the cultural result that the last day before Lent has been a time of wild partying. Shrove Tuesday, as it is called in English, is Mardi Gras ('fat Tuesday') in French, notably in New Orleans, and Carnival ('goodbye, meat') in the Hispanic culture of the Caribbean.

The English term 'Lent' is a reference to the season, when the days are 'lengthening'. Lent begins on Ash Wednesday, so named because in some Christian traditions the foreheads of the worshippers are daubed with ashes from the palm-leaf decorations used for the preceding year's Palm Sunday—the last Sunday before Easter. The palm branches used to decorate churches recall the greenery that decorated Jesus' processional route into Jerusalem as he began the last week of his life. The Hebrew ritual exclamation *hosanna*, 'O save now', with which Jesus was greeted, expresses the optimism of this day.

In four brief days, the mood of Jesus' followers in Jerusalem shifted from enthusiasm to foreboding, and this is reflected in the course of Holy Week. Thursday, the day of Jesus' last Passover supper with his disciples, is called Maundy Thursday in English, after the commandment (in Latin, *mandatum*) to love one another that (in *John* 13) Jesus gives on that occasion. In various traditional churches, a bishop or ranking priest re-enacts Jesus' washing of his disciples' feet by washing the feet of a dozen priests or of a group of poor people.

The Friday of Holy Week is known as **Good Friday**. Although it has been suggested that the name is a reference to the 'good' that Jesus' self-sacrificing death did for humanity, a more convincing explanation is that the original term was 'God's Friday'. This most solemn day of the Christian year is marked by services recalling Jesus' Passion—his suffering on the cross. Services generally run from noon till three in the afternoon (more or less matching the hours of the crucifixion according to three of the gospels). Some follow the narrative of the Passion as told in one or another of the gospels; others follow the seven 'last words' or utterances of Jesus from the cross.

Easter day itself commemorates the disciples' discovery, on the morning after the Sabbath, that Jesus has risen from the dead. Among the layers of meaning that Christian worshippers find on Easter is a sense of cosmic triumph over sin and death.

Like Passover, Easter is a spring festival associated with the renewal of life. In popular Christian culture, some traditional symbols connoting fertility probably originated in the pre-Christian era: the egg, for instance, and the rabbit. The English word 'Easter' itself comes from Eostre, a pagan goddess; in most other European languages, though, the name is derived from Pesach, the Hebrew name for Passover (e.g., the French Pâques) .

Pentecost

The fiftieth day after Easter is **Pentecost**, from the Greek for 'fifty'. In the Jewish tradition this was the festival of Shavuoth, the Feast of Weeks celebrating the end of the grain harvest and the giving of the ten commandments to Moses. But Christianity celebrates the event recounted in *Acts* 2, when the Holy Spirit enabled the apostles to speak in diverse languages; therefore Pentecost marks the emergence of the Church as a missionary movement with a message for all people. In England, Pentecost is often called Whitsunday, on account of the white garments formerly worn by persons baptized on that day. In Latin countries, it is generally known as the feast of the Holy Spirit.

✤ CULTURAL EXPRESSIONS

Early Christian Art

The Cross

The cross is the central symbol of Christianity. Yet it did not come into widespread use until the reign of Constantine. The crucifixion of criminals was abolished, now that the crucified saviour was seen as glorified, and the symbol went wherever Christians did, acquiring many variations in form and decoration.

The Latin cross has a vertical bar somewhat longer than the single horizontal bar. The Greek cross has two horizontal bars. In Ireland and Scotland, the cross of the Celts has a circle superimposed on it. A cross with twin flared points at the ends of four arms of equal length is associated with Malta. And the Copts of Egypt sometimes represented the top arm of the cross as a loop, thus associating the cross with the ancient Egyptian *ankh*, a symbol of life.

Devout Anglicans, Catholics, and Orthodox Christians touch their face, chest, and shoulders to make the sign on their own bodies. Medieval warriors placed crosses on their shields, a practice that survives in the heraldry of arms and in national flags. The flags of Switzerland, Greece, and all the Scandinavian countries feature crosses, and Britain's flag, the Union Jack, consists of three superimposed crosses, one of them the diagonal Cross of St Andrew, representing the Scots.

The hot cross buns traditional in the English-speaking world around Easter are descended from the cross-marked cakes that pre-Christian Saxons ate at the spring festival of Eostre, their goddess of light. Instead of fighting that custom, the Christian clergy in England introduced their own cross-marked cakes, made from the same dough as the Eucharistic wafer and distributed to the congregation at the close of the Easter service.

Constantine's cross-like monogram, called the *labarum*, is used in both the Latin and Greek Christian worlds. It superimposes X and P, *chi* and *rho*, the first two letters of the name 'Christ' in Greek.

Other Symbols

Among the oldest of the Christian symbols is the fish. Stylized fish designs can be seen in the catacombs, outside Rome. Many interpreters see the fish symbol as a kind of code spelling out a Christian declaration of faith, since the Greek word for 'fish', *ichthus*, is made up of the initial letters of the Greek phrase *Iesous Christos, Theou huios, soter* ('Jesus Christ, son of God, saviour'). Others believe that the fish is a reference either to the story in which Jesus multiplies a few loaves of bread and fishes to feed a crowd or to his description of his disciples as 'fishers of humanity'. Another sort of symbol or monogram consists of the letters IHS: the first three letters of the name 'Jesus' in Greek. Latin speakers, however, offered their own interpretations: *in hoc signo* ('in this sign [you shall conquer]'), associated with reports of Constantine's vision of a cross in the heavens, and *Iesus hominum Salvator* ('Jesus, humanity's saviour').

The first and last letters of the Greek alphabet, alpha and omega, together refer to *Revelation* 22: 13: 'I am Alpha and Omega, the beginning and the end, the first and the last.' A lamb represents Jesus as the sacrificial lamb of God who takes away the sins of the world, while a dove represents God's Holy Spirit. The spirit can also be represented by a male figure, sometimes youthful, sometimes mature, often equipped with birds' wings. An orb (a ball with a cross at the top), represents the world; when it appears with God the Father in royal attire, it signifies his role as creator, sustainer, and judge of the world or universe. During the years of persecution before Constantine, symbols such as these may have served as a code, allowing Christians to affirm their faith without attracting attention. Some scholars have suggested that they may also reflect the resistance to picture-making that can be found in the rabbinic literature (although ancient synagogues actually had pictorial decoration). Whatever their origin, symbols were capable of surviving times when pictorial images were not tolerated (in eighth-century Byzantium, for example, or sixteenth-century Reformation Germany).

Jesus in Art

Archaeologists often find funerary art—such as the elaborately carved stone sarcophagi created to hold the remains of wealthy or venerated Christians—to be better preserved than other types of artwork because it is buried intact. Often such carvings depict scenes from the biblical narrative or visions of the final judgment.

Central to many of these tableaux is the figure of Jesus. In early representations he is portrayed as a simple shepherd, sometimes carrying a lamb across his shoulders. Such images were clearly intended to evoke Jesus' description of himself as the good shepherd (in *John* 10), but their actual form seems to derive from earlier Roman representations of the god Hermes (Mercury) as a shepherd. In some other early images, Jesus is a beardless young man wearing the simple attire of a pilgrim or ascetic.

Byzantine Art

The influence of the Byzantine imperial tradition can be seen in pictorial representations of Jesus. After Constantine made Christianity respectable, Jesus began to appear not as the young shepherd of the early centuries, but as an older, bearded man, a king or a judge, attired in robes reflecting the dignity of his office. It was also around this time that he came to be depicted with a halo or nimbus representing the glory and radiance of the sun. (Halo imagery goes back a long way: third- to seventh-century Sasanian kings were portrayed with halos; similar imagery was used throughout Asia in representations of the Buddha.)

By the sixth century, Byzantine mosaics were depicting Christ enthroned in heaven as the ruler of creation. Usually located in a place of honour, such as directly above an altar, these formal, frontal Byzantine representations position Christ in the centre, flanked by attendant figures in a kind of heraldic symmetry. The cosmic ruler-Christ generally has a far more mature and distinguished appearance than the carpenter from Nazareth who was crucified in his early thirties.

Icons in the Orthodox Church

The Orthodox churches, such as the Greek and the Russian, developed a distinctive form of portraiture for depicting Jesus, Mary, and other religious figures. These portraits are known as icons, from the Greek word for image. An icon might be an entirely two-dimensional painting, often on a piece of wood, or it might be overlaid in low relief, in wood or precious metal and ornamented with jewels. While the robes clothing the figure were executed in relief, the hands and face were typically two-dimensional, so that the parts of the image representing flesh appeared to exist on a different plane from the material world around them. Nevertheless, in the seventh and eighth centuries these images became the subject of a heated dispute known as the iconoclastic controversy.

Pitting a faction called the iconoclasts ('icon breakers') against one called the iconodules ('icon worshippers'), the controversy served in part as a vehicle for other antagonisms (political, regional, etc.). But points of principle were also at stake, and Byzantine intellectuals engaged in serious theological discussions concerning the role of images in worship. In the end the Second Council of Nicaea in 787 decided that icons were permissible and could be venerated, as long as the faithful did not actually worship them.

Some historians continue to wonder whether the dispute might also have had something to do with the success of Islam, which rejects any kind of iconography, since the iconoclastic movement seems to have been particularly strong in the regions bordering Syria. In any event, their opponents prevailed in the end, and Eastern Christendom retained its distinctive tradition.

In Orthodox sanctuaries today, a massive screen in front of the altar shields it from the main portion of the sanctuary. The screen is called an iconostasis ('place for icons') and is designed to hold a row of large icons. Smaller icons are hung in private homes; some, as small as a pocket diary, are equipped with folding covers so that they can be carried on the person, especially when travelling.

Church Architecture

Since the earliest Christians did not have separate ecclesiastical buildings, some probably gathered in synagogues to preach their new message. Some may also have met in secret places such as the catacombs (a third-century underground tomb complex on the outskirts of Rome), at least from time to time. Most often, though, small groups met in private homes.

The early church buildings that have survived, such as the Christian building in the eastern Syrian frontier town of Dura-Europos, took the same form as Roman houses, with rooms off an interior atrium or courtyard. To ensure privacy, the room for worship was probably out of the direct line of sight from the street door.

With imperial patronage, Christians began to build more ambitious large-scale sanctuaries in the fourth century. Constantine's mother, Helena, is said to have visited Palestine herself to identify the sites of Jesus' birth and his crucifixion and have large sanctuaries (the Church of the Nativity in Bethlehem and the Church of the Holy Sepulchre in Jerusalem) erected in the appropriate locations.

Christianity repudiated the religion and temples of the Roman Empire as pagan. Instead, it adopted the building style of civil law courts and tribunals, known as the 'basilica' (from the Greek meaning 'royal'). The classic basilica had a dais raised a few steps at the end of the hall farthest from the entrance, and a nave or hall usually two storeys high, with clerestory windows to admit light. In the hands of the Christians, the sides of the basilica were extended by arms ('transepts') that gave the overall floor plan the shape of a cross. From Byzantium to Rome to northern Europe, this plan became standard for the interior space of Christian sanctuaries, especially cathedrals, throughout the Middle Ages.

Not every church was built on the cruciform plan, however. A second pattern that was influential from the fourth or fifth century onward was the circle or octagon. Over the centre, where a shrine object could be situated, was a dome resting on a polygon or circle of columns and arches. This radial plan, used in the Eastern Roman Empire, served as the prototype for Islam's masterpiece, the Dome of the Rock in Jerusalem, which was constructed at the end of the seventh century.

Hagia Sophia, the Church of Divine Wisdom in Istanbul (Constantinople), is a treasure of Byzantine architecture completed under the emperor Justinian in 537. For centuries it was the largest church in the world; its dome was a work of engineering genius, and its interior was sumptuously decorated with gilded mosaics. When Sultan Mehmet II conquered Constantinople in 1453, he had such respect for the magnificent building that at first he refused to enter it. Later he had it converted to a mosque, but since 1953 it has been a museum.

Medieval Church Architecture

In the western Mediterranean, as in Byzantium, the round arch was standard. In northern Europe, however, a new style of arch came into fashion around the twelfth century. This 'Gothic' arch had two curved sides rising to a point at the top, and it enabled architects to build churches with increasingly high interior spaces; in some cases the nave of a Gothic cathedral reached a height five times its width. Many writers on Gothic architecture have suggested that the great height of these structures directed the thoughts of worshippers heavenward.

In any case, the architects were pushing the capacity of their material—stone—to the limits. Many Gothic churches had to be buttressed from outside

Flying buttresses support the walls of the Cathedral of Notre Dame in Paris (Andrew Leyerle).

to keep the weight of the roof from forcing the upper parts of the walls outward. When these supports stood free of the wall and were bridged to it with half-arches, they were called 'flying buttresses'.

The exteriors of Gothic churches were usually much more elaborate than their Byzantine or Romanesque counterparts, and their interiors were often full of ornamental detail. Carvings in stone and wood, usually brightly painted, depicted events in the life of Christ and the lives of the saints. Above the altars in the side aisles of a church there might also be paintings, often in the form of a triptych. Another feature that developed in the Middle Ages was the stained-glass window, made up of thousands of pieces of coloured glass—especially in deep, clear blues and reds—joined by strips of lead. Whether in sculpture, painting, tapestry, or stained glass, scenes from the Bible were often arranged in sequence like the panels of a comic strip, to serve as teaching aids in an era when literacy was limited and written texts were the almost exclusive preserve of the clergy. The only way for most lay people to learn the stories of the faith was by listening and 'reading' the stories told in the visual art that decorated the churches.

A feature unique to Roman Catholic churches is a sequence of fourteen paintings, plaques, sculptures, or (in austerely decorated churches), simply Roman numerals or crosses, usually located along the side of the nave, representing the '**Stations of the Cross**': the sequence of events from Jesus' trial to the placing of his body in the tomb. During Lent, the individual worshipper proceeds from one station to the next, meditating on Jesus' final suffering. This practice developed in medieval Jerusalem, when pilgrims would retrace Christ's steps through the streets of the city to the Church of the Holy Sepulchre on Good Friday, and was promoted by the Franciscans, the order that was made responsible for sites in the Holy Land. The present list of the fourteen stations was finalized only within the past two centuries.

Protestant Art and Architecture

Protestant architecture in northern Europe was not markedly different from earlier Catholic forms, since in many cases Protestants took over existing churches. Within the sanctuary, however, Reformed Churches rearranged the furniture to suit their sacramental theology. Instead of an altar that the priest faced with his back to the worshippers, Protestants adopted a communion table behind which the minister stood, facing the congregation.

The sixteenth-century reformers had little patience with images, especially those of Mary and the saints, and they preferred an empty cross to a crucifix with the suffering Jesus on it. Statues and paintings were destroyed with fanatical zeal, though stained-glass windows were generally spared. Denominations that condemn what they consider image worship have kept their church interiors bare and austere. Other Protestants, who regret the loss of so much fine art, retain at least an aesthetic affection for Renaissance paintings of Mary with the infant Jesus. Mary does appear in Protestantism at the Christmas season, but she is clearly subordinated to the figure of Jesus himself and is associated mainly with his childhood.

Music

From the beginning, music was part of Christian worship, for the Church inherited from Judaism the biblical psalms that had been sung in the temple. The fact that hymn-like passages were incorporated into the text of the New Testament (in the opening chapters of Luke's gospel, for instance) suggests additional compositional activity.

Catholic Music

In medieval Europe, the entire Latin mass had been chanted in a melodic musical form known as plainsong. With the Renaissance, Europeans made increasing use of polyphony, in which different musical lines were sounded at the same time by different instruments or voices. Since polyphonic music was better suited to groups than to individuals, it was used for choral or congregational responses rather than for the solo parts of the mass said by the officiating clergy.

Choral settings of the Latin mass generally consist of the following sections:

- the Kyrie: '*Kyrie eleison, Christe eleison*' (Greek for 'Lord, have mercy; Christ, have mercy')
- the Gloria: a long section that begins '*Gloria in excelsis Deo . . .* ' (Latin for 'Glory to God in the highest')
- the Credo: the entire Nicene Creed, beginning '*Credo in unum Deum . . .* ' ('I believe in one God')
- the Sanctus: '*Sanctus, sanctus, sanctus, Dominus Deus sabaoth . . .* ' ('Holy, holy, holy, Lord God of hosts')
- the Benedictus: '*Benedictus qui venit in nomine Domini; hosanna in excelsis*' ('Blessed in the name of the Lord is he who comes; hosanna in the highest')
- the Agnus Dei: '*Agnus Dei, qui tollis peccata mundi, miserere nobis; dona nobis pacem*' ('Lamb of God, who takest away the sins of the world, have mercy upon us; give us peace').

Among the many settings of the mass in the choral literature are five by Johann Sebastian Bach, seven by Franz Joseph Haydn, and seventeen by Wolfgang Amadeus Mozart. Franz Schubert composed six but omitted from the 'Credo' section of each of them the phrase 'and [I believe] in one holy catholic and apostolic Church.'

European composers also produced many substantial choral settings for parts of the requiem mass (the mass for the dead), which has a different Latin text. Another Latin text frequently set to music was the hymn of praise that begins *Te Deum laudamus, Te Dominum confitemur* ('We praise you, O God; we acknowledge you to be the Lord'). Also popular among Catholic composers was a long medieval Latin devotional poem that describes Mary's grief at the crucifixion and is known as the *Stabat Mater*. Here is a literal translation of two of its stanzas:

> The mother stood sadly
> By the cross, in tears
> As her son hung there.
> Have me truly weep with thee
> To share the grief of the crucified one
> As long as I live . . .

Protestant Music

In music Protestantism was much less austere than in the visual arts, often taking over the tunes of folk songs and dances for use in worship. Perhaps the most widely cherished Protestant hymn of all was composed by Martin Luther, and since the rapprochement of Protestants and Roman Catholics in the 1960s it has been widely used by Catholics as well. Here is the first stanza:

> A mighty fortress is our God, a bulwark
> never failing;
> Our helper he amid the flood of mortal ills
> prevailing.
> For still our ancient foe doth seek to work
> us woe;
> His craft and power are great; and armed
> with cruel hate, on earth is not his equal.

Often tuneful and musically simple, Protestant hymns express a wide range of religious emotions, from praise of God as creator, to the longing for social justice and world peace, to hopes for individual strength and divine guidance.

In the sixteenth century, the Calvinists in Switzerland and Scotland produced a collection of musical settings of the biblical psalms known as the 'psalter'. The psalms were also the principal focus of congregational song in the Church of England following the Reformation.

From the middle of the eighteenth to the end of the nineteenth century, many hymns evoke the personal experience of conversion. An example is 'Amazing Grace', which is usually sung to a familiar early American tune. The words date from 1779:

> Amazing grace—how sweet the sound—
> that saved a wretch like me!
> I once was lost, but now am found,
> was blind, but now I see.

🦁 INTERACTION AND ADAPTATION

The Enlightenment

By the end of the eighteenth century, Christianity was no longer at the centre of Western civilization and the ties between Church and state had been significantly loosened. The intellectual movement responsible for those changes is generally known as the Enlightenment. At the heart of the Enlightenment was a growing confidence in human reason.

The precise beginning of the Enlightenment is hard to identify, but a crucial early moment came in 1543, when the Polish astronomer Nicolaus Copernicus proposed that the universe revolved around the sun rather than the earth. Half a century later, the Italian mathematician Galileo Galilei confirmed that theory through observation. The Church responded by adding Copernicus' book to its list of prohibited writings and, in 1633, bringing Galileo to trial before the Inquisition. Found guilty of heresy, he was forced to 'abjure, curse, and detest' his supposed errors, and to live the remaining eight years of his life under house arrest. Three and a half centuries later, in 1992, the Church finally admitted the truth of Galileo's findings and retracted its condemnation.

Galileo on Scripture and Reason

In 1613, Galileo wrote to his former student Benedetto Castelli explaining his decision to pursue his scientific research even though his findings were not consistent with the Bible.

. . . I think it would be the part of wisdom not to allow any one to apply passages of Scripture in such a way as to force them to support, as true, conclusions concerning nature the contrary of which may afterwards be revealed by the evidence of our senses or by necessary demonstration. Who will set bounds to man's understanding? Who can assure us that everything that can be known in the world is already known? . . .

I am inclined to think that the authority of Holy Scripture is intended to convince men of those truths which are necessary for their salvation, and which being far above man's understanding cannot be made credible by any learning, or any other means than revelation by the Holy Spirit. But that the same God has endowed us with senses, reason, and understanding, does not permit us to use them, and desires to acquaint us in any other way with such knowledge as we are in a position to acquire for ourselves by means of those faculties, *that* it seems to me I am not bound to believe, especially concerning those sciences about which the Holy Scriptures contain only small fragments and varying conclusions. . . (Von Gebler 1879).

Deism

The growing importance of science was reflected in the rise of Deism, a philosophical position that gained a considerable following in England in the seventeenth and eighteenth centuries. Recognizing that the universe manifests regular patterns or 'laws of nature', the Deists were unable to accept the idea that those laws could be suspended by divine intervention. On the other hand, they were willing to think of the universe as the product of a divine intelligence. The creator God of the Deists was envisioned as a divine clockmaker, who assembles or shapes the universe and then leaves it to run on its own.

In his *Natural Theology*, published in 1802, the English philosopher William Paley offered the following example of the Deist position. If we found a watch on a desert island, we would not need to have seen any other watch in order to posit the existence of a maker; the watch would not even have to work perfectly, nor would we have to

understand the function of every part. The same is true of the universe as evidence for God: even if the creation is imperfect, or not fully comprehensible, humans can still reasonably posit the existence of a perfect creator deity.

For scientists in the eighteenth century, the 'clockmaker' analogy was persuasive. To see the universe as a mechanism that obeyed regular laws was not in itself antithetical to religious faith. Indeed, the religious climate of the eighteenth century was highly favourable to the investigation of natural mechanisms, as each new discovery was received as another example of the marvels of God's creation.

Philosophy

At the same time, the eighteenth century was a period of philosophical skepticism about claims for the transcendent. Particularly decisive were the critiques of the Scotsman David Hume and the German Immanuel Kant. Thomas Aquinas's argument for God as the First Cause cannot be proved; as Kant argued, causality is not part of the data of the physical world but part of the framework of thought by which human minds interpret it.

But what Kant showed to be in principle unprovable is by the same token not disprovable. Whereas earlier thinkers sought to prove the existence of the divine or transcendent itself, many philosophers of religion since Kant have focused instead on experience and feeling—that is, the human response to the transcendent. In the early nineteenth century, the German philosopher Friedrich Schleiermacher characterized religion as an 'intuitive sense of absolute dependence': if we cannot prove the existence of what we intuitively feel that we depend on, at least we can describe that intuition. In the same vein, the twentieth-century German philosopher of religion Rudolf Otto coined the word 'numinous' for what people perceive as an overpowering mystery.

Schleiermacher also contributed to a 'subjective' understanding of Christ's atonement. In the traditional Christian understanding, it is through Christ's sacrifice that humanity is saved and restored to its proper relationship with God. For Schleiermacher, however, Jesus functions as a moral example, an embodiment of human awareness of God. For Schleiermacher, salvation comes first as a change in spiritual awareness and then atonement follows as a divine–human reconciliation.

Meanwhile, the nineteenth-century Danish philosopher Søren Kierkegaard pioneered the line of inquiry called existentialism. In existentialism, the focus shifts from knowledge, already limited by Kant's strictures, to commitment. It is no accident that many modern defenders of religion compare it with love, which likewise rests on commitment rather than argument.

Commitment-based theologies have been influential, but they do not rule out one powerful argument against religious faith, which is at least as ancient as the biblical book of *Job*. This argument is the problem of evil and suffering: how can one regard as both powerful and good, and hence worthy of worship, a deity that would allow either the evil that results from some human actions or the suffering that results from accident or chaos in nature? Even in a mechanistic theory, where the deity merely creates the world and does not intervene in it thereafter, the creator does not escape responsibility. The modern world has clearly not eliminated evil and suffering as objections to theistic faith, nor has it come up with any striking new ways to resolve the problem. If anything, the modern world has only added new instances of human brutality to the inventory of grievances that those who would defend the goodness of God must answer.

Sociology

The nineteenth century brought a growing tendency to look at religious institutions and identities in a social context. The French philosopher Auguste Comte, who coined the term 'sociology', saw history as progressing from a theological stage, in which everything is governed by will, through a metaphysical stage that understands causes, to a 'positive' stage in which law-like generalizations constitute knowledge. Comte expected a scientific intellectual élite to replace institutional clergy.

Arguably the most influential contributor to the new field of sociology was Émile Durkheim, whose family had expected him to become a rabbi. Studying with a social historian of the classical world in Paris, he turned his interest to social rather than traditional explanations of religious faith and practice. In his mature work *The Elementary Forms of the Religious Life*, first published in 1912, he located the origin and essence of religion in the identity of the clan or tribal group: 'The god of the clan . . . can be nothing else than the clan itself, personified and represented to the imagination under the visible form of the animal or vegetable which serves as totem' (Durkheim 1915: 206).

Not all sociologists were as eager as Durkheim to reduce religion to social components. The

German Protestant Max Weber, mentioned earlier in connection with the Puritan ethic, chose to discuss the functions of religious leadership and motivation rather than to speculate on the essence and origin of religion itself.

Psychology

The twentieth century has revised our view of the way the self functions. The Austrian psychoanalyst Sigmund Freud assembled evidence of a domain of personality operating below the level of conscious thought and volition. Under Freud's influence, many people came to see the human self not as a static entity, but as an arena in which conscious intellect and choice are in battle with unconscious impulses, drives, fantasies, and emotions. From the Freudian perspective, a seemingly ordered and rational personality is only superficially stable, like the thin crust of the earth resting on a deep interior of churning molten rock.

In Freud's own life, the concrete instances of religion that he experienced ran counter to his instincts as a scientist. For fostering obscurantist mythology, moral injustice, and intergroup hostility, religion earned little respect from him. The shaping of Freud's attitudes began in a secular Jewish family, where about the only traditional observance was the annual Passover celebration. He encountered strident anti-Semitism in the society of late nineteenth-century Vienna.

But it was the expectations and inhibitions Freud observed in his patients that led him to see religion as infantile dependency and wishful thinking. Religion, for Freud, was simply a mechanism for tolerating infantile helplessness.

The Swiss psychoanalyst Carl Gustav Jung broke with Freud, in part over religion. The son of a Protestant pastor, Jung found rich meaning in religious symbolism, including magic and alchemy. Nevertheless, Jung agreed with Freud to the extent that he saw religion as a product of psychological processes. The challenge for modern religious thought is to make a convincing case for the idea that something that meets profound psychic needs is not necessarily or merely the product of those needs.

Evolution

At the beginning of the nineteenth century, most biology in England was 'creationist'. Scientists held that every species on earth had been created by God with specific characteristics. This view was definitively overturned by Charles Darwin, whose theory of evolution proposed that new types of organisms were not created by a deity but developed over time through a process he called natural selection.

Darwin's epoch-making study, *On the Origin of Species*, was published in 1859, more than twenty years after he had worked out the basics of his theory. Refining his argument clearly took time, but Darwin may have been especially cautious because he had studied theology and was well aware of the resistance he would encounter. He needed not merely to make a credible case for evolution, but to refute the doctrine of biological creationism. He also knew that natural selection was antithetical to the theological argument from design. If the natural world was completely self-regulating, there was no need for a supervising deity. Although, in the *Origin*, he referred to the laws of nature as 'secondary causes', established in the beginning by the Creator, he left the door open for readers to infer that the laws he described would operate on their own, without a creator. Darwin had said little in the *Origin* about the human species, but in *The Descent of Man* (1871) he stressed the continuities between humans and other animals. For Darwin, human intellectual activity, including language and social morality, was the adaptively advantageous product of natural selection.

Thanks to Darwin, modern Christian theologians assessing the place of human life in the universe have tended to locate human distinctiveness not in a special physical creation but in a unique intellectual and spiritual capacity for transcendence. For religious thinkers persuaded by Darwin's discoveries, what matters is not so much where we came from as where we are going.

New American Denominations

With the Protestant emphasis on the individual's relationship with God came a bewildering diversity of expression, which was illustrated by the new denominations that emerged on the American scene in the nineteenth century. To explain this phenomenon, many historians point to the disorienting economic and social changes that were taking place at the time. This was particularly true of upstate New York, which—like California in the following century—became a hotbed of new movements.

Disciples of Christ

Following Presbyterian opposition to a revival in Kentucky in 1804, Barton Stone left the Presbyterians to become a 'Christian only', and gained a number of followers. Meanwhile, when Thomas Campbell, a Presbyterian from Northern Ireland, became disaffected with the sectarian character of his church, he and his son Alexander joined Baptist associations, calling themselves Reformers. In 1832, the Stone and Campbell movements merged.

Stone's followers called themselves the Christian Church, while the Campbells preferred the name Disciples of Christ. The merged movement, which used both names as well as 'Churches of Christ', spread with the westward expansion of the United States. Although the generic names they chose suggest a protest against sectarianism, the movement itself soon became another denomination. An influential periodical called the *Christian Century*, created by the Disciples, continues to reflect a pan-Protestant vision today, as do educational institutions such as Texas Christian University.

Seventh-Day Adventists

In 1831, in upstate New York, a Baptist lay minister called William Miller began to preach that the second coming of Christ—the 'advent'—was imminent. Interpreting a reference to 2,300 days (in *Daniel* 8:14) as 2,300 years, he predicted that the apocalypse would take place in or around the year 1843. When that did not happen (a 'great disappointment'), Miller's followers revised their **millenarian** calculations several times, but eventually gave up trying to predict a specific date. The movement's name reflects both its emphasis on the 'advent' and its belief that the true Sabbath is the seventh day (Saturday) rather than Sunday.

From the 1840s until her death in 1915, the Adventists were guided by the 'gift of prophecy' of Ellen Gould Harmon White, whose husband James was an Adventist preacher. As early as 1866, the Adventists began to promote health cures, opening a sanatorium in Battle Creek, Michigan. In the 1880s, they began sending medical missionaries around the world, and in the twentieth century their ranks grew dramatically in the Third World. At the same time, Adventist intellectuals and scholars in the United States were becoming more willing to ask critical questions about biblical interpretation and the claims of Ellen White. By the late twentieth century, the Adventists had completed the transition from millenarian sect to established denomination.

Jehovah's Witnesses

The Witnesses are another millenarian group centred on the belief that the Advent is imminent. Their founder was Charles Taze Russell. Born in 1852 and raised near Pittsburgh, Russell was exposed from an early age to forecasts of the end of the world and the return of Christ. He became intensely interested in Bible study, but was largely self-taught. He formed a study group and in 1879 began publishing *Zion's Watch Tower and Herald of Christ's Presence*. Initially Russell and his followers expected the world to end in 1914; when that prediction proved false, they came to believe that 1914 was the year when Jehovah's Kingdom was inaugurated in anticipation of the end, which they subsequently predicted for 1918, 1920, 1925, 1941, and 1975.

Russell himself died in 1916. It was under his successor, J.F. Russell, that the movement adopted the name Jehovah's Witnesses, using the version of the tetragrammaton 'YHWH' introduced by the translators of the King James Bible. Their principal activity is door-to-door missionary work distributing their publications *Awake!* and *The Watchtower*. They reject the doctrine of the Trinity and regard Jesus Christ as a created being (as Arius did), although they believe that in dying he gave humanity a second chance to choose righteousness and escape the punishment expected at the end. They also refuse to salute flags or serve in armies, not because they are pacifists but because they see themselves as citizens of another kingdom and therefore reject the authority of secular states.

Witnesses call their meeting places Kingdom Halls rather than churches. They have their own version of the Christian Eucharist or mass, which they call the Memorial of Christ's Death. Whereas most Christian churches celebrate this ritual regularly, Witnesses observe it only once a year. They reject holidays such as Christmas because of their 'pagan' origins, and they do not celebrate birthdays because there is no reference to them in the Bible.

Some countries have treated Witnesses harshly, but in the United States their demands for exemption from state allegiance and service have often been upheld in the courts. They also refuse blood transfusions and some medical treatments for their children, but on this issue the courts have tended to place the child's right to health ahead of the parents' right to religious expression.

Christian Science

The Church of Christ, Scientist, was founded in Boston in 1879 by Mary Baker Eddy, a New England woman who in 1862 had received help for a spinal condition from a mental healer named Phineas Quimby. Believing that Quimby's method was the same one that Jesus had used, she began to write articles on non-medical healing. After Quimby died in 1866, her condition returned and she suffered a bad fall. But after reading the New Testament, she recovered and began to write about spiritual healing; her *Science and Health*, which was published in 1875, came to be regarded by her followers as an inspired text, second in authority only to the Bible.

Mary Baker Eddy had come from a New England Congregationalist background with Puritan affinities and a longing for spiritual presence in tune with the thought of Jonathan Edwards and the Great Awakening. But she departed from the standard Protestant view in several respects. She believed that the material world and its evils—sickness, suffering, even death—could be transcended, and that spiritual existence was possible in the here and now. The quest to live those beliefs has occupied most of Christian Scientists' energy, and although it is active in publishing activity, the Church has not played a conspicuous role in social projects.

Mrs Eddy founded the Massachusetts Metaphysical College in Boston in 1881 and taught there until it closed in 1889. From 1883 the Church published the *Christian Science Journal* and from 1898 the *Christian Science Sentinel*, but it is the Church's newspaper, the *Christian Science Monitor* (founded in 1908 and known for the integrity of its journalism) that has gained it the widest public respect. Apart from a religion page, the *Monitor* devotes little direct attention to the Church's teachings; but, perhaps in deference to its heritage, its coverage of world events is sometimes more hopeful in tone than comparable stories in the commercial press. For years, the *Monitor* refused to report that people had 'died'; instead, they had 'passed'.

Mormons (Church of Jesus Christ of Latter-day Saints)

The Church of Jesus Christ of Latter-day Saints was founded in 1830 by Joseph Smith, Jr, who claimed that in 1820, as a boy in upstate New York, he had experienced a vision of God and Jesus in which he was told not to join any of the existing denominations. Subsequent visions persuaded him that he had been divinely chosen to restore the true Church of Christ.

The textual basis for Smith's new faith was an account of God's activity in the Western hemisphere, paralleling the Bible's account of events in the East, entitled *The Book of Mormon*, which Smith said he had translated from gold plates, inscribed in 'reformed Egyptian', that had been divinely entrusted to him. Under the leadership of one of his disciples, Brigham Young, the main branch of the Mormons settled in Utah, but smaller groups are found in Illinois and elsewhere.

Whether Mormonism is a new form of Christianity or a new religion, emerging out of Christianity, depends on one's perspective. For a more detailed discussion, see Chapter 7 of this volume.

Pentecostal Churches

Protestant congregations that cultivate the practice of 'speaking in tongues' call themselves Pentecostal, after the feast during which the apostles received the miraculous gift of speaking in foreign languages, which enabled them to communicate with people outside their own community. But the 'tongues' that modern Pentecostals speak are not intelligible human languages: rather, they are understood to represent the mystical language of heaven.

Charismatic tongue-speaking was promoted in London as early as the 1830s by a Scottish Presbyterian named Edward Irving, and in the United States in 1901 by Charles Fox Parham, who taught at a Bible college in Topeka, Kansas, but the modern Pentecostal movement is generally believed to have originated in a revival led by William J. Seymour at a church in Los Angeles in 1906. The son of former slaves, Seymour had been influenced by Parham's work in Topeka. Newspaper coverage described the sounds of Seymour's meetings as a 'weird babble'. At the outset Blacks and Whites worshipped together, but as Pentecostalism diversified, it developed segregated congregations.

With its emphasis on immediate personal experience rather than textual or doctrinal tradition, Pentecostalism can take a much greater range of forms than more established varieties of Christianity, and is more accessible to people with little formal education. It also has a strong cross-cultural appeal. Pentecostal missionaries have had remarkable success in Latin America and Africa, and Pentecostalism has been identified as the fastest-growing segment of Christianity today.

Protestant Missions

The colonial policies of the northern European nations and the missionary efforts of Protestants peaked in the second half of the nineteenth century. In Africa (one of their main objectives), the aims of Church and state went hand in hand. The British established themselves on large stretches of the African coastline, moving into the interior of the continent by river and road, and later by rail. Although formerly active in slave trading from West Africa to the New World, Britain outlawed slavery in 1834, and by mid-century its opposition to the ongoing slave trade in East Africa had become one of the arguments it used to justify its colonization efforts. Even the Scottish missionary David Livingstone made an explicit connection between evangelism and empire. On a return visit to Britain from East Africa in 1857, he told a Cambridge audience:

> [Africa] is now open; do not let it be shut again! I go back to Africa to try to make an open path for commerce and Christianity. Do you carry on the work I have begun. I leave it with you (Livingstone 1858: 24).

Elsewhere in the world there were comparable opportunities. A missionary to the southwestern Pacific reported in 1837 that at least '150,000 persons, who a few years ago were unclothed savages, are now wearing articles of British manufacture.' And though an atheist himself, Sir Harry Johnston, a British colonial administrator, considered missionaries essential to the colonial enterprise:

> As their immediate object is not profit, they can afford to reside at places till they become profitable. They strengthen our hold over the country, they spread the use of the English language, they induct the natives into the best kind of civilization, and in fact each mission station is an essay in colonization (Oliver 1957: 297).

But missionaries sometimes opposed colonial policy; for that reason, the British East India Company excluded missionaries from its trading concessions in India until 1813, when Church pressure in Britain forced it to allow them into the country.

Opinion on the subject of missionaries remained mixed: even Rudyard Kipling, who has often been stereotyped as a supporter of British cultural domination in India, criticized the missionary enterprise in a letter to a clergyman:

> . . . it seems to me cruel that white men . . . should amaze and confound their fellow creatures with a doctrine of salvation imperfectly understood by themselves and a code of ethics foreign to the climate and instincts of those races whose most cherished customs they outrage and whose gods they insult (Faber 1966: 106–7).

Many Protestant missionaries from Canada and the United States likewise (if unconsciously) conveyed political and cultural messages along with the gospel. Even among the great Asian cultures, where missionaries attracted relatively few converts, Protestant medical and educational institutions served as channels for significant transfers of technology and culture. From the 1870s to at least the 1950s, colleges and universities founded by missionaries in China, India, and the Middle East had a visible influence: it has been said of the delegates at the founding conference of the United Nations in 1945 that more had been educated at the American University of Beirut than at any other university in the world.

Missionaries often insisted that rejection of the old ways was a precondition for receiving the benefits of the new. By the 1930s, however, it was becoming clear that this approach was not particularly effective in Africa and Asia. Liberal Protestants began to move towards a view of missionary work as a low-key matter of sharing with the target community, rather than a high-pressure confrontation aimed at rescuing 'the other' from ignorance and damnation.

Contextualizing the Bible

Until the nineteenth century, most Christians believed that the Bible was the word of God, a factual account of the creation of the world, the origins of the human race, and the emergence of the Israelite nation; then a set of converging circumstances took the Bible off its special pedestal and turned it into a book like other books, the word of human beings.

A historical context for ancient Israel was pieced together. Until the nineteenth century, the only stories of the ancient world that Europeans knew, apart from the Greek epics, were the narratives of the Bible. The Egyptians, the Babylonians, the Assyrians, the Hittites, the Canaanites or Phoenicians were the naughty neighbours of Israel, merely the supporting cast in the biblical drama.

In 1798, however, when Napoleon led a campaign to Egypt (to try to counter British influence in India), he took with him scientists who began to investigate the ancient Egyptians' own monuments and documents. Over the decades that followed, European archaeologists excavated the stratified city-mounds of Mesopotamia (now Iraq), on the trail of the Babylonians and Assyrians. By the end of the nineteenth century, historians were able to situate the Bible in a specific cultural context.

That context was not necessarily consistent with the Bible. The civilizations of Mesopotamia and Egypt were already ancient before the Hebrews appeared on the scene, and they had larger populations than Israel. The Hebrews, it now appeared, were a minor group on the receiving end of ideas and technology from the major centres of empire. Mesopotamia and Egypt had had writing systems for nearly two thousand years before Moses. What's more, their literatures contained prototypes of stories told in the Bible.

The Mesopotamian epic *Gilgamesh*, for instance, tells of an ancient sage named Utnapishtim, who has survived a primeval flood. Utnapishtim tells Gilgamesh how he built a boat and took pairs of animals aboard in order to survive the all-submerging deluge. When the flood waters receded, says Utnapishtim, he sent out birds to see whether there was dry land; at first they returned, but then they did not. The fact that the Mesopotamian narrative was clearly the source of the biblical account of Noah and his ark presented a challenge both to the originality of the Noah story and to the historicity of Noah himself. (If that weren't enough, a flood covering everything in sight was far more likely to have occurred on the flat plains of ancient Mesopotamia than in the hill country where the Hebrews lived.)

Admittedly, archaeological work is unlikely either to confirm or to contradict biblical accounts, especially when it comes to miraculous events. In general, though, historians now operated on the assumption that biblical events could be understood in a human, historical context, without reference to divine intervention. Literary criticism of the Bible, which was centred in Protestant circles but eventually became influential in Catholic and Jewish circles as well, treated the text not as the gift of God but as the product of human beings. Though scholars continue to debate detail, the main outlines of nineteenth-century biblical criticism have stood the test of time and have been incorporated into contemporary Christians' understanding of their own tradition.

The Quest for the Historical Jesus

Before he became famous as a medical missionary to Africa, Albert Schweitzer was a theologian who published a ground-breaking book entitled *The Quest for the Historical Jesus* in 1906. He was hardly the first to argue that the Jesus of history was not necessarily the same as the 'Christ' of Christian theology and belief. Thomas Jefferson had disputed the historicity of the miracles reported in the gospels, and in the 1700s the German philosopher H.S. Reimarus argued that most of the details of the gospels were forged by Jesus' followers, disappointed that the kingdom of God had not come during his lifetime, or soon afterwards.

During the nineteenth century many scholars had argued that Jesus was a great moral teacher. But Schweitzer's book raised the theological discussion to a new level by reviewing earlier studies and bringing all the issues together. He suggested that the Jesus presented in the gospel accounts was less a moral teacher than an apocalyptic fanatic who believed the current world order would come to a dramatic end within the lifetime of his listeners.

A 'New Quest' or 'Second Quest' began in the 1950s, initiated by German New Testament scholars who used literary criticism and related critical methods to distinguish the 'Jesus of history' from the 'Christ of faith'. Founded in 1985, the 'Jesus Seminar' brought together scholars in a collaborative effort to reach a consensus by reviewing all the stories about Jesus, and all the sayings attributed to him, in both canonical and non-canonical gospel material. Although criticized by fundamentalists and conservatives, the Seminar established important benchmarks and clear criteria for determining whether particular sayings and stories were historical or not. The Seminar was in general skeptical about the apocalyptic sayings ascribed to Jesus, but more sympathetic to the 'wisdom' material (parables, maxims, etc.).

Evangelicalism

Protestant evangelicalism is a multifaceted emphasis or movement cutting across the major denominations. It is not a denomination as such, although some denominations are solidly evangelical. It draws on earlier themes, notably the assurance of God's grace and acceptance that characterized Reformation Pietism on the European continent and the revivalist movements of England and North America. Evangelicals refer to this assurance of grace as a spiritual rebirth, an experience of being 'born again'. As their name (from the Greek for the gospel or 'good news') indicates, evangelicals are typically active in spreading their message, and they often do so with the conviction that it, and no other, is valid.

Because the Reformation thinkers had put so many of their eggs in the basket of scriptural authority in their critique of the institutional Church, biblical criticism was bound to provoke a sharp reaction among evangelical Protestants. Committed to the literal authority of the Bible, evangelicals fought a rearguard battle against both modern biblical criticism and the Darwinian theory of human evolution. By 1920, some were beginning to label the most deeply conservative advocates of the inerrancy of scripture 'fundamentalist'. (**Fundamentalism** will be discussed in our concluding chapter.)

In the twentieth century, a number of evangelical preachers—heirs to the revivalist tradition—became famous for their 'crusades', preaching to massive audiences and calling on them to make a 'decision for Christ': to convert from a lapsed or inactive form of the faith to a revitalized one.

Radio was the first medium to make it possible to preach to a widely dispersed, unseen audience. In the United States, the faith healer Aimee Semple McPherson was a pioneer in the use of radio in the 1920s. Charles E. Fuller conducted 'The Old-Fashioned Revival Hour' on radio in the 1940s;

Gospel music evokes the personal experience of conversion (Getty Images North America).

the scattered 'congregation' of his listeners could make their offerings by mail. (Fulton J. Sheen pioneered Roman Catholic broadcasting in the same years.) Among the most successful evangelical preachers from 1949 on was the Southern Baptist Billy Graham. His pioneering use of television gave rise to a succession of 'televangelists' who made the electronic audience their primary 'congregation' and solicited contributions by mail and telephone. Several highly entrepreneurial preachers who operated outside established denominations built what amounted to personal empires. Financial and marital scandals brought a few of the most visible televangelists into disrepute in the late 1980s, but audience ratings remain high, particularly for the success-oriented *Hour of Power* broadcast from the Crystal Cathedral of Robert Schuller in southern California.

Modern Roman Catholicism

For Roman Catholics, modernity has posed challenges on various matters of faith and practice. These include (to name only a few) philosophical justifications for doctrine, the status of Mary and the saints, the theology of the sacraments, clerical celibacy, and the rules that lay Catholics are expected to follow in the area of sexuality and reproduction.

A focus in all these issues—arguably the heart of the matter for many committed Catholics—is the authority of the institutional church and, in particular, its head, the pope. Just as Protestants committed to the principle of scriptural authority saw that principle threatened by modern historical criticism, so Catholics committed to the infallibility of the *magisterium*—the Church's teaching authority—saw that principle threatened by the modern world. Historically, the Catholic Church has often traced its authority to Jesus' disciple Peter, even though the New Testament accounts show Peter as clearly fallible: after Jesus' arrest, he denies knowing him, and Jesus even calls him

Satan. But as the centuries passed, the Church came to see its connection to Peter as establishing absolute authority.

A central tenet of Christian faith is that God guides the Church through the continuing presence of the Holy Spirit. Catholics have held that such guidance includes the formulation and maintenance of its doctrines. It may follow that the Church's doctrines, having been formulated with divine guidance, must be infallibly true. Surprisingly, though, no formal claim of infallibility has ever been made on behalf of the Church itself, even though a council was convened at the Vatican to address the matter in 1869–70, during the papacy of Pius IX. We know that the council considered a draft statement asserting that the Church was enabled 'to conserve in its entirety and without alteration the already revealed Word of God contained in Scripture and Tradition', and that the keeping of Christ's revelation intact was the collective responsibility of the apostles and their successors, not the sole responsibility of the pope. But that document was never ratified before the outbreak of the Franco-Prussian War forced the council to close.

Instead, the First Vatican Council devoted its political energies to defining a monarchical role for the pope, in the context of which the doctrine of papal infallibility was extrapolated from ecclesiastical infallibility. The first to propose papal infallibility was a thirteenth-century Franciscan named Peter John Olivi, and his views were condemned as the work of the devil by Pope John XXII in 1324. Nor did the Council of Trent specify that the pope was infallible. The classic view was that individual heads of the Church might err from time to time, but the Church as a whole would not go astray. Thus Vatican I (the First Vatican Council) broke new ground when it announced that the pope 'when he speaks *ex cathedra* [i.e., when speaking officially, 'from the seat of authority']' on matters of faith and morals 'is possessed of that infallibility with which the divine Redeemer willed his Church to be endowed . . . and therefore such definitions of the Roman Pontiff are irreformable of themselves and not from the consent of the Church'.

In this way the doctrine of papal infallibility, a disturbing innovation when Olivi proposed it six centuries earlier, became conservative tradition in 1870. A few years later, in 1879, the theological system of Thomas Aquinas, also a disturbing innovation six centuries earlier, was given official status by Pope Leo XIII. A small group of German, Austrian, and Swiss Catholics who refused to accept the new doctrine of papal authority broke away from Rome and came to be known as Old Catholics. But the Catholic Church as a whole had to wait nearly a century for the winds of reform and renewal to blow.

Vatican II

When the Italian cardinal Angelo Giuseppe Roncalli was elected pope in 1958, few had any inkling of the changes that lay in store for the Roman Catholic Church. Though already in his late seventies, John XXIII (the name he chose upon his election) proved to have a vision for his Church and a fearless openness to change, as well as great human warmth. Calling for *aggiornamento*, Italian for 'updating', John XXIII convoked the Second Vatican Council, which met from 1962 to 1965.

The changes set in motion at the council ushered in a new era for Catholicism. Latin was replaced as the language of the mass by the vernacular, and the officiating priest now turned to face the congregation (although the doctrine of transubstantiation was retained). The dress of priests and nuns was modernized and in many cases secularized. In contrast to Vatican I, which had emphasized the monarchical aspect of the pope's role, Vatican II emphasized the more collegial nature of his role in council with the bishops (although the doctrine of papal infallibility was also retained). Efforts were made to improve relations with people of other religions, including Protestants, the Eastern Orthodox, and Jews. An institution that had barely assimilated

either the Reformation or the Enlightenment now had to try to swallow both in one gulp.

Nearly fifty years later, the council's agenda still has not been completed. The priesthood today is under serious threat, with declining numbers of recruits. Clearly, the requirement of celibacy, on which the Church has not budged, has reduced the appeal of the priesthood for modern Roman Catholics. Another problem may be that the traditional ritual activities of priests and ministers are no longer perceived to offer a sufficient intellectual challenge. A major breach developed in the Church shortly after the council, in 1968, when John's successor, Pope Paul VI, in his encyclical *Humanae Vitae* ('On human life') prohibited the use of artificial birth control by Catholics. The gap between the Church's official stand on sexuality and the actual practice of the faithful has only widened in the intervening decades. Many Catholics have ceased to follow some of the teachings they consider out of date.

But the matter had other implications as well. *Humanae Vitae* intensified the theological tension between the reform-minded and traditionalist wings in the Church's hierarchy. Progressive Catholics saw the encyclical—which did not have the status of an *ex cathedra* statement, but nonetheless came from the pope alone, without the consensus of bishops in council—as an attempt to turn the clock back to Vatican I. The Swiss theologian Hans Küng, who held a post in the Roman Catholic theological faculty of the University of Tübingen, Germany, responded by publishing a controversial book on the issue entitled *Infallible? An Inquiry* (1970). Nine years later, when a student of his published a doctoral thesis on the same subject with an introduction by Küng, the Church revoked his status as a theological teacher (though Küng remained a priest and continued in a professorship in the university). This move on the part of the Church reflected a 'fundamentalism' of ecclesiastical authority parallel to the Protestant fundamentalism of scriptural authority.

Ecumenism

The historical divisions within Euro-American Christianity made little sense when they were exported to Africa and Asia. What did it matter in India or China whether someone was Anglican or Presbyterian, Baptist or Congregationalist? From 1910 onward, the mainline Protestant denominations began to overcome four centuries of separation.

Part of the movement towards union was rooted in missionary collaboration. Denominational mission boards agreed to divide overseas territories among the various denominations to reduce redundant competition. Also significant was collaboration in youth work, through organizations such as the interdenominational Student Christian Movement. And in the United States, the Federal Council of Churches was particularly devoted to collaboration on economic and social issues.

By mid-century, a generation of Church leaders who had grown up with interdenominationalism had moved into positions of responsibility in their denominations. The time was ripe for worldwide collaboration, and in 1948 the World Council of Churches was formed with representation from most major Protestant and Orthodox bodies.

Ecumenism (from the Greek meaning 'inhabited world') offered a climate of mutual acceptance and common purpose, an emphasis on unity within diversity. Protestants agreed to continue disagreeing on many issues (such as Church discipline and Eucharistic theology) that had historically separated them. It was much easier to affirm one another's agendas regarding social justice (or, later, ecological concern) than to take communion together.

Nonetheless a number of denominational mergers did take place in the twentieth century. In 1925, Canadian Methodists, Congregationalists, and a majority of the country's Presbyterians formed the United Church of Canada. A similar group of churches joined to form the Uniting Church in Australia in 1977. In England in 1972, the Presbyterians and Congregationalists merged to form the United Reformed Church. In the United States, a multiple merger in 1961 produced the United Church of Christ.

But more ambitious twentieth-century attempts at Church union remain unconsummated. Consultations in the United States and New Zealand involving Anglicans, Presbyterians, and others were unable to resolve differences over ordination and the Eucharist. And Anglicans hesitated to rush into union with Reformed Churches, partly because they wanted to conduct conversations also with Lutherans and with the Roman Catholic Church. However, the Church of South India was formed in 1947 by a variety of Protestant denominations, including Anglicans, and it was followed by a number of regionally defined unions in North India, Pakistan, and Bangladesh. And Episcopalians and Lutherans in the United States moved part of the way towards union in 1999.

For years, the goal of ecumenism for Catholics had been what they termed the return of 'separated brethren' to the Roman Church. This frequently amounted to a unilateral stipulation of terms, but there were hints that concessions might be made. The Belgian cardinal Désiré-Joseph Mercier sponsored ground-breaking conversations with Anglicans in his city, Malines, from 1921 to 1926. Elsewhere as well, intellectual, spiritual, and personal contacts were replacing political confrontation.

Rome's twentieth-century move into ecumenism is associated primarily with the papacy of John XXIII (1958–63). A permanent Secretariat for the Promotion of Christian Unity was established in 1960. An important item on the agenda of the Second Vatican Council was the drafting of documents and declarations that might bring about a rapprochement with other Christians.

The spirit of reunion was in the air. By the end of the 1960s, Protestant and Catholic institutions for the study of theology and the training of clergy

From the Vatican's Declaration on Relations with Non-Christian Religions, 1965

The statement entitled Nostra Aetate *was proclaimed by Pope Paul VI in October 1965, shortly before the conclusion of the Second Vatican Council.*

3. The Church regards with esteem . . . the Moslems. They adore the one God, living and subsisting in Himself; merciful and all-powerful, the Creator of heaven and earth, who has spoken to men; they take pains to submit wholeheartedly to even His inscrutable decrees, just as Abraham, with whom the faith of Islam takes pleasure in linking itself, submitted to God. Though they do not acknowledge Jesus as God, they revere Him as a prophet. They also honour Mary, His virgin Mother; at times they even call on her with devotion. In addition, they await the day of judgment when God will render their desserts to all those who have been raised up from the dead. Finally, they value the moral life and worship God especially through prayer, almsgiving, and fasting.

Since in the course of centuries not a few quarrels and hostilities have arisen between Christians and Moslems, this sacred synod urges all to forget the past and to work sincerely for mutual understanding and to preserve as well as to promote together for the benefit of all mankind social justice and moral welfare, as well as peace and freedom.

4. As the sacred synod searches into the mystery of the Church, it remembers the bond that spiritually ties the people of the New Covenant to Abraham's stock.

Thus the Church of Christ acknowledges that, according to God's saving design, the beginnings of her faith and her election are found already among the Patriarchs, Moses, and the prophets. She professes that all who believe in Christ—Abraham's sons according to faith—are included in the same Patriarch's call, and likewise that the salvation of the Church is mysteriously foreshadowed by the chosen people's exodus from the land of bondage. The Church, therefore, cannot forget that she received the revelation of the Old Testament through the people with whom God in His inexpressible mercy concluded the Ancient Covenant. Nor can she forget that she draws sustenance from the root of that well-cultivated olive tree onto which have been grafted the wild shoots, the Gentiles. Indeed, the Church believes that by His cross Christ, Our Peace, reconciled Jews and Gentiles, making both one in Himself (*NOSTRA AETATE* 1965).

were entering into collaborative arrangements of all sorts, while their students were attending the same lectures and reading the same books. No matter how hard conservative Protestants or Catholics might try to reverse these trends, it would be impossible to unscramble the ecumenical omelet. A gulf that had separated Western Christendom for four centuries was being bridged.

Reforming Society

The denominations influenced by Puritanism emphasized personal morality, which they expected to bear fruit in society. To Quakers, English Congregationalists, and some Methodist-derived movements such as the Salvation Army (organized by William Booth in London after 1865), one test of any renewal was whether it improved living conditions—food, clothing, shelter, education— for the population at large.

In the middle of the nineteenth century, the United States was torn apart by the issue of slavery. When that issue erupted politically in the Civil War of 1861–5, its effects were felt in the Christian denominations. Some, such as the Presbyterians, separated into northern and southern churches that took a century to reunite. By and large, the Christian conscience was anti-slavery, but there were more interests to be offended in southern White constituencies than in their northern counterparts.

Political issues around race erupted again in the mid-twentieth century. When the civil-rights movement developed during the early 1960s, the Black community had few institutional structures other than churches, with the result that almost all the early Black leaders emerged from the ranks of the ministry. Martin Luther King, Jr, and his Southern Christian Leadership Conference were the pivotal leaders in the movement, but the support of White religious leaders was also important.

Religion has been invoked on both sides of the race issue. Some conservative Protestants have argued that God created different races and clearly meant for them to remain separate; the Mormons in America long resisted even Black membership, let alone leadership. The Afrikaner population of South Africa, whose National Party came to power in 1948, had a Dutch Calvinist background, and they put forward theological as well as practical reasons for its policy of apartheid (segregation). Vehement condemnation of that policy by members of the United Nations and the British Commonwealth brought about South Africa's withdrawal from the Commonwealth in 1961 and its expulsion from the UN. But within South Africa there was equally vocal opposition to the policy from both Black and White Christians, many of them Anglicans. By 1994, when Blacks first voted in South African elections, even

Reformed Church leaders had begun to repudiate apartheid.

Similarly, Christians have not been of one mind on economic policy. During the Industrial Revolution, for instance, the ownership and managerial classes in many parts of the English-speaking world were largely Protestant, while the industrial workers were largely Roman Catholic.

Many religious institutions were indebted to the philanthropy of wealthy families such as the Rockefellers and Vanderbilts in the United States or the Eatons in Canada. It was sometimes hard for churches to bite the hand that fed them, with the result that affinities between the political right and the religious right continued to be evident during the presidencies of Ronald Reagan and George W. Bush.

From the 1860s onward, socialism in Europe addressed the growing gulf between owners and workers. On the continent, socialism was largely anti-Church, but in Britain there was a significant Christian socialist movement, which was inspired by two Anglicans, the theologian Frederick Denison Maurice and the clergyman–novelist Charles Kingsley. The influence also spread across the Atlantic.

A principal moral concern of late nineteenth-century Protestants had been alcoholism; thus temperance movements enlisted many of their energies. But as the twentieth century opened, broader issues of social and economic justice moved to the fore. For example, the Canadian Methodist board of Temperance, Prohibition, and Moral Reform was renamed Evangelism and Social Service.

In the decade before the First World War, Christian critics of the civic and corporate order in the United States called for the Christianization of the economy. The leading theologian of the 'social gospel' movement was Walter Rauschenbusch. While he was a Baptist pastor in New York City, he supported a radical candidate for mayor, and later, as a theology professor in Rochester, New York, he

From Martin Luther King, Jr, 'Letter from Birmingham Jail'

In the spring of 1963 the Baptist minister and civil-rights leader Martin Luther King, Jr, was arrested and imprisoned for leading a protest against racial segregation in Birmingham, Alabama. When eight fellow clergymen criticized him for taking part in the protest, King responded with an open letter that came to be known as the 'Letter from Birmingham Jail'.

You express a great deal of anxiety over our willingness to break laws. . . . One may well ask: 'How can you advocate breaking some laws and obeying others?' The answer lies in the fact that there are two types of laws: just and unjust. . . . One has not only a legal but a moral responsibility to obey just laws. Conversely, one has a moral responsibility to disobey unjust laws. I would agree with St Augustine that 'an unjust law is no law at all'. . . .

I have beheld the impressive outlines of [the South's] massive religious-education buildings. Over and over I have found myself asking: 'What kind of people worship here? Who is their God? . . . Where were they when Governor Wallace gave a clarion call for defiance and hatred? Where were their voices of support when bruised and weary Negro men and women decided to rise from the dark dungeons of complacency to the bright hills of creative protest?'. . .

There was a time when the church was very powerful—in the time when the early Christians rejoiced at being deemed worthy to suffer for what they believed. In those days the church was not merely a thermometer that recorded the ideas and principles of popular opinion; it was a thermostat that transformed the mores of society. Whenever the early Christians entered a town, the people in power became disturbed and immediately sought to convict the Christians for being 'disturbers of the peace' and 'outside agitators'. . . .

But the judgment of God is upon the church as never before. If today's church does not recapture the sacrificial spirit of the early church, it will lose its authenticity, forfeit the loyalty of millions, and be dismissed as an irrelevant social club with no meaning for the twentieth century. Every day I meet young people whose disappointment with the church has turned into outright disgust. . . .

I hope the church as a whole will meet the challenge of this decisive hour. . . .

Let us all hope that the dark clouds of racial prejudice will soon pass away and the deep fog of misunderstanding will be lifted from our fear-drenched communities, and in some not too distant tomorrow the radiant stars of love and brotherhood will shine over our great nation with all their scintillating beauty (King 1964: 76–95).

campaigned to make the gas company, the transit system, and the public schools more responsive to people's needs. Another leader was Washington Gladden, a Congregational minister who served on the city council in Columbus, Ohio, coordinated social service agencies, mediated in labour disputes, and lobbied the US Congress to create a commission on industrial relations.

In Canada, the Nova Scotian Presbyterian George M. Grant (1835–1902), who became head of Queen's University in Kingston, Ontario, in 1877, was a spokesman for interdenominational and national unity as well as a social conscience in public affairs. A more dramatic voice was that of the Manitoba Methodist James S. Woodsworth, the son of a mission superintendent. For criticizing the use of churches as recruiting centres during the First World War, he was ousted from his position with the Methodists' Bureau of Social Research. Later he left the ministry to become a Vancouver long-shoreman and eventually one of the founders of the Co-operative Commonwealth Federation, the forerunner of the New Democratic Party. Thus the roots of Canada's political left can be located not only in secular socialism but in Christian calls for economic justice, especially during the Depression of the 1930s. Christians have often been divided by issues of war, peace, and international justice. Pacifist refusal to participate in wars on grounds of conscience or ideology has generally been a minor-ity position, more common among individualist denominations such as Quakers and Anabaptists than among the more 'establishment' Catholics, Lutherans, and Anglicans. When the justification for fighting seemed relatively simple, as in the two world wars, most served in the military when called; an American popular song about an artil-lery chaplain in the Second World War had the refrain, 'Praise the Lord and pass the ammunition.'

After the Second World War, the Cold War be-tween the West and the Soviet bloc often evoked simplistic responses. The communist world was portrayed as formally atheist, even if only debat-ably diabolical. Religious support of American national policy during the 1960s, however, was fragmented when the US found itself mired in an ambiguous war in Vietnam. On an unprecedented scale, American Christians opposed this particular war, if not all war, in the name of religion. But more than a few leaders who were 'doves' on Viet-nam were 'hawks' when it came to Israel's con-quests in 1967.

Christians spoke out in increasing numbers against Washington's encouragement of regimes around the world that they judged repressive. Such criticism could often be selective, one per-son's terrorist being another's freedom fighter. Atti-tudes also depended on personal affinities and the information available, often conditioned by the varying media coverage given to Latin America,

Africa, the Middle East, or Southeast Asia. Still, the Christian ideals for society continue to be peace, justice, and reconciliation.

Marxism in Theory and Practice

The thought of Karl Marx (1818–83), including his critique of traditional religion, remains a ma-jor intellectual development of the modern world. We may still be too close to the collapse of So-viet and eastern European communism in 1989 to judge the extent to which Marx's ideas remain in play. China remains officially communist, though popular sentiment there favours more democracy.

Marx was raised in Germany in a secular Jew-ish family. The prevailing climate was one of so-cial emancipation and assimilation, so much so that Marx was baptized a Christian at the age of six. In the mid-1840s, after having written a doctoral dissertation on the philosophy of G.W.F. Hegel, Marx came to know Friedrich Engels, the Calvinist son of a wealthy German industrialist who owned cotton mills in England. After the publication of Engels's *The Condition of the Work-ing Class in England*, the two began collaborating in Brussels, and in 1848 they published *The Com-munist Manifesto*. As a result, Marx was no longer welcome in either Belgium or his Prussian home-land, and he spent the next three decades as an exile in London, where with Engels he pursued his writing and took part in the movement to or-ganize industrial labourers.

Marx's atheism is evident in his conviction that the divine is a projection of human powers and at-tributes. The implication of this view, put forward by Ludwig Feuerbach in his 1841 work *Essence of Christianity*, was that humankind, rather than the divinity, had to come first if humanity was to be fulfilled.

Although Marx wrote as an atheist, his critique of religion is primarily social rather than philo-sophical. Popularizing a phrase describing religion as the 'opium of the people', he argued that the function of institutional religion is to numb people to the injustices they suffer, promising pie in the sky after death instead of working for their material betterment in the here and now.

The Marxist criterion of success for any institution was whether it actually improved the conditions of human existence. By this criterion Marx found religion wanting. Before the twentieth century ended, many in eastern Europe and the Soviet Union found the socialist system wanting, by the same criterion. Marx judged religion by its achievements, not its ideals; and the world would judge Marxism similarly.

There are striking affinities between Marx's thought and the Judeo-Christian religious heritage. Both protest against social injustice. Both look forward to the end of the present world order and to a radical reshaping of things that will compensate those who currently suffer. This ideal has resonated in Latin America. The Latin American Council of [Catholic] Bishops, meeting in 1968 in Colombia, called for the Church to identify with the poor rather than the ruling élite.

Some South American churchmen, such as the Peruvian priest Gustavo Gutiérrez and the Uruguayan Jesuit Juan Luis Segundo, are proponents of liberation theology, which makes use of Christian biblical and theological resources that parallel Marxist thought. Like Marxism, it asks on behalf of the rural peasantry and the urban working class for a share in the material benefits of economy and society. It offers a rationale for social action that addresses an enduring problem, and has attracted the attention of concerned Christians, Catholic and otherwise, outside Latin America as well.

Recent Theology

'I believe because it's absurd,' said the third-century Latin theologian Tertullian, but theologians in the Latin Middle Ages regarded faith and reason as mutually confirming.

In the twentieth century a number of Roman Catholic theologians and philosophers explored the Aristotelian principles and methods of Thomas Aquinas for modern purposes. One

of the most innovative and wide-ranging was the German Jesuit Karl Rahner. Another influential Jesuit concerned with the theory of knowledge was the Canadian Bernard Lonergan, who taught in Rome for half his career. Jacques Maritain was a French neo-Thomist with conservative views on many issues who converted to Catholicism while a student and taught in Paris, Toronto, and Princeton. Widowed at the age of 78, he joined the Dominicans in a French monastery for his last years.

Tradition-based theologies also continued to command adherents among Protestants. A commentary on Paul's New Testament letter to the Romans propelled the Swiss theologian Karl Barth into prominence at the end of the First World War—a time of disillusionment with the idea of inevitable human progress. Barth's theology is termed dialectical because it draws a sharp distinction between what humans can do or know by themselves and the gift of saving grace offered by God; the Barthian position has been popular in conservative Protestant circles.

For existentialist thought, the unprovability of religion is irrelevant: what matters is individual commitment and experience. Existentialism has been particularly important among theologians trained in Europe. The German Paul Tillich, who settled in the United States in the 1930s, characterized religious awareness as moving not from God downwards, as Barth did, but from the human experience upwards: in Tillich's words, religion is 'ultimate concern'. Tillich's formulations were widely influential during the second half of the century.

A distinctly American movement is process theology. Drawing on the process thought of Alfred North Whitehead, it appeals to people who associate change with modernity. Whitehead was one of the century's relatively few English-speaking philosophers to make a substantial contribution to metaphysics (the branch of philosophy that speculates on the nature of ultimate reality). Whitehead saw reality as dynamic rather than as static:

It is as true to say that God is permanent and the world fluent, as that the World is permanent and God is fluent. . . . It is as true to say that the World is immanent in God, as that God is immanent in the World (Whitehead 1929: 410–11).

For the principal process theologians, such as the American Charles Hartshorne, creation is unfinished and God is developing too. The idea of God is the idea of a dynamic power open to virtually unlimited possibility.

In recent decades, few systematic thinkers have had as significant an influence as Barth and Tillich had among Protestants at mid-century, or as Rahner had among Catholics at the time of Vatican II. With few exceptions, progressive theological thinkers have had little success in presenting the meaning of scripture, tradition, and religious experience to the public. Statements of Christianity's classic message have been less important than applications of it: theologies of social liberation, feminist empowerment, global ecology, and so on. In particular, recent liberal theology has seemed reactive in its relationship to modern life, shifting and rethinking its priorities in response to the demands of the culture.

By contrast, fundamentalism in both its Protestant and Catholic forms is a defensive reaction against modernity that promises a return to the basics of Christian faith. The two varieties differ in what they look to as the ultimate authority: scripture in one case and the tradition of the church itself in the other. But both offer systematic formulations that seem easy to pin down, solid rather than shifting. Thus a liberal stance can be considerably more demanding than a fundamentalist one, because it is more likely to require a rethinking of the priorities of faith and tradition.

Women and Gender

The twentieth century, particularly in its second half, brought dramatic changes in the cultural expectations of women in society. The notion that females are subordinate to, or inferior to, or the property of, males has been discredited and is now in rapid retreat.

Liberal Protestant denominations in North America were ordaining women as clergy by the middle of the twentieth century, and the Anglican communion began doing so not long after that. Several American and Canadian denominations have had women as presiding officers. A Black woman, Barbara Harris, became an Episcopalian bishop in Massachusetts in 1989. Lois Wilson, a minister and also moderator of the United Church of Canada, served as one of the presidents of the World Council of Churches from 1983 to 1991, as did Madeleine Barot, from France, from 1954 to 1960.

The Roman Catholic and Eastern Orthodox churches, however, do not yet ordain women as priests, let alone admit women to the senior hierarchy. (The Old Catholics, who broke away from the Roman Catholic Church after Vatican I, began ordaining women in 1996.) Both the Greek and Latin Churches put special emphasis on historical precedent, and the tradition of women's subordination is so entrenched in them that it has proven particularly difficult to overturn. In the past, Rome did not allow women to take degrees in theology, and even though Catholic women, lay and religious, have made substantial contributions to the field as scholars in recent decades, they are still conspicuous as a minority.

Efforts to redress the patriarchal bias of two millennia of Christian tradition have run along several lines. First, attention has been given to the role of the feminine principle, along with female figures and symbols in the history and psychology of religion. Comparative studies have suggested parallels between the mother goddesses of various other religions and the function of Mary as archetypal mother in Roman Catholic piety.

Some theologians suggest that the real problem is the traditional conception of the Christian God as male. They see the deity as equally masculine and feminine, and therefore they address their prayers to 'Our Father and Mother'. Others point out that a gender-balanced God is still anthropomorphic—a deity in human form—and argue that the God who transcends the world must necessarily transcend gender.

Second, there has been an effort to emphasize the contribution made by gifted women in the history of Christianity, particularly in devotional spirituality. Female mystics such as Julian of Norwich, Teresa of Ávila, and Marie de l'Incarnation have attracted significantly more research attention in recent years than male mystics have.

Third, critics have heaped both blame and praise on Christianity for Western culture's treatment of human sexuality. Some praise the Church for its ideals of fidelity and equal partnership in marriage, or point to the difference Christianity made to social mores in the Roman Empire, where the male head of a household would formerly have slept freely with the slave girls. Clearly, though, Christians too have sometimes fallen short of the ideal.

Others accuse Christianity of imposing psychologically repressive and socially restrictive standards of sexual behaviour. The Christian rejection of bodily appetites as sinful has been blamed for a 'pathologization of sex'. The standard teaching that the only purpose of sexuality is reproduction has undoubtedly caused many people, men and women alike, to feel intense guilt for enjoying what comes naturally. And the continuing rejection of birth control by the Roman Catholic Church may be not only unrealistic but irresponsible in the face of global population forecasts.

Finally, the movement towards 'inclusive language' since the early 1980s has caused a major shift in the popular understanding of biblical language. Formerly accustomed to thinking of phrases such as 'the salvation of man' as referring to humankind in general, many English-speaking Christians have come to feel that such expressions are not sufficiently inclusive. For this reason many efforts have been made to substitute gender-neutral terms such as 'humanity'. The English texts of hymns have been revised, with non-rhyming but politically correct language sometimes prevailing over the original rhymes. Inclusive language is considered especially important in texts used in worship, so that women in the congregation can feel they have an equal share in the words that are spoken or sung.

Christianity and Pluralism

By the beginning of the third millennium, diversity had become part of the national fabric not only of societies built on immigration—like Canada, the United States, and Australia—but also, increasingly, of European societies where until recently the great majority of citizens shared a common cultural background, including the Christian faith. At the same time those societies have become more and more secular.

Many factors have contributed to the process of secularization. The most obvious is science, but there is good reason to think that Christianity itself has played a part. Certainly the first modern attempts to create secular states took place in Christian societies: England, France, the United States. The distinction between sacred and secular, which was fundamental to Christianity from the beginning, has been reflected in a general recognition of the right to freedom of religion.

Thus Christianity has largely ceased to play a significant official role in the public life of these secular societies. Many Christians remain convinced that the truth of their gospel leaves no room for other beliefs. Nevertheless, Christians have no choice today but to live as one faith group among many. And even if that were not the case, Jesus' commandment to love our neighbours as ourselves would demand full openness to the identities of our fellow human beings. The plural nature of religious life today is a fact that must be accepted. To see that fact as desirable is to embrace what has come to be known as pluralism.

Christianity and Change

In the past century, many denominations have formulated new statements of affirmation that can be used instead of the Apostles' Creed in worship. A particularly successful example—fresh, direct, and open to modern critical thought—was the statement introduced by the United Church of Canada in 1968:

> Man is not alone, he lives in God's world. We believe in God: who has created and is creating, who has come in the true man, Jesus, to reconcile and make new, who works in us and others by his spirit. We trust him. He calls us to be his church: to celebrate his presence, to love and serve others, to seek justice and resist evil, to proclaim Jesus, crucified and risen, our judge and our hope. In life, in death, in life beyond death, God is with us. We are not alone. Thanks be to God.

But time does not stand still. In only twenty years, it became necessary to revise the first sentence of this statement with the gender-neutral wording 'We are not alone, we live in God's world.'

What has modernity meant for the Christian tradition? It has opened new perspectives on the nature of thought and knowledge; brought new insights into the physical universe, living creatures, and the structure of personality; stimulated new understandings of human culture, history, and society. Above all, it has meant change. As Wilfred Cantwell Smith, an eminent Canadian scholar of religion, put it:

> We live, if I may coin a phrase, in a time of transition. The observation is a platitude; but the transitions themselves through which we are moving, the radical transformations in which we find ourselves involved, are far from hackneyed. Rather, there is excitement and at times almost terror in the newness to which all our cherished past is giving way. In area after area we are becoming conscious of being participants in a process, where we thought we were carriers of a pattern (Smith 1963: 115).

We have sampled the elaboration and differentiation of Christian traditions over 2,000 years. Their diversity is a reflection of the fact that they have been shaped by individuals in response to the new needs that have presented themselves in their own times. Some Christians may feel nostalgic for the comfortable, self-contained Christian world of an earlier era, but that world is no more. Change has been and will be a feature of Christian history in every age.

Sites

Bethlehem The traditional birthplace of Jesus.

Nazareth Jesus' home in youth and manhood.

Jerusalem The site of Jesus' crucifixion and centre of the earliest Jewish Christian community; capital of the Latin Christian Kingdom in the Holy Land from 1099 to 1187.

Rome The capital of the Roman Empire, where Peter introduced Christianity and the Roman Catholic Church eventually established its headquarters in Vatican City—the world's smallest independent country.

Anatolia A region (corresponding to modern-day Turkey), evangelized by Paul, that became an important centre of the early Church; the location of the famous councils of Chalcedon, Nicaea, and Constantinople.

Constantinople The capital of the Byzantine Empire and headquarters of the Orthodox Church; conquered by the Ottoman Turks in 1453 and renamed Istanbul.

Wittenberg The German town where Martin Luther posted his 95 theses, beginning the Protestant Reformation.

Worms The German city where an imperial council ('diet') tried Luther for political subversion.

Trent (Trentino in Italian) Site of the Council of Trent (1545–63) and centre of the Catholic Church's response to Protestantism, known as the Counter-Reformation.

Geneva The city in which John Calvin attempted to translate his vision of Christianity into a practising community.

Münster A town in northwestern Germany that became a centre of the Anabaptist movement.

Valladolid City in Spain; the site of a great debate in 1550 in which Bartolomé de las Casas defended the rights of the indigenous peoples of the New World.

Salt Lake City, Utah Founded by the Mormons in 1847; the headquarters of the Church of Jesus Christ of Latter-day Saints.

Glossary

Advent The beginning of the Christian liturgical year, a period including the four Sundays immediately preceding Christmas.

apocalypse, **apocalyptic** Cataclysmic events marking the transition from one era to another; a name of the last book of the New Testament, which describes such events.

apostles The first generation of Jesus' followers.

atonement Christ's restoration of humanity to a right relationship with God, variously interpreted as divine victory over demonic power, satisfaction of divine justice, or demonstration of a moral example.

baptism Sprinkling with or immersion in water; the ritual by which a person is initiated into membership in the Christian community. Baptism is considered a cleansing from sin.

bishop The supervising priest of an ecclesiastical district called a diocese.

canon A standard; a scriptural canon is the list of books acknowledged as scripture; the list of acknowledged saints is likewise a canon. Canon law is the accumulated body of Church regulations and discipline. Clergy subject to the rule of a particular cathedral or congregation are also sometimes termed canons.

charismatic Characterized by spiritual gifts such as **glossolalia**.

Christ From the Greek *Christos,* a translation of the Hebrew word for messiah, 'anointed'.

conversion Spiritual rebirth, accompanied by certainty of divine forgiveness and acceptance.

cosmological argument An argument that infers the existence of God from the fact of creation, based on the assumption that every effect must have a cause and that there cannot be an infinite regress of causes.

creeds Brief formal statements of doctrinal belief, often recited in unison by congregations.

crucifix A cross with an image of the suffering Jesus mounted on it.

dogma A church doctrine defined as indisputable and necessary to the faith.

Eastern-rite Catholic churches Churches in the Eastern Orthodox world and farther east that are aligned with the Roman Catholic Church but retain many Orthodox elements, including married clergy.

ecumenism The movement for reunion or collaboration between previously separate branches of Christianity.

Eucharist The ritual re-enactment of Jesus' sacrifice of himself, patterned after his sharing of bread and wine as his body and blood at the final Passover meal with his disciples. Orthodox Christians term it the liturgy, Catholics the mass, and Protestants the Lord's Supper or Holy Communion.

Evangelical In Germany, a name for the Lutheran Church; in the English-speaking world, a description of conservative Protestants with a confident sense of the assurance of divine grace and the obligation to preach it.

excommunication Formal expulsion from the Church, particularly the Roman Catholic Church, for doctrinal error or moral misconduct.

friar A member of a Latin mendicant order such as the Dominicans, Franciscans, or Carmelites.

fundamentalism A twentieth-century reaction to modernity, originally among Protestants who maintained the infallibility of scripture and doctrine.

glossolalia Speaking in 'tongues'; a distinguishing feature of **charismatic** movements.

Gnosticism An ancient movement that believed the material world to be the evil result of a fall from pure spiritual existence. Christian Gnostics viewed Jesus as the bearer of a secret, saving knowledge.

Good Friday The solemn holy day, two days before Easter, that commemorates the Passion or suffering and death of Jesus on the cross.

gospel 'Good news' (*evangelion* in Greek); the news of redemption that the Hebrew prophets had promised. The gospels are the accounts of Jesus' life attributed to his disciples Mark, Matthew, Luke, and John.

Holiness Churches Protestant churches that believe their members have already received 'holiness' (spiritual perfection) as a gift from God.

icon From the Greek for 'image'; a distinctive Byzantine form of portraiture used to depict Jesus, Mary, and the saints.

Immaculate Conception The doctrine that the virgin Mary was without sin from the moment she herself was conceived; defined as Roman Catholic dogma in 1854.

incarnation The embodiment of the divine in human form.

indulgences Releases from time in purgatory; the selling of indulgences was one of the abuses that led to the Protestant Reformation.

justification by faith alone The Lutheran belief that humans are saved not by 'works'—specifically, the Catholic rituals of confession and penance—but only by faith.

Lent The period of forty days, not counting Sundays, leading up to Easter; the season for the most serious Christian spiritual reflection.

logos 'Word' in the sense of eternal divine intelligence and purpose.

Manichaeism An intensely dualistic religion, founded by Mani in the third century, that grew out of Syrian Christianity under the influence of Gnosticism.

mass The Roman Catholic name for the Eucharist.

mendicant orders Medieval religious orders operating in the cities and towns.

millenarianism The belief that the current world order will come to an end and be replaced by a new era.

Monophysites Fifth-century advocates of the view that Christ's nature was fully divine.

mysticism A tradition cultivating an intensely felt spiritual union with the divine.

Nestorians Fifth-century advocates of the view that the incarnate Christ was two separate persons, one divine and one human.

ontological argument The eleventh-century theologian Anselm's argument based on logic holding that God must necessarily exist.

original sin The sinfulness, or tendency towards sin, supposedly innate

in human beings as a consequence of Adam's Fall.

orthodoxy Literally, the 'straight way', meaning correct belief; in any church, the accepted doctrine.

parables Stores about everyday life told to illustrate a point.

Passion The suffering and death of Jesus on the cross.

patriarchs The five bishops who together represent supreme authority in the Eastern Orthodox tradition.

Pentecost The fiftieth day after Easter, commemorated as the dramatic occasion when Jesus' followers experienced the presence of the Holy Spirit.

Pentecostal Churches Modern Protestant groups that emphasize speaking in 'tongues' as a mark of the Holy Spirit's presence and of the individual's holiness or spiritual perfection.

Pietism A movement that originated in late seventeenth-century Lutheran Germany, expressing a spontaneity of devotion and a confident certainty of forgiveness.

pope From *papa*, 'father'; the bishop of Rome, supreme authority in the Roman Catholic tradition.

predestination The notion that God anticipates or controls human actions and foreordains every individual to either salvation or damnation.

purgatory In Catholic doctrine, the realm to which the soul proceeds after death for some unspecified period in preparation for entering heaven.

Puritanism A Calvinist-inspired movement (1558–1660) that sought to 'purify' the Church of England of Catholic influences.

Reformed Churches Churches that are Calvinist in doctrine and often Presbyterian in governance; strong in the Netherlands and Scotland and also found in France, Switzerland, and Hungary.

rosary A string consisting of 58 beads and a small crucifix, used in Catholic devotion to keep count when repeating 'Our Father' and 'Hail Mary' prayers.

sacrament A ritual action seen as signifying divine grace. The most widely accepted sacraments are baptism and the Eucharist, although the Catholic Church also recognizes five others.

Stations of the Cross Fourteen locations marked in the nave of some churches, recalling events along the route in Jerusalem from Jesus' trial to his crucifixion.

syncretism The combination of elements from more than one religious tradition.

teleological argument From Greek *telos*, 'end' or 'purpose'; an argument inferring the existence of God from the perception of purpose or design in the universe.

transubstantiation The Catholic doctrine that in the Eucharistic service, the bread and wine are miraculously transformed into the body and blood of Christ.

Trinity The concept of God as having three 'persons' or manifestations: as father, as son, and as Holy Spirit.

Further Reading

Barrett, C.K. 1989. *The New Testament Background: Selected Documents*. Rev. ed. San Francisco: Harper & Row. Provides a context for understanding Christian origins.

Beilby, James, ed. 2009. *The Historic Jesus: Five Views*. Five scholars write on their view of the historic Jesus.

Bettenson, Henry S., and Maunder, Chris, eds. 1999. *Documents of the Christian Church*. 3rd ed. London: Oxford University Press. Strong on the early Church and Anglicanism.

Cross, F.L., and Livingstone, E.A., eds. 2005. *The Oxford Dictionary of the Christian Church*. 3rd ed. New York: Oxford University Press. The best general one-volume reference handbook.

Farmer, David Hugh. 2004. *The Oxford Dictionary of Saints*. New York: Oxford University Press. Comprehensive guide to Christian saints.

Hastings, Adrian. 2000, 2007. *A World History of Christianity*. Grand Rapids: Eerdmans Publishing. A detailed history including Orthodox, Asian, African, Latin American, and North American Christianity.

Jenkins, Philip. 2007. *The Next Christianity: The Coming of Global Christianity*. New York: Oxford University Press. Projects that the majority Christian population will shift to Africa and Asia.

Küng, Hans. 1976. *On Being a Christian*. London: Collins; New York: Doubleday. A comprehensive review of Christian theology by a leading progressive Roman Catholic thinker.

MacCulloch, Diarmaid. 2010. *Christianity: The First Three Thousand Years*. New York: Viking Adult. A large, recent work by a noted Reformation historian.

McGinn, Bernard. 2006. *The Essential Writings of Christian Mysticism*. New York: Modern Library. A wide-ranging anthology of Christian mystics' writing.

McManners, John, ed. 1990. *The Oxford Illustrated History of Christianity*. Oxford: Oxford University Press. Comprehensive; well-written chapters by reliable authors.

The New Catholic Encyclopedia. 2nd ed. 15 vols. 2003. Detroit: Thomson Gale Group. A good place to start for many medieval and Roman Catholic topics.

Sakenfeld, Katharine Doob. 2009. *New Interpreter's Dictionary of the Bible*. 5 vols. Nashville: Abingdon Press. A good reference work on Biblical topics.

Spong, John Shelby. 2008. *Jesus for the Non-Religious*. New York: HarperOne. One of many attempts to recover the real Jesus and his role for moderns.

Roeder, Helen. 1951. *Saints and Their Attributes*. London: Longmans, Green. A useful guide to Christian iconography.

Ruether, Rosemary R., and Eleanor McLaughlin, eds. 1979. *Women of Spirit: Female Leadership in the Jewish and Christian Traditions*. New York: Simon and Schuster. One of the best feminist collections.

Tomkins, Steven. 2006. *A Short History of Christianity*. Grand Rapids: Eerdmans Publishing. A brief but comprehensive introduction to Christian history.

Ware, Timothy. 1993. *The Orthodox Church: New Edition*. 2nd ed. New York: Penguin. A readable introduction to Orthodox Christian thought and practice.

Recommended Websites

www.christianity.com

www.ncccusa.org
    Site of the National Council of Churches USA.

www.oikoumene.org/
    Site of the World Council of Churches.

www.religionfacts.com/christianity/index.htm
    A wide-ranging source of information on Christianity as well as other religions.

www.vatican.va/phome_en.htm
    English-language version of the official Vatican site.

http://virtualreligion.net/forum/index.html
    Site of the Jesus Seminar.

www.wicc.org
    Site of the Women's Inter-Church Council of Canada.

www.worldevangelicals.org
    A global association of evangelical Christians.

References

Bainton, Roland H. 1974. 'Reformation'. In *Encyclopaedia Britannica*, vol. 15, 547–57. Chicago: Encyclopaedia Britannica Inc.

Bettenson, Henry, ed. 1967. *Documents of the Christian Church*. 2nd ed. Oxford: Oxford University Press.

Bowie, Fiona, and Oliver Davies, eds. 1990. *Hildegard of Bingen: Mystical Writings*. New York: Crossroad.

Cohen, J.M., trans. 1957. *The Life of St Teresa of Avila by Herself*. London: Penguin.

Colgrave, Bertram, ed. 1969. *Bede's Ecclesiastical History of the English People*. Oxford: Clarendon Press.

Durkheim, Émile. 1915. *The Elementary Forms of the Religious Life*. London: Allen & Unwin.

Faber, Richard. 1966. *The Vision and the Need: Late Victorian Imperialist Aims*. London: Faber.

Frend, W.H.C. 1965. *The Early Church*. Oxford: Blackwell.

King, Martin Luther, Jr. 1964. *Why We Can't Wait*. Reprinted by arrangement with The Heirs to the Estate of Martin Luther King Jr., c/o Writers House as agent for the proprietor New York, NY. Copyright 1963 Dr. Martin Luther King Jr.; copyright renewed 1991 Ciretta Scott King.

Livingstone, David. 1858. *Cambridge Lectures*. Cambridge: Deighton.

McManners, John, ed. 1990. *The Oxford Illustrated History of Christianity*. Oxford: Oxford University Press.

Meyendorff, John. 1964. *A Study of Gregory Palamas*. London: Faith Press.

Meyer, Robert T., trans. 1950. *Athanasius, Life of St. Anthony*. Westminster, MD: Newman Press.

New English Bible. 1970. New York: Oxford University Press; Cambridge: Cambridge University Press.

NOSTRA AETATE. 1965. 'Declaration on the Relation of the Church to Non-Christian Religions'. Accessed 26 Feb. 2010 at <http://www.ewtn.com/library/councils/v2non.htm>.

O'Brien, Elmer. 1964. *Varieties of Mystic Experience*. New York: Holt, Rinehart and Winston.

Oliver, Roland. 1957. *Sir Harry Johnston and the Scramble for Africa*. London: Chatto & Windus.

Outler, Albert C., trans. 1955. *Augustine: Confessions and Enchiridion*. Philadelphia: Westminster Press; London: SCM Press.

Radice, Betty, trans. 1986. 'Moriae encomium'. In *Collected Works of Erasmus*, vol. 27. Toronto: University of Toronto Press.

Smith, Wilfred Cantwell. 1963. *The Faith of Other Men*. New York: New American Library.

Stevenson, J., ed. 1957. *A New Eusebius*. London: SPCK.

Stokes, Francis G., trans. 1909. *Epistolae obscurorum virorum*. London: Chatto & Windus.

Von Gebler, Karl. 1879. 'Letter to Castelli (excerpt)'. Accessed 26 Feb. 2010 at <http://www.law.umkc.edu/faculty/projects/ftrials/galileo/lettercastelli.html>.

Whitehead, Alfred North. 1929. *Process and Reality*. Cambridge: Cambridge University Press; New York: Macmillan.

Notes

I am indebted to Alan Segal for allowing me to incorporate parts of the adaptation of Will Oxtoby's chapter on Christianity that he prepared for *A Concise Introduction to World Religions* (2007).

1. For a discussion of the many parallels between Buddhism and early Christianity, see Roy C. Amore, *Two Masters, One Message*.

2. The words in brackets (a doxology, or short hymn of praise) do not appear in the earliest editions of the gospels, but were recited as part of the prayer by early Christians. As a result not all Christian churches include them as part of the prayer.

Chapter 5

Muslim Traditions

❦ Amir Hussain ❦

Islam is the last of the three historic monotheistic faiths that arose in the Middle East, coming after Judaism and Christianity. Its name means 'submission' in Arabic and signifies the commitment of its adherents to live in total submission to God. A person who professes Islam is called a Muslim, meaning 'one who submits to God'. An older term, rarely used today, is 'Mohammedan', which misleadingly—and to Muslims offensively—suggests that Muslims worship the Prophet Muhammad himself.

Who is a Muslim? The Qur'an, the Islamic scripture, presents Islam as the universal and primordial faith of all the prophets from Adam to Muhammad, and of all those who have faith in God, the one sovereign Lord, creator, and sustainer of all things. According to the Qur'an, Islam is God's eternal way for the universe.

Inanimate things, plants and animals, even the angels, are all *muslims* to God by nature or instinct. Only human *islam* is an *islam* of choice. Human beings may voluntarily accept or wilfully reject faith, but on the Day of Judgment they will face the consequences of their choice. They can expect to be rewarded for their faith or punished for their rejection of it.

Most Muslims are born into Muslim families. But it is also possible to become a Muslim simply by repeating before two Muslim witnesses the **shahadah**, or profession of faith: 'I bear witness that there is no god except God, and I bear witness that Muhammad is the messenger of God.' Anyone who does this becomes legally a Muslim, with all the rights and responsibilities that this new identity entails.

❧ ORIGINS

Jewish and Christian communities existed in Arabia long before the emergence of Islam in the seventh century. The city of Mecca, where Muhammad was born, was dominated mainly by one tribe, the Quraysh, but it was open to a broad range of cultural and religious influences, including Jewish and Christian moral and devotional ideas. There were desert hermits who practised holiness and healing, and a group of Meccan Arabs known as **hanifs** ('pious ones') who concurred with Judaism and Christianity in their ethical monotheism. The majority of the society, however, was polytheistic, and many of the images of the gods and goddesses they worshipped were housed in an ancient

Hadith: A saying of the Prophet

The Messenger of God (may God bless him and give him peace) said: 'Whoever has faith in God and the Last Day should not hurt their neighbour, and whoever has faith in God and the Last Day should serve their guest generously, and whoever has faith in God and the Last Day should speak what is good or keep quiet' (*Sahih al-Bukhari*, vol. 8, book 73).

◀ In the courtyard of the Rustem Pasha mosque in Istanbul, Turkey (Andrew Leyerle).

Timeline

622	Muhammad's *hijrah* from Mecca to Medina
632	Muhammad dies; leadership passes to the caliph
642	Birth of al-Hasan al-Basri, early Sufi ascetic (d. 728)
661	Damascus established as capital of Umayyad caliphate
680	Death of Husayn at Karbala', commemorated as martyrdom by Shi'is
711	Arab armies reach Spain
762	Baghdad established as 'Abbasid capital
922	al-Hallaj (born c. 858) executed for claiming to be one with the Truth
1058	Birth of al-Ghazali, theological synthesizer of faith and reason (d. 1111)
1071	Seljuq Turks defeat Byzantines in eastern Anatolia
1165	Birth of Ibn 'Arabi, philosopher of the mystical unity of being (d. 1240)
1207	Birth of Jalal al-Din Rumi, Persian mystical poet (d. 1273)
1258	Baghdad falls to Mongol invaders
1492	Christian forces take Granada, the last Muslim stronghold in Spain
1529	Ottoman Turks reach Vienna (again in 1683)
1602	Muslims officially expelled from Spain
1703	Birth of Ibn 'Abd al-Wahhab, leader of traditionalist revival in Arabia (d. 1792)
1924	Atatürk, Turkish modernizer and secularizer, abolishes the caliphate
1930	Iqbal proposes a Muslim state in India
1947	Pakistan established as an Islamic state
1979	Ayatollah Khomeini establishes a revolutionary Islamic regime in Iran
2001	Osama bin Laden launches terrorist attacks on America
2004	Madrid train station bombings
2005	London transit bombings

structure called the Ka'ba, believed to have been built by Abraham and his son Ishmael.

The Life of Muhammad (570–632 CE)

Muhammad was born into the Quraysh tribe around the year 570. His father died before his birth and his mother died a few years later. Muhammad thus grew up an orphan and was cared for first by his paternal grandfather, 'Abd al-Muttalib, and then, after his grandfather's death, by his uncle Abu Talib.

Little is known about Muhammad's youth. He worked as a merchant for a rich widow, Khadijah, whom he married in his mid-twenties. Muhammad is described in the early biographical sources as a contemplative, honest, and mild-mannered

Traditions at a Glance

Numbers
There are more than 1 billion Muslims around the world; approximately 600,000 in Canada; and between 6 and 7 million in the United States.

Distribution
Although Islam originated in Arabia, the largest Muslim populations today are in Indonesia, Pakistan, India, and Bangladesh. Muslims are the second largest religious community (behind Christians) in many Western countries, including Canada, Great Britain, France, and Germany.

Principal Historical Periods
570–632 Lifetime of the Prophet Muhammad
632–661 The time of the four caliphs
661–750 Umayyad caliphate
750–1258 'Abbasid caliphate
1517–1924 Ottoman caliphate

Founder and Principal Leaders
All Muslims place authority in Muhammad as the last prophet. Shi'i Muslims give special authority after Muhammad to his son-in-law 'Ali and 'Ali's descendants.

Deity
Allah is Arabic for 'the God' and is cognate with the Hebrew *'Eloh* (plural *'Elohim*), 'deity'. Muslims believe Allah to be the same God worshipped by Christians, Jews, and other monotheists.

Authoritative Texts
The essential text is the Qur'an (literally, 'The Recitation'), believed to have been revealed by God to Muhammad between the years 610 and 632 CE. Second in importance are the sayings of Muhammad, known as the *hadith* (literally, 'narrative').

Noteworthy Doctrines
Islam, like Judaism and Christianity, is a faith based on ethical monotheism. Its prophetic tradition begins with the first created human being (Adam) and ends with the Prophet Muhammad. Muslims believe that the first place of worship dedicated to the one true God is the Ka'ba in Mecca, built by Abraham and his son Ishmael.

young man. He was called al-Amin ('the faithful' or 'trustworthy') because of the confidence he inspired in people.

Once a year, during the month of **Ramadan**, Muhammad spent days in seclusion in a cave on Mount Hira, a short distance from Mecca. Tradition reports that it was during one of those retreats he received the call to prophethood and the first revelation of the Qur'an.

As Muhammad was sitting one night in the solitude of his retreat, an angel—later identified as Gabriel (Jibril in Arabic)—appeared. Taking hold of him and pressing him hard, the angel commanded, 'Recite [or read]!' Muhammad answered,

'I cannot read.' After repeating the command for the third time, the angel continued, 'Recite in the name of your Lord who created, created man from a blood clot. Recite, for your Lord is most magnanimous—who taught by the pen, taught the human being that which s/he did not know' (Q. 96: 1–5). Shivering with fear and apprehension, Muhammad ran home and asked the people of his household to cover him.

Yet the angel returned to him often, saying, 'O Muhammad, I am Gabriel, and you are the Messenger of God.' Khadijah consoled and encouraged him, and eventually took him to her cousin, a learned Christian named Waraqah bin Nawfal. Waraqah confirmed Muhammad in his mission, declaring him to be a Prophet sent by God with a sacred law like that of Moses.

The idea of a prophet—*nabi* in both Arabic and Hebrew—was not unfamiliar to Muhammad's people. For twelve years Muhammad the Prophet of God preached the new faith in the One God to his people with little success. The Meccans did not wish to abandon the ways of their ancestors, and they feared the implications of the new faith both for their social customs and for the religious and economic status of the Ka'ba.

Muhammad's message was not only religious but also moral and social. He instructed the Meccans to give alms, to care for the orphaned, to feed the hungry, to assist the oppressed and destitute, and to offer hospitality to the wayfarer. He also warned of impending doom on the day of the last judgment. The first to accept the new faith were the Prophet's wife Khadijah, his cousin and son-in-law 'Ali bin Abi Talib, his slave Zayd bin Harithah—whom he later freed and adopted—and his faithful companion Abu Bakr.

Similar to the first followers of Jesus, Muhammad and his followers were often vilified. Around 615, one group of Muslims without tribal protection faced such severe persecution from the polytheistic Meccans that the Prophet advised them to migrate across the Red Sea to the Christian country of Abyssinia (Ethiopia), where they were well received. And in 619 the Prophet himself was left without support or protection when his wife Khadijah and his uncle Abu Talib both died within the space of barely two months. It was soon after these losses that he experienced what came to be known as the **mi'raj** or 'night journey', travelling from Mecca to Jerusalem in the course of one night and then ascending to heaven. There he met some of the earlier prophets and was granted an audience with God. For Muslims, these miraculous events confirmed that the Prophet still had the support of God. Even so, it would be another three years before the Prophet was able to find a place for the Muslims to establish their own community, free of the persecution they suffered in Mecca.

The First Muslim Community

Finally, in 622, an invitation was offered by the city of Yathrib, about 400 kilometres (250 miles) north of Mecca. The migration (**hijrah**) to Yathrib, which thereafter came to be known as 'the city of the Prophet' or Medina ('the city'), marked the beginning of community life under Islam, and thus of Islamic history. In Medina Muhammad established the first Islamic commonwealth: a truly theocratic state, headed by a prophet whose rule was believed to follow the dictates of a divine scripture.

Islamic Dates

The migration to Medina provided the starting-point for the dating system used throughout the Muslim world. Years are counted backwards or forwards from the *hijrah* and accompanied by the abbreviation AH, from the Latin for 'year of the *hijrah*'. Because Muslims use the lunar year—which is 11 days shorter than the solar year—*hijri* dates gain one year approximately every 33 solar years. Thus the year 1400 AH was reached in 1979 CE, and the new year of 1432 AH was celebrated in 2010 CE.

Medina was an oasis city with an agricultural economy. Its social structure was far more heterogeneous than Mecca's, for its population included a substantial Jewish community as well as two feuding Arab tribes, the Aws and the Khazraj, whose old rivalries had kept the city in a continuous state of civil strife. Muhammad was remarkably successful in welding these disparate elements into a cohesive social unit. In a brief constitutional document known as the covenant of Medina, he stipulated that all the people of the city should form a single Muslim commonwealth. The covenant granted the Jews full religious freedom and equality with the Muslims, on condition that they support the state and refrain from entering into any alliance against it, whether with the Quraysh or with any other tribe.

The Qur'an's narratives and worldview are closely akin to the prophetic view of history laid out in the Hebrew Bible. The Prophet expected the Jews of Medina, recognizing this kinship, to be natural allies, and he adopted a number of Jewish practices, including the fast of the Day of Atonement (Yom Kippur). But the Medinan Jews rejected both Muhammad's claim to be a prophet and the Qur'an's claim to be a sacred book. The resulting tension between the two communities is reflected in the Qur'an's treatment of the Jews. Some references are clearly positive; for example: 'Among the People of the Book are an upright community who recite God's revelations in the night, prostrate themselves in adoration, believing in God and the Last Day . . . these are of the righteous, whatever good they do, they shall not be denied it' (3: 113–15). Others are just as clearly negative: 'Take not the Jews and Christians for friends' (5: 51). Increasingly, Islam began to distinguish itself from Judaism, so that within two years of the Prophet's arrival in Medina, the fast of Ramadan took precedence over the fast of Yom Kippur and the *qiblah* (direction of prayer) was changed from Jerusalem to the Ka'ba in Mecca.

In the Qur'an the people of Medina are called Ansar ('helpers') because they were the first supporters and protectors of Islam and the Prophet. As the flow of Muslim immigrants from Mecca increased, however, a new social group was added to an already diverse society. The new immigrants, along with those who came with or shortly after the Prophet, were called Muhajirun ('immigrants').

The Conversion of Mecca

The Muslims who had fled Mecca for Medina had left all their goods and property behind. Without the means to support themselves in their new home, they began raiding Meccan caravans returning from Syria. In 624, when the Meccans sent an army of roughly a thousand men to Medina, they were met at the well of Badr by a 300-man detachment of Muslims.

Though poorly equipped and far outnumbered, the Muslims were highly motivated, and they inflicted a crushing defeat on the Meccans. Thus the Battle of Badr remains one of the most memorable events in Muslim history. It is celebrated in the Qur'an as a miraculous proof of the truth of Islam: 'You [Muhammad] did not shoot the first arrow when you did shoot it; rather God shot it' (Q. 8: 17); 'God supported you [Muslims] at Badr when you were in an abased state' (Q. 3: 123).

To avenge their defeat, however, the Meccans met the Muslims the following year by Mount Uhud, not far from Medina, and this time they prevailed. Following the Battle of Uhud, the Jews of Medina were expelled from the city on the grounds that they had formed alliances with the Meccans against the Muslims. The real reason for the decision, however, may have been to free the Muslim state of external influences at a critical stage in its development.

The Muslims were growing in strength. Meanwhile, they continued to raid the caravans of the Quraysh, and before long they received word that the Meccans were planning to attack Medina itself. On the advice of Salman the Persian, a former slave, the Prophet had a trench dug around the exposed parts of the city, to prevent the Meccan cavalry from entering. Thus when the Quraysh, along with a large coalition of other tribes, tried to invade Medina in 627, the city was able to withstand the attack. The 'Battle of the Trench' marked a tipping point in relations between the Muslims and the Meccans, and in 628 the latter were impelled to seek a truce.

Two years later, when the Quraysh breached the truce, the Prophet set out for Mecca at the head of a large army. But there was no need to fight. When the Muslims arrived, the Meccans surrendered to them and accepted Islam en masse.

Whenever an individual or tribe accepted Islam, all hostilities were to cease and enemies were to become brothers in faith. Therefore the Prophet granted amnesty to all in the city. Asked by the Meccans what he intended to do with them, the Prophet answered, 'I will do with you what Joseph did with his brothers. Go; you are free.' Then he quoted Joseph's words to his brothers: 'There is no blame in you today; God forgive you' (Q. 12: 92).

Muhammad took no credit for the conquest of Mecca, attributing the victory solely to God, as prescribed in the Qur'an: 'When support from God comes, and victory, and you see people enter into the religion of God in throngs, proclaim the praise of your Lord and seek God's forgiveness, for God is truly relenting' (Q. 110). He returned to Medina and died there two years later, in 632, after making a farewell pilgrimage to Mecca and its sacred shrine, the Ka'ba.

Muhammad was always known as *rasul Allah* ('the Messenger of God') rather than as a ruler or military leader. But he was all of these. He waged war and made peace. He laid the foundations of a community (**ummah**) that was based on Islamic principles. He firmly established Islam in Arabia and sent expeditions to Syria. Within eighty years the Muslims would administer the largest empire the world had ever known, stretching from the southern borders of France through North Africa and the Middle East into India and Central Asia.

At the time of his death, however, no one could have foreseen that future. The majority of Muslims—the **Sunni**, meaning those who follow the

The Dome of the Rock in Jerusalem, built between 687 and 691 by Caliph 'Abd al-Malik b. Marwan, is not a mosque but a shrine. It stands on the site of the Hebrew temple destroyed by the Romans in 70 CE (Zafer Kizilkaya/ Ponkawonka.com).

sunnah (traditions) of the Prophet—believed that he had not even designated a successor or specified how one should be chosen. But a minority community, known as the Shi'a (from the Arabic meaning 'party'), believed that Muhammad had in fact appointed his son-in-law 'Ali to succeed him. Muhammad's death therefore precipitated a crisis, which grew into a permanent ideological rift.

A *khalifah* is one who represents or acts on behalf of another. Thus after Muhammad's death, his close companion Abu Bakr became the *khalifat rasul Allah*—the 'successor' or 'representative' of the Messenger of God—and Abu Bakr's successor, 'Umar ibn al-Khattab, was at first referred to as the 'successor of the successor of the Messenger of God'.

From the beginning, the institution of the caliphate had a worldly as well as a religious dimension. As a successor of the Prophet, the **caliph** was a religious leader. At the same time, as the chief or administrative head of the community, he was the *amir* or commander of the Muslims in times of peace as well as war. Perhaps conscious of this temporal dimension of his office, 'Umar is said to have adopted the title 'commander of the faithful' in place of his cumbersome original title. Nevertheless, the caliph continued to function as the chief religious leader ('imam') of the community. In all, there were four caliphs who ruled after Muhammad, from 632 to 661. From 661 to 750, the Muslim world was ruled by a hereditary dynasty, known as the Umayyads. The Umayyads, in turn, were defeated by the 'Abbasid dynasty, which ruled from 750 to 1258.

 CRYSTALLIZATION

Prophets and Messengers

According to the Qur'an, God operates through prophets and messengers who convey God's will in revealed scriptures and seek to establish God's sacred law in the lives of their communities. From the Islamic point of view, therefore, human history is prophetic history.

Islamic tradition maintains that, from the time of Adam to the time of Muhammad, God sent 124,000 prophets into the world to remind people of every community of their obligation to the one and only sovereign Lord and warn them against heedlessness and disobedience: 'There is not a nation but that a warner was sent to it' (Q. 26: 207). The Qur'an mentions by name 26 prophets and messengers. Most are well-known biblical figures, among them Abraham, Moses, David, Solomon, Elijah, Jonah, John the Baptist, and Jesus. It also mentions three Arabian prophets: Shu'ayb, Hud, and Salih.

Islamic tradition distinguishes between prophets and messengers. A prophet (*nabi*) is one who conveys a message from God to a specific people at a specific time. A messenger (*rasul*) is also a prophet sent by God to a specific community; but the message he delivers is a universally binding sacred law (**shari'ah**). The Torah given to Moses on Mount Sinai was an example of the latter: though delivered to the ancient Hebrews, it remained binding on all those who knew it, Hebrews and others, until the arrival of the next revelation—the gospel of Jesus. In other words, every messenger is a prophet; but not every prophet is a messenger. Among the messenger-prophets, five—Noah, Abraham, Moses, Jesus, and Muhammad—are called *ulu al-'azm* ('prophets of power or firm

---

Abraham

In the Qur'an, it is the innate reasoning capacity of the Hebrew patriarch Abraham—Ibrahim in Arabic—that leads him away from his people's tradition of idol worship and towards the knowledge of God. Even as a youth he recognizes that idols made of wood or stone cannot hear the supplications of their worshippers, and therefore can do them neither good nor harm.

One night, gazing at the full moon in its glory, Ibrahim thinks that it must be God. But when he sees it set, he changes his mind. He then gazes at the bright sun and thinks that, since it is so much larger, it must be the real God. But that night the sun too sets, leading Ibrahim to declare: 'I turn my face to the One who originated the heavens and the earth, a man of pure faith, and I am not one of the Associators [those who associate other things or beings with God]' (Q. 6: 77–9).

From the Qur'an: Abraham Destroys the Idols

When [Abraham] said to his father and his people, 'What are these idols that you so fervently worship?' they said, 'We found our fathers worshipping them.'

He said, 'Both you and your fathers are in manifest error.' They said, 'Have you come to us with the truth, or are you one of those who jest?'

He said, 'Your Lord is indeed the Lord of the heavens and the earth, for your Lord originated them; and to this I am one of those who bear witness. By God, I shall confound your idols as soon as you turn your backs.'

He thus destroyed them utterly except for the chief one, so that the people might turn to it [for petition].

They said, 'Who did this to our gods? He is surely a wrongdoer.'

Some said, 'We heard a youth called Abraham speaking of them.'

Others said, 'Bring him here in the sight of the people, so that they may all witness.'

They said, 'Did you do this to our gods, O Abraham?'

He said, 'No, it was their chief who did it. Question them—if they could speak.'

The people then turned on one another, saying, 'Indeed you are the wrongdoers!' Then they bowed their heads in humiliation, saying, 'You know well, [O Abraham], that these do not speak.'

He [Abraham] said, 'Would you then worship instead of God a thing that can do you neither good nor harm? Shame on you and on what you worship instead of God; do you not reason?'

They said, 'Burn him and stand up for your gods, if you would do anything.'

We [God] said, 'O fire, be coolness and peace for Abraham'

They wished evil for him, but We turned them into utter losers. And We delivered him and Lot to a land that We blessed for all beings. We also granted him Isaac and Jacob as added favour, and We made them both righteous. We made them all leaders guiding others by our command. We inspired them to do good deeds, perform regular worship, and give the obligatory alms; and they were true worshippers of Us alone (Q. 21: 51–73).

resolve', Q. 46: 35). Their special significance lies in their having received universally binding revelations from God.

In the context of Muslim piety, respect for Muhammad is shown by speaking (or writing) the phrase 'peace [and blessings of God] be upon him' every time his name or title is mentioned. In writing, the formula is often abbreviated as PBUH.

When the prophets as a group, culminating in Muhammad, are mentioned, the formula changes to 'peace be on them all'.

The Qur'an

The Qur'an was revealed (literally, 'sent down') to the prophet Muhammad over a period of 23 years. According to both the Qur'an and Muslim tradition, the angel Gabriel appeared to him, often in human guise, transmitting the *ayahs* (verses) and **surahs** (chapters) that came to constitute the Qur'an.

The Prophet's role as transmitter of revelation is reflected in the Qur'an's characteristic phrasing as God ('We') instructs the Prophet ('you') to 'say' something to the people (that is, to deliver a particular message to them). Yet the first instruction, as we have seen, was the command that Muhammad himself 'recite' or 'read' (*iqra*'). The term Qur'an is derived from the same root: *q–r–*', meaning 'to read' or 'recite'.

In size the Qur'an is nearly as long as the New Testament. The individual portions revealed to Muhammad vary in length and content from short verses on a single theme or idea to fairly lengthy chapters. The early Meccan *surahs* are generally brief admonitions couched in terse and powerful verses, while the later ones are didactic narratives or illustrative tales of earlier prophets and their communities. Through stories, parables, and exhortations urging good conduct and dissuading evil and indecent behaviour, the Qur'an aims to create an *ummah*: a 'community' (that is, a society united by faith).

The *surahs* revealed in Medina are fewer in number but longer, presenting didactic arguments, discourses, and legal pronouncements, often in response to questions or situations arising in the life of the community.

The Status of the Qur'an

Muslims believe that the Qur'an is an immutable heavenly book containing the eternal Word of God. In fact, there is an interesting theological parallel with Christian understandings of Jesus, who in the prologue to John's gospel is proclaimed to be the eternal Word of God made incarnate at a certain moment in history. For Christians Christ is the Word of God made flesh, while for Muslims the Qur'an is the Word of God made into a book.

Muslims understand the Qur'an to have been revealed specifically in the Arabic language—not surprising, given that Arabic was the language of its first audience. Hence any translation is considered to constitute an interpretation, not the Qur'an itself. Even in places where few if any Muslims speak the language, the Qur'an is always recited in Arabic. Of course, each passage is usually followed by a translation in the appropriate language.

The words of the Qur'an are recited in a newborn child's ear as a blessing. They are also recited to bless and seal a marriage contract or a business deal, to celebrate a successful venture, or to express sorrow and give solace in times of misfortune. Throughout the Muslim world, the Qur'an is recited on most special public occasions and daily on radio and television. Qur'anic recitation is an

From the Qur'an: On the Day of Judgment

This short surah *(chapter) is known by the title 'The Earthquake'.*

When the earth shall be shaken with a great quake, and the earth yields up her burdens, and the human being exclaims, 'What has happened to her!' On that day the earth shall recount her tidings—as her Lord had inspired her. Whoever does an atom's weight of good shall then see it, and whoever does an atom's weight of evil shall then see it (Q. 99).

art of great virtuosity and hypnotic power. For private devotional recitation over the course of a month, the Qur'an has been divided into 30 parts of equal length. The words of the Qur'an, in the form of calligraphy, have also been a central motif in Islamic art, and are used to decorate Muslim homes, mosques, and public buildings.

Compiling the Qur'an

When the Prophet died in 632, there were many people who had committed the Qur'an to memory. The only physical records, however, were fragments written on stones, bones, palm leaves, and animal parchment, which were held in a variety of private collections. In some cases the same material existed in several versions, and since the vowel marks were not added until later, different readings of certain words or phrases were possible. These variants became identified with specific readers through the generations of Muslim scholars.

The process of producing an official text of the Qur'an was completed under the third caliph, 'Uthman ibn 'Affan, within twenty years of the Prophet's death. One of the first copies of the complete text was given to Hafsah, a widow of the Prophet.

As an earthly book, the Qur'an has been shaped by Muslim history. Tradition maintains that the verses of each individual *surah* were arranged by the Prophet at Gabriel's instruction, but that the order of the *surahs* in relation to one another—roughly in decreasing order of length—was fixed by a committee that 'Uthman appointed to compile an official version. Of the 114 *surahs*, 113 are preceded by the invocation *bism-illahi ar-rahman ar-rahim* ('in the name of God, the All-merciful, the Compassionate'); the exception is the ninth *surah*, which commentators generally believe to be a continuation of the eighth.

Qur'anic Commentary (Tafsir)

The term for commentary on the Qur'an, **tafsir**, means 'unveiling' or elucidating the meaning of a text. Any such interpretation is based on one of three authoritative sources: the Qur'an itself, Prophetic **hadith** (tradition), and the opinions of the Prophet's Companions and their successors. Like the Qur'an and the *hadith*, the earliest commentaries were transmitted orally, but by the tenth century Qur'anic interpretation had developed into a science with several ancillary fields of study.

In fact, every legal or theological school, religious trend, or political movement in Muslim history has looked to the Qur'an for its primary support and justification. The result has been a wide range of interpretations reflecting the diversity of the sects, legal schools, and mystical and philosophical movements that emerged as the Islamic tradition developed.

The Qur'an's Concept of God

The Qur'an presents its view of the divinity in direct and unambiguous declarations of faith in the one and only God, creator, sustainer, judge, and sovereign Lord over all creation. For Muslims, it is a sin to associate any other being with God or to ascribe divinity to any but God alone.

'Allah' is not the name of a particular deity but the Arabic word for God, 'the Lord of all beings' (Q. 1: 2), who demands faith and worship of all rational creatures. It was used in the same sense by the pagan Arabs before Islam, and is still used in that sense by Arab Jews and Christians today.

Islamic theology holds that God's essence is unknowable, inconceivable, and above all categories of time, space, form, and number. Materiality and temporality cannot be attributed to God. Nor, properly speaking, can masculinity or femininity, although references to God in the Qur'an and throughout Islamic literature use masculine pronouns, verbs, and adjectives.

God is known through attributes referred to in the Qur'an as the 'most beautiful names' (sometimes translated as 'wonderful names'). These divine attributes are manifested in creation in power and mercy, life and knowledge, might and wisdom. The Qur'an (59: 22–3) declares:

> God is God other than whom there is no god, knower of the unknown and the visible. God is the All-merciful, the Compassionate. God is God other than whom there is no god, the King, the Holy One, Peace, the Faithful, the Guardian, the Majestic, the Compeller, the Lofty One.

Faith and Action

Righteousness as it is expressed in the Qur'an has several components. In addition to faith in God, God's angels, books, and prophets, and the judgment of the last day, it includes good works: Muslims should give of their wealth, however cherished it may be, to orphans and the needy or for the ransoming of slaves and war captives. It also includes patience and steadfastness in times of misfortune or hardship and war, and integrity in one's dealings with others.

Because all men and women belong ultimately to one humanity, they are all equal before God, regardless of race, colour, or social status. They may surpass one another only in righteousness: 'Humankind, We have created you all of one male and one female and made you different peoples and tribes in order that you may know one another. Surely, the noblest of you in God's sight is the one who is most aware of God' (Q. 49: 13).

The Arabic word *iman* means faith, trust, and a personal sense of safety and well-being in God's providential care, mercy, and justice. On this level of inner personal commitment, *iman* is synonymous with *islam*: total surrender of the human will and destiny to the will of God. The opposite of *iman* is **kufr**, rejection of faith. To have faith is to know the truth and assent to it in the heart, profess it with the tongue, and manifest it in concrete acts of charity and almsgiving. *Kufr*, on the other hand, means knowing the truth but wilfully denying or obscuring it by acts of rebellion against the

law of God. The word *kufr* literally means 'to cover up, deny, or obscure'.

The Qur'an also makes an important distinction between Islam and faith. Outwardly, Islam is a religious, social, and legal institution, whose members constitute the worldwide Muslim *ummah*, or community. *Iman*—faith—is an inner conviction whose sincerity God alone can judge, a commitment to a way of life in the worship of God and in moral relations with other persons. This is described beautifully in the Qur'an (49: 14), where the Bedouin come to Muhammad and say, 'we have faith'. Muhammad is commanded to respond: 'Do not say that you have faith, rather, say that you have submitted [you have *islam*], for faith has not yet entered your hearts.' Faith, as a comprehensive framework of worship and moral conduct, is explicitly depicted in the answer that the Prophet is said to have given to the question 'What is faith?': 'Faith is seventy-odd branches, the highest of which is to say "There is no god except God" and the lowest is to remove a harmful object from the road.'

Above Islam and *iman* stands *ihsan* (doing good or creating beauty). On the level of human inter-relations, *ihsan* is a concrete manifestation of both Islam and *iman*. On the level of the personal relationship of the man or woman of faith with God, *ihsan* constitutes the highest form of worship, expressed in this hadith: 'Ihsan is to worship God as though you see God, for even if you do not see God, God sees you.'

Religious Sciences

In Arabic a learned person is termed an *'alim*. The plural, *'ulama'*, refers to the religio-legal scholars, or religious intellectuals, of the Islamic world as a group. What Muslims call the 'religious sciences' were part of a comprehensive cultural package—including theology, philosophy, literature, and science—that developed as Islam expanded geographically far beyond the religio-political framework of its Arabian homeland. Cosmopolitan, pluralistic Islamic cultural centres like Baghdad, Córdoba, and Cairo offered ideal settings for intellectual growth. Beginning in the eighth century, the development of philosophy, theology, literature, and science continued in different parts of the Muslim world well into the seventeenth.

Islam is a religion more of action than of abstract speculation about right belief. Hence the first and most important of the religious sciences, Islamic law, stresses that the essence of faith is right living. The Prophet characterizes a Muslim thus: 'Anyone who performs our prayers [i.e., observes the rituals of worship] and eats our ritually slaughtered animals [i.e., observes the proper dietary laws] is one of us.' For Muslims, inner submission to the will of God is God's way for all of humankind. At both the personal and the societal level, Islam is a way of life that is to be realized by living within the framework of divine law, the *shari'ah*: that is, a way of life based on moral imperatives.

The Sources of Islamic Law

The Qur'an
The Qur'an and hence the *shari'ah* are centrally concerned with relationships among individuals in society and between individuals and God. The most particular and intimate human relationship is the one between husband and wife; the second is the relationship between parent and child. The circle then broadens to include the extended family, the tribe, and finally the *ummah* and the world.

Islam has no priesthood. Every person is responsible both for his or her own morality and for the morality of the entire Muslim *ummah*: 'Let there be of you a community that calls to the good, enjoins honourable conduct, and dissuades from evil conduct. These are indeed prosperous people' (Q. 3: 104).

The Qur'an places kindness and respect to parents next in importance to the worship of God. These are followed by caring for the poor and the needy through alms giving. Usury is prohibited as

a means of increasing one's wealth. But renunciation of material possessions is no more desirable than total attachment to them. Rather, the Qur'an enjoins the faithful to 'Seek amidst that which God has given you, the last abode, but do not forget your portion of the present world' (Q. 28: 77).

In short, the Qur'an is primarily concerned with moral issues in actual situations. It is not a legal manual. Of its 6,236 verses, no more than 200 are explicitly legislative.

The *Sunnah*
The life-example of the Prophet includes not only his acts and sayings but also his tacit consent. His acts are reported in anecdotes about situations or events to which he reacted or in which he participated. In situations where he expressed neither approval nor objection, his silence is taken to signify consent. Thus the *sunnah* of consent became a normative source in the development of Islamic law.

Accounts that report the Prophet's *hadiths* (sayings) must go back to an eyewitness of the event. The *hadith* literature is often called 'tradition' in English, in a quite specific sense. Islamic 'tradition' (or 'Prophetic tradition') is the body of sayings traced to the Prophet Muhammad through chains of oral transmission. *Hadith* is the most important component of *sunnah* because it is the most direct expression of the Prophet's opinions or judgments regarding the community's conduct.

To qualify as a *hadith*, a text must be accompanied by its chain of transmission, beginning with the compiler or last transmitter and going back to the Prophet. The aim of the study of *hadith* is to ascertain the authenticity of a particular text by establishing the completeness of the chain of its transmission and the veracity of its transmitters.

There are six canonical collections of *hadiths*. The earliest and most important collectors were Muhammad b. Isma'il al-Bukhari (810–70) and Muslim bin al-Hajjaj al-Nisaburi (c. 817–75). As their names suggest, the former came from the city of Bukhara in Central Asia and the latter from Nishapur in northeastern Iran. Although the two men did not know each other, they were contemporaries and both spent many years travelling across the Muslim world in search of *hadith* traditions. The fact that their independent quests produced very similar results suggests that a unified *hadith* tradition was already well established.

Both men are said to have collected hundreds of thousands of *hadiths*, out of which each selected about 3,000, discounting repetitions. Their approach became the model for all subsequent *hadith* compilers. Their two collections, entitled simply *Sahih* (literally, 'sound') *al-Bukhari* and *Sahih Muslim*, soon achieved canonical status, second in authority only to the Qur'an. Within less than half a century, four other collections—by Abu Dawud al-Sijistani, Ibn Majah, al-Tirmidhi, and al-Nasa'i—were produced. It is worth noting that, like al-Bukhari and Muslim, these four also came from Central Asia and Iran. Each of these collections is entitled simply *Sunan* (the plural of *sunnah*).

As legal manuals, all six collections are organized topically, beginning with the laws governing the rituals of worship and then continuing with the laws regulating the social, political, and economic life of the community.

The Scope of Islamic Law

For Muslims God is the ultimate lawgiver. The *shari'ah* is sacred law, 'the law of God'. It consists of the maxims, admonitions, and legal sanctions and prohibitions enshrined in the Qur'an and explained, elaborated, and realized in the Prophetic tradition.

The term *shari'ah* originally signified the way to a source of water. Metaphorically it came to mean the way to the good in this world and the next. It is 'the straight way' that leads the faithful to paradise in the hereafter. Muslims believe the *shari'ah* to be God's plan for the ordering of human society.

Within the framework of the divine law, human actions range between those that are absolutely obligatory and will bring rewards on the Day of Judgment, and those that are absolutely forbidden and will bring harsh punishment. Actions are classified in five categories:

- lawful (**halal**), and therefore obligatory;
- commendable, and therefore recommended (*mustahabb*);
- neutral, and therefore permitted (*mubah*);
- reprehensible, and therefore disliked (*makruh*); and
- unlawful (**haram**), and therefore forbidden.

These categories govern all human actions. The correctness of an action and the intention that lies behind it together determine its nature and its consequences for the person who performs it.

Jurisprudence (Fiqh)

Jurisprudence, or **fiqh**, is the theoretical and systematic aspect of Islamic law, consisting of the interpretation and codification of the *shari'ah*, or sacred law. A scholar who specializes in this exacting science is called a *faqih* ('jurist').

Islamic jurisprudence, as it was developed in the various legal schools (Hanafi, Maliki, Shafi'i, and Hanbali), is based on four sources. Two of these, the Qur'an and *sunnah*, are its primary sources. The other two are secondary sources: the personal reasoning (**ijtihad**) of the scholars, and the general consensus (**ijma'**) of the community. The schools of Islamic law differed in the degree of emphasis or acceptance that they gave to each source.

Personal reasoning is the process through which legal scholars deduced from the Qur'an and *sunnah* the laws that are the foundations of their various schools of thought. The term *ijtihad* signifies a scholar's best effort in this endeavour, which is based on reasoning from analogous situations in the past: modern software piracy, for instance, would be considered analogous to theft.

Finally, the principle of consensus (*ijma'*) is meant to ensure the continued authenticity and truth of the three other sources. In the broadest sense, *ijma'* refers to the community's acceptance and support of applied *shari'ah*. More narrowly, it has encouraged an active exchange of ideas among the scholars of the various schools, at least during the formative period of Islamic law. Consensus has remained the final arbiter of truth and error, expressed in the Prophet's declaration that 'my community will not agree on an error.'

Yet even this important principle has been the subject of debate and dissension among the scholars of the various schools. Among the many questions at issue are whether the consensus of earlier generations is binding on the present one, and whether the necessary consensus can be reached by the scholars alone, without the participation of the community at large.

Islamic Philosophy and Theology

An important subset of the religious sciences (also known as the transmitted sciences) contained the 'rational' sciences of philosophy and theology. Theology is discourse about God, God's attributes, and God's creation and nurture of all things. It is also concerned with human free will and predestination, moral and religious obligations, and the return to God on the Day of Resurrection for the final judgment. Insofar as theology addresses human faith and conduct, it is part of the science of *fiqh*, or jurisprudence.

In time, however, Islamic theology also came to concern itself with more philosophical questions about the existence of God, creation, and the problem of evil and suffering. In these areas Islamic theology reflects the influence of Hellenistic philosophy, whose principles and rationalistic methodology it adopted.

The rapid spread of Islam out of Arabia into Syria and Mesopotamia brought Muslims into contact with people of other faiths and ethnic backgrounds, including Hellenized Jews and Christians. With the rise of the 'Abbasid dynasty in the mid-eighth century, interest in Greek philosophy, science, and medicine increased, and Arabic translations of Greek works began to appear.

The quest for knowledge reached its peak in the next century under the caliph al-Ma'mun (r. 813–33), whose Bayt al-Hikmah ('House of Wisdom') in Baghdad was the first institution of higher

Muhammad ibn Idris al-Shafi'i

A decisive stage in Muslim jurisprudence came in the ninth century with Muhammad ibn Idris al-Shafi'i (767–820). Having travelled widely and studied in various centres of learning across the Muslim world, he spent his last years in Egypt, where he wrote the first systematic treatise on the subject. This work radically changed the scope and nature of Islamic jurisprudence. Rejecting personal opinion in favour of absolute dependence on the two primary sources, the Qur'an and *sunnah*, Shafi'i based his system on a vast collection of *hadith* and legal traditions entitled *Kitab al-Umm*, which he compiled in order to write his work. In opposition to the majority of jurists of his time, he argued that they should not base their judgments on the opinions of people, but should rely exclusively on the Book of God and the *sunnah* of his Prophet.

Although Shafi'i's legal system was later adopted as the basis of a school of thought bearing his name, he himself expressly opposed the idea. He saw himself not as the founder of a new legal school, but as the reformer of Islamic law. The Shafi'i school took root early in Egypt, where its founder lived and died. It then spread to southern Arabia and later followed the maritime trade routes first to East Africa and then to Southeast Asia, where it remains the dominant legal school.

learning not only in the Islamic world but any-where in the West. Christian scholars had already translated many Greek medical, philosophical, and theological treatises into Syriac and commented on them, but the House of Wisdom, which housed an impressive library of Greek manuscripts, pro-vided additional support for their work. Families of translators worked in teams, rendering into Arabic the ancient treasures of Hellenistic science and philosophy. Smaller centres of philosophical and medical studies in Syria and Iran also made notable contributions.

The Early Period

Early Islamic philosophy had a distinctive char-acter: Aristotelian in its logic, physics, and meta-physics; Platonic in its political and social aspects; and Neoplatonic in its mysticism and theology. Two figures stand out in this early period. The first was the Iraqi theologian-philosopher Abu Yusuf Ya'qub al-Kindi (d. 870), who used philosoph-ical principles and methods of reasoning to defend fundamental Islamic teachings such as the exis-tence and oneness of God, the temporal creation of the universe by God's command out of noth-ing, the inimitability of the Qur'an, and the ne-cessity of prophets. In his argument for the latter, Al-Kindi underlined the distinction between the philosopher who acquires his knowledge through rational investigation and contemplation and the prophet who receives his knowledge instanta-neously, through divine revelation.

In sharp contrast to al-Kindi, Abu Bakr Zakari-yah al-Razi ('the one from Rayy, Iran'; c. 865–926) was a thoroughgoing Platonist who rejected the doctrine of creation out of nothing. Rather, draw-ing on the theory that Plato elaborated in his *Timaeus*, al-Razi argued that the universe evolved from primal matter, floating gas atoms in an abso-lute void. The universe or cosmos came into being when God imposed order on the primeval chaos, but it will return to chaos at some distant point in the future, because matter will revert to its pri-meval state.

The Flowering of Islamic Philosophy

Abu Nasr al-Farabi (c. 878–950), who moved to Baghdad from Turkestan, in Central Asia, was not only a great philosopher but an important musical theorist and an accomplished instrumentalist. His Platonic philosophical system was comprehensive and universal. According to al-Farabi, God is pure intellect and the highest good. From God's self-knowledge or contemplation emanates the first intellect, which generates the heavenly spheres and a second intellect, who then repeats the pro-cess. Each subsequent intellect generates another sphere and another intellect.

Al-Farabi agreed with al-Kindi that a prophet is gifted with a sharp intellect capable of receiv-ing philosophical verities naturally and without any mental exertion. He then communicates these truths to the masses, who are incapable of com-prehending them on the philosophical level.

Although al-Farabi was called 'the second teacher', after Aristotle, even he was excelled by 'the great master' Ibn Sina (known in Latin as Avicenna, 980–1037). Ibn Sina, who was born in Bukhara, Iran, was a self-taught genius who mas-tered the religious sciences at the age of ten and by the age of eighteen had become a leading physi-cian, philosopher, and astronomer. His encyclope-dic manual of medicine, *al-Qanun fi al-Tibb* ('The canon of medicine'), and his philosophical ency-clopedia, *al-Shifa'* ('The book of healing'), were studied in European universities throughout the Middle Ages.

Ibn Sina built on al-Farabi's Neoplatonic ideas to produce a comprehensive system of mystical philosophy and theology. He accepted and de-veloped al-Farabi's emanationism, placing it in a more precise logical and philosophical frame-work. Although he affirmed the prophethood of Muhammad, the revelation of the Qur'an, and the immortality of the soul, he rejected the Qur'anic traditions of the resurrection of the body, the re-ward of paradise, and the punishment of hell.

According to a widely accepted Prophetic tradition, at the beginning of every century God raises a scholar to renew and strengthen the faith of the Muslim community. Such a man is known as a *mujaddid* ('renovator') of the faith. Abu Hamid Muhammad al-Ghazali (1058–1111) of Tus, in Iran, has been regarded as the *mujaddid* of the sixth Islamic century. His work went far beyond theology and philosophy, encompassing mysticism and all the religious sciences.

In 1091 al-Ghazali was appointed a professor of theology and law at the prestigious Nizamiyah college in Baghdad, where he tirelessly defended mainstream Sunni Islam against the innovations of the theologians and the heresies of the philosophers. Four years later, however, he suffered a deep psychological crisis and gave up teaching. After a long quest, he determined that true knowledge could not be attained through either the senses or the rational sciences, but only through a divine light that God casts into the heart of the person of faith. His reason thus enlightened, al-Ghazali produced one of the most ambitious works in the history of Islamic thought. Appropriately entitled *Ihya' 'ulum al-din* (The Revivification of the Religious Sciences), this magnum opus examines all religious learning from a deeply mystical point of view.

In his book *The Incoherence* [or 'Collapse'] *of the Philosophers*, al-Ghazali rejected the philosophical principle of causality (which said, for example, that created things could be the efficient causes of events) and in its place proposed a theory of occasionalism, according to which the only cause of anything in the universe is God. Al-Ghazali's critique itself would be the subject of a critique by the Andalusian Aristotelian philosopher Ibn Rushd.

Ibn Rushd (known in Latin as Averroës, 1126–98), who was born in Córdoba, Spain, was the greatest Muslim commentator on Aristotle. He came from a long line of jurists, and was himself a noted scholar of Islamic law. His legal training decisively influenced his philosophy. In his critique of al-Ghazali, entitled *The Incoherence of the Incoherence*, Ibn Rushd methodically criticizes al-Ghazali for misunderstanding philosophy and Ibn Sina for misunderstanding Aristotle. The first to construct a true Aristotelian philosophical system, Ibn Rushd essentially shared his Eastern predecessors' belief in the primacy of philosophy over religion. In his famous double-truth theory, however, he argued that both were valid ways of arriving at truth: the difference was that philosophy was the way of the intellectual elite, while religion was the way of the masses.

The great thirteenth-century philosophermystic Ibn 'Arabi will be discussed later, in the context of Sufism. A more empirical philosopher than any of those mentioned so far was the Tunisian-born 'Abd al-Rahman Ibn Khaldun (1332–1406). Through his extensive travels and the positions he held as a jurist and political theorist, Ibn Khaldun gained insight into the workings both of nations and of political and religious institutions. This led him to write a universal history. The most important part of this work is its introduction (*Muqaddimah*), in which Ibn Khaldun presents the first social philosophy of history in the Western world.

Islamic philosophy had a lasting influence on medieval and Renaissance thought in Europe, particularly through its interpretation of Aristotelianism. Europeans came to know many Muslim philosophers by Latinized forms of their names: Rhazes for al-Razi, Alpharabius or Avennasar for al-Farabi, Avicenna for Ibn Sina, Algazel for al-Ghazali, Averroës for Ibn Rushd.

DIFFERENTIATION

Shi'ism

As we have seen, the Muslim community was permanently divided soon after the death of the Prophet when a political party (*shi'ah*) formed around his cousin and son-in-law 'Ali in support of his right to succeed Muhammad as leader, or Imam.

'Shi'ism' is a broad term covering a variety of religio-political movements, sects, and ideologies. What they share is a general allegiance to 'Ali and his descendants, and their right to spiritual and temporal authority in the Muslim community after Muhammad.

For Sunni Muslims, the term 'imam' refers to anyone who serves as the leader of prayer at the mosque, a role that the caliph sometimes performed. For **Shi'is**, by contrast, 'Imam' is the title given to the one individual held to be the rightful, divinely mandated leader of the Muslim community.

In general, Shi'ism has always been characterized by absolute devotion to the Prophet's household. To Shi'is, the Qur'an underlines the high status of Muhammad's family ('the people of the house'): 'Surely, God wishes to take away all abomination from you, O people of the House, and purify you with a great purification' (Q. 33: 33). Furthermore, Muhammad is prompted to declare that he wishes no reward for his work in conveying God's revelation 'except love for [my] next of kin' (Q. 42: 23). The expressions 'people of the house' (*ahl al-bayt*) and 'next of kin' (*al-qurba*) are usually interpreted as referring to the Prophet's daughter Fatimah, her husband 'Ali, and their two sons, Hasan and Husayn.

The foundation of the Shi'i claim is a *hadith* according to which the Prophet, on his way back from Mecca to Medina, stopped at a place called Ghadir Khumm, took 'Ali by the hand, and made the following declaration:

> O people, hear my words, and let him who is present inform him who is absent: Anyone of whom I am the master, 'Ali, too, is his master. O God, be a friend to those who befriend him and an enemy to those who show hostility to him, support those who support him and abandon those who desert him.

On the basis of this and other sayings in which they believe the Prophet directly or indirectly designated 'Ali as his successor, Shi'i specialists on the Prophetic oral tradition constructed an elaborate legal and theological system based on the doctrine of *imamah*, according to which the source of all legitimate authority is the office of the Imam.

Ashura

In the year 680 the Prophet's grandson Husayn (the son of 'Ali) was leading an uprising against the Umayyad Caliph Yazid when he was killed in battle at Karbala' in Iraq. The anniversary of his death, on the tenth day of the month of Muharram, has become a focal point for the Shi'i community's hopes and frustrations, messianic expectations, and highly eschatological view of history.

'Ashura' ('ten'), as the anniversary came to be known, is still commemorated by the Shi'i community throughout the Muslim world. Blending sorrow, blessing, and mystery, it has inspired a rich devotional literature, as well as numerous popular passion plays re-enacting the events leading up to the death of Husayn. Above all, it is observed by the Shi'i community as a day of suffering and martyrdom. Its symbolism is expressed in a variety of devotional acts, including solemn processions, public readings, and a pilgrimage to the sacred ground of Karbala'. Sunni Muslims commemorate 'Ashura' with a day of fasting.

Imami ('Twelver') Shi'ism

According to the doctrine of *imamah* as elaborated by the Shi'i tradition, the Prophet appointed 'Ali as his viceregent. 'Ali in turn appointed his son Hasan to succeed him as Imam, and Hasan appointed his brother Husayn. Thereafter, each Imam designated his successor, usually his eldest son.

Mainstream Shi'is believe that the line of imams descended from Husayn continued until 874, when the twelfth Imam, Muhammad ibn Hasan al-'Askari, disappeared at the age of four. Twelver Shi'is believe that he went into hiding ('occultation') and thereafter communicated with his Shi'ah through four successive deputies until 941. At that point the Imam entered a new phase known as the 'greater occultation', which will continue until the end of the world. Then, before the Day of Resurrection, he will return as the **Mahdi**, 'the rightly guided one', who with Jesus will establish universal justice and true Islam on earth.

Shi'is agree with Sunni Muslims on the centrality of the Qur'an and *sunnah* as the primary sources of Islamic law. However, they understand the *sunnah* to include not only the life-example of the Prophet Muhammad and his generation, but the life-examples of the Imams—the men they believe to be his rightful successors. Hence the period of the *sunnah* for Twelver Shi'i Muslims extends over three centuries, until the end of the lesser occultation of the twelfth Imam in 941.

'Sevener' or Isma'ili Shi'ism

The majority of Shi'is accepted the line of Husaynid Imams down to Ja'far al-Sadiq (d. 765), the sixth in the succession. But a major schism occurred when Ja'far's oldest son and successor, Isma'il, died about ten years before him. Ja'far then appointed a younger son, Musa al-Kazim, as his successor.

Many of Ja'far's supporters considered this appointment irregular and insisted that the seventh Imam should be Isma'il's son Ahmad. For this reason they came to be known as Isma'ilis or 'Seveners'. The largest faction, called Nizaris, carried on the line of imams through Ahmad and his descendants down to the present.

Basic to Isma'ili faith and worldview is the doctrine of the divine mandate of the Imam and his absolute temporal and religious authority. Over the centuries Isma'ili philosophers and theologians developed this fundamental teaching into an impressive esoteric system of prophetology. The Isma'ilis have played a very conspicuous intellectual and political role in Muslim history.

For centuries they lived as an obscure sect in Iran, Syria, East Africa, and the Indo-Pakistani subcontinent. Since 1818 their leader, or Imam, has been known as the Agha Khan, an Indo-Iranian title signifying nobility. The third Agha Khan (1877–1957) initiated a movement for reconciliation with the larger Muslim community, and efforts to resolve differences have continued under his Harvard-educated successor, Karim Agha Khan (b. 1936). In modern times Isma'ilis have migrated in large numbers to the West. Prosperous and well-organized, the Isma'ilis now number roughly 15 million and are the best-integrated Muslim community in the West.

Sufism: The Mystical Tradition

The early Muslim mystics were said to wear a garment of coarse wool over their bare skin in emulation of Jesus, who is represented in Islamic hagiography as a model of ascetic piety. For this reason they became known as Sufis (from the Arabic word meaning 'wool'). Asceticism was only one element in the development of Sufism, however.

At least as important was the Islamic tradition of devotional piety. Since the ultimate purpose of all creation is to worship God and sing God's praises (see Q. 17: 44 and 51: 56), the pious are urged to 'remember God much' (33: 41), 'in the morning and evening' (76: 25), for 'in the remembrance of God hearts find peace and contentment' (13: 28). The Prophet's night vigils and other devotions, alluded to in the Qur'an (73: 1–8) and greatly embellished by hagiographical tradition, have served as a living example for pious Muslims across the centuries. *Hadith* traditions, particularly the 'divine sayings' (*hadith qudsi*) in which the speaker is God, have also provided a rich source of mystical piety. Above all, the *mi'raj*—the Prophet's miraculous journey to heaven—has been a guide for numerous mystics on their own spiritual ascent to God.

The early Muslim ascetics were known as *zuhhad*, meaning 'those who shun [the world and its pleasures]'. One of the earliest champions of this movement was a well-known theologian and traditionist named al-Hasan al-Basri, who was born in Medina in 642 and lived through both the crises and the rise to glory of the Muslim *ummah*. In a letter addressed to the pious caliph 'Umar ibn 'Abd al-'Aziz, Hasan likened the world to a snake: soft to the touch, but full of venom.

The early ascetics were also called weepers, for the tears they shed in fear of God's punishment and in yearning for God's reward. Significantly, this early ascetic movement emerged in areas of mixed populations, where other forms of asceticism had existed for centuries: places such as Kufa and Basra in Iraq (long the home of Eastern Christian asceticism); northeastern Iran, particularly the region of Balkh (an ancient centre of Buddhist ascetic piety, now part of Afghanistan); and Egypt (the home of Christian monasticism as well as Gnostic asceticism).

Asceticism for its own sake, however, was frowned on by many advocates of mystical piety.

Among the critics was the sixth Imam, Ja'far al-Sadiq, who argued that when God bestows a favour on a servant, God wishes to see that favour manifested in the servant's clothing and way of life. Ja'far's grandfather 'Ali Zayn al-'Abidin is said to have argued that God should be worshipped not out of fear of hell or desire for paradise, but in humble gratitude for the gift of the capacity to worship God.

What transformed ascetic piety into mysticism was the all-consuming love of the divine exemplified by an early woman mystic named Rabi'a al-'Adawiyah of Basra (c. 713–801). Born into a poor family, Rabi'a was orphaned and sold into slavery as a child, but her master was so impressed with her piety that he set her free. She lived the rest of her life in mystical contemplation, loving God with no motive other than love itself:

Rabi'a al-'Adawiyah

When Rabi'a's fellow Sufis urged her to marry, she agreed in principle, but only on the condition that the prospective husband—a devout man named Hasan—answer four questions. In the end she remained unmarried, free to devote all her thoughts to God.

'What will the Judge of the world say when I die? That I have come forth from the world a Muslim, or an unbeliever?'

Hasan answered, 'This is among the hidden things known only to God. . . .'

Then she said, 'When I am put in the grave and Munkar and Nakir [the angels who question the dead] question me, shall I be able to answer them [satisfactorily] or not?' He replied, 'This is also hidden.'

'When people are assembled at the Resurrection and the books are distributed, shall I be given mine in my right hand or my left?' . . . 'This also is among the hidden things.'

Finally she asked, 'When mankind is summoned (at the Judgment), some to Paradise and some to Hell, in which group shall I be?' He answered, 'This too is hidden, and none knows what is hidden save God—His is the glory and the majesty.'

Then she said to him, 'Since this is so, and I have these four questions with which to concern myself, how should I need a husband, with whom to be occupied?' (Smith 1928: 11).

Farid al-Din 'Attar

Farid al-Din 'Attar lived in Iran at the turn of the thirteenth century. In this extract, the words 'Ask not' echo a phrase used by theologians to express paradox—bila kayf, 'without asking how'—but here they evoke the mystic's sense of ineffability.

His beauty if it thrill my heart
If thou a man of passion art
Of time and of eternity,
Of being and non-entity,
   Ask not.

When thou hast passed the bases four,
Behold the sanctuary door;
And having satisfied thine eyes,
What in the sanctuary lies
   Ask not....

When unto the sublime degree
Thou hast attained, desist to be;
But lost to self in nothingness
And, being not, of more and less
   Ask not.

    (Arberry 1948: 32–3)

My Lord, if I worship you in fear of the fire, burn me in hell. If I worship you in desire for paradise, deprive me of it. But if I worship you in love of you, then deprive me not of your eternal beauty. (Smith 1928)

Mystics of all religious traditions have used the language of erotic love to express their love for God. Rabi'a was perhaps the first to introduce this language into Islamic mysticism. She loved God with two loves, the love of passion and a spiritual love worthy of God alone.

The love that Rabi'a spoke of was the devotional love of the worshipful servant for his or her Lord. A more controversial tradition within Sufism pursued absolute union with God. Among the proponents of this ecstatic or 'intoxicated' Sufism was Husayn bin Mansur al-Hallaj (c. 858–922), whose identification with the divine was so intense as to suggest that he made no distinction between God and himself. For this apparent blasphemy he was brutally executed by the 'Abbasid authorities.

Al-Hallaj had been initiated into Sufism early in life and travelled widely, studying with the best-known Sufi masters of his time. But in time he broke away from his teachers and embarked on a long and ultimately dangerous quest of self-realization. It began when he went one day to see his teacher Abu Qasim al-Junayd. When the latter asked who was at the door, Al-Hallaj answered, 'I, the absolute divine truth' (*ana al-Haqq*)—calling himself by one of the 99 'wonderful names' of God mentioned in the Qur'an. Al-Junayd reprimanded his wayward disciple and predicted an evil end for him.

At its core, al-Hallaj's message was moral and intensely spiritual, but it was interpreted as suggesting that God takes the form of a human person (as Christians believe of Jesus)—an idea that most Muslims of his time found deeply shocking. Whereas a less extreme predecessor, Bayazid Bistami, had preached annihilation of the mystic in God, al-Hallaj preached total identification of the lover with the beloved:

I am He whom I love, and He whom I love
   is I.
We are two spirits dwelling in one body.
If thou seest me, you see Him; and if thou
   seest Him, you see us both
   (Nicholson 1931: 210–38).

After eight years in prison, al-Hallaj danced to
the gallows, where he begged his executioners to
'Kill me, O my trusted friends, for in my death
is my life, and in my life is my death.' For many
Muslims, al-Hallaj lives on as the martyr of love
who was killed for the sin of intoxication with God
by the sword of God's own *shari'ah*.

The Crystallization of Sufism

The mystical life is a spiritual journey to God. The
novice who wishes to embark on such an arduous
journey must be guided by a master who becomes
in effect his or her spiritual parent. As Sufism grew,
however, many well-recognized masters attracted
too many disciples to allow for a one-to-one relationship. By the eleventh century, therefore, teaching manuals were being produced to impart the
ideas of great masters to eager disciples. A high
point in this process of crystallization was al-
Ghazali's *Revivification of the Religious Sciences*.

Roughly half a century after al-Ghazali, Shihab
al-Din Suhrawardi (c. 1155–91) became known as
the great master of illumination (*shaykh al-ishraq*).
He grew up in Iran and eventually settled in northern Syria. Drawing on a verse in the Qur'an (24:
35) that speaks of God as the light of the heavens
and the earth, Suhrawardi described a cosmos of
light and darkness populated by countless luminous angelic spirits.

The most important Sufi master of the thirteenth century was Muhyi al-Din Ibn 'Arabi
(1165–1240), who was born and educated in
Muslim Spain and travelled widely in the Middle
East before finally settling in Damascus. The central theme of Ibn 'Arabi's numerous books and
treatises is the 'unity of being' (*wahdat al-wujud*).

According to this doctrine, God in God's essence
remains in 'blind obscurity', but is manifested in
the creation through an eternal process of self-
disclosure. Thus even as human beings need God
for their very existence, God also needs them in
order to be known.

Ibn 'Arabi's doctrine of the unity of being had
many implications, among them the idea that, if
God alone really is, then all ways ultimately lead to
God. This means that all the world's religions are
in reality one. Ibn 'Arabi says:

My heart has become capable of every
   form: it is a pasture for gazelles and a
   convent for Christian monks,
And a temple for idols, and the pilgrim's
   Ka'ba, and the tables of the Tora and the
   book of the Koran.
I follow the religion of Love, whichever
   way his camels take. My religion and my
   faith is the true religion
   (Nicholson 2002 [1914]: 75).

Ibn 'Arabi remains one of the greatest mystic
geniuses of all time.

Rumi

The most creative poet of the Persian language was
Jalal al-Din Rumi (1207–73). Like Ibn 'Arabi, he
was the product of a multicultural, multi-religious
environment. Rumi was born in Balkh, Afghanistan, but as a child fled with his parents from the
advancing Mongols. At last they settled in the city
of Konya in central Anatolia (Turkey), a region that
had been part of the Roman Empire.

In 1244 Rumi met a wandering Sufi named
Shams of Tabriz. The two men developed a relationship so intimate that Rumi neglected his teaching duties because he could not bear to be separated
from his friend. In the end, however, Shams disappeared, leaving Rumi to pour out his soul in heart-
rending verses expressing his love for the 'Sun' (the
name Shams means 'sun' in Arabic) of Tabriz.

Jalal al-Din Rumi

Here Rumi expresses the mystic's experience of union with God in terms of the dissolution of individual identity.

I died as mineral and became a plant
I died as plant and rose to animal,
I died as animal and I was Man.
Why should I fear? When was I less by dying?
Yet once more I shall die as Man, to soar
With angels blest; but even from angelhood
I must pass on: all except God doth perish (Q. 28: 88).
When I have sacrificed my angel-soul,
I shall become what no mind e'er conceived.
Oh, let me not exist! for Non-existence
Proclaims in organ tones, 'To him we shall return' (Q. 2: 151)
    (Nicholson 1950: 103).

Rumi's greatest masterpiece is his *Mathnawi* ('Couplets'), a collection of nearly 30,000 verses. The spirit of this vast panorama of poetry is clearly expressed in its opening verses, which evoke the haunting melodies of the reed flute telling its sad tale of separation from its reed bed. In stories, couplets of lyrical beauty, and at times even coarse tales of sexual impropriety, the *Mathnawi* depicts the longing of the human soul for God.

Sufi Orders and Saints

The religious fraternity is an ancient and widespread phenomenon. The earliest Sufi fraternities were established in the late eighth century, and by the thirteenth century a number of these groups were becoming institutionalized. Usually founded either by a famous **shaykh** (master) or by a disciple in the *shaykh*'s name, Sufi orders began as teaching and devotional institutions located in urban centres, where they would often attach themselves to craft or trade guilds in the main bazaar.

It became a common custom for lay Muslims to join a Sufi order. Lay associates provided a good source of income for the order, participated in devotional observances, and in return for their contributions received the blessing (*barakah*) of the *shaykh*.

The truth and authenticity of a *shaykh*'s claim to spiritual leadership depended on his or her spiritual genealogy. By the thirteenth century, Sufi chains of initiation (similar to chains of **isnad** in *hadith* transmission) were established. Such chains began with the *shaykh*'s immediate master and went back in an unbroken chain to 'Ali or one of his descendants, or in some cases to other Companions of the Prophet or their successors.

Through this spiritual lineage, a *shaykh* inherited the *barakah* of his masters, who inherited it from the Prophet. In turn, the *shaykh* bestowed his *barakah*, or healing power, on his devotees, both during his life and, with even greater efficacy, after his death.

The *shaykh*s of Sufi orders are similar to the saints of the Catholic Church in that the faithful ascribe miracles or divine favours (*karamat*) to them. Unlike Christian saints, however, they are recognized through popular acclaim rather than official canonization.

Devotional Practices

The most characteristic Sufi practice is a ritual called the **dhikr** ('remembrance') of God, which may be public or private. The congregational *dhikr* ritual is usually held before the dawn or evening prayers. It consists of the repetition of the name of God, Allah, or the *shahadah*, 'There is no god except God' (*la ilaha illa Allah*). The *dhikr* is often accompanied by special bodily movements and, in some Sufi orders, by elaborate breathing techniques.

Often the performance of the *dhikr* is what distinguishes the various Sufi orders from one another. In some popular orders it is a highly emotional ritual (similar to charismatic practices in some Pentecostal churches) intended to stir devotees into a state of frenzy. By contrast, in the sober Naqshbandi order (founded by Baha' al-Din al-Naqshbandi in the fourteenth century), the *dhikr* is silent, an inward prayer of the heart.

Another distinctly Sufi practice is the *sama'* ('hearing' or 'audition'), in which devotees simply listen to the often hypnotic chanting of mystical poetry, accompanied by various musical instruments. As instrumental music is not allowed in the mosque, *sama'* sessions are usually held in a hall adjacent to the mosque, or at the shrine of a famous *shaykh*.

Music and dance are vital elements of devotional life for members of the Mevlevi (Mawlawi) order, named after Mawlana ('our master') Rumi and founded by his son shortly after his death. As practised by the Mevlevis—also known as the 'Whirling Dervishes'—dance is a highly sophisticated art symbolizing the perfect motion of the stars; the haunting melodies of the reed flute and the large orchestra that accompanies the chanting

Dervishes at the Galata Mevlevihanesi (Mevlevi Whirling Dervish hall) in Istanbul (Images & Stories/Alamy).

poetry echo the primordial melodies of the heavenly spheres.

Sufism has always shown an amazing capacity for self-reform and regeneration. It was the Sufis who preserved Islamic learning and spirituality after 1258, when Baghdad fell to Mongol invaders, and Sufis who carried Islam to Africa and Asia. Today in the West it is primarily Sufi piety that is attracting non-Muslims to Islam.

Women and Sufism

Women have played an important role in the Sufi tradition, often serving as positive role models for both men and women. This may help to explain part of the historical tension between orthodox Islam and Sufism. One of the most beloved stories about Rabi'a, the early female Sufi, has her roaming the streets of Basra carrying a bucket of water and a flaming torch, ready to put out the fires of Hell and set fire to the gardens of Paradise so that people will worship God for the sake of Love alone.

The Sufi tradition provided one of the few outlets for women to be recognized as leaders. Since the Sufis believed the Divine to be without gender, the gender of the worshipper did not matter. After Rabi'a, women could be Sufi leaders even though they were prohibited from training as imams. In addition, the shrines of Sufi saints, whether male or female, are often cared for by women. As places where women have some measure of control, they tend to attract more women than men, inverting the usual gender breakdown of attendance at mosques. It isn't hard to imagine how some men, accustomed to thinking of public space as male space, might feel threatened by a public space where women are the dominant presence.

✤ THE SPREAD OF ISLAM

Islam, like Christianity, is a missionary religion. Muslims believe that the message of their faith is intended for all humankind, to be practised in a community transcending geographical, cultural, and linguistic borders.

Islam is ideologically and historically a post-Jewish, post-Christian religion. Ideologically, it sees itself as one of the religions of the Book, one that confirms the scriptures that preceded it, notably the Torah and the Gospel. Historically, Muslims from the beginning responded to and interacted with the communities of other faiths, particularly Christians and Jews. It was therefore necessary for Islam as a religio-political power to regulate its relations with non-Muslim citizens.

The Qur'an regards Jews and Christians as People of the Book. They were promised full freedom to practise their faith in return for paying a poll tax that also guaranteed them physical and economic protection and exemption from military service. Legally such communities came to be known as **dhimmis** ('protected people'). In the course of time, this designation was expanded to encompass other communities with sacred scriptures, including Zoroastrians in Iran and Hindus in India.

In its first century Islam spread through conquest and military occupation. Much of the Byzantine and Roman world and all of the Sasanian Persian domains yielded to the Arab armies and came under Umayyad rule. In subsequent centuries, politico-military regimes continued to contribute to Islam's dominance, especially in regions under Arab, Persian, or Turkish rule.

Over time, however, the influence of mystics, teachers, and traders has reached farther and endured longer than the power of caliphs and conquerors. It was principally through the preaching and the living examples of individual Muslims that Islam spread to China, Southeast Asia, and East and West Africa. In modern times, migration and missionary activity have carried Islam to the Western hemisphere as well.

North Africa

After conquering what came to be the historical heartland of Islam—Syria, Egypt, and Persia—the

Map 5.1 Language and Culture in the Spread of Islam

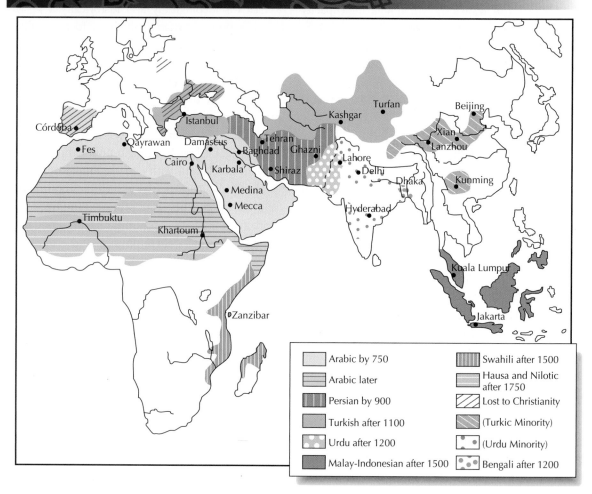

	Arabic by 750		Swahili after 1500
	Arabic later		Hausa and Nilotic after 1750
	Persian by 900		Lost to Christianity
	Turkish after 1100		(Turkic Minority)
	Urdu after 1200		(Urdu Minority)
	Malay-Indonesian after 1500		Bengali after 1200

Muslims moved into North Africa in the second half of the seventh century. Before that time North Africa had been first an important Roman province and then an equally important home of Latin Christianity. With its indigenous Berber, Phoenician, Roman, and Byzantine populations, North Africa was rich in cultural and religious diversity, and it has always maintained a distinct religious and cultural identity that reflects its ancient heritage.

The Umayyads had established their capital in Damascus in 661. With the shift of the capital from Damascus to Baghdad under the 'Abbasids in 762, the main orientation of the eastern Islamic domains became more Persian than Arab, more Asian than Mediterranean. Meanwhile, the centre of Arab Islamic culture shifted from Syria to the western Mediterranean: to Qayrawan, the capital of North Africa, in what is today Tunisia; and to Córdoba, Islam's western capital, in Spain, which rivalled Baghdad and Cairo in its cultural splendour. North African mystics, scholars, and philosophers were all instrumental in this remarkable achievement. In the nineteenth and twentieth centuries, North African religious scholars and particularly Sufi masters played a crucial role in the region's struggle for independence from European colonial powers. They helped to preserve the religious and cultural identity of their people and mobilized them to resist Italian and French colonization in Libya and Algeria. In spite of the deep influence of the French language and secular culture, North African popular piety still reflects the classical Islamic heritage.

Spain

When Arab forces arrived on the Iberian Peninsula in 711, Jews who had lived in Spain for centuries were facing harsh restrictions imposed by rulers recently converted to Catholic Christianity. They welcomed the Arabs as liberators.

With astonishing rapidity, Umayyad forces conquered the land of Andalusia, or al-Andalus, as the Arabs called southern Spain, and laid the foundations for an extraordinary culture. Arab men married local women, and a mixed but harmonious society developed that was Arab in language and expression and Arabo-Hispanic in spirit. Muslims, Christians, and Jews lived together in mutual tolerance for centuries before fanatical forces on all sides stifled one of the most creative experiments in interfaith living in human history.

Arab Spain produced some of the world's greatest minds, including not only Ibn 'Arabi, Ibn Tufayl, and Ibn Rushd but the jurist and writer Ibn Hazm (994–1064), and the mystic-philosopher Ibn Masarrah (d. 931). Islamic Spain was the cultural centre of Europe. Students came from as far away as Scotland to study Islamic theology, philosophy, and science in centres of higher learning such as Córdoba and Toledo. It was in these centres that the European Renaissance was conceived, and the great universities in which it was nurtured were inspired by their Arabo-Hispanic counterparts.

In Muslim Spain the Jews enjoyed a golden age of philosophy and science, mysticism, and general prosperity. Jewish scholars, court physicians, and administrators occupied high state offices and served as political and cultural liaisons between Islamic Spain and the rest of Europe. Arab learning penetrated deep into western Europe and contributed directly to the rise of the West to world prominence.

In addition to symbiotic creativity, however, the 900-year history of Arab Spain (711–1609) included the tensions and conflicts typical of any multi-religious, multicultural society ruled by a minority regime. In the end, Islamic faith and civilization were driven out of Spain and failed to establish themselves anywhere else in Europe.

Sub-Saharan Africa

Islam may have arrived in sub-Saharan Africa as early as the eighth century. As in other places where it became the dominant religion, it was spread first by traders, and then on a much larger scale by preachers. Finally jurists came to consolidate and establish the new faith as a religious and legal system. Sufi orders played an important part both in the spread of Islam and in its use as a motivation and framework for social and political reform.

Islam always had to compete with traditional African religion. Muslim prayers, for example, had to show themselves to be no less potent than the rain-making prayers or rituals of the indigenous traditions. In the fourteenth century, the Moroccan Muslim traveller Ibn Battutah wrote a vivid account of the efforts of Muslims in the Mali Empire of West Africa to adapt the new faith to local traditions.

In East Africa Islam spread along the coast, carried mainly by mariners from Arabia and the Gulf trading in commodities and also in slaves. From the sixteenth century onward, after Portuguese navigators rounded the southern cape of Africa, the cultural and political development of East African Islam was directly affected by European colonialism as well.

Unlike the populations of Syria, Iraq, Egypt, and North Africa, the peoples of East Africa did not adopt the Arabic language. But so much Arabic vocabulary penetrated the local languages that at least one-third of the Swahili vocabulary today is Arabic, and until recently, most of the major African languages were written in the Arabic script.

An important element of East African society has been the Khoja community. Including both Sevener (Isma'ili) and Twelver Shi'is, the Khojas immigrated from India to Africa in the mid-1800s. They have on the whole been successful business people with Western education and close relationships with Europe and North America. These relationships have been strengthened by the migration of many Khojas to Britain, the United States, and Canada.

Iran and Central Asia

Central Asia had a cosmopolitan culture before Islam. Buddhism, Gnosticism, Zoroastrianism, Judaism, and Christianity existed side by side in mutual tolerance. The Arab conquest of the region took more than a century: beginning in 649, less than two decades after the Prophet's death, it was not completed until 752.

Under the Samanid dynasty, which ruled large areas of Persia and Central Asia in the ninth and tenth centuries, Persian culture flourished, as did classical *hadith* traditionists, historians, philosophers, and religious scholars working in the Arabic language. Particularly important centres of learning developed in the cities of Bukhara and Samarkand, located in what is now Uzbekistan, which owed much of their prosperity to trade with India, China, and the rest of the Muslim domains. With the first notable Persian poet, Rudaki (c. 859–940), Bukhara became the birthplace of Persian literature.

While their contemporaries the Buyids promoted Shi'i learning and public devotions in the region that is now Iraq, the Samanids firmly established Sunni orthodoxy in Central Asia. Many Sunni theologians and religious scholars lived and worked in Bukhara and Samarkand under Samanid patronage. Among the great minds of the tenth and eleventh centuries were the theologian

al-Maturidi, the philosopher Ibn Sina, the great scholar and historian of religion Abu Rayhan al-Biruni, and the famous Persian poet Ferdowsi. In this intellectual environment, Islam was spread by persuasion and enticement rather than propaganda and war.

Early in the eleventh century, the Samanids were succeeded by the Seljuq Turks in the Middle East and the Karakhanid Mongols in Persia and Central Asia. The Mongols profoundly altered the situation in that region as they did in the Middle East a century later. The devastating consequences of the Mongol conquest of Persia and Central Asia were compounded by the loss of trade revenues when the traditional caravan routes were abandoned in favour of sea travel to India and China. Central Asia never recovered from the resulting decline in culture and prosperity.

The Turks

As Turkic tribal populations from Central Asia moved into parts of the Middle Eastern Muslim heartland, they were converted to Islam mainly by Sufi missionaries. They became influential from the tenth century onward in Central Asia, Armenia, Anatolia, and Syria. Mahmud of Ghazna in Afghanistan (r. 998–1030), of Turkish descent, broke away from the Persian Samanid dynasty; his successors, the Ghaznavids, extended Muslim power in northern India. Mahmud was the first person to be called 'sultan', a term that until his time had referred to the authority of the state.

The Seljuqs, another Turkic family, prevailed in Iran and farther west a generation after Mahmud. The second Seljuq sultan, Alp Arslan, inflicted a crushing defeat on the Byzantines at Manzikert, in eastern Anatolia, in 1071. Bit by bit, eastern Anatolia (today's Turkey) fell to the Seljuqs, who ruled until they were conquered by the Mongols in 1243.

In 1299 Osman I took over the caliphate from the 'Abbasids, establishing a dynasty—the

'Ottomans'—that was to endure until 1924. In the fourteenth century they absorbed former Seljuq territory in eastern Anatolia and took western Anatolia from the Byzantines, and they reached the height of their power in the sixteenth century, occupying the Balkans as far north as Vienna, the Levant (i.e., the Syro-Palestinian region), and all of northern Africa except Morocco. So widespread was their empire that Christian Europe until the nineteenth century thought of Islamic culture as primarily Turkish.

As their imperial symbol the Ottomans adopted the crescent, an ancient symbol that the Byzantines had also used. Conspicuous on the Turkish flag, the crescent was considered by Europeans and eventually by Muslims themselves to be the symbol of Islam. Turkic languages continue to prevail in much of the region of Central Asia ruled by the Soviet Union for much of the twentieth century. From Azerbaijan to Uzbekistan and Turkmenistan, a dominant element in the population is Turkic. The same is true of Chinese Central Asia, in the vast region of Xinjiang.

China

Islam may have made contact with China as early as the eighth century, although the first written sources referring to Islam in China do not appear till the seventeenth century. For earlier information we have to rely on Chinese sources, which unfortunately focus on commercial activities and have little to say about the social and intellectual life of Chinese Muslims.

The extent of the Muslim presence in any area may often be gauged by the number of mosques. There seem to have been no mosques in the main inland cities of China before the thirteenth century. Along the coast, however, the minaret of the mosque in Guangzhou (Canton) and various inscriptions in the province of Fujian suggest that maritime trade was under way considerably earlier, in 'Abbasid times.

From the beginning, Persian and Arab merchants were allowed to trade freely so long as they complied with Chinese rules. But it was not until the thirteenth century that Muslim traders began settling in China in numbers large enough to support the establishment of mosques. The presence of Islam in China before that time was probably limited.

Muslim communities in China prospered under the Mongol (1206–1368) and Ming (1368–1644) emperors. After the Mongol period Chinese Muslims were assimilated culturally but kept their distinct religious identity. Since it was through trade that they kept in touch with the rest of the Muslim *ummah*, however, the decline of the overland trade with Central Asia in the 1600s had the effect of isolating the Chinese Muslim community. It became virtually cut off from the rest of the world, so that our information about Muslims in China after the seventeenth century is largely a matter of conjecture.

Unlike Buddhism, centuries earlier, Islam never came to be seen as culturally Chinese. The Uighurs—the Muslim population of Xinjiang (Chinese Turkestan), in the far northwest of the country—are an identifiable minority in Chinese society, distinguished by their language as well as their religion. Yet even the Chinese-speaking Muslims in the principal eastern cities of 'Han' China are set apart by their avoidance of pork—a staple of the Chinese diet. The presence of *halal* (ritually acceptable) restaurants and butcher shops is a sure sign of a Muslim neighbourhood.

Chinese Muslims experienced their share of repression under the Communist regime, particularly during the Cultural Revolution of 1966–76. While the overall situation for Muslims has improved since then, Uighur demands for independence have been met with a severe crackdown, and Chinese authorities often describe Uighur nationalists as 'terrorists'. Today there are approximately 50 million Muslims in China. Like other religious communities in contemporary China, they face an uncertain future, but the ethnic base of the minorities in China's Central Asian interior is not likely to disappear soon.

South Asia

Islam arrived early in India, carried by traders and Arab settlers. Umayyad armies began moving east into India in the early eighth century, and since that time Islam has become an integral part of Indian life and culture.

The Muslim conquest of India was a long process. In the second half of the tenth century the city of Ghazni, in what is today Afghanistan, became the base from which the armies of the sultan Mahmud the Ghaznavid and his successors advanced over the famous Khyber Pass onto the North Indian Plain. By the fourteenth century most of India had come under Muslim rule, with the exceptions of Tamil Nadu and Kerala in the far south.

The Muslim rulers of India came from Iran and Central Asia. Thus maintaining and expanding Muslim power over a large Hindu population meant continuous warfare. For Hindus, the Muslim regime was undoubtedly repressive; yet Indian Islam developed a unique and rich religious and intellectual culture.

India was something new in the history of Islam's territorial expansion. For the first time, the majority of the conquered population did not convert to the new faith. In ancient Arabia Islam had been able to suppress and supplant polytheism; but in India it had to learn to coexist with a culture that remained largely polytheistic.

At the same time Islam was something new to India. In a land where people often had multiple religious allegiances, and community boundaries were fluid, Islam's exclusive devotion to the one God and clear delineation of community membership represented a dramatically different way of life.

Together, the three countries of the Indian subcontinent—India, Bangladesh, and Pakistan —have the largest Muslim population in the world. The Muslims of India alone make up the world's third-largest Muslim population (after Indonesia and Pakistan), numbering between 100 and 120 million. Even so, they are a minority whose future appears bleak in the face of rising Hindu nationalism.

Southeast Asia

Southeast Asia, when Islam arrived there, consisted of small kingdoms and settlements that were home to a wide variety of languages and cultures, and its religious life had been strongly influenced by the Hindu and Buddhist traditions. These influences can still be seen in the ancient Hindu culture on the island of Bali and the great Buddhist stupa complex of Borobudur in Indonesia.

There is no evidence for the presence of Islam in Southeast Asia before the tenth century. But Yemeni traders are reported to have sailed into the islands of the Malay archipelago before the time of the Prophet, and this suggests that the Malay people may have been exposed to Islam at an early date. Scattered evidence from Chinese and Portuguese travellers, as well as passing references by Ibn Battutah, indicate that by the fifteenth century Islam had spread widely in Southeast Asia. Two centuries later, when British and Dutch trading companies arrived in the region, Islam was the dominant religion and culture of the Malay archipelago.

Muslim communities in small states ruled by sultans are widely reported by the thirteenth century. The earliest of these was Pasai, a small kingdom on the east coast of northern Sumatra. Some of the states that emerged in the fifteenth century gained considerable prominence both culturally and economically. In every case, prosperity attracted Muslim religious scholars from India to these states. In an effort to expand and strengthen his realm, the sultan Iskandar Muda of Acheh (r. 1607–36) became the first Muslim ruler in Southeast Asia to establish alliances with European powers. Acheh also produced noteworthy Islamic scholarship, which is still used in the Malay world today.

In Southeast Asia even more than elsewhere, Sufi orders played a crucial part in the process of Islamization. They were also prominent in later political and social struggles for reform and liberation. In the late nineteenth and early twentieth centuries, Modernist reform movements in the Middle East inspired similar movements in Indonesia and other countries of the region. At present Islam is the majority religion in Malaysia, Brunei, and Indonesia (the largest Muslim country in the world today, with at least 180 million Muslims), and there are Muslim minorities in all the other countries of Southeast Asia. Today Southeast Asia can claim at least one-third of the world's Muslims.

 PRACTICE

The Five Pillars of Islam

Individual faith and institutional Islam converge in the worship of God and service to others. According to well-attested tradition, the Prophet himself said that Islam was built on five 'pillars'. With the exception of the first (the *shahadah*, the profession of faith through which one becomes a Muslim), the pillars are all rites of worship, both personal and communal. The Five Pillars are:

- to declare, or bear witness, that there is no god except God, and that Muhammad is the Messenger of God;
- to establish regular worship;
- to pay the **zakat** alms;
- to observe the fast of Ramadan; and
- to perform the **hajj** pilgrimage.

The Five Pillars are the foundations on which Islam rests as a religious system of faith and social responsibility, worship, and piety. Acts of worship are obligatory for all Muslims. Each of the Five Pillars has both an outer or public obligatory dimension and an inner or private voluntary dimension.

Bearing Witness

The first pillar is the *shahadah*: 'I bear witness that there is no god except God, and I bear witness that Muhammad is the messenger of God.' It consists of two declarations. The first, affirming the oneness of God, expresses the universal and primordial state of faith in which every child is born. The Prophet is said to have declared, 'Every child is born in this original state of faith; then his parents turn him into a Jew, Christian, or Zoroastrian, and if they are Muslims, into a Muslim.'

The second declaration, affirming Muhammad's role as messenger, signifies acceptance of the truth of Muhammad's claim to prophethood, and hence the truth of his message.

Prayer

The second pillar consists of the obligatory prayers (**salat**). These are distinguished from voluntary devotional acts, such as meditations and personal supplicatory prayers (which may be offered at any time), in that they must be performed five times in a day and night: at dawn, noon, mid-afternoon, sunset, and after dark. The *salat* prayers were the first Islamic rituals to be instituted.

The *salat* prayers must always be preceded by ritual washing. *Wudu'* ('making pure or radiant') or partial washing involves washing the face, rinsing the mouth and nostrils, washing the hands and forearms to the elbows, passing one's wet hands over the head and feet, or washing the feet to the two heels.

Five times a day—on radio and television, through loudspeakers, and from high minarets—a **mu'adhdhin** chants in a melodious voice the call to prayer inviting the faithful to pray together either in a mosque or at home. Whether a Muslim prays alone or behind an imam in congregation, he or she is always conscious of countless other men and women engaged in the same act of worship.

Each phrase of the call to prayer is repeated at least twice for emphasis:

> God is greater. I bear witness that there is no god except God, and I bear witness that Muhammad is the Messenger of God. Hasten to the prayers! Hasten to success or prosperity! [Shi'i Muslims add: Hasten to the best action!] God is greater. There is no god except God.

The prayers consist of cycles or units called *rak'ahs*, with bowing, kneeling, and prostration. The dawn prayers consist of two cycles, the noon and mid-afternoon prayers of four each, the sunset prayer of three, and the night prayers of four cycles.

Apart from some moments of contemplation and personal supplication at the end of the *salat*, these prayers are fixed formulas consisting largely of passages from the Qur'an, especially the opening *surah* (*al-Fatihah*):

> In the name of God, the All-merciful, the Compassionate:
> Praise be to God, the All-merciful, the Compassionate, King of the Day of Judgment. You alone do we worship, and to you alone do we turn for help. Guide us to the straight way, the way of those upon whom you have bestowed your grace, not those who have incurred your wrath, nor those who have gone astray (Q. 1: 1–7).

The **Fatihah** for Muslims is in some ways similar to the Lord's Prayer for Christians. It is repeated in every *rak'ah*—at least seventeen times in every 24-hour period.

Unlike Judaism and Christianity, Islam has no Sabbath specified for rest. Friday is the day

The hours of prayer are posted on the door of a small mosque in Paris (Andrew Leyerle).

designated for *jum'ah* ('assembly'), for congregational prayers. In the Friday service the first two *rak'ah*s of the noon prayers are replaced by two short sermons, usually on religious, moral, and political issues, followed by two *rak'ah*s. The place of worship is called the *masjid* ('place of prostration in prayer') or *jami'* (literally, 'gatherer'). The English word 'mosque' is derived from *masjid*.

Other congregational prayers are performed on the first days of the two major festivals, **'Id al-Fitr** and 'Id al-Adha, at the end of Ramadan and the *hajj* pilgrimage, respectively.

Faithful Muslims see all things, good or evil, as contingent on God's will. Hence many take care to preface any statement about hopes for the future with the phrase *in-sha' Allah*, 'if God wills'.

Almsgiving

The third pillar of Islam reflects the close relationship between worship of God and service to the poor and needy. Traditionally, all adult Muslims who had wealth were expected to 'give alms' through payment of an obligatory tax called the *zakat* (from a root meaning 'to purify or increase').

Offering alms in this way served to purify the donor, purging greed and attachment to material possessions.

The *zakat* obligation was 2.5 per cent of the value of all accumulated wealth (savings, financial gains of any kind, livestock, agricultural produce, real estate, etc.). During the early centuries of Islam, when the community was controlled by a central authority, the *zakat* revenues were kept in a central treasury and disbursed for public educational and civic projects, care of orphans and the needy, and the ransoming of Muslim war captives. Now, however, the Muslim world is divided into many independent nation-states, most of which now collect some form of income tax, and as a consequence the *zakat* obligation has become largely voluntary. Many ignore it; others pay through donations to private religious and philanthropic organizations.

In addition to the obligatory *zakat* alms, Muslims are expected to practice voluntary almsgiving (**sadaqah**). The Qur'an calls *sadaqah* a loan given to God, which will be repaid in manifold measure on the Day of Resurrection (Q. 57: 11). *Sadaqah* giving is not bound by any consideration of race,

A Muslim Ritual: The Call to Prayer

It is Friday afternoon, a few minutes before the start of the weekly congregational prayer. In this mosque in Southern California, perhaps 200 men and 30 women are gathered; the difference in numbers reflects the fact that this prayer is obligatory for men but optional for women. A young man walks to the front of the large men's section (the women are seated in a second-floor gallery), raises his hands to his ears, and begins the call to prayer: 'Allahu akbar, God is greater. . .'. When he has finished, the people behind him line up in rows and wait for the imam—the person who will lead the prayer—to begin.

Were this service in a different location, the call to prayer might already have been sounded in the traditional way, broadcast from minarets (towers) beside the mosque. But there are no minarets here, as the mostly non-Muslim residents of this neighbourhood wanted a building that would 'fit in' with its surroundings. Nor does this mosque have the characteristic dome. Instead it is a two-storey building designed to look more like a school than a mosque. In this non-traditional context, the function of the call to prayer has changed. Instead of being broadcast outside, to let the community know that it is time to pray, the call is broadcast inside to those already assembled for the prayer. This is one of the ways in which the Muslims who come to this mosque have adapted to their surroundings.

colour, or creed: the recipient may be anyone in need.

The Ramadan Fast

The fourth pillar of Islam is the month-long fast of Ramadan. Fasting is recognized in the Qur'an as a universal form of worship, enjoined by scriptures of all faiths. In addition to the Ramadan fast, the Prophet observed a variety of voluntary fasts, which are still honoured by many pious Muslims.

The Ramadan fast is mandated in just one passage of the Qur'an:

> O you who have faith, fasting is ordained for you as it was ordained for those before you, that you may become aware of God. [. . .] Ramadan is the month in which the Qur'an was sent down as a guidance to humankind, manifestations of guidance and the Criterion. Therefore whosoever among you witnesses the moon, let them fast [the month], but whosoever is sick or on a journey, an equal number of other days (Q. 2: 183, 185).

According to this passage, Ramadan was the month in which the Qur'an was revealed to the Prophet.

Ramadan is a month-long fast extending from daybreak till sundown each day. It requires complete abstention from food, drink, smoking, and sexual relations. The fast is broken at sunset, and another light meal is eaten at the end of the night, just before the next day's fast begins at dawn.

With respect to the rules governing the fast, the Qur'an notes that 'God desires ease for you, not hardship' (2: 185). Therefore the sick, travellers, children, and women who are pregnant, nursing, or menstruating are exempted from the fast, either altogether or until they are able to make up the missed days.

Before Islam, the Arabs followed a lunar calendar in which the year consisted of only 354 days. To keep festivals and sacred months in their proper seasons, they (like the Jews) added an extra month every three years. The Qur'an abolished this custom, however, allowing Islamic festivals to rotate throughout the year. When Ramadan comes in the summer, particularly in the equatorial countries of Asia and Africa, fasting can be a real hardship. But when it comes in winter, as it did in the 1990s in the northern hemisphere, it can be relatively tolerable.

Ramadan ends with a festival called 'Id al-Fitr, a three-day celebration during which people exchange gifts and well-wishing visits. Children receive gifts and wear brightly coloured new clothes, and people visit the graves of loved ones, where special sweet dishes are distributed to the poor.

Beginning the Fast

Ms Becker teaches fourth grade in a public elementary school. Eleven of the school's pupils are Muslim, and one of them is in Ms Becker's class. This year, seven of the Muslim students have decided that they will fast during the month of Ramadan. Some of them have fasted before, but for the nine-year-old in Ms Becker's class this will be the first time.

There is no set age at which Muslim children are expected to begin observing the fast. It may be as early as age 8 or 9, or as late as adolescence. In certain Muslim cultures, girls begin at an earlier age than boys, who are usually exempted on the grounds that they 'aren't strong enough'. While their non-Muslim classmates have lunch, those who are fasting gather in Ms Becker's classroom to work quietly on school projects. They are also excused from their physical education classes, and instead do a writing assignment about physical fitness. In this way, a public school accommodates the needs of its Muslim students.

Before the first breakfast after the long fast, the head of every family must give special alms for breaking the fast, called *zakat al-fitr*, on behalf of every member of his household. Those who are exempted from fasting for reasons of chronic illness or old age must feed a poor person for every day they miss.

The fast of Ramadan becomes a true act of worship when a person shares God's bounty with those who have no food with which to break their fast. True fasting means more than giving up the pleasures of food and drink: it also means abstaining from gossip and anger, and turning one's heart and mind to God in devotional prayers and meditations.

The Pilgrimage to Mecca

The fifth pillar of Islam is the *hajj* pilgrimage, instituted by Abraham at God's command after he and his son Ishmael were ordered to build the Ka'ba. Thus most of its ritual elements are understood as re-enacting the experiences of Abraham, whom the Qur'an declares to be the father of prophets and the first true Muslim.

Before the pilgrims reach the sacred precincts of Mecca, they exchange their regular clothes for two pieces of white linen, symbolic of the shrouds in which Muslims are wrapped for burial. With this act they enter the state of consecration. They approach Mecca with the solemn proclamation: 'Here we come in answer to your call, O God, here we come! Here we come, for you have no partner, here we come! Indeed, all praise, dominion, and grace belong to you alone, here we come!'

Once in Mecca, the pilgrims begin with the lesser *hajj* ('umrah). This ritual is performed in the precincts of the Great Mosque and includes the *tawaf* (walking counter-clockwise around the Ka'ba) and running between the two hills of al-Safa and al-Marwa. In the traditional narrative, Hagar, Abraham's handmaid and the mother of his son Ishmael, ran between these two hills in search of water for her dying child. After the seventh run, water gushed out by the child's feet, and Hagar contained it with sand. The place, according to Islamic tradition, is the ancient well of Zamzam ('the contained water'). The water of Zamzam is considered holy, and pilgrims often take home containers of it as blessed gifts for family and friends.

The *hajj* pilgrimage proper begins on the eighth of Dhu al-Hijjah, the twelfth month of the Islamic calendar, when throngs of pilgrims set out for 'Arafat, a large plain, about 20 kilometres (13 miles) east of Mecca, on which stands the goal of every pilgrim: the Mount of Mercy (Jabal al-Rahmah). In accordance with the Prophet's *sunnah* (practice), many pilgrims spend the night at Mina, but others press on to 'Arafat. As the sun passes the noon meridian, all the pilgrims gather for the central rite of the *hajj* pilgrimage: the standing (*wuquf*) on the Mount of Mercy in 'Arafat.

In this rite, the pilgrims stand in solemn prayer and supplication till sunset, as though standing before God for judgment on the last day. The *wuquf* recalls three sacred occasions: when Adam and Eve stood on that plain after their expulsion from paradise, when Abraham and his son Ishmael performed the rite during the first *hajj* pilgrimage, and when Muhammad gave his farewell oration, affirming the family of all Muslims.

The sombre scene changes abruptly at sundown, when the pilgrims leave 'Arafat for Muzdalifah, a sacred spot a short distance along the road back to Mecca. There the pilgrims observe the combined sunset and evening prayers and gather pebbles for the ritual lapidation (throwing of stones) at Mina the next day. The tenth of Dhu al-Hijjah is the final day of the *hajj* season, and the first of the four-day festival of sacrifice ('Id al-Adha). The day is spent at Mina, where the remaining pilgrimage rites are completed.

Tradition says that on his way from 'Arafat to Mina, Abraham was commanded by God to sacrifice that which was dearest to him—his son Ishmael. Satan whispered to him three times, tempting him to disobey God's command. Abraham's response was to hurl stones at Satan, to drive him away. Thus at the spot called al-'Aqabah, meaning the hard or steep road, a brick pillar has been erected to represent Satan. Pilgrims gather early in the morning to throw seven stones at the pillar, in emulation of Abraham. Three other pillars in Mina, representing the three temptations, are also stoned.

Following the ritual of stoning, the pilgrims offer a blood sacrifice—a lamb, goat, cow, or camel—to symbolize the animal sent from heaven with which God ransoms Abraham's son (Q. 27: 107). After this, to mark the end of their state of consecration, pilgrims ritually clip a minimum of three hairs from their heads (some shave their heads completely). The *hajj* ends with a final circumambulation of the Ka'ba and the completion of the rites of the lesser *hajj* ('*umrah*) for those who have not done so.

Tradition asserts that a person returns from a sincerely performed *hajj* free from all sins, as on the day when he or she was born. Thus the *hajj* is regarded as a form of resurrection or rebirth, and its completion marks a new stage in the life of a Muslim. Every pilgrim is henceforth distinguished by the title *hajji* or *hajjah* before his or her name.

CULTURAL EXPRESSIONS

Islamic Architecture

The functions of the mosque include not only prayer, implied in the Arabic *masjid* ('kneeling place'), but other community activities, implied in Arabic *jami'* ('gatherer'). Early mosques functioned as treasuries, where financial records were kept; as law courts, where judges heard cases; and as educational centres, where classes and study circles

The Sultan Ahmet or Blue Mosque in Istanbul, built in 1609–16 (Andrew Leyerle).

were held. In time these other activities moved into their own buildings, but the functions of public assembly and prayer continued to dictate the architectural form of mosques. Two other types of buildings with religious functions—the *madrasah* or religious school, and the tomb or mausoleum—drew on much the same repertory of styles that mosques did.

Every mosque includes four essential features: a fountain for washing hands, face, and feet upon entering; a large area for kneeling and prostration in prayer; a pulpit (*minbar*) from which the leader of Friday noon worship delivers the sermon; and an imageless niche in the middle of the wall closest to Mecca, indicating the *qiblah* (direction of prayer). Not part of the earliest mosques in Arabia but characteristic of Islam in many places is the minaret, the tower from which the *mu'adhdhin*

delivers the call to prayer. The Turks in the sixteenth century made much use of the dome, an important feature of church architecture among the Byzantines who had preceded them. A high central dome, resting on four semi-dome apses, enclosed the prayer space. Some major Turkish mosques had four or more minarets, marking the corners of the mosque. Central dome architecture, though often simpler and without minarets, is also characteristic of mosques in Malaysia and Indonesia, where the rainy climate dictates that the prayer space must be roofed over.

Ultimately, Islamic architecture tends to reflect the distinctive idioms of different geographic regions. The keyhole arch, for instance, though it appears in the great mosque of Damascus, is characteristic mainly of North Africa and Islamic Spain. A shallow pointed arch emerged in Iraq, became

Inside the bin Yousuf madrasa (religious school) in Marrakech, Morocco (Jonathan Brown). Dating from the sixteenth century, the building was restored in 1982. There are no animal or human figures in the decoration: only inscriptions and either geometric or floral patterns.

the predominant form in Iran, and spread to Central Asia and India. The bud or onion domes of Indo-Muslim architecture have been picked up in Southeast Asia. In China many mosques are built like Chinese temples, with tiled roofs resting on wooden columns and bracket structures. A number of Chinese minarets are built in the form of East Asian Buddhist pagodas.

Islamic Art

Islamic art is rich, elaborate, even exuberant. Three elements are particularly distinctive: calligraphy (the decorative use of script and units of text); geometrical decoration (particularly the interlaced motifs called arabesques in the West); and floral designs (especially common in Iran). All three are more abstract than pictorial and therefore point beyond themselves in a way that pictorial images may not. Design using these elements captures the viewer's attention and directs it to the larger structure on which the decoration appears, whether a page of the Qur'an, a prayer rug, or the tiled entrance of a mosque. Religious content is most obvious in the decorative use of calligraphy in mosques, where the texts used are often passages from the Qur'an, but even the craft items sold in bazaars are often adorned with some of the 99 'wonderful names' or attributes of God.

Three-dimensional sculpture is prohibited in Islam, but the two-dimensional representation of living creatures is highly developed. Some Persian carpets include animals in their garden scenes. Persian and Indian manuscripts are illustrated with miniature paintings of legendary heroes and current rulers. Among Iranian Shi'a, portraits of 'Ali are a focus of popular piety. While representations of the Prophet himself are avoided, Buraq—the steed that carried him on his heavenly journey—is portrayed in popular art as a winged horse with a human head; this is a common motif on trucks and buses in Afghanistan and Pakistan.

Mohamed Zakariya

Mohamed Zakariya (b. 1942) is the most celebrated Islamic calligrapher in the United States. Born in Ventura, California, he moved to Los Angeles with his family and saw Islamic calligraphy for the first time in the window of an Armenian carpet store. Travelling to Morocco in his late teens, he became fascinated with Islam and Islamic calligraphy. On his return to the United States he converted to Islam.

He made other journeys to North Africa and the Middle East, and spent some time studying manuscripts in the British Museum in London. After studying with the Egyptian calligrapher Abdussalam Ali-Nour, Zakariya in 1984 became a student of the Turkish master calligrapher Hasan Celebi. In 1988 he received his diploma from Celebi at the Research Center for Islamic History, Art and Culture in Istanbul, the first American to achieve this honour. He received his second diploma, in the *ta'lik* script, from the master calligrapher Ali Alparslan in 1997.

Zakariya lives with his family in Arlington, Virginia. His work has been displayed in various museums and galleries, and is in a number of private collections. He was the artist commissioned by the United States Postal Service to design its Eid stamp, which made its debut on 1 September 2001.

In addition to teaching calligraphy according to the Ottoman method, producing new work, and exhibiting it around the world, Zakariya writes contemporary instructional material and translates classic texts. In 2009, he was commissioned by US President Barack Obama to create a piece of calligraphy that was presented to King Abdulaziz of Saudi Arabia. Mohamed Zakariya's work shows that American Islam has become an integral part of the Muslim world. Now students from that world travel to the United States to study with an American master of an ancient Islamic art.

In addition, Arabic calligraphy has been used ingeniously to create the outlines of birds and animals, as well as crescents, mosques, minarets, and other forms to the present day.

❧ INTERACTION AND ADAPTATION

Islam and Modernity

Throughout the history of Islam, many individuals and groups have taken it on themselves to reform the rest of the Muslim community. An external impetus for reform has been Muslim interaction with Western Christendom. The first major Western challenges to Muslim power and Islam's capacity to rally its people in a universal struggle to defend the integrity of its domains were the crusades. Fired by a spirit of Christian holy war to liberate Jerusalem from Muslim domination, the armies of the first crusade captured the Holy City in 1099 after massacring its Jewish and Muslim inhabitants. For nearly two centuries, Frankish Christian kingdoms existed side by side with Muslim states along the eastern Mediterranean shores, sometimes peacefully, but most of the time at war.

In the end the crusaders returned home, and those who remained were assimilated. But the spirit of the crusades lived on, as did the distorted images of Islam and its followers that the crusaders took back with them. The equally distorted images of Christianity and Western Christendom that the crusades left in Muslim lands have also lived on, and have been reinforced and embellished in response to Western imperialism and its aftermath.

Premodern Reform Movements

We shall examine Islam in the modern era from two perspectives: internal reform and the challenge of the West.

Common to all reform movements has been the call to return to pristine *islam*, the *islam* of the Prophet's society and the normative period of his 'rightly guided' successors. Among those who championed this cause was the Egyptian religious scholar Ibn Taymiyah (1263–1328), a jurist who fought relentlessly against Shi'i beliefs and practices, Sufi excesses, and the blind imitation of established legal traditions, while fighting to revive the practice of *ijtihad*. He exerted a powerful and long-lasting influence on subsequent reform movements.

Some four centuries later, Ibn Taymiyah's ideas became the basis of the reform program advocated by the Wahhabi movement, named for its founder Muhammad Ibn 'Abd al-Wahhab (1703–92). Significantly, this uncompromising and influential revivalist movement began in the highlands of Arabia, the birthplace of Islam. Ibn 'Abd al-Wahhab's long life allowed him to establish his movement on a firm foundation. He allied himself with Muhammad 'Al Sa'ud, a local tribal prince, on the understanding that the prince would exercise political power and protect the nascent movement, which would hold religious authority. This agreement remains operative today: the kingdom of Saudi Arabia is a Wahhabi state, ruled by the descendants of 'Al Sa'ud.

The Wahhabis preached a strictly egalitarian Islam based solely on a direct relationship between the worshipper and God. They repudiated the widely cherished hope that the Prophet and other divinely favoured individuals would intercede with God for the pious to grant them blessing and succour in this life and salvation in the next. The Wahhabis regarded the veneration of saints, including the Prophet, as a form of idolatry. They even advocated the destruction of the sacred black stone of the Ka'ba, on the grounds that it stood as an idol between faithful Muslims and their Lord.

The Wahhabis held all those who did not share their convictions to be in error. They waged a violent campaign aimed at purging Muslim society of what they considered to be its un-Islamic beliefs and practices. They destroyed the Prophet's tomb in Medina and levelled the graves of his Companions. They attacked the Shi'i sacred cities of Najaf and Karbala', massacred their inhabitants, and demolished the shrines of 'Ali and his son Husayn. They also went on a rampage in Arab cities, desecrating the tombs of Sufi saints and destroying their shrines.

The basic ideals of Wahhabism have appealed to many revivalists and played an especially significant role in eighteenth- and nineteenth-century Sufi reforms. In the present day, however, a number of extremist groups influenced by Wahhabi ideology, including Al-Qaeda and the Taliban, have transformed the internal struggle to 'purify' Islam into an external war against all perceived enemies, Muslim and non-Muslim alike.

Nineteenth-Century Revivalism

Jihad—Arabic for 'struggle'—has two components. Inner *jihad* is the struggle to make oneself more Islamic; outer *jihad* is the struggle to make one's society more Islamic.

A number of Sufi *jihad* movements arose in the nineteenth century, partly in response to Wahhabi reforms and partly in reaction against European colonial encroachment on Muslim domains. Several of these movements were able to establish short-lived states, among them those led by Usman ('Uthman) dan Fodio (the Sokoto caliphate, 1809–1903) in Nigeria, Muhammad al-Sanusi (the Sanusi movement, 1837–1969) in Libya, and Muhammad Ahmad al-Mahdi (the Mahdi rebellion, 1881–9) in Sudan. Common to all these movements was an activist ideology of militant struggle against external colonialism and internal decadence. They also strove for reform and the revival of *ijtihad*.

Because of their broad appeal, these Sufi reform movements exerted a lasting influence on most subsequent reform programs and ideologies. In North Africa in particular, Sufi *shaykhs*

and religious scholars not only helped to preserve their countries' religious, linguistic, and cultural identity but in some cases spearheaded the long and bloody struggles for independence from French and Italian colonial rule. In the nineteenth century, for example, the Sufi *shaykh* Abdelkader ('Abd al-Qadir) played an important political role in the long campaign for Algeria's independence. King Muhammad V of Morocco, who negotiated his country's independence from France in 1956, was himself a Sufi *shaykh* and a 'venerable descendant' (*sayyid*) of the Prophet. And the grandson of al-Sanusi, Idris I, ruled Libya as king from independence in 1951 until he was overthrown in a revolution in 1969.

The movement begun by al-Sanusi in Libya promoted reform and Muslim unity across North and West Africa. By contrast, the goal of al-Mahdi's movement in Sudan was more eschatological: its founder saw himself as God's representative on earth and set out to establish a social and political order modelled on that of the Prophet. He regarded the Ottoman–Egyptian occupation of Sudan to be un-Islamic and waged a war of *jihad* against it. In 1885 he triumphed over Egyptian forces and established an Islamic state based on strict application of the *shari'ah* law. Although al-Mahdi himself died within a few months, the regime lasted until 1889, when it was overthrown by British and Egyptian forces.

Ahmadiyah

The career of Mirza Ghulam Ahmad (1835–1908) reflects both the social and the religious diversity of the Punjab in the 1880s, a time of various movements for renewal of Hindu and Muslim identity, as well as a growing emphasis on self-definition among the Sikhs. To this mix Ghulam Ahmad contributed several volumes of commentary on the Qur'an and claims of his own leadership status.

In 1889 he accepted from his followers the homage reserved for a prophet like Muhammad.

Ahmadis, as they are known, have also revered him as the *mujaddid* (renewer) ushering in the fourteenth century of Islam, as the Mahdi of Shi'i expectation, as the tenth incarnation of the Hindu deity Vishnu, and as the returning Messiah of Christianity (Ahmadis also maintain that Jesus did not die in Palestine but went to Afghanistan, in search of the ten lost tribes of Israel, and was buried in Srinagar, Kashmir).

Active proselytizers, Ghulam Ahmad and his followers preached in the streets, engaged in debates, and published translations of the Qur'an. The movement has spread widely. Including 4 million in Pakistan, Ahmadis now total at least 10 million, or 1 per cent of the world's Muslims. Leadership since the founder's death in 1908 has been termed *khilafat al-Masih* (succession of the Messiah). Although the successor is chosen by election, since 1914 the title has stayed in Ghulam Ahmad's family, held first by a son and then by two grandsons. Because they identified themselves as Muslims, on the partition of India in 1947 the Ahmadis were displaced from Qadian and relocated their centre across the border in Rabwah, Pakistan, west of Lahore.

Many Muslims, however, have not accepted the Ahmadis as fellow Muslims. As early as 1891, Ghulam Ahmad's claim to prophethood was rejected by orthodox Muslim authorities. In Pakistan Ahmadis have been the target of riots and demonstrations; in 1984 they were declared to be a non-Muslim minority (hence ineligible for opportunities accorded Muslims); and they have been prohibited from calling themselves Muslims or using Islamic vocabulary in their worship and preaching.

Ahmadiyah's future, therefore, may lie in its diaspora. Missions have been notably successful in lands not historically Islamic, such as West Africa, the Caribbean, and the overseas English-speaking world. The largest mosque in North America, opened in 1992, is the Ahmadi Baitul Islam mosque in the Toronto-area suburb of Maple.

Modernist Reformers

As the nineteenth century opened, European influence in the Muslim world was growing. Napoleon, who landed on Egyptian shores in 1798, brought with him not only soldiers but also scholars and the printing press; in this way the Middle East discovered Europe. The great Ottoman Empire, which in the early decades of the sixteenth century had threatened Vienna, had by the nineteenth become 'the sick man of Europe'. Meanwhile, the British Empire was extending its rule in India and its control over much of the Muslim world.

Muslim thinkers everywhere were awed by the West and resentful of the political inertia into which the Muslim *ummah* had apparently fallen. Even so, many areas of the Islamic east did experience an intellectual and cultural revival in the nineteenth century. Egypt, for instance, was the home of an Arab intellectual renaissance. Owing to unsettled social and political conditions in the Levant, a number of Western-educated Syro-Lebanese Christians immigrated to Egypt, where they established newspapers and cultural journals and participated actively in the recovery of the Arabo-Islamic heritage.

The Arab renaissance of the nineteenth century was largely stimulated by the cultural and intellectual flowering that was taking place in the West. Undermined first by the Protestant Reformation and then by the Enlightenment, religious faith and institutions were now giving way to secularism and romantic nationalism. These ideas similarly appealed to eastern Mediterranean Muslims, and in the end they led to the rise of Arab nationalism. The same ideas also influenced Muslims in other regions, so that nationalistic identities came to compete with, and in some cases even supersede, Islamic identities.

These and other Western influences were reinforced by the proliferation of Western Christian missionary schools and institutions of higher learning throughout the Muslim world. In short,

Islamic reform movements of the nineteenth and twentieth centuries in Asia, Africa, and the Middle East arose in a context of widespread cultural and intellectual ferment.

The Indian Subcontinent

The Mughal dynasty was founded in India by Babur in 1526. It reached its peak during the reign (1556–1605) of Akbar, who was Babur's grandson. With the decline of the Mughal Empire in the seventeenth century, calls for reform along traditional lines intensified. One of the strongest voices for reform was that of Ahmad Sirhindi (1564–1624), who called for a return to the *shari'ah*, regarded Sufis as deviants, and condemned Ibn 'Arabi in particular as an infidel.

The most important movement of Islamic reform on the Indian subcontinent in modern times was begun by Shah Wali Allah of Delhi (1702–62). Although he was a disciple of Ibn 'Abd al-Wahhab, he was a Sufi himself, and instead of rejecting Sufism he sought to reform it. Shah Wali Allah was a moderate reformer with encyclopedic learning. He also attempted to reconcile Shi'i–Sunni differences, which had been (and sometimes are still) a source of great friction on the Indian subcontinent in particular.

Shah Wali Allah's grandson Ahmad Barelwi transformed his program into a *jihad* movement against British rule and the Sikhs. In 1826 he established an Islamic state based on the *shari'ah* and adopted the old caliphal title 'commander of the faithful'. Although he was killed in battle in 1831, his *jihad* movement lived on. For Barelwi, India ceased to be an Islamic domain after the end of Mughal rule, and therefore Muslims should wage a *jihad* to liberate it. If independence from infidel

The Badshahi or great Mosque in Lahore, Pakistan, was built by the Emperor Aurangzeb in 1673–4 (Christine Osborne/Alamy).

sovereignty was not possible, Muslims should undertake a religious migration (*hijrah*) to an area where Muslims did rule.

The shock that Indian Muslims suffered with the consolidation of British rule was intensified by the fact that the British tampered with Islamic law itself. The result was a mixture of Islamic law and Western humanistic rulings known as Anglo-Muhammadan law.

At the opposite end of the spectrum of reaction to British rule from *jihad* movements like Barelwi's was the approach of Sayyid Ahmad Khan (1817–98). Like all reformers, Khan called for modern *ijtihad* or rethinking of the Islamic heritage, but unlike most of them he rejected *hadith* tradition as a legitimate basis for modern Islamic living. He founded the Aligarh Muhammadan College (later Aligarh Muslim University), where he attempted to apply his ideas in a modern Western-style program of education.

Muhammad Iqbal

The ideas of Sayyid Ahmad Khan and his fellows culminated in the philosophy of Muhammad Iqbal (1876–1938), the greatest Muslim thinker of modern India. Central to Iqbal's work is the idea of an inner spirit that moves human civilization.

Iqbal argued that Western science and philosophy were rightfully part of the Islamic heritage and should be integrated into a fresh *Reconstruction of Religious Thought in Islam* (the title of his only major work in English, published in the 1930s). A poet as well as a philosopher, Iqbal frequently repeated this call for a dynamic rethinking of Islamic faith and civilization in his verse.

Twentieth-Century Secularism

Many of the early Muslim reformers were at once liberal modernists and traditional thinkers. For this reason they are known as *salafis*: reformers who sought to emulate the example of 'the pious forebears' (*al-salaf al-salih*). This important ideal of equilibrium between tradition and modernity

disappeared by the 1920s. Thereafter, Islamic reform meant either revivalism, apologetics, or secularism.

Following the Ottoman defeat in the First World War, a young army officer named Mustafa Kemal Atatürk (1881–1938) launched a movement for national liberation. After gaining power, he abolished the caliphate in 1924, transforming the Turkish state from a traditional Islamic domain into a modern secular republic, of which he became the first president. Although for centuries the caliphate had been a shadowy office without any power, it had nevertheless embodied the only hope for a viable pan-Islamic state. Its disappearance therefore had far-reaching consequences for Islamic political thought.

Atatürk banned Sufi orders, dissolved Islamic religious institutions, replaced the Arabic alphabet (in which Turkish had traditionally been written) with the Latin, and mounted a nationwide campaign for literacy in the new script. His express aim was to westernize the Turkish republic and cut it off from its Islamic past. He encouraged the adoption of Western-style clothing and even went so far as to ban the fez—the brimless conical red hat that, like all traditional Muslim headgear, allowed the faithful to touch their foreheads to the ground during prayer.

Though Atatürk's ideology has remained the official state policy in Turkey, his program largely failed, for the people's Islamic roots were not easily destroyed. Islamic faith and practice remain strong among the people of Turkey, and the country has its own powerful revivalist movements.

Twentieth-Century Islamic Revivalism

Islamic reform movements generally seem to have experienced a loss of nerve after the international upheavals of the First World War and the break-up of the Ottoman Empire. Despite their differences, the various reform movements of the nineteenth century shared a dynamic and courageous spirit of progress. The premature stifling of that spirit may have reflected the lack of a coherent program of reform that post-colonialist Muslim thinkers could implement or build upon. In any event, the liberal reform movements of the nineteenth century were transformed in the twentieth into traditional revivalist movements.

On the eve of Atatürk's abolition of the caliphate in 1924, Muhammad Rashid Rida (1865–1935) published an important treatise on the Imamate, or Supreme Caliphate, in which he argued for the establishment of an Islamic state that would be ruled by a council of jurists or religious scholars. Such a state would recognize nationalistic sentiments and aspirations, but would subordinate them to the religio-political interests of the larger community. Rida's Islamic revivalism and Arab nationalism came to represent a major trend in twentieth-century Muslim thinking, and his political plan for a council of jurists would be implemented in Iran following the revolution of 1978–9.

Contemporary Revivalist Movements

It remains the ideal of Islamic reform to establish a transnational Islamic caliphate. The reality, however, has been a proliferation of local movements reflecting local needs and ideas.

Common to most revivalist movements in the second half of the twentieth century was the ideal of an all-inclusive and self-sufficient Islamic order. This ideal had its roots in the Society of Muslim Brothers (Jam'iyat al-Ikhwan al-Muslimin), founded in 1928 by an Egyptian schoolteacher named Hasan al-Banna. The aim of this society was to establish a network of Islamic social, economic, and political institutions through which the total Islamization of society might in time be achieved. Working through social and educational facilities such as schools, banks, cooperatives, and clinics, the Muslim Brothers penetrated all levels of Egyptian society.

The political and militaristic aspects of revivalism also had their beginnings in the Muslim Brothers, particularly after the assassination of the populist and generally peaceful al-Banna in 1949. He was succeeded by hard-line leaders who advocated active *jihad* against the Egyptian state system, which they regarded as un-Islamic. Among the products of the Muslim Brothers' ideology were the young officers, led by Gamal Abdel Nasser, behind the 1952 socialist revolution that abolished monarchical rule in Egypt.

A charismatic proponent of Arab nationalism in the 1950s and 1960s, Nasser nevertheless clashed with the Muslim Brothers, and in the mid-1960s he imprisoned, exiled, or executed most of their leaders. One of those leaders was Sayyid Qutb, who is important as a link to modern Islamist groups. As a theoretician he influenced Islamist ideology; and as an activist whose defiance of the state led to his execution he provided younger militants with a model of martyrdom to emulate. Following the Arab defeat in the six-day Arab–Israeli war of June 1967 and the death of Nasser three years later, the Muslim Brothers were driven underground and superseded by more powerful revivalist movements under Anwar Sadat and his successor Hosni Mubarak, some of which advocated the use of violence to achieve their goals. Although suppressed in Egypt, the Brotherhood has spread in other Arab countries; but in exile, without its social infrastructure, it has been more influential on the level of ideology than of social action. A similar organization, the Jama'at-i Islami (Islamic Society), was established in 1941 by Mawlana Sayyid Abu al-A'la Mawdudi. Like Hasan al-Banna, Mawdudi was committed to pan-Islamic unity. But also like al-Banna, he concentrated his efforts on his own community—in this case the Muslims of India and (after 1947) Pakistan. The influence of both organizations spread far beyond their original homes.

While most contemporary revivalist movements, including the two organizations noted above, have been open to modern science and technology, they have rejected many Western values and practices—including capitalist democracy, women's liberation, and the free mixing of the sexes—as decadent. Therefore, unlike the nineteenth-century reformers who looked to the West for ideas and models, contemporary revivalist reformers have insisted on finding Islamic alternatives. Mawdudi, for example, wishing to distinguish his Islamic state model from Western democracies, described it as a 'theodemocracy' based on the broad Qur'anic principle of consultation (*shura*) and the *shari'ah* law.

State Islam and the Islamic Revolution

Following a coup in 1969, Gaafar Mohamed el-Nimeiri made *shari'ah* the law in Sudan. The result was a bloody conflict between the Muslim north and the generally Christian south that has continued for decades, reducing a formerly rich agricultural country to famine. Likewise in Pakistan, which for three decades had been a constitutionally Islamic but modern state. The introduction of *shari'ah* by General Mohammad Zia-ul-Haq following a coup in 1977 led to violent social and political conflict.

In Egypt and Algeria, revivalist movements continue to resort to violent means in their quest to establish Islamic states. Again, the results are social strife and instability.

In almost every Muslim country there is at least one revivalist movement advocating some form of Islamic state. In countries like Malaysia and Indonesia, the governments themselves espouse Islamic national policies in order to silence extremist demands for radical reform. Nevertheless, in most Muslim countries feelings continue to run high between Islamic movements made up of educated middle-class men and women and despotic regimes determined to hold on to power at any cost.

In such highly charged social and political conditions, religion serves as a powerful moral, social,

and spiritual expression of discontent—not only for Islamic activists, but for a broad spectrum of the community as well. It was on precisely such mass discontent that Imam Ruhollah Khomeini (1901–89) and his fellow Shi'i *mullahs* (religio-legal functionaries) built the Islamic Republic of Iran, in which social, political, economic, and religious life are all under the control of a religious hierarchy headed by a supreme Ayatollah (*ayat Allah*, 'sign of God').

Throughout the long period of Shi'i secular rule in Iran (1501–1979), the authority of the religious '*ulama*' operated in more or less continuous tension with the secular authorities. This tension was greatly increased during the reign of Shah Mohammad Reza Pahlavi, who sought to westernize the country and obscure its Islamic identity by emphasizing Iran's pre-Islamic cultural past. In 1963, during the Muharram observances of Husayn's martyrdom, matters came to a head when the Shah's dreaded secret police ruthlessly put down mass demonstrations led by the '*ulama*'. Khomeini, already a prominent religious leader, was sent into exile, where he elaborated his religio-political theory, according to which the jurist should have all-embracing authority in the community. In 1979 Khomeini returned to Iran at the head of the Islamic revolution. The Islamic republic he founded has had a turbulent history, including an eight-year war with Iraq (1980–8), out of which it emerged greatly weakened but still intact. Pro-democracy protests and challenges to the authority of the '*ulama*' came to international attention with the controversy that surrounded the 2009 election.

Islam in Western Europe

The Islamic presence in western Europe began with the establishment of Umayyad rule in southern Spain in 711. Commercial, political, and cultural relations were initiated with both Latin and Byzantine states, but medieval Europe would not tolerate a permanent Muslim community on its soil. The campaign to drive the Muslims out of Spain succeeded in 1492 with the conquest of Granada. As a result, the Muslim communities in western Europe today are a relatively recent phenomenon.

In the twentieth century some Muslims migrated to Europe from various colonies as students, visitors, and merchants. Many also went as menial labourers and factory workers, especially after the Second World War. The majority of these post-war immigrants were men ranging in age from their teens to their forties.

The ethnic makeup of the Muslim communities in Europe was largely determined by colonial ties. Muslims from the French colonies in North Africa, for example, went to France. Indian and, later, Pakistani and Bangladeshi Muslims tended to go to Britain. Those from Turkey and the former Soviet Turkic republics went to Germany and the Netherlands, while Bosnians went to Austria. These patterns were established in the early decades of the twentieth century and continued in spite of many restrictions.

Muslim communities in Europe tend to reflect ethnic and linguistic rather than sectarian affiliations. In recent years hundreds of mosques and cultural centres have been established in European cities, and Muslim communities have become a dynamic religious and intellectual force in European society. France and Britain no longer confine Muslims to the status of 'guest workers', as most other European countries do. Yet even there, the long histories of European racism, ethnocentrism, and colonialism have ensured that many Muslims continue to be treated as second-class citizens. This has created serious problems.

After the Islamic revolution of 1978–9, many Iranians immigrated to Europe, adding yet another layer of ethnic and religious diversity to European Muslim society. The 15-year Lebanese civil war of 1975–90, as well as the disturbances in other Arab countries, including the Gulf War of 1991, also sent many political and economic refugees to the West. Meanwhile, intermarriage and conversion have infused new blood into the Muslim community in the Western world.

Many Muslims born in Europe to foreign-born parents are assimilating into European society and culture. On the other hand, most European countries have taken legal measures to limit immigration, and since the mid-1980s a number of them have repatriated some of their Muslim immigrants. Such actions may have been prompted in part by economic considerations, but also perhaps by nationalistic fears that Muslim immigrants might alter the social and ethnic character of these countries. At the end of 2009, for example, Swiss citizens voted into their constitution a ban on minarets for new mosques—even though, of the approximately 150 mosques and Islamic centres in Switzerland, only four have minarets. At the same time, European discrimination against ethnic minorities and the Islamic awakening precipitated by the Iranian revolution have made Muslims more aware of their own religious and cultural identity.

Islam in North America

When the first Muslims arrived on American shores is a matter of conjecture. Suggestions that Muslims from Spain and West Africa may have sailed to America long before Columbus should not be discounted, but they are far from conclusive. It is very likely that the fall of Granada in 1492 and the harsh treatment imposed on Muslims and Jews by the Inquisition led many to flee to America soon after Columbus's historic voyage. Scattered records point to the presence of Muslims in Spanish America before 1550.

In the sixteenth and seventeenth centuries, hundreds of thousands of Africans were taken as slaves to the Spanish, Portuguese, and British colonies in the Americas. Although the majority were from West Africa, Muslims made up at least 20 per cent of the total. And among the slaves taken from Senegal, Nigeria, and the western Sudan, the majority were Muslims, many of whom were well educated in Arabic and the religious sciences. Some were able to preserve their faith and heritage, and some tried to maintain contact with Muslims in their home areas, but many others were quickly absorbed into American society, adopting their masters' religion and even family names.

Islamic customs and ideas can still be traced in the African-American community, and today efforts are underway to reconstruct the story behind them from slave narratives, oral history, and other archival materials, including observations of Islamic activities by white travellers in the mid-1800s.

Beginning in the late nineteenth century, African-Americans made conscious efforts to recover their Islamic heritage. In the early 1930s, Elijah Muhammad (born Elijah Poole, 1897–1975) became a follower of Wallace D. Fard and founded the Nation of Islam in America. He saw Islam as a religion of Black people only, misrepresenting the universalistic and non-racial nature of Islam. But his sons and successors, after travelling in the Muslim world and observing the international and multiracial character of the *hajj* pilgrimage, have drawn closer to classical Islam. African-American Muslims often refer to themselves as Bilalians, after Bilal, an African Companion of the Prophet's time and community. Islam continues to be the fastest-growing religion in America, particularly among African-Americans.

Before the revival of Islam in the African-American community early in the twentieth century, small numbers of Muslims travelled to Canada and the United States, mainly from Syria and Lebanon. These early immigrants were uneducated men who intended only to work in North America for a few years and then return home. Instead, many married Canadian or American women and were soon completely assimilated.

The first Muslim missionary in America was Muhammad Alexander Webb, a jeweller, newspaper editor, and diplomat who converted to Islam in 1888, while travelling in India. On his return, Webb created an Islamic propaganda movement, wrote three books on Islam, and founded a periodical entitled *The Muslim World* (not to be confused with the academic journal of the same name). He travelled widely to spread the new faith and established Islamic study circles or Muslim brotherhoods in many northeastern and midwestern American cities. With his death in 1916, however, his movement died as well.

The numbers of Muslim immigrants coming to Canada and the United States increased markedly during the twentieth century. Most were of South Asian origin. Many were students who later chose to stay, or well-educated professionals who came in search of better opportunities. But others came to escape persecution in their homelands on account of their religious or political activities. Interestingly, many recent newcomers have arrived as staunch anti-Western revivalists but have soon forgotten their hostility and taken up life as peaceful, responsible, and law-abiding citizens.

Although these and other religiously committed Muslim immigrants may have moderated their political convictions, they retained a high degree of religious zeal, which they put to good use in the service both of their own community and of the society at large. They have played a crucial role in preserving the Islamic identity of fellow immigrants and promoting a better understanding of Islam through media activities and academic meetings.

The first mosque in the United States was built in 1915 in Maine by Albanian Muslims; another followed in Connecticut in 1919. Other mosques were established in the 1920s and 1930s in South Dakota and Iowa. In 1928, Polish Tatars built a mosque in Brooklyn, New York, which is still in use. The first Canadian mosque was built in Edmonton, Alberta, in 1938, and a number of smaller towns in Alberta also have Muslim communities. In Toronto, the first Muslim organization was the Albanian Muslim Society of Toronto, founded in 1956. In 1968, this organization purchased an unused Presbyterian Church and converted it into a mosque. Toronto currently has the largest population of Canada's Muslims.

The exact numbers of Muslims in Canada and the United States are a matter of debate. The 2001 Canadian census counted almost 600,000 Muslims, making Islam the second-largest religion in the country. The United States has not had a religious census since 1936, but the current Muslim population there is estimated to be between 6 and 7 million. Whatever the numbers may be, Islam in North America is no longer an exotic rarity: it is the faith of many people's co-workers and neighbours.

Women and the Family

Islam strictly forbade the practice of female infanticide, and it required that those who had killed their daughters in pre-Islamic times (often by burying them alive) make expiation for their crime. The Qur'an states that on the Day of Resurrection, it will be asked of the child who was buried alive, 'For what sin was she slain?' (Q. 81: 8–9). Victims are to be vindicated and recompensed on the Day of Judgment for the wrong done them in this life.

Marriage under Islam is essentially a contractual relationship negotiated between the prospective husband and the woman's father or guardian. But the Qur'an emphasizes that the true contract is between the husband and the wife, based on mutual consent: the woman's father or guardian, 'he in whose hand is the tie of marriage' (Q. 2: 237), is expected to act on her behalf and, ideally, in her interest. Divorce is allowed, but only as a last resort, to be used only after every effort has been made to save the marriage.

The Qur'an allows polygyny (simultaneous marriage to more than one wife). But it places two significant restrictions on such marriages. First, it limits to four the number of wives that a man can have at one time, whereas before Islam the number was unlimited. Second, it demands strict justice and equality in a man's material and emotional support for all his wives. If this is not possible, the Qur'an stipulates, 'then only one'. The Qur'an further insists, 'You cannot act equitably among your wives however much you try' (Q. 4: 3 and 129). As a result, the vast majority of Muslim marriages are monogamous.

Even more significantly, the Qur'an changes the nature of polygyny from an entitlement to a social responsibility. The verses dealing with this subject open with the proviso, 'If you [men] are afraid that you would not act justly towards the orphans [in your care], then marry what seems good to you of women: two, three, or four' (Q. 4: 3). This statement may be interpreted in two ways. It may mean that a man could marry the widowed mother of orphans in order to provide a family for them. It may also mean that a man could marry two, three, or four orphan girls after they have attained marriageable age, again to provide a home and family for them. In either case, marriage to more than one wife was explicitly allowed as a way of providing for female orphans and widows in a traditional society beset with continuous warfare, where a woman could find the love and security she needed only in her own home.

In addition the Qur'an allows women to own property and dispose of it as they please. Women may acquire property through bequest, inheritance, and bride dowry. Judged by today's social and economic needs and circumstances, these rights may seem inadequate. Yet the Qur'an undeniably recognizes in women a human dignity and a social and emotional personality that were denied until recently in many societies.

Islamic law and social custom have been not been so generous and forward-looking, however. In general, they have tended either to restrict the rights laid out in the Qur'an or to render them virtually inoperative. Of all the social and political issues that are currently being debated within the Muslim community, one of the most important is the age-old question of women's rights, with all its ramifications.

The Qur'an does not refer at all to the **hijab** or veiling of women as we know it today. It only demands that women avoid wearing jewellery and that they dress modestly; and in the very next verse it also demands modesty of males. The *hadith* tradition indicates that Muslim communities adopted the practice of veiling during the time of the caliphate, probably under the influence of Eastern Christian and ancient Greek customs. An extreme extension of the practice, which may also be attributable to non-Arab influences, is the seclusion of women. Under the South Asian system of *purdah*, for instance, women are not only veiled but isolated from men. And seclusion became a hallmark of Turkish life under the *harim* system of the Ottoman aristocracy. In Afghanistan, the *burqa* covers the entire body; even the woman's eyes (and her vision) are obscured by a screen.

In the twenty-first century, the *hijab* has become a powerful—and powerfully ambiguous—symbol, widely condemned (especially by non-Muslims)

as a limitation on women's rights, but often defended by Muslim women themselves as a freely chosen affirmation of their Islamic identity. The question at issue is to what extent women can be excluded from public life. A closely related issue, of course, is access to education for both women and men. Increasingly, social and economic conditions throughout the world call for equal participation and equal rights for women and men alike.

Sexual Diversity

Issues of gender equality and sexual diversity are rarely discussed within the largest of the Muslim political and religious organizations in North America (such as the Islamic Society of North America), partly because those groups tend to

'Miss Dia', a Pakistani-American college student and DJ, at the Inner-city Muslim Action Network (IMAN) in Chicago. The mural was an interfaith project involving Christian and Jewish as well as Muslim youth (© 2007 Kauthar Umar, *isl.am.erica*).

emphasize traditional interpretations of Islam, and partly because they have been preoccupied with matters such as community-building, immigration policy, discrimination, and (to some extent) foreign policy. But as the size of their constituencies has grown, and the range of perspectives within those constituencies has increased, there has been growing pressure to address matters involving gender and sexuality.

Diasporic communities in large urban centres tend to become more open to questions about traditional religious and cultural ideas as they become more deeply rooted (or 'assimiliated') in their new societies. As contact with the 'host' community intensifies, those who question traditional ideas are likely to have much easier access to information and networks of like-minded people than their counterparts in their countries of origin. Some will 'exit' their communities of origin and seek full assimilation to the dominant society; but in large communities particularly, some will remain connected and mobilize their challenges to traditionalism from within.

In general, Muslims born and raised in North America are more open to diversity than those born abroad, especially if their communities are not sufficiently homogeneous to support their own separate social institutions (such as schools). The likelihood of dissent is further amplified in the Muslim communities of North America by relatively high levels of education. In general, high education increases openness to diversity, as well as to equity claims by women and sexual minorities. The fact that Muslim minorities in North America are less economically marginalized than those in Europe also reduces the likelihood of strict adherence to religious belief.

On the other hand, the great majority of Muslims in Canada and the United States are still relatively recent immigrants from places where social norms regarding gender and sexuality are starkly conservative, and the mosques and Islamic centres to which new immigrants become attached are almost invariably conservative on moral questions. Groups seeking to challenge conservative ideas are

developing, as we shall see in Chapter 8, but homosexual Muslims in particular continue to face condemnation from mainstream Muslim society.

Islam and the Future

A major development in the history of Islam is now underway in the West. Muslims who, through migration, have moved from majority to minority status are being spurred to define the priorities of their faith. Their decisions about what to pass on to their Western-born children will shape the contours of Islam in the twenty-first century and beyond. At the same time, the Western emphasis on open discussion calls on Muslims from different cultural and regional backgrounds to think clearly about what they do and do not share. Perhaps Muslims living in the West will use Western technology and democratic institutions to revitalize the Muslim communities in their countries of origin, as well as the rest of the Muslim *ummah*. The speed of modern travel and communications may contribute to this process.

For a time it seemed that political developments might contribute to it as well. Many hoped that the end of the cold war in 1989 and the moves made in the 1990s towards ending the long and bitter conflict between Israelis and Palestinians might allow for better relations between the Western and Muslim worlds in general. But the Israeli–Palestinian conflict has only deepened, and new conflicts have emerged in recent years.

One major political development was the Iranian revolution of 1979. Three decades later, the prospect of an Iran with nuclear weapons has only increased the tensions between the Islamic regime and the West. A second development can also be traced to 1979, when the Soviet Union invaded Afghanistan. Muslims from around the world volunteered to fight with the Afghans for their liberation, and the United States contributed heavily to their training. They were called *mujahidin* (the word is derived from *jihad*), and at the time—before the end of the cold war—they were seen as 'freedom fighters' by much of the world, including the American president, Ronald Reagan.

Among the other contributors to Afghanistan's 'holy war' was Osama bin Laden, the son of a wealthy Saudi Arabian family, who created Al-Qaeda ('the base') to help fund and train *mujahidin*. The Soviet troops were withdrawn in 1988. But Al-Qaeda was not disbanded. In 1996 bin Laden issued a **fatwa** (religious legal opinion) calling for the overthrow of the Saudi government and the removal of US forces in Arabia, and in 1998 he declared war against Americans generally. A series of terrorist actions followed, culminating in the attacks on the United States of 11 September 2001. In response, the United States and its allies went to war, first in Afghanistan and then in Iraq.

Muslims around the world have repeatedly condemned terrorist activity. Muslim leaders have pointed out that the use of suicide bombers violates mainstream Islamic teachings that prohibit both suicide and the killing of civilians during war, and in March 2005, on the first anniversary of the 2004 Al-Qaeda train bombing in Madrid, Spanish clerics issued a *fatwa* against bin Laden himself. Unfortunately, extremists seem impervious to mainstream Muslim opinion.

Muslims can accomplish much in the West if they work with their non-Muslim neighbours to promote justice and moral consciousness. But many non-Muslims see 'Islam' and 'the West' as mutually exclusive realities, and do not recognize their shared heritage. If future generations of Muslims are to remain active as Muslims in pluralistic Western societies, it is more important than ever to change old images and ideas.

Sites

Mecca Home to the Ka'ba, the first place of monotheistic worship. Also the place where Muhammad was born and received his first revelations.

Medina The home of the first Muslim community and the place where Muhammad was buried.

Jerusalem The area of the ancient city called Haram al-Sharif (the 'Noble Sanctuary'; also known to Jews and Christians as the Temple Mount) contains two sacred buildings: the Masjid al-Aqsa—the 'farthest mosque', from a passage in the Qur'an (17: 1) referring to Muhammad's miraculous journey—and the Dome of the Rock, a sanctuary built on the spot from which tradition says Muhammad made his ascent to heaven.

Karbala' The city in Iraq where Imam Husayn (the third Imam and the grandson of Muhammad) was martyred; of special importance to Shi'i Muslims.

Cairo Home of Al-Azhar University, the oldest university in the Western world and an important centre of Sunni learning.

Istanbul Captured by the Turkish ruler Muhammad II in 1453, Istanbul had been called Constantinople under the Byzantines. It became the capital of the Ottoman Turkish Empire and the centre of the sultan's power. It contains many imperial buildings, including the famous Topkapi Palace and the Western-influenced Dolmabahce Palace.

Glossary

caliph From the Arabic *khalifah* ('one who represents or acts on behalf of another'). The caliph was the Prophet's successor as the head of the Muslim community; the position became institutionalized in the form of the caliphate, which lasted from 632 to 1924.

dhikr 'Remembering' God's name; chanted in Sufi devotional exercises, sometimes while devotees dance in a circle.

dhimmis 'Protected people': non-Muslim religious minorities (specifically Jews and Christians, as 'People of the Book') accorded tolerated status in Islamic society.

faqir A Sufi ascetic, from the Arabic word for 'poor'; the corresponding Persian word is *darvish*.

Fatihah The short opening *surah* of the Qur'an, recited at least 17 times every day.

fatwa A ruling issued by a traditional religio-legal authority.

fiqh Jurisprudence, or the theoretical principles underpinning the specific regulations contained in the *shari'ah*.

hadith The body of texts reporting Muhammad's words and example, taken by Muslims as a foundation for conduct and doctrine; a *hadith* is an individual unit of the literature.

hajj The annual pilgrimage to Mecca.

halal Ritually acceptable; most often used in the context of the slaughter of animals for meat; also refers generally to Muslim dietary regulations.

hanifs 'Pious ones'; a group of pre-Islamic Arabs who shared the ethical monotheism of Jews and Christians.

haram 'Forbidden', used especially in reference to actions; similar in its connotations to 'taboo'.

hijab A woman's veil or head covering.

hijrah The Prophet's migration from Mecca to establish a community in Medina in 622 CE. In dates, the abbreviation AH stands for 'year of the *hijrah*' (the starting-point of the Islamic dating system)

'Id al-Fitr The holiday celebrating the end of the Ramadan fast; the festival traditionally begins following the sighting of the new moon.

ijma' The consensus of religio-legal scholars; one of the two secondary principles used in jurisprudence; some legal schools give it more weight than others.

ijtihad Personal reasoning applied to the development of legal opinions.

Imamis ('Twelvers') Shi'is who recognize twelve imams as legitimate heirs to the Prophet's authority; the last, in occultation since 874, is expected to return some day as the **Mahdi**.

Isma'ilis ('Seveners') Shi'is who recognize only seven imams; named after the last of them, Isma'il, whose lineage continues to the present in the Agha Khan.

isnad The pedigree or chain of transmission of a *hadith*, with which the individual unit begins.

jihad Struggle in defence of the faith; some *jihads* are military, waged in response to threats to the community's security or welfare; others are spiritual, waged to improve moral conduct in society.

jinn Spirits or demons (the singular is *jinni*).

kufr Rejecting belief; implies lack of gratitude for God's grace.

Mahdi The Shi'i twelfth Imam, understood in his role as the 'rightly guided one' who will emerge from hiding at some unspecified future date to restore righteousness and order to the world.

mi'raj The Prophet's miraculous journey to heaven.

mu'adhdhin The person who calls people to prayer.

qiblah The direction of prayer, marked in mosques by a niche inside the wall nearest Mecca.

Ramadan The month throughout which Muslims fast during daylight hours.

sadaqah Alms given voluntarily, in addition to the required *zakat*.

salat The prescribed daily prayers, said five times during the day.

shahadah The Muslim profession of faith in God as the only god, and in Muhammad as God's prophet.

shari'ah The specific regulations of Islamic law (jurisprudence, or theoretical discussion of the law, is *fiqh*).

shaykh The Arabic term for a senior master, especially in the context of Sufism.

Shi'is Muslims who trace succession to the Prophet's authority through imams in the lineage of 'Ali; the smaller of the two main divisions of Islam, accounting for about one-sixth of all Muslims today.

sunnah The 'life-example' of Muhammad's words and deeds, based mainly on the Hadith literature; the primary source of guidance for Muslims.

Sunnis Muslims who trace succession to the Prophet's authority through the caliphate, which lasted until the twentieth century; the larger of the two main divisions of Islam, accounting for about five-sixths of all Muslims today.

surah A chapter of the Qur'an; there are 114 in all, arranged mainly in decreasing order of length except for the first (the **Fatihah**).

tafsir Commentary on the Qur'an.

taqlid Following the **ijtihad** or legal opinion of a particular jurist.

ummah The Muslim community.

zakat The prescribed welfare tax; 2.5 per cent of each Muslim's accumulated wealth, collected by central treasuries in earlier times but now donated to charities independently of state governments; see also **sadaqah**.

Further Reading

Ahmed, Leila. 1992. *Women and Gender in Islam: Historical Roots of a Modern Debate*. New Haven: Yale University Press. A frequently cited contribution on this topic.

Alvi, Sajida Sultana, et al., eds. 2003. *The Muslim Veil in North America: Issues and Debates*. Toronto: Women's Press. A good collection of essays about the issues surrounding *hijab*.

Coulson, N.G. 1964. *A History of Islamic Law*. Edinburgh: Edinburgh University Press. Traces the development of Islamic jurisprudence from its inception in the ninth century through to the influence of modern Western legal systems.

The Encyclopedia of Islam, rev. ed. 1963–. Leiden: E.J. Brill. (First published in 4 vols, 1913–38.) Vast and technical, but authoritative. Entries appear under Arabic head-words, sometimes in unfamiliar transliterations, and so pose a challenge for the beginner.

Esposito, John, ed. 2009. *The Oxford Encyclopedia of the Islamic World*. New York: Oxford University Press. An indispensable reference.

Grabar, Oleg. 1973. *The Formation of Islamic Art*. New Haven: Yale University Press. Concentrates on Islamic art in the Middle East in the early Islamic centuries.

Haddad, Yvonne Y., and Jane I. Smith, eds. 1994. *Muslim Communities in North America*. Albany: State University of New York Press. An examination of Islamic tradition and identity in the modern Western diaspora.

Mottahedeh, Roy. 2002. *The Mantle of the Prophet: Religion and Politics in Iran*. Oxford: Oneworld Publications. One of the best single-volume studies of the events leading up to the Iranian revolution.

Peters, Francis E. 1994. *A Reader on Islam*. Princeton: Princeton University Press. An anthology of historical source readings.

Qureshi, Emran, and Michael A. Sells, eds. 2003. *The New Crusades: Constructing the Muslim Enemy*. New York: Columbia. An excellent collection of essays on Western representations of Islam and Muslim lives.

Safi, Omid, ed. 2003. *Progressive Muslims: On Justice, Gender and Pluralism*. Oxford: Oneworld. A collection of essays by Muslim scholars of Islam on these contemporary topics.

Schimmel, Annemarie. 1975. *Mystical Dimensions of Islam*. Chapel Hill: University of North Carolina Press. A survey of Sufism by one of its most respected Western interpreters.

Taylor, Jennifer Maytorena. 2009. *New Muslim Cool*. Documentary film. Educational DVD available from Seventh Art Releasing at <http://www.7thart.com>. The story of Hamza Perez, a Puerto Rican American hip hop artist who converted to Islam.

Watt, W. Montgomery. 1962. *Islamic Philosophy and Theology*. Edinburgh: Edinburgh University Press. A masterly survey of Muslim religious intellectuals, especially in the first six centuries of Islam.

Recommended Websites

www.uga.edu/islam/
> The best academic site for the study of Islam, presented by Professor Alan Godlas of the University of Georgia.

www.cie.org/index.aspx
> The Council on Islamic Education offers useful resources for teachers.

http://acommonword.com/
> An interfaith initiative supported by a wide range of Muslim scholars and leaders.

www.msawest.net/islam/
> An excellent selection of resources on Islam, including searchable translations of both the Qur'an and the Hadith literature, presented by the Muslim Students Association.

References

Arberry, Arthur J. trans. 1955. *The Koran Interpreted*. London: Allen and Unwin.

Nicholson, Reynold A. 1931. 'Mysticism'. In *The Legacy of Islam*, ed. T. Arnold and Alfred Guillaume, 210–38. London: Oxford University Press.

———, trans. 1950. *Rumi: Poet and Mystic*. London: G. Allen and Unwin.

———. 2002 [1914]. *The Mystics of Islam*. Bloomington: World Wisdom.

Smith, Margaret. 1928. *Rabi'a the Mystic*. Cambridge: Cambridge University Press.

Chapter 6

Indigenous Traditions

ᔐ Ken Derry ᔐ

S o.
   In the beginning, there was nothing. Just the water.
Coyote was there, but Coyote was asleep. That Coyote was asleep and that Coyote was dreaming. When that Coyote dreams, anything can happen.
        I can tell you that.
—Thomas King (1993: 1), **Cherokee/Greek**

Anything can happen. The possibilities, the complexities, of religions seem to be endless. This is particularly true of Indigenous traditions, which constitute the majority of the world's religions. They are interwoven with the entire history of humanity, they encompass the whole earth. And they are almost unimaginably diverse. So where to begin?

Perhaps it is best to start with ourselves. Let us approach the task of generalizing about Indigenous traditions with humility, and with the understanding that there are exceptions to every rule. We should also keep in mind that many past interpretations of these traditions have proven to be deeply mistaken. Looking through the lenses of their own assumptions and cultural biases, scholars can easily be tricked into seeing things that are not there, or missing what is right in front of them.

Coyote would not be surprised.

'INDIGENOUS RELIGION'

Definitions

There is a shared sense of Aboriginality nationally (and internationally with other Indigenous peoples), regardless of the geographical location or socio-economic experience of the individual.
—Anita Heiss (2001: 207), **Wiradjuri**

There is no definitive, agreed-on understanding of 'Indigenous religion'. In fact, the meanings of the words 'Indigenous' and 'religion' themselves are open to debate; some have even questioned whether they mean anything at all. You might think that trying to define a term made up of two elements that may be meaningless is doomed to failure. But we are going to try anyway.

'Religion'

Many of the difficulties surrounding the word 'religion' stem from the effort to find common patterns in such a variety of human practices. Are religions always about gods? (No.) Do all religions have a sacred text, believe in life after death, or promote the same basic values? (No again.) So what exactly are we talking about when we refer to 'religion'? Although scholars generally concede that we are unlikely to develop a single definition on which all can agree, they also point out that all definitions are themselves constructs. In other words, often what is most important is simply to be clear about which construct we are using.

The view of religion underlying this chapter is one that focuses on the beliefs, experiences, and practices of specific communities with respect to non-falsifiable realities (Cox 2007: 88). A proposition that is falsifiable is one that can be scientifically proven untrue. Religious propositions are of a different kind. It may not be possible to prove them true, but it is equally impossible to prove them false. Rather, religious propositions traffic in the unseeable, the untouchable, the unmeasurable. Whenever we step outside of material reality to address questions of spirit, meaning, or divinity, I would say, we are dealing with religion.

This definition is not perfect, of course. Among other potential weaknesses, it implies a distinction

◀ Young Pondo women from Transkei in South Africa during their initiation to become sacred healers (Daniel Lainé).

Timeline

Although most of the dates below relate to developments in Indigenous traditions since contact with non-Indigenous people, the histories of those traditions began many millennia earlier. Archaeological evidence can at least identify the presence of *Homo sapiens* communities, but dates remain approximate at best. Also note that the events listed here relate only to the cultures discussed in this chapter—a tiny fraction of the thousands that have existed.

c. 190,000 BCE	Earliest evidence of Indigenous people in Africa
c. 70,000 BCE	Earliest evidence of Indigenous people in Australia, Europe, and Asia
c. 12,500 BCE	Earliest evidence of Indigenous people in the Americas
616 CE	First Muslims arrive in Africa (Ethiopia)
c. 1250	First contact between the Ainu and the Japanese
c. 1300	First Indigenous settlers arrive in New Zealand (from Polynesia)
1444	Portuguese exploration of sub-Saharan Africa begins
c.1480	Atlantic slave trade begins
1492	Christopher Columbus (Italian) arrives in the West Indies, initiating Spanish colonization of the Americas
1642	Dutch explorer Abel Janszoon Tasman arrives in New Zealand
1788	British First Fleet arrives in Sydney, Australia
1799	Handsome Lake experiences his first vision
1819	British and Xhosa (led by Nxele) fight Battle of Grahamstown
c.1840	Canada establishes residential school system
1856–7	Nongqawuse's vision leads to Xhosa cattle massacre
1869	Australia begins taking Aboriginal children from their families, producing the first of many 'Stolen Generations'
1883	Pauline Johnson (Mohawk) publishes first poems; US bans Sun Dance
1884	Canada bans potlatch
1885	European powers partition Africa at Congress of Berlin; intensive Christian missionary efforts begin in non-Muslim areas of Africa; earliest recorded 'cargo cult' begins in Fiji
1889	Wovoka revives the Ghost Dance
1890	US Cavalry massacres more than 300 Lakota Sioux at Wounded Knee, North Dakota
1899	Japan appropriates Ainu lands, denies Ainu status as Indigenous people
1934	US lifts ban on Sun Dance and potlatch
1951	Canada lifts ban on potlatch
1956–65	Beginning of African post-independence era

Continued

1958	Chinua Achebe (Igbo) publishes *Things Fall Apart*
1969	Kiowa novelist N. Scott Momaday's *House Made of Dawn* wins Pulitzer Prize for Fiction
1970	US returns 194 km² of land to Taos Pueblo
1985	Maori novelist Keri Hulme's *The Bone People* wins the Booker Prize for Fiction
1990	Oka Crisis in Quebec, Canada
1992	Australian High Court overturns *terra nullius* ruling
1994	Nelson Mandela (Xhosa) elected president of South Africa
2007	United Nations adopts Declaration on the Rights of Indigenous Peoples
2008	Australia apologizes for 'Stolen Generations'; Canada apologies for residential school system; Japan formally recognizes Ainu as an Indigenous group

between religion and science—as if religion had no scientific components, or science could not function as a religion for some people. This is not a reasonable distinction, in my opinion: religion and science may often overlap. Nor do I mean to imply that scientific knowledge supersedes other forms of knowledge or ways of knowing. Scientists have been proven wrong about aspects of our world that some Indigenous cultures have long been right about.

Still, I believe that the focus on 'non-falsifiable realities' as a basis for defining religion can work quite well. In particular—and most relevantly—it is a good fit for the examples of Indigenous religion that this chapter will examine.

'Indigenous'

The term 'Indigenous' is also problematic, for it obliges us to ask which cultures and people are 'Indigenous' and which are not. This is not just an academic question, but one loaded with legal and political implications. It has a direct and severe impact on the lives of millions of people around the world. If we cannot identify a particular group as Indigenous, for example, how can its members assert their treaty rights, or see their land claims settled fairly?

Unfortunately, it is usually non-Indigenous governments that impose the definitions, and those definitions themselves tend to change over time. In Canada, for instance, it was for many years the case that a 'status Indian' woman who married a 'non-status' man was no longer legally Indigenous; she automatically forfeited all the rights that the (legally defined) Indigenous people of Canada are entitled to. When this law was reversed after years of protest, not only these women but also their children suddenly 'became' Indigenous, virtually overnight.

Other definitions are also problematic. Almost invariably, 'Indigenous' is understood to mean 'original to the land'. Yet many places in the world, including India and Africa, have very ancient histories of migration and interaction between various groups. How could anyone possibly determine the 'original' inhabitants of such lands?

Furthermore, we again run into the difficulty of finding religious patterns. Some cultures that may be considered Indigenous recognize a single supreme being; some recognize a variety of deities; and some do not bother themselves at all with such things. Among those Indigenous people who do believe in a god or god(s), there are some who pray to those higher powers and some

Traditions at a Glance

Numbers

Reliable statistical information on Indigenous religions is virtually impossible to come by. According to the United Nations, there are approximately 370 million Indigenous people in the world; on average perhaps 15 to 20 per cent practise their ancestral traditions, but the figures would be much higher in some communities and much lower in others.

Distribution

Indigenous religious traditions can be found almost everywhere: there are more than 5,000 distinct Indigenous cultures in some 90 countries around the world. By far the largest Indigenous populations are in Asia and Africa; fewer than 10 per cent live in Central and South America, approximately 2 per cent in North America and Oceania, and just a small fraction in Europe.

Recent Historical Periods

Written records of most Indigenous traditions begin only after contact with non-Indigenous people, so the only developments we can trace with any certainty are those that have taken place since then. It's important to keep in mind, however, that Indigenous religions had been changing and adapting for millennia before that time.

600–700	First contact between Muslims and Indigenous Africans
1450–1850	First contact between Europeans and Indigenous people of Africa, North America, and Oceania; development of Atlantic slave trade and other colonial practices that devastated Indigenous populations
1930–1960	Several governments begin to reduce restrictions on Indigenous people and religion
1960–present	Revival of many Indigenous traditions around the world; development of global pan-Indigenous movements

Founders and Leaders

Few pre-contact Indigenous traditions identify a human founder, although most attribute key features of their religious life to superhuman ancestors. Virtually all traditions also contain religious authority figures such as elders, as well as ritual specialists such as diviners and healers who invoke spiritual powers to aid their communities. In response to colonialism, several new movements were founded by specific people, such as Wovoka (Paiute) or Nongqawuse (Xhosa).

Deities

Indigenous traditions vary widely in their conceptions of deities. Some recognize a single, supreme deity as the source of all life and power. Others do not recognize such a being, but attribute creation to a series of gods, spirits, or ancestors. Almost all Indigenous traditions, however, believe that personal deities (or spirits or ancestors) have an active, ongoing impact on the world.

Authoritative Texts

Most pre-contact Indigenous religions passed along their sacred stories orally. These stories often include accounts of the creation of the present world and/or the origins of the community. Many also recount the ongoing activity of personal spiritual forces in the world. New tales continue to be told (and written), particularly about the trickster figure, and some post-contact movements (such as the Handsome Lake religion of the Iroquois) have their own sacred texts.

Noteworthy Teachings

Indigenous traditions are typically bound to specific places where important spiritual forces have manifested themselves (e.g., where acts of creation occurred). They also tend to be more concerned with what happens during life than after death; therefore they place greater emphasis on behaviour than on belief, and assess actions in terms of whether they benefit the community or cause it harm. Indigenous traditions frequently understand time as rhythmic rather than linear, linking the past to the present in a way that responds to changing circumstances; in this conception, the sacred interacts with the world on an ongoing basis, in ways that are both old and new.

who do not. Given the immense diversity of these traditions, how reasonable is it to group them all together?

That said, there is at least one definition that avoids some of these problems by focusing on two elements of central importance to cultures that have typically been considered Indigenous both by themselves and by others: kinship and location. To be 'Indigenous' (or its synonym, 'Aboriginal') in this sense is to belong to a community that is defined both by its members' geneological *relations* to one another, and by its connection to a particular *place*. The people who make up this community may or may not be the first or 'original' inhabitants of this place. They may not even inhabit it now. Yet they see themselves as belonging to it in critical ways, and they distinguish themselves from people who do not share this connection.

Putting our two terms together, then, 'Indigenous religion' refers to the beliefs, experiences, and practices concerning non-falsifiable realities of peoples who (a) identify themselves as Indigenous and (b) rely (at least in part) on kinship and location to define their place in the world.

Change and Syncretism

One other problem we need to consider from the outset is the fact that Indigenous religions no longer exist as they did before contact with the 'outside' world. This situation is partly the result of **syncretism**, the merging of elements from different religions. Many Native North American traditions have been deeply influenced by Christianity; some African rituals have incorporated elements of Islam; the sacred oral stories of Japanese Shinto became written texts under the influence of Chinese Buddhism. Does this mean that 'real' Indigenous religions have disappeared?

Definitely not. Change and syncretism have taken place among *all* religions throughout history. It is true that Indigenous religions today are not the same as they were a hundred, or five hundred, or ten thousand years ago. But the traditions as they exist now are no less authentic than they were in the past. The forms of Christianity practised in the contemporary United States have likewise been variously influenced by the religious beliefs and practices of many cultures, including African and Native American. These American forms in turn are quite different from the European Christianity that Martin Luther knew in the sixteenth-century, or the Hellenized Christianity that Paul taught in the first century—a tradition which of course began life as the Palestinian Judaism practised by Jesus. Like everything else in the world, religions change, and none of them are exactly what they used to be.

Map 6.1   North American Indigenous Language Families

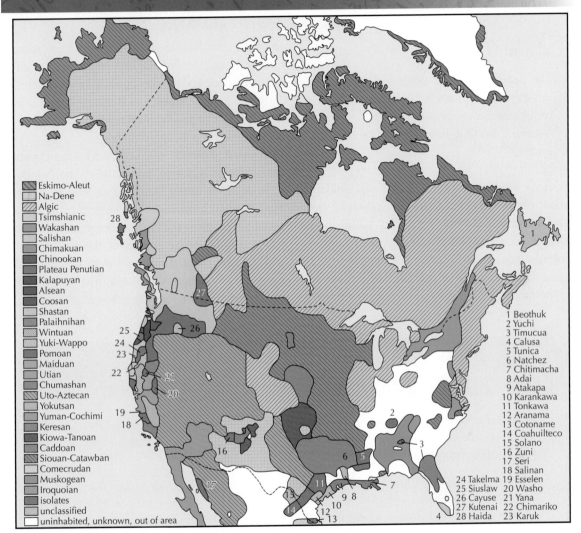

Eskimo-Aleut
Na-Dene
Algic
Tsimshianic
Wakashan
Salishan
Chimakuan
Chinookan
Plateau Penutian
Kalapuyan
Alsean
Coosan
Shastan
Palaihnihan
Wintuan
Yuki-Wappo
Pomoan
Maiduan
Utian
Chumashan
Uto-Aztecan
Yokutsan
Yuman-Cochimi
Keresan
Kiowa-Tanoan
Caddoan
Siouan-Catawban
Comecrudan
Muskogean
Iroquoian
isolates
unclassified
uninhabited, unknown, out of area

1 Beothuk
2 Yuchi
3 Timucua
4 Calusa
5 Tunica
6 Natchez
7 Chitimacha
8 Adai
9 Atakapa
10 Karankawa
11 Tonkawa
12 Aranama
13 Cotoname
14 Coahuilteco
15 Solano
16 Zuni
17 Seri
18 Salinan
19 Esselen
20 Washo
21 Yana
22 Chimariko
23 Karuk
24 Takelma
25 Siuslaw
26 Cayuse
27 Kutenai
28 Haida

This map shows the distribution of North American language families north of Mexico at the time of European contact (to the extent that scholars can determine). Language borders are given for the sake of clarity but were in reality much fuzzier than this image suggests. The map points to the tremendous diversity of Native North American cultures, since each language *family* may contain dozens of distinct *languages*. The family of Romance languages, for instance, contains Italian, French, Spanish, Portuguese, Romanian, and Catalan, as well as many regional languages.

These days, Indigenous religious practices can be found anywhere: **Anishinaubae** drumming ceremonies in Toronto, Canada; **Yoruba** funeral rites in London, England; and **Maori** purification rituals at the opera house in Sydney, Australia. Indigenous people and their religions may be connected to history, but they are not bound (or buried) by it.

The 'Patterns' section below will offer a basic overview of some additional features that seem to be common to many, if not all, Indigenous religions, both past and present. Before we can say much more about what Indigenous religions are, however, we first need to briefly consider what they are not. That means breaking down some of the key misconceptions about these religions that many non-Indigenous people have held, and often continue to hold.

'Us' and 'Them'

> The people who have control of your stories, control of your voice, also have control of your destiny, your culture.
> —Lenore Keeshig-Tobias, Anishinaubae (in Lutz 1991: 81)

Most of what most people know, or think they know, about Indigenous cultures has come from non-Indigenous people. This reality points to one further element common to Indigenous traditions: **colonialism**. The effects of colonialism will be discussed in some detail later in this chapter, but at the moment it is important to say a few words about one facet of colonialism: namely, academic work on Indigenous people and cultures.

Scholars with Weapons

Over the past few decades, there has been some opposition to the efforts of non-Indigenous scholars to 'explain' Indigenous people. The main concern is that, even though such theories often bear little relation to reality, they tend to have significant social and political influence.

A classic example was outlined by the **Oglala** Sioux lawyer, historian, and activist Vine Deloria, Jr, in his book *Custer Died for Your Sins: An Indian Manifesto*. Anthropologists seeking to explain the social ills plaguing the Oglala community ignored the 'real issue, white control of the reservation', and theorized that the people were simply 'warriors without weapons' (Deloria, Jr, 1988 [1969]: 90). In other words, the Oglala were incapable of

From *Custer Died for Your Sins*, by Vine Deloria, Jr (Oglala Sioux)

Looking at a variety of Native American issues including colonialism, religion, and even humour, and appearing in the early days of the American Indian Movement, Custer Died for Your Sins *remains one of the most influential works of Indigenous non-fiction ever written.*

From lack of roads to unshined shoes, Sioux problems were generated, so the anthros discovered, by the refusal of the white man to recognize the great desire of the Oglala to go to war. Why expect an Oglala to become a small businessman, when he was only waiting for that wagon train to come around the bend?

The very real and human problems of the reservation were considered to be merely by-products of the failure of a warrior people to become domesticated. . . . What use would roads, houses, schools, businesses, and income be to a people who, everyone expected, would soon depart on the hunt or warpath? . . .

The question of the Oglala Sioux is one that plagues every Indian tribe in the nation, if it will closely examine itself. Tribes have been defined as one thing, the definition has been completely explored, test scores have been advanced promoting and deriding the thesis, and finally the conclusion has been reached—Indians must be redefined in terms that white men will accept, even if that means re-Indianizing them according to the white man's idea of what they were like in the past and should logically become in the future (Deloria, Jr, 1988 [1969]: 92).

adapting to a market-economy lifestyle because, deep in their souls, they remained violently primitive. Accordingly, attention was diverted away from the pressing needs of the people in this community—credit, employment, housing, medical services—and focused instead on figuring out how to make 'modern Indians' out of them (Deloria, Jr, 1988 [1969]: 92).

Today it is not unusual for concern to be expressed when non-Indigenous scholars speak about Indigenous people. The main objection might seem to be that 'outsiders' lack the 'insider' knowledge and insight required to speak with authority about a particular community, culture, or tradition. As Deloria suggests, however, the real problem is not so much a matter of accuracy as it is one of *power* and *control*. The fact is that such scholars historically have been in a privileged position of authority to define Indigenous people not only to other non-Natives, but even to Native people themselves.

Unacceptable Terms

Another important problem with academic work about Indigenous people is that it tends to reinforce the idea that 'they' are different from 'us'. Thus the study of Indigenous religions has produced many terms and concepts that typically are applied only to those traditions, and not to world religions more broadly. Such terms include:

- animism
- fetish
- mana
- myth
- shaman
- taboo
- totem

This chapter will rarely use any of the above terms, in part because they are not necessary for an introductory understanding of Indigenous religions—but also because they are not used in reference to the other religions discussed in this book, even when they might be relevant. For example, the origin stories of Indigenous people are usually labelled 'myth', while the stories recounted in texts like the Hebrew Bible or Buddhist sutras are referred to as 'sacred literature'. Similarly, the rule that prohibits an African mask carver from coming into contact with a woman during his work would normally be called a 'taboo'; yet that term is not applied to the rule that forbids a priest from pouring unused communion wine down the drain. In short, it is important not to perpetuate the notion that Indigenous religions are of a different order from non-Indigenous religions.

'Primitives' and the Problem of History

> If I press any anthros in a prolonged discussion on exactly why they study Indians and other tribal peoples and why they study anthropology at all, I am almost always informed that tribal people represent an earlier stage of human accomplishment and that we can learn about our past by studying the way existing tribal peoples live.
> —Vine Deloria, Jr (1997: 214), Oglala Sioux

The More Things Change

For many years non-Indigenous people assumed that Indigenous people and cultures had changed very little over time—at least until the two groups met and colonization began. Until relatively recently, in fact, only anthropologists studied Aboriginal people: historians (including historians of religion) did not, because they assumed there was no Aboriginal history to look at.

The development of anthropology as an academic field can be traced to the European Enlightenment of the seventeenth and eighteenth centuries. Among other factors that led to this development, the Enlightenment was an age of exploration, during which reports were regularly sent back to Europe describing encounters with previously unknown cultures—cultures that were primarily oral in nature, for example, and that used simpler technology.

Assuming that such cultures had remained essentially unchanged from their beginnings, the Europeans referred to them as 'primitive' (from the Latin *primus*, meaning 'first'). For those people, history was assumed to have begun only when they first encountered 'modern/civilized' cultures.

This assumption was supported by the fact that the majority of Europeans at the time of contact were Christians who believed both in the (God-given) superiority of their own culture, and in the divine imperative to spread their religion to those who had not yet heard the gospel. Indigenous cultures were seen as ideal recipients of the Word of God, blank slates with no real history—or religion—of their own. This missionary worldview often went hand in hand with academic inquiry, and tended to colour the scholars' interpretation (in some cases, fabrication) of the details of Indigenous lives.

We know now that those long-standing assumptions about Indigenous cultures as static and ahistorical were completely untrue. All the available evidence shows that Indigenous peoples had dynamic, eventful histories long before they were 'discovered'. They have also been quite conscious of their histories, using stories, songs, or physical markings to record all manner of past events and conditions, changes in the culture or the land, family genealogies, remarkable natural phenomena, and so on.

A Persistent Problem

One example of the persistent notion that Indigenous cultures are 'primitive' is the tendency to think of them as non-literate. This notion is deeply problematic in several ways, which will be discussed in the next section ('Transmission'). For now I simply wish to state three points. First, writing is not inherently more 'advanced' than orality. Second, many Indigenous cultures (such as the Mayans) did use a form of writing before

contact with non-Indigenous people. Third, of course, the simple fact is that the vast majority of contemporary Indigenous cultures are fully literate; to ignore this fact is to continue to think of these cultures only in the past tense.

Another example of the tendency to regard Indigenous people as 'primitive' is the belief that they do not distinguish between the 'religious' and the 'non-religious' aspects of their lives—that they consider everything to be sacred. Sometimes this idea is supported by pointing to practices such as the **Navajo** enactment of the 'Blessingway' ceremony before a new dwelling is occupied (see p. 357). Commentators claim that for the Navajo, this ceremony transforms the home into a sacred site in a manner that renders every single act of daily life that occurs within it—eating, sleeping, arguing, laughing—equally sacred. This notion is both inaccurate and patronizing. Essentially, Indigenous people are understood to resemble young children, who often believe that everything—trees, stuffed animals, bits of clothing—is alive and sentient.

The fact is that Indigenous cultures are no less able than non-Indigenous ones to form distinctions in relation to the category of religion. Observant Muslims may take their prayer mats wherever they go, but they use the mats only at specific, established times; other times are not for prayer. Similarly, an Australian **Aborigine** knows the difference between a mountain that is sacred and one that is not, and that certain acts are performed only during particular ritual contexts, and not at any other time.

Many non-Indigenous scholars have come to realize that Indigenous cultures were (and are) just as complex and innovative as their own, and that the idea of the 'primitive' says much more about the person who holds it than about the people it is applied to. For example, it typically suggests a belief in one's own superiority. As such, it provides justification for the 'improvement' of Indigenous cultures through the introduction of writing, technology, or a market economy. In a similar fashion, those who romanticize 'primitive' cultures often do so as a way of expressing the belief that their own 'civilized' culture has alienated people from themselves, or from the natural world. Again, the concept tells us more about such people—and their culture—than it tells us about the people they imagine to be 'primitive'.

Still, the idea of the 'primitive' is a stubborn one, and it continues to have deeply negative consequences. It is one reason why many world religions courses still ignore Indigenous traditions altogether. It also helps to explain why literary scholars often ignore modern Indigenous writers, while anthropologists continue to pore over transcriptions of ancient tales. As the Anishinaubae author Daniel David Moses has commented: 'This image of traditional Native storytelling places Native people in the museum with all the other extinct species' (Moses and Goldie 1992: xiii).

Patterns

> The knowledge imposes a pattern, and falsifies . . .
> The only wisdom we can hope to acquire
> Is the wisdom of humility: humility is endless.
> —T.S. Eliot (1959: 23–4), Euro-American

Eating and Seeing

Dr Clare Brant, a **Mohawk** from southern Ontario, has recounted an experience from the 1970s when his band invited a group of James Bay **Cree** to a sporting tournament they were hosting (Ross 1992: 2–3). The Mohawk—who developed agriculture long before meeting Europeans—had a tradition of always setting out more food than their guests could eat, in order to demonstrate their wealth and generosity. Unfortunately the Cree had a very different tradition. Coming from a culture of hunting and gathering they were accustomed to living with scarcity; as a result they would eat all the food offered, thus showing their respect for the skill and generosity of those who provided it.

Of course these two traditions did not mix well. The Cree thought the Mohawk were deliberately forcing them to overeat to the point of severe discomfort, while the Mohawk thought the Cree were grossly self-indulgent and bizarrely determined to insult their hosts. Thus even though both groups were trying their best to be polite, each was seen by the other as intentionally disrespectful.

This story highlights two important points. First, it tells us that not all Indigenous cultures are alike. Even people who live very close to one another can sometimes think or act in very different ways. Consider that New Guinea and its surrounding islands contain more ethnographic diversity than anywhere else on earth, approximately one-fourth of the world's cultures (and languages and religions). It would be the height of arrogance for us to imagine that these cultures are essentially identical simply because the same label ('Indigenous') has been applied to them. The second point is that anyone attempting to understand another culture is in a position similar to that of the Mohawk and the Cree. The eyes we see through are the ones we have inherited from our own cultures, and so we must never forget to use them with caution and humility.

Common Elements

With the above points in mind, in the rest of this chapter we will try to identify some patterns and elements common to many (if not necessarily all) Indigenous religions. Among them are the following patterns:

- importance of orality
- connection to specific places
- emphasis on community and relationship
- sense of time as rhythmic
- greater emphasis on what happens during life than after death
- behaviour more important than belief
- authority of **elders**
- **complementary dualism**

- a view of the sacred as ongoing process rather than static revelation
- meaning and value of gender roles

This last point requires some comment at the outset. Traditionally, everyone in an Indigenous community had clearly defined roles, and often these roles were gendered. In general, hunting and warfare were male occupations, while food preparation and healing were the responsibility of women. Maori carvers were men, and Maori weavers were women. The **Bunu** Yoruba men were responsible for growing cotton, and the women for turning it into cloth. In this way, men and women were dependent on one another, and yet also independent in certain important ways.

A similar balancing can often be seen in regard to political and social power. The heads of most Indigenous societies have typically been male. Yet in many instances women have been inherently involved with any decisions that affect the entire community. And in some instances such decisions are normally made by women, then carried out by men.

It is also important to note that gender classification could be somewhat fluid in many Indigenous societies. Sometimes women might participate in men's work, and vice versa. Sexual roles and orientations could also be fluid. Accounts of men identifying as women, wearing female clothes and taking on women's roles in the community, are not unusual. There are also accounts of Indigenous women identifying as men and becoming hunters or warriors.

There is no definitive gender pattern with respect to kinship. Some Indigenous societies are matrilineal, tracing ancestry primarily through the mother's family, while others are patrilineal, focusing on the father. Similarly, important spirits and gods—including the supreme being—may be either male or female.

It was also not uncommon for Indigenous societies to separate the religious practices of women and men. Although the idea of gender-specific shrines and rituals seems simple enough, most studies of these societies have focused on the male practices only—whether because male scholars were not permitted to study the women's religious practices, or because they assumed that the Indigenous men were the most important members of their communities and that the men's religious practices were the only ones worth investigating. It is only relatively recently that scholars have begun to understand, and correct, this error.

Final Concerns

Most of the examples examined below come from three vast regions of the world—Africa, Oceania, and North America—though a few come from Asia and South America. It is important to emphasize that the very idea of the world as composed of these regions was a European invention: their diverse Indigenous inhabitants thought in much more local terms.

Still, this (mis-)perception of the world as made up of a few large regions, rather than thousands of small communities, can serve a useful political purpose for Indigenous people; for example, it gives them a stronger and more unified voice on issues such as land claims or self-government. These and many other matters of general concern are articulated in the 2007 United Nations Declaration on the Rights of Indigenous Peoples, a resolution that would not have been possible without a global understanding of what it means to be Indigenous.

Finally, regarding another kind of boundary, please note that the aspects of Indigenous religious life discussed in the next three sections—'Transmission', 'Practice', and 'Cultural Expressions'—are in reality not as cleanly demarcated as those headings might suggest. As is the case with all religions, there is a good deal of overlap. Oral stories are also ritual performances, for example, while rituals may require, or produce, works of art, which in turn may evoke stories that are at the heart of a community's religious tradition.

The last point to keep in mind is that the examples in this chapter represent only a tiny sample of the religious traditions of the world's Indigenous people. As such, they say as much about me as they do about Indigenous religions themselves. They represent what I know and what I think is important, arranged into the patterns that I see. An author with different views, experience, or knowledge would have made different choices, and would perhaps have constructed quite a different picture overall. All this is true of any work on any subject, of course, which is why a good dose of skepticism is always helpful. Nothing should be taken at face value. But this point is especially important in relation to Indigenous people, who have consistently been misrepresented, often with harmful results. I have done my best to avoid grievous errors, and I apologize upfront for any mistakes that appear despite these efforts.

❧ TRANSMISSION

The Power of Speech

> When you dig in the earth, you find stone and earthen implements, but not words—not the words of our ancestors. Words aren't buried in the ground. They aren't hanging from the branches of trees. They're only transmitted from one mouth to the next.
> —**Ainu** elder (in Shigeru 1994: 154–5)

Orality may not be a defining characteristic of Indigenous religions, but it remains a vital one for the vast majority of them. Even though some Indigenous cultures in the past did have writing, and virtually all of them have it now, most often the things of critical importance to them—including the values and beliefs that would be classified as religious—were (and are still) passed on orally. Typically this transmission happens through stories.

Writing versus Speaking

Unfortunately, many people in contemporary non-Indigenous societies continue to think of orality as 'primitive' and writing as a defining characteristic of 'civilization'. To these people, the development of writing represents a key evolutionary advance that allows for philosophical, abstract thought, while oral cultures remain attached to the present, material world, incapable of sophisticated analysis or extended self-reflection. Writing frees humans to develop science, whereas reliance on speaking alone limits us to magic.

Such views are both incorrect and self-interested, and (as mentioned above) they contribute to the construction of Indigenous cultures as primitive. Furthermore, all cultures—including all other world religions—have many crucial oral dimensions. Both the Qur'an and the stories of Jesus in the New Testament gospels were passed along in oral form for many years before they were recorded as texts.

In addition, although in non-Indigenous cultures writing is often assumed to be more important than speaking, things that are *said*, in certain contexts, still have a power that the written word does not. There is a world of difference between words on paper and those same words delivered by a skillful comedian, actor, preacher, or politician. Shakespeare's plays literally come alive when the words are voiced, while the sermons of Martin Luther King, Jr, affected the course of history in a way that would have been impossible had they appeared only in print.

There is also the obvious fact that books and newspapers are no longer the standard communications media in many non-Indigenous cultures today. People in these cultures tend to prefer video, film, or television—media that have more in common with Indigenous storytelling than they do with written texts. In keeping with the high value that non-Indigenous societies place on the written word, this preference is usually lamented as proof of civilization's decline.

There may be another explanation, though. Perhaps we are simply more easily and strongly engaged by narratives that are performed than by those that just sit on a page. Perhaps technology has finally caught up with modern living arrangements, and non-Indigenous people can once again readily experience stories in their full power, as Indigenous people have been experiencing them all along.

Stories

> I can recall lying on the earth and wondering what it was all about. The stars were a beautiful mystery and so was the place where the eagle went when he soared out of sight. Many of these questions were answered in story form by the older people. How we got our pipestone, where corn came from and why lightning flashed in the sky, were all answered in stories.
> —Luther Standing Bear, **Lakota** (in Beck et al. 1992 [1977]: 59)

Although in many cultures stories often serve as vehicles for the transmission of beliefs and values, it is not always easy to determine what is being passed along. This is as true for Indigenous tales as it is for the New Testament parables of Jesus. There are many factors that may undermine our ability to interpret the meaning of a particular story.

The Afterlife

Stories about the afterlife often appear to reveal a culture's beliefs about what literally happens following death, but the truth may be more complex. In a **Kewa** tale from Papua New Guinea, for instance, a young man goes into the bush and finds a tunnel that leads to the underworld. He recognizes many of his dead kinsmen there, living together in a large house. The men give him many tools and other valuable items to distribute among the people of his village, but warn him not to say where the items came from. The young man gives everything away but breaks his promise not to speak, and when he returns to the tunnel he finds it sealed.

There is also the Anishinaubae story of a man whose beloved dies just before they are to be married. Distraught, he journeys for months in search of the Path of Souls, so that he may see his love one last time. The people in his community try to dissuade him; they say the quest is hopeless, and that even if he were to succeed, seeing her would only bring more pain. When he finds the path at last, the old man who guards the land of the dead agrees to let him enter only if he promises to return to his regular life once his wish is fulfilled. The man agrees, journeys through a misty forest and across a turbulent river, and finds the woman he loved. Then he turns his canoe around and returns home as instructed, heartbroken but prepared now to continue with his life.

What do these stories tell us about the Kewa and the Anishinaubae? Do they believe that the dead live underground, or on the other side of a forest? Perhaps. But in each case the story seems to have more to do with relationships than with metaphysics. In the Kewa tale, ancestors help their descendants, and the young man helps his community but breaks his promise to his dead kinsmen; as a result, life becomes a little harder for everyone. Similarly, the Anishinaubae story depicts the difficulty and necessity of pushing through loss and returning to life after tragedy.

In short, these stories may tell us more about how we should live than about what happens when we die. Even the places where the dead are found have a this-worldly quality to them: our ancestors have not disappeared into some far-off, inaccessible alternative dimension, but are (relatively) nearby, and can affect our lives in direct, material ways.

Truth in Storytelling

As the above afterlife tales suggest, we should not assume that all stories are thought to be literally true by the people who tell them, or that the literal meaning of the story is the most important aspect. Some may well be understood to be fiction, or true only in a figurative or symbolic sense. The Kewa, for example, clearly distinguish between true stories called *ramani* (oral *history*) and fictional tales called *lidi* (oral *literature*). Among their many classifications of oral form, the **Nyanga** of Zaire similarly contrast *nganuriro* (true stories) with *karisi* (epic poems). Not all Indigenous people make this kind of distinction, of course, but many of them do.

We must also recognize that what others see as factual history may include elements that seem fictional to us. One Kewa story classified as *ramani*, for instance, concerns a leper who removes his diseased skin before attending a ceremonial dance, in order to appear healthy and beautiful.

To further complicate the issue, we must be careful about assuming that a particular story is an authorized or transparent reflection of a culture. It may be only a single storyteller's version, and the narrative details may reflect the teller's own preferences as much as they do the values or worldview of his or her culture. In other words, the story may be 'true' only to the person who is sharing it.

Context

Perhaps the most important point to remember about interpreting Indigenous stories is that we almost never encounter them in their natural form: spoken to a group in their original language. Instead, most of us read them silently, to ourselves, in a colonial language such as English, in a time and a place that are usually far removed from the circumstances in which they would normally have been performed. It is hard to overestimate the effect of these differences. It would be something like the contrast between reading 'Close your eyes and I'll kiss you . . .', and being part of the shrieking studio audience when the Beatles sang 'All My Loving' during their first American television appearance on *The Ed Sullivan Show* in February 1964.

The shift from community performance to solitary reading has the potential to transform the meaning of a story. The act of telling is itself a ritual—many stories are told only in a particular place and time, and only by certain people. Similarly, not all stories are for everyone—some may be just for women, some for men, and some for children. When we lose all this context and tradition, what else is lost?

Writing the Spoken

Writing also diminishes the capacity of an oral story to change with the teller and the time. The same story told by a cheerful woman on a sunny day will likely seem much different if it is told by an angry man on a rainy night. And the stories themselves can alter or evolve in response to changing circumstances or needs, producing significant variations. But what happens when a story is committed to ink on paper? Is it fixed in place forever?

Perhaps, in certain ways. But writing may be less 'fixed in place' than we tend to think. This fact becomes evident when we look at different written accounts of the same oral story. In various collections of Anishinaubae tales, for example, Basil Johnston has several times recounted the fight between the **trickster** Nanabush and his father Epingishmook (the spirit being who represents the West, old age, and death). In one version the two appear equally matched, and the battle ends only when Nanabush manages to cut his father with a piece of flint; in another, Epingishmook is the clear winner and stops the fight when Nanabush falls to the ground, exhausted and expecting to be killed by his father at any second.

Together, the two versions of the story emphasize that Nanabush is both a brave, strong warrior and a weak, cowardly one in a way that might not be so clear in a single story that showed him behaving differently in different circumstances. In addition, the stories together raise the question of what is true about them, whether literally or symbolically.

Multiple versions of the same story also pose an important challenge: how are we to make sense of them all? Generally speaking, every Indigenous culture has thousands of stories, and every story may have many variations. There is no possible way to do justice to such variety here. Instead, we will consider just a few examples of two types of stories: those that in some way explain origins, and those featuring 'trickster' figures. Doing so will highlight some of the points already mentioned, and also with luck show both the challenges and rewards of trying to understand what these stories may be saying to (and about) the people who tell them.

Origin Stories

No matter if they are fish, birds, men, women, animals, wind or rain. . . . All things in our country here have Law, they have ceremony and song, and they have people who are related to them.
—Mussolini Harvey, **Yanyuwa** elder (in Swain and Trompf 1995: 24)

North America

Among the best-known origin stories are the Native North American 'Earth Diver' tales. Several of their key elements are common to cultures across the eastern woodlands areas of Canada and the United States. Typically, the story begins with the world destroyed by flooding; then an animal or deity brings a bit of earth up from beneath the waters to begin rebuilding the land.

In one version Sky Woman, a spirit being, descends to earth during the flood. Seeing that she is pregnant, the giant turtle offers to let her rest on his back. She then asks the other animals to dive for some soil. Many try but fail, and they drown. In the end, it is one of the lowliest animals, the muskrat—who has been ridiculed by the others for offering to help—that succeeds.

Sky Woman breathes life into the soil, which spreads across the turtle's back to become what is now called North America. Her breath infuses the earth with the spirit of life, nourishment, shelter, and inspiration for the heart and mind. She gives birth to twins—the ancestors of the people who tell this story—and she awards joint stewardship of the land to all beings who live there, whether human, spirit, or animal.

Africa

The African **Dogon** people also refer to a form of pregnancy in their origin stories, which tell how the supreme being, Amma, created the world (and humanity) essentially by accident. Out of loneliness, Amma transformed himself into a womb holding four new beings called Nummo; two of these were mostly male but partly female, and the other two were mostly female but partly male. Before their 60-year gestation period was complete, one of the males became impatient to be with his sister, and tore away part of the womb searching for her. This torn part became the earth.

Life began when Amma sacrificed the sister, scattering the pieces of her body on the ground in order to purify the earth. After the departure of their transgressing brother, the two remaining Nummo clothed the earth with vegetation and infused it with a creative, universal life force called *nyama*. Amma and the Nummo also created eight beings who were placed in separate celestial chambers and prohibited from eating a certain type of grain. They became lonely and their food ran out, however, and so they gathered together and cooked the forbidden grain. When they were expelled from the heavens and crashed to earth, the world as we know it was created, including human life, culture, and speech.

Australia

The origin stories of the Australian Aborigines centre around events that occurred in a time and place unique to Australian conceptions, a time that was famously (mis-)translated as '**The Dreaming**' by nineteenth-century anthropologists; a more accurate translation might be 'The Uncreated'. Anthropologists understand The Dreaming as archaic time; however, Aborigines themselves have traditionally given the impression that the events of The Dreaming occurred just a few generations before their own time. In other words, those events are out of reach of living memory, but they are not fixed in time. They are also recent enough to remain vital and meaningful to the communities that speak of them.

Unlike most Africans and Native North Americans, Australian Aborigines generally do not recognize a single divine authority from whom all life, values, rules, and so on, derive. Instead, stories of origin usually concern the first ancestors, whose actions shaped both the physical world and the cultural practices of their descendants.

There are countless stories of The Dreaming, but many tales reflect some basic patterns. 'Love Magic', for instance, explains how several elements important to the community—including the love magic ritual and a specific sacred site—originated in the actions of two ancestors, while reinforcing its prohibitions on incest and rape. The metamorphosis of the ancestors into physical formations on the land is typical of Dreaming tales.

Meanings

What do these origin stories mean? It is certainly possible that they were (and perhaps still are) understood to be straightforward historical accounts. I have met many Native people in Canada who refer to North America as 'Turtle Island' and who regard it as sacred. But to my knowledge none of them think that the continent was actually formed from a clump of mud on the back of a giant reptile.

'Love Magic' (Australian Aborigine)

Ngarlu *has three meanings in this story from central Australia. It is the flower of the* ngarlkirdi *(witchetty grub tree) as well as the name of a sacred site and of the ceremonies performed there. A 'subsection' is a kinship group, while 'hairstring' is string made from human hair, used to make many different items, from belts to wrappings for spears.*

There was a Dreaming man named *Linjiplinjipi* of the Jungari subsection at this site. He had adorned his body with *Ngarlu* and was spinning hairstring. The whirling sound of his spinning tool [made of crossed sticks] attracted a woman of the Ngapangardi subsection [and therefore his mother-in-law]. He climbed the hill and as he was watching her she stopped to urinate. Sexually aroused, he continued to attract her with the noise. Finally, he caught her, forced her legs apart and raped her. Upon ejaculation, however, she closed her legs and her tight vagina dismembered his penis.

Today, at *Ngarlu* her vagina remains transformed into rock and the severed stone-penis is still embedded in it. *Linjiplinjipi* himself, in agony, went to the other side of the hill where he turned into a large boulder which has paintings upon it depicting his hairstring cross and his erect penis. *Yilpinji* ['love magic'] is performed modelled on *Linjiplinjipi's* methods of attracting his mother-in-law, using sticks from *Ngarlu* and adorning the torso with the flowers of the witchetty grub tree (Swain and Trompf 1995: 22–3).

In any case, we should also consider what other aspects of these stories might be important. First, as in the Kewa and Anishinaubae 'afterlife' stories, relationships are central. Creation in each case results from a desire for community or companionship. Similarly, the central beings in each story are the ancestors of the people to whom it belongs.

Second—and along the same lines—the stories typically underline the inherent relatedness of all aspects of existence. Just as the Australian Aborigines are related to The Dreaming ancestors who are related to the landscape, for example, all of existence is connected along a network of various pathways and intersections. The world in its entirety is infused with the spirit of the ancestors. Specific communities, however, would be more strongly joined to certain stories, and therefore to the specific elements of those stories (locations, rituals, beliefs, etc.).

Third, origin stories typically do not imagine the beginning of time. Instead, they presuppose the existence of the universe, and focus on the origin of certain elements within it—language, culture, landscape—that remain present, connecting us to the actions of our ancestors. Past and present are forever linked, and stories of origin remain deeply meaningful to our contemporary lives.

Finally, it is worth noting that these stories rarely present a simple, idealized picture of nature. They tell us that the world we live in is (at least in part) the product of violence: the result of a torn womb, an attempted rape, a devastating flood. The Dogon tradition associates the creation of humans with loneliness and disobedience, while in North America many animals sacrificed themselves in their efforts to help Sky Woman and her baby. In other words, order, creation, and life in Indigenous origin stories are almost always connected to chaos, destruction, and death.

And, speaking of chaos . . .

Tricksters

'You know what I noticed? Nobody panics when things go according to plan, even if the plan is horrifying. If tomorrow I tell the press that, like, a gangbanger will get shot, or a truckload of soldiers will be blown up, nobody panics. Because it's all part of the plan. But when I say that one little old mayor will die, well then *everyone loses their minds.*'

—Joker, in *The Dark Knight* (2008)

The concept of the trickster was developed by scholars to categorize a certain type of character that appears in the stories of many cultures, including those of the non-Indigenous 'West'; Loki was the trickster in Norse mythology, while the ancient Greeks had Hermes. Although the people who told these stories did not conceive of such characters as 'tricksters', and many trickster figures do not actually seem to have very much in common, the label has stuck.

Tricksters are sometimes referred to as 'culture heroes', typically because they are the central figures in many (if not most) of a community's stories, and also because they often serve to teach the most important lessons in history, ethics, and relationships. Once again, however, the ways in which these lessons are transmitted are not always simple or obvious.

Shape-changers

As their name implies, tricksters are hard to pin down. For one thing, they can usually shape-shift, and many tricksters are explicitly 'zoomorphic'— that is, they take the form of animals. Examples include

- badger (Japan)
- coyote (North America)
- crow (North America)
- fox (South America)

- rabbit (Africa and North America)
- raven (North America)
- spider (Africa)
- tortoise (Africa)
- wolf (South America)

In addition, many tricksters can change genders. Invariably the change is from male to female, and in some cases it is biological, though in others the trickster simply puts on women's clothing and uses prosthetics to mimic female sexual

'Red Willows' (Anishinaubae)

Nanabush was wandering in the far north. He was hungry. Nanabush was always hungry.

He was with his mother at the time. That old lady is known by many names. Some call her 'Dodomum' or 'Dodum'; others call her 'Gushiwun' or 'Gushih.'

They wandered until Nanabush chanced to meet a bear. 'Ha!' he announced. 'I'm going to eat you!'

'Oh no you don't,' replied the bear. 'I will fight back if you try to kill me. Get out of here, Nanabush.'

Nanabush would not leave. 'Listen,' he pleaded, 'I'm hungry. Can't you see that? I'm hungry. I've eaten next to nothing for about three days. Maybe four days! I'm going to kill you.'

They started fighting somewhere over there, somewhere near Kenora. They battled tooth and nail. They fought in a number of different places along the way, even where Sault Ste Marie now stands. At the rapids. That really happened. That was all land then. At that time there was no channel of water flowing there.

First, Nanabush would hit the bear; then the bear would hit Nanabush. One time, Nanabush threw the bear so hard against the ground he broke the earth, and water began to flow through. That in fact is the reason the water now flows past Sault Ste Marie.

Finally, Nanabush said to his mother, 'You go on ahead and stay there. When I get there too, I will kill this bear.' As soon as the word was given, she was gone.

She could hear them battling in the distance. At one point, the bear sent Nanabush flying with such force that he landed on his mother, causing her to fall backwards onto her rump. That is why the lake there is called 'The Old Lady Sat Down'.

They fought all along the way. The evidence of it is still there. At the place that is now called Sudbury they hurled rocks at one another.

Where they pulled boulders up from the earth, ore was later found. Where they dragged each other along the ground, depressions were made in the land.

Eventually, Nanabush killed the bear, in the general vicinity of Parry Sound.

Meanwhile, his mother came along behind, carrying supplies. She made a fire and put a pot of water over it. Nanabush butchered the bear. When it was cooked, he ate and ate. But he ate too much and very soon suffered the runs.

'Oh!' He ran over there. 'Ah!' Such discomfort. He could not stop going to the toilet. When he sat down to defecate, blood also flowed. He couldn't find anything to use to wipe himself, so he grabbed a sapling and used that. Then he stuck the sapling—with the blood and feces on it—into the earth, somewhere near Parry Sound.

A red willow grew at that spot. Its colour came from the blood of Nanabush.

That is how the red willows came to be (Johnston 1995: 33–7).

characteristics. In one Cree story, Wichikapache physically transforms himself into the perfect woman in order to teach a lesson to a conceited young man, who refuses to marry because he cannot find anyone good enough for him. The trickster even becomes pregnant, but when the children are born as wolf cubs the trick is revealed and the young man is humiliated.

The various changes in the trickster's outer form are reflected in other inconstancies. Tricksters are typically related to both the spirit and material/human worlds; though in general they are more than human, they are almost always less than gods. They can be selfless or greedy, kind or cruel, funny or deadly serious. They may be fools, but they may also reveal fools. And while very often their behaviour is scandalous, explicitly violating the social order, this is not always a bad thing. Sometimes the social order *needs* to be violated, and sometimes the most effective way to make this point is through laughter.

Self and Others

So how do we know when to imitate the trickster's example and when to take the opposite course? Often the main clue is the trickster's motivation: whether a particular action is intended to help others or is driven by self-interest alone. In other words, our judgment depends on understanding what is good for the community. One of the most common scenarios centres on the male trickster's efforts to satisfy his enormous sexual appetite. These efforts often result in some kind of disaster, either for the trickster himself or for his victim(s). Such stories testify to the understanding that unrestrained (male) sexuality poses a serious threat to society.

In contrast, the Anishinaubae story 'Red Willows' shows Nanabush displaying obvious consideration for his mother. He tells her to get out of harm's way while he fights a bear, and he keeps his promise to rejoin her when the battle is done. Presumably these are admirable qualities, as he defeats the bear and assuages his (and his

mother's) hunger. However, he also appears to be exclusively concerned with his own hunger, and he shows no self-restraint when eating the bear—a transgression for which he immediately pays a painful price.

Like many trickster stories, 'Red Willows' explains the origins of certain elements of the physical world that was home to the community connected to the tale, from the river at Sault Ste Marie to the rugged terrain around Sudbury. And since those (colonial) towns are named, we know that this is either a modern retelling of an old tale or one of the new stories of Nanabush that continue to appear. Finally, we learn that the red willows got their colour from Nanabush's bloody feces. Here we have another wonderful illustration of a view of nature that is not naively idealized, and that recognizes holistic connections between the beautiful and the ugly or painful.

'Red Willows', by contemporary Anishinaubae artist David Johnson (with permission of the Royal Ontario Museum).

Chaos and Order

Like the origin stories, trickster tales such as 'Red Willows' also attribute the creation of aspects of our world to violent, destructive activity. In other stories the trickster invents the bow and arrow; breaks the teeth in women's vaginas to make intercourse possible; initiates pregnancy and menstruation; and introduces death. Despite his association with chaos, then, the trickster also brings a kind of order to the world.

The Yoruba trickster, Eshu, is an explicit example of such activity. Eshu delights in chaos, and is constantly playing pranks on the Yoruba in the hope that disorder will result. But his tricks work only when the people, forgetting the importance of community stability, become greedy or lazy, or behave stupidly. In one story Eshu wears a special hat, black on one side and red on the other, while walking between two friends; each seeing only one side of the hat, the friends fight over what colour it is and wind up bitter enemies for no reason at all.

Thus trickster stories, like tricksters themselves, can play many roles: they can show us how we *should* behave, or should *not*; they can help to explain the origins of the world, and connect a community more deeply to specific locations; and whether they are funny or scary, thoughtful or silly, simple or complex, they are almost always entertaining and highly provocative. They embody the extremes of humanity, and all of our contradictions: our weaknesses and strengths; our selfishness and compassion; our humiliations and our triumphs. But it is in the specific ways in which they embody humanity that tricksters are critical to understanding the people who tell their stories, as well as the people to whom the stories are told.

In this regard it is worth noting again that, while there is greater gender diversity in newer stories, almost all the traditional trickster figures we know of are male. Here too, one reason may be that trickster stories were, until relatively recently, recorded only by male European academics. It is possible that those men had no interest in female trickster stories. It is also possible that if such stories did exist, they were the preserve of women and the male scholars never inquired about them, presuming that any important cultural knowledge was carried by the community's men.

On the other hand, it may be that most of the trickster's typical activities—hunting, travelling, unrestrained sex—were in fact associated mainly or even exclusively with men. If so, we might be justified in supposing that even though tricksters are specialists in social transgression, gender roles may represent one boundary that (until recently) even these cagey figures have had difficulty transcending.

🦁 PRACTICE

Ritual

> If you ask what is the greatest thing
> I will tell you
> It is people, people, people.
> —Maori proverb (in Webber-Dreadon
> 2002: 258)

Rituals perform the same functions in Indigenous cultures that they do in every culture. They identify and remind us of what is important in life—or more precisely, what the culture we live in understands to be important. In religious terms, their explicit purpose is to communicate in some way with gods, ancestors, or spirits. Ultimately, though, rituals are rooted in human needs and relationships.

Varieties

Around the world, followers of virtually every religious tradition affirm their faith through the performance of daily domestic rituals. Many of these rituals involve food—one of the most common and vital elements of life. Thus Jews and Muslims observe kosher and halal regulations; many Buddhists set a portion of each meal aside in a shrine for their ancestors; and the Anishinaubae traditionally put a small amount of food in a dish for the spirits. Australian Aborigines practise rites aimed at maintaining the balance and abundance of the animal species they rely on for food; these ceremonies are often very simple, and may involve nothing more than singing the song of the ancestor while rubbing a pile of stones.

Other rituals are more complex and much less frequent, marking critical moments in the life of individuals (birth, marriage, death), the community (departure of a powerful leader, liberation from slavery, completion of a great project), or the natural world (annual cycles, great disasters, rich harvests). Sometimes these rituals mark transformations, and sometimes they help to bring transformation about. It is this less frequent, more dramatic type of ritual that will be discussed in detail in this section.

Meaning and Structure

When someone who has been ill recovers after a ritual healer asks an ancestor spirit to remove the illness, does the healer (or the patient, or the community) believe that the illness has actually been removed by the spirit? Those of us who are not Indigenous may ask the same questions about our own rituals. To what extent does a young Jewish girl change objectively, at the moment of her Bat Mitzvah, into an adult woman? How many Catholics believe they drink the literal blood of Christ when they take communion?

It seems evident that many people, past and present, have believed in the literal truth of their religious stories and rituals. Once again, though, we often separate Indigenous traditions from other world religions by treating their ritual practices as 'magic' rather than 'religion', implying that 'they' believe in things that obviously are not true, whereas 'we' do not. In fact, many Indigenous and non-Indigenous people alike believe in the literal truth of at least some of their religious traditions, and many others in both groups take a more figurative approach.

In either case, when we look closely at the rituals of any Indigenous culture, what we find is a system of formal yet creative activities through which the members of the community relate to the world and to one another. Such activities tap into the people's deepest beliefs about the origins of the world, the existence of order, and the creation of life. Repeating them therefore serves in some way to recreate key aspects of the world, of order, of life. In this sense, we can see ritual as an indicator both of the human need for meaning and structure in a world that is often random and frightening, and of the human capacity to create such meaning and structure.

Rites of Passage

All people who go to the sacred bush benefit from it. They may be observers; they may be priests; they may be the initiate. Only we concentrate on the initiate most. Yet everybody is involved, particularly the priests, for there is a belief . . . that we are reborning ourselves. Even we priests, we are getting another rebirth.

—Ositola, Yoruba (in Drewal 2002: 133)

The Journey

Many cultures around the world regard life as a journey or quest; this perspective forms the central metaphor of a huge number of pop/rock songs ('Like a Rolling Stone', 'Proud Mary', 'Born to Run', 'Road to Nowhere'), and is also indicated by the sacred Yoruba text in the box on the next page. Rituals highlight points along the way, but they also constitute journeys on their own. This understanding is most clearly evident in rites of passage, rituals that explicitly mark a change of state and that often involve *literal* journeys.

Typically, such rituals take participants away from their community—the site of social order and familiarity—to a new place with unfamiliar rules, where some sort of transformation occurs. The participant then returns home, often with a physical change, such as a tattoo, scar, or missing

Yoruba Verse

This verse from the sacred literature of the Yoruba (known as the Odu Ifa) describes life as a quest.

A small child works his way off the edge of his sleeping mat.
A bird soars high above it all.
They divined for our elderly people,
When they were preparing to leave heaven to go to the world.
They said, what are we going to do?
They asked themselves, where are we going?
We are going in search of knowledge, truth, and justice.
In accordance with our destiny,
At the peak of the hill
We were delayed.
We are going to meet success.
We will arrive on earth knowledgeable.
We will arrive on earth in beauty.
We are searching for knowledge continuously.
Knowledge has no end (Drewal 2002: 129).

body part to symbolize their new mode of being. While away, he or she exists in a kind of in-between state, after the death of the old self but before the birth of the new, neither the person they once were nor the person they will become.

In South Africa, for example, young **Pondos** are moved into a special, separate hut during their long initiation to become sangomas, or sacred healers. If they go into town before the ritual is completed, their faces and bodies must be covered in white—the colour of transformation throughout most of Africa—to indicate that they are in the midst of a journey between the realms of the living and the ancestors (see photo on p. 323). This initiation is most often undertaken by women, and is complete only when the initiates receive a dream of a particular animal, the incarnation of the ancestor who will authorize them to become a sangoma.

Many Anishinaubae undertake a similar initiation, known as a **vision quest**. After years of guidance and preparation for this ritual, a young man on the verge of adulthood travels far from home to a designated site in the wilderness where the spirits dwell. Typically, this is the first time he has ever been completely alone in his life.

The boy has no food, only water. He endures cold and hunger, as well as fear of the wilderness and of harmful unseen forces. With luck, the spirits will give him dreams or visions that reveal his true self and the role he is to play in his community. After several days, an adult male will arrive with food and take the initiate home. If the religious leader determines that true spirit visions were indeed experienced during the quest, the ritual is complete and the boy is accepted into the group as an adult man.

Behind the Curtain

The rite of passage for Wiradjuri males in eastern Australia also involves a literal journey, along with fear and pain. At the appointed time, the women and children of the village are covered with branches and blankets. A roaring sound is heard, identified as the voice of the spirit being Daramulun, and burning brands are thrown about. Daramulun takes the boys away to the bush, where he will devour them and regurgitate them back as men. The boys are led away looking only at the ground, with the roaring all about them. While they are covered with blankets, each one has an incisor tooth knocked out. Then fires appear again and the boys are told that Daramulun is coming to burn them.

At the height of their terror, however, the boys receive a shock. Their blankets are removed and the men of the village reveal that they have been acting as Daramulun all along. It was the men who took the boys' teeth, who set the fires, and who made the voice of the spirit being using bullroarers. It is much like Toto pulling aside the curtain to show Dorothy that the Great and Powerful Oz is simply an old man, except in this case the deceivers reveal themselves.

When the boys return to the village, therefore, they are truly transformed. They have been initiated into a secret (male) knowledge about the spirit world. They have also formed a bond with one another through their shared experiences of fear and revelation. When they return to the village they do so as men, are given new adult names, and take up residence outside their parents' homes.

In revealing that the initiates have been tricked, doesn't this ritual expose the community's religious beliefs as false? Not necessarily. Sam Gill argues that its point is to demonstrate that what is genuinely meaningful lies beyond the surface of reality, beyond what we can see, hear, feel, taste, and touch. By exposing their trickery, the men produce 'a disenchantment with a naive view of reality, that is, with the view that things are what they appear to be' (Gill 1982: 81). In this way, the boys experience a true death of their old selves—their youthful view of the world.

Sacrifice

We are imitating what the gods or holy people have done. It is a return to the beginning.
—Blackhorse Mitchell, Navajo (in Beck et al. 1992 [1977]: 76)

In Mel Gibson's film *Apocalypto* (2006), Mayan priests cut out the beating hearts of captured villagers, cook them, and make offerings of them to appease the gods and end the famine that is afflicting the people. Although it is true that some Indigenous cultures did perform human sacrifices, there are still several problems with the scenario presented by Gibson. Aside from the historical inaccuracies that some scholars have pointed out, *Apocalypto* perpetuates common misunderstandings about the nature of sacrifice itself. These issues become clearer when we consider some real examples of the practice.

Japan, North America, Africa

Sacrificial rituals are extremely common among Indigenous cultures. At one time the central religious ceremony of the Ainu of northern Japan, for example, was bear sacrifice. They would capture a young cub, raise it for two or three years, shoot it with ceremonial arrows, and then finally kill it. The carcass was specially prepared—often the head was emptied out and filled with flowers—and then the animal was cooked and eaten by the entire village.

Among the Aboriginal peoples of the North American plains, the **Sun Dance** is an annual ritual lasting several days. Inside a specially created lodge, people who have vowed to take part in the ritual dance to exhaustion while the community provides support and encouragement. In some cultures, such as the Sioux, the Sun Dance includes self-sacrifice: male dancers fast, pierce their bodies, and attach themselves to a pole through holes in their chest or back. They may be partially or entirely suspended off the ground, and they dance until they pass out or their fastenings tear loose.

In Africa, the **Nuer** regularly sacrifice an ox for purposes that range from celebration to healing to atonement for moral transgressions. The **Xhosa** people perform a similar but more complex ritual when a young woman falls ill and a **diviner** determines that she is being punished by an ancestor spirit. To restore good relations between the woman's home and the ancestor, a cow is consecrated and then speared. The cry of the animal opens up the path of communication with the spirit world, along which the words of the ritual elder requesting help can travel. Inside the woman's home, a special piece of the animal is cooked. One part is given to the woman, who sucks it and throws it to the back of the house as a sign that she is throwing away her illness. The woman is given a second piece of meat, which she holds while being chastised for behaving in a manner displeasing to the ancestor(s). She consumes the meat and is congratulated for having 'eaten the ancestor'. Then the rest of the cow is cooked and eaten by the entire community in group celebration.

Community and Ritual Action

When we compare these rituals to the sacrifice in *Apocalypto*, two major differences become clear. First, there is no real social significance to the film's ritual, no communal participation beyond a sense of general bloodlust. For the Ainu, the Sioux, and the Xhosa, however, communal participation is crucial. Even though the sacrifice itself is performed by designated people, everyone becomes involved in some way, whether by providing guidance and support to the dancers during their ordeal or simply by sharing in the group meal. The ritual ultimately brings people together. By contrast, the priests in the film are portrayed as corrupt and the ritual ultimately helps to tear the community apart.

The second difference is that *Apocalypto* presents the sacrifice as a simple offering made to the gods or spirits in return for some reward. The Mayans in the film want food, and apparently the gods want human hearts—it's a simple exchange. Yet in many cultures, the object of sacrifice itself is clearly not of such central importance. When necessary, the Nuer can replace the ox with a cucumber. Similarly, if no suitable cow is available to the Xhosa, beer is used instead.

The fact that such substitutions are possible suggests that the item used is far less meaningful than the ritual actions themselves. When the Xhosa do sacrifice a cow, for example, why don't they just kill and eat it? Why go through all the complex stages? What appears to be primarily at stake here is the woman's behaviour in relation to notions of social order set down by the ancestors and reinforced by (male) ritual elders. The community thus shares both in naming the transgression that led to her illness, and in the meal generated by the ritual that heals her.

Why is a special lodge built for the Sun Dance? The creation of the lodge replicates the creation of the world, and is accompanied by songs that tell of this creation. The pole used in the dance is a newly-cut cottonwood tree; in its state between life and death and its physical positioning at the centre of the lodge, it links this world to the world of the spirits. Physically attached to this tree, the dancers are thus also tied to the spirits and to the earliest times.

Why did the Ainu fill the bear's head with flowers? Because, in their eyes, the animal was not a regular bear but the mountain god in disguise, and the ritual killing of his bear form was necessary to release the god's spirit back to his own realm. The Ainu were not offering a bear to the god; rather, from primordial times onward the god became a bear, over and over again, as a gift to the Ainu. The flowers were an expression of the community's gratitude.

In each case, the ritual actions relate to the spiritual and sometimes physical establishment of the community, or of the world itself. Like rites of passage, sacrificial practices thus play a key role in (re-) creating order and meaning. In re-enacting ancient events, these rituals clearly join people to the past, and yet they also respond to current situations and needs. Thus they reflect and re-establish the common Indigenous sense of time as rhythmic, neither purely linear nor entirely cyclical. Individuals and communities are always changing over time; nothing ever repeats exactly. But in the course of their journeys, people do need to be replenished, and through ritual they return to a source that sustains them.

✥ CULTURAL EXPRESSIONS

The array of art forms traditionally produced by Indigenous cultures is extraordinarily rich and diverse, including (among others) architecture, songs, baskets, clothing, statues, paintings, drums, pipes, mats, headdresses, amulets, masks, and tapestries. In each community, some art forms will exist almost entirely for religious purposes; some will be entwined with religion at specific times only; and others may have very little to do with religion.

What You See

> If you don't live the things that go with it, then it's only a design. It's not a *moko* [traditional Maori tattoo].
> —George Tamihana Nuku, Maori (in Mitchell 2003)

With a good deal of Indigenous creative work, what you see is not at all what you get. In some cases, you don't see (or get) anything at all by the time the work is done, because the piece has been consumed by the same process that brought it into being.

A key element of the *malagan* death rituals of Papua New Guinea, for example, is the creation and burning of delicate sculptures made from fibre, wood, bark, and feathers. Likewise, the beautiful and complex sand paintings created by the Navajo must be erased the day they are made if they are to perform their healing function; through ceremony, the cosmic pictures become identified with the patient's sickness, and it is only through the sand painting's destruction that health can be restored.

Other works, like those discussed below—cloth, totem poles, **mbari** shrines—are created from natural materials that decay over time. The works are very often understood as living things, which can (and should) dissolve back into the world when their time is done. Even when the work remains, it may still be relatively bereft of meaning (and life) when we look at it, especially if it is completely removed from its native context. Without knowing what an African mask or Native American basket is used for, and why, we can hardly have any idea what it represents.

In this respect, 'art' in Indigenous cultures is fundamentally about relationships. There is a network that connects an object to the person or people who created it; to the ritual in which it is used; to the community it is meant to serve; to the stories that underlie their worldview. These relationships are in many ways vital to the culture in question, and, depending on the context, some or even all aspects of the network—object, creation, ritual, stories—may be considered religious. To illustrate the varied, complex ways in which Indigenous art forms are related to Indigenous religion, we will consider three examples: weaving, carving, and building.

Weaving

It all starts from the beginning with roots. How the basket makes itself. Like two people meeting. . . . What I'm talking about

when I'm talking about my baskets is my life, the stories, the rules, how this things is living, what they do to you.
—Mabel McKay, **Pomo** (in Sarris 1992: 23–4)

The relationships that are central to Indigenous creative work are well symbolized by weaving. To weave is to intertwine, to connect. Even in modern English, we speak of the 'social fabric', the 'warp and weft' of history, friendships, or community life. In most cultures, traditional weaving is a social activity; weavers work together, helping (and watching) one another, sharing stories, passing on their skills to younger generations. In addition, the products of weaving often have both a religious meaning and a practical purpose. These functions reflect and reinforce the bonds among the people of a community, as well as the bonds between the people and their environment, their ancestors, and their gods.

Sacred Thread

In Maori tradition, all weavers are female. A prospective weaver is selected as a baby and a special prayer is spoken over her. As she grows up, she learns from her mother, her aunts, her grandmothers, until the art becomes a natural part of her. But her destiny is not fixed. The more she learns, the more the women *discourage* her from weaving. This is a test. The girl must persevere, to demonstrate her true commitment. When her elders are satisfied, she is at last initiated into the *whare pora* ('house of weaving'), which is not a physical building but the collective of weavers in the community. Only then does she come to understand why the weft used to create the pattern and design in Maori weaving is *te aho tapu*—'the sacred thread'.

The *whare pora* women are the caretakers of the weaving traditions. These include not only the physical techniques and skills, but the rituals that are essential to every aspect of the craft. For example: materials used in weaving must be specially prepared; sex is prohibited the night before dyeing fibres; no food is allowed during weaving; fine garments must be woven during daylight; and no strangers can view any work until it is completed.

To weave is to be part of an ancient trust, a gift brought to humanity by Niwareka, daughter of the lightning god Uetonga. The patterns and techniques that she gave the Maori people became the foundation of all future works. The goddess of weaving is Hine-te-iwaiwa, who also presides over healing and childbirth and is often associated both with the moon and with menstruation.

The traditional colours used in Maori weaving—black, red, and white—symbolize the basic

A Maori girl performing a *poi* (a mainly female ritual that involves swinging a ball on a cord) and wearing a traditional dress woven of the three sacred colours: black, red, and white (Seth Mazow).

forces of creation. Black represents the realm of potential being, the darkness from which the earth emerged; white represents the process of coming into being, the energies that make life possible; and red represents the realm of being and light, the physical world itself. The sacred thread thus runs not only through all garments, which join the members of the community together, but also through time, linking past and present, and through the various realms of existence, entwining people in the divine nature of the cosmos itself.

Undying Cloth

Of course it not just the process of weaving that has religious significance, but the final product itself. Around the world, a key function of clothing is to declare who we are, how we fit into the 'social fabric'. Are we Muslim or Hindu, artist or lawyer, man or woman, heterosexual or homosexual, poor or rich? And yet clothing literally has two sides: it can hide as much as it reveals, helping us to construct a public face while obscuring certain aspects of both our bodies and our identities.

Lady Gaga is a great (if perhaps extreme) example of the double-sided nature of clothing. Her costumes and masks hide her private self from view, but reveal those aspects of her identity that she wishes to make public. Part of the woman is Lady Gaga the performance artist, but another part is Stefani Germanotta, graduate of a Catholic private school in Manhattan. In addition, Gaga's apparel announces her individuality while also showing her connection and indebtedness to a community of modern pop figures that includes Madonna and Michael Jackson, and even—through the crown she wears in her 'Bad Romance' video—the artist Jean-Michel Basquiat.

In virtually all societies, special cloths are also associated with important rituals—baptisms, graduations, weddings, funerals. These cloths help to set such occasions apart from everyday life. Ideally, the outer form of the cloth reveals (rather than hides) one's true self at these moments, as it announces to the community that a genuine inner

change has taken place. Given that rites of passage represent a symbolic death and rebirth, it is fitting that the Bunu Yoruba, of central Nigeria, consider the special cloth worn for them to be a kind of womb, enveloping the body as if it were a fetus waiting to be born.

The Bunu have a key saying in this regard: 'Cloth only wears, it does not die' (Renne 1995: 9). The saying reflects a belief that, just as old cloth is continually replaced by new, so the spirits of the ancestors are reborn into the bodies of children. A special ritual cloth, *orun pada*, is used to divine the identity of such ancestors. Once a child is understood to be a reborn spirit, he or she may wear the *orun pada* used in the ritual at any time.

Many people picture very colourful fabrics when they think of African textiles—such as the famous Kente cloth from Ghana—but in fact the most common traditional cloth is white. There are various reasons for this, but among the Bunu Yoruba one important reason has to do with religious meaning. The Bunu understand white to represent any colour from transparent to light grey; thus 'white' describes a range of items, from human secretions (milk, semen) to aspects of nature (air, water), and religious phenomena (spirits, heaven).

White cloth—traditionally woven by Bunu women only—is thus used in many instances to bridge the gap between the physical world and the spirit world, between living people and their ancestors. For example:

- wearing white cloth remedies certain types of disorder caused by destructive spirits (miscarriage, anger, illness);
- wrapping white cloth around the trunks of sacred trees may appease the spirits living inside them;
- a white cloth is wrapped around a pot of objects used to help bring rain;
- at burial, people are wrapped in white cloth to facilitate rebirth as an ancestor; and
- the supreme being *Olorun* is sometimes described as 'The One clothed in white'.

For the Bunu Yoruba, then, white cloth plays a key role in helping members of the community cope with—and find meaning in—the disruptions and pain of disease, drought, conflict, and even death. From the outside, one would likely never suspect that this simple-looking substance could have such meaning and power.

Spirit Baskets

Basket weaving is one of the oldest and most widespread of all the arts. Because the tradition goes back so far, and because the baskets themselves decay into nothingness, much of the history of basket weaving cannot be traced. Baskets come in a staggering variety of patterns, colours, materials, sizes, and shapes. They may also be used to hold an enormous array of items, from food and babies to spirits and prayers, and have been used in ceremonies for all stages of life from birth to death.

Baskets also figure in the sacred stories of many cultures. The Hebrew Bible tells how Moses' mother put him in a basket and set it in the river, to be found later by Pharaoh's daughter (Exodus 2: 3–5). Tane, the Maori god of light and wisdom, climbed to heaven to bring three baskets of knowledge back to earth (knowledge of all ritual matters; of acts of harm and aggression among people; and of peace and well-being). A Navajo story describes the origin of birds such as wrens, warblers, and titmice: a woman plucked the feathers of several winged monsters and put them in her basket, but when she passed through a forbidden territory filled with sunflowers, the feathers were transformed into tiny birds and flew out of the basket.

Mabel McKay (1907–91) was a traditional healer of the Pomo people, and one of the most famous basket makers in the world. Her work is collected in various museums, including the Smithsonian. In addition to holding jobs as a washerwoman, factory employee, and seasonal fruit picker, for much of her adult life Mabel gave lectures on baskets and Native American culture at universities in California.

Mabel's basket making was interwoven with her healing practices, as she would give each patient a tiny basket for health and protection, or instruction in making one. Some of her miniature baskets were the size of a pea, and it was impossible to see their intricate patterns without a magnifying glass.

In Pomo communities, men traditionally wove the heavy baskets used for work like hunting and fishing; women were responsible for the baskets that had more explicitly religious purposes, and therefore had to follow specific rules in creating them. As in most Indigenous communities, rituals were prescribed for obtaining and preparing the materials to be used, and the weaving process was surrounded by restrictions. Thus weavers were forbidden to make baskets at all when menstruating or consuming alcohol. They were also forbidden to include representations of humans in their designs, or to reproduce the designs of medicine weavers such as Mabel.

This last rule reflected the fact that those designs were the product of personal spiritual visions. Such visions were for the weaver alone, and were relevant to particular situations. Although Mabel followed the traditions of her culture, and wove with respect for the people, history, and stories of her community, her baskets were always individual, unique. Even more than usual, then, her baskets were living things, which both reflected and communicated her sacred visions. Thus, when asked if she had been taught to weave baskets by her grandmother or mother, she replied: 'No, spirit teach me, since I was small child' (Sarris 1992: 25).

Carvings

What annoys me is that a lot of totem poles that go up have no plaque or information. People who come by wonder, 'Who did this? What's it all about?' Every time I carve a totem pole, there's always a kind of signature to identify my family or my nation, the Nisga'a.

—Norman Tait (1993: 11), **Nisga'a**

Masks

The difference that context makes in understanding the meaning of cultural objects is well illustrated by African masks. Non-Africans usually encounter these masks only in museums, where they exist as shadows of their former selves. Used as intended, the masks come alive as part of the community's most important ritual activities: initiations, weddings, hunting celebrations, funerals, harvests, war preparations. There is no comparison between the lifeless husk stuck on a post behind glass, and the fully animate ritual object that links its wearer with the world of spirits, ancestors, and gods.

Across Africa there are thousands of mask designs, created from a great variety of materials including wood, brass, ivory, bronze, copper, glazed pottery, and textiles. Some aspects of their meaning may be apparent even to the outsider, but we always need to be cautious in our interpretations. Typically, masks are meant to bring a spirit into the community; however, it is important to remember that in African traditions the supreme being is never represented by any physical object: therefore masks can relate only to lesser deities.

Also, the fact that certain masks clearly represent certain animals does not mean (as was once assumed) that the people who use them worship those animals. In Mali, both the Dogon and Bamana cultures use antelope masks in agricultural ceremonies that have little to do with actual antelopes. And even in this instance, the symbolic meaning is not identical: for the Dogon the antelope represents hard work, whereas for the Bamana the animal's horns symbolize tall sprouts of grain.

When we focus only on the form of a mask, without reference to the context in which it is used, we can easily miss the meaning of certain critical elements. The Epa masks of the Yoruba, for example, are not only complex and intricately carved, but also extremely heavy. The weight reflects their function in rituals celebrating the male passage into adulthood. The strength required to dance with such a mask is a literal representation

Indigenous carvings: a traditional Dogon mask, totem poles in Vancouver's Stanley Park, and a Maori figure of Tihori from Waitangi, New Zealand (left: Ferdinand Reus; centre: Peter Graham; right: Kahuroa).

of the wearer's ability to take on his responsibilities as an adult member of the community.

Another unseen—but equally important— aspect of the mask is the process of its creation. Carvers have traditionally been male, trained as apprentices to master carvers who hold positions of high esteem in their societies. Ritual formalities are no less central in the creation of a mask than they are in the final ceremony for which it is made. Typically, for example, carvers must work in isolation, while fasting, abstaining from any sexual activity, and avoiding contact with women and with anything connected to death.

Totem Poles

Produced by the Aboriginal peoples of the Pacific Northwest Coast, totem poles pose similar challenges of context and symbolism. As with the masks, the various markings and carving styles are highly specific to particular communities and locations; someone familiar with these traditions would immediately know, when encountering a totem pole, whose territory they had entered.

Yet for many years now, totem poles have been removed from their homes. Poles with little or no connection to one another, from different cultures and with different functions, are often gathered together in a kind of outdoor museum such as Stanley Park in Vancouver, Canada. Some groups have fought this trend—in 2006 the Haisla of northern British Columbia successfully retrieved from Sweden's Museum of Ethnography a sacred totem pole that had been stolen from them almost 80 years earlier.

Ironically, the word 'totem' is derived from the Anishinaubae word *dodaem*, which has been variously translated as 'heart', 'nourishment', and 'kinship group'. But the Anishinaubae (who live thousands of kilometres to the east) never made totem poles, and the cultures of the Pacific Northwest themselves never used the word 'totem'. The **Tsimshian** people—to pick just one example— call such a pole a *ptsan*.

Normally carved from a single cedar tree, a pole can survive for a century or so. It is traditionally regarded as a living thing and is allowed to rot naturally; some believe that to physically preserve a totem pole is to interfere with the natural order of the world. Certain communities even forbid the 'preservation' of poles in drawings or photographs.

The meaning of a particular totem pole depends on its intended use. Some were designed primarily to serve as supporting structures or grave markers; others, as symbols of status or power. Most, however, tell stories. Some stories are mainly historical, recounting achievements, murders, arguments, victories, defeats, marriages, ancestral lineages, and so on. But other stories are more explicitly religious, relating to particular beliefs, or to the tales of great figures such as Raven or Thunderbird (among the most powerful of all North American spirits, Thunderbird is responsible for great storms).

The photo on page 352 shows two totem poles. The one in front may appear more ornate than the other but is actually much simpler, depicting only two main figures. Grizzly Bear is at the base, holding a human, which usually represents self-preservation or survival. Thunderbird, a symbol of strength, is at the top. The pole's relative simplicity reflects the fact that it was one of a pair created to serve as house posts, holding the roof beam of a building.

The pole behind it, carved by Norman Tait (with Robert and Isaac Tait), tells a more complicated story. The family is first of all represented by the man at the top, who is holding Eagle to signify their clan. There are five disembodied faces on the pole representing five ancestral brothers who one day saw two beavers emerge from their home, remove their skin, and become men (the two figures beside the hole at the base of the pole). The figures told the five brothers that they were being slaughtered by the humans, so the brothers sang a sad song which froze the river, protecting the beavers (who can be seen climbing the pole). This is how the Tait family came to adopt the Beaver for their crest.

Moko

Maori carvings are less likely than totem poles or masks to be displayed outside their original physical context. This is because many of them are an integral part of the ancestral meeting house, or *whare whakairo* (literally, 'carved house'), for which they were created. The figures that decorate these houses are ancestors such as Tihori, of the Ngati Awa in Bay of Plenty, New Zealand (see the photo on p. 352). Tihori is shown holding a *taiaha*, a weapon used in hand-to-hand combat, which symbolizes his role and accomplishments as a warrior.

Tihori is also covered with traditional Maori tattoos, or **moko** (literally, 'to strike' or 'to tap'). Originally chiselled (not just inked) into the skin, these markings identify both the individual and his or her relationship to the community. Some *moko* elements may signify education level, personal and family rank, tribal history, or ancestral connections; other designs may simply be marks of beauty or ferocity in battle. Traditionally, women were allowed tattoos only on or around their lips and chin, while men could receive markings on their entire face.

A key design that is repeated on Tihori's face and arms is the *koru*, or frond/spiral, the most common (and important) of all *moko* elements. A Maori proverb helps explain its meaning: 'As one fern frond dies, another is born to take its place'. This suggests that the *koru*'s primary meaning has to do with birth, regeneration, and sustainability, but that it can also represent the ancestors themselves, who gave birth to the Maori and who continue to sustain them.

Beyond this symbolism, the art of *moko* itself is directly linked to the Maori ancestors. Uetonga, the god of lightning, developed *moko* in imitation of the marks that his grandfather Ru, god of earthquakes, had left on the face of the primal parent, the earth. One day Uetonga's daughter Niwareka (who brought weaving to humanity) journeyed to the world of the living and fell in love with the Maori ancestral chief Mataora. The two married and lived together until Mataora, in a jealous rage, hit Niwareka and she fled home. In sorrow, Mataora followed her and came upon Uetonga tattooing a man by cutting deep patterns into his flesh. When Mataora asked to have his own story marked on his face in the same way, Uetonga agreed.

To ease the pain of the carving, Mataora sang of his loss and regret, and the sound reached Niwareka, who forgave her husband. The couple reunited and received permission to return to the surface world. But Mataora neglected to leave an appropriate offering for the guardian of the portal between the two realms, and so from then on living humans were forbidden from entering the underworld. *Moko*—in fact, all traditional carvings—thus remind Maori people of their ancestors, of the importance of meeting one's obligations, of the need to treat one another with respect, of the power of the natural world, and of the boundaries between life and death.

Buildings

> The way into the shrine was a round hole at the side of a hill, just a little bigger than the round opening into a henhouse. Worshippers and those who came to seek knowledge from the god crawled on their belly through the hole and found themselves in a dark, endless space in the presence of Agbala.
> —Chinua Achebe (1996 [1958]: 12), **Igbo**

Ancestral Houses

The Maori meeting house (*whare whakairo*) is part of a larger complex called a **marae**, a cleared area containing several other structures such as a dining room, shelters, and a site where the recently deceased are placed to lie in state. The *marae* is the religious and social home of a Maori person, the site of ritual ceremonies such as weddings, funerals, family celebrations, and formal welcomes for visitors. Authority on the *marae* is held by the community's elders, who use the space to pass on traditions, stories, and arts such as weaving and carving.

As in the case of African masks, the builders and carvers of the *whare whakairo* were traditionally male; women and the rest of the community were banned from the site until the work was officially declared complete at a public ceremony. The workers themselves operated under a number of ritual restrictions and obligations from the moment the first trees for the building were cut down. Traditionally, *marae* artists were held responsible to such a degree that they could be put to death if the community did not judge the completed work to be acceptable.

The location of the *marae* is critical: it must be a place where previous generations carried out the religious and social activities that continue to define and restore the world itself. This connection to the land is not merely metaphorical, as it is Maori custom to bury the placenta in the ground at birth, as well as the bones after death. The *marae* is also identified with a single common ancestor to whom all members of the community are ostensibly connected.

This identification is given physical form in the *whare whakairo*, which represents the body of the ancestor. On the front of the house, where the roof slopes meet, is the mask-head of the ancestor; the boards along the front of each side of the roof are his arms; the central ridge of the roof is his spine, with ribs/rafters spreading out from it; the front door is his mouth; and the window is his eye. Non-Maori may be able to appreciate the beauty and intricacy of the *whare whakairo*'s construction, but they cannot grasp what such a building truly means to a community without a deeper understanding of its cultural roots.

The interior of a Maori *whare whakairo* (meeting house) in Waitangi, New Zealand (Phil Whitehouse).

Three Points, and a Shrine

That said, the attention to detail in the construction of the *whare whakairo* is so great that even a casual observer might still be able to recognize that such a building is imbued with religious significance. Many other Indigenous religious structures—including the majority of those in Africa and North America—are so plain that it may be difficult for outsiders to understand how they could have any deeper meaning.

There are three main points at issue here. First, the majority of Indigenous people throughout history have performed all or most of their rituals out of doors, in the natural world. Specific locations can be critically important; when the object of the ritual is to make contact with particular gods or spirits, for example, the ritual must generally be performed where they dwell or intersect with our world. Although some communities may erect a simple structure to mark such sites, to do anything more elaborate would in many instances simply hold no meaning to them, it would not be in keeping with their religious worldview.

Second, it may be helpful to think about the functions of the elaborate religious structures erected by various non-Indigenous groups. One reason the Catholic Church blanketed Europe with grand cathedrals, for example, was the simple fact that for a very long time it was the ultimate authority in that part of the world. Such buildings symbolized the Church's wealth and political power. Small Indigenous communities that did not rule entire continents had no occasion (or resources) for such displays.

Finally, we come back to the point made at the beginning of this section: that what you see is often not what you get. An African shrine may contain nothing more than a couple of small, plain, human-shaped carvings, but if the community understands that particular ancestors or spirits from time to time inhabit those figures, then they become at those times the visible manifestations of the gods.

Other shrine statues may have quite a different meaning, however. Consider the *mbari* shrine in the photo below. How would you interpret these figures? Are they gods? Which one is the most important? Who is the man sitting in front of the statues, and why is he there?

The statues actually represent the founder of the community in the lower middle, with his wife above and servants on either side. He was renowned as a great healer approximately two hundred years ago, but was attacked by another community and forced to flee across the marshes, carrying his wife. Relics of the healer are kept with the statues and protect members of the society from disease. Because most of the *mbari* shrines in this region have been destroyed, an elder stands guard here at all times.

The guard signifies the presence not only of religious conflict in this region but also religious change. The idea of defending or preserving this particular type of religious building is actually a modern development. Traditionally, *mbari* shrines

A *mbari* shrine from southeastern Nigeria (Daniel Lainé).

were formed out of earth and clay, and—like totem poles—were never repaired after their ceremonial unveiling; after several rains, they would simply dissolve back into the earth.

Hogans

The Navajo **hogan** is our final example of a structure that is much more than it appears. It is also the only one that is not 'explicitly' religious: although many ceremonies are performed here a hogan is also simply a traditional dwelling, the kind of building in which any Navajo family might live. As such it is the site of all the daily activities that go on in a home, some of which are religious and some of which are not.

Before a newly constructed hogan is occupied the community will perform the Blessingway ceremony. This ritual includes a song that begins by referring to 'a holy home' (Gill 1982: 10), although this term merely hints at what the hogan represents. The point becomes slightly clearer when we learn that the Blessingway ceremony is in many ways the foundation of Navajo religious thought and practice. Before any other ritual can be conducted, for example, some version of the Blessingway must be performed.

The Blessingway song names four divine beings: Earth, Mountain Woman, Water Woman, and Corn Woman. But the song also speaks of everyday things: vegetation, fabrics, long life, happiness. In this way it represents a joining of perspectives, the cosmic with the mundane.

The cosmic–mundane connection is furthered by the song's identification of the four deities with the four main supporting poles of the hogan. And in Navajo cosmology, the same deities provide support for the world itself. In fact, the Navajo understand the creation of the world to have begun

The Navajo hogan is a traditional living space, as well as the site of many key rituals (PRA).

From the Nightway Prayer (Navajo)

Like the Blessingway song performed as part of the creation of a new hogan, the first part of this prayer connects the ordinary with the extraordinary through the central symbol of the home. And like the Yoruba verse in the box on page 345, its concluding section envisions life as a journey.

In *Tse 'gíhi*
In the house made of the dawn
In the house made of the evening twilight
In the house made of the dark cloud
In the house made of the he-rain
In the house made of the dark mist
In the house made of the she-rain
In the house made of pollen
In the house made of grasshoppers
Where the dark mist curtains the doorway
The path to which is on the rainbow
. . .

In beauty (happily) I walk
With beauty before me, I walk
With beauty behind me, I walk
With beauty below me, I walk
With beauty above me, I walk
With beauty all around me, I walk
It is finished (again) in beauty
It is finished in beauty
It is finished in beauty
It is finished in beauty
    (Matthews 1995 [1902]: 143–5)

with the building of a structure; which is to say that the world *is* a structure—a hogan. It should come as no surprise that creation was accompanied by the first performance of the Blessingway ritual. Thus to build a hogan is to reproduce the origin of all things, and to fulfill one's ongoing (sacred) responsibility to continually make and re-make the world.

Despite its apparent simplicity, then, the Navajo hogan—like Pomo baskets and Nisga'a totem poles, like Yoruba white cloth and Dogon shrines, like Maori tattoos and *whare whakairo*—is a vital link between present and past, between community and place, between our world and the world of the spirits.

🌿 COLONIALISM

'Colonialism' refers both to the process in which people from one place establish and maintain a settlement in another, and to the effects of this process on any people who were already there. Typically, those effects include their subjugation if not removal and the imposition of new laws, economies, and social practices that are controlled by, and often modelled on, those of the colonists' home territory.

An enormous amount of colonial activity occurred between the fifteenth and twentieth centuries, when western Europeans were exploring parts of the world such as Africa, North and South America, Australia, and the islands of the Pacific Ocean. Until this activity began, western Europe was a relatively insignificant region in terms of global influence; afterwards, it was the centre of the world.

The quests for power and profit have often been the key factors driving colonialism. Religion has also played a critical role, however, both as a motivating factor and as a justification for the conquest of other peoples. The consequences for the religious traditions of the conquered peoples have been profound. It is not possible to understand Indigenous traditions today, therefore, without understanding colonialism.

Invasion

> They do not bear arms, and do not know them, for I showed them a sword, they took it by the edge and cut themselves out of ignorance. . . . They would make fine servants. . . . With fifty men we could subjugate them and make them do whatever we want.
>
> —Christopher Columbus, Italian (in Zinn 1995: 1)

Columbus

The journals of Christopher Columbus offer an insider's account of the start of the most devastating colonial project in history. His first contact with the **Arawaks** foretells much of what happened later: 'As soon as I arrived in the Indies, on the first Island which I found, I took some of the natives by force in order that they might learn and might give me information of whatever there is in these parts' (Zinn 1995: 1).

What was it that Columbus most wanted to learn from his captives? He wanted to know where the gold was. Unfortunately for the Arawaks, there was very little gold for the Europeans to find, but Columbus was not deterred. Those who managed to bring him a specified amount of gold were given a copper token to hang around their necks; then those who were found without a token had their hands cut off and were left to bleed to death.

Eventually Columbus came to see that the islands' most valuable 'resources' were the people themselves, and he sent them back to Europe by the boatload. Thus he exclaimed: 'Let us in the name of the Holy Trinity go on sending all the slaves that can be sold' (Zinn 1995: 4). Within two years of his arrival, roughly half of the original estimated population of 250,000 had been either exported or killed. A century later, all of the Arawaks were gone.

Genocides

Colonial efforts elsewhere—in Africa, Australia, New Zealand, the Americas—were similarly catastrophic. Millions upon millions of people, representing thousands of distinct cultures, were wiped out entirely.

In Africa, as in the West Indies, the chief source of wealth for the Europeans was the population itself. By the late nineteenth century, upwards of 20 million Africans had been taken from their homes and sent to the Americas as slaves, though only about 11 million made it there alive. Scholars estimate that by the time the trans-Atlantic slave trade ended, the population of Africa had been reduced by half.

In Australia, less than half of the original population of about 500,000 remained after just a few years of contact with Europeans. The southeast—where the First Fleet arrived in 1788—was hit the hardest. During the first year of colonization, approximately two-thirds of the estimated 250,000 Aboriginals in this region were killed by a smallpox epidemic. By 1850, 96 per cent were dead.

In the Americas, records suggest that by 1600 as many as 90 million Indigenous people—more than 90 per cent of the original population—had died as a direct result of the arrival of the Europeans. More people had been killed than existed in all of Europe at the time (approximately 60 to 80 million). The destruction of the original inhabitants of the Americas was a genocide on a scale that has not been seen in human history before or since.

The biggest single cause of the depopulation of both Australia and the Americas was disease, but other factors included military action, mistreatment (including torture and forced labour) starvation or malnutrition, loss of will to live (e.g., suicide, abortion), and slavery. And the destruction has not ended yet. Most South American countries continue to move or kill their Indigenous citizens whenever the governments want more land.

Of course, humans have been killing and conquering other humans for as long as humans have existed. This, sadly, is what we do. Indigenous people are no exception to the rule; violence and warfare certainly existed in North America, Africa, and Oceania before the Europeans showed up. But it did not exist on nearly the same scale.

'Masters of the Continent'

Almost everywhere the Europeans went, they occupied the land they found. In many parts of North America, this occupation was initially accomplished through relatively peaceful negotiations with the original inhabitants. After all, the first settlers were greatly outnumbered, and the Indigenous people possessed valuable knowledge and skills. As the settler population grew, however, and the Indigenous population declined, the negotiation process became less friendly. Eventually it ceased entirely in most instances, and Native people living on land that Europeans wanted were either forcibly removed or simply killed.

Colonists justified this behaviour in many ways, some of which were explicitly religious. Many equated their situation with that of the Jews who were ordered by God to destroy the native inhabitants of Canaan. Only then could they inherit the Promised Land.

The notion of **terra nullius** ('no one's land') was also frequently invoked by European settlers in several places, including New Zealand, western Canada, and (most notably) Australia. Colonists argued variously that Indigenous people were not 'really' using the land; or that they could not own the land because they did not have any concept of ownership; or that because of their 'primitive' nature, they simply did not count as people.

By the late nineteenth century, it was widely assumed that the Indigenous people of North America were on the way to extinction. A newspaper editor in South Dakota named L. Frank Baum—the future author of *The Wizard of Oz*—wrote an editorial in December 1890 that carried the theory of the 'vanishing Indian' to a brutally logical conclusion:

> The Whites, by law of conquest, by justice of civilization, are masters of the American continent, and the best safety of the frontier settlements will be secured by the total annihilation of the few remaining Indians. Why not annihilation? Their glory has fled, their spirit broken, their manhood effaced; better that they die than live the miserable wretches that they are (Baum 1890).

In effect, Baum was calling for his fellow Euro-Americans to complete the genocide begun by Columbus.

Just nine days after Baum's editorial, the US Calvary moved to relocate an encampment of Lakota Sioux near Wounded Knee Creek, South Dakota, in order to free up the land for colonial settlers. The result was a massacre. More than three hundred Sioux were killed, among them unarmed women and children; some were shot as they tried to run away.

Around the world, Wounded Knee remains a powerful symbol of colonialism and its consequences for Indigenous people. A similar conjunction of land acquisition and extreme violence can be found at some point in the history of virtually every encounter between colonial interests and Indigenous people.

Conversion

I thought I was being taken just for a few days. I can recall seeing my mother standing on the side of the road with her head in her hands, crying, and me in the black FJ Holden wondering why she was so upset. . . . . . I see myself as that little girl, crying myself to sleep at night, crying and wishing I could go home to my family. Everything's gone, the

loss of your culture, the loss of your family, all these things have a big impact.
—Lyn Austin, Australian Aborigine (in Cooke 2008)

As a result of colonialism, the majority of Indigenous peoples in the world were converted to the religion of one colonial power or another. That religion was usually some form of Christianity, but other missionary religions took hold in some areas of the world, notably Islam in parts of Africa and Buddhism throughout Asia.

Accurate information on adherence to Indigenous religions is virtually impossible to come by. Such data are normally obtained from national censuses. On the topic of religion, however, many countries have run into serious problems either with their census questions or with the answer choices they offer. In Indonesia, for example, adherence to an Indigenous religion is simply not recognized by law; as a result Indigenous people are counted as Muslims since Indonesia's dominant tradition is Islam. As well, Indigenous people in many parts of the world have expressed justifiable concern about what they reveal to government officials, and so may give what they think are the desired census answers in order to avoid any possible reprisals or repercussions.

That said, the general pattern is that approximately 70 per cent of Indigenous people in the world today identify with a colonial religion, while only 15 to 20 per cent continue to practise an Indigenous religion. The rest declare adherence either to an alternative tradition or to none at all.

Loss of Religion

In the early years of contact, some European missionaries tried to persuade Indigenous communities that Christianity simply made more sense than their own traditions, but that approach was rarely successful. A more effective strategy was to demonstrate the 'superiority' of Christian beliefs in practical terms. In many cases, that task was accomplished through the association of military strength with religious authority. The message was simple: Our people are stronger than your people because our god is stronger than yours.

Another major factor in the decline of Indigenous religions was the people's belief that, in order to integrate themselves into the new system, they needed the education that in most cases was available only through missionaries. Then, as colonial abuses accumulated, many oppressed Native people looked to the missionaries for *protection* from the new system. In both situations, Christianity flourished at the expense of traditional beliefs and practices.

Sometimes colonial governments simply made the practice of Indigenous religions illegal. This was invariably the case whenever such religions were suspected of involvement with any sort of anti-colonial resistance. And sometimes such laws were put into effect in a more pre-emptive manner.

In 1883, for example, the United States imposed a federal ban on many Native ceremonies, including the Sun Dance. The next year, Canada amended its **Indian Act** and criminalized the **potlatch**. In both cases the governments claimed that their motive was not to regulate religion but to protect citizens—from physical harm in the case of the Sun Dance, and from economic hardship in the case of the potlatch, which was depicted as driving people into poverty.

Finally, it is important to note that the conversion of Indigenous people had an enormous impact on gender relations, which in turn has had repercussions in all areas of life. Most colonial powers brought a form of patriarchy with them that resulted in the gendered stratification of the local societies, and the devaluation of women and their roles. As the Métis author Maria Campbell has pointed out, this devaluation was often supported at the deepest levels by colonial religious teachings: 'The missionaries had impressed upon us the feeling that women were a source of evil. This belief, combined with the ancient Indian recognition of the power of women, is still holding

From *Things Fall Apart*, by Chinua Achebe (Igbo)

Achebe's 1958 novel—which focuses on an Igbo man named Okonkwo from a fictional village in Nigeria in the late 1800s—is the most influential work of African literature ever written. In this passage Okonkwo has just returned home after a seven-year exile, and his best friend Obierika is explaining the dramatic changes that have taken place during his absence as a result of colonialism.

'Perhaps I have been away too long,' Okonkwo said, almost to himself. 'But I cannot understand these things you tell me. What is it that has happened to our people? Why have they lost the power to fight?'

'Have you not heard how the white man wiped out Abame?' asked Obierika.

'I have heard,' said Okonkwo. 'But I have also heard that Abame people were weak and foolish. Why did they not fight back? Had they no guns and machetes? We would be cowards to compare ourselves with the men of Abame. Their fathers had never dared to stand before our ancestors. We must fight these men and drive them from the land.'

'It is already too late,' said Obierika sadly. 'Our own men and our sons have joined the ranks of the stranger. They have joined his religion and they help to uphold his government. If we should try to drive out the white men in Umuofia we should find it easy. There are only two of them. But what of our own people who are following their way and have been given power? They would go to Umuru and bring the soldiers, and we would be like Abame.' He paused for a long time and then said: 'I told you on my last visit to Mbanta how they hanged Aneto.'

'What has happened to that piece of land in dispute?' asked Okonkwo.

'The white man's court has decided that it should belong to Nnama's family, who had given much money to the white man's messengers and interpreter.'

'Does the white man understand our custom about land?'

'How can he when he does not even speak our tongue? But he says that our customs are bad, and our own brothers who have taken up his religion also say that our customs are bad. How do you think we can fight when our own brothers have turned against us? The white man is very clever. He came quietly and peaceably with his religion. We were amused at his foolishness and allowed him to stay. Now he has won our brothers, and our clan can no longer act like one. He has put a knife on the things that held us together and we have fallen apart' (Achebe 1996 [1958]: 124–5).

back the progress of our people today' (Campbell 1973: 168).

Loss of Language

As a result of colonialism, an untold number of Indigenous languages have disappeared forever. It has been estimated that Australia had almost three hundred distinct Aboriginal languages at the time of first contact; today all but twenty are either extinct or endangered. According to the United Nations, as many as 90 per cent of all existing languages are in danger of becoming extinct within 100 years; the vast majority of these languages are Indigenous.

For cultures that rely heavily on oral traditions to transmit their beliefs and values, this loss of language constitutes a devastating blow to their religion. In his memoir *Our Land Was a Forest*, Kayano Shigeru tells a story about the last three fluent Ainu-speakers in his town, one of whom

The Potlatch

A ritual dating back thousands of years, the potlatch is practised by many peoples of the Pacific Northwest, including the Haida, Kwakwaka'wakw, Salish, Tlingit, and Tsimshian. To a significant extent the ceremony is about demonstrating hospitality and redistributing wealth; it typically consists of a feast at which the hosting family presents the guests with gifts. Before contact with Europeans, these gifts included items such as tools, blankets, carvings, and dried food (e.g., pemmican); gifts today usually consist of manufactured goods, especially practical household items, as well as artwork and cash.

Each community has its own way of potlatching, but the practice typically marks important moments such as marriage, childbirth, or death, and may include music, theatre, and ceremonial dancing. The potlatch also frequently serves to indicate social status: families demonstrate their wealth and importance by giving away (or even destroying) more resources than other families.

Christian missionaries saw the potlatch as useless and 'uncivilized', but also recognized it as a central element of many Native cultures. Getting rid of the practice, they thought, would facilitate assimilation. Their governments agreed: the potlatch was made illegal in Canada in 1884, and banned in the United States a few years later.

In October 1886, the anthropologist Franz Boas recorded a famous comment about the potlatch ban by Chief O'waxalagalis of the Kwakwaka'wakw people on Vancouver Island:

> We will dance when our laws command us to dance, and we will feast when our hearts desire to feast. Do we ask the white man, 'Do as the Indian does'? No, we do not. Why then do you ask us, 'Do as the white man does'? It is a strict law that bids us dance. It is a strict law that bids us distribute our property among our friends and neighbours. It is a good law. Let the white man observe his law, we shall observe ours. And now, if you come to forbid us dance, be gone. If not, you will be welcome to us (Bunn-Marcuse 2005: 322).

As it turned out, the law was hard to enforce. Indigenous communities were large and widespread, and so could often hold potlatches in secret. Even when non-Natives discovered a potlatch, it was not easy for them to distinguish this event from a regular (legal) feast. In addition, many non-Natives—including the government agents tasked with enforcing the ban—regarded the law as harsh and unnecessary. The potlatch ban was finally lifted in the US in 1934 and in Canada in 1951.

was Shigeru's father. The three agreed that the first among them to die would be the luckiest, because the other two would be able to perform the death ritual for him in the Ainu language and thereby ensure that he would 'return to the realm of the gods' (Shigeru 1994: 107).

What has caused this situation? In many cases, as communities died their languages died with them. In other cases, the process of language loss was accelerated by government programs designed specifically to promote assimilation. Thus in Canada Aboriginal children were taken from their families, often by force, and placed in church-run **residential schools** where they were forbidden to speak their own languages. In Australia children were sent either to foster homes or (much more often) to government- or church-run institutions, where they remained as wards of the state until they reached the age of 18. Record-keeping was often either inadequate or non-existent, with the result that some children never found their families, never returned to their homes.

In both countries, agents of the institutions involved—including teachers and administrators, priests and nuns—inflicted physical, psychological, and/or sexual abuse on many Indigenous children. Taken from their families and told they were worthless, heathen, primitive, these children grew up with no knowledge of their language and culture; at the same time they were deprived of the social knowledge required to establish healthy relationships and raise their own families. It is no wonder that Aboriginal children in Australia who endured such practices for more than a century have been termed the 'Stolen Generations'.

Loss of Land

We have already noted how closely Indigenous religions are tied to specific locations: the sacred places where gods, spirits, and ancestors become present in the lives of each community. Limiting or preventing access to such locations, therefore, undermines the very foundations of Indigenous religion.

Around the world, thousands of Indigenous religious sites have been taken over or destroyed as a result of colonialism; no doubt there are many more such sites that we know nothing of, because the people who held them sacred have themselves been destroyed. Yet even where both the people and the land survive, gaining recognition of land rights is an ongoing problem.

Canada and Australia have particularly poor track records in this respect. When these countries became independent from Great Britain, they essentially refused to recognize any titles granted to Indigenous people by the British. In 1971, an Australian judge, upholding the concept of *terra nullius*, went so far as to rule that Aborigines had no land rights at all—a decision that was not overturned until 1992.

In the United States, more than 90 per cent of the land had been taken from its Indigenous inhabitants by 1890. A key (negative) moment in the Native Americans' struggle to reclaim some of this territory came almost a century later, when the Forest Service proposed putting a paved road through the Chimney Rock area of the Six Rivers National Forest in Northern California, in order to open the space for commercial logging. The project would effectively destroy the centre of religious existence for two Native communities, the **Yurok** and the **Karuk.**

The case was brought to the Supreme Court. The Natives were not asking that the land in question be returned to them—only that they retain access to it. The court, however, found that their attachment to the disputed territory was no different from the attachment that any individual might feel for any space. Thus to agree to their request would set a precedent allowing anyone to request protection of any site on religious grounds. The petition was denied.

This case highlights two central problems in the understanding that many non-Indigenous people have of Indigenous religions. The first problem is that religion in general is frequently seen primarily as an individual commitment to a set of beliefs. Indigenous religions, by contrast, are communal and are as much about practice as they are about belief.

The second problem is the difficulty that non-Indigenous people have in understanding why Indigenous practices are often bound to particular sites—unlike, say, Christian prayer or Buddhist meditation, which can be performed anywhere at all. This difficulty in turn is related to the difference between religions that see the world as a unity—all people are loved equally by Jesus, or have equal access to the Four Noble Truths—and religions that see the world in more particular, or locative, terms. For most Indigenous people, specific places are related, and sacred, to specific people, not to everyone in the world.

Appropriation

We lost most of our land, most of our 'Aboriginal' rights, many of our languages, most of our traditional cultural ways, our religion, our relationship to the land and the spirits of the land, and, it seems, that

we've even lost control of much of our identity through the process of 'trade-marking' images of us, and elements of our culture.
—Philip Bellfy (2005: 30), Chippewa

Identity

For some people, it's not just a baseball game when the Cleveland Indians play the Atlanta Braves: it's a stark reminder of the ongoing legacy of colonialism, of all that has been taken from Indigenous people and all that continues to be taken from them. Adding insult to injury, the Braves' fans are known for doing the 'tomahawk chop', while the Indians' mascot is a degrading caricature named 'Chief Wahoo'.

Of course this phenomenon is not limited to baseball. Many North American sports teams—such as the Chicago Blackhawks and Washington Redskins—have taken Indigenous-oriented names. And many other types of companies have used 'Indigenous' names or logos to market their products, from Eskimo Pie ice cream to the Ford Thunderbird. In effect, the dominant colonial culture has appropriated Indigenous identities and reconstructed them to evoke whatever 'primitive' stereotype is best suited to the product they wish to sell: the primal 'warrior' for a sports team, the noble 'chief' for tobacco, or the pure, natural 'Indian maiden' for a line of dairy products or even beer.

Such appropriation is thus not simply arrogant, impolite, or politically incorrect. It serves to perpetuate an image of Indigenous people that is far removed from current reality and, in so doing, helps to blind non-Indigenous people to ongoing injustices. To the extent that these people continue to see Indigenous cultures as primitive, savage, and uncivilized, as vanished or vanishing, they will

The logo of the Jacob Leinenkugel Brewing Company of Chippewa Falls, Wisconsin (Jacob Leinenkugel Brewing Company).

have difficulty recognizing the reality of modern communities and their concerns. Whether they are celebrating or protesting, laughing or grieving, practising Indigenous traditions or Christianity, Indigenous people should at least have the right to ownership and control of their own identity.

Religion in the Movies

From the 'Indian burial ground' of Stephen King's *Pet Sematary* to the baboon 'shaman' Rafiki in *The Lion King*, to Betty White's 'tribal' chanting in *The Proposal*, American films are filled with false ideas about Indigenous religious life. The best-known portrayals of Native culture likely remain those from the classic Hollywood Westerns—most of which used Italian or Spanish actors to play the 'Indians'. Again and again, Indigenous people are portrayed either as fierce/savage warriors or as the noble/dying people of a lost age.

Similar patterns are evident in movies from both Oceania and Africa. In the highest-grossing Australian film of all time, *Crocodile Dundee*, the extinction of Indigenous culture is signalled by Dundee's Aboriginal friend Neville, who is repeatedly shown to have left his roots behind ('God, I hate the bush', he mutters). More disturbingly, Dundee himself proclaims that 'Aborigines don't own the land. They belong to it.' It is precisely this view of traditional Aboriginal conceptions of place that the Australian government used to help deprive people of their land rights.

The Gods Must Be Crazy remains the most commercially successful movie about Indigenous people ever made. Released in 1980, the film grossed over $100 million worldwide and focused directly on the (imagined) religious beliefs of the (real) Jul'hoansi people, in the Kalahari Desert in southern Africa. The movie presents them as 'noble savages' living in a simple, idyllic society whose peace is shattered when a Coke bottle falls out of a plane and upsets the balance of Indigenous life, prompting the film's hero, Xi, to set off for the end of the world in order to return the offending object to the gods who sent it. In other words, the movie

presents the Jul'hoansi as naive, superstitious, and innocent, and then uses them to criticize modern non-Indigenous culture.

Catching Dreams and Burning Men

Around the world, sacred Indigenous items continue to be turned into souvenirs for cultural tourists. There is a lot of money to be made by selling cheap versions of African masks to non-Africans. Imitation Maori *moko* have attained a similar level of popularity among non-Indigenous tattoo enthusiasts, and were even used on fashion models for a 2007 Jean Paul Gaultier collection. Even more striking is the proliferation of dream catchers. Originally used in Anishinaubae culture to help protect children from nightmares, they are now sold by the thousands to non-Native people for use as decorative knick-knacks. Often they can be seen hanging from a rearview mirror like a pair of fuzzy dice.

Indigenous opinion concerning the commercial use of religious objects and symbols is divided. Some people see it as disrespectful and damaging; others argue that it has some value, not only in economic terms but in helping to educate the public about Indigenous culture. Still, there are forms of appropriation that almost all can agree are clearly inappropriate. Some of these are part of what is often referred to as the **New Age** movement.

Many New Age teachings that seem to reflect Indigenous religions in reality turn them upside down. Thus elements of a locative and communal tradition are co-opted to promote notions of universal truth and individual fulfillment. Non-Indigenous people are often willing to pay New Age 'shamans' lots of money for the opportunity to get in touch with a 'primal' part of themselves and overcome their own psychological and emotional problems. To this end they engage in all manner of pseudo-Indigenous rituals: they tell stories, chant, pass around the talking stick, bang drums, yell in a forest, and dance.

These imitative practices are not simply misguided, but can actually be quite dangerous. In

Statement by Chief Arvol Looking Horse (Lakota) on the Sweat Deaths in Arizona

Chief Looking Horse's statement was issued on 16 October 2009, one day prior to the third death resulting from this incident.

As Keeper of our Sacred White Buffalo Calf Pipe Bundle, I am concerned for the two deaths and illnesses of the many people that participated in a sweat lodge in Sedona, Arizona that brought our sacred rite under fire in the news. I would like to clarify that this lodge and many others are not our ceremonial way of life, because of the way they are being conducted. My prayers go out for their families and loved ones for their loss.

Our ceremonies are about life and healing. From the time this ancient ceremonial rite was given to our people, never has death been a part of our *inikaga* (life within) when conducted properly. . . .

Our First Nations People have to earn the right to pour the *mini wiconi* (water of life) upon the *inyan oyate* (the stone people) in creating *Inikaga* by going on the vision quest for four years and four years Sundance. Then you are put through a ceremony to be painted, to recognize that you have now earned that right to take care of someone's life through purification. They should also be able to understand our sacred language, to be able to understand the messages from the Grandfathers, because they are ancient, they are our spirit ancestors. They walk and teach the values of our culture; in being humble, wise, caring, and compassionate.

What has happened in the news with the makeshift sauna called the sweat lodge is not our ceremonial way of life. . . .

At this time, I would like to ask all Nations upon Grandmother Earth to please respect our sacred ceremonial way of life and stop the exploitation of our *Tunka Oyate* (Spiritual Grandfathers).

In a Sacred Hoop of Life, where there is no ending and no beginning, *namahu yo* (hear my words).

Chief Arvol Looking Horse,
19th Generation Keeper of the Sacred White Buffalo Calf Pipe Bundle
(Looking Horse 2009)

October 2009, three people died and eighteen more were hospitalized when self-help guru James Arthur Ray conducted a New Age **sweat lodge** ceremony in Arizona. In the traditional practice, participants sit in an enclosed space and water is poured over rocks heated in a fire to create steam. The ritual is used for various medicinal and religious purposes, including purification and reconnection to the spirits. Many Native communities, including the Anishinaubae, Lakota, **Crow**, and **Chumash** conduct sweat lodge ceremonies safely in enclosures covered with hides, dirt, or blankets, but it seems that Ray's lodge was covered with plastic sheeting. On 3 February 2010, Ray was arrested and charged with manslaughter for the three deaths.

The largest and most famous Indigenous-themed New Age event is the week-long Burning Man festival held every summer in northern Nevada. The festival takes its name from its central ceremony, when a large wooden effigy is set aflame. Since 2007 well over 40,000 people have attended each year to take part in activities that range from making art and music to self-expression, communal living, gift giving, and public nudity.

On occasion, some have complained about the degree to which Burning Man (and/or its participants) seem to be appropriating Indigenous cultures. For example, in April 2009 organizers of an offshoot Burner party in Oakland, California, circulated an online flyer encouraging participants to 'GO NATIVE' and offering a discount to anyone who showed up 'in Native costume'. In addition, the party was to feature four 'elemental rooms': 'Water: Island Natives (Maori); Air: Cliff Natives (Anasazi); Earth: Jungle Natives (Shipibo); Fire: Desert Natives (Pueblo)'.

Given the immense popularity of Burning Man and its related events, it is impossible to underestimate the degree to which such appropriation influences the views of non-Natives about Native people—and thereby affects the actual lives of Native people.

❧ RECENT DEVELOPMENTS

There are references to Gen. Custer and the US Cavalry, to John Wayne and to US policies toward Indians over the years, but *Smoke Signals* is free of the oppressive weight of victim culture; these characters don't live in the past and define themselves by the crimes committed against their people.
—Roger Ebert (1998), Euro-American

Given that Indigenous traditions are the world's oldest religions, changes that have taken place since the emergence of colonialism a few hundred years ago certainly qualify as 'recent developments'. As a result of colonialism, the religious

traditions of Indigenous people have also changed perhaps more dramatically over the last centuries than the traditions of any other cultures in the world. That said, in what follows it is important to bear two key points in mind.

First, there is a critical difference between recognizing that awful things have been done (and continue to be done) to Indigenous people in the name of colonialism and defining Indigenous people as 'victims', a label that robs them of full humanity. Second, and relatedly, Indigenous people were never simply the passive objects of colonialism: they engaged with it at every step, and they have remained active agents in their histories, including recent developments in their religions.

Interaction and Adaptation

I picture oppressors . . . coming into our garden of Eden like a snake. Satan used the snake as his instrument to tempt God's people and to try to destroy God's plan for his people. The bad influence came in breaking our relationship with God, with man, and the Land. We never dreamed that one day the bulldozers would come in.
—Djiniyini Gondarra, **Yolngu** (in Swain and Trompf 1995: 107)

Dualisms

In most Indigenous religions, the process of change began soon after contact with Europeans. Typically, Indigenous people would gradually incorporate some elements of the colonial religion into their own traditions. One of the most important examples of this process was the shift in worldview that sometimes took place from the more typically Indigenous one of complementary dualism (seeing the universe as necessarily including both creative and destructive forces, which can work together), to the 'Western' one of **conflict dualism** (seeing the universe as divided between good and evil forces that are in constant battle with one another).

Such a shift occurred in the late sixteenth and early seventeenth centuries among many of the Indigenous people of Peru, people who previously had no real concept of 'evil'. In certain regions, the invading Spanish characterized the local populations as the demonic enemies of Christ, giving them licence to use extreme violence in order to subjugate and convert the people. The plan worked: many of the Indigenous Peruvians who suffered great cruelty at the hands of the invaders did adopt basic Christian beliefs, including the good–evil dualism promoted by the Spanish. However, while they came to regard Jesus as a positive and humane figure, they saw the Spanish as the true embodiments of evil.

A similar change took place among the **Iroquois** in the late eighteenth century. A man in his sixties named Ganioda'yo, or Handsome Lake, experienced a series of visions in which he met Jesus as well as four angels sent by the creator, Tarachiawagon. As a result of these visions, Handsome Lake taught the Iroquois that they should publicly confess their sins; that they should avoid evil (including witchcraft and alcohol); and that they should worship only Tarachiawagon, not his malevolent brother, Tawiskaron. This division of the world between the good and evil brothers represented a potent fusion of Indigenous religion with Christian conflict dualism. Ganioda'yo's teachings were so influential that today approximately a third of all Iroquois practise what came to be called the Handsome Lake or Longhouse religion.

The Diaspora and the Diviner

The Atlantic slave trade carried African traditions to the Americas, where they mixed with elements of both Christianity and Native American religions. Many relocated Africans continued to worship Yoruba gods under the guise of praying to Christian saints, but in time elements of the traditions often merged in fact, giving rise to new religions such as Macumba (in Brazil), Voudou (in Haiti), and Santeria (in Cuba).

Many Africans who blended elements of traditional and colonial religion also moved towards a mode of conflict dualism. In the early nineteenth century, in the region that became South Africa, a Xhosa diviner named Nxele experienced what he understood to be an intervention by Christ. Although he continued to practise divination, he also began preaching a message that echoed the teachings of the nearby Christian missionaries.

Like the Indigenous Peruvians, however, Nxele came to see the Europeans as Christ's betrayers. Preaching that the god Mdalidiphu, who lived underground with the ancestors, was on their side, Nxele led 10,000 warriors against the British at Grahamstown. The attack failed and Nxele was imprisoned. He later drowned off the Cape coast while attempting to escape.

Cargo Cults

One of the most famous examples of an Indigenous religion changing in response to contact with outsiders is also one of the most recent: the **cargo cult**. Most cargo cults developed in the region of the southwest Pacific Ocean, although a few similar groups have also appeared in Africa and the Americas. The cargoes that gave rise to these groups were the regular shipments of supplies and manufactured goods that arrived for non-Indigenous foreigners.

Colonists and missionaries first appeared on many of the Pacific islands in the late nineteenth and early twentieth centuries, but activity intensified during the Second World War as the Japanese and then the Allied forces set up (and then abandoned) military bases. The local people believed that the goods arriving for these groups were provided by deities or ancestors, and that in order to receive shipments themselves they should imitate the newcomers. Thus they painted military insignia on their bodies, marched like soldiers, and constructed mock buildings and equipment, making guns from wood and radios from coconuts. Some Indigenous groups built replicas of airplanes, control towers, and headphones, waved landing signals, and lit torches along runways at night, all in the hope that the gods would send more cargo.

This hope was fuelled by two related goals. First, attaining the desired goods would allow for reciprocal exchanges with the Europeans—a practice that for many Indigenous cultures was central to establishing relationships. Second, cargo cults often came to believe that attaining these goods would bring about a new age of social harmony, a harmony that had been deeply upset by the arrival of the colonists in the first place.

Unfortunately, this focus on obtaining cargo eclipsed other elements of the local religions. Even though the Indigenous participants followed the content of their traditions (which explained the cargo as originating with gods or ancestors), they radically changed its form (their ritual behaviour). In the end, many of those traditions disappeared.

Paths of Resistance

Not all Indigenous religions changed so dramatically or so quickly. For many years after first contact with Europeans, several Australian communities did not mix their tradition with the colonial one; but neither did they reject one or the other. Instead, they were able to declare the simultaneous, contradictory truth of both Christian and Indigenous views of existence. The Aborigines referred to this way of thinking as having 'Two Laws'. Some have suggested that the Aborigines were better able than most to entertain two radically different cosmologies because their own cultural heritage had accustomed them to paradoxes and non-linear thinking.

In a number of instances where the two were combined, it was Christianity that was subsumed by the Indigenous tradition. The Warlpiri of Central Australia, for example, used ritual song and dance to tell Bible stories, just as they did with Dreaming tales. They also tended to conflate events, as if Adam, Abraham, and Jesus had lived at the same time as the Warlpiri's own ancestors.

In effect, by telling the biblical stories in their own way, they reconfigured the stories to focus on place rather than the chronological order of events.

This emphasis on place is a clear indication that the Aboriginal worldview took precedence over the Christian. To most Christians, for example, it is theologically critical to understand the sequence in which the stories of Adam, Abraham, and Jesus occur. For the Aborigines, however, this sequence was irrelevant; the biblical figures were thus easily incorporated into their universe. In contrast to the cargo cult practitioners, in other words, they kept the form of key elements of their traditional religion (how stories were told), even though aspects of its content had been altered (those stories now included biblical references). It is possible that, because of this approach, these Aborigines were able to resist conversion longer than many other communities.

'The End Is Near'

> They [the Ghost Dancers] danced in rings, the men outside circling to the right, the women and children inside circling to the left. Some of the songs came from Siletz [a community in Oregon], others were dreamed by the people when they were in a trance. All the songs were wordless. The dancers wore the old-time dress. Most of them went crazy and then they would see the dead.
> —Robert Spott, Yurok (in Beck et al. 1992 [1977]: 176)

In the wake of the destruction wrought by Europeans, many Indigenous cultures experienced a religious crisis. One response was to understand colonialism as punishment for inadequate observance of native traditions. Among the people who took this view were some who reasoned that if they repented they might help to usher in a new golden age. In some cases this view may have reflected the influence of Christian eschatology—the idea that the end of the world was near and the kingdom of God would soon arrive. Of course, it may also have derived from the fact that the world as Indigenous people had known it really was coming to an end.

The Cattle Massacre

In the mid-1800s—a time when the Xhosa were suffering greatly under the British—a young woman named Nongqawuse had a vision in which her ancestors told her that, because some of her people had practised witchcraft, the British had been sent to punish them all. If the Xhosa renounced witchcraft and destroyed their food supplies, then the Europeans would be destroyed, the ancestors would return, their food would be replaced, and their land would be restored to them.

Many Xhosa responded by burning their granaries and slaughtering their cattle; in fact, almost half a million cows were ultimately killed. As a result, thousands of Xhosa died of starvation—their population declined within a year from 105,000 to 27,000—and any hope of resisting the British died with them. Many blamed the tragedy on those who had failed to heed Nongqawuse's prophecy, although there was a later backlash against Nongqawuse herself. In the end, most of the survivors turned to Christianity.

The Ghost Dance

Nongqawuse's vision shares some basic similarities with a vision promoted in 1889 by a **Paiute** religious leader named Wovoka in the region that is now Nevada. Reviving a movement from two decades earlier, he prophesied that in a few years the ancestors would return, the buffalo herds would be restored, and the settlers would disappear. To hasten the coming of this new world, Wovoka was told that his people must live peacefully, and that they must perform a ritual focused on the spirits of their ancestors. The Lakota Sioux termed this ritual the 'spirit dance', which the Euro-Americans translated as '**Ghost Dance**'.

Delegates from various Native communities were sent to hear Wovoka. The Navajo, who were enjoying a period of relative stability, were not convinced. But the Lakota were on the verge of starvation after the US government had broken a treaty and given away their fertile reservation lands to white settlers. With the bison gone, crops scarce, and government supplies running low, the Lakota were strongly attracted to Wovoka's message, in particular the idea that the whites could be made to disappear. They danced with greater urgency as their situation deteriorated, and many took to wearing 'Ghost Shirts', which they believed would repel bullets.

Alarmed, the Bureau of Indian Affairs dispatched thousands of US Army troops to the Lakota territory to put an end to the dancing and protests and force any remaining Sioux to leave areas that had been set aside for white settlers. Among the consequences of this response were the death of Sitting Bull and the massacre at Wounded Knee.

From Earth to Sky

The British arrived in Australia in 1788 at the site that would become Sydney, and proceeded to devastate the Indigenous people and appropriate their lands so rapidly that, within a decade, the Aborigines in the region were desperate to be rid of them. They consequently developed a number of rituals to bring about this event, including ceremonial rebellions against mock recreations of the European murder of Aborigines and calling on the serpent Mindi to (fittingly) destroy the British with an outbreak of smallpox.

When these efforts failed to produce the desired results, and as the British continued to destroy the bonds between local people and their ancestral lands, a religious crisis developed. Some Aborigines came to believe not only that the world would soon end, but that the source of sacred power and authority had moved from the earth to the sky, a heavenly utopia beyond the clouds.

Evidence suggests that these beliefs were a direct result of exposure to Christianity.

Traditionally, the Aborigines had understood that after death their spirits would return to their homelands. Now, in a sad irony, they found comfort in the colonizers' notion that their spirits would instead journey to a paradise in the sky. The only difference was that, for the Aborigines, this paradise would be free of Europeans.

Autonomy and Equality

'If God be for us, who can be against us?'
—Archbishop Desmond Tutu, Xhosa (quoting *Romans* 8: 31; in Allen 2008: 334)

After various unsuccessful efforts to resist colonialism, many Indigenous people eventually found more effective ways of pursuing autonomy, equality, and fair treatment. In one way or another, religion has often been at the heart of these efforts.

Non-Indigenous Religions

Often the religion involved in the quest for equity has been Indigenous, but not always. Many Indigenous Christians, for example, have fought passionately against colonial (and Christian) abuses using ideas from the imported religion itself. Like Archbishop Desmond Tutu of South Africa, they have drawn on biblical notions of justice, of sympathy for the oppressed, and of deliverance from evil to support their work for equality and redress.

By the same token, some Indigenous Christians have also incorporated Indigenous views into their critiques of colonial attitudes and practices. To this end Desmond Tutu has frequently cited the African concept of *Ubuntu*, according to which all human beings are interconnected and therefore to harm others is to harm oneself. Stan McKay (Cree), an ordained minister in the United Church—and the first Native person in Canada to head up a mainline denomination—similarly draws on Aboriginal notions of the inter-relatedness of all life in his censure of Christianity's contributions to current environmental problems. In contrast to such Aboriginal notions, McKay writes, Christian theology for hundreds of years 'denied the integrity of creation' (McKay 1996: 55).

Land Claims

McKay's position combines a general concern for the environment with more specific concerns related to the appropriation and destruction of sacred Indigenous lands and efforts to reclaim such lands wherever possible. Some of these efforts have failed completely, some have done well, and others have had more complex results.

One early success came in 1970, when 194 square kilometres (48,000 acres) of land in New Mexico were returned to the Taos **Pueblo** by President Richard Nixon. Originally confiscated by President Theodore Roosevelt and designated the Carson National Forest, the region includes Blue Lake, which Taos tradition holds to be the site of creation.

In Canada, a major land dispute erupted in the summer of 1990 between the Mohawk community of Kanesatake and the town of Oka, Quebec. At issue was the town's plan to expand a golf course onto land containing sites sacred to the Mohawk, including a cemetery. After a court ruling allowed construction to proceed despite the Natives' objections, members of the Mohawk community erected a barricade denying access to the disputed territory.

The 78-day standoff eventually pitted Native people from across North America against the Canadian army. The federal government ultimately purchased the land and stopped the golf course development. But the Mohawk regarded this victory as only partial, since ownership of the land still did not rest with them.

Australian Aborigines have perhaps had more success at reclaiming land than any other Indigenous group. Since a High Court case in 1992 overturned the idea of Australia as *terra nullius*, Aborigines have successfully negotiated approximately 3,000 land claims. In the Northern

Territory, for example, most of the coastline and more than 40 per cent of the land area is now (once again) owned by Indigenous people.

Other Victories

Most countries have also repealed their laws inhibiting the practice of Indigenous religions. The bans on the Sun Dance and potlatch were lifted decades ago. Much more recently, when a local government in Florida outlawed animal sacrifice in an effort to stop the practice of Santeria and Voudou, the US Supreme Court ruled the legislation unconstitutional.

On a much larger scale, South Africa's apartheid laws were eliminated and its colonial regime overturned in 1994, and in 2008 Australia's Prime Minister Kevin Rudd officially apologized to the Aboriginal people for the policies and practices that had created the Stolen Generations. Later that same year, Canada's prime minister, Stephen Harper, issued an official apology for the residential school system, acknowledging that 'it was wrong . . . to separate children from rich and vibrant traditions.'

Such victories are reflected in more local but equally important changes in attitude. School teams in countries around the world, for example, have replaced their Indigenous-themed names or mascots. An especially imaginative solution was devised in 2006 for the Syracuse Chiefs, a triple-A baseball team in New York State, which kept its name but changed its logo from an 'Indian chief' to a silver locomotive (with a 'chief engineer'). The change actually made the team's name more relevant to the town's history as a railway hub.

In April 2009, when several Native people got wind of the 'GO NATIVE' party in Oakland, California, promoting the Burning Man festival, they decided to attend and use the occasion to explain why they believed the event was harmful to all. They reportedly spent more than four hours lecturing the participants about colonialism and the history of invasion, genocide, and appropriation associated with it. Apparently they made their point: most of those present apologized for their actions, and several broke down sobbing with regret and embarrassment.

Contemporary Indigenous Traditions

The people nowadays have an idea about the ceremonies. They think the ceremonies must be performed exactly as they have always been done. . . . But long ago when the people were given these ceremonies, the changing began, if only in the aging of the yellow gourd rattle or the shrinking of the skin around the eagle's claw, if only in the different voices from generation to generation, singing the chants. You see, in many ways, the ceremonies have always been changing.

—Betonie, a character in the novel *Ceremony* by Leslie Marmon Silko (1977: 132), Laguna Pueblo

Resurgence

Not surprisingly, with increasing legal and social recognition of Indigenous traditions has come an increase in the actual practice of those traditions. Most of the varieties of religious expression discussed in this chapter have experienced a resurgence in recent decades, from carving masks in Africa to telling Dreamtime stories in Australia to performing the Sun Dance in North America.

The revival of the Maori *moko* tradition is considered by some to be especially significant, symbolically. As we saw, *moko* is said to have originated in the underworld, and was then brought to the surface. When the practice was abolished by colonial rulers, the tradition returned underground in a political and figurative way; and thus its modern 'resurfacing' can be seen as re-enacting the ancestral story.

The resurgence of Indigenous religions is seen at least in part as a way of coping with the cultural damage done by colonialism. At the same time some people—Indigenous and non-Indigenous—have pointed out that the more 'material' consequences of colonialism must be addressed as well. For many Indigenous people around the world, these consequences include extreme poverty and deprivation; therefore it is important not to focus on 'spiritual' issues at the expense of economics and politics. Ideally, the aim is to channel the positive effects of revitalized religious practices in ways that will also contribute to the improvement of Indigenous living conditions.

It is also important to remember that Indigenous people themselves are not of one mind on the revival of traditional religions. There are many who do not wish to return to these traditions, whether because they do not find value in them or because they now practise another religion. Nevertheless, growing numbers of Indigenous people do seem eager to make traditional practices and beliefs an important part of their lives.

Always Been Changing

The ways in which Indigenous traditions are practised today are generally not identical with the ways in which they were practised in the past, for several reasons. First, of course, all religions—and cultures—change over time. Second, the disruptions caused by colonial practices have been so severe that in many instances it is not possible to recover pre-colonial traditions in full or even in part. Third, Indigenous traditions are typically interested in the manifestation of the sacred in the here and now; the intersection of spirits and ancestors with the world did not end sometime in the ancient past but is an ongoing reality that necessitates adaptation.

A couple of simple changes in Yoruba practice may illustrate the above points. For one thing, the roles of many traditional spirits have altered somewhat. Thus the Yoruba god of iron and war, Ogun, has come to be associated with the protection of welders, car mechanics, and chauffeurs. Also, as a result of the lifestyle upheavals caused

by colonialism, very little cloth is now woven by hand. Mass-produced fabric is thus used for many rituals, and at times younger people in particular will wear American clothing to ceremonial events. Some communities such as the Bunu, however, still ascribe to handwoven cloth great religious and social value, and so continue to produce it for the most important occasions.

Trickster stories also frequently embody the ways in which Indigenous religions have continued to respond to historical developments. New tales are always appearing. When colonization began, for example, some tricksters used their powers to get the better of the newcomers; others imitated colonizing practices—for example, negotiating worthless agreements—to fool the Indigenous people into giving them things they wanted. Tricksters in modern stories may appear in any number of non-traditional guises, from politician to bartender to university teacher. In addition, there are now many female tricksters.

Gender shifts are evident in other areas of Indigenous life as well. In the past, men and women often had quite different but interdependent functions, but because of the severe disruptions to traditional lifestyles over the past few hundred years, the same role differentiation is often no longer possible. For example, if at one time women in a community were responsible for preparing the food that the men killed or grew, the whole arrangement fell apart once their land was taken. This dissolution combined with the advent of colonial patriarchies to put severe stress on Indigenous gender relations.

Some communities are now addressing this situation by moving towards more balanced gender representation in similar roles, many of them related to religious practices. Thus increasing numbers of Native American men are weaving ritual baskets. Similarly, there are now several female *moko* artists, and it is no longer uncommon for women to receive full *moko* themselves (not just on their lips or lower face). Such changes are among the ways in which Indigenous people are working to overcome the gender hierarchies that developed under colonialism.

Cultural Expressions

One of the most noticeable recent developments in Indigenous religions is their presence in art forms that originated in non-Indigenous cultures, including film, written literature, oil painting, and electronic music. Works *by* Indigenous people *about* Indigenous people are appearing with increasing frequency and receiving much attention and acclaim. Religion may be employed in these works in the service of engaging issues arising from colonialism (past or present), or to highlight/explore aspects of Indigenous life on their own terms.

An example of the latter approach is the painting 'Red Willows' by David Johnson (Anishinaubae), which appears on page 342. The work is clearly modern, produced in the mid-1990s to accompany Basil Johnston's retelling of the traditional story. The pairing of art and text adds meaning to both, often in a way that highlights the religious aspects of the tale. Thus the significance of the colour red in the painting is revealed only by the text, while the branch that appears both inside and outside the man suggests the interrelatedness of all things, a theme that readers of the story—distracted by its vivid, humorous physicality—could easily miss.

Prominent recent films that focus primarily on Indigenous religion include *Atanarjuat: The Fast Runner* (Canada, 2001), *Whale Rider* (New Zealand, 2002), and *Ten Canoes* (Australia, 2006). Two notable documentaries that consider the appropriation of Indigenous religion are *White Shamans and Plastic Medicine Men* (US, 1996), which looks at the theft and commercialization of Native American traditions by non-Natives, and *Reel Injun* (Canada, 2009), which explores the depictions of Native people in movies.

Several other films refer to Indigenous religion while focusing primarily on the consequences of colonialism, among them *Dance Me Outside* (Canada, 1994), *Rabbit-Proof Fence* (Australia, 2002), *Moolaadé* (Senegal/France/Burkina Faso/Cameroon/Morocco/Tunisia, 2004), and perhaps most famously, *Once Were Warriors* (New Zealand, 1994). Directed by Lee Tamahori (Maori) and starring mostly Maori actors, *Once Were Warriors* presents a complex picture of the return to Indigenous traditions. For some key female characters, this return is beneficial, helping them to regain a sense of dignity, community, and self-worth in the wake of the personal and cultural havoc wreaked by colonialism. For a number of male characters, however, the return is clouded by anger and misunderstanding, and sadly helps to perpetuate the domestic and communal violence resulting from colonialism.

Literature

One of the first Indigenous writers to be recognized internationally was the poet Pauline Johnson (Mohawk), who began publishing in 1883. In fact, she was described by critics of her time as 'perhaps the most unique figure in the literary world on this continent', and even 'the greatest living poetess' (Francis 1992: 113). In 1961 Johnson also became the first Canadian writer, the first Canadian woman, and the first Canadian Aboriginal person to be honoured by a commemorative stamp. Her poetry covered a range of topics but very often returned to the sacred theme of place, as in her most famous work, 'The Song My Paddle Sings'.

The modern era of Indigenous literature began in earnest in 1958 with the appearance of Chinua Achebe's *Things Fall Apart*. Focusing on the life and family of Okonkwo, an Igbo man from a fictional village in Nigeria around the turn of the nineteenth century, the novel depicts the effects of British colonialism, and particularly Christian missionaries, on the life and religion of the Indigenous people of Africa. *Things Fall Apart* was a landmark, undeniably the most influential work of modern African literature to date, and regularly appears high in the lists of the top 100 books of

From *The Bone People*, by Keri Hulme (Maori)

Published in 1984, this Booker Prize–winning novel follows three interconnected characters—Simon, Joe, and Kerewin—whose experiences are symbolically linked to Maori religious beliefs and practices. These characters are briefly introduced in the book's prologue.

He walks down the street. The asphalt reels by him.
It is all silence.
The silence is music.
He is the singer.
The people passing smile and shake their heads.
He holds a hand out to them.
They open their hands like flowers, shyly.
He smiles with them.
The light is blinding: he loves the light.
They are the light.

. . .

He walks down the street. The asphalt is hot and soft with sun.
The people passing smile, and call out greetings.
He smiles and calls back.
His mind is full of change and curve and hope, and he knows it is being lightly tapped. He laughs.
Maybe there is the dance, as she says. Creation and change, destruction and change.
New marae from the old marae, a beginning from the end.
His mind weaves it into a spiral fretted with stars.
He holds out his hand, and it is gently taken.

. . .

She walks down the street. The asphalt sinks beneath her muscled feet.
She whistles softly as she walks. Sometimes she smiles.
The people passing smile too, but duck their heads in a deferential way as though her smile is too
    sharp.
She grins more at the lowered heads. She can dig out each thought, each reaction, out from the grey
    brains, out through the bones. She knows a lot.
She is eager to know more.
But for now there is the sun at her back, and home here, and free wind all round.
And them, shuffling ahead in the strange-paced dance. She quickens her steps until she has reached
    them.
And she sings as she takes their hands.

. . .

They were nothing more than people, by themselves. Even paired, any pairing, they would have
    been nothing more than people by themselves. But all together, they have become the heart and
    muscles and mind of something perilous and new, something strange and growing and great.
Together, all together, they are the instruments of change (Hulme 1983: 3–4).

all time (including *Newsweek's* 2009 'meta-list', on which it ranked number 14).

Achebe's novel was part of the first wave of a flood of modern Indigenous writing around the world. Hundreds of authors have since produced a huge variety of compelling works of fiction, poetry, autobiography, and drama. Some of these authors include:

- José María Arguedas (Quechua)
- Maria Campbell (Métis)
- Jack Davis (Noongar)
- Louise Erdrich (Anishinaubae)
- Tomson Highway (Cree)
- Keri Hulme (Maori)
- Thomas King (Cherokee)
- N. Scott Momaday (Kiowa)
- Sally Morgan (Palku)
- Leslie Marmon Silko (Laguna Pueblo)
- Wole Soyinka (Yoruba)

Religion is consistently a central issue in the works of most Indigenous authors. The very title of Momaday's breakthrough novel *House Made of Dawn*—winner of the 1969 Pulitzer Prize for Fiction—is taken from the Navajo Nightway Prayer.

Keri Hulme's novel *The Bone People* similarly displays elements characteristic of the resurgence of Indigenous traditions in general and Maori traditions in particular. Many of these elements are evident even in the book's brief prologue:

- a rhythmic sense of time, the past connected to the present;
- complementary dualism (the 'dance' of 'creation and change, destruction and change');
- allusion to the central *koru* (spiral) element of Maori *moko*; and
- the importance of community, of rebuilding the *marae*.

Like other works of contemporary Indigenous art, *The Bone People* taps into the existential possibility of Indigenous religions, applying traditional views and practices to current situations. With both pathos and humour, it shows us characters struggling with their place in the world as individuals and as part of a community. Some of them manage better than others, some of them make terrible mistakes. But nothing is forever, and, as in many Indigenous stories—both past and present—when we get to the end, we are also very clearly at a beginning. For there are always new stories to tell.

Sites

Given the centrality of place in Indigenous traditions, it is no surprise that there are innumerable sacred sites around the globe. Often connected with acts of creation, these are places where gods, spirits, or ancestors intersect with our world. Thousands of sites have been destroyed or appropriated in the process of colonization, but many remain. Listed below are just a few of the places sacred to Indigenous peoples that are still in use.

Bandiagara Escarpment In the Dogon creation story, the supreme being Amma sacrificed one of the Nummo (his four children) and scattered the body's remains on the earth. The Bandiagara escarpment in Mali is one of the sites where the Dogon people erected shrines to house the pieces. Other such sites can be found throughout Western Africa.

Continued

Bighorn Medicine Wheel In general, a medicine wheel or sacred hoop is a circular arrangement of stones with radial lines from the centre to the rim, designed to facilitate communication with spirits. Located in Wyoming at an elevation of roughly 3,000 metres (almost 10,000 feet), the Bighorn Medicine Wheel is arguably the most important sacred hoop in North America. Blackfoot, Crow, Cheyenne, Sioux, and Arapahoe communities continue to use the site for vision quests, healing rituals, and prayers for guidance and wisdom.

Blue Lake The site of creation for the Taos Pueblo in New Mexico. Part of the 194 square kilometres of land confiscated in 1906 to create the Carson National Forest, it was returned to the Taos people in 1970.

Ife The ancient site in Nigeria where the Yoruba deities Oduduwa and Obatala began the creation of the world. Many Yoruba communities still celebrate this act at the annual Itapa festival in Ife—now a city of roughly 500,000.

Kanesatake The home of the Mohawk community that objected when the neighbouring town of Oka, Quebec, planned to expand a golf course onto land the Mohawk considered sacred, resulting in armed confrontation. After a 78-day standoff in the summer of 1990, the government of Canada bought the site and stopped the development.

Nibutani The site where the Ainu god Okikurmikamuy arrived on earth, at the midpoint of the Saru River in Hokkaido, Japan. This is also the site where the Ainu author Kayano Shigeru built the Nibutani Museum of Ainu Cultural Resources, dedicated to preserving and revitalizing his people's culture.

Saut d'Eau A group of waterfalls about 95 kilometres (60 miles) from Port-au-Prince, Haiti, where Yoruba spirits are understood to dwell along with several Catholic saints. Voudou adherents make an annual pilgrimage to Saut d'Eau in June, a journey that is required of those seeking to join the priesthood.

Tanna An island belonging to the archipelago nation of Vanuatu in the South Pacific Ocean, and home to one of the last remaining Melanesian cargo cults. The Jon Frum movement began in the 1930s urging a return to traditional practices, and evolved into a cargo cult during the Second World War when approximately 300,000 American troops were stationed in Vanuatu. Its followers still hold a military-style parade every year on 15 February.

Tiwanaku The most sacred place for the Aymara people of Bolivia. Located roughly 70 kilometres (45 miles) west of La Paz, it is the centre of the world, the site of humanity's creation, and the place where the local Indigenous people go to communicate with their ancestors. Because Tiwanaku is considered a major archaeological site, access to it has been severely restricted; even the Aymara must pay an entrance fee.

Uluru An enormous sandstone formation in central Australia that is sacred to the local Aboriginal people, the Pitjantjatjara and Yankunytjatjara. These communities conduct ceremonies along the rock's base and in its caves, where ancestral markings from Dreamtime events are evident. Uluru itself was the result of such an event, when the earth rose up in grief after a bloody battle.

Glossary

Aborigine An Indigenous person. Often the term specifically indicates an Indigenous person of Australia.

Ainu The Indigenous people of northern Japan; not officially recognized as such by the government of Japan until 2008. Current population estimates range widely, from about 25,000 to as high as 200,000.

Anishinaubae The term (roughly translating as 'the people') traditionally used by the Odawa, Ojibwe, and Algonkin peoples to refer to themselves. The Anishinaubae are located mainly around the Great Lakes area in Canada and the US.

Arawak The Indigenous people encountered by the Spanish (led by Columbus) in the West Indies in 1492. Most Arawaks were killed by the Spanish or died from other results of colonialism, but a few small populations remain in northeastern South America.

Bunu One of four Yoruba groups in central Nigeria, living near the city of Lokoja where the Niger and Benue Rivers converge.

cargo cults Religious movements, mainly in Melanesia, inspired by the shipments of goods that local Indigenous people saw arriving for foreigners; founded on the belief that one day the spirits would send similar shipments to them, initiating a new age of peace and social harmony.

Cherokee The largest federally recognized Native American group in America, with more than 300,000 members. Most currently live in the southeastern US, with band headquarters in Oklahoma and North Carolina.

Chumash Native American people traditionally based along the southern California coast, from Morro Bay to Malibu. Although only about 200 Chumash remained in 1900, recent estimates put their numbers at around 5,000.

colonialism The process of establishing and maintaining colonies in one place by people who are from another, and the effects of this process on the people who were already there. Historically, these effects have often included the destruction of Indigenous cultures and people.

complementary dualism A worldview in which the universe necessarily comprises both creative and destructive forces, and the two can work together; a feature of many Indigenous religions.

conflict dualism A worldview in which the universe is divided between good and evil forces that are in constant battle with one another; a feature of many Western religions.

Cree The largest Indigenous group in Canada, with a population over 200,000. Formerly based in central Canada, Cree populations are now well established in every province from Alberta to Quebec, as well as parts of the northern US such as Montana.

Crow A Siouan-speaking Native American people historically residing in the Yellowstone River valley, and now concentrated in Montana.

diviner A religious specialist who uses various ritual tools and practices to gain insight into the hidden or spiritual aspects of particular circumstances, events, problems, etc.

Dogon A West African people living mainly in the central region of Mali, with a population of about half a million. Their first contact with Europeans was in 1857, but the Dogon have been more successful than many other Indigenous Africans at holding on to their traditional religious practices.

The Dreaming The term that anthropologists gave to the time and place of Australian Aboriginal origin stories. Although often thought to refer to the archaic past, The Dreaming is actually understood by many traditional Aborigines to lie just out of reach of living memory.

elder A man or woman whose wisdom and authority in cultural matters are recognized by their community. Elders are not necessarily elderly per se, but are understood to possess greater knowledge of tradition than others, and often to be more closely in touch with spiritual forces.

Ghost Dance A religious movement that emerged in the western US in the late nineteenth century in response to the colonial destruction of American Indigenous people and cultures. Begun in 1869 by Wodziwob and revived in 1889 by Wovoka, the Ghost Dance was practised to hasten both the removal of the settlers and the restoration of what Native people had lost. Smaller, modified Ghost Dance revivals occurred periodically throughout the twentieth century.

hogan A traditional Navajo home. The first hogan was the earth itself, and so building a new home reproduces the creation of the world. This structure is at the centre of the community's domestic, social, and religious life. If anyone dies inside a hogan it is never used again, and in fact is often burned.

Igbo One of the largest Indigenous groups in Nigeria, living principally in the southeastern region of the country. Worldwide population estimates range between 20 million and 40 million.

Indian Act Canadian federal legislation created in 1876 that defines and regulates Native people and their lands and outlines the federal government's responsibilities towards them. The act is administered by the Department of Indian and Northern Affairs and has undergone several amendments and revisions.

Iroquois Also known as the Six Nations; a Native North American confederacy based in the northeastern US and southeastern Canada, originally composed of five Iroquoian-speaking groups (Mohawk, Oneida, Onondaga, Cayuga, and Seneca) and joined in 1722 by the Tuscarora.

Karuk A Native American community from the region of the Klamath River in northwestern California, with a population of about 3,500. Karuk translates as 'upstream people', in contrast to their neighbours the Yurok, or 'downstream people'.

Kewa Indigenous people from the Southern Highlands province of Papua New Guinea, with a current estimated population of about 65,000.

Lakota The largest of the three Native American groups that make up the Sioux Nation (the others are the Eastern and Western Dakota). The Lakota were originally based near the Great Lakes, but moved to the Great Plains region in response to the influx of European settlers.

Maori The Indigenous people of New Zealand, who appear to have arrived there in the late thirteenth century from elsewhere in Polynesia. Current estimates put the Maori population at around 700,000.

marae The religious and social home of a Maori community, consisting of a cleared area bordered with stones or wooden posts, and containing several structures including the *whare whakairo* ('carved house'), dining room, shelters, and a site where the dead are placed in state.

mbari A mode or style of Igbo cultural practice, especially architecture; principally identified with the Owerri Igbo of Nigeria.

Mohawk Native North American people based near Lake Ontario and the St Lawrence River; the most easterly of the Iroquoian Six Nations.

moko Traditional Maori tattoos originally chiselled into the skin (*moko* literally means 'to strike' or 'to tap'). These markings identify both the individual and his or her relationship to the community. Brought up to earth from the underworld by ancestors long ago, *moko* was abolished by colonial rulers but has 'resurfaced' with the revival of other Maori practices.

Navajo The second-largest Native American group in the US (after the Cherokee), with an estimated population of almost 300,000. The Navajo occupy extensive territory in Arizona, New Mexico, and Utah.

New Age A common term for Western spiritual movements concerned with universal truths and individual potential. New Age teachings are drawn from a wide range of religions and philosophies, including astrology, Buddhism, metaphysics, environmentalism, and Indigenous traditions. The term was used in the early 1800s by William Blake and gained wide popularity in the mid-1970s.

Nisga'a Indigenous people of the Nass River valley of northwestern British Columbia. In 1998 the Nisga'a reached a historic settlement with the provincial and federal governments acknowledging their sovereignty over 2,000 square kilometres of land; the Nisga'a agreement was the first formal treaty signed by a Native group in British Columbia since 1854.

Nuer A confederation of peoples in southern Sudan and western Ethiopia; the largest Indigenous group in East Africa, with a population of about 33 million. The Nuer successfully fought off colonial forces in the early twentieth century and have largely resisted conversion to Christianity.

Nyanga Indigenous people from the highlands of east-central Zaire, near the borders of Rwanda and Uganda. Part of the larger Bantu group in Africa, their current population is about 35,000.

Oglala One of seven groups that make up the Lakota Sioux, the Oglala are based at the Pine Ridge Indian Reservation in South Dakota, the second-largest reservation in the US.

Paiute Two related Native American groups, the Northern Paiute (based in California, Nevada, and Oregon) and the Southern Paiute (based in Arizona, California, Nevada, and Utah). Wovoka, the leader of the 1889 Ghost Dance movement, was a member of the Northern group.

Pomo Native American people of the northern California coast who, though connected by geography and marriage, traditionally lived in small separate bands rather than as a large unified group. The Pomo linguistic family once comprised seven distinct languages, but few Pomo speakers now remain.

Pondo South African Indigenous group who speak the Xhosa language and live along the southeastern coast of Cape Province.

potlatch A ritual practised by many Indigenous groups of the Pacific Northwest Coast (e.g., Haida, Salish, Tlingit, Tsimshian), in which a family hosts a feast and offers guests a variety of gifts. The ritual typically marks important moments such as marriage, childbirth, or death, and may include music, theatre, and ceremonial dancing.

Pueblo Native American people from the southwestern US, particularly New Mexico and Arizona, who traditionally lived in small villages ('pueblos' in Spanish). Approximately 25 separate Pueblo communities remain, including the Hopi, Taos, and Zuni.

residential schools Church-run schools, funded by the Canadian federal government, designed to facilitate the assimilation and Christian conversion of Indigenous people. Families were forced to send their children to the schools, where they remained for months or even years at a time, forbidden to speak their own languages and often subjected to neglect or abuse. The system was established in the 1840s and the last school did not close until 1996.

Sioux Native American people with reserves in the Dakotas, Minnesota, Montana, Nebraska, Manitoba, and southern Saskatchewan, and comprised of three main groups: the Lakota, Eastern Dakota, and Western Dakota. The Sioux have been centrally involved in many key moments of American colonial history, including the Battle of Little Bighorn, and Sioux writers and political leaders remain among the most influential members of the larger Native North American community.

Stolen Generations The generations of Australian Aborigines who as children were taken from their families by the government and sent either to foster homes or to government- or church-run institutions. Because records were frequently lost or not kept, many children were never able to reconnect with their families. The practice continued from approximately 1869 to the early 1970s.

Sun Dance Annual summer ritual practised by peoples of the North American plains (e.g., Blackfoot, Cheyenne, Crow, Kiowa, Sioux). The details of the ritual vary among different communities, as does the meaning of the solar symbolism. In the late nineteenth century the Sun Dance was severely discouraged by the Canadian government and outlawed in the US; it has experienced a revival since the 1960s.

sweat lodge A structure traditionally covered with skins, blankets, or dirt, used to induce sweating by pouring water over heated stones to create steam. Sweat lodge ceremonies are performed by several Native North American communities for various medicinal and religious purposes, including purification and reconnection to the spirits.

syncretism The combination of elements from two or more different religious traditions. Too often the term is used negatively to suggest that the 'purity' of a particular religion has been compromised or contaminated.

terra nullius Latin for 'no one's land', referring to territory over which no person or state has ownership or sovereignty; a concept invoked in several instances by European colonists to claim land occupied by Indigenous people. In Australia, the High Court invalidated this justification in a 1992 ruling.

trickster Term coined by scholars to classify a variety of usually superhuman figures who appear in the stories of cultures around the world; tricksters disrupt the norms of society and/or nature and often serve to teach important lessons about what kinds of behaviour a particular community considers appropriate.

Tsimshian Indigenous people of the Pacific Northwest Coast, from British Columbia to southeast Alaska. The current Tsimshian population is approximately 10,000.

Ubuntu African concept that all human beings are interconnected, employed most famously by Nelson Mandela and Archbishop Desmond Tutu as one of the founding principles of the new South Africa. *Ubuntu* has since also gained prominence in the US.

vision quest Fasting ritual undertaken by members of many Native North American communities to induce visions through contact with spirits. A vision quest typically lasts several days and involves a solitary journey away from home into the wilderness; it may be undertaken as a rite of passage to adulthood or during other key life events, such as preparation for war.

Wiradjuri The largest Indigenous group in New South Wales, Australia, who have lived in the central region of the state for more than 40,000 years. Evidence indicates that no native speakers of the Wiradjuri language remain.

Xhosa Indigenous people living mainly in southeast South Africa. There are currently about 8 million Xhosa, and their language is the second most common in South Africa after Zulu. Nelson Mandela and Archbishop Desmond Tutu are both Xhosa.

Yanyuwa A small group of Australian Aborigines located mainly in the Northern Territory. Fewer than ten speakers of the Yanyuwa language currently remain.

Yolngu Aboriginal Australian community from northeastern Arnhem Land in the Northern Territory. For more than fifty years, Yolngu leaders have been centrally involved with land claims in Australia.

Yoruba One of the largest Indigenous groups in west Africa, with a population of approximately 30 million based mainly in Nigeria. Yoruba traditions have had an enormous influence on the religions of African communities around the world; because so many African slaves were Yoruba, their impact has been especially significant in the Americas.

Yurok Native American community, with a population of about 6,000, who have lived near the northern California coast for more than 10,000 years. Yurok translates as 'downstream people', in contrast to their neighbours the Karuk, or 'upstream people'.

Further Reading

Ballinger, Franchot. 2004. *Living Sideways: Tricksters in American Indian Oral Traditions.* Norman: University of Oklahoma Press. An excellent, engaging introduction to the roles, meanings, and diversity of Native American trickster figures; focuses on traditional (oral) stories but also includes references to contemporary literature.

Baum, Robert M. 1999. *Shrines of the Slave Trade: Diola Religion and Society in Precolonial Senegambia.* New York: Oxford University Press. This detailed study is one of the few to examine the pre-contact history of any African Indigenous religion.

Bell, Diane. 1983. *Daughters of the Dreaming.* Melbourne: McPhee-Gribble. An accessible (and best-selling) work of groundbreaking scholarship on the religious lives of Aboriginal women in central Australia.

Bockle, Simon. 1993. *Death and the Invisible Powers: The World of Kongo Belief.* Bloomington: Indiana University Press. An insider's introduction to the religious life of the Kongo people of Lower Zaire and to African religions generally, focusing on views and behaviours concerning death.

Deloria, Vine, Jr. 1994 (1972). *God Is Red: A Native View of Religion.* 2nd ed. Golden: Fulcrum. Indispensable overview of Native American religious perspectives, particularly regarding the importance of sacred places and the effects of colonialism.

Francis, Daniel. 1992. *The Imaginary Indian: The Image of the Indian in Canadian Culture.* Vancouver: Arsenal Pulp. A detailed, accessible discussion of the ways in which non-Natives in Canada have appropriated Native identity.

Gill, Sam D. 1982. *Beyond the 'Primitive': The Religions of Nonliterate Peoples.* Englewood Cliffs, NJ: Prentice-Hall. Still one of the best general introductions to Indigenous traditions; especially useful on what religious practices mean to their communities.

Jacobs, Sue-Ellen, Wesley Thomas, and Sabine Lang, eds. 1997. *Two-Spirit People: Native American Gender Identity, Sexuality, and Spirituality.* Urbana and Chicago: University of Illinois Press. A vital collection of essays examining the connections between Native North American religions and constructions of gender and sexuality, from the traditional acceptance of diversity in many communities to current efforts to reclaim that acceptance.

LeRoy, John, ed. 1985. *Kewa Tales.* Vancouver: University of British Columbia Press. A valuable collection of traditional oral narratives from Papua New Guinea, catalogued to highlight various story patterns.

Mead, Hirini Moko. 2003. *Tikanga Maori: Living by Maori Values.* Wellington, NZ: Huia. A useful overview of Maori *tikanga* ('way of doing things'), especially the connections between religion and the creative arts; promotes *tikanga* as a guide for non-Maori people.

Olajubu, Oyeronke. 2003. *Women in the Yoruba Religious Sphere.* New York: State University of New York Press. Examines women's roles—along with issues of gender and power relations—in both traditional and contemporary Yoruba thought and practice.

Olupona, Jacob K., ed. 2004. *Beyond Primitivism: Indigenous Religious Traditions and Modernity.* New York: Routledge. One of the very few works to look at the contemporary situation of Indigenous religions; contributors from a broad range of backgrounds consider traditions from across America, Africa, Asia, and the Pacific.

Renne, Elisha P. 1995. *Cloth That Does Not Die: The Meaning of Cloth in Bùnú Social Life.* Seattle: University of Washington Press. A clear, insightful look at the role of a key material object in the culture (and especially religion) of the Bunu Yoruba people.

Rosaldo, Renato. 1980. *Ilongot Headhunting 1883–1974: A Study in Society and History.* Stanford: Stanford

University Press. An influential analysis of the meaning and function of headhunting for the Ilongot people in the Philippines; discredits the notion that Indigenous societies were/are static, as opposed to European societies that changed over time.

Ryan, Allan. 1999. *The Trickster Shift: Humour and Irony in Contemporary Native Art.* Vancouver: University of British Columbia Press. The first book-length study of the influence of trickster conceptions in modern Native art, with photos of recent work alongside commentaries from the artists.

Shigeru, Kayano. 1994. *Our Land Was a Forest: An Ainu Memoir.* Trans. Kyoko Selden and Lili Selden. Boulder: Westview. A moving personal account by an Ainu man who has spent much of his life documenting his people's culture and history, as well as creating a school to ensure the continuation of the Ainu language.

Smith, Jonathan Z., et al., eds. 1995. *The HarperCollins Dictionary of Religion.* San Francisco: HarperCollins. The following entries provide an excellent brief introduction to particular topics relevant to the study of Indigenous religions: 'Africa, traditional religions in'; 'Australian and Pacific traditional religions'; 'circumpolar religions'; 'Mesoamerican religion'; 'Native Americans (Central and South America), new religions among'; 'Native Americans (North America), new religions among'; 'non-literacy'; 'North America, traditional religions in'; 'Religions of Traditional Peoples'; 'South American religions, traditional'; 'traditional religions, Western influence on'.

Swain, Tony, and Garry Trompf. 1995. *The Religions of Oceania.* London: Routledge. The first (and possibly best) book in English on the religions of the southwest Pacific as a whole; provides clear interpretive tools and general information on the history and content of these traditions, from before colonialism through to modernity.

Wright, Ronald. 1992. *Stolen Continents: The 'New World' through Indian Eyes.* Boston: Houghton Mifflin. Powerful, accessible account of the colonization and survival of five American civilizations—Aztec, Maya, Inca, Cherokee, and Iroquois—that includes much Indigenous testimony.

Recommended Websites

http://cwis.org/wwwvl/indig-vl.html
  Center for World Indigenous Studies Virtual Library: a list of websites offering further information on Indigenous cultures and current issues, organized by region.

www.everyculture.com
  Countries and Their Cultures: contains brief but substantive information on most Indigenous cultures, including an overview of religious beliefs and practices, and a bibliography for further research on each group.

http://indigenouspeoplesissues.com/
  Indigenous Peoples Issues and Resources: articles, updates, and information on current issues affecting Indigenous communities around the world, provided by a global network of scholars, activists, and organizations.

www.hanksville.org/sand/index.html
  A Line in the Sand: information and resources about (and critiques of) the appropriation of Indigenous cultural property, particularly religious images and practices.

www.nativewiki.org
  NativeWiki: a library of information about Indigenous cultures and peoples, past and present, to which users can also contribute. As yet, most of the material on the site concerns Native North Americans.

References

Achebe, Chinua. 1996 (1958). *Things Fall Apart*. Oxford: Heinemann.

Allen, John. 2008. *Desmond Tutu: Rabble-Rouser for Peace: The Authorized Biography*. Chicago: Lawrence Hill.

Baum, L. Frank. 1890. *Aberdeen (South Dakota) Saturday Pioneer*, 20 December.

Beck, Peggy V., Anne Lee Walters, and Nia Francisco. 1992 (1977). *The Sacred: Ways of Knowledge, Sources of Life*. Redesigned ed. Tsaile: Navajo Community College Press.

Bellfy, Philip. 2005. 'Permission and Possession: The Identity Tightrope'. In Ute Lischke and David T. McNab, eds. *Walking a Tightrope: Aboriginal People and Their Representations*, 29–44. Waterloo: Wilfrid Laurier University Press.

Bunn-Marcuse, Kathryn. 2005. 'Kwakwaka'wakw on Film'. In Ute Lischke and David T. McNab, eds. *Walking a Tightrope: Aboriginal People and Their Representations*, 305–34. Waterloo: Wilfrid Laurier University Press.

Campbell, Maria. 1973. *Halfbreed*. Halifax: Goodread.

Cooke, Dewi. 2008. '"Sorry" Statement Should Acknowledge Cultural Loss, Says State Leader'. *The Age* (1 February). Accessed 11 Oct. 2009 at <http://www.theage.com.au/articles/2008/01/31/12017141 53311.html>.

Cox, James L. 2007. *From Primitive to Indigenous: The Academic Study of Indigenous Religions*. Aldershot: Ashgate.

Deloria, Vine, Jr. 1988 (1969). *Custer Died for Your Sins: An Indian Manifesto*. Norman and Lincoln: University of Oklahoma Press.

———. 1997. 'Conclusion: Anthros, Indians, and Planetary Reality'. In Thomas Biolsi and Larry J. Zimmerman, eds. *Indians and Anthropologists: Vine Deloria, Jr., and the Critique of Anthropology*, 209–21. Tucson: University of Arizona Press.

Drewal, Margaret Thompson. 2002. 'The Ontological Journey'. In Graham Harvey, ed. *Readings in Indigenous Religions*, 123–48. London: Continuum.

Ebert, Roger. 1998. Review of *Smoke Signals*. rogerebert. com (3 July). Accessed 17 Jan. 2010 at <http://rogerebert.suntimes.com/apps/pbcs.dll/article?AID=/19980703/REVIEWS/807030303/1023>.

Eliot, T.S. 1959. *Four Quartets*. London: Faber and Faber.

Francis, Daniel. 1992. *The Imaginary Indian: The Image of the Indian in Canadian Culture*. Vancouver: Arsenal Pulp.

Gill, Sam D. 1982. *Beyond the 'Primitive': The Religions of Nonliterate Peoples*. Englewood Cliffs: Prentice-Hall.

Heiss, Anita. 2001. 'Aboriginal Identity and Its Effects on Writing'. In Armand Garnet Ruffo, ed. *(Ad)dressing Our Words: Aboriginal Perspectives on Aboriginal Literatures*, 205–32. Penticton, BC: Theytus.

Hulme, Keri. 1983. *The Bone People*. Wellington: Spiral.

Johnston, Basil. 1995. *The Bear-Walker and Other Stories*. Illustrated by David Johnson. Toronto: Royal Ontario Museum.

King, Thomas. 1993. *Green Grass, Running Water*. Toronto: HarperCollins.

Looking Horse, Arvol. 2009. 'Concerning the deaths in Sedona.' *Indian Country Today* (16 Oct.). Accessed 20 Feb. 2010 at <http://www.indiancountrytoday.com/opinion/columnists/64486777.html>.

Lutz, Hartmut. 1991. *Contemporary Challenges: Conversations with Canadian Native Authors*. Saskatoon: Fifth House.

McKay, Stan. 1996. 'An Aboriginal Christian Perspective on the Integrity of Creation'. In James Treat, ed. *Native and Christian: Indigenous Voices on Religious Identity in the United States and Canada*, 51–5. New York: Routledge.

Matthews, Washington. 1995 (1902). *The Night Chant: A Navaho Ceremony*. Salt Lake City: University of Utah Press.

Mitchell, Ryan. 2003. 'Maori Chief on Facial Tattoos and Tribal Pride.' *National Geographic News* (14 Oct.). Accessed 21 Mar. 2009 at <http://news.nationalgeographic.com/news/pf/84577710.html. 2009>.

Moses, Daniel David, and Terry Goldie. 1992. 'Preface: Two Voices'. In Daniel David Moses and Terry Goldie, eds. *An Anthology of Canadian Native Literature in English*, xii-xxii. Toronto: Oxford University Press.

Renne, Elisha P. 1995. *Cloth That Does Not Die: The Meaning of Cloth in Bunu Social Life*. Seattle: University of Washington Press.

Ross, Rupert. 1992. *Dancing with a Ghost: Exploring Indian Reality*. Markham: Octopus.

Sarris, Greg. 1992. '"What I'm Talking about When I'm Talking about My Baskets": Conversations with Mabel McKay.' In Sidonie Smith and Julia Watson, eds. *De/Colonizing the Subject: The Politics of Gender in Women's Autobiography*, 20–33. Minneapolis: University of Minnesota Press.

Shigeru, Kayano. 1994. *Our Land Was a Forest: An Ainu Memoir*. Trans. Kyoko Selden and Lili Selden. Boulder: Westview.

Silko, Leslie Marmon. 1977. *Ceremony*. New York: Penguin.

Swain, Tony, and Garry Trompf. 1995. *The Religions of Oceania*. London: Routledge.

Tait, Norman. 1993. Foreword to Hilary Stewart, *Looking at Totem Poles*, 9–11. Vancouver: Douglas & McIntyre.

Webber-Dreadon, Emma. 2002. 'He Taonga Tuku Iho, Hei Ara: A Gift Handed Down as a Pathway'. In Graham Harvey, ed. *Readings in Indigenous Religions*, 250–9. London: Continuum.

Zinn, Howard. 1995. *A People's History of the United States: 1492–Present*. New York: HarperPerennial.

Note

I would like to express my very great thanks to all those who read, commented upon, or inspired any part of this chapter: Ted Chamberlin, Michel Desjardins, Graham Harvey, Amir Hussain, Agnes Jay, Kelly Jay, Daniel Heath Justice, Sarah King, Sally Livingston, Jennifer Mueller, Michael Ostling, Keren Rice, and Mark Ruml. I also wish to dedicate this chapter to Willard Oxtoby, who defined much of my time at the University of Toronto and who was always generous with both his scholarship and his humour.

Chapter 7

New Religions and Movements

≈ Roy C. Amore ≈

The youngest of the Abrahamic religions covered in this volume is well over a thousand years old, but innovations in religion did not end with Islam. The early nineteenth century saw the emergence of many new faiths, and more have developed since then. This chapter will explore a selection of those newer religions. First, though, we need to consider what distinguishes a 'religion' from a 'sect' or a 'cult'.

DEFINING NEW RELIGIONS, SECTS, AND CULTS

What is a 'new religion'? The question might be easier to answer if scholars could agree on what constitutes a religion. But there are hundreds, if not thousands, of ideas on that subject. Even a definition as seemingly basic as 'belief in a god or goddess' would not take into account non-theistic traditions such as Buddhism and Jainism. Fortunately, it is not our task here to define religion, but to understand what is meant by the terms 'sect' and 'cult', and how those terms are applied to new religious movements.

Sociologists of religion such as Max Weber, writing in the early 1900s, used the word '**sect**' to refer to Christian splinter groups, new institutionalized movements that had broken away from mainstream denominations, usually in order to practise what they considered to be a purer form of the faith. Often the breakaway group would denounce the parent institution and adopt stricter rules, new modes of worship, or distinctive clothing to set itself apart. With the passage of time, however, sectarian movements usually either faded away or moved back towards the mainstream. In other words, new movements would begin as sects (or sectarian movements) and evolve into churches (new denominations). A similar process can be seen in the history of many other religions.

As for '**cult**', it was originally a neutral term, used as a synonym for 'worship' or even 'religion'. Today, however, its connotations—at least in the popular media—are almost always negative: a cult is generally assumed to be a small group under the control of a charismatic leader who is suspected of brainwashing followers—especially young people—and promoting self-destructive, illegal, or immoral behaviour.

A movement that is accepted by outsiders as a 'new religion' will enjoy all the constitutional protections and tax exemptions afforded to established religions. One that gets labelled a cult is likely to attract scrutiny if not harassment from legal authorities and taxation officials. In divorce cases where custody of the children is in dispute, it is not unusual for one parent to use association with a 'cult' to argue that the other parent is unfit. And in the 1994 race for the California Senate, one candidate received damaging media attention because his wife was thought to be associated with a cult (Lewis 2003: 208).

Yet the definitional lines between a cult and a sect (or new religion) are quite vague. By the usual definitions, for example, the **Hare Krishna** movement was a sect of Hinduism in India, but in the West its members' unusual practice and dress soon led to their branding as a cult. This suggests that the 'cult' label has less to do with the nature of the movement itself than with how sharply it differs from the mainstream religious culture—in other words, that one person's religion is another person's cult.

At the same time, it is possible to identify several traits that many cults seem to share. Cults typically claim to have some special knowledge or insight, sometimes based on a new interpretation of an old scripture or revealed through contact with spirits (or even aliens). Their practice

◀ The Baha'i House of Worship in Wilmette, Illinois (Andrew Leyerle).

often includes rituals designed to promote ecstatic experiences, and they tend to focus more on individual spiritual experience than institutional organization (see Dawson 2006: 28–9).

Perhaps the most widely shared characteristic, however, is a charismatic individual leader who demands extreme loyalty. Adherents may be required to work long hours for little or no pay, cut ties with family and friends from the past, denounce former religious beliefs and practices, or even submit sexually to the leader. In extreme cases, leaders may go so far as to demand that followers be willing to die for the cause. The mass suicide, forced or voluntary, of more than 900 members of the Peoples Temple at Jonestown, Guyana, in 1978 is one famous example. Others include the succession of murders and suicides in the mid-1990s associated with the Solar Temple cult, in which more than 70 people in Switzerland, France, and Canada died; the suicides of 37 Heaven's Gate adherents in California in 1997, and the murder-suicide of 780 members of a breakaway Catholic cult called the Movement for the Restoration of the Ten Commandments in Uganda in 2000 (Dawson 2006: 13). (The 1993 murder-suicide of 80 people at the Branch Davidian compound near Waco, Texas, was somewhat different in that it was precipitated by an assault on the compound by law enforcement officers.) In most of these mass suicides, whether coerced or voluntary, the underlying belief was that the current world order was about to end and be replaced by a new order in which the cult's members would be rewarded for their loyalty. That is, the movements had a **millenarian** belief in an imminent 'End of Time' leading to the dawning of a 'New Age'.

What gives rise to new religious movements? It has often been noted that new religions tend to appear at times of serious cultural disruption or change. The Indigenous prophetic movements discussed in Chapter 6 are classic examples, emerging in societies whose traditional cultures were breaking down under the pressure of European colonization. Similarly, the massive cultural changes of the 1960s gave rise to several new religions in North America.

Hundreds of new religions and movements have established themselves in the West over the past two centuries. This chapter will focus on a small selection of the ones that have been most successful or have attracted the most attention. We will discuss them in three groups, organized according to their spiritual roots: traditional Asian religions, Abrahamic traditions, and other forms of spirituality.

NEW RELIGIONS FROM THE EAST

Soka Gakkai

Soka Gakkai was founded in Japan in the years leading up to the Second World War and emerged as an important force only after the war—a period that saw a flowering of new Japanese religions. However, its roots lie deep in Buddhist history, in the tradition of the controversial thirteenth-century monk Nichiren.

The dominant tradition of Nichiren's day was the Pure Land school of Mahayana Buddhism, which taught its followers to trust in the saving power of Amida Buddha. Nichiren, however, believed that a Mahayana scripture called the *Lotus Sutra* represented the culmination of all Buddhist truths, and warned that Japan would be doomed if the people ignored its teachings. At the same time he became increasingly critical of the Pure Land sects of his day, so angering their leaders that they persuaded the emperor to exile him to a remote island. While in exile, he continued to write tracts criticizing other Buddhist sects and promoting his own.

Nichiren's prophecies of impending doom seemed to come true when the Mongols attempted to invade Japan in 1274. Thus he was allowed to return from exile and, with his followers, establish a sect based on his teachings, together with the *Lotus Sutra*. It is to this sect, eventually known as Nichiren Shoshu, 'True Nichiren', that Soka Gakkai traces its roots.

Soka Gakkai ('Association for Creating Values') was established in 1930 as a lay organization within Nichiren Shoshu. Its founder was a reform-minded schoolteacher named Makiguchi Tsunesaburo, who wanted to promote moral values among young people. Many of its leading figures were imprisoned during the Second World War because they refused to recognize the divinity of the Emperor as required by the officially Shinto Japanese state, and Makiguchi himself died in prison before the war ended.

The organization's new leader, Toda Josei, adopted an aggressive recruitment strategy based on an ancient Buddhist missionary principle. To break down resistance to their message, Soka Gakkai members might gather outside the home of a potential convert and chant all day and all night, or point out to shop-owners that their business would improve if they converted because Soka Gakkai members would shop at their stores. Although critics complained that these tactics amounted to harassment and coercion, the approach was effective, and Soka Gakkai grew exponentially under Toda's leadership. Meanwhile, small groups of practitioners began to establish themselves throughout much of Asia, Europe, and the Americas. Often the leaders of these local groups were ethnic Japanese, but the majority of the members were not. As usual with new religious movements, young people made up the majority of the converts.

Today Soka Gakkai International (SGI)—founded in 1975 as a worldwide organization under the umbrella of Soka Gakkai in Japan—claims 12 million members. Most 'new religions' in Japan promise this-worldly happiness, and Soka Gakkai is no exception. In particular, it stresses the benefits of chanting for passing tests, getting promotions, and improving one's outlook on life. Soka Gakkai is also active in youth activities and the enjoyment of nature, sponsoring summer camps designed to give urban youth a taste of Japan's natural beauty and a chance to experience life in a more traditional setting.

At the core of Soka Gakkai is the belief that, through the practice of Nichiren Buddhism, a personal transformation or 'human revolution' can be achieved that will empower the individual to take effective action towards the goals of peace, justice, social harmony, and economic prosperity. An example of the organization's economic perspective can be seen in a 2008 speech by SGI President Daisaku Ikeda, in which he called for 'humanitarian competition' in a new economic order that would avoid both the excessive greed of capitalism and the lack of competition historically associated with socialism (Ikeda 2008).

An emphasis on social engagement had been a central feature of Soka Gakkai from the beginning, and in 1964 it led some prominent members to form a political party. Known as **Komeito**, the new party was not officially affiliated with Soka Gakkai, but its unofficial association with the organization was well recognized. It had socialist leanings, took a strong stand against corruption in Japanese politics, and worked with several other parties in opposition to the long-ruling Liberal Democratic Party (LDP). Finally, in 1993, the LDP government was replaced by a short-lived centre–left coalition of which Komeito was part. When the coalition fell apart, however, the LDP returned to power and Komeito itself soon fragmented as well. The New Komeito party, formed in 1998 through a union with the New Peace party, is more conservative than its predecessor, with a platform of reducing the size of central government, increasing transparency, and promoting world peace through nuclear disarmament.

Meanwhile, in 1991, Nichiren Shoshu had officially severed its links with Soka Gakkai. It was the most dramatic event in recent Japanese religious history, and the climax of a long dispute between the conservative clergy and the reform-minded lay organization. Following the split, the priests of Nichiren Shoshu even tore down the Grand Hall that Soka Gakkai had built on the grounds of the main Nichiren temple.

The profile of Soka Gakkai in Japan has been somewhat diminished because of the split. But the international organization has continued to grow, even establishing a university in California in 1995, and the split has not affected Soka Gakkai's practice. Members continue to follow the religious teachings of Nichiren Shoshu, studying the *Lotus Sutra* and chanting the sacred mantra *namu-myoho renge-kyo*: 'homage to the Lotus Sutra'. The emotional power of the mantra grows with repetition as the pace and volume increase, rising to a crescendo.

Falun Dafa (Falun Gong)

Falun Dafa ('Energy of the Wheel of Law'), popularly known as Falun Gong, arose out of a Buddhist Qigong tradition in China in the early 1990s. The term *qi* (pronounced 'chi' and often spelled *chi* in the older transliteration system) refers to unseen energy flowing through the body, while *qigong* refers to various techniques of breathing and movement designed to permit energy to flow properly through the body, promoting healing, health, and long life. Although Western science has been reluctant to incorporate the flow of energy into its worldview, the belief in *qi* and the various ways to strengthen it have been part of Chinese and other East Asian cultures for centuries. In addition to exercise techniques designed to enhance the flow of *qi*, the Chinese have developed eating patterns that are thought to maintain the proper balance between the *yin* (feminine, cold, wet, dark) and *yang* (masculine, warm, dry, light) forces in the body. Even skeptics have trouble explaining why acupuncturists are able to anesthetize patients by inserting needles at various energy points in the body.

A man named Li Hongzhi brought Falun Dafa to prominence in China in 1992. He explains it as a system of Buddhist cultivation passed down through the centuries, and considers himself only the most recent in a long line of teachers. The system's Buddhist roots are reflected in its name, for the *falun* or Dharma Wheel and its symbols, among them the swastika, are auspicious symbols in Buddhism. Li's teachings of compassion and self-development are based on Buddhist principles and he uses Buddhist symbols and terms, but Falun Dafa is not officially recognized as a traditional school of Chinese Buddhism. As a consequence, the Chinese government has been able to outlaw Falun Dafa without contravening its policy on the five religions it does recognize.

Although Falun Dafa has traditional roots, Li Hongzhi was the first to turn it into a popular practice adapted to everyday life, and the practice spread quickly among the people of China, for whom it was simply a new variation on a familiar theme. Unfortunately, its rapid growth in popularity attracted the attention of the Communist Party, which in 1999 counted a total party membership

The Falun Dafa symbol (Courtesy of Falun Dafa Association). Note the Daoist *yin–yang* (*taiji*) symbols and Buddhist rotating swastikas. The outer symbols rotate individually, and together they rotate around the central swastika, first in one direction and then in the other. The colours are said to vary depending on the level of visions experienced by the practitioner.

of just over 63 million. With as many as 70 million members in that year, Falun Dafa was seen as a threat to the party, and the fact that it was increasingly popular among younger party members and their children was particularly disturbing. When some senior party officials began expressing alarm over Falun Dafa in 1998 and early 1999, the leaders of Falun Dafa made a fateful decision. They organized a demonstration in April 1999 in the section of Beijing where the top government officials live and work. Sitting silently in well organized rows, without banners or placards, they intended to show that Falun Dafa was not a political threat to the government or the social order. But their silent demonstration had the opposite effect. The government was alarmed by the sudden presence of so large a gathering in the heart of Beijing.

In 2001, Falun Dafa held a candlelight vigil in Washington, DC, to mark the second anniversary of the Chinese government's crackdown (Alex Wong/Getty Images). Members spelled out both the organization's name and the Chinese characters for their three guiding principles: Truthfulness, Benevolence, and Forbearance.

Government officials persuaded the Falun Dafa leadership to send the demonstrators home. Then, three months later, the organization was banned on the grounds that it was an unregistered religion and had the effect of discouraging people from seeking proper medical attention. Falun Dafa members throughout China were arrested, fired, imprisoned, sent to prison camps, tortured, or killed.

Under pressure from the government, Li Hongzhi had left China two years before the ban was imposed. He now lives in New York City, which has become the base of a worldwide organization claiming more than a hundred million followers in over one hundred countries. Its literature has been translated into more than forty languages.

Practice

Whereas some people practise *qigong* purely for its physiological benefits, Falun Dafa practitioners seek both physical and spiritual purification through meditation and *qigong* exercises. The organization describes Falun Dafa as 'a high-level cultivation practice guided by the characteristics of the universe—Truthfulness, Benevolence, and Forbearance' ('Introduction'). And Li Hongzhi himself refers to it specifically as a 'buddhist practice' (Li 2000).

Practitioners are said to develop a *falun* or 'law wheel' in the abdomen. This is not the same as the *qi*, which is naturally present in everyone. Once acquired, the *falun* spins in synchrony with the rotation of the planets, the milky way, and other objects in the universe. When rotating clockwise, the *falun* absorbs and transforms energy from the universe, and when rotating counter-clockwise, it dispenses salvation to oneself, to others, and to the universe. According to Li, healing comes not from the *qi* but from the *falun* when it is rotating counter-clockwise. The *falun* changes its rotational direction according to its own dynamics, and it continues to rotate even when one is not actually practising the Dafa exercises. Li writes that this is a unique feature of Dafa practice, setting it apart from other cultivation systems. The energy cluster emitted by the *falun* is called *gong*—hence the alternative name Falun Gong. The *gong* is said to glow like light.

Li divides Falun Gong practices into five sets, with names such as 'Buddha showing a thousand hands', which is the foundational set of exercises. It is repeated three times and is meant to open the body's energy channels. When it is done properly, the body will feel warm; this is said to indicate that the energies have been unblocked and that energy is being absorbed from the universe.

Reflecting the practice's Buddhist background, one of its goals is to cultivate 'mind-nature' (*xinxing*); that is, to build a character that is kinder, more honest, and more patient.

Although Falun Dafa teaches and practises non-violence, along Buddhist lines, practitioners have faced serious persecution in China, and therefore it remains an underground movement, regularly denounced as an evil cult working against the good of the people. Curiously, it has not been banned in Hong Kong, which has been a part of China since 1997. However, when the organization wanted to hold a major international rally there in 2007, Beijing blocked the event by refusing to grant visas to Falun Dafa members from abroad.

Outside China, Falun Dafa is openly practised and has mounted a campaign of severe criticism of the Chinese government. According to Falun Dafa many practitioners are imprisoned in long-term work camps, where they are used as what amounts to slave labour to produce various goods that are sold in the West. The organization also claims that organs are involuntarily removed from prisoners to be used for transplants. Organizations such as Amnesty International have lent some credence to these accusations (Amnesty International).

International Society for Krishna Consciousness (ISKCON)

In September 1965 a seventy-year-old Hindu holy man arrived by freighter in New York City with virtually nothing but a short list of contacts. A few weeks later, he sat under a now famous tree in Tompkins Square Park and began to chant:

Hare Krishna Hare Krishna,
Krishna Krishna Hare Hare,
Hare Rama Hare Rama,
Rama Rama Hare Hare.

He had learned this *Maha Mantra*, 'great mantra', from his guru in India, who learned it from his guru, and so on—it was said—all the way back to a sixteenth-century Hindu mystic named Chaitanya, who was reputed to enter a state of mystical ecstasy while chanting the three names of the god: Krishna, Hare, Rama. Within a year of his arrival, A.C. Bhaktivedanta Swami Prabhupada had established the International Society for Krishna Consciousness (ISKCON) and the 'Hare Krishna' movement began to take root in America.

The Hare Krishna movement was new to the West, but it was not a new religion. Rather, it was a Western mission of **Vaishnava** Hinduism, the school that emphasizes devotion to Vishnu. Traditional Vaishnavas worship Vishnu both as the Supreme Godhead and in the forms of his ten major avatars—the animal or human forms he has assumed at different times to 'come down' (*avatara*) to earth to save humanity. In this system, Krishna, 'the dark-complexioned one', is the eighth avatar. However, Prabhupada belonged to a regional (Bengali) variant known as Gaudiya Vaishnava, in which the Cowherd (Gopala) Krishna is the Supreme Godhead—the source of everything, including other divine forces. As the Supreme Personality, Krishna is understood to encourage a very personal relationship between the devotee and himself. Like other forms of Hinduism, ISKCON teaches that the soul is eternal and subject to reincarnation according to the individual's karma; however, those who practise loving devotion to Krishna will go to his heaven when they die and thus escape from the cycle of rebirth. The fundamental texts for ISKCON are the *Bhagavad Gita* and

Hare Krishna devotees in New York's Central Park in May 1978 (Ernst Haas/Hulton Archive/Getty Images).

a collection of stories about Krishna's life called the *Srimad Bhagavatam*.

Between the founding of ISKCON in 1966 and his death only eleven years later, Srila Prabhupada travelled throughout North America and around the world spreading his version of Hinduism. His recorded addresses and voluminous writings laid down the fundamental beliefs and practices of the movement. Soon the Hare Krishna movement was establishing centres in cities across North America and abroad. Schools were started to educate the children of devotees in Vedic culture, and some devotees studied 'Vedic architecture'. Each centre included a temple with an altar area featuring images of Krishna and his consort Radha, as the male and female aspects of the divine, as well as pictures of the guru, Prabhupada. In addition to the temples, located mostly in large cities, farms

were established that undertook to work the land in traditional ways consistent with Vedic (ancient Hindu) ways.

It is not uncommon for new religions to undergo a difficult period of institutional adjustment after the death of the charismatic founder/leader. Following Prabhupada's death, ISKCON vested authority not in a new guru, but in a Governing Body Commission (GBC). Eleven devotees who had risen to high positions under Prabhupada's leadership were recognized by the GBC as gurus, each of whom was authorized to ordain recruits and oversee operations in one of eleven regional zones. Some of the eleven got into trouble with the law over matters including illegal guns, drugs, child abuse, and murder, and by the 1980s six of the original eleven had quit or been removed from office by the GBC. Those who were following in the tradition of Prabhupada had to deal with the bad publicity attracted by those who were not.

Practice

In the *Gita*, Krishna is the charioteer for a heroic royal leader named Arjuna. On the eve of a great battle between two factions of the royal family, Arjuna is troubled at the thought of fighting his own kin. His charioteer counsels him, and in the course of their conversation he reveals his identity. He tells Arjuna that he, Krishna, is the highest of all gods, and informs him that although the yoga (spiritual practice) of good karma actions and the yoga of spiritual wisdom are both valid paths, the best and highest path is **bhakti** yoga: loving devotion to Krishna.

These ideas—that Krishna is the supreme God and that devotional faith is the best spiritual path—combined with Chaitanya's mystical practices of chanting the praises of Krishna while dancing in ecstasy, are at the heart of the tradition that Prabhupada introduced to the West. Devotional services, *pujas*, to Krishna are held several times a day. One male or female devotee acting as *pujari*, the *puja* leader, stands near the altar and makes offerings of fire and vegetarian food to the images on the altar, which include, in addition to Krishna himself, his consort Radha and his brother Balarama. While the *pujari* performs these rituals, the other devotees play music and chant. As the pace of the chanting builds, the music becomes louder and the devotees raise their arms over their heads while dancing feverishly. As the chanting reaches its crescendo, many devotees jump high into the air.

Devotees are given a Sanskrit name by the guru. They wear saffron-coloured robes and show their devotion to Krishna by adorning their bodies with painted marks called *tilaka*, made of cream-coloured clay from the banks of a holy lake in India associated with the life of Krishna. Two vertical marks represent the feet of Krishna, or the walls of a temple, and below them is a leaf representing the sacred *tulasi* (basil) plant. The diet is strictly vegetarian, including a prohibition on eating fish or eggs. Recreational drugs of all kinds, including alcohol and caffeine, are avoided.

Great effort is put into keeping the temple clean, and every activity is to be done 'for Krishna', as an act of devotional service. In this way the mental state known as Krishna consciousness is developed. Some devotees are congregational members, living away from the temple and attending only for main temple activities, but others live in or near the temple. Single male and female devotees have separate living quarters, while married couples and families often live in nearby houses or apartments. Sexual activity is allowed only within marriage, for the purpose of procreation. Some devotees have outside employment and turn their wages over to the temple. Others work full time for the movement.

Most temple-based male devotees shave their heads except for a pigtail at the back of the head. Women are required to dress very modestly. Devotees carry a small bag containing a string of 108 chanting beads (*japa mala*), similar to a Christian rosary, made from the *tulasi* plant. The number 108 is sacred in India partly because it represents the multiple of the 12 zodiac houses and 9 planetary bodies as understood in Indian astrology. Using the beads if their hands are free, devotees chant the Hare Krishna mantra hundreds of times each day as they go about their duties around the temple.

ISKCON has a full cycle of festivals, including Gita Jayanti, celebrating the conversation between Krishna and Arjuna. They have staged some lavish festival parades in India and abroad, following the style of traditional Indian religious processions.

The Hare Krishna movement provoked strong reactions, both positive and negative. On the positive side was the enthusiasm shown by celebrities like George Harrison of the Beatles. Harrison's 1970 song 'My Sweet Lord' contributed greatly to the acceptance of the movement. But there were many negative reactions as well. One reason was simply that the movement was so foreign to Western culture and that its members were so keen to adopt Indian styles of dress, music, and worship. The practice of chanting in public places such as airports while trying to raise money generated bad publicity. Another reason was the fact that in the early years ISKCON discouraged any contact between devotees and their former friends and family. As a consequence, the media quickly branded the movement a 'cult', and a new profession known as 'deprogrammer' came into existence. Hired by concerned parents to kidnap their offspring from the movement, deprogrammers would hold their subjects in a motel room for days and try to break the 'cult program' that had been 'brainwashed' into them. Sometimes these efforts succeeded, but many young people returned to the Hare Krishnas as soon as they were free to do so.

The schools operated by ISKCON for children of devotees have also generated controversy, initially from concerned outsiders and eventually from former students. Efforts were made to correct the problems and address the concerns of former students. But in 2000 a class action suit (Children of ISKCON vs ISKCON) was filed in Dallas by a group of 44 former students who claimed to have been victims of physical, emotional, and sexual abuse in ISKCON-operated schools in the United States and India. Although the case was initially dismissed on technical grounds, it was refiled in another court. By the time the final settlement was reached, hundreds of others had joined the list of plaintiffs and ISKCON had been forced to seek bankruptcy protection. The claims, totalling $20 million, were settled by 2008, and ISKCON emerged from bankruptcy protection.

ISKCON now runs approximately 350 temples and centres worldwide. It has been especially

Indian ISKCON devotees celebrate Ratha Yatra, the festival of chariots, in Hyderabad (Noah Seelam/AFP/Getty Images).

successful in the former states of the Soviet Union, including Russia. South America has also proven receptive to ISKCON. The spread of ISKCON back to India has been a remarkable development. After starting his mission in America, Prabphupada frequently returned to India, where he established temples in Mumbai as well as various places associated with either Krishna or Chaitanya. Having established a strong presence in the West, ISKCON has been welcomed in India as a movement reviving Gaudiya Vaishnava devotion. Indian devotees now may outnumber Western ones. New temples have been built and major festivals have been organized.

🌺 RELIGIONS ARISING FROM THE ABRAHAMIC LINEAGE

We now turn our attention to some new religions arising from the three Abrahamic religions. The Church of Latter-day Saints can be classed either as a branch of Protestant Christianity or as a new religion developing out of Christianity. Our second example, the Baha'i Faith, originated in Iran in the context of Shi'i Islam. The Kabbalah Centre draws on a Jewish mystical tradition that is centuries old, while the Nation of Islam was established in the United States by leaders raised in the Christian tradition.

Church of Jesus Christ of Latter-day Saints (Mormons)

The founder of the Church of Jesus Christ of Latter-day Saints, Joseph Smith, Jr (1805–44), claimed that in 1820, as a boy in upstate New York, he had experienced a vision of God and Jesus in which he was told not to join any of the existing denominations. In subsequent visions, he said, an angel of God named Moroni had persuaded him that he had been divinely chosen to restore the true Church of Christ. The new Church was founded in 1830.

As a textual basis for the enterprise, Smith published the *Book of Mormon*, which he said he had translated from gold plates inscribed in 'reformed Egyptian' that had been entrusted to him by Moroni during a hilltop meeting near Palmyra, New York. Though subsequent editions referred to Smith as the 'translator', the title page of the 1830 first edition declared him 'author and proprietor'. He said that he was aided in translating the *Book* by two special stones he called 'Urim and Thummin'—the names given in the Old Testament to two unidentified objects used by the Hebrew high priests to determine the will of God.

The *Book of Mormon* uses the language and format of the 1611 King James translation of the Bible to tell the previously unknown, and otherwise undocumented, story of two groups, both descended from one of the lost tribes of Israel, that supposedly migrated from the Near East to the New World around 600 BCE and became the ancestors of the indigenous peoples of the Americas. Including accounts of visitations by Christ sometime after his crucifixion, the book is understood by **Mormons** to be a scriptural account of God's activity in the western hemisphere, parallel with the Bible and its account of divine events in the eastern hemisphere.

Also scriptural for Mormons are Smith's *The Pearl of Great Price*, a book of revelations and translations, and *Doctrine and Covenants*, a collection of his revelatory declarations. Passages in the latter work address specific moments in the Church's early years. General reflection is interspersed with guidance for particular circumstances in a manner reminiscent of the letters of Paul or certain *surahs* of the Qur'an.

Smith and his small band of followers faced ridicule and persecution from mainstream Christians in New York, and so Smith led them westward in search of a safer place. They established settlements in Ohio and Missouri, and, when driven out of Missouri in 1839, moved on to Nauvoo, Illinois, on the Mississippi River. By now the Mormons were calling themselves the Church of Jesus Christ of Latter-day Saints. It was in Nauvoo that Smith secretly introduced 'plural marriage' (polygamy), rumours of which added to the suspicions of outsiders. He also declared himself a candidate for the American presidency in the 1844 elections, advocating a blend of democracy and religious authority he called 'theodemocracy'. Some of these innovations caused strife between factions of the Latter-day Saints. In 1844 Smith and his brother were killed by an anti-Mormon mob.

A number of the traditionalist, anti-polygamy Mormons stayed in the Midwest as the Reorganized Church of Latter-day Saints, with headquarters in Independence, Missouri. For years, this branch of the Mormons was led by descendants of Smith, and they prided themselves on remaining true to his legacy. In 2001 they renamed themselves the Community of Christ. Although relatively small in numbers, the Community of Christ is very active in spreading its message around the world. Its members continue to regard the *Book of Mormon* and the *Doctrine and Covenants* as scripture, but emphasize the Bible and its teachings about Jesus. It sees itself not as a 'new religion', but as a branch of Christianity in the line running from the Hebrew prophets through Jesus to Joseph Smith.

The larger branch of the Mormons, the Church of Jesus Christ of Latter-day Saints, has a separate history. In 1847 most of them moved to Utah under the leadership of Brigham Young, who had been president of an inner council of twelve that Smith had organized on the pattern of the apostolic Church and who continued to lead the Mormons for the next thirty years. Although they were unsuccessful in their bid to make Utah a Mormon state, they dominated the region and Young was chosen by the United States government to serve as governor of the Utah Territory.

Practice

The Mormons set their community apart with a code of behaviour that included not only a rigid sexual morality but strict abstinence from stimulants, including tea and coffee as well as alcohol and tobacco. Young adults are expected to serve as volunteer missionaries for two years after completing high school—a practice that has helped spread awareness of the faith and attract new members around the world. Distinctive Mormon doctrines include the notion that God is increasing in perfection as human beings improve. Distinctive practices include the augmentation of the spiritual community through baptism (by proxy) of the deceased; because of this practice, Utah has become a world centre for genealogical research. (Mormons have also taken a keen interest in western-hemisphere archaeology, in the hope that physical evidence of the events described by the *Book of Mormon* will be found.)

The most controversial Mormon practice, however, was plural marriage, which was officially adopted in 1852 and officially dropped in 1890 after the federal government threatened to abolish it. The practice soon faded among mainstream LDS members. But a few congregations refused to accept the change and broke away from the Church of Jesus Christ of Latter-day Saints to form independent sects known collectively as 'Fundamentalist Mormons'. The largest of these sects, the Fundamentalist Church of Jesus Christ of Latter-day Saints (FLDS) in particular is known for allowing its male leaders to have multiple wives. Because the women involved are often quite young, FLDS congregations have come under intense scrutiny by government officials and concerned women's organizations. In 2007, FLDS leader Warren Jeffs was sentenced to ten years in prison for being an accomplice to rape.

Whether the Mormons constitute a new religion or merely a new denomination of Christianity is open to question. Joseph Smith saw himself as reforming the Christian Church, and the fact

The Tabernacle in Salt Lake City, Utah, home to the famous Mormon Tabernacle Choir, is renowned for its acoustics (Jed Jacobsohn/Getty Images).

that Mormons keep the Bible as scripture argues for inclusion under the umbrella of Christianity. On the other hand, the Mormons' belief in new, post-scriptural revelations, new scriptures, and new modes of worship (e.g., using water rather than wine for the communion sacrament) suggests a new religion. The issue came into focus during the lead-up to the 2000 electoral primaries, when Massachusetts governor Mitt Romney was seeking nomination as the Republican party's candidate for president. Some conservative Christians who admired his strong family values were nevertheless reluctant to support his candidacy because of his Mormon faith.

The Baha'i Faith

Baha'i developed out of Islam in the mid-nineteenth century, when Islam was already more than

1,200 years old. Although it has many elements in common with Islam, it gives those elements a new and more nearly universal configuration. The main point of divergence is that Baha'is believe that their leader, Baha'u'llah, was a new prophet, whereas Muslims believe there can never be another prophet after Muhammad.

The roots of Baha'i lie in the particular eschatology of Iranian Shi'ism. Ever since the last imam disappeared in 874, Twelver Shi'a had been waiting for a figure known as the **Bab** ('gateway') to appear and reopen communication with the hidden imam. After ten centuries, most people no longer expected this to happen anytime soon. But seeds of messianic expectation germinated in the soil of political unrest.

Thus in 1844 Sayyid 'Ali Muhammad declared himself to be the Bab, the gateway to a new prophetic revelation. Although he himself was imprisoned in 1845, his followers, the Babis, were not discouraged. They repudiated the Islamic *shari'ah* law and in 1848 the Bab proclaimed himself the hidden Imam. He was executed by a firing squad in 1850, but he left behind a number of writings that have been considered scriptural.

The leadership momentum passed to Mirza Husayn 'Ali Nuri (1817–92), whose religious name was Baha'u'llah, 'Glory of God'. He had not met the Bab personally, but had a profound experience of divine support while imprisoned in Tehran in 1852. On his release the following year he was banished from Iran to Baghdad in Turkish-controlled Iraq, where he became a spiritual leader of Babis in exile. Then, since he was still near enough to Iran to be seen as a threat, in 1863 he was moved to Istanbul. Before going, he declared himself to be 'the one whom God shall manifest' as foretold by the Bab. He also claimed to have had a 'transforming' twelve-day mystical experience in 1862.

This transfer to the Mediterranean world expanded the sphere of Baha'u'llah's spiritual activity well beyond the horizons of Iranian Shi'ism. Now he was in a position to address the entire Otto-man Empire. Although he was banished to Acre in Palestine a few years later, his following continued to grow. Nearby Haifa, today in Israel, remains the world headquarters of the Baha'i faith today.

Baha'u'llah wrote prolifically throughout his years in Acre, producing more than a hundred texts. Baha'is believe his writings to be God's in-spired revelation for this age. Among the most im-portant are *Kitab-i Aqdas* ('The Most Holy Book', 1873), containing Baha'i laws; *Kitab-i Iqan* ('The Book of Certitude', 1861), the principal doctrinal work; and *Hidden Words* (1858), a discourse on ethics. *The Seven Valleys* (1856), a mystical treatise, enumerates seven spiritual stages: search, love, knowledge, unity, contentment, wonderment, and true poverty and absolute nothingness.

For 65 years after Baha'u'llah's death in 1892, authority in interpreting the tradition was passed on to family heirs. His son 'Abbas Effendi was con-sidered an infallible interpreter of his father's writ-ings, and on his death the mantle of infallibility was bequeathed to his grandson, Shoghi Effendi Rabbani. Shoghi Effendi appointed an Interna-tional Baha'i Council, and from 1963 leadership was vested in an elected body of representatives called the Universal House of Justice.

Baha'i teachings are based on Baha'u'llah's writ-ings. The soul is believed to be eternal, a mystery that is independent both of the body and of space and time; it can never decay. Yet it becomes in-dividuated at the moment of the human being's conception.

The Baha'i notion of prophethood is in line with the Abrahamic religions. Prophets are sent by God to diagnose spiritual and moral disorder and to prescribe the appropriate remedy. Islam af-firms that God sent prophets to various peoples before Muhammad with a message to each. Simi-larly, Baha'is believe that the world has known a sequence of prophets. They do not believe the prophets' messages to have been community-specific, however: instead, they understand the prophets to speak to the entire world. They also believe that the series remains open; according to their doctrine of 'progressive revelation', more prophets will come in future ages.

It may well be their ideal of world community that has done the most to energize Baha'is and make their tradition attractive to serious searchers. Baha'u'llah himself wrote that he came to 'unify the world', and Baha'is have asserted the unity of religions. Over a doorway to one Baha'i house of worship is the inscription, 'All the Prophets of God proclaim the same Faith.' Various religions are seen as corroborating the Baha'i faith itself.

But there is more to unity than doctrinal teach-ing; Baha'is actively advocate economic, sexual, and racial equality. Extremes of poverty and wealth are to be eliminated, and slavery rooted out—along with priesthood and monasticism. Women are to enjoy rights and opportunities equal to men's, marriage is to be strictly monogamous, and divorce is frowned on. Baha'is have consultative status with the United Nations as an official NGO (non-governmental organization). World peace is to be achieved through disarmament, democ-racy, and the rule of law, along with the promo-tion of international education and human rights. Although these goals are clearly compatible with modern secular values, they have a spiritual qual-ity for Baha'is, who cite Baha'u'llah as saying that human well-being is unattainable until unity is firmly established, and Shoghi Effendi as saying that 'Nothing short of the transmuting spirit of God, working through His chosen Mouthpiece [Baha'u'llah], can bring it about.'

Unity of the races in the human family is ac-tively proclaimed, and interracial marriage wel-comed. In recent decades this emphasis has been a major factor in the appeal of the Baha'i Faith to African-Americans. Once the United States elimi-nates racism at home, some Baha'is claim, it will be the spiritual leader of the world.

Practice

Bahai'is strive to live a peaceful and ethical life. Personal spiritual cultivation is encouraged, and recreational drugs and alcohol are forbidden. Since the Baha'i Faith sees itself as the fulfillment of other religions, Baha'is are unusually open to dialogue with other faiths.

Baha'is follow a distinctive calendar, in which the number 19 (which figured in the tradition's early mystical thinking) plays an important role. Beginning with the spring equinox, Iran's traditional time for the new year, there are 19 months of 19 days each, with four additional days (five in leap years) to keep up with the solar year. Local Baha'i societies assemble for a community feast on the first day of each month, and the final month, in early March, is devoted to dawn-to-dusk fasting, as in the Muslim observance of Ramadan.

Although the 19-day calendar does not recognize the seven-day week, Sunday gatherings for study and reflection have become common among Baha'is in the West. Important days in the annual cycle are essentially historical, marking events in the founding of the religion: several days in April and May are associated with Baha'u'llah's mission, for instance. In addition, the Bab's birth, mission, and martyrdom are commemorated, as are the birth and passing (or ascension) of Baha'u'llah.

Baha'i devotions at the monthly feasts feature a cappella singing but no instrumental music. Prayers are in Farsi (Persian), Arabic, or other languages. Readings are mainly from Baha'i scriptural writings by Baha'u'llah or the Bab, but they may be supplemented with devotional readings from other traditions. Among life-cycle rituals there is a simple naming ceremony, and many who grow up as Baha'is may make a personal profession of faith at the age of fifteen. Converts simply sign a declaration card. Baha'i weddings vary depending on the tastes of the couple, but always include the declaration 'We will all, truly, abide by the will of God.' At funerals there is a standard prayer for the departed, which is virtually the only prayer said in unison by Baha'is.

Personal devotions are similar to Islamic practice. As in Islam, the faithful wash their hands and face before praying. Set prayers are said at five times of the day. Also reminiscent of Islam is the practice of repeating the phrase *Allahu-'l Abha* ('God is the most glorious'). These similarities notwithstanding, the Baha'i faith has gone its own way. Its revelation does not conclude with the Qur'an, and its ideals for society depart from those reflected in the *shari'ah*. There have also been political tensions with Islam. Muslims have tended to see the Baha'is as Israeli sympathizers, and in Iran the Baha'i community suffered serious losses in lives and property after the Islamic revolution of 1979.

Since the end of the nineteenth century, the Baha'i Faith has spread around the world. It now claims some 7 million adherents in 235 countries. These include 750,000 in North America and several times that number in India. More than one-quarter of local councils are in Africa and a similar number in Asia. There are nearly as many councils in the southwestern Pacific as in Europe.

The Nation of Islam

It is estimated that at least 20 per cent of the Africans taken as slaves to the Americas were Muslims. One early promoter of Islam—or a version of it—among African-Americans was Noble Drew Ali, who in 1913 founded the Moorish Science Temple of America in Newark, New Jersey. By the time of his death in 1929, major congregations had been established in cities including Chicago, Detroit, and Philadelphia.

Whether Wallace D. Fard was ever associated with the Temple is unclear; his followers say he wasn't. But the idea that Islam was the appropriate religion for African Americans was in the air when he established the Nation of Islam (NOI) in Detroit in 1930. Fard's version of Islam bore little resemblance to either the Sunni or the Shi'i tradition. For Muslims, who understand Allah to be a purely spiritual entity, the most fundamental difference lay in the NOI's claim that Allah took human form in the person of Fard himself. In fact, Fard was identified as the second coming of Jesus as well.

These claims may have originated in Fard's first encounter with Elijah Poole, a young man who had felt called to a religious mission of some kind, but did not think of it as a Christian one and had stopped attending church before his fateful 1923 meeting with Fard. He later described the meeting:

> when I got to him I . . . told him that I recognized who he is and he held his head down close to my face and he said to me, 'Yes, Brother.' I said to him: 'You are that one we read in the Bible that he would come in the last day under the name Jesus.' . . . finally he said; 'Yes, I am the one that you have been looking for in the last two thousand years' (quoted in Sahib 1951: 91–2).

Fard was so impressed with the young man—who later changed his name to Elijah Muhammad—that he authorized him to teach Islam with his blessing. Elijah quickly became Fard's favourite disciple.

The men who developed the theology of the Nation of Islam were more familiar with the Bible than the Qur'an, but the story they told was no more familiar to mainstream Christians than it was to Muslims. They maintained that all humans were originally black and had lived in harmony as one tribe called Shabazz for millions of years, until an evil man named Yakub rebelled and left Egypt for an island where he created a white race by killing all dark babies. Eventually, the evil white race returned to Egypt and subjugated the blacks, bringing oppression and disunity to humankind. God sent Moses to try to redeem them, but that effort failed. Now the blacks needed to undergo a 'resurrection' and recognize themselves as proud members of the Shabazz people who once had a great and peaceful society.

Martha Lee has argued that the Nation of Islam is a millenarian movement (1996: 3). In the NOI version of history, white rule has lasted more than six thousand years and is approaching the 'end time', when the Mother of Planes—a huge aircraft base in the sky—will destroy the 'white devils'. The 'Fall of America' is to be expected soon. In fact, Elijah Muhammad originally prophesied that the fall would occur in the mid-1960s. When that prediction failed to come true, NOI thinking about the 'end time' became less literal.

An economic as well as a religious movement, the NOI advocates black economic self-sufficiency and teaches a strict ethical way of life. It follows the Islamic prohibitions on pork and alcohol, but does not practice Friday prayers (services are generally held on Sunday) and does not follow the shari'ah law. Although Elijah Muhammad called for a separate state, such a demand was too impractical to pursue seriously.

The Nation of Islam came to the attention of the authorities in Detroit when it was rumoured that Fard had promised life in heaven for anyone who killed four whites. This was most likely not true, although he was known to have preached that anyone who killed four devils would go to heaven. In any event, Fard disappeared after he was arrested and expelled from Detroit in 1933. Elijah Muhammad took over the leadership but the movement fragmented, and some factions were quite hostile to him. Leaving Detroit in 1935, he settled in Washington, DC, where he preached under the name Elijah Rasool (Lee 1996: 26).

In 1942, however, he was convicted of sedition for counselling his followers not to register for the draft. He spent four years in prison, but his wife, Clara, directed the organization in his absence, and after his release in 1946 the NOI's numbers soon began to grow. Much of the credit for the movement's expansion in the 1950s has been given to a convert named Malcolm X.

Malcolm X

Malcolm Little (1925–65) was born in Nebraska but spent much of his childhood in Lansing, Michigan. When he was six, his father was run over by a streetcar; the coroner ruled it a suicide, but the Little family believed he had been killed by a white supremacist group. After his father's death the family was impoverished and his mother suffered a nervous breakdown, so the children were put in foster care. Later, Malcolm moved to Boston and became involved with criminals. It was while he was serving time for theft that he was encouraged by his brother to join the NOI. He read widely and after release in 1952, he became a key disciple of Elijah Muhammad. Like other converts at that time, he took the surname X to protest the absence of an African name and to recall the X branded on some slaves. Before long Malcolm X had become the leader of the Harlem temple. His eloquence brought him national attention as an advocate for Black Power, and he came to symbolize the black defiance of white racism in America.

Despite his success, however, Malcolm X became increasingly alienated from the movement. Finally in 1964 he broke away from the NOI and founded Muslim Mosque, Inc. Increasingly aware of the differences between NOI theology and that of traditional Islam, he converted to Sunni Islam and made the pilgrimage to Mecca, where he learned that Islam was not an exclusively black religion, as the NOI had taught. It was a life-changing experience. Changing his name to El Hajj Malik El-Shabazz, he began to teach an understanding of Islam as a religion for all races. Less than a year later, in February 1965, he was assassinated while giving a speech in New York. Three members of the NOI were convicted of the murder, although some people suspected that the FBI's Counter Intelligence Program might have played a role in instigating the assassination (Lee 1996: 44).

Wallace Muhammad

The early 1970s also saw a softening of the NOI's attitude towards whites and an increasing willingness to work with other black organizations. When Elijah Muhammad, known as the Messenger, died in 1975, the leadership passed to his son Wallace, who took the NOI further towards the mainstream. He declared an end to the idea that all whites were devils; withdrew the demand for a separate black state; and helped put the NOI on a more solid financial basis. He also renamed the temples, adopting the Arabic word for mosque, 'masjid'. This, together with a new emphasis on studying the Qur'an, moved the NOI closer to Sunni Islam. In 1975 Wallace renamed the organization the World Community of al-Islam in the West, or WCIW.

Louis Farrakhan

Not all members of the former NOI agreed with these reforms, however. Among the dissenters was Minister Louis Farrakhan. In 1978 he broke with WCIW and formed a new organization modelled on the NOI. He restored the original name, reinstituted the Saviour's Day festival—formerly the most important holiday—and attracted a large number of members.

In 2001 a former member of the revived NOI published an account of his experience that was particularly critical of Farrakhan's financial dealings. According to Vibert L. White, Jr, members were pressured to donate large sums, and many struggling black-owned businesses were left with unpaid bills for their services to the organization, even as substantial amounts of money were finding their way to various members of the Farrakhan family (White 2001).

At the same time, Farrakhan appears to have courted African Muslim leaders including Libya's Muammar Khadafi for support. Perhaps this helps to explain why he has moved the NOI towards the Islamic mainstream by encouraging Islamic-style daily prayers and the study of the Qur'an. The most difficult change he made was to drop the doctrine that identified Fard as Allah and Elijah Muhammad as his Messenger. In a 1997 conference, Farrakhan publicly affirmed that Muhammad was the last and greatest prophet of Allah (Walker 2005: 495).

In 1995 Farrakhan organized a 'Million Man March' on Washington, DC, to draw attention to the role of the black male and to unite for social and economic improvement. The March was a joint effort sponsored by many black organizations, and most of the participants had a Christian background. As the main organizer, however, Farrakhan set the agenda. As Dennis Walker writes:

> The March was an Islamizing event. A range of Muslim sects were allowed to appear before the multitude and recite the Qur'an in Arabic on a basis of equality with the Christian and black Jewish clerics whom Farrakhan had inducted. It was a recognition in public space of Islam as part of the being of blacks that had had no precedent (Walker 2005: 508).

Although the March was criticized for excluding black women and promoting a Muslim agenda, as well as its lack of transparency in accounting, it did bring several African-American organizations into fuller cooperation and helped draw public attention to the challenges faced by African Americans.

The Kabbalah Centre

The Kabbalah Centre in Los Angeles teaches a new form of spirituality based on traditional Jewish mysticism. As an organization, it traces its roots to a centre for Kabbalah studies founded in Jerusalem in 1922 by Rabbi (or Rav) Yehuda Ashlag. But the tradition stretches back through the sixteenth-century master Isaac Luria to the (probably) thirteenth-century text called the *Zohar* and beyond. The Centre itself claims that its teachings go back some four thousand years.

The National Institute for the Research of Kabbalah (later renamed the Kabbalah Centre) was founded in 1965 by Rabbi Philip S. Berg. Raised in New York City, he had trained as a rabbi but was not practising when, during a trip to Israel in 1962, he met Rabbi Yehuda Brandwein, the Kabbalist dean of a *yeshiva* in Jerusalem's Old City, and a descendant of many famous Hasidic scholars. With Brandwein as his mentor, Berg became an active Kabbalist.

Berg's followers claim that he succeeded Rabbi Brandwein as leader of the entire Kabbalah movement, including leadership of the Jerusalem *yeshiva*. At the *yeshiva* itself, however, Brandwein's son Rabbi Avraham Brandwein is considered the leader, and the **Kabbalah** taught there is in no way new.

In itself, Berg's Kabbalah is not new either, but his approach to it is radically different. Traditionally, the study of Kabbalah was restricted to mature male Jews, aged 40 or older, who had already completed years of Talmudic studies. Yet Berg taught Kabbalah to his secretary, who would later become his wife and a leading figure in the movement herself. Within a few years, the Bergs set out to make Kabbalah available to the world at large: young and old, male and female, Jews and Goyim alike. This was the new dimension of Berg's Kaballah, and it sparked a great deal of controversy in traditional Jewish circles.

On its website the Centre defines Kabbalah as 'ancient wisdom and practical tools for creating joy and lasting fulfillment now'. The emphasis on 'practical tools' is significant, for the purpose of Kabbalah study, as the Centre presents it, is to unlock the human potential for greatness. In fact, it is a fundamental tenet of Kabbalah (as it is of Eastern traditions such as Hinduism and Buddhism) that humans will be reincarnated over and over again, returning to this world as many times as necessary 'until the task of transformation is done' (Kabbalah Centre).

Another fundamental principle is that the reality perceived by our five senses is only a tiny portion of the totality, and that events occurring in the knowable 1 per cent of reality are the product of events in the unknown 99 per cent. Berg's followers maintain that their teachings enable people to perceive the 99 per cent of reality that normally remains unknown.

Practice

Kabbalists experience God in the world as the energy that underlies and imbues all things. As the sixteenth-century Kabbalist Moses Cordovero put it, even a stone is 'pervaded by divinity'. (A similar

Kabbalah: Thoughts on God

God's only desire is to reveal unity through diversity. That is, to reveal that all reality is unique in all its levels and all its details, and nevertheless united in a fundamental oneness (Kabbalist Aharon Ha-Levi Horowitz, 1766–1828; in Levi 2009: 929).

The essence of divinity is found in every single thing—nothing but It exists. Since It causes everything to be, no thing can live by anything else. It enlivens them. *Ein Sof* exists in each existent. Do not say, 'This is a stone and not God.' God forbid! Rather all existence is God, and the stone is a thing pervaded by divinity (Moses Cordovero, 1522–70; in Levi 2009: 937).

Shards of Light are drawn out of the destructive entities that reside within my being. Their life force is cut off and I am then replenished with Divine energy. Life grows brighter each and every day as billions of sacred sparks return to my soul! ('Focus in Front').

idea can be found in the non-canonical Christian Gospel of Thomas, which quotes Jesus as saying, 'Li[f]t the stone and there you will find me. Split the wood and I am there'; Saying 30 + 77b [pOxy. 1.23–30]).

To illustrate the way God and the material world interrelate, Kabbalah uses a diagram usually referred to as the Tree of Life. The space above the tree represents God as *Ein Sof*, 'The Endless'—a common Kabbalah term calling attention to the infinite nature of God. The tree itself pictures the ten **spherot**, shining circles of fire, representing the ten attributes of God in the world. The topmost circle represents the Crown (*Keter* or *Kether*). Below it the other nine circles are arranged in three sets, each with a circle in the left, centre, and right columns. Read from top down, these three sets represent the spiritual, intellectual, and material (earth-level) qualities of creation. The *spherot* in the right-hand column represent masculine attributes of God and those on the left feminine attributes. The *spherah* in the centre of the nine *spherot* is 'Glory', which brings harmony and interconnectedness among the lower nine *spherot*.

Lines connecting the *spherot* illustrate the ways they interact.

The 10 *spherot* are numbered from top to bottom, and the 22 connecting lines are numbered 11 to 32, also from top to bottom. The total number of connecting lines corresponds to the number of letters in the Hebrew alphabet.

In an interesting twist on most theological systems, Kabbalah practitioners believe that their practices using the tree facilitate the flow of divine energy into the world. Whereas mainstream Judaism, Christianity, and Islam stress the absolute power of God, in Kabbalah God needs human effort to work in the world.

Kabbalists do not attempt to interpret the Bible literally; instead, they use a complex kind of numerology. The ancient Hebrews used regular letters as numbers, assigning their numerical value according to their position in the 22-letter Hebrew alphabet. Totalling the numbers in certain words could reveal hidden connections between them and lead to new interpretations. For example, it turns out that the numerical values of YHWH, the name for God revealed to Moses, and *aleph*, the

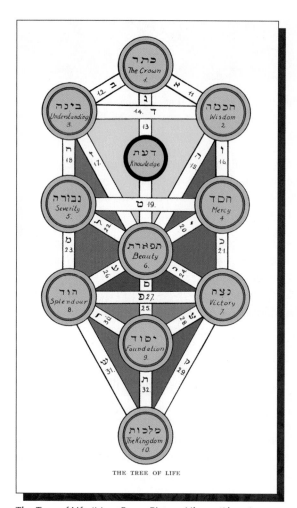

The Tree of Life (Mary Evans Picture Library/Alamy).

72 letters in Hebrew, and developed 72 names of God by combining them into triads of three letters each. To get the first name, they took the first letter of verse 19, the last of verse 20, and the first of verse 21. The next name is composed of the second letter of verse 19, the second from last of verse 20, and the second of verse 21, and so on for a total of 72. These 72 names are then arranged in a grid with 8 columns and 9 rows. According to the Kabbalah Centre, the 72 Names of God 'work as tuning forks to repair you on the soul level'; each three-letter sequence 'act[s] like an index to specific, spiritual frequencies. By simply looking at the letters, as well as closing your eyes and visualizing them, you can connect with these frequencies' ('72 Names').

Traditional Kabbalah employs a dualistic symbolism of light and darkness, and many of the Centre's teachings focus on moving from darkness to light. For example, it stresses that instead of running away from adversaries, one should confront and learn from them, just as the biblical Jacob wrestled with the angel and gained light from the experience. Kabbalists see Jacob's angel as a personification of the personal darkness with which every individual must struggle in order to reach the light. The ego is seen as covered with a garment of darkness. Kabbalah practice helps to remove the darkness that covers the ego so as to reveal the light, the spark.

Like many other religious institutions, the Kabbalah Centre claims that its spiritual understanding fulfills other religions. In sharp contrast to most, however, it does not require its members to give up their former religious identities.

Like **Scientology** (see below), the Kabbalah Centre has benefitted from the media attention attracted by some of its adherents. At the head of the celebrity list is Madonna, who has sometimes included references to Kabbalah in her lyrics (Huss 2005). However, with this notoriety, and the large sums of money donated by celebrities, have come questions about the Kabbalah Centre's finances and accounting.

first letter of the alphabet, are both 26. For Kabbalists, this is significant because one of the words for Lord or Master in Hebrew, *aluph*, is based on the word *aleph*. Inspired by the numerological practices of ancient Kabbalah, modern Kabbalists maintain that determining the numerical value of one's name can lead to new insights.

One of those practices involves meditating on the 72 names for God, based on combinations of Hebrew letters that Kabbalah finds hidden in *Exodus* 14: 19–21, the biblical account in which Moses calls to God for help before leading the people into the sea, as the Egyptian army pursues them. Kabbalists took these three verses, each having

Many Kabbalists wear a bracelet of red wool string on the left wrist that is thought to provide protection against the 'evil eye' and other malevolent forces (David Silverman/Getty Images).

Some Jews have accused the Centre of exploiting Kabbalah for worldly gain, which the Kabbalist tradition explicitly forbids. Other criticisms have focused on the Centre for going too far in linking worldly happiness with Kabbalah practice. One leader of the Centre in London, England, was heavily criticized for seeming to suggest that the 6 million Jews killed in the Holocaust died because they did not follow Kabbalah practices to unblock the light.

RELIGIONS INSPIRED BY OTHER FORMS OF SPIRITUALITY

Not all new religions are offshoots of established mainstream religious traditions. We turn now to a selection of new religions deriving from unconventional sources. **Wicca** is a modern phenomenon inspired by pre-Christian European traditions, with a significant feminist component. Scientology and the Raëlian Movement draw on more secular sources, including science fiction and new forms of depth psychology. Finally, we will look at some spiritual manifestations of the New Age movement.

Wicca: The Witchcraft Revival

In the late Middle Ages, after centuries of condemning the remnants of 'pagan' tradition in northern Europe as 'witchcraft', the Roman Catholic Church mounted a systematic campaign to eradicate those remnants once and for all. Although accusations of witchcraft were frequent well into the 1700s, by the early twentieth century witchcraft was widely considered a thing of the past in industrialized societies: a matter of historical curiosity, but not in any way a living tradition.

Around the time of the Second World War, however, a movement emerged in England that claimed witchcraft to be the original religion of Britain and sought to revive the tradition. The leading figures in this movement were two men, Gerald B. Gardner and Aleister Crowley, but women's interest increased after 1948, when Robert Graves published *The White Goddess*, a work on myth that posited a mother goddess in European prehistory. In 1953, Doreen Valiente was initiated into the movement and wrote *The Book of Shadows*, a kind of a liturgical handbook for witchcraft.

The first modern use of the Old English word 'Wicca' is attributed to Gardner in 1959. Within a few years, an Englishman named Alex Sanders, who claimed descent from witches in Wales, was attracting media attention to the movement; a 1969 film entitled 'Legends of the Witches' was based on his writing. Sanders also initiated many witches who in turn founded covens (assemblies of witches) in Great Britain and continental Europe, but it is a Gardner initiate named Ray Buckland who is credited with introducing Wicca to the United States. Soon people with no connection to the Gardner lineage were establishing covens, and the name Wicca was becoming known outside the movement or 'Craft' itself.

It is difficult to estimate the current size of the Wicca movement, but publications sales and various claims regarding coven attendance suggest there are at least 85,000 adherents in North America, and perhaps four times as many around the world. The Covenant of the Goddess, which was organized in California in 1975, is a kind of umbrella organization, but it enlists no more than one coven out of every twenty in the United States.

The feminist movement had a major impact on Wicca in North America. Zsuzsanna Budapest established a coven for women only in 1971; her book *The Holy Book of Women's Mysteries* (1980) focuses on goddesses and rituals for women.

Journalist Margot Adler became interested in the movement after listening to a tape sent by a witchcraft circle in Wales. Investigating other women's involvement in the Craft, she found that the visionary or aesthetic element played an important part, along with the mysteries of birth and growth, a concern for the natural environment, and particularly a sense of feminist empowerment. Feminism was also central to Starhawk (Miriam Simos), for whom the religion of the Goddess is the pulsating rhythm of life, and human sexuality a reflection of the fundamentally sexual nature of the earth itself. At a lake high in the Sierra Nevada Mountains of California, she writes,

> it seems clear that earth is truly Her flesh and was formed by a sexual process: Her shakes and shudders and moans of pleasure, the orgasmic release of molten rock spewing forth in fiery eruptions, the slow caress of glaciers, like white hands gently smoothing all that has been left jagged (Starhawk 1982: 136).

In general, this kind of neopagan witchcraft seeks a return to primal nature and repudiates the classical Western religions that it holds responsible for repressing human sexuality. At the same time, its feminist emphasis challenges the patriarchal traditions of Judaism and Christianity. Although men can take an active part in it, Wicca is particularly empowering for women, and this has surely been part of its appeal.

Practice

Wiccans celebrate as many as eight *sabbats* (festivals) during the annual cycle or 'wheel of the year'. Four have fixed dates: Candlemas (1 February), May Day (1 May), Lammas (1 August), and Hallowe'en. The other four mark the important days of the solar cycle: the Spring and Autumn equinoxes and the Fall and Winter solstices.

Ideally, every Wiccan service would be held in the open air, but this is not always possible. Although practices vary in their details, standard activities include healing rituals and celebration of important life-cycle events: birth, coming of age, marriage, death. Among the most important symbols are the circle, the four directions, and the four elements (earth, water, fire, air). Some of the rituals are symbolically sacrificial, paralleling (or parodying) the Christian Eucharist. Some covens announce upcoming services only by word of mouth and require that strangers be introduced by a trusted friend.

In 1993, members of the Covenant of the Goddess took part in the centennial World's Parliament of Religions in Chicago. In an age of interfaith acceptance, Wiccan priestesses and priests sought public and governmental recognition of their work as institutional chaplains, in hospitals, prisons, universities, and military units, but they could not provide any formal documentation of clerical training. To obtain the necessary credentials, some Wiccan leaders enrolled in Unitarian theological seminaries. Since then, the term 'witch' has begun to be used to distinguish credentialled clergy (group leaders) from lay adherents.

Scientology

The Church of Scientology was founded in 1954 by L. Ron Hubbard (1911–86). Official biographies emphasize the breadth of his experience and learning. As a boy in Montana, for instance, he was exposed to the traditional teachings of the Blackfoot nation. In his youth he was introduced to Freudian psychology by a mentor who had trained with Freud and, travelling to Asia with his family, learned about a variety of ancient spiritual traditions. As an adult he not only became a prolific author in various genres, including science fiction, but served as a naval officer in the Second World War and, severely wounded, assisted his return to health by discovering how to remove deep-seated blocks in his mind. Following his recovery he began to advocate a new theory of what the soul does to the body. He called this theory **dianetics**, from the Greek *dia* (through) and *nous* (mind or soul).

Hubbard's 1950 book *Dianetics: The Modern Science of Mental Health* sold millions of copies. Soon followers were forming groups across the US, and in 1954 they became the first members of the Church of Scientology. The Church's official website defines Scientology—a word derived from the Latin *scio* (knowing) and the Greek *logos* (study)—as 'knowing about knowing' and describes it as an 'applied religious philosophy'.

The Creed of Scientology begins with several generic statements about human rights, including freedom of expression, association, and religion. Reflecting Hubbard's belief that the underlying principle of all life forms is the drive to survive, it asserts that all humans have the right to survive and defend themselves, and the duty to protect others. At the same time it affirms that 'the laws of God forbid' humans to destroy or enslave the souls of others; that the spirit can be saved; and that the spirit alone can heal the body.

Scientologists understand the universe to consist of eight intersecting planes or 'dynamics', beginning with the self, the family, and so on at the bottom and moving up to the spiritual universe (the seventh dynamic) and the Supreme Being or Infinity (the eighth). The nature of the Infinity or God dynamic is not clearly defined. However, it seems to have less in common with the 'personal God' of Christianity, who knows, wills, and acts like a (super) human person, than with 'impersonal' principles or divinities such as the Dao of Daoism, the Brahman of the Hindu *Upanishads*, and the transcendent cosmic Buddha of some forms of Mahayana Buddhism.

Scientology uses the term '**thetan**' (pronounced 'thay-tan') for the soul. Each thetan is thought to be billions of years old. Like the atman of Hindu belief, the thetan is reincarnated, passing from one body to another at death.

Scientologists prefer to think of the movement as originating with its practitioners rather than with Hubbard himself. But he was its inspiration, he gave it direction from the first, and his writings and lectures constitute its religious literature. In a sense, the spread of Scientology began with the publication of *Dianetics* and its translation into numerous languages, even before the official founding of the Church in 1954. Various publications helped to spread Scientology to Britain and Europe. Today Scientologists have an organized presence in most countries.

As a strategy for spreading their influence Hubbard decided to focus on high-profile celebrities. 'Celebrity Centers' featuring posh facilities for practice and training, established in major cities of North America and Europe, succeeded in attracting several celebrities, whose names have added credibility to the organization.

Credibility was important because the movement was haunted by controversy. Several Scientologists, including Hubbard's wife, Mary Sue, were convicted of criminal activity involving the infiltration of various government agencies and theft in an effort (referred to by Scientology leaders as Operation Snow White) to remove documents thought to reflect badly on the operation. L. Ron Hubbard was named as an unindicted co-conspirator (United States vs Mary Sue Hubbard et al., 1979).

After Hubbard's death in 1986, the leadership passed to David Miscavige. As a boy growing up in Philadelphia, Miscavige had suffered from allergies and asthma, but was apparently cured following a dianetics training session. He joined Scientology in 1976, right at the time of Operation Snow White, and within three years rose from a cameraman filming Hubbard to an executive role, restructuring the various divisions so as to better conform to various laws and to protect Hubbard from personal liability. In the aftermath of the trial, Mary Sue Hubbard resigned from her leadership role and a new division was created under the leadership of Miscavige, who became chairman of the board of the Religious Technologies Center, charged with protecting the integrity of Hubbard's teachings. From this power base, he has served as the organization's paramount leader since 1986,

although his role is that of an administrator rather than a spiritual leader.

As early as 1982, some dissenting followers of Hubbard were beginning to form alternative organizations outside the Church of Scientology. This activity increased after Hubbard's death. These 'heretical' organizations are known collectively as the 'Free Zone'. The name comes from Hubbard himself, who claimed that planet earth, under the galactic name Teegeeack, had been declared a 'free zone' millions of years ago. In that context, 'free' meant free of political or economic interference from other planets in the galaxy, but in the organizational context it meant free to follow the teachings of Hubbard without either payment to or interference from the Church of Scientology. RON's Org was one of the first of the Free Zone groups. Other Free Zone groups sprung up in Germany and elsewhere. The Church of Scientology tries to maintain exclusive rights to Hubbard's practices and refers to any unauthorized scientological practices as 'squirreling' and to **Free Zoners** as 'squirrels', which corresponds to the term *heretics* in Christianity. On the other hand, Free Zoners such as The International Free Zone Association claim that it is the Free Zoners who are faithful to the original teachings and practices of Hubbard.

Practice

In the 1960s Hubbard developed a step-by-step method for clearing the mind, or thetan, of mental blocks (called **engrams**) and restoring it to a state referred to as 'clear'. Engrams are the result of traumatic experiences, and they remain with the thetan until they are cleared, even carrying over from one life to the next. In some ways they are comparable to bad karma in the religions of India. Hubbard's process for clearing engrams, called 'auditing', involves the use of a device called an '**E-meter**', which is supposed to indicate when an engram blockage has been discovered in the mind. The E-meter (electro-psychometer) was originally developed by a polygraph expert named Volney

Mathison, who had noticed while doing lie detection sessions that subjects tended to give readable responses to words that triggered unconscious as well as conscious thoughts. Mathison and Hubbard knew each other because they both wrote science fiction, and Hubbard began to use the 'Mathison E-meter' in his dianetics practice. Although Mathison later distanced himself from Hubbard, the latter was able to get a patent on a modified version of the device. The Hubbard E-meter is manufactured at the movement's California headquarters and sold to members for their use in auditing.

Another important practice—the equivalent of scriptural study—is the study of Hubbard's thought and writings (an area in which the movement works hard to preserve orthodoxy). This study is known as 'training' and students are encouraged to continue it, striving to reach ever-higher levels. Progress is termed 'moving along the bridge' to total freedom, and it can take years of expensive auditing. After sufficient progress has been made to be called a Clear, the 'advanced training' begins. This instruction introduces some of Hubbard's imaginative science fiction concepts, among them the idea that an extraterrestrial named Xenu, the ruler of a galactic confederation, came to Teegeeack (earth) 75 million years ago, bringing with him thousands of aliens who had tried to revolt against his leadership. He put these political prisoners around volcanoes in which he detonated H-bombs. Then he captured the souls of the dead, now known as Thetans, and subjected them to brainwashing, implanting in them various ideas that we now associate with other religions. However, traces of their essences remain to this day, and some of their souls accumulated on the few bodies that were left. They are known as 'body thetans'. Those who complete all seven levels of this training are known as Operating Thetans (OTs).

Scientologists try to minimize the formation of new engrams in themselves or others. For example, Scientologist women are encouraged (though not required) to give birth in silence, in order to minimize the trauma of birth and therefore the creation of engrams in the baby thetan. Gestures are used for communication between the mother and attendants, and the mother is urged to minimize her cries of pain. Since Scientology prohibits drugs, the mother is also encouraged to give birth without the aid of painkillers.

Since Scientology does not anticipate any form of divine judgment after death, funeral services focus on celebrating the life of the deceased and wishing his or her thetan well in the next incarnation. After the funeral, friends and relatives of the deceased are encouraged to undergo auditing to rid themselves of the engrams resulting from grief. Scientologists may opt for cremation or burial. Hubbard was cremated, and before his death he discouraged the building of any elaborate memorials to him.

Scientology has come under intense public scrutiny and criticism for several reasons. Professional psychologists and other scientists are not sympathetic to the underlying claims of dianetics, and the fact that every step along the bridge costs additional money has given rise to accusations that it is just a pyramid scheme designed to bilk money from the rich and gullible. Some observers have claimed that Hubbard once suggested to a meeting of science-fiction writers that, instead of writing for a penny a word, they could make millions by starting a new religion.

Marc Headley, a former Scientology believer and employee, broke with the movement after fifteen years, escaping on a motorcycle with security personnel chasing him in a van until he crashed. Later he returned to rescue his Scientologist wife as well. In 2009 Headley published an autobiographical exposé of his years in Scientology. In *Blown for Good: Behind the Iron Curtain of Scientology* he describes his early years as a child of Scientologists who sent him to Scientology schools whenever they could afford it. Eventually he took a job with the organization. Promoted to the headquarters where the tapes, E-meters, and other equipment were manufactured, he happened to be chosen as the subject on whom Tom Cruise would practise auditing. In an interview with *The Village Voice*, Headley explained that, as Cruise's trainee, he was instructed to tell inanimate objects such as bottles or ashtrays to move in a certain way; then, when they did not move, Headley was instructed to move the objects himself and then thank them for moving. The purpose of this exercise, according to Headley, was to rehabilitate the mind's ability to control things and be controlled (Ortega 2009). He also claimed that employees lived and worked in sub-standard conditions for little or no pay, and were not allowed to leave the premises. In Scientology circles, critics such as Headley are known as Suppressive Persons, or SPs.

Despite the controversies that surround it, Scientology has been recognized as a valid new religion in several countries, including South Africa, Spain, Portugal, and Sweden. According to Headley, when the Internal Revenue Service of the United States granted Scientology tax-free status as a religious organization in 1993, Miscavige held a big meeting to announce that 'the war' was over.

The movement has had problems elsewhere, however, especially in France. In 1977 five Scientology leaders were found guilty of fraudulently coercing money from members, and the next year Hubbard himself was found guilty of fraud. A well-known owner of a computer company lost a large order from the ministry of education after the French media ran a story about his Scientology affiliation in 1991, and in 2009 six leaders of the Scientology Celebrity Center of Paris were convicted of fraud and fined almost one million dollars, although the court stopped short of banning the organization, as the prosecution had requested, on the grounds that the law regarding fraud did not extend that far (Erlanger 2009). In such cases, even the prosecution is careful to focus on Scientology's money-raising tactics rather than its spiritual beliefs.

Although it was founded only in the mid-twentieth century, Scientology now claims more than 12 million followers in over one hundred countries. Critics who believe that number to be grossly exaggerated suggest that it is based on the numbers of people who have ever bought a book or taken a Scientology course since its inception. Based on the quantities of E-meters and other supplies shipped during his time with the organization, Headley estimates that there were roughly 10,000 to 15,000 active Scientologists in the 1990s.

The Raëlian Movement

The Raëlian Movement traces its origins to a winter day in 1973 when a French journalist and racing enthusiast named Claude Vorilhon impulsively decided to drive to the site of an old volcano where he had enjoyed family picnics in the past. There he saw a small flying saucer hovering near the ground. An extraterrestrial creature—approximately 1.2 metres (4 feet) tall and resembling a bearded human with a greenish skin tone—then walked over and spoke to Vorilhon in French. In the course of this and subsequent encounters, the alien—whom Vorilhon came to know as Yahweh—recounted details of Vorilhon's own life and explained that he had telepathically drawn the Frenchman to this spot. Yahweh invited him inside the spaceship and told him that all life on earth was originally created in a laboratory by aliens called Elohim—the plural form of the word for a god in biblical Hebrew (*eloh*), frequently used in the Torah to refer to the one God. The International Raëlian Movement translates 'Elohim' as 'those who came from the sky', replacing the traditional idea of creation by a deity with creation by sky people.

Yahweh explained that a few weeks earlier he had used telepathy to urge Vorilhon to refresh his memory of the book of *Genesis* because he wanted to talk to him about it; now Vorilhon understood why he had recently, for no apparent reason, purchased a Bible and started to read it. The alien interpreted the reference to God's creation of heaven and earth (in *Genesis* 1: 1) as a reference to the aliens 'from the sky', and the verse (*Genesis* 1: 2) saying that the spirit of God moved over the face of the earth as a reference to the alien spacecraft. Continuing to instruct Vorilhon on the proper interpretation of *Genesis*, Yahweh said that a 'day' in the context of the six days of creation was equal to 2,000 earth years; that since the earth at that time was covered in water, the aliens had caused explosions in order to form the continents; and that they had used advanced scientific techniques to create the first plants and animals on earth in such a way that they would be able to reproduce themselves thereafter.

Despite minor differences in physical appearance (explained as the result of differences in the methods used by the various teams of Elohim scientists to create each group), the humans were formed 'in the image of' the Elohim themselves. This alarmed the Elohim back on the home planet, who feared that humans' intelligence might someday allow them to travel to the alien planet and cause trouble. Therefore it was decided to keep the scientific knowledge of humans at a very primitive level. The team of scientists working in what is now Israel, however, had created an unusually intelligent group of humans, and wanted to give them greater scientific knowledge. That team, Yahweh explained, was what *Genesis* refers to as the 'serpent' that tempted Eve, and the 'Garden' from which Adam and Eve were expelled was in fact the laboratory of the Elohim. Similarly, the idea of the Jews being a 'chosen people' was a reflection of the way the Elohim scientists had realized their genius. However, *Genesis* 6: 4—in which 'the sons of Elohim' mate with the daughters of men—is interpreted literally.

The story of Noah and the flood in *Genesis* 7 is also given a novel twist. In the Raëlian interpretation, the flood is the result of nuclear explosions set off by the Elohim on the home planet who fear that humans have been given too much knowledge, and Noah thwarts their plan by taking cells of each creature aboard an orbiting satellite. Then, after the flood, Noah waits for the nuclear fallout to settle before returning to earth with a cargo that includes a pair of humans from each of the races created by the Elohim scientists.

The biblical story of the Tower of Babel gets a new interpretation as well. Traditionally, the Tower was built by a great king to reach to the heavens—a symbol of arrogance, which God punished by making humans (who until then had all spoken the same language) unable to understand one another. In the alien's account, the 'Tower of Babel' is the name of a spaceship built by the Hebrews in partnership with the Elohim scientists who had been banished to earth for making humans too intelligent. This project so alarms the Elohim on the home planet that they thwart the progress of human science by scattering the Hebrews throughout the world. Similarly, the cities of Sodom and Gomorrah are destroyed not by normal fire in punishment for sexual sin, but by nuclear explosion in response to the threat posed to the home planet by scientific progress on earth. And God's order that Abraham sacrifice his son is translated into a test by the Elohim to see if the leader of the Hebrew scientists was still loyal to them. The New Testament gets some novel interpretations as well: for example, the resurrection of Jesus is attributed to cloning.

Yahweh told Vorilhon that he had been chosen to receive the truth because he had a religious background, with a Jewish father and a Catholic mother, and was a free-thinking opponent of traditional religion. As a result of his UFO encounter, Vorilhon was told to change his name to Raël, 'messenger of the Elohim'. Feeling called to prophecy, he was told to write down the message in book form, and to spread the word in anticipation of the Elohim's return.

Two years after his initial encounter, Raël reports, he was taken aboard a spaceship and transported to the planet of the Elohim, where he received further instruction and met with past religious leaders. He wrote an account of the visit in his book *They Took Me to Their Planet*.

In 1974 Raël called a press conference in Paris, at which he introduced his movement to the media. By 1980 the International Raëlian Movement had taken on most of the features of an organized religion: scripture, rituals, festival days, a communal building. It is organized hierarchically on the model of the Roman Catholic Church, with Raël himself at the pinnacle, like a pope, and various lesser officials with titles such as Bishop Guide and Priest Guide. Susan Jean Palmer (1995) notes that although the movement advocates gender equality and is libertarian about sexuality and gender roles, women are not well represented in the leadership hierarchy, especially at the upper levels.

The leadership hierarchy may reflect Roman Catholicism, but the Raëlian cosmology is nothing like that of traditional Christianity. Not only does it reject belief in gods of any kind, but it teaches that the whole of the observable universe is just a small atom of a larger structure, which is itself part of a larger one, and so on infinitely. At the same time every atom is itself a universe on the next smaller scale, with structures descending in size scale infinitely. Time and space are infinite in this cosmology, which runs on scientific principles without any need for divine command or intervention.

The Elohim are expected to return by 2035, but only on condition that humans are ready to welcome them, have tolerance for one another, and show respect for the environment. The Movement hopes one day to create an 'embassy' that would function as a place for the Elohim to interact with humans in a helpful way; ideally, this embassy would be located in Israel.

Raëlians reject the theory of evolution. Instead, they believe that the Elohim brought all life to earth from another planet 25,000 years ago, and that just as the Elohim were themselves created by previous entities, we earthlings may someday take life to yet another planet. The term 'Intelligent Design', which some conservative Christians have promoted as an alternative to Darwinian evolution, has been adopted by Raëlians. But whereas for conservative Christians Intelligent Design is a way to get God and creationism back into the post-Darwinian picture, for Raëlians the term represents a third option for those who, like themselves, reject both evolution and creation by a god. The latest collection of Raël's writings about his UFO encounters has been published under the title *Intelligent Design: Message from the Designers*. In a postscript, Raël calls his approach a Third Way, between Darwin and *Genesis*. Since Raël holds that humans were created in a laboratory, he is confident this Third Way will one day be replicated in a laboratory by humans.

The Raëlian symbol is a swastika—best known today as the symbol of Nazism in Hitler's Germany—inside a six-pointed star that is said to be based on a design of interlocking triangles displayed on the spaceship during Raël's UFO encounter. In fact, though, it seems identical to the Star of David—the symbol of Judaism. To avoid offending Jews, the symbol was changed for a few years to a swirling galaxy image inside the hexagram. But now the movement has returned to the original symbol. Raëlians claim that their swastika has nothing to do with Nazism, and point out that for thousands of years before its adoption by Hitler, it was a symbol of good luck and prosperity used in Buddhist, Jaina, and other religious traditions. They say that the symbol as a whole stands for the Elohim, while the swastika part represents infinite time and the hexagram infinite space. It reflects the Raëlian belief that the universe is cyclical, without beginning or end.

Practice

During Raël's second encounter with the Elohim he was taught a spiritual technique known as 'sensual meditation' or 'meditation of all senses', in which the meditator turns inward to experience the lesser universes within the atoms of his or her own body, and then turns outward to experience the greater universes beyond our own; eventually, the most adept will be able to visualize the planet of the Elohim. The goal is to awaken humans' highest spiritual potential by first awakening their physical sensibilities.

There are four main Raëlian holidays: the first Sunday in April, celebrated as the day the Elohim created Adam and Eve; 6 August, the day of the Hiroshima bombing, which for Raëlians is the beginning of the Apocalypse; 7 October, the date that Raël met with Jesus, Buddha, and other past prophets aboard a spaceship during the second encounter; and 13 December, the day when Raël first encountered the Elohim.

Raëlians are expected to avoid mind-altering drugs, coffee, and tobacco, and to use alcohol either in moderation or not at all. They celebrate sensuality, advocate free love, and discourage traditional marriage contracts. The movement's liberal policy regarding marriage and sexual partners has made it an attractive religious home for gays and lesbians.

Becoming a Raëlian involves two ceremonies. First, initiates must renounce all ties to theistic religions. After this 'Act of Apostasy' comes a baptismal ceremony in which information about the initiate's DNA is supposedly transmitted to the Elohim.

As part of his effort to free humans from the constraints imposed by traditional religions, Raël has called for a massive 'de-baptism' campaign across Africa or (as he prefers to call it) the

Raël with a full-scale model of the spaceship he encountered in 1973 (AFP/AFP/Getty Images).

United Kingdom of Kama. He argues that 'spiritual decolonization' is a prerequisite for future development. The Movement has also been active in denouncing the practice of clitorectomy that is common in some parts of Africa, and has started a fundraising effort to pay for restorative surgery.

Although Raëlians reject the concept of the soul, they believe that a kind of everlasting life can be attained through cloning. Clonaid, a Raëlian enterprise founded in France in 1997, claims to be the world's first human cloning company. Since then, it has announced the births of several cloned babies; none of these claims have been substantiated, however.

Because Raëlians do not believe in gods, the International Raëlian Movement is not officially classified as a religion, although some jurisdictions do recognize it as a non-profit organization (the first to do so was the province of Quebec, in 1977). Important religious leaders such as Jesus and Buddha are recognized as prophets, however, inspired by the Elohim to communicate as much of the truth as humans were able to absorb in their time. Raël himself is identified with Maitreya, the future Buddha who is expected to come when the world needs him, although Buddhists themselves do not accept this idea.

Despite their partial recognition of traditional religious leaders, the Movement is exclusivistic in terms of allegiance, as the Act of Apostasy indicates. Just as Christianity sees itself as completing Judaism, and as Islam sees Muhammad as the 'seal of the prophets', Raëlians see their Movement as the culmination of earlier religions, which incorrectly understood the role of the Elohim.

According to Raël, the Elohim told him that only 4 per cent of humans were advanced enough to understand the truth about them, so it is not surprising that the Raëlian mission has not made converts by the millions. Nevertheless, the movement claims more than 65,000 members in 84 countries.

✵ THE NEW AGE MOVEMENT

The expression 'New Age' has a wide range of connotations, including the biblical notion of an apocalypse in which God will intervene to restructure society, reward the righteous, and (in some scenarios) smite the wicked with long-overdue punishment. The nineteenth century saw the rise of several millenarian Christian movements, among them the Jehovah's Witnesses, that looked forward to the literal fulfillment of the prophecies in the biblical books of *Daniel* and *Revelation*. On the whole, the idea of a 'new age' for these movements meant a reconstitution of society. For the Nation of Islam, however, the 'new age' would be one in which African Americans would emerge strong and triumphant. And various loosely defined organizations have emerged under the generic name New Age. As we will see, New Age draws on both Eastern and Western traditions.

The term 'New Age' was in use as early as 1907 as the title of a progressive British political and literary journal that introduced its readers to topics such as Freudian psychoanalysis. With the 'consciousness revolution' of the 1960s came expectations of a different sort of 'new age', however. The transpersonal psychology movement, for instance, emphasized spiritual insights and therapeutic techniques that were diametrically opposed to the mechanistic approach of orthodox Freudianism. One centre of transpersonal psychology was the Esalen Institute in Big Sur, California, founded in 1962 as a retreat centre offering seminars, workshops, and encounter groups.

Not all New Age seekers were so disciplined. In 1967 the musical *Hair!* popularized the idea that the dawning of the Age of Aquarius would usher in a universal religion to replace the Christianity of the Piscean age. To some, the Aquarian age meant little more than freely available rock music or drugs. Those expectations came together in 1969, when as many as half a million young people congregated in a farmer's field near Woodstock, New York. By the late 1980s, 'New Age' had become a kind of shorthand term for a cluster of trends that included a quest for individual spiritual insight, expectations of both personal transformation and worldly success, the pursuit of physical healing and psychological peace through various self-help disciplines, and in some cases reliance on astrology and psychic powers. Many New Age enthusiasts have published accounts of their personal transformation through some combination of New Age disciplines, diets, and cures.

Scholars looking for the historical roots of New Age spirituality often point to Emanuel Swedenborg, an eighteenth-century Swedish mystic who wrote about the evolution of the human soul; the nineteenth-century American Transcendentalist Ralph Waldo Emerson; or the Russian founder of the Theosophical movement, Helena P. Blavatsky, who claimed to have discovered the wisdom of the ages in Asian teachings such as Hindu Vedanta. Those looking for antecedents of New Age therapeutic techniques, for their part, often point to the Swiss physician Paracelsus (Philippus Aureolus Theophrastus Bombast von Hohenheim; 1493–1541), who claimed that humans were subject to the magnetism of the universe. Two centuries later, the German physician Franz Anton Mesmer postulated that healing takes place through a kind of magnetism in bodily fluids analogous to ocean tides, and sought to manipulate these with magnets or the wave of a wand or a finger. The effort to direct their flow, called mesmerism after him, was reflected in the development of hypnosis in the nineteenth century. As for what New Agers call 'channelling', the roots can be traced back at least as far as the nineteenth-century practice of the séance, in which the bereaved sought to make contact with their deceased loved ones through a 'spirit medium'. The use of gems and crystals was promoted in the first half of the twentieth century by the medium Edgar Cayce.

None of these earlier developments in itself constituted the New Age. But together they fertilized the spiritual soil of the English-speaking world, so that after the 1960s the New Age fascination with the exotic, the occult, the experiential, the curative, and the futuristic could take root and spread rapidly. Subjects that had been left on the sidelines of a scientific and technological age—astrology, hypnosis, alternative healing—were resurrected and, at a time of growing interest in subjects such as nutrition, ecology, and altruistic business ethics, entered the mainstream. All these could be seen as alternatives to orthodox religion, medicine, and society generally, and perhaps also to the exclusivist claims made by mainstream orthodoxies.

The metaphysical and therapeutic resources sketched so far came from outside or, at best, the margins of the major religious traditions discussed in this book. How did the New Age movement come to be so closely associated with religion? At least part of the answer can be found in its connections with Eastern religious traditions.

A prominent feature of the search for alternative modes of consciousness in the 1960s was a fascination with depths of awareness that traditions of Muslim Sufism, Hindu yoga, and Japanese Zen Buddhism in particular were believed to offer. The *Yijing* (or *I Ching*), an ancient Chinese divination manual, became a bestseller, and many people were introduced to Asian religious symbolism through the writings of the Swiss psychologist Carl G. Jung and the Jungian comparative-religion scholar Joseph Campbell. 'Exotic' religions seemed to offer something that the familiar traditions of the West did not.

Across North America and Europe, practitioners turned to Chinese *qigong* and acupuncture, Indian yoga and ayurvedic medicine, and Buddhist meditation techniques. In India, Maharishi Mahesh Yogi's Transcendental Meditation movement attracted high-profile entertainers, including the Beatles, Mia Farrow, and Clint Eastwood, as devotees. Deepak Chopra, an endocrinologist practising in the West, returned to his native India to explore traditional ayurvedic medicine and proceeded to write and lecture about its compatibility with modern Western medicine. The Thailand-born and Western-educated Chinese master Mantak Chia, working in New York, has written extensively on the potential of Daoist techniques for healing and sexual energy. And the list goes on.

A recurring temptation, in the promotion of Asian disciplines and therapies, is to divorce the techniques from a comprehensive understanding of the cultural vocabularies in which they had developed. It is a temptation not only for consumers of these wares, but also for their providers. For example, **Eckankar**, a new religion introduced in the 1960s by the American Paul Twitchell, takes its name from 'Ik Onkar' ('the one om-expression'), a name for the transcendent God in the Sikh tradition. But though Twitchell claimed to have studied with a Sikh master in India, it was only one episode in a lifetime of 'soul travel' to supposed invisible worlds on levels above our earthly one. Eckankar holds that there has always been a living Eck master on earth, among whom have been ancient Greek and Iranian Muslim figures, and that Twitchell was the 971st in the series.

The New Age movement is thoroughly eclectic, and its diversity is part of its appeal. It is open to many possibilities, including exploration, expression, and leadership by women. As such, it stands in sharp contrast to the male-dominated structures of the established religions and professions. This may constitute one of its lasting contributions.

Is there an any single word that sums up the spirit of the New Age? One candidate would be 'holistic'. Implying a quest for wholeness, sometimes with an overtone of holiness, it was coined in the context of evolutionary biology to refer to the whole as something more than the sum of its parts. Thus holistic diets and therapies seek to treat the whole person, body and mind, and holistic principles are fundamental to the ecological movement; the Gaia hypothesis, for instance, sees the earth as a single organism whose survival depends on the interaction of all its components (a perspective central to James Cameron's film *Avatar*). New ages yet to come are bound to view ecological holism as an increasingly urgent goal.

CONCLUSION

The new religions we have discussed cover the spiritual landscape, from East to West to outer space. None of these new religions is seriously challenging the traditional religions for influence. Some of them seem to have already peaked in numbers, at least in North America. Since new religions typically need a strong, charismatic leader, most such organizations have trouble sustaining their growth and unity after their founders' death. But others are still making significant gains in numbers, wealth, and influence.

The few that survive and prosper eventually become established as normal parts of the religious landscape. They become just 'religions' rather than 'new religions'. Judaism, Christianity, and Islam made this transition long ago. The Baha'i Faith and the Mormons have made it more recently. Which, if any, of the new religions that emerged in the late twentieth century will survive into the twenty-second is impossible to tell from this vantage point, but is surely an interesting topic for debate.

Glossary

Bab The individual expected to appear as the 'Gateway' to the new prophet in the Baha'i Faith.

bhakti Devotional faith, the favoured spiritual path in ISKCON.

cult Term for a new religion, typically demanding loyalty to a charismatic leader.

dianetics Hubbard's term for the system he developed to clear mental blocks.

Eckankar A new religion based on the teachings of Paul Twitchell.

E-meter A device used in Scientology to detect mental blocks.

engrams Scientology's term for mental blocks.

Falun A 'law wheel' said to be acquired through Dafa practice.

Free Zoner Person or group teaching Hubbard's thought independently of Scientology International.

Hare Krishnas Informal name for the members of ISKCON, based on their chant.

ISKCON International Society for Krishna Consciousness.

Kabbalah Traditional Jewish mysticism.

Komeito A Japanese political party loosely associated with Soka Gakkai.

Mormons Another name for members of the Church of Jesus Christ of Latter-day Saints.

millenarian Term used to refer to the belief that the current social order will soon come to an end.

qi Spiritual energy (*qi* or *chi*).

qigong Excercises to cultivate *qi*.

Scientology A new religion devoted to clearing mental blockages.

sect A sociological term for a group that breaks away from the main religion.

spherot The ten attributes of God in Kabbalah.

thetan Scientology's term for the soul or mind.

Vaishnava A Hindu who worships Vishnu and related deities.

Wicca A name for witchcraft or the Craft.

Further Reading

Baha'u'llah. 1952. *Gleanings from the Writings of Baha'u'llah,* rev. ed. Wilmette, IL: Baha'i Publishing Trust. A good selection of Baha'i writings.

Barrett, David V. 2003. *The New Believers: A Survey of Sects, Cults and Alternative Religions.* London: Octopus Publishing Group. A good place to start on the topic of cults versus new religions.

Dan, Joseph. 2005. *Kabbalah: A Very Short Introduction.* Oxford: Oxford University Press. A useful introduction.

Drew, A. J. 2003. *The Wiccan Bible: Exploring the Mysteries of the Craft from Birth to Summerland.* Franklin, NJ: Career Press. An overview of Wicca.

Esslemont, John E. 1979. *Bahá'u'lláh and the New Era: An Introduction to the Bahá'í Faith.* 4th ed. Wilmette, IL: Baha'i Publishing Trust. The standard survey recommended by Baha'is.

Gallagher, Eugene V., William M. Ashcraft, and W. Michael Ashcraft, eds. 2006. *An Introduction to New and Alternative Religions in America.* 5 vols. Westport: Greenwood Press. Scholarly introductions to religious movements from colonial era to present.

Headley, Marc. 2009. *Blown for Good: Behind the Iron Curtain of Scientology.* Burbank: BFG Books. An autobiography of a former Scientologist turned critic.

Hubbard, L. Ron. 1956. *Scientology: The Fundamentals of Thought.* 2007. Los Angeles: Bridge Publications. Basic book by Scientology's founder.

Lewis, James R., and J. Gordon Melton, eds. 1992. *Perspectives on the New Age.* Albany: State University of

New York Press. One of the best assessments of the New Age phenomenon.

Li Hongzhi. 2000. *Falun Gong*. 3rd ed. New York: University Publishing Co. Master Li's introduction to Falun Dafa.

Miller, William McElwee. 1974. *The Baha'i Faith: Its History and Teachings*. Pasadena: William Carey Library. An outsider's view of Bahai.

Muster, Nori J. 2001. *Betrayal of the Spirit: My Life behind the Headlines of the Hare Krishna Movement*. Champaign: University of Illinois Press. A former member's critical view of ISKCON.

Ostling, Richard, and Joan K. Ostling. 2007. *Mormon America—Revised and Updated Edition: The Power and the Promise*. New York: HarperOne. An overview of the issues.

Porter, Noah. 2003. *Falun Gong in the United States: An Ethnographic Study*. N.p.: Dissertation.Com. Argues against the 'cult' label based on interviews and publications.

Seager, Richard H. 2006. *Encountering the Dharma. Daisaku Ikeda, Soka Gakkai, and the Globalization of Buddhist Humanism*. Berkeley: University of California Press. A scholarly overview.

Shinn, Larry D. 1987. *The Dark Lord: Cult Images and the Hare Krishnas in America*. Philadelphia: Westminster Press. An objective overview based on extensive interviews.

Starhawk. 1982. *Dreaming the Dark*. Boston: Beacon Press. One of many works by an important Wicca leader.

White, Vibert L., Jr. 2001. *Inside the Nation of Islam: A Historical and Personal Testimony by a Black Muslim*. Gainesville: University Press of Florida. An account made more interesting because it is written by someone involved in the movement and in organizing the 1995 March.

Recommended Websites

www.bahai.org
> Site of the Baha'i religion.

www.falundafa.org
> Site of the Falun Dafa.

www.finalcall.com
> News site of the Nation of Islam.

www.internationfreezone.net
> Portal for the Free Zoner alternative to Scientology.

www.iskcon.org
> Site of the International Society for Krishna Consciousness.

www.kabbalah.com
> Site of the Kabbalah Centre International.

www.lds.org
> Site of the Church of Jesus Christ of Latter-day Saints, the Mormons.

www.komei.or.jp
> Site of the New Komeito party, loosely affiliated with Soka Gakkai.

www.rael.org
> Site of the International Raëlian Movement.

www.scientology.org
> Site of the international Scientology organization.

www.sgi.org
> Site of Soka Gakkai International.

www.wicca.org
> Site of the Church and School of Wicca.

References

Amnesty International. 'Human Rights in China'. Accessed 10 March 2010 at <http://www.amnesty.ca/blog2.php?blog=keep_the_promise_2&page=7>.

Dawson, Lorne L. 2006. *Comprehending Cults: The Sociology of New Religious Movements*. Toronto: Oxford University Press.

Erlanger, Steven. 2009. 'French Branch of Scientology Convicted of Fraud'. *New York Times*. Accessed 10 March 2010 at <http://www.nytimes.com/2009/10/28/world/europe/28france.html?_r=1>.

'Focus in Front'. Accessed 10 March 2010 at <http://www.kabbalah.com/newsletters/weekly-consciousness-tune-ups/focus-front>.

Huss, Boaz. 2005. 'All You Need is LAV: Madonna and Postmodern Kabbalah.' *Jewish Quarterly Review* 95, 4: 611–24.

Ikeda, Daisaku. 2008. 'Toward Humanitarian Competition: A New Current in History'. Accessed 10 March 2010 at <www.sgi.org/peace2009sum.html>.

'Introduction: What Is Falun Dafa?'. Accessed 10 March 2010 at <http://www.falundafa.org/eng/intro.html>.

Kabbalah Centre. 'Reincarnation'. Accessed 10 March 2010 at <http://www.kabbalah.com/node/434>.

Lee, Martha F. 1996. *The Nation of Islam: An American Millenarian Movement*. Syracuse: Syracuse University Press.

Levi, Jerome M. 2009. 'Structuralism and Kabbalah: Sciences of Mysticism or Mystifications of Science?' *Anthropological Quarterly* 82, 4 (Fall).

Lewis, James R. 2003. *Legitimating New Religions*. Rutgers: Rutgers University Press.

Li Hongzhi. 2000. *Falun Gong*. 3rd ed. New York: University Publishing Co.

Ljungdahl, Alex. 1975. 'What Can We Learn from Non-Biblical Prophet Movements'. In *New Religions*, ed. Haralds Biezais. Stockholm: Almqvist & Wiksell International.

Olyan, Saul M., and Gary A. Anderson. 2009. *Priesthood and Cult in Ancient Israel*. Sheffield: Sheffield Academic Press.

Ortega, Tony. 2009. 'Tom Cruise Told Me to Talk to a Bottle: Life at Scientology's Secret Headquarters'. *The Village Voice*. Accessed 10 March 2010 at <http://blogs.villagevoice.com/runninscared/archives/2009/11/tom_cruise_was.php>.

Palmer, Susan Jean. 1995. 'Women in the Raelian Movement: New Religious Experiments in Gender and Authority.' In *The Gods Have Landed: New Religions from Other Worlds*, ed. James R. Lewis. Albany: State University of New York Press.

Sahib, Hatim A. 1951. 'The Nation of Islam'. Master's thesis. University of Chicago. Cited in Lee 1996: 23.

'72 Names of God, The'. Accessed 15 March at <http://www.kabbalah.com/node/432>.

Starhawk. 1982. *Dreaming the Dark*. Boston: Beacon Press.

Walker, Dennis. 2005. *Islam and the Search for African-American Nationhood: Elijah Muhammad, Louis Farrakhan and the Nation of Islam*. Atlanta: Clarity Press.

White, Vibert L., Jr. 2001. *Inside the Nation of Islam: A Historical and Personal Testimony by a Black Muslim*. Gainesville: University Press of Florida.

Note

Parts of this chapter, especially in the sections on the Mormons, the Baha'i Faith, Wicca, and New Age movements, incorporate material written by the late Will Oxtoby for earlier editions of the work.

Chapter 8

Current Issues

Amir Hussain ❧ Roy C. Amore

Most of the chapters in this volume have concentrated on individual religious traditions. In this concluding chapter we will widen our focus and look at the way different traditions are handling some important current issues.

RELIGION AND POLITICS

Once upon a time, many in the West regarded religion as a kind of cultural fossil. Aesthetically rich, anthropologically intriguing? Yes. But relevant to today's hard-nosed world of economics and politics? Hardly at all. Those of us who studied religion were often asked how we could waste our lives on something that had so little to do with the modern world. In the secular intellectual climate of the 1960s, some philosophers and even theologians announced that God was dead. That announcement proved to be premature.

Religion has been a major factor in many of the events that have shaken the world over the last thirty years. One such event occurred in 1979, when the Shah of Iran was deposed in an 'Islamic Revolution'. That a nation of 40 million people would be ready to sacrifice lives and livelihoods to defend religious values was a concept utterly alien to development economists and politico-military strategists in the West. Meanwhile, not only in Iran but elsewhere, Muslims were turning their backs to modernity and secularism in general and to the modern West in particular. In increasing numbers, Muslim men from Algeria to Zanzibar started to grow beards and wear turbans, and more Muslim women than ever before adopted the *hijab* (head scarf).

A second event of 1979 that was to have profound repercussions was the Soviet Union's invasion of Afghanistan. From across the Muslim world, volunteers were taken to Afghanistan and trained by the United States to fight for the country's liberation. They were called *mujahidin*, and at

the time—before the end of the cold war—they were widely seen as what US President Ronald Reagan called 'freedom fighters'.

Among the supporters of Afghanistan's 'holy war' was Osama bin Laden (b. 1957), a wealthy Saudi who helped fund and train *mujahidin*. The Soviet troops were withdrawn in 1988, but bin Laden emerged as the leader of Al-Qaeda ('the base'), an extremist organization. In 1996 bin Laden issued a *fatwa* (religious legal opinion) calling for the overthrow of the Saudi government and the removal of US forces in Arabia; in 1998 he declared war against Americans generally; and in 2001 he was accused of masterminding the 9/11 attacks. In response to those attacks, the United States went to war first in Afghanistan and then in Iraq. To understand the modern world, we now realize, we need to take into account the meanings that traditional religions have for their adherents.

Another eventful year was 1989, when the communist order of eastern Europe and the Soviet Union began to crumble. Hopes for democracy, peace, and progress were high. But when the restraints of the socialist order were loosened, old identities resurfaced, and with them passions that most outsiders had assumed to be long dead. Feuds and ethno-religious divisions in the Balkans, the Caucasus, and Central Asia erupted into bitter conflict. Samuel Huntington, in his book *The Clash of Civilizations*, argued that the old world order based on the conflict between communism and capitalism had been replaced by a new one based on the differences among civilizations—and civilizations are defined mainly along religious lines.

Islam is not the only religious tradition that has experienced a revival in recent years. In India, advocates of Hindu nationalism have formed

◀ **Buddhist monks in northeast Thailand constructed the Wat Pa Maha Chedi Kaew temple complex entirely of recycled bottles** (Bronek Kaminski/Barcroft Media Ltd).

At a protest in New Delhi in 2009, Tibetans in exile called for the release from Chinese detention of Gedhun Choekyi Nyima (b. 1989), recognized by the Dalai Lama as the Panchen Lama—Tibet's second-highest spiritual leader (REUTERS/Arko Datta).

governments at both the state and the national level. In Sri Lanka, the struggle of Hindu Tamil separatists to establish an independent homeland sparked a resurgence of Buddhist fervour among the Sinhalese majority, which—for the first time in history—elected several monks to parliament. And in China religious minorities such as the Muslim Uighurs and the Buddhist Tibetans have renewed their struggles against the repressive tendencies of the national government.

✾ FUNDAMENTALISM

In most cases the leading figures in the resurgence of religious fervour have come from the ultraconservative or 'fundamentalist' end of the religious spectrum. A brief review of the rise of fundamentalism may help to explain why.

The term 'fundamentalism' originated in the United States, where a series of booklets entitled *The Fundamentals* was published in 1910. Affirming the 'inerrancy' (infallibility) of the Bible and traditional Christian doctrines, the booklets were distributed free to Protestant clergy, missionaries, and students through the anonymous sponsorship of 'two Christian laymen' (William Lyman Stewart and his brother Milton, both of whom were major figures in the Union Oil Company of California). By 1920 advocates of inerrancy were being described as 'fundamentalists'.

Fundamentalism is a modern phenomenon, a reaction against the values associated with secularism and modernity. Above all, perhaps, what fundamentalists reject is the modern tendency to locate ultimate authority in human institutions such as courts and legislatures rather than divine scriptures and religious leaders. If they interpret their scripture as condemning homosexuality, for example, they resist all efforts to legalize same-sex marriage as a human right. Fundamentalists do not necessarily denounce science, but on specific issues where science differs from their interpretation of scripture, they side with scripture as the ultimate authority. For Christian fundamentalists, the main conflict with science has centred on the perceived conflict between the biblical stories of creation and the consensus of modern science. They understand the Bible to affirm that the world was created by God in six days, only a few thousand years ago, and that everything that exists originated at that time. By contrast, science maintains that the universe has existed for many billions of years, that our planet formed some time later, and that all life on earth was the product of evolution through countless generations.

The test case for fundamentalism came in 1925, when a high-school teacher named John T. Scopes was brought to trial for violating a newly enacted Tennessee law that banned the teaching of evolution on the grounds that it contradicted the Bible. The court found for the prosecution, conducted by the famed orator William Jennings Bryan (1860–1925) against the defence of Clarence Darrow (1857–1938), and fined Scopes $100. So extensive was the news coverage of the case, however, that fundamentalism itself was effectively put on trial in the court of public opinion, where Darwin, Scopes, and Darrow emerged the clear victors. In particular, it was the idea that humans were not the special creations of God but a species of primate descended from the same common ancestor as gorillas and chimpanzees that underlay the Scopes case and earned it the nickname the 'monkey trial'. Scopes's conviction was overturned in 1927 on the technical grounds that the fine was too high, although it would be another forty years before the Tennessee law banning the teaching of evolution was repealed.

The word 'fundamentalism' can have various meanings, but almost all of them are pejorative: even conservative Protestants tend to describe their own views as evangelical and use 'fundamentalist' only to refer to more extreme views. In addition to denoting an orthodoxy based on the inerrancy of scripture, 'fundamentalism' generally suggests orthopraxy—conformity to a straitlaced code of social and personal conduct—and a militant defence of their tradition as they understand it. Fundamentalists have been known to attack as diabolical those they believe to be subverting that tradition by expressing doubt or taking more liberal positions on some issues.

Fundamentalists perceive a struggle between good and evil forces in the world, and they have a greater-than-average readiness to believe that evil is tangibly manifested in social groups and forces with which they take issue, such as advocates of homosexual rights or free choice in abortion. They also tend to believe that the apocalypse—a final battle between the forces of good and evil in this world—is imminent.

Since the 1970s the term 'fundamentalist' has been widely used to describe ultraconservative movements in religious traditions other than Christianity—especially those that have taken their beliefs into the political realm. Some scholars object to the use of a term with specifically Christian roots to refer to different traditions. Nevertheless, from the popular perspective there are enough similarities among the various ultraconservative movements around the world to justify the term's extension to other cultures.

Bioethics

Another important challenge facing religious communities in the twenty-first century is the unprecedented power over human life and death made available by developments in biological research and medical technology. This power is especially troubling for the Western religions, which have traditionally considered humans to be sacred, set apart from all other beings. In Islam, for example, the human being is created expressly to serve as God's representative on earth:

> Behold, your Lord said to the angels: 'I will create a vicegerent on earth.' They said: 'Will You place therein one who will make mischief there and shed blood while we celebrate Your praises and glorify Your holy name?' God said: 'I know what you do not' (Q. 2: 30).

Central to the notion of the human being as sacred is the notion of the soul. The Christian understanding of the soul was economically expressed by the Anglican writer C.S. Lewis: 'You don't have a soul, you are a soul. You have a body.' Hinduism likewise teaches that the soul (*atman*) is the eternal and therefore the more important part of the human being; in fact, one of the Hindu terms for soul is *dehin*, meaning 'that which possesses a body'. In Islam, the soul is believed to enter the body at a certain stage of its development in the womb:

'And truly We created the human being out of wet clay, then we made it a drop in a firm resting place, then We made the seed a clot, then We made the clot a lump of flesh, then We made (in) the lump of flesh bones, then We clothed the bones with flesh, then We caused it to grow into another creation, so blessed be God, the best of the creators' (Q. 23: 12–14).

Modern Muslims take great pride in the history of science and medicine associated with Islam. Following an injunction of the Prophet Muhammad 'to seek knowledge even unto China' (that is, to the end of the then-known world),[1] Muslims never really experienced the kind of tension between religion and science that Western Christianity did. To discover scientific truths about the world was to learn more about God who created the world. Thus universities were established in the Islamic world as early as the ninth century; one of the earliest accounts of the duties of the doctor was written by a ninth-century physician named Ishaq ibn Ali Rahawi; and in the tenth century another Muslim physician named al-Razi (known in the West as Rhazes) wrote numerous treatises on medicine, pharmacy, and medical ethics.

The Islamic system of moral deliberation is even older. Jonathan Brockopp, in his edited volume *Islamic Ethics of Life: Abortion, War and Euthanasia* (2003), identifies the sources of Islamic ethics as the Qur'an and the traditions of the Prophet Muhammad (*hadiths*), together with the commentaries on those texts written over the centuries. Traditionally, the scholars and jurists who interpret these texts in order to rule on the ethical questions brought before them have tended to prefer cases and examples over abstract principles.

Perhaps this traditional preference for the specific over the general helps to account for Muslims' reluctance to approach medical issues from the perspective of 'bioethics' (as is usually done in the West). Rather, the tradition has been to let God and the family decide. Although advances in medicine are welcomed and the doctor's expertise is honoured, the wishes of the individual or the family have taken priority over the opinions either of doctors or of Islamic religious scholars. And because it is impossible to know God's will, Muslims have preferred what Brockopp calls a 'stance of humility' when it comes to deciding questions of life and death.

In the West, arguments for the patient's right to die are often based on the concept of human dignity. Among Muslims, however, human life is valued not for its own sake but because it is a trust given by God; similarly, human dignity is not inherent in the individual but a product of his or her relationship with God. While active euthanasia (mercy killing) would be forbidden, therefore, a brain-dead patient kept alive only by medical technology could be removed from artificial life support if that were the family's wish.

Nevertheless, 'Let God and the family decide' is not always adequate to the conditions under which most North Americans, including Muslims, now live and die. Amyn Sajoo, in his book *Muslim Ethics: Emerging Vistas* (2004), writes not only as an academic but as an insider to the Muslim tradition, and he shows it responding to medicalized death in a more activist mode. Sajoo reprints extracts from the *Islamic Code of Medical Ethics* adopted by the Islamic Organization for Medical Sciences in 1981. The organization upheld the traditional position on euthanasia: 'A doctor shall not take away life even when motivated by mercy.' With respect to the artificial prolongation of life, however, it advised the doctor

> to realize his limit and not transgress it. If it is scientifically certain that life cannot be restored, then it is futile to diligently keep on the vegetative state of the patient by heroic means of animation or preserve him by deep-freezing or other artificial methods.

Thus in cases where the family wishes to continue life support even when there is no hope of recovery, it may not necessarily have the final word: the doctor may become the primary decision-maker.

Another organization that is working to bring traditional religious standards and ideals into modern medical situations is the Islamic Medical Association of North America (IMANA). IMANA has developed a number of principles and policy statements (available on its website) to guide Muslim medical practice and help to answer questions about current controversial issues. This organization may not represent a universal Muslim consensus about such issues, but it is a vivid example of accommodation and creative adaptation to new circumstances.

The situation with Eastern religious traditions is somewhat different. One reason is that modern medical technologies have only recently arrived in Asia, and still are not readily available to many people. Abortion, however, has long been an issue for Buddhists and Hindus. All Eastern traditions condemn the practice, but abortion is relatively common in most Asian countries, especially Japan, India, and South Korea.

The Buddhist scriptures have little to say about abortion itself, but the Buddhist ethic of nonviolence has been understood to apply to abortion no less than to any other form of harm. In the Theravada countries of Southeast Asia abortion is typically illegal, but covert abortions are common. Japanese Buddhists have developed a special memorial service, called *mizuko kuyo*, for aborted fetuses, and some temples set aside special areas where family members may go to honour their memory.

As well as all the usual motivations for abortion, Hindus in India face two additional pressures. One is the persistence of an unusually onerous dowry system under which the family of a bride is expected to provide the groom's family with generous compensation. Because the family can rarely afford to pay the entire debt before the wedding, the payments are often spread over several years, like a mortgage. The dowry system is not sanctioned in traditional Hindu law, but neither governmental legislation nor the condemnation of Hindu leaders has been able to put an end to it. Thus the birth of a daughter means that the family faces the prospect of a terrible burden when she comes of marital age. Not only will it have to pay for both the wedding and the dowry, but after marriage the girl will go to live with—and work for—the groom's family. Conversely, a baby boy brings the prospect not only of receiving a significant financial reward when he marries, but of gaining an additional labourer or income earner in the form of his wife.

Under these circumstances it is hardly surprising that many families use modern medical technology to find out the sex of a prospective child before birth, and that some give in to the temptation to abort female fetuses. The other factor contributing to the rise of abortion in India is the government's ongoing effort to address overpopulation problems. Unlike China, India has not resorted to forced birth control, but it has put in place incentives to limit reproduction. For example, a village that manages to keep its birth rate low is eligible to receive special grants for community development projects, such as roads, wells, or community centres. Thus community leaders sometimes put heavy pressure on women who already have children to undergo sterilization in order to prevent additional pregnancies. This approach may have the unintended effect of encouraging abortion.

THE ENVIRONMENT

After creating the first humans, according to the Bible (*Genesis* 1: 28), God gave them 'dominion . . . over all the earth': the fish of the sea, the birds of the air, and every living thing. This verse was traditionally interpreted as a grant of power and a licence for unlimited exploitation of the earth's resources, but today it is generally understood differently, as a command to take responsibility for the environment.

An influential early advocate of this 'greener' interpretation was Lynn White, who in 1967 published an article entitled 'The Historical Roots of Our Ecologic Crisis', in which he argued that the traditional reading of Genesis had played a significant part in the degradation of the earth. This article prompted a shift in attitude among many Jews and Christians, towards an understanding of 'dominion over the earth' that emphasized stewardship of God's creation rather than exploitation of it. This awareness can be seen in churches such as the Canadian Memorial Church in Vancouver, which has embraced an environmental mission 'To cultivate a spiritual understanding of Creation, and to adopt and promote awareness of a spiritually-principled approach to planetary sustainability.'

According to the Qur'an, God offered the responsibility for this universe as 'a Trust to the heavens and the earth and the mountains; but they refused to undertake it, being afraid thereof' (Q. 33: 72). Thus the 'Trust' passed to the one part of creation that was willing to take it: the human being. The verse concludes with the following words: 'The human being was indeed unjust and foolish.' In suggesting that we would behave foolishly and without justice to the earth, this passage underlines the necessity of wisdom and justice in the exercise of the profound responsibility that humans have been given.

Faced with the evidence of humans' failure to serve as responsible stewards, Muslims today, like Jews and Christians, are reflecting on their fundamental religious teachings and discovering in them the bases for a new environmental ethic. So, for example, the web page of the Muslim group Green Deen (deen is the Arabic word for religion), based in southern California, states that its mission is 'to raise awareness and change the current environmental conditions by promoting a healthier, greener and more environmentally conscious lifestyle'.

In sharp contrast to their Western counterparts, most Eastern religious traditions have never made any radical distinction between humans and other animals. Hinduism understands all animals to have a soul (atman), and reincarnation may take place in either a human or an animal body. Jainism goes even further, teaching that plants as well are animated by a kind of soul. Jainism and Buddhism alike emphasize the ethic of non-violence and denounce any human activity that causes unnecessary harm to living things.

A number of Buddhists, including the Dalai Lama and Sulak Sivaraksa, have applied the Buddhist ethic of moderation to environmental issues. Sulak argues that human greed is responsible for the redirection of vast quantities of natural resources to support the demand for cash crops, causing suffering on the part of local people as well as harm to the environment. One of the first to bring these ecological concerns to wide public attention

Appa Sherpa, a Nepali high-altitude guide, holds a vase filled with Buddhist offerings that he planned to carry to the summit of Mount Everest in an effort to restore the sanctity of the Himalayas and raise awareness about climate change (REUTERS/Gopal Chitrakar).

was the economist E.F. Schumacher, in his book *Small Is Beautiful* (1973). Schumacher called for a 'Buddhist economics' designed to meet the needs of all the planet, as opposed to a traditional business economics designed to maximize profits. But of course this approach is not confined to Buddhism: M.K. Gandhi's preference for small-scale, locally based technology, together with his call for all to work for the benefit of all, has inspired many organizations around the world dedicated to environmental responsibility and human-centred development.

GENDER AND SEXUALITY

In 2000, two advertising campaigns in Los Angeles featured images of veiled women. One campaign was for the opening of the renovated Aladdin Hotel and Casino in Las Vegas, a day's drive across the desert. Billboards featured the head and shoulders of an attractive Middle Eastern woman with an enticing smile, wearing a delicate veil that covered her hair and lower face. The image was a classic example of the 'erotic Orient' myth—the harem girl whose sensuality so shocked (and sometimes titillated) the Victorians.

The other campaign was for the *Los Angeles Times*. Entitled 'Connecting Us to the Times', it included television commercials as well as print ads and billboards. In each case, an image of bikini-clad women on a beach was juxtaposed with an image of women covered from head to toe in full black robes. In many ways, this campaign was more troubling than the first example. It's no surprise that a Las Vegas casino would use sex to sell itself, but why would a respected newspaper choose that approach? In this case, the veiled women suggested a suppressed sexuality that underlined the overt sexuality of the women in bikinis. The ads were criticized not only by Muslim groups, but also by two hundred *Times* employees who objected to the use of women's bodies—covered or uncovered—to sell their product. As a result, the *Times* cancelled the campaign.

These examples are recent and specifically North American, but the distorted images they present point to a tendency to distort the image of Muslim women that is rooted in prejudice and misunderstanding.

When discussing the roles and lives of Muslim women today, it is essential to keep in mind that individual circumstances vary just as widely for them as for any other group. To be a woman in North America is a very different experience for a university professor than it is for an unemployed mother of four who never finished high school. Or look at the roles of women in political life. Both in Canada and the United States, women are theoretically equal to men, yet neither country has elected a female leader. (Kim Campbell's short stint as prime minister in 1993 was the result of the midterm resignation of Brian Mulroney, not a national election.) By contrast, Indonesia, Pakistan, Bangladesh, and Turkey—all with predominantly Muslim populations—have elected women as leaders. It would be no less simplistic to assume that North America is necessarily progressive in its treatment of women than it would be to assume that the Muslim world is necessarily oppressive.

Another issue centred on gender made headlines in 2005, after Dr Amina Wadud led a mixed-gender Muslim prayer service in New York City. The event caused a great deal of controversy, not only because it broke the Islamic convention that women may lead prayer only among other women or within their own family, but because men and women sat beside one another rather than in separate rows, and because some of the women left their hair uncovered, contrary to the rule that women should veil themselves for prayer. Since then a number of similar events have been held in Toronto as well as New York City. This is a classic example of the issues centred on gender roles and expectations that are likely to become increasingly important for North American Muslims.

Karva Chauth is a North Indian Hindu festival celebrating married women's devotion to their husbands. Participants observe a 24-hour fast, during which they pray for their husbands' well-being (REUTERS/Ajay Verma).

Many religious traditions are also beginning to rethink their positions on sexuality. Islam is among the majority of Western religious traditions that recognize only heterosexual relationships as valid, and Muslims often speak out against homosexuality. However, there are Muslims who identify themselves as gay–lesbian–bisexual–transgendered–intersex–questioning (GLBTIQ), and they are forming support groups. One such group, with branches in several Canadian cities including Toronto and Vancouver, is Min al-Alaq, which takes its name from a Qur'anic phrase (96: 2) that translates literally as 'from the clot'. The implication is that members consider all believers, whatever their sexual orientation, to come 'from the same clot of blood'.

According to its founder, Min al-Alaq does not openly advertise its meetings, or even its existence, for fear of attracting the attention of homophobes within the Muslim community. Instead, information is passed along to 'fellow travellers', and counselling and support are offered on an individual basis. A conversation with another member of Min al-Alaq underlined the tremendous religious isolation that comes with being a gay Muslim in North America. While his partner was a Christian member of an 'affirming congregation' open to all, regardless of sexual orientation, this man had no 'affirming mosque' that he could attend. Although he could pray with other Muslims in the mosque, he could feel 'welcomed' religiously only in his partner's church.

Al-Fatiha ('the opening') is a group for GLBTIQ Muslims based in Los Angeles. A non-Muslim who hosted a meeting at his home in Los Angeles in 2001 later said he was interested to hear the group discussing 'gay Sunni Muslims versus gay Shi'i Muslims'. A few years earlier, he said, 'they were all just "gay Muslims", but now they can be more divisive . . . along the same lines as gay Christians who are now gay Baptists, gay Methodists, [or] gay Adventists.'

An increasingly important source of support for gay Muslims is the Internet. With access to the Net (and the anonymity that it provides), people around the world can have access to groups such as the South Asian Gay and Lesbian Association of New York (its site includes a description of the first GLBTIQ Muslim conference, held in Boston in 1998) and Queer Jihad. Based in West Hollywood—an area where gay people have a strong voice in local government and community affairs—Queer Jihad defines itself as 'the queer Muslim struggle for acceptance: first, the struggle to accept ourselves as being exactly the way Allah has created us to be; and secondly, the struggle for acceptance and tolerance among Muslims in general'.

Homosexuality has played a major role in Christian church politics as well. The international family of churches led by the Archbishop of Canterbury, the head of the Church of England, has been particularly hard hit by controversy over homosexuality. Until recently these churches constituted one big family known as the Anglican Communion, but in recent years a major split has taken place, largely over the question of whether or not the Church should bless same-sex marriages and ordain persons openly living in same-sex relationships. James Packer, a well-known conservative Anglican theologian, officially resigned his membership in a Vancouver-area diocese in 2008 because its head favoured allowing the ritual blessing of same-sex unions. Earlier that year several conservative congregations broke away from the Anglican Church of Canada to form the Anglican Network of Canada. They recognize a South African bishop as their spiritual head and pride themselves on adhering to biblical tradition, which in their view considers homosexuality a sin. (In fact, although some local divisions of the Anglican Church of Canada have endorsed same-sex blessings, so far the Church as a whole has not done so.)

Most Eastern traditions are just beginning to discuss such issues. In fact, it is only recently that India has officially recognized the existence of homosexuality within its borders. Buddhist ordination rules prohibit the admission to the sangha of a category of persons that has been understood to include homosexuals and transsexuals. But most sanghas insist that monks and nuns remain celibate in any case, so questions about sexual orientation rarely arise. (The one exception is Japan, where married Buddhist priests are common.) In general, Buddhist societies in Asia are socially conservative and frown on homosexual relationships, although the Buddhist culture of Thailand has a long tradition of accepting males who cross-dress as females.

A major factor in India's movement towards greater openness has been the Bollywood film industry. Just a few years ago, the leading lady in an Indian film could not be kissed on camera, but now physical expressions of affection—even suggestions of gay or lesbian sexuality—are increasingly common. Still, many traditionally minded Hindus and Muslims are shocked by the new openness.

🦋 RELIGIOUS DIVERSITY

'Aren't all religions pretty much the same?' Most students of religion will be asked this question, or some version of it, more than once in their careers. As scholars we might want to unpack the proposition: what aspect of religion are we talking about—teachings? practices? implications for society? Still, it would probably be safe to assume that the questioner considers all religions to be of equal value and deserving of equal respect. And in the multicultural society of twenty-first-century North America, most of us would probably agree. This was not the case a hundred years ago, when North American society was overwhelmingly Christian and most of the Christian churches were actively engaged in missionary work. Missionary activity presumes a difference among religions—a difference so consequential that believers cannot keep silent about it, but must spread the word.

For its first three centuries, Christianity was an affinity-based movement whose members were not born into it but actively chose to join. In the early fourth century, however, with the imperial favour of the emperor Constantine (r. 306–37), the missionary religion became a state religion as well. Christianity converted several entire populations by first converting their rulers. In its earlier centuries, Islam likewise succeeded in persuading a significant number of nations to convert, perhaps partly because it offered improved juridical status, including especially tax exemption, to those who became Muslims. Christianity's spread after the

1490s was closely associated with European military and cultural expansion. Priests accompanied soldiers in Mexico and Peru, and the sponsoring Spanish and Portuguese regimes took it as their responsibility to save the souls of the indigenous peoples whose bodies they enslaved. The cultural-religious imperialism of Catholic countries in the sixteenth century was matched in the nineteenth by that of Protestant England, notably in Africa.

Muslim rule in northern India began with the establishment of the Delhi sultanate in the thirteenth century. This was the first region where Islam did not succeed in converting the entire population. Only in the Indus Valley, Bengal, and the mid-southern interior did Muslims become the majority; the rest of the subcontinent remained predominantly Hindu.

In the later centuries of its expansion, Islam grew not through military conquest, but through trade and the missionary activity of the Sufis in

Missionary Religions

The fact that a mere three traditions—Buddhism, Christianity, and Islam—claim the allegiance of over half the world's population reflects the success of their missionary activities. All three are 'universal' rather than 'ethnic' religions: that is, they direct their messages to all human beings, regardless of heredity or descent. And all three were strongly motivated from the start to spread their messages far and wide.

By the time Buddhism emerged in what is now northern India, Indian society was already stratified into four broad social classes. Whether those distinctions had ethnic connotations in the time of the Buddha may be debated. What is clear is that Buddhism set caste and class status aside as irrelevant to the achievement of spiritual purity and liberation.

Christianity began as a sect of Judaism, a religion focused almost exclusively on the relationship of one particular nation to God. But the early Christians decided that it was not necessary to be a Jew in order to become a Christian. Early Christian teaching understood the new covenant to apply to all humans who accepted Jesus as their Lord, regardless of ethnicity.

Islam believes the Prophet Muhammad to have been the last in a long line of prophets sent by God to different peoples. And although the Qur'an explicitly addresses the people of Arabia, it was understood from the start to incorporate the messages delivered to other groups by earlier prophets and to represent God's final revelation to humanity at large. It is not ethnic identity but submission to the One God that renders humans acceptable in the sight of God. Thus the community established by the Prophet could expand far beyond Arabia.

particular. The devotional life of the Sufis resonated with the Hindu and Buddhist meditational piety already present in Southeast Asia and provided Islam with an entrée to that region, in which it became dominant. Similarly in Africa south of the Sahara, traders and Sufis were the principal vehicles of Islam.

In general, Buddhist, Muslim, and Christian missionaries have been more successful in recruiting converts from the traditional religions of small-scale tribal societies than from the other major religions. The reasons may have something to do with the material culture and technologies—including writing systems—of the major civilizations, which have conferred powerful advantages on those who possess them. Scriptural literatures have given the major traditions a special authority among cultures that were primarily oral, allowing them to use the content of their scriptures to shape social values. The early missionary spread of Theravada Buddhism is credited to King Ashoka. We do not know enough about the indigenous traditions in many of the regions where Theravada spread to determine why its teachings were accepted. In the case of China, however, it seems that the Daoist interest in magic and healing techniques may have helped Mahayana Buddhism gain an initial foothold.

In the twentieth century, some Christian denominations began to curtail their missionary activity, partly because the returns on the resources invested were too small. Generations of European missionary effort in the eastern Mediterranean had made almost no inroads into Islam. And in the years around 1960, when many African countries were struggling for independence from European rule, Christian missionaries in West Africa particularly suffered from identification with colonial interests as well as the former slave trade. Thus Christian missionaries in Africa were largely replaced by an emerging generation of indigenous church leaders. Another factor in the Christian churches' retreat from missionary work, however,

was an increasing respect for other communities and traditions.

Dialogue in a Pluralistic Age

Today we often use the term 'pluralism' to denote a combination of two things: the fact of diversity, and the evaluation of that diversity as desirable. This use of the word, which has become standard since the mid-twentieth century, reflects a convergence of developments and trends.

But let us be clear about what we mean by it. First, pluralism is not the same thing as diversity. People from many different religions and ethnic backgrounds may be present in one place, but unless they are constructively engaged with one another, there is no pluralism.

Second, pluralism means more than simple tolerance of the other. It's quite possible to tolerate a neighbour about whom we know nothing. Pluralism, by contrast, demands an active effort to learn.

Third, pluralism is not the same thing as relativism, which can lead us to ignore profound differences. Pluralism is committed to engaging those differences, to gain a deeper understanding both of others' commitments and of our own. It is also important to recognize that pluralism and dialogue are happening around the world, not just in North America.

The current situation has been shaped by increasingly intimate intercultural contact. Within the lifetimes of people still alive today, transportation and communication have been transformed almost beyond recognition. As late as 1950, travel between North America and East Asia was rare, but now tens of thousands of people fly across the Pacific every day. And new technologies allow us to be in touch with almost any part of the world in an instant. Migration has also increased significantly. Since the end of the Second World War, the demographic profile of European and North American cities has been transformed by the arrival of populations from other parts of the world who have brought their Muslim, Hindu, Buddhist, and other traditions with them. Though apprehensive at first, Western societies have made some progress towards understanding those traditions.

Change in the evaluation of diversity is reflected in many aspects of contemporary life, large and small. In some cases old institutions have been retained, but with new rationales. For instance, Sunday—the Christian day of religious observance—remains the day of reduced business activity in many jurisdictions. The arguments for legislation preserving Sunday store closing, however, now involve fairness, family time, and opportunities for recreation.

We should distinguish pluralism from secularism. Secularism means the exclusion (in principle) of all religious groups, institutions, and identities from public support and public decision-making. Pluralism, on the other hand, means equal support, acceptance, and participation in decision-making for multiple religious groups. Whereas recreational arguments for Sunday closing are secularist, arguments for school holidays on the Jewish New Year or the Muslim festival ending the Ramadan fast are pluralist. Up to a point, secularism and pluralism go hand in hand in the West because both seek to limit the role that Christianity can play in setting the society's standards. Where they differ is in what they propose as alternatives. Pluralism places a parallel and a positive value on the faith and practice of different communities. It often does so on the assumption that any religion is beneficial to society so long as it does no harm to other religions. It can also presume that the effort to understand a neighbour's religion—whatever it may be—is beneficial to society. Essentially, pluralism downplays the differences between religions and focuses instead on the values they share. In its scale of priorities, the value of harmony in the society as a whole is more important than the commitments of any particular religion.

Interfaith Dialogue

The word 'dialogue' comes from a Greek root meaning to argue, reason, or contend. Some Christian writers have pointed to the apostle Paul as an early proponent of interfaith dialogue because he is described as 'arguing and pleading about the kingdom of God' with the Jews (*Acts* 19: 8–9). Paul was a missionary, however, and missionaries—by definition—believe they are possessed of a truth that it is their mission to spread. Missionary argumentation therefore bears little resemblance to dialogue in the modern sense, which demands openness to other points of view.

Dialogue is also a literary form, almost always designed to advance the author's point of view. The Greek philosopher Plato was a master of the dialogue form, using questioners and objectors as foils (or comedic 'straight men') to demonstrate the invincible logic of his own ideas and those of his mentor Socrates.

The Hindu *Upanishads* also take the form of dialogues, and they too were composed to advance specific arguments. The early Christian writer Justin Martyr in his dialogues with the Jew Trypho; the Buddhist sage Nagasena who answers the questions of King Milinda (Menander); and the Khazar king in the *Kuzari* of Yehuda Ha-Levi—in each case the questioner is like a puppet whose only function is to bring out the views that the author is already committed to.

True openness to alternative points of view is rare in any of the premodern traditions, but we do find instances of it. One highly significant example is the Mughal Indian emperor Akbar (r. 1556–1605). As a Muslim ruler of a mainly Hindu population, Akbar could have taken a tolerant stance towards Hindu spirituality on purely practical grounds, but he was a genuine seeker of religious insight. Therefore he summoned to his court representatives of all the religious communities within his domain and pursued conversations with them late into the night. From those conversations Akbar drew the components of an eclectic new religion that he called Din-i Ilahi ('divine faith'). Although Akbar's synthesis did not endure for long after his death, it reflected a remarkable phenomenon in his society: a widespread perception that despite their communal boundaries, Hindus and Muslims shared a devotional spirituality.

Conservative Muslims disapproved of Akbar's openness to heretical views. This is nothing new. Traditional religions may encourage disputation when the outcome is not in question. But Akbar's explorations were open-ended. A dialogue in which both sides are equal is something that orthodoxy cannot control. To those committed to a fixed position, such dialogue implies a threat.

The World's Parliament of Religions, convened in Chicago in 1893, was an adventure in dialogue that brought together representatives of many—though not all—of the world's faiths to present their religious goals and understandings. The conference reflected the existing religious scene and at the same time affected its future development by creating opportunities for Vedanta to present itself as the definitive form of Hinduism, Zen to claim to represent Buddhism, and the Baha'i faith to appear as an overarching synthesis of religion.

Understanding of interfaith dialogue has grown considerably since 1948, when the World Council of Churches was formed. Experienced dialogue participants emphasize that such exercises require both parties to set aside their claims to exclusivity: each must work to understand the other on his or her own terms. Both participants must also be open to the possibility of revising their views in the light of what they learn in the encounter—though this is easier said than done. Even the best-intentioned participants may be tempted to read their own views into others'. The influential Roman Catholic theologian Karl Rahner (1904–84), for instance, referred to people of other faiths as 'anonymous Christians'—Christians who simply did not recognize the fact. By the same token, could not Rahner himself have been an anonymous Buddhist?

The goal of dialogue in the modern sense is 'understanding'. But 'understanding' can be a slippery term in the context of religion. Academic students of religion understand particular traditions by explaining them: by describing as accurately as possible what they require of their adherents and how they have developed to become what they are. For those people, understanding may be informed by sympathy, but it is not the same as participation or identification. Similarly, the participants in dialogue understand each other by identifying one another's commitments, but that is not to say that they identify with those commitments. Particularly in the area of Jewish–Christian–Muslim dialogue, there have been calls for complete solidarity on complex and hotly debated issues, characterized by one critic as 'ecumenical blackmail'. Does true understanding of Judaism require uncritical endorsement of

Archbishop Desmond Tutu of South Africa meeting with the Dalai Lama in Vancouver in 2004 (REUTERS/Lyle Stafford).

Israel's policies towards the Palestinians? If one truly 'understands' Islam, must one agree with Iran's theocratic government and its suppression of democracy? Does understanding Hinduism mean accepting polytheism or animal sacrifice? No. Real understanding is not a matter of agreement or acquiescence, but a quest for a patient and appreciative relationship that can persist despite disagreement.

The Question of Value

For more than three decades, the 1978 Jonestown tragedy—in which 914 members of a religious community called the Peoples Temple died in a mass suicide—has stood as a challenge to the idea that all religions are equally valuable and deserving of respect. The community's founder, the Reverend Jim Jones (1931–78), who took his own life alongside his followers, had aspirations to overhaul the world order that were compatible with a reformist and utopian strand in Protestant (and Marxist) thought; one of his objectives in founding the movement had been to improve the living standards of the poor. But he also sought from his followers an uncritical dedication to his personal leadership that many found disturbing. Having moved the community from the US to rural Guyana in 1972, Jones ordered the mass suicide when he became convinced that evil forces were closing in and the only honourable escape was death.

History repeats itself. The Jonestown story recalls the Jewish Zealots at the fortress of Masada who are said to have committed mass suicide when they were surrounded by Roman troops in 73 CE. Suicide and the psychology of martyrdom have been linked at various times by Christian groups, and in other traditions as well. A similar interpretation has been applied to the conduct of the followers of David Koresh (Vernon Wayne Howell, 1959–93), 85 of whom perished with him when their heavily armed religious commune outside Waco, Texas, was stormed by US law enforcement forces for firearms violations in 1993.

To approve of Masada's defenders while condemning the 'Branch Davidians' at Waco would amount to deciding what constitutes a provocation worth resisting to the death.

Jim Jones and David Koresh were both leaders of movements that sought to recruit and retain converts. That is not unusual in missionary religions: Buddhism, Christianity, and Islam have all done the same, as have numerous 'new religious movements' since the late 1960s. If modern pluralistic society proclaims the freedom to preach or follow religion without state intervention, fairness demands that the same freedom be extended to all.

Nevertheless, my freedom to practise or promote a religion is limited by the freedom of others to know what I am offering and to refuse it if they so choose. In a pluralistic society, religious groups forfeit their right to acceptance if they engage in coercion (psychological or physical) or illegal activities (such as narcotics abuse, firearms abuse, or tax fraud). Critics of movements such as the Unification Church (the 'Moonies'), or the International Society for Krishna Consciousness (the Hare Krishna movement), or the Church of Scientology are particularly alarmed when recruits are instructed to sever all ties with their families—even though there have been parallels to such demands in the early Christian movement and in some religious orders, and the families of such recruits have often resorted to equally coercive methods to retrieve and 'deprogram' them.

By the early twenty-first century, some of the new religions had achieved a degree of institutional maturity and public acceptance. Most of these organizations were compatible with mainstream religions in that they helped their members cope with their lives and encouraged good citizenship. Like mainstream religions, in one way or another they addressed the human condition.

The last point is important. Religions are not all the same, but many may be humanly acceptable if they in fact benefit human beings; an appropriate test is suggested by Jesus' words in the

Sermon on the Mount: 'you shall know them by their fruits' (*Matthew* 7: 16). On some occasions, when they have lived up to their ideals, all the major traditions have passed that test; on other occasions, when they have fallen short of their ideals, the same traditions have failed. Typically, though, the various traditions see their distinguishing features as eminently valuable in themselves. If all religions were of equal worth, if there were no fundamentally important differences, why would anyone choose one of them over another? Pluralism may be socially desirable, but it poses a serious theological challenge. Does it really require us to modify our own doctrinal claims?

We personally are convinced that it does. Affirmations of religious 'truth' that used to be understood as statements of fact are now increasingly regarded as perspectival—true 'for me'—rather than universal claims. Today, thinkers from various backgrounds are presenting their traditions as symbolic accounts of the world and metaphorical narratives of the past. What is more, they argue that this is the way the various traditions should have been seen all along, and that literal interpretation has always been a mistake.

Pluralism demands that religious traditions adapt to a world that is becoming ever more interconnected. Here we think of the work of Wilfred Cantwell Smith (1916–2000), perhaps the greatest Canadian scholar of religion in the twentieth century. Professor Smith founded the Institute of Islamic Studies at McGill University in Montreal. He then moved to Harvard University, where he directed the Center for the Study of World Religions. One of his most important books was *Towards a World Theology: Faith and the Comparative History of Religion* (1981). In it he argued that our various religious traditions were best understood in comparative context, 'as strands in a . . . complex whole':

> What they have in common is that the history of each has been what it has been in significant part because the history of the others has been what *it* has been. This truth is newly discovered; yet truth it is, truth it has throughout been. Things proceeded in this interrelated way for many centuries without humanity's being aware of it; certainly not fully aware of it. A new, and itself interconnected, development is that currently humankind *is* becoming aware of it, in various communities.

Although current events make us painfully aware of the differences that separate the world's religions, it is more crucial today than ever to appreciate the complex connections they share. That is exactly what we are trying to do in this book: to deepen understanding of our interconnected religious worlds.

References

Brockopp, Jonathan. 2003. *Islamic Ethics of Life: Abortion, War and Euthanasia*. Columbia: University of South Carolina Press.

Sajoo, Amyn. 2004. *Muslim Ethics: Emerging Vistas*. London: I.B. Tauris in association with The Institute for Ismaili Studies.

Schumacher, E.F. 1973. *Small Is Beautiful: Economics as if People Mattered*. New York: Harper and Row.

Smith, Wilfred Cantwell. 1981. *Towards a World Theology: Faith and the Comparative History of Religion*. London: Macmillan, and Philadelphia: Westminster.

Note

1. Some Islamic scholars have questioned the authenticity of this *hadith*.

Credits

Index